NeXTSTEP™ GENERAL REFERENCE

Volume 2

NeXTSTEP Developer's Library
NeXT Computer, Inc.

Release 3

Addison-Wesley Publishing Company
Reading, Massachusetts · Menlo Park, California · New York · Don Mills, Ontario
Wokingham, England · Amsterdam · Bonn · Sydney · Singapore · Tokyo · Madrid
San Juan · Paris · Seoul · Milan · Mexico City · Taipei

This manual describes NeXTSTEP Release 3.

Written by NeXT Publications.

This manual was designed, written, and produced on NeXT computers. Proofs were printed on a NeXT 400 dpi Laser Printer and NeXT Color Printer. Final pages were transferred directly from a NeXT optical disk to film using NeXT computers and an electronic imagesetter.

2 3 4 5 6 7 8 9–AL–96959493
Second printing, April 1993

ISBN 0-201-62221-1

Contents

Appendices

4 *Database Kit*

4 *Database Kit*

Library: libNeXT_s, libsys_s

Header File Directory: /NextDeveloper/Headers/dbkit

Import: dbkit/dbkit.h

Introduction

The Database Kit provides a comprehensive set of tools, classes, and protocols for building applications that use a high-level entity-relationship model to manipulate database servers such as those provided by Oracle or Sybase. The kit provides services that include:

- Communication with client-server databases.
- Modeling properties (attributes and relationships) of each database.
- Record management and buffering.
- Data flow between record managers and the application user interface.
- User interface objects for display and editing.

Tools for Building a Database Application

To build a database application in NeXTSTEP, in addition to Project Builder and Interface Builder, you must have:

- An *adaptor* for each type of database you will use.
- A *model* (built with DBModeler) for each database you will use, specifying the entities available to your application and their properties (attributes and relationships).
- A *palette* of database accessories to supplement Interface Builder's standard palettes.

Adaptors

The Database Kit includes adaptors for ORACLE® and for SYBASE®. The supplied adaptors are installed in the directory **/NextLibrary/Adaptors**. Each is a bundle having a name that ends in the extension ".adaptor". Adaptors may also be installed in the application's own bundle, or in directories on a standard search path, searched in the following sequence:

- The application bundle
- **~/Library/Adaptors**
- **/LocalLibrary/Adaptors**
- **/NextLibrary/Adaptors**
- **/usr/local/lib/Adaptors**

Additional adaptors may be supplied by NeXT or by third parties; it's possible to build your own, but directions for doing so are outside the scope of this manual (see *NeXTSTEP Development Tools and Techniques*, Chapter 7, "DBModeler").

The adaptor is necessary not only for communicating with the database when your application runs, but also for building the data model and testing its user interface during development with Interface Builder.

Linking the Adaptor

When your application uses one of the separately-provided adapters, you must include a directive that will require the compiler to link symbols required by the adaptor as well as those from your own application. This can be done by including the following in the file **Makefile.preamble**:

```
OTHER_LDFLAGS = -u libNeXT_s -u libsys_s
```

(The effect of this statement is to undefine the symbols **libNeXT_s** and **libsys_s**. The undefined references force the loading of the corresponding object files.)

Models

Before you can start building the application, you must have a model of the entities you will use and their properties (attributes and relationships).

To create a model, you need access to the database you will model. When you have the authorization (which may require an account name and password), launch the DBModeler application (it's in the **/NextDeveloper/Apps** directory). To create a new model, select "Model" and then "New." DBModeler first asks you to select an adaptor from among those currently installed; the list should include the OracleAdaptor and SybaseAdaptor, plus any others that have been installed in your home directories or on the host you are using. Then it asks you to identify the database you want and to supply login information. DBModeler connects to the database by way of the adaptor you chose. (If the connection failed, you may need to set up your database server. In general, if you can connect with Sybase's **isql** or Oracle's **sqlplus**, then you should be able to connect from DBModeler.)

When connected, DBModeler automatically reads from the data dictionary a list of the database's entities and their attributes. This is called the *default model*.

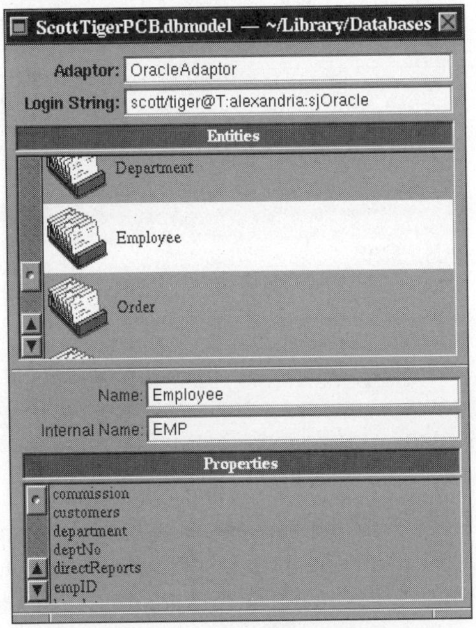

In the display, each entity is represented by a card-tray icon in the upper scrollable window. For the selected entity, the name you assign, the internal name, and the list of its properties appear below. DBModeler allows you to extend and edit the default model. To begin with, you can replace the database's internal names for entities with names by which they'll be known in your application.

Relationships

Note: If your application is going to use relationships formed by joining entities in the database, this is where you define them: in the model, rather than in the application itself.

To create a new relationship, from the Property submenu select New Relationship. Select the Inspector menu item and, in the Inspector, name the relationship. You now need to specify which entity the relationship maps to (that is, which table to join to). To do this, select a second entity and drag its icon to the empty framed area in the Inspector.

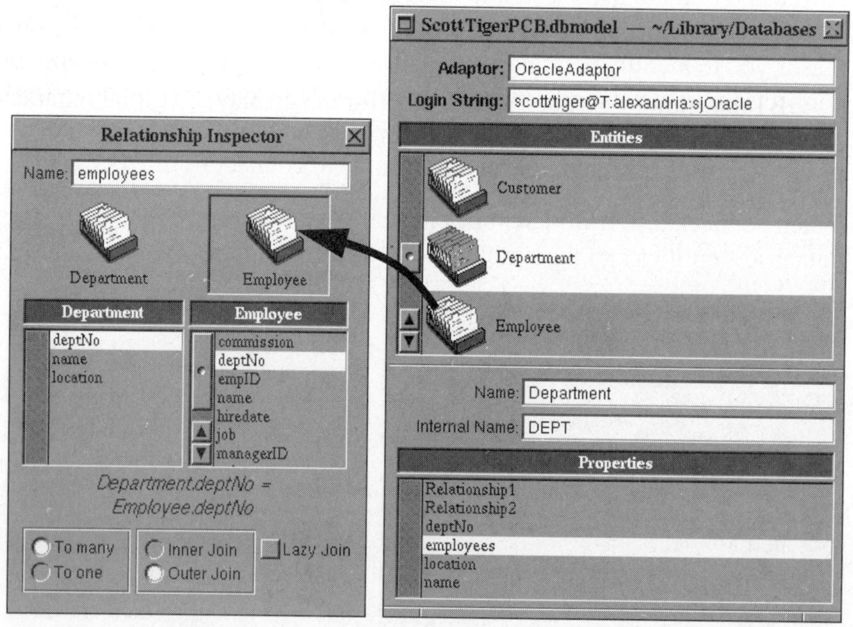

The Inspector's browser should now be populated with attributes of that entity you dragged in. Select an attribute in the left browser and one in the right browser to indicate which columns of each table should be joined. Set the radio buttons to indicate whether the relationship is "to one" or "to many."

A saved model resides in a bundle whose name ends in the ".dbmodel" extension. To be found by Interface Builder when you're building the application, or by the application itself when it's running, the model file must be located in a standard place. Directories are searched in the following order:

- The application bundle
- **~/Library/Databases**
- **/LocalLibrary/Databases**
- **/NextLibrary/Databases**
- **/usr/local/lib/Databases**

Database Palette for Interface Builder

The first time you use Interface Builder to build a database application, you'll need to load the database palette. Choose Load Palette from the Tools menu; in the file browser, select **/NextDeveloper/Palettes/DatabaseKit.palette**. (Thereafter, Interface Builder remembers that you want it and loads it automatically.)

The DatabaseKit palette includes three new objects for work with databases:

DBModule	The file-cabinet icon represents your application's access to a database. Double-clicking opens a browser that displays its contents.
DBTableView	A scrollable view for the display of textual (character or numeric) data from the database.
DBImageView	A view for TIFF or EPS data from the database.

While you're building a database application with Interface Builder, you drag into the application's file window the icon that represents a DBModule. When you double-click that icon, Interface Builder opens a browser that shows the entities defined in the model and their attributes. You select one of those entities. (If you need to make use of several entitites, drag a new DBModule icon for each.)

When you save the application's nib file, your DBModule object is included in what's saved. At run time, the DBModule and relevant portions of the model file are loaded into the application. Because the DBModule continues to refer back to the model file, the finished application will continue to require access to the model. If you subsequently edit the model file to which the application refers (for example, to use the same model with a different database), the application's behavior will change accordingly.

You could construct a simple application using instances from the three classes DBModule, DBTableView and DBImageView, creating the need instances just by dragging them from the database palette. A DBModule provides target/action methods. Since the methods include requests to fetch data, when you test the interface with Interface Builder's Test Interface command, it can actually connect to the database and fill the views with real data.

Since your application probably won't be limited to connecting to the database and scrolling through its data, the rest of the kit provides methods that allow you to customize and control the exact behavior.

Levels of Detail in a Database Application

The Database Kit's classes can be roughly grouped into levels by the amount of detail they conceal and automate, or (conversely) the amount of control they give to the application. If you work at the higher levels, you will never need to make explicit use of many of the kit's classes, protocols, or methods.

High Level: Interface Builder Palette Objects Only

At the highest level (that is, least visible detail), it's possible to construct an application solely by connecting objects dragged from the Interface Builder palettes. The application has no source other than its nib file; its objects are generated at run time when the application loads the interface file. Because it depends only on its nib file, it can be run in Interface Builder's test mode even without compiling it. In addition to a model and an adaptor (essential to every database application), such an application needs:

- One or more DBModule objects, dragged from Interface Builder palette. Each module represents one entity in the database.
- One or more View objects (for example, instances of Browser, TextField, DBTableView, or DBImageView.
- One or more controls (for example, instances of Button).

The outlets of the controls are connected to the DBModule's target/action methods in the usual way (by Control-dragging between them, and selecting action methods in the Connections Inspector). For example, to connect to a TextField, a Form, or a Matrix of FormCells or TextField cells, drag the database field to the user interface object you with to connect. The DBModule object contains several action methods, such as **fetchAllRecords:**, **nextRecord:**, **previousRecord:**, **saveChanges:**, and **deleteRecord:**. In a large application, these methods are often called programmatically, but to get started, it's convenient to invoke them from a Button or a Menu.

If you want the DBModule to pick up any editing the user does, you'll need to connect the **textDelegate** outlet of the text-editing user interface object to the DBModule. (Otherwise the DBModule will have no way of finding out when the user edits a text value.)

To connect to a Rich Text editor, simply make a database connection as usual. In order to store actual rich text (RTF) in the database, however, the database field must be of type "object," class "NXData," and format "RTF."

To connect a display object (for example, an NXBrowser), open the DBModule's browser by double clicking the DBModule icon. Within the browser, navigate to select the database, entity, and attribute you want. (Note that there's a distinct icon for each of these levels.) Drag an attribute icon from the DBModule browser to the NXBrowser object. If you want the action of selecting a row in the NXBrowser to move the DBRecordList cursor to that row, then connect the target of the NXBrowser to **takeValueFrom:** of the DBModule.

To connect a DBTableView, drag off a DBTableView from the Database Kit palette and drag database field objects from the DBModule editor to the column you wish to connect. To add extra columns, deposit the field icon on any part of the DBTableView other than a column (the scroll bars, for example).

Mid Level: The DBModule's Fetch Groups

For each DBModule that you drag from the palette to the application, at run time the Database Kit creates one or more DBFetchGroups. The role of the fetch groups is to synchronize the fetching of data when one part of the display is dependent on another, and in particular when you have included a one-to-many relationship. For example, you might have in one DBTableView a display of the firm's departments, and in another DBTableView beside it, the employees within a department. Each time the user selects a record in the higher level display (that is, selects a particular department), you want the display of employees to show that department's employees. The fetch group for the subordinate level (employees) is notified each time there's a change in selection, and issues a fetch command to get the appropriate new data. Thus the set of DBFetchGroups corresponds to the nodes of the tree of data dependencies for the module. There's always at least one fetch group, called the root fetch group, and as many others as necessary for all the dependent displays that use the same DBModule.

Qualifiers and Custom Associations

Most database applications will need a way to select a subset of records by sending a query to the database server. Since most NeXTSTEP database applications are built using DBModules dragged from the Interface Builder palette, you need a way to ask the DBModule to fetch a subset of records. To constrain the records retrieved, you create a custom object, and in it define a method that creates a DBQualifier object and uses it as an argument of the method **fetchContentsOf:usingQualifier:**. In most cases, this method's first argument is **nil**, meaning that the source is the database entity corresponding to the DBModule. (The first argument can also be a DBValue object containing a record-key or relationship value from some other DBRecordList.). The second argument is the qualifier for the fetch.

In addition to connecting DBModules to the standard NeXTSTEP interface objects, you can also connect DBModules to objects of your own. The process is the same: drag a database field off the DBModule editor and deposit it one of your objects. You will have to compile the application in order for the code for your objects to be linked in. When you run the application, a DBAssociation will be made between your object and one of the module's DBFetchGroups. When the application is running, the DBFetchGroup will call any of the following methods that your object implements:

– associationContentsDidChange:
– associationSelectionDidChange:
– associationCurrentRecordDidDelete:
– association:setValue:
– association:getValue:

Of these, the most important is **association:setValue:**. It will be called any time the database field value changes (for example, when the data is first fetched, when the user selects a different record, or when the user changes that value in the user interface).

Custom associations are most useful for implementing your own user interface objects (such as Custom Views) or passing information through the nib file owner or some Custom Object of your own.

Low Level: The Data Access Layer

The Database Kit Access Layer is a collection of Objective C objects and protocols designed to work with the Interface Builder to allow relatively painless access to a variety of "external" sources of data. There are seven basic classes in this group:

- DBDatabase
- DBValue
- DBRecordStream
- DBRecordList
- DBQualifier
- DBExpression
- DBBinder

DBDatabase

A DBDatabase object represents two important aspects of an external source of data: the structure that the information takes, and the nature of the application's connection to that database. Each application typically has a single instance of the DBDatabase class communicating with any given database. An application can have many DBDatabase objects, communicating with multiple "backed" databases; in special situations, there can also be several DBDatabase objects communicating with the same database (but embodying different views of it).

A DBDatabase object represents the view onto a given database from the perspective of the Database Kit. This view, or data model, represents the various components of information available from the database in the form of Objective C objects. For instance, a database containing employee information might contain attributes such as an employee's name or address. Within the DBDatabase object that corresponds to the employee database, information about these pieces of data is assigned to objects; the objects contain such things as the Objective C type or the string "employeeName" for the employee's name. The actual classes of objects used to represent a data model are not specified by the Database Kit; the only requirement placed on them is that they obey the DBProperties protocol.

DBProperties

DBProperties represent what is commonly called the "schema" of a database. This schema can come from one of two places: a representation that has been stored in the file system as a "bundle file," or from the DBDatabase object itself (a representation of that database's "data dictionary"). Although the default data model that is provided by a DBDatabase object is often sufficient to build applications, there are several advantages to storing a reusable representation of a database's schema. Once stored in this way, the database representation can be easily accessed by name. In addition, special components such as complicated queries or relationships between particular pieces of data can be designated as a part of the data model and reused. Finally, multiple data models can be supported for a given database; these models can be tailored to the needs of the design perspective or permissions of the application programmer. DBProperties can be obtained directly from a DBDatabase object by name.

DBExpression

A DBExpression encapsulates a database expression as an object. A database expression specifies the attributes of data to be returned from an entity in the database. The simplest expression contains just the name of an existing attribute (just as the simplest expression in algebra is simply the name of a variable). A slightly more complex expression provides the name of a database attribute, but specifies a type for the data to be delivered (perhaps requiring a type conversion). A more complex expression (called a *derived* expression) defines a new property by some operations on one or more of the entity's existing attributes. For example, the expression "((salary / manager.salary) * 100.0)" might define a new property, the employee's salary stated as a percentage of the manager's salary. Data resulting from such an expression is derived from data in the database, but doesn't exist as a separate item anywhere in the database. Because a DBExpression may be simple, typed, or derived, the fields of a DBRecordList can be described by a list of DBExpressions, one DBExpression for each static field. In databases that support the notion, an expression can represent aggregate or composite types of information, such as "the average age of customers."

DBValue

Once you've procured or created an object that conforms to the DBProperties protocol, you can use this object in conjunction with a DBValue object to extract actual values from the "data-bearing" objects of the kit. The information represented by and contained in Database Kit objects can never be accessed directly; this makes sense, since the "real" data resides externally. Instead, DBValue objects are used as proxies for extracting, inserting, circulating, or modifying the external information.

The DBValue is a simple, generic container for many different kinds of data. It provides an easy and universal way for objects in the Database Kit to refer to many different kinds of raw data. DBValues can be set and read using familiar methods such as **setStringValue:** and **intValue**. Additionally, they can perform basic type conversions automatically, such as converting integer-valued contents into their string representation, much as some Application Kit objects do. DBValues can be used to hold both Objective C objects and arbitrary ranges of opaque bytes; because of this, the Database Kit is able to archive and unarchive Objective C objects and complex structured data (such as TIFF images) to and from remote data sources.

Transferring Information Between Application and Database

How is information actually retrieved from or sent back to the database? There are three important objects for this purpose:

- DBRecordStream
- DBRecordList
- DBBinder

All of these objects link "external" pieces of data to "internal" Objective C variables or objects; of the three, the DBRecordList and the DBRecordStream are more commonly used, since they provide a much higher level of abstraction than the DBBinder. The DBBinder is useful in certain more advanced situations, notably when passing data directly into Objective C object classes or when doing very sophisticated operations with the underlying query language for a given database.

If your application relies on objects dragged from the Database palette, you need only create one or more DBTableViews. At run time, when your nib file is loaded, to support the DBTableViews, supporting DBRecordLists are created for you, along with a DBFetchGroup for each node of the data you've requested, and DBAssociations to map the link from fetch group to a vector (static column or row) of the display. In this situation, the principal intermediate storage for the data being transferred is the DBRecordList. Your application may also create and manage DBRecordLists explicitly.

For an application characterized by systematic sequential processing of an entire set of records (without a browsing display, perhaps with no display at all), it is more efficient to create a DBRecordStream instance. You can manipulate its fields in the same way as those of a DBRecordList, but you can look at only one record (the *current* record), and the only way to change the cursor is to move ahead by one, to the *next* record.

DBRecordList

The DBRecordList is an object that is organized into repeating rows of data. The layout is specified by a list of DBProperties, and is identical for each row. The rows of data in a DBRecordList can be created from scratch by an Objective C program and inserted into a DBDatabase, or, conversely, they can be created when a DBRecordList receives their contents from a database. The rows in a DBRecordList can be manipulated, modified, deleted, and eventually resubmitted to the database; the DBRecordList takes care of the housekeeping necessary to identify where the individual pieces belong.

The value for any individual DBProperty can be retrieved from a given row into a DBValue, and directly manipulated or modified by an application. DBValues can even be used as "sources" for other DBRecordLists. For example, in an orders database, the DBValue representing an "order" might be used as the source for a DBRecordList full of "line items."

DBRecordStream

DBRecordStream is the superclass of DBRecordList, and is a simpler and more efficient object. Again, it is organized into repeating rows of identical records; in the DBRecordStream these rows are abstracted as a continuous, unidirectional stream. There is no random access to the records, as there is in the DBRecordList. Instead, the DBRecordStream has a "cursor" through which only the current record may be accessed and modified. This object is especially useful in situations where there is an indeterminately large number of records to be accessed in order, such as batch filtering or updates to a database.

DBBinder

The third data-bearing component of the Database Kit is the DBBinder. This object represents specific Objective C objects or variables that have been directly "pinned" to corresponding DBProperties for the database. The objects and variables in question can have their values placed into the database, or filled in from the database. Both DBRecordList and DBRecordStream are implemented by using DBBinder objects, but in a way that is transparent to the application. Explicit use of a DBBinder is appropriate only for applications that for some reason cannot make effective use of DBRecordList or DBRecordStream.

When data is fetched to a DBBinder, it is stored in a container: an object (usually a List object) that conforms to the DBContainers protocol. The container serves as an unstructured repository. To make the data available as Objective C objects, the DBBinder offers two alternate strategies:

- To return each record as a generic record, with self-describing components that incorporate the properties
- To return each record as an instance of an application-supplied prototype class

If you provide a prototype class, you can specify that attributes of the data are mapped to instance variables declared in the class (by **associateRecordIvar:withProperty:**) or are made available by "set" and "return" methods declared in the class (by the method **associateRecordSelectors::withProperty:**).

The Database's Query Language

In many cases, programs built using the Database Kit in conjunction with Interface Builder will never have to involve themselves with the underlying query language for a database, since both the DBRecordList and the DBBinder cooperate with their DBDatabases' adaptors to generate query expressions automatically. These queries are available to the programmer; you can choose to override them. When you need access to the query language, however, there are two objects that support it in a simple way: DBExpression and DBQualifier.

DBRecordList, DBRecordStream, and DBBinder can restrict the set of data that they are manipulating through the use of DBQualifier objects. A qualifier has (associated with it) an expression in some query language, for example, "lastname = 'Smith'" or "age > 72 AND hatsize < 6.5." Typically, a given database has its own unique query language; the DBQualifier object is a way to pass the complete expressivity of any ASCII-based query language through to the programmer of the Database Kit. A wide range of expressions can be built using a DBQualifier, from simple strings to complex trees of Objective C objects. Furthermore, the values contained in a DBQualifier can be obtained "lazily" from other Objective C objects; this allows very dynamic database applications to be easily built and configured.

In order to be meaningful in the context of a given data-bearing object, the "owners" of every DBExpression or DBQualifier that are used within a query must match. It would make very little sense, for example, to ask for the DBProperty "employee.age" (the age of an employee) in a DBRecordList that was qualified with the DBQualifier "department is accounting," unless the department being specified was that of the employee in question. Because of this, DBExpressions and DBQualifiers are always created "relative to" some entity in the DBDatabase.

The four types of components that have been described make up a generalized framework for communicating with and manipulating data that exists "outside" of a program. There is an object to represent the external database (DBDatabase), several objects that can be used together to identify specific items in that database (DBProperties, DBExpressions, and DBQualifiers), objects that stand in for the specified set of items (DBRecordStream, DBRecordList, and DBBinder), and finally, an object that represents the concrete value for a specific item (DBValue).

Formatting and Editing

The DBTableView class displays data using the DBFormatter class, whose subclasses are DBImageFormatter, DBTextFormatter (for read-only applications) and DBEditableFormatter (for applications in which the user may edit the display). Details of the appearance of a data field are governed by the DBTableVectors protocol. For a DBTableView, each "cell" (the field at the intersection of a particular row and column) is formatted by calling the formatter appropriate to its row and its column.

Classes and Protocols

The Database Kit comprises sixteen public classes, ten protocols, and an additional five informal protocols. (To review, in the Objective C language, a class may have instances that contain data; each instance is able to perform all the instance methods defined for its class. Like a class, a protocol defines a set of methods; however, a protocol can't be instantiated. When a class conforms to a protocol, it thereby gains the ability to perform any of the protocol's methods. An informal protocol is a set of related methods—usually defined as a category of Object—but without a formal procedure for conforming to them as a whole.)

Inheritance Hierarchy

Most of the Database Kit's classes inherit only from Object. The two database view classes inherit from Control, View, and Responder, and from ScrollView, View, and Responder respectively. The three formatter classes inherit from the abstract superclass DBFormatter.

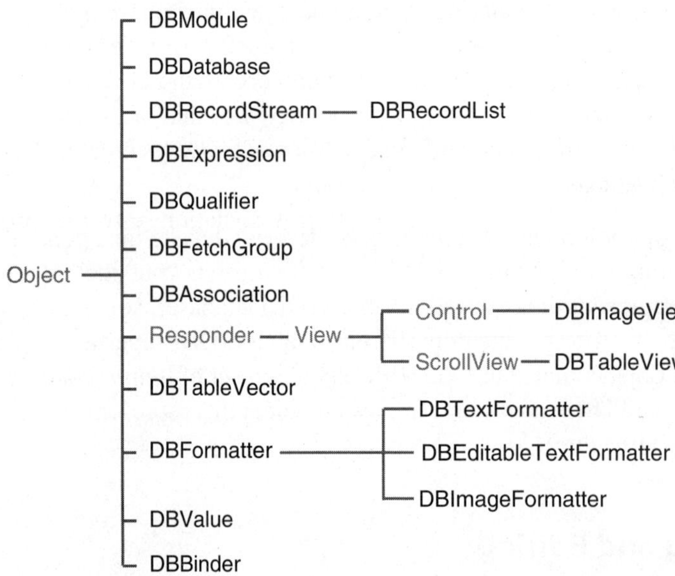

The Database Kit's public classes and protocols may be roughly grouped by function as follows:

High level	DBModule DBValue DBTransactions (protocol)

User interface	DBImageView
	DBTableView
	  DBTableVector
	    DBTableVectors (protocol)
	  DBFormatter
	    DBImageFormatter
	    DBTextFormatter
	  DBEditableFormatter
	    DBFormatterViewEditing (protocol)
	    DBFormatterValidation (informal protocol)

Objectifying database access	DBDatabase
	    DBEntities (protocol)
	    DBProperties (protocol)
	DBQualifier
	DBExpression
	    DBExpressionValues (protocol)
	DBTypes (protocol)

Record buffering	DBRecordStream DBRecordList DBTableDataSources (informal protocol)
View/fetch coordination	DBAssociation DBCustomAssociation (informal protocol) DBFetchGroup

Explicit control of data transfer	DBBinder
	    DBContainers (protocol)
	    DBCursorPositioning (protocol)

Conversion to database formats	DBFormatConversion (protocol) DBFormatInitialization (protocol)

Classes

DBAssociation

Inherits From: Object

Declared In: dbkit/DBAssociation.h

Class Description

A DBAssociation object is the link between a property in a DBRecordList and a user interface object—called the *destination*—that displays and lets the user manipulate values for that property. DBAssociation objects are created and owned by DBFetchGroup objects; a DBFetchGroup automatically creates and configures a DBAssociation for each interface object that it (the DBFetchGroup) manages, so that you never need to create DBAssociation objects directly. In addition, you should rarely need to create a subclass of DBAssociation. (However, if you create your own user interface class to display database values, that class will need to implement some of the DBCustomAssociation category methods.)

You retrieve DBAssociation objects through DBModule's **associationForObject:** method (DBModules manage DBFetchGroups), as explained in the specification for the DBModule class. Once you've gotten a DBAssociation, you should only send it querying messages; you never alter a DBAssociation directly.

Instance Variables

None declared in this class.

Method Types

Initializing	– initFetchGroup:expression:destination:
Querying the object	– destination – fetchGroup – expression

Manipulating the object	– contentsDidChange – setDestination: – currentRecordDidDelete – endEditing – selectedRowAfter: – selectionDidChange – validateEditing – getValue: – setValue:

Instance Methods

contentsDidChange

– contentsDidChange

Notifies the DBAssociation that the destination's contents have changed. You never invoke this method directly; it's invoked automatically by an internal mechanism.

currentRecordDidDelete

– currentRecordDidDelete

Notifies the DBAssociation that the current record (in the associated DBRecordList) has been deleted. You never invoke this method directly; it's invoked automatically by an internal mechanism.

destination

– destination

Returns the user interface object that's associated with this DBAssociation.

endEditing

– endEditing

Tells the DBAssociation to disallow further editing in the user interface object. You never invoke this method directly; it's invoked automatically by an internal mechanism.

expression

– **expression**

Returns the DBExpression that represents the property associated with this DBAssociation.

fetchGroup

– **fetchGroup**

Returns the DBFetchGroup that owns this DBAssociation.

getValue:

– **getValue:***value*

Instructs the DBAssociation to copy the value from its destination into *value*. You never invoke this method directly; it's invoked automatically by an internal mechanism.

initFetchGroup:expression:destination:

– **initFetchGroup:***aFetchGroup* **expression:***anExpr* **destination:**aDest

Initializes an instance of DBAssociation such that *anExpr*, a DBExpression object that represents a property in a DBRecordList, is associated with the destination *aDest*. The DBAssociation will be owned by *aFetchGroup*. You never invoke this method directly; it's invoked automatically by the owning DBFetchGroup object.

setDestination:

– **setDestination:***newDestination*

Sets the DBAssociation's destination. You should rarely need to invoke this method directly. Returns **self**.

selectedRowAfter:

– (unsigned int)**selectedRowAfter:**(unsigned int)*previousRow*

Returns the index of a row in the DBAssociation's destination to which this association is linked. You never invoke this method directly; it's invoked automatically by an internal mechanism.

selectionDidChange

– **selectionDidChange**

Notifies the DBAssociation that there has been some sort of change in the current row of the DBFetchGroup. You never invoke this method directly; it's invoked automatically by an internal mechanism.

setValue:

– **setValue:***value*

Sets a value in the DBAssociation's DBRecordList. You never invoke this method directly; it's invoked automatically by an internal mechanism.

validateEditing

– **validateEditing**

Invokes validation for the DBAssociation's destination after editing. You never invoke this method directly; it's invoked automatically by an internal mechanism.

DBBinder

Inherits From: Object

Conforms To: DBCursorPositioning

Declared In: dbkit/DBBinder.h

Class Description

The DBBinder class provides a mechanism for connecting individual data items in a database to particular objects, variables, and methods in your application. Most applications benefit by avoiding DBBinders and working instead with higher-level classes such as DBRecordList or DBRecordStream. You should create and use DBBinder objects only if your application needs to augment or modify the functionality provided by DBRecordStream or DBRecordList.

Preparing a DBBinder

To access a database, a DBBinder must be initialized and associated with a database model through a DBDatabase object, as shown below:

```
/* Initialize the DBBinder through the init method.  */
DBBinder *myBinder = [[DBBinder alloc] init];

/* Associate it with a DBDatabase through the setDatabase: method.  */
[myBinder setDatabase:myDB];
```

Furthermore, the DBBinder must be informed of which properties in which tables in the database it should accommodate. There are two ways to do this:

- If you can determine the list of properties that you're interested in, you should inform the DBBinder through the **setProperties:** method. As a convenience, the **initForDatabase:withProperties:andQualifier:** method lets you initialize the DBBinder and set its DBDatabase and property list (and an optional property qualifier) in a single breath. An example of this method is given in the next section.

- Alternatively, you can describe the properties that you want as an expression in the database's query language, passing the expression (a string) as the argument to the **evaluateString:** method, as shown below:

```
/* Select all the properties in the "Weight" table.  */
[myBinder evaluateString:"select * in Weight"];
```

The optional qualifier described as part of the **initForDatabase:...** method can be set separately, through the **setQualifier:** method. The qualifier, of which there can be but one at a time per DBBinder, is used to filter properties when the DBBinder is told to select data from the database. (See the "Qualification" section, below for more on the qualifier.)

Records and Containers

The pith of a DBBinder is a collection of objects that hold records from a database table. Each object, called a *record*, holds one record from the database. The collection of a DBBinder's record-holding objects is stored in a *container* object. Record and container objects, however, aren't built into the DBBinder class—you have to specify what sorts of objects you want to assume these two roles.

Specifying a container is easy, you invoke the **setContainer:** method, passing an object that conforms to the DBContainers protocol. That object will be used by the DBBinder to store record objects when the DBBinder fetches from the database. Barring any specialized requirements, a DBBinder is well served using a List object as its container (DBBinder defines a List category that allows a List to pose as a DBContainers-conforming object). You can also use a DBBinder without setting its container. For a container-less DBBinder, fetching data is done one record at a time and can only step forward through the database.

Setting a record object takes a bit more thought. There are two general approaches: You can specify an object yourself that will be copied for each record, or you can let the DBBinder create and assemble a class dynamically, instances of which it will then create to store records.

The first approach centers around the **setRecordPrototype:** method. To this method you pass an object that will be copied as records are fetched from the table, one copy per record. But you're not done yet. To actually get a record's property values into a copy of the prototype record object, you must create an association between each property and one of the record object's instance variables, or between a property and a pair of methods, one to set and the other to retrieve the property's value. These associations are created through the **associateRecordIvar:withProperty:** and **associateRecordSelectors::withProperty:** methods. You can mix and match associations within a record object such that some properties are associated with instance variables and others are associated with method pairs, but a single property can only be associated with one variable or one pair of methods.

For example, let's say you want to access a table that contains information about convicted felons. Furthermore, you're only interested in a felon's name and the length of his or her sentence. To accommodate the records in the table you create a class called FelonRecord, for which the interface file might look like this:

```
@interface FelonRecord : Object
{
   char *name;
   float sentence;
}
...
@end
```

Having connected to the database and the table (as described in the DBDatabase class and DBEntities protocol descriptions), you would create a DBBinder object, set the record prototype, and associate the appropriate properties with the designated instance variables:

```
DBDatabase myDB;
id felonTable;
id nameProp, sentenceProp;
List *propList = [[List alloc] initCount:2];
DBBinder *aBinder;

/* Get the database, entity, and properties.  */
myDB = [DBDatabase findDatabaseNamed:"Crime Data" connect:YES];
felonTable = [myDB entityNamed:"Convicts"];
nameProp = [felonTable propertyNamed:"Name"];
sentenceProp = [felonTable propertyNamed:"Sentence Length"];
[propList addObject:nameProp];
[propList addObject:sentenceProp];

/* Initialize the binder.  */
aBinder = [[DBBinder alloc] initForDatabase:myDB
                            withProperties:propList
                            andQualifier:nil];

/* Set the container, record prototype, and associations.  */
[aBinder setContainer:[[List alloc] init]];
[aBinder setRecordPrototype:[[FelonRecord alloc] init]];
[aBinder associateRecordIvar:"name" withProperty:nameProp];
[aBinder associateRecordIvar:"sentence" withProperty:sentenceProp];
```

The DBBinder is now ready to fetch records from the table (as described in the following section).

The other approach to creating a record object prototype requires less work and is more adaptable, but it's also less controllable. It centers around the method **createRecordPrototype**. When a DBBinder receives a **createRecordPrototype** message, it creates and assembles, while you wait, a class (by default, a subclass of Object) that will be used to create record objects. This new class defines a set of instance variables that match, in number, name, and type, the properties that the DBBinder knows about (as set through the methods described in the previous section, and possibly modified by **addProperty:** and **removePropertyAt:**). When a record is fetched, an instance of the class is created and its instance variables are bound to the record's properties. Fetching (through the **fetch** method) automatically invokes **createRecordPrototype**, thus you needn't invoke it yourself.

You can prepare the dynamic record class through two DBBinder class methods:

- **setDynamicRecordClassName:** takes a string argument that's used to name the class that DBBinder will create; by default, DBBinder gives the class an arbitrary, but unique, name. The argument that you pass must itself be a unique class name—it *mustn't* name an existing class.
- **setDynamicRecordSuperclassName:** also takes a string argument that names a class, but for this method the named class *must* exist. It's used as the superclass for the class that DBBinder will create (which, as mentioned above, is Object by default). This is of particular use if you've created a class whose set of instance variables are known to match, to some extent, the properties in the table that you're binding to. If the set isn't complete, the subclass (the class that DBBinder will create) will be given a sufficient number of additional instance variables.

Warning: Since these are class methods, invoking either of them will affect all subsequent invocations of **createRecordPrototype** for all DBBinder instances. Classes that were previously created are unaffected.

Of the two approaches, the **setRecordPrototype:** method takes priority. Reinforcing this, you shouldn't send **createRecordPrototype** to a DBBinder that has previously received a **setRecordPrototype:** message.

Using a DBBinder

The point of all this, of course, is to gain access to the data in the actual database. Having set up your DBBinder, you can command it to retrieve data through the **select**, **selectWithoutFetching**, and **fetch** methods (**select** performs a select and a fetch; **selectWithoutFetching** just selects). The **insert**, **update**, and **delete** methods write data back to the database. In addition, the **evaluateString:** method can be used to command the adaptor associated with the DBBinder's DBDatabase to evaluate the given string, and thereby produce data or modify data.

After fetching data into a DBBinder's record objects, you can point to a particular record by positioning the "cursor" in the container. This is done through the DBCursorPositioning protocol methods such as **setNext** and **setTo:**. (If the DBBinder doesn't have a container, then only the **setNext** method can be used; in this case, **setNext** causes a fetch to be performed.)

Having positioned the cursor, you can retrieve a DBValue object from the pointed-to record for a particular property through the **valueForProperty:** method. You can then examine and modify the DBValue; any changes you make will be imprinted on the record in the DBBinder and will be written back to the database when the DBBinder receives an **update** message.

The DBBinder class also provides an asynchronous fetch mechanism, provoked by the **fetchInThread** method. When the DBBinder receives a **fetchInThread** message, it creates a separate thread in which the fetch is performed. (Note that asynchronous fetching requires containers.) To check on the progress of a threaded fetch, use the method **checkThreadedFetchCompletion:**.

Qualification

You can give a DBBinder a DBQualifier object through the **setQualifier:** or **initForDatabase:withProperties:andQualifier:** method. The DBQualifier is applied to data that's obtained through DBBinder's fetch and select methods; note, however, that it isn't used by **evaluateString:**.

Instance Variables

id **database**;
id **recordPrototype**;
id **container**;
id **delegate**;

database	The DBDatabase object with which this DBBinder is associated.
recordPrototype	A template for the DBBinder's record objects.
container	The repository for record objects.
delegate	The receiver of notification messages.

Adopted Protocols

DBCursorPositioning	– setFirst – setNext – setPrevious – setLast – setTo: – currentPosition

Method Types

Initializing	– init – initForDatabase:withProperties:andQualifier: – free
Connecting to a database	– database – setDatabase:
Managing properties	– getProperties: – setProperties: – addProperty: – removePropertyAt:
Managing the qualifier	– qualifier – setQualifier:
Managing the container	– container – setContainer: – setFlushEnabled: – isFlushEnabled – setFreeObjectsOnFlush: – areObjectsFreedOnFlush
Managing the record prototype	+ setDynamicRecordSuperclassName: + setDynamicRecordClassName: – setRecordPrototype: – createRecordPrototype – ownsRecordPrototype – recordPrototype – associateRecordIvar:withProperty: – associateRecordSelectors::withProperty: – valueForProperty:

Ordering and ignoring records	– addRetrieveOrder:for: – removeRetrieveOrderFor: – retrieveOrderFor: – positionInOrderingsFor: – ignoresDuplicateResults – setIgnoresDuplicateResults:
Accessing the database	– fetch – select – selectWithoutFetching – insert – update – delete – evaluateString: – adaptorWillEvaluateString:
Fetching in a thread	– fetchInThread – cancelFetch – checkThreadedFetchCompletion
Limiting a fetch	– setMaximumRecordsPerFetch: – maximumRecordsPerFetch – recordLimitReached
Using the shared cursor for several binders	– setSharesContext: – sharesContext
Managing general resources	– reset – flush – scratchZone
Appointing a delegate	– delegate – setDelegate:
Archiving	– read: – write:

Class Methods

setDynamicRecordClassName:

+ **setDynamicRecordClassName:**(const char *)*aName*

Sets the name of the record class that's dynamically created and assembled by the **createRecordPrototype** method. The argument must *not* name an existing class; if it does, invocations of **createRecordPrototype** will fail. An argument of NULL erases the previously established class name. Lacking the instruction provided by this method, the DBBinder class creates a class name that's arbitrary and unique. The dynamic record class mechanism only applies to DBBinder objects that have no prototype record objects; in other words, it applies only to DBBinders that haven't received a **setRecordPrototype:** message. See the class description above for a detailed description of the dynamic record class mechanism. Returns **self**, regardless of the viability of the argument.

See also: + **setDynamicRecordSuperclassName:**, – **setRecordPrototype:**

setDynamicRecordSuperclassName:

+ **setDynamicRecordSuperclassName:**(const char *)*aName*

Identifies, by name, the class that's used as the superclass of the record classes that are created by **createRecordPrototype**. The argument must name an existing class; if it doesn't, invocations of **createRecordPrototype** will fail. By default, dynamic record classes are subclasses of Object; an argument of NULL to this method will return the superclass to the default. The dynamic record class mechanism only applies to DBBinder objects that have no prototype record objects; in other words, it applies only to DBBinders that haven't received a **setRecordPrototype:** message. See the class description above for a detailed description of the dynamic record class mechanism. Returns **self**, regardless of the viability of the argument.

See also: + **setDynamicRecordClassName:**, – **setRecordPrototype:**

Instance Methods

acceptValues:forProperty:

– **acceptValues:**(BOOL) *flag* **forProperty:**(id <DBProperties>)*aProperty*

Establishes whether the given property will accept values from the database. By default, all properties are set to accept values. This method is typically invoked by the adaptor that's associated with the DBBinder's DBDatabase to proclaim that certain properties don't correspond to actual categories in the database—for example, a property that represents a relationship (as created by a database model file) would be set to not accept values.

See also: – **propertyAcceptsValues:**, – **provideValues:forProperty:**, – **qualifyValues:forProperty:**

adaptorWillEvaluateString:

– (BOOL)**adaptorWillEvaluateString:**(const unsigned char *)*aString*

Returns YES if the adaptor associated with the DBBinder's DBDatabase object will accept the given string for evaluation, otherwise returns NO. (This is determined by sending a **binder:willEvaluateString:** message to the DBDatabase.)

See also: – **binder:willEvaluateString:** (DBDatabase)

addProperty:

– **addProperty:***anObject*

Adds the given object (which should conform to the DBProperties protocol) to the DBBinder's list of properties that it's interested in. The list can't contain duplicates; if the property is already present, the addition isn't performed. The return value should be ignored.

Typically, you only use this method if you're building the DBBinder's property list incrementally, and so will rely on the DBBinder to create a record class dynamically. If you're setting your own prototype record object (through **setRecordPrototype:**), you should, rather than use this method, inform the DBBinder of its properties all at once, through **initForDatabase:withProperties:andQualifier:** or **setProperties:**.

See also: – **setProperties:**, – **getProperties:**, – **removePropertyAt:**

addRetrieveOrder:for:

– **addRetrieveOrder:**(DBRetrieveOrder)*anOrder* **for:**(id <DBProperties>)*aProperty*

Establishes the order in which records are retrieved from the database (and stored in the DBBinder's container). Using the value of the *aProperty* property as a retrieval "key," records are retrieved in least-to-greatest or greatest-to-least order, as *anOrder* is DB_AscendingOrder or DB_DescendingOrder. If *anOrder* is DB_NoOrder, the default, the property is removed from the retrieval order scheme. Returns **self**.

You can invoke this method for as many properties as you choose, but the order in which the invocations are performed is important: The first invocation establishes the primary retrieval order property, the second establishes the secondary such property, and so on. If two or more records have the same value for their primary properties, their order is determined according to the values of their secondary properties. If they still can't be distinguished, the decision falls to the tertiary properties, and so on.

Note well that it's the adaptor—not the DBBinder—that retrieves records. If the adaptor that you're using doesn't support the notion of an ordered retrieval, then this method is for naught.

See also: – **retrieveOrderFor:**, – **removeRetrieveOrderFor:**, – **positionInOrderingsFor:**

areObjectsFreedOnFlush

– (BOOL)**areObjectsFreedOnFlush**

Returns YES if the objects in the DBBinder's container are freed when the DBBinder is flushed, otherwise returns NO. Flushing is explained in the description of the **flush** method. By default, the objects are freed.

See also: – **setFreeObjectsOnFlush:**, – **setFlushEnabled:**

associateRecordIvar:withProperty:

– **associateRecordIvar:**(const char *)*variableName*
  withProperty:(id <DBProperties>)*aProperty*

Associates the record object instance variable named *variableName* with the given property such that when a record is fetched from the database, the value of the named instance variable (in the record object that's created to hold the record) is set to the value at the property. The property's value is coerced, if possible, to match the data type of the instance variable. If *aProperty* isn't in the DBBinder's list of properties, the association isn't made and **nil** is returned, otherwise non-**nil** is returned.

You should only invoke this method if you're setting your own prototype record object (through the **setRecordPrototype:** method). Furthermore, the prototype record must already be set when you invoke this method, and it must contain an instance variable with the given name. Failing these, the association isn't made (although the return value will still be non-**nil**).

Rather than associate a property with an instance variable, you can associate it with a pair of instance methods, through the **associateRecordSelectors:withProperty:** method. However, a single property can be associated with only one instance variable or one method pair; invoking this method with a particular property undoes the effect of a previous invocation of this or of the **associateRecordSelectors:withProperty:** method for that property.

See also: – **associateRecordSelectors::withProperty:**

associateRecordSelectors::withProperty:

– **associateRecordSelectors:**(SEL)*set*
:(SEL)*get*
withProperty:(id <DBProperties>)*aProperty*

Associates the record object instance methods *set* and *get* with the given property such that when a record is fetched from the database, the value at the property is set through the *set* method, and when the record is written back to the database, the value is retrieved through the *get* method. Either or both of the selector arguments may be NULL. If non-NULL, the *set* method must take exactly one argument, the value that's being set; the *get* method must take no arguments. The data type of the value returned by the *get* method should match that of the *set* method's argument.

You should only invoke this method if you're setting your own prototype record object (through the **setRecordPrototype:** method). Furthermore, the prototype record must have already been set, and the object must respond to the *set* and *get* methods (if they're non-NULL). If it doesn't respond, or if *aProperty* isn't in the DBBinder's list of properties, the association isn't made and **nil** is returned. Otherwise, the method returns non-**nil.**

Rather than associate a property with a pair of methods, you can associate it with an instance variable, through the **associateRecordIvar:withProperty:** method. However, a single property can be associated with only one instance variable or one method pair; invoking this method with a particular property undoes the effect of a previous invocation of this or of the **associateRecordIvar:withProperty:** method for that property.

See also: – **associateRecordIvar:withProperty:**

cancelFetch

– **cancelFetch**

Interrupts an asynchronous fetch. You can also use this method after a successful synchronous fetch to ensure that idle resources are reclaimed.

See also: – **fetchInThread**, – **fetch**, – **fetchDone:** (DBDatabase)

checkThreadedFetchCompletion:

– **checkThreadedFetchCompletion:**(double)*timeout*

If you're not using the Application Kit's event loop, you should invoke this message after an asynchronous fetch to ensure that the delegate message **binderDidFetch:** is sent. The argument is the maximum amount of time, in seconds, to wait before returning. Returns

nil (and the message isn't sent) if the time limit expires before the fetch completes, otherwise returns **self**.

See also: – **fetchInThread**

container

– (id <DBContainers>)**container**

Returns the DBBinder's container object, as set through **setContainer:**. The container, which must conform to the DBContainers protocol, holds the record objects that are created when the DBBinder fetches data. A DBBinder has no default container and can operate without one, although this impedes some of the object's functionality. Lacking a container, a DBBinder can't perform an asynchronous fetch, and its cursor can only be positioned through the **setNext** method.

See also: – **setContainer:**

createRecordPrototype

– **createRecordPrototype**

Creates and assembles a class that's used to create record objects. The class is given sufficient instance variables to hold the DBBinder's properties (one instance variable per property). By default, the name of the class that's created is arbitrary and unique and its superclass is Object. You can change these settings through the **setDynamicRecordClass:** and **setDynamicRecordSuperclass:** class methods. This method has no effect and returns **nil** under the following conditions:

- If the DBBinder's current prototype record object isn't **nil**.
- If the DBBinder has no properties.
- If the name set through **setDynamicRecordClass:** names an existing class.
- If the class named by **setDynamicRecordSuperclass:** doesn't exist.

Upon success, this method returns the class that it created.

This method is automatically invoked when the DBBinder fetches data, thus you needn't invoke it directly. In general, it's a good idea to never invoke this method; however, if you do—for example, to examine the return value—you should send a **setRecordPrototype:nil** message to the DBBinder before the next fetch to ensure that the correct class will be assembled.

See also: + **setDynamicRecordClass:**, + **setDynamicRecordSuperclass:**

database

– (DBDatabase *)**database**

Returns the DBDatabase object that's associated with the DBBinder.

See also: – **initForDatabase:withProperties:andQualifier:**, – **setDatabase:**

delegate

– **delegate**

Returns the object that will receive notification messages for the DBBinder.

See also: – **setDelegate:**

delete

– **delete**

Deletes from the database each of the DBBinder's record objects.

Before the operation begins, a **binderWillDelete:** message is sent to the DBBinder's delegate (with the DBBinder as the argument); if the delegate message returns NO, then the deletion isn't performed and this method returns **nil**. After all the records have been processed, the DBBinder is flushed. If the records were successfully deleted, a **binderDidDelete:** message is sent to the delegate and **self** is returned, otherwise the delegate message isn't sent and **nil** is returned.

As each record is deleted, one of two messages is sent to the container's delegate (if the DBBinder has a container, if the container has a delegate, and if the delegate implements the method):

- **binder:didAcceptObject:** if the record was deleted.
- **binder:didRejectObject:** is sent if the record couldn't be deleted.

For both methods, the first argument is the DBBinder and the second is the record object. The values returned by these methods are ignored.

See also: – **deleteData:** (DBDatabase)

evaluateString:

– (BOOL)**evaluateString:**(const unsigned char *)*aString*

Tells the adaptor to evaluate and execute the commands that are encoded in *aString*. The DBBinder's qualifier *isn't* applied to the evaluation.

Before the evaluation is performed, a **binder:willEvaluateString:** message is sent to the DBBinder's delegate. If the delegate message returns NO, then the evaluation isn't performed and this method immediately returns NO.

The evaluation itself is performed by sending an **evaluateString:using:** message to the DBDatabase, passing *aString* and **self** as the arguments. Before the message is sent, the DBBinder is flushed. If the DBDatabase message returns NO, then this method returns NO, otherwise a **binder:didEvaluateString:** message is sent to the delegate and YES is returned.

See also: – **evaluateString:using:** (DBDatabase)

fetch

– **fetch**

Fetches data from the database and places it in the DBBinder's record objects. If the DBBinder has a container, the container is filled with record objects until it contains the number of records set by **setMaximumRecordsPerFetch:** or there's no more data to fetch. If the binder has no container, a single record is fetched from the database (however, in that case you should use the **setNext** method, rather than this one, to fetch data).

Before the fetch begins, the DBBinder's delegate is sent a **binderWillFetch:** message; after, it's sent **binderDidFetch:**. If **binderWillFetch:** returns NO, the fetch isn't performed and this method immediately returns **nil**.

The DBDatabase method **fetchData:** is invoked—iteratively if there's a container—to perform the fetch. As each record of data is fetched, a copy of the DBBinder's prototype record object is created to hold the data. If the DBBinder's prototype record hasn't been set, a class is dynamically assembled to fill the need, as explained in the description of **createRecordPrototype**.

The fetch continues until there's no more data to retrieve, or until the previously set record limit (as set through the **setMaximumRecordsPerFetch:** method) has been reached. If the fetch ended because the record limit was reached, the next fetch will continue where the previous one ended.

After the fetch has ended, the DBBinder's cursor is set to the first record in the container (or to the single fetched record if there is no container) and **self** is returned. If there was no data to fetch, or if there's a fetch in progress (and the DBBinder has a container), the cursor isn't set, **fetchDone:** is sent to the DBDatabase, and **nil** is returned.

If the fetch ended by exhausting the source data—in other words, it didn't end because the record limit was reached—you should then invoke **cancelFetch** to reclaim resources that were used during the fetch. Use the **recordLimitReached** method to test whether the fetch ended because it reached the limit while there was more data to fetch.

fetchInThread

– **fetchInThread**

Fetches data asynchronously from the database by performing the fetch in a separate thread. The general mechanism and conditions are as described in the **fetch** method, but with these differences:

- An asynchronous fetch only works if the DBBinder has a container.
- You shouldn't invoke **cancelFetch** after invoking this method unless you actually want to abort the fetch.
- The record limit set through **setMaximumRecordsPerFetch:**has no effect on an asynchronous fetch.

If there is no container, or if the **binderWillFetch:** delegate message returns NO, then the fetch isn't performed and this method returns **nil**. Otherwise, this method returns **self** while the fetch proceeds in the background. When the fetch is complete, the **binderDidFetch:** method is sent to the delegate.

If you're not using the Application Kit's main event loop, you should follow this method with an invocation of **checkThreadedFetchCompletion:** to synchronize the fetch thread with the main thread and to ensure that the **binderDidFetch:** message is sent.

To be used in an asynchronous fetch, the DBBinder's container must be thread-safe (it must be re-entrant). Alternatively, if you limit yourself to DBCursorPositioning methods, such as **setTo:** and **setNext:**, you can access the container regardless of the type of fetch employed.

See also: – **fetch**, – **cancelFetch**, – **checkThreadedFetchCompletion:**

flush

– (BOOL)**flush**

If flushing is enabled, this empties the DBBinder's container. Furthermore, if the DBBinder has been told to free-on-flush, the records that were in the container are freed and the prototype record object is set to **nil**. By default, both flushing and free-on-flush are enabled. Returns YES if flushing is enabled, NO if not.

This method always interrupts a fetch, if one is in progress, whether or not flushing is enabled.

The following DBBinder methods may cause **flush** to be invoked:

- – evaluateString:
- – selectWithoutFetching
- – insert
- – update
- – delete
- – setProperties:
- – reset
- – free

See also: – **setFlushEnabled:**, – **setFreeOnFlush:**

free

– **free**

Frees the DBBinder and its records. If the DBBinder owns the prototype record object, it too is freed.

getProperties:

– (List *)**getProperties:**(List *)*aList*

Fills *aList* with the DBBinder's properties, then returns the List directly and by reference. The order of the properties in the List is that by which they were added to the DBBinder. You mustn't free the contents of *aList*, although you may free the List itself.

See also: – **initForDatabase:withProperties:andQualifier:**, – **setProperties:**, – **addProperty**

ignoresDuplicateResults

– (BOOL)**ignoresDuplicateResults**

Returns YES if the DBBinder is set to ignore duplicate records during a select. The default is YES. The instruction to ignore duplicate results is implemented by including a SELECTDISTINCT in the SQL expression sent to the adaptor. It's up to the adaptor to support this (the Oracle and Sybase adapters supplied with the Database Kit do).

See also: – **setIgnoresDuplicateResults:**

init

– init

The designated initializer for the DBBinder class, **init** initializes and returns the DBBinder. All the objects that the DBBinder owns or knows of, such as its container, properties, DBDatabase, and DBQualifier are set to **nil**. Its boolean attributes are set as follows:

Attribute	Value
flushing enabled?	YES
frees properties on flush?	YES
ignores duplicates?	YES
shares context?	NO

See also: **– initForDatabase:withProperties:andQualifier**

initForDatabase:withProperties:andQualifier:

– initForDatabase:*aDBDatabase*
    withProperties:(List *)*propertyList*
    andQualifier:(DBQualifier *)*aDBQualifier*

Invokes **init** and then sets the DBBinder's DBDatabase, properties, and DBQualifier as given by the arguments. The properties in *propertyList* are added to the DBBinder's own List, thus the argument may be freed.

See also: **– init**

insert

– insert

Inserts into the database each of the DBBinder's record objects.

Before the operation begins, a **binderWillInsert:** message is sent to the DBBinder's delegate (with the DBBinder as the argument); if the delegate message returns NO then the insertion isn't performed and **nil** is immediately returned by this method. After all the records have been processed, the DBBinder is flushed. If the records were successfully inserted, a **binderDidInsert:** message is sent to the delegate and **self** is returned, otherwise the delegate message isn't sent and **nil** is returned.

As each record is inserted, one of two messages is sent to the container's delegate (if the DBBinder has a container, if the container has a delegate, and if the delegate implements the appropriate method):

- **binder:didAcceptObject:** if the record was inserted.
- **binder:didRejectObject:** is sent if the record couldn't be inserted.

For both methods, the first argument is the DBBinder and the second is the record object. The values returned by these methods are ignored.

See also: – **insertData:** (DBDatabase)

isFlushEnabled

– (BOOL)**isFlushEnabled**

Returns YES if the DBBinder has flushing enabled, otherwise return NO. The default is YES. See the description of the **flush** method for more information. (Note that sharing a cursor is incompatible with flushing, so **setSharesContext:** has the side effect of disabling flushing.)

See also: – **flush**, – **setFlushEnabled:**, – **setSharesContext:**

maximumRecordsPerFetch

– (unsigned int)**maximumRecordsPerFetch**

Returns the maximum number of records that will be retrieved during a synchronous fetch, as set through the **setMaximumRecordsPerFetch:** method. By default, this limit is set to DB_NoIndex, which imposes no limit.

See also: – **setMaximumRecordsPerFetch:**, – **recordLimitReached**, – **fetch**

ownsRecordPrototype

– (BOOL)**ownsRecordPrototype**

Returns YES if the DBBinder owns its prototype record object—in other words, if it will create a record class for you (when **createRecordPrototype** is invoked). If you've set the prototype record object yourself, through **setRecordPrototype:**, then this returns NO.

positionInOrderingsFor:

– (unsigned int)**positionInOrderingsFor:**(id <DBProperties>)*aProperty*

Returns an integer that indicates the level (primary, secondary, tertiary, and so on) at which the given property is used to order the records that are retrieved from the database. The ordering position of a particular property is the order in which it was added to the ordering mechanism (amongst the currently "active" ordering properties) through the **addRetrieveOrder:for:** method. A return of DB_NoIndex means that the property isn't used in the ordering mechanism.

See also: – **addRetrieveOrder:For:**

qualifier

– (DBQualifier *)**qualifier**

Returns the DBQualifier object that was set through **setQualifier:** or **initForDatabase: withProperties:andQualifier:**. The qualifier is used to qualify values during a select.

See also: – **setQualifier:**, – **initForDatabase:withProperties:andQualifier:**

read:

– **read:**(NXTypedStream *)*stream*

Reads the DBBinder from the typed stream *stream*. Returns **self**.

recordLimitReached

– (BOOL)**recordLimitReached**

If the previous fetch was stopped because the DBBinder's record limit (as set through the **setMaximumRecordsPerFetch:** method) was reached, then this returns YES. By default, this returns NO; the **flush** method will also set this to return NO, whether or not flushing is enabled. See the description of the **fetch** method for an example of the use this method.

See also: – **setMaximumRecordsPerFetch:**, – **maximumRecordsPerFetch**, – **fetch**

recordPrototype

– **recordPrototype**

Returns the DBBinder's prototype record object. If you've set the object yourself, through **setRecordPrototype:**, then that object is returned. Otherwise, this returns **nil** unless you've previously invoked **createRecordPrototype** directly, or unless this is called from within a subclass implementation of **fetch**.

See also: – **setRecordPrototype**, – **createRecordPrototype**

removePropertyAt:

– **removePropertyAt:**(unsigned int)*index*

Removes the property at the given index. To find the index of a particular property, get the DBBinder's List of properties through the **getProperties:** method, and then ask for the index by sending **indexOf:** to the List, passing the property as the argument. Returns the property (or **nil** if there was none).

See also: – **setProperties:**, – **addProperty:**

removeRetrieveOrderFor:

– **removeRetrieveOrderFor:**(id <DBProperties>)*aProperty*

Removes the given property from the list of properties that are used to sort records as they're being fetched. The property's retrieve order constant is set to DB_NoOrder. Returns **nil** if the property hadn't previously been added to the record-sorting list (if it hadn't previously received an **addRetrieveOrderFor:** message), otherwise **self** is returned.

See also: – **addRetrieveOrderFor:**, – **positionInOrderingsFor:**

reset

– **reset**

Restores the DBBinder to a virgin state. The DBBinder is first flushed (which cancels a fetch, if one is in progress), then the objects that it has allocated, and any that you've allocated in the scratch zone, are freed. The **setProperties:** and **free** methods automatically cause a reset.

See also: – **flush**, – **scratchZone**

retrieveOrderFor:

– (DBRetrieveOrder)**retrieveOrderFor:**(id <DBProperties>)*aProperty*

Returns a constant that indicates the order in which records are retrieved when *aProperty* is used as a retrieval key (see the **addRetrieveOrder:for:** method for a further explanation). The retrieval order constants are:

Constant	Meaning
DB_NoOrder	The property isn't part of the ordering scheme
DB_AscendingOrder	Least to greatest
DB_DescendingOrder	Greatest to least

See also: – **addRetrieveOrder:for:**, – **positionInOrderingsFor:**

scratchZone

– (NXZone *)**scratchZone**

Returns the zone in which the DBBinder allocates the objects that it owns. The objects in the zone are freed during a reset; the zone is made public so you can use it to allocate your own supporting objects and have them freed during a reset as well. Note that the zone may be different after each reset.

See also: – **reset**

select

– **select**

Selects and fetches data from the database. First, **selectWithoutFetching** is invoked; if that returns **nil**, then this returns **nil**. If the method was successful, then **fetch** is invoked; the value returned by **fetch** is returned by this method.

See also: – **selectWithoutFetching**, – **fetch**

selectWithoutFetching

– **selectWithoutFetching**

Selects records from the database, using the DBBinder's qualifier (as set through **setQualifier:** or **initForDatabase:withProperties:andQualifier:**) to qualify the records that are selected.

Before the operation begins, a **binderWillSelect:** message is sent to the DBBinder's delegate (with the DBBinder as the argument); if the delegate message returns NO, then the select isn't performed and **nil** is immediately returned by this method. Otherwise, the DBBinder is flushed, and a **selectData:** message is sent to the DBDatabase. If **selectData:** returns NO, then this method returns **nil.** If the select was successful, a **binderDidSelect:** message is sent to the delegate and **self** is returned, otherwise the delegate message isn't sent and **nil** is returned.

If the DBBinder is set to ignore duplicate results and the adaptor supports this feature (both the Oracle and the Sybase adaptors do), then only the first of duplicate records will be selected.

See also: – **select**, – **setIgnoreDuplicateResults**, – **selectData:** (DBDatabase)

setContainer:

– **setContainer:**(id <DBContainers>)*anObject*

Sets the container that's used to store record objects. The argument must either adopt the DBContainers protocol, or it can be a List object—DBBinder defines a category of List that allows its instances, and those of its subclasses, to pose as DBContainers-conforming objects. Most DBBinders are well served using a List as a container. For more on the theory and practice of containment, see the class description, above.

Returns the previous container.

setDatabase:

– **setDatabase:**(DBDatabase *)*aDatabase*

Sets the DBBinder's database. Returns the previous DBDatabase object.

setDelegate:

– **setDelegate:***anObject*

Sets the object that receives notification messages for the DBBinder.

setFlushEnabled:

– **setFlushEnabled:**(BOOL)*flag*

Establishes whether the DBBinder is capable of being flushed, as explained in the description of the **flush** method. The default is YES.

See also: – **flush**, – **setFreeObjectOnFlush:**

setFreeObjectsOnFlush:

– **setFreeObjectsOnFlush:**(BOOL)*flag*

Establishes whether the DBBinder will free its records when it's flushed. Setting this to YES is effective only if the DBBinder is capable of being flushed, as established by the **setFlushEnabled:** method. The default is YES (the default flush-enablement is also YES).

See also: – **flush**, – **setFlushEnabled:**

setIgnoresDuplicateResults:

– **setIgnoresDuplicateResults:**(BOOL)*flag*

Establishes whether duplicate records are ignored during a select. The default is YES.

The instruction to ignore duplicate results is implemented by including a SELECTDISTINCT in the SQL expression sent to the adaptor. It's up the adaptor to support this; the Oracle and Sybase adapters supplied with the Database Kit do.

See also: – **ignoresDuplicateRecords**, – **selectWithoutFetching**

setMaximumRecordsPerFetch:

– **setMaximumRecordsPerFetch:**(unsigned int)*limit*

Sets, to *limit*, the maximum number of records that will be retrieved during a synchronous fetch. When the limit is reached, the fetch is stopped but the "pointer" into the selected data isn't reset, thus the next fetch will start where the previous one ended. The limit only applies to synchronous fetches; the asynchronous fetch method **fetchInThread** ignores the record limit.

See also: – **maximumRecordsPerFetch**, – **recordLimitReached**, – **fetch**

setProperties:

– (List *)**setProperties:**(List *)*aList*

Resets the DBBinder and then adds to it the properties in *aList*. Returns the argument.

See also: – **getProperties:**, – **addProperty:**, – **removePropertyAt:**

setQualifier:

– **setQualifier:**(DBQualifier *)*aQualifier*

Sets the qualifier that's used during a select. Returns **self**.

See also: – **qualifier**

setRecordPrototype:

– **setRecordPrototype:***anObject*

Sets the object that's copied to store the results of a fetch. See the class description for a full explanation of the record prototype object.

See also: – **recordPrototype**, – **createRecordPrototype**

setSharesContext:

– **setSharesContext:**(BOOL)*flag*

Determines whether the DBBinder shares its cursor with other DBBinders that have done so. The default is NO. Making a DBBinder share its cursor disables flushing. Returns **self**.

Shared cursor behavior depends on the implementation of the adaptor rather than the database; it's provided in both the Oracle and the Sybase adaptors as a way of achieving atomic updates. Sharing the cursor also provides a slightly more efficient use of memory.

See also: – **sharesContext**

sharesContext

– (BOOL)**sharesContext**

Returns YES if the DBBinder shares its cursor with other DBBinders, otherwise returns NO.

See also: – **setSharesContext:**

update

– **update**

Updates the records in the database by sending an **updateData:self** message to the DBDatabase for each of the DBBinder's record objects.

Before the operation begins, a **binderWillUpdate:** message is sent to the DBBinder's delegate (with the DBBinder as the argument); if the delegate message returns NO, then the update isn't performed and **nil** is immediately returned by this method. After all the records have been processed, the DBBinder is flushed. If the records were successfully updated, a **binderDidUpdate:** message is sent to the delegate and **self** is returned, otherwise the delegate message isn't sent and **nil** is returned.

As each record is updated, one of two messages is sent to the container's delegate (if the DBBinder has a container, if the container has a delegate, and if the delegate implements the appropriate method):

- **binder:didAcceptObject:** if the record was updated.
- **binder:didRejectObject:** is sent if the record couldn't be updated.

For both methods, the first argument is the DBBinder and the second is the record object. The values returned by these methods are ignored.

See also: – **updateData:** (DBDatabase)

valueForProperty:

– (DBValue *)**valueForProperty:**(id <DBProperties>)*aProperty*

Returns a DBValue object for the given property of the currently pointed-to record. Use the DBCursorPositioning methods, such as **setNext** and **setTo:**, to set the cursor to point to a particular record. The object that's returned is owned by the DBBinder and shouldn't be freed.

write:

– **write:**(NXTypedStream *)*stream*

Writes the DBBinder to the typed stream *stream*. Returns **self**.

Methods Implemented by the Delegate

binder:didEvaluateString:

– **binder:***aBinder* **didEvaluateString:**(const unsigned char *)*aString*

Invoked after the given string has been successfully evaluated by DBBinder's **evaluateString:** method. The return value is ignored.

binder:willEvaluateString:

– (BOOL)**binder:***aBinder* **willEvaluateString:**(const unsigned char *)*aString*

Invoked before the given string is evaluated by DBBinder's **evaluateString:** method. A return of NO will thwart the evaluation.

binderDidDelete:

– **binderDidDelete:***aBinder*

Invoked after the DBBinder has successfully deleted records through the **delete** method. The return value is ignored.

binderDidFetch:

– **binderDidFetch:***aBinder*

Invoked after the DBBinder has successfully fetched records through the **fetch** or **fetchInThread** method. The return value is ignored.

binderDidInsert:

– **binderDidInsert:***aBinder*

Invoked after the DBBinder has successfully inserted records through the **insert** method. The return value is ignored.

binderDidSelect:

– **binderDidSelect:***aBinder*

Invoked after the DBBinder has successfully selected data through the **selectWithoutFetching** method. The return value is ignored.

binderDidUpdate:

– **binderDidUpdate:***aBinder*

Invoked after the DBBinder has successfully updated the database through the **update** method. The return value is ignored.

binderWillDelete:

– (BOOL)**binderWillDelete:***aBinder*

Invoked before the DBBinder attempts to delete records from the database through the **delete** method. A return of NO will thwart the attempt.

binderWillFetch:

– (BOOL)**binderWillFetch:***aBinder*

Invoked before the DBBinder attempts to fetch data through the **fetch** or **fetchInThread** method. A return of NO will thwart the attempt.

binderWillInsert:

– (BOOL)**binderWillInsert:***aBinder*

Invoked before the DBBinder attempts to insert records into the database through the **insert** method. A return of NO will thwart the attempt.

binderWillSelect:

– (BOOL)**binderWillSelect:***aBinder*

Invoked before the DBBinder attempts to select data from the database through the **selectWithoutFetching** method. A return of NO will thwart the attempt.

binderWillUpdate:

– (BOOL)**binderWillUpdate:***aBinder*

Invoked before the DBBinder attempts to update the database through the **update** method. A return of NO will thwart the attempt.

DBDatabase

Inherits From: Object

Declared In: dbkit/DBDatabase.h

Class Description

A DBDatabase object acts as a representation of an external database. Your application sends messages to the DBDatabase object as if it were the database; the DBDatabase object then forwards them to an adaptor that knows how to translate and format the messages appropriately for the type of database the application is using. In a high level application—that is, one built by dragging one or more DBModules from Interface Builder's database palette—the DBModules will in fact make use of a DBDatabase as their intermediary for communication with the database, but your application will not need to create or address DBDatabase objects directly.

A DBDatabase object maintains:

- A connection to the database
- A model of the database's entities
- The use of transactions to treat a sequence of operations as an indivisible "atom"

Only if your application needs more specific control of any of those areas should it make explicit use of a DBDatabase object. For example, you might want to regulate the database connection directly, to discover the database's entities independently of their description in the model file, or to establish your own transaction boundaries.

Class methods in DBDatabase can supply the names of databases that are available in your computing environment. The class gets this information by scanning standard directory paths for database models and database adaptors, residing in bundles identified by the extensions ".dbmodel" and ".adaptor".

To use a database, your application (either explicitly, or through its DBModule) creates a DBDatabase object. The application opens a connection to the database and reads or writes data by sending messages to the DBDatabase object. If your application uses several different databases, or several models of the same database, it will need a separate DBDatabase object for each model of each database.

The DBDatabase's Adaptor and its Model

To gain access to data in the database, each DBDatabase object must have:

- An *adaptor* that manages communication with the database
- A *model* of the data that the database contains

An adaptor is specific to a type of database or DBMS product. It acts as a sort of delegate for your DBDatabase object (or objects). The adaptor contains the DBMS-specific code for accessing a particular vendor's client library. You communicate with the database primarily by sending messages to a DBDatabase object, which passes them to the adaptor you have designated, which in turn translates them and relays them to the database server.

A model contains data dictionary information, as well as other information used to map the Database Kit's high-level model to the lower-level database structure. The model defines what you can talk about in framing requests to the database. It lists the entities in a particular database, and their attributes and relationships. The model doesn't have to describe everything in the database; it's only required to cover the entities, attributes, and relationships your application may use.

When first instantiated, a DBDatabase has no data model and no adaptor. There are two main ways the DBDatabase object can obtain its model:

- By loading a previously prepared model from a model file
- By asking the database to supply a model (called the *default* model)

In addition to the list of entities and attributes, a model file may contain other useful information about the database and its use. This typically includes the name of the adaptor that the database requires, a default login string for connecting to it, and perhaps specific login strings for individual users of the application.

The DBDatabase's Records

To access data in the database, the usual procedure is to create an instance of DBRecordStream (for sequential access) or its subclass DBRecordList (for random access). The sections on those two classes describe their methods to fetch, save, or update data. Those methods makes use of an intermediate class called DBBinder. Many applications will require never need to make any explicit mention of a DBBinder. However, to support applications that choose to deal directly with their DBBinders, the DBDatabase class provides certain methods that typically are invoked from a DBBinder and therefore identify the sending DBBinder in their argument.

Delegate

Before executing certain database operations, the DBDatabase object notifies its delegate; if you implement the corresponding methods in the delegate, the delegate can insert a check on those operations before they're passed to the database. It can also receive notification of commands to commit or roll back a transaction. The delegate may also implement a logging system. When logging is enabled, the delegate writes a record of each command sent to the database.

Instance Variables

id **delegate**;

delegate	The object that receives notification messages

Method Types

Initializing the class	+ initialize
Reporting what's available	+ adaptorNames + databaseNamesForAdaptor:
Initializing an instance	– initFromFile:
Describing the model source	– directory – name – setName: – currentAdaptorName – defaultAdaptorName – defaultLoginString – currentLoginString – loginStringForUser:
Describing the database model	– entityNamed: – getEntities:
Revising the data dictionary	– emptyDataDictionary – loadDefaultDataDictionary

Connecting to the database	+ findDatabaseNamed:connect: – connect – connectUsingString: – connectUsingAdaptor:andString: – disconnect – disconnectUsingString: – isConnected – connectionName
Managing transactions	– beginTransaction – rollbackTransaction – commitTransaction – isTransactionInProgress – areTransactionsEnabled – enableTransactions:
Using a delegate	– delegate – setDelegate:
Evaluating an arbitrary string	– evaluateString:
Controlling the user interface	– arePanelsEnabled – setPanelsEnabled:
Archiving	– read: – write:

Class Methods

adaptorNames

+ (const char **)**adaptorNames**

Returns a list of the names of adaptors available to the DBDatabase class.

The DBDatabase class maintains a list of adaptor names. It initially constructs the list by searching the application's bundle and then the directories **~/Library/Adaptors**, **/usr/local/lib/Adaptors**, **/LocalLibrary/Adaptors**, and finally **/NextLibrary/Adaptors**. It searches for bundles whose names have the extension ".adaptor". The list returned contains the set of distinct adaptor names, without the extension or the path. (Thus a local adaptor shadows another adaptor of the same name.)

databaseNamesForAdaptor:

+ (const char **)**databaseNamesForAdaptor:**(const char *)*anAdaptorName*

Returns a list of the names of databases that the named adaptor serves. Typically, an adaptor class serves a single type of database, but might be used with any of several databases of the same type. An adaptor instance connects to a single database.

A DBDatabase object can be identified either by its **id** or by an arbitrary name. Assigning a name to a DBDatabase object (through the **setName:** method) adds that name to a table maintained by the DBDatabase class. Each name in the table identifies exactly one DBDatabase. The class initially constructs the list by searching the application's bundle and then the directories **~/Library/Databases**, **/usr/local/lib/Databases**, **/LocalLibrary/Databases**, and finally **/NextLibrary/Databases**. It searches for bundles whose names have the extension ".dbmodel".

If the argument is NULL, the method returns the names of databases for all available model files.

findDatabaseNamed:connect:

+ **findDatabaseNamed:**(const char *)*aName*
  connect:(BOOL)*flag*

Returns the already instantiated DBDatabase having the specified name, if one exists. If no DBDatabase of that name has been instantiated, the method searches the table maintained by the DBDatabase class, and then (if it finds no match there) through a standard sequence of directory paths for a file named *aName*.**dbmodel**. The path sequence is **~/Library/Databases**, **/LocalLibrary/Databases**, and finally **/NextLibrary/Databases**.

If the method finds *aName* for which no DBDatabase object has yet been instantiated, it creates a new DBDatabase object, initializes it and then loads into it the database description it finds in the model file.

When *flag* is YES and there is not yet a connection to the database, the method makes the connection, using the default login string and the adaptor identified in the database description just loaded.

Returns the DBDatabase object (whether previously existing or just created). However, returns **nil** if *aName* wasn't found, or if *flag* was YES but the method wasn't able to connect to the database. When the method attempts to connect but is unsuccessful, the method also frees the DBDatabase object, so that subsequent use of the same method with the same database bundle will require a new DBDatabase object (and a fresh loading of the database description). A DBDatabase object returned by **findDatabaseNamed:connect:** should never be freed.

initialize

+ **initialize**

Initializes the class object. The **initialize** message is sent for you before the class object receives any other message; you never send an **initialize** message directly. Returns **self**.

Instance Methods

arePanelsEnabled

– (BOOL)**arePanelsEnabled**

Reports whether (when connecting to a remote database) the DBDatabase object will prompt the user for required items that it didn't find in the database bundle. Items for which the DBDatabase may prompt the user include login string, user name, password and alert panels.

An application designed for interactive use will usually run with panels enabled, whereas one that is run as a batch or background job without a user interface must run with panels disabled.

Returns YES if panels are enabled, NO otherwise. The default at initialization is YES.

areTransactionsEnabled

– (BOOL)**areTransactionsEnabled**

Reports whether the transaction facility is enabled in the adaptor through which the database is connected. Returns YES if the database is connected and transactions are enabled.

beginTransaction

– (BOOL)**beginTransaction**

Signals the adaptor that a transaction is about to begin. The database then takes whatever action it provides for safeguarding a transaction; typically, it groups all changes that follow so that they can be combined in a single operation. If it subsequently must roll back the changes, the original data remains intact.

Returns YES if there is a connection to the database, the adaptor has the transactions facility enabled, and no transaction is already in progress.

See also: – commitTransaction, – rollbackTransaction

commitTransaction

– (BOOL)**commitTransaction**

Causes a transaction started with **beginTransaction** to be committed. Any changes to the data that have been queued up since the previous **beginTransaction** will be irreversibly made in the database. Returns YES if the transaction was committed: that is, if a transaction was in progress and the database was able to commit it successfully. If the database server supports referential integrity and these integrity checks fail, this method returns NO.

Important: A return of NO does *not* mean that the transaction has been closed. It remains open. That way, the application retains the option to take remedial action before trying again to commit. The transaction will remain open until **rollbackTransaction** is called.

If the delegate implements **db:log:** (to maintain a log file), each use of **commitTransaction** generates a log entry containing the name of the method and text indicating whether the cancellation succeeded or failed.

See also: – **rollbackTransaction**

connect

– (BOOL)**connect**

Opens a connection to the database, using the default login string. If no adaptor has been specified, the connection is established through the default adaptor. Returns YES if the connection was successfully established or already existed. Invoking this method is equivalent to invoking **connectUsingString:** with *aString* set to NULL.

If the delegate implements **db:log:** (to maintain a log file), each use of **connect** generates a log entry containing the name of the method and language-specific text indicating success or failure.

See also: **connectUsingString:**

connectionName

– (const unsigned char *)**connectionName**

Returns the name of the adaptor's current connection to a database, or NULL if there is no adaptor or the adopter is not connected to a database. When an adaptor establishes a connection to a database, it retains the name of the database to which it is connected.

connectUsingAdaptor:andString:

– (BOOL)**connectUsingAdaptor:**(const char *)*aClassname*
andString:(const unsigned char *)*aString*

Opens a connection to the database by way of the adaptor identified by *aClassname*, using the login string *aString*. When the connection is established (or already exists), the method asks the database for its default data dictionary and loads it into the DBDatabase object.

If *aClassName* is the same as the name of the adaptor that the DBDatabase is already using, this method simply continues to use it. But if *aClassName* differs from the name of the current adaptor, or there is no current adaptor, the method instantiates one from the adaptor bundle named *aClassName*, replacing the former instance, if any. (The DBDatabase class maintains a list of known adaptor bundles and database bundles; see the discussion of **adaptorNames**.) If the login string *aString* is NULL, the method uses the default login string.

Returns YES if the connection is made (or already existed). If the delegate implements **db:log:** (to maintain a log file), each use of **connectUsingAdaptorNamed:andLoginString:** generates a log entry containing the name of the method and language-specific text indicating success or failure.

See also: **connectUsingString:**

connectUsingString:

– (BOOL)**connectUsingString:**(const unsigned char *)*aString*

Instructs the adaptor to connect to the database, using the login string *aString*. If *aString* is NULL, uses the default login string.

Returns YES when the method makes a new connection to the database, and NO if the database is already connected (or no connection can be made). If the delegate implements **db:log:** (to maintain a log file), each use of **connectUsingString:** generates a log entry containing the name of the method and language-specific text indicating success or failure.

See also: **connectUsingAdaptorNamed:andLoginString:**

currentAdaptorName

– (const char *)**currentAdaptorName**

Returns the name of the current adaptor, or NULL if none has been set.

(The name of an adaptor to be used by default is among the items stored in the bundle from which the DBDatabase object was initialized; however, the method **connectUsingAdaptorNamed:andString:** can specify a different adaptor.)

currentLoginString

– (const unsigned char *)**currentLoginString**

Returns the text of the current login string, or NULL if none has been set.

defaultAdaptorName

– (const char *)**defaultAdaptorName**

Returns the name of the adaptor that will be used by default. (The name of the default adaptor is among the items stored in the bundle from which the DBDatabase object was initialized.)

defaultLoginString

– (const unsigned char *)**defaultLoginString**

Returns the text of the login string that will be used by default when the adaptor connects to the database. (The default login string is among the items stored in the bundle from which the DBDatabase object was initialized.)

delegate

– **delegate**

Returns the DBDatabase object's delegate.

directory

– (const char *)**directory**

Returns the path to the directory containing the bundle from which the DBDatabase object was initialized.

disconnect

– (BOOL)**disconnect**

Closes the connection to the database. The DBDatabase object then loads the default data dictionary. Returns YES if the connection was successfully closed. Invoking the **disconnect** method is equivalent to invoking **disconnectUsingString:** with *aString* set to NULL.

See also: disconnectUsingString:

disconnectUsingString:

– (BOOL)**disconnectUsingString:**(const unsigned char *)*aString*

Closes the connection to the database by sending it the command *aString*. The DBDatabase object then loads the default data dictionary. Returns YES if the connection was successfully closed.

See also: disconnect

emptyDataDictionary

– **emptyDataDictionary**

Frees the DBDatabase object's currently loaded data dictionary. The entity names, adaptor name, and login string are zeroed. Returns **self**.

enableTransactions:

– (BOOL)**enableTransactions:**(BOOL)*flag*

Controls the right to use transactions—that is, permits use of the methods **beginTransaction**, **commitTransaction**, and **rollbackTransaction**—according to the value of *flag*. If the database supports transactions, transactions are enabled by default. Returns YES if the adaptor is able to comply, NO otherwise.

If the delegate implements **db:log:** (to maintain a log file), each use of **enableTransactions** generates a log entry containing the name of the method, the argument (YES or NO) and language-specific text indicating whether the adaptor was able to comply.

entityNamed:

– (id <DBEntities>)**entityNamed:**(const char *)*aName*

Returns the entity named *aName* from the DBDatabase object's list of entities, or **nil** if *aName* is invalid. The length and spelling of *aName* must exactly match the name of an entity; entities are supposed to have unique names.

evaluateString:

– (BOOL)**evaluateString:**(const unsigned char *)*aString*

Passes the adaptor a request to evaluate the string *aString*. This method is most useful to an application that sets up its own DBBinders to transfer data to and from the database. The method makes it possible to pass SQL directly to the database, for example to call stored procedures or to pass SQL data definition statements.

Warning: If the evaluation fetches data, note that this method bypasses the Databse Kit's standard procedures for describing the data to be fetched. As a consequence, fetched data won't be automatically accessible by its properties. This method can be used to fetch data only in an application that sets up its own DBBinders to receive the fetch, and its own mappings from the binder's container to objects that encapsulate the data.

Returns YES if the string is successfully evaluated. If the delegate implements the method **db:willEvaluateString:usingBinder:**, the evaluation is permitted only if the delegate returns YES to that notification.

If the delegate implements **db:log:** (to maintain a log file), each use of **evaluateString:** generates a log entry containing the name of the method, the return value, and the string proposed for evaluation.

getEntities:

– (List *)**getEntities:**(List *)*aList*

Fills *aList* with references to all of the entities in the database's model. This is the only way to get a complete list of entities from the DBDatabase object. Returns *aList*.

initFromFile:

– **initFromFile:**(const char *)*aPath*

Initializes the DBDatabase object from the database model information in the bundle identified by the path *aPath*. Model information (database name, login string, adaptor name, and entities) are read from the file. Returns **self**.

isConnected

– (BOOL)**isConnected**

Returns YES if the database connection is currently open (ready to fetch or store data).

isTransactionInProgress

– (BOOL)**isTransactionInProgress**

Returns YES if a transaction has been started (by **beginTransaction**) and has not yet been committed or rolled back.

loadDefaultDataDictionary

– **loadDefaultDataDictionary**

Reads the data dictionary of the database ands fills the list of entities with the information thus obtained. This method has no effect if the DBDatabase object is not connected to a database or if it already has a non-empty list of entities or attributes.

Returns **self**.

loginStringForUser:

– (const unsigned char *)**loginStringForUser:**(const char *)*aUser*

Returns the login string for the user identified by *aUser*, as recorded in the database bundle from which the DBDatabase object was initialized. However, if *aUser* does not exactly match the name of a user as recorded in the bundle's string table, the method returns the default login string.

name

– (const char *)**name**

Returns the name assigned to the DBDatabase object in the table maintained by the DBDatabase class.

See also: **– setName:**, **– findDatabseNamed:**

read:

– **read:**(NXTypedStream *)*stream*

Standard archiving method for retrieving a DBDatabase object from a typed stream.

Returns **self**.

rollbackTransaction

– (BOOL)**rollbackTransaction**

Causes the database to roll back all changes since a preceding **startTransaction**. Returns YES if the rollback was successful. Returns NO is the database could not roll back the transaction or there was no transaction in progress.

If the delegate implements **db:log:** (to maintain a log file), each use of **rollbackTransaction** generates a log entry containing the name of the method and text indicating whether the cancellation succeeded or failed.

See also: dbWillRollbackTransaction

setDelegate:

– **setDelegate:***anObject*

Makes *anObject* the delegate of the DBDatabase. Returns **self**.

setName:

– (BOOL)**setName:**(const char *)*aString*

Sets the name of the database to *aString*. Returns YES.

setPanelsEnabled:

– **setPanelsEnabled:**(BOOL)*flag*

Causes panels to be enabled or disabled. Panels are used to inform the user of unusual conditions or prompt the user to supply parameters that have not been stored (for example, a password). If the application is to run unattended or as a program without an Application object, it's essential to suppress panels. By default, a new DBDatabase is initialized to show panels. Returns **self**.

Note that when panels are enabled, a request for an attention panels (but not for a login or password panel) is forwarded to the delegate if the delegate implements **notificationFrom:message:code:**.

See also: arePanelsEnabled, notificationFrom:message:code:

write:

– **write:**(NXTypedStream *)*stream*

Archives the DBDatabase object to the stream identified by *stream*. Returns **self**.

Methods Implemented by the Delegate

db:log:

– **db:***aDatabase* **log:**(const char *)*fmt, ...*

Logs the notifications of database commands. The method receives a format string and a variable number of arguments, to be used with **vsprintf()**. The following fragment illustrates a possible implementation:

```
@implementation Control (DatabaseDelegate)
- db:aDatabase log:(const char*)format, ...
{
  va_list args;
  static char buf[1024];
  va_start(args, format);
  vsprintf(buf, format, args);
  if ([self respondsTo:@selector(setStringValue:)])
      [self setStringValue:buf];
  else
      syslog(LOG_NOTICE, buf);
  return self;
}
@end
```

db:notificationFrom:message:code:

– (BOOL)**db:***aDatabase*
  notificationFrom:*anObject*
  message:(const unsigned char *)*msg*
  code:(int)*n*

Invoked when the database encounters an exceptional situation. If your application appoints a delegate and it responds to this method, the method replaces a call to the generic attention panel.

This message originates from an object (often the adaptor) that wishes to notify the user of some unusual condition. The argument *msg* is a string supplied by the object that sent the message (and should have been selected from the strings for the appropriate language). The argument *code* is a numeric indication of the type of problem (usually, as supplied by the database vendor). The delegate method may choose to interpret the value of *code*. However, if the delegate doesn't implement this method, the message is handled by the default attention panel, which ignores *code*. (The ability to put up panels is by default enabled; you can explicitly enable it with **setPanelsEnabled:**.) The panel's only message is the text specified by *msg*, and its only button is labeled "OK." Returns YES if the panel was successfully displayed and acknowledged by the user.

db:willEvaluateString:usingBinder:

– (BOOL)**db:***aDb*
  willEvaluateString:(const unsigned char *)*aString*
  usingBinder:*aBinder*

Invoked before database control string (for example, in SQL) is sent to the database. Returning YES permits the string to be sent.

dbDidRollbackTransaction:

– **dbDidRollbackTransaction:***aDatabase*

Invoked when the database has rolled back the current transaction.

dbDidCommitTransaction:

– **dbDidCommitTransaction:***aDatabase*

Invoked when the database has committed the current transaction.

dbWillRollbackTransaction:

– **dbWillRollbackTransaction:***aDatabase*

Invoked when the database is about to roll back a transaction.

dbWillCommitTransaction:

– **dbWillCommitTransaction:***aDatabase*

Invoked when the database is about to commit a transaction.

DBEditableFormatter

Inherits From: DBFormatter : Object

Declared In: dbkit/DBEditableFormatter.h

Class Description

DBEditableFormatter is one of three subclasses of DBFormatter that support the display and editing of data in DBTableView. The others are DBTextFormatter and DBImageFormatter. DBEditableFormatter supports user revisions of the displayed data. Although DBTextFormatter is capable of faster character-based display, it's limited to read-only use. See the description of the superclass, DBFormatter.

Instance Variables

id **font**;
id **editView**;
id **drawCell**;

font	The current font
editView	The view now being edited
drawCell	The TextField cell that's being edited

Method Types

Initializing	– init – free
Manipulating the font	– font – setFont:

Displaying and editing	– drawFieldAt::inside:inView:withAttributes:: usePositions:: – editFieldAt::inside:inView:withAttributes:: usePositions::onEvent: – abortEditing – endEditing
Archiving	– write: – read: – finishUnarchiving

Instance Methods

abortEditing

– **abortEditing**

Forces an end to the current editing (if any), discarding any changes the user may have made. Returns **self**.

drawFieldAt::inside:inView:withAttributes::usePositions::

– **drawFieldAt:**(unsigned int) *row*
:(unsigned int)*column*
inside:(NXRect *)*frame*
inView:*aView*
withAttributes:(id <DBTableVectors>) *rowAttrs*
:(id <DBTableVectors>) *columnAttrs*
usePositions:*useRowPos*
:(BOOL)*useColumnPos*

Draws one field of data. You never invoke this method directly; it's invoked automatically by the DBTableView that's using this DBEditableFormatter when a field needs to be displayed.

editFieldAt::inside:inView:withAttributes::usePositions::onEvent:

– (BOOL)**editFieldAt:**(unsigned int)*row*
:*column*
inside:(NXRect *)*frame*
inView:*view*
withAttributes:(<DBTableVectors>)*rowAttrs*
:(<DBTableVectors>)*columnAttrs*
usePositions:(BOOL)*useRowPos*
:(BOOL)*useColumnPos*
onEvent:*theEvent*

Prepares the DBEditableFormatter for editing. You never invoke this method directly; it's invoked when the user acts on the DBTableView.

endEditing

– (BOOL)**endEditing**

Invoked to terminate editing in the current field, usually when the user clicks in a different field (thereby indicating that editing in this one is complete). Returns YES if successful (this, if the method is able to make the window that sent the message the first responder).

finishUnarchiving

– **finishUnarchiving**

Invoked after a DBEditableFormatter's instance variables have been unarchived (using **read:**) as a final step in initialization. Your application should not need to invoke this method explicitly. Returns **self.**

font

– **font**

Returns the DBEditableFormatter's Font object.

free

– **free**

Frees the DBEditableFormatter instance..

init

– **init**

Initializes the DBTextFormatter instance. In the course of initializing, the display font is set to the user's default font at 12.0 point. Returns **self**.

read:

– **read:**(NXTypedStream *) *stream*

Restores the values of the object's instance variables from the archive *stream*, including its font and delegate. Returns **self**.

setFont:

– **setFont:***aFont*

Sets the current font to the Font object *aFont*. Returns **self**.

write:

– **write:**(NXTypedStream *) *stream*

Writes the DBTextFormatter's instance variables to *stream*, including its font and its delegate.

Closes the connection to the database by sending it the command *aString*. The DBDatabase object then loads the default data dictionary. Returns YES if the connection was successfully closed.

See also: disconnect

DBExpression

Inherits From: Object

Conforms To: DBProperties
DBExpressionValues

Declared In: dbkit/DBExpression.h

Class Description

A DBExpression encapusulates a database expression as an object. A database expression specifies a property of data to be returned from an entity in the database. A fetch is governed by a list of DBExpressions, one for each of the properties to be returned (and also by a DBQualifier that specifies which records are to be included.)

The DBExpression class provides methods that let you refer to existing properties, specify the type of data to be returned for a property, and combine existing properties to create a new one.

Every DBExpression is relative to an entity; the entity is specified in the **initForEntity:...** methods:

- initForEntity:fromDescription:
- initForEntity:fromName:usingType:

You can change the entity or description of an existing DBExpression by sending it a **setEntity:andDescription:** message.

Format of a DBExpression's Description

The text of a DBExpression is called its *description*. The description is constructed in much the same way as a **printf** statement. That is, it consists of a quoted string containing the symbols needed to construct the expression with placeholders for the various values, followed by the names of the objects to be substituted for the placeholders. The following substitution symbols may occur within the quoted string:

Symbol	Expected value
%s	A constant string (**const char ***).
%p	A (**const char ***) that names one of the entity's properties.
%d	An **int**.
%f	A **double** or **float**.
%@	An object that conforms to the DBExpressionValues protocol, or a property object created by the Database Kit. (The former includes DBExpression, allowing you to created a nested expression.)
%%	No value—this passes a single '%' literally.

The rest of the format string should comprise query-language operators and symbols, the names of properties, and whitespace. For example, suppose you have a **boxes** entity that has properties named "height", "width", and "depth." To create a DBExpression that calculates the volume of a box, you would do the following:

```
id h = [boxes propertyNamed:"height"];
id w = [boxes propertyNamed:"width"];
id d = [boxes propertyNamed:"depth"];

DBExpression *volume = [[DBExpression alloc] initForEntity:boxes
                         fromDescription:"%@ * %@ * %@", h,w,d];

/* Setting the name isn't essential, but it's a good idea. */
[volume setName:"volume"];
```

To evaluate a DBExpression, you send it an **expressionValue** message. The return is a string in the query language used by the adaptor, representing the expression.

Using a DBExpression

A DBExpression object adopts the DBProperties protocol, and so can be used in any situation that requires a property. To retrieve data for a DBExpression, before executing a fetch, you add the DBExpression to the list of expressions maintained by the object that you're using to fetch data (a DBRecordList, DBRecordStream, or DBBinder). You can use a DBExpression to get the value for a property from a record by passing it to methods such as DBBinder's **valueForProperty:** or DBRecordList's **getValue:forProperty:**.

The two most important differences between a DBExpression that you've created and a property that you've retrieved from an entity are these:

- You can't write the value for a self-created DBExpression back to the source.
- You create it, you free it.

Instance Variables

None declared in this class.

Adopted Protocols

DBExpressionValues	– expressionValue – isDeferredExpression
DBProperties	– name – setName: – entity – matchesProperty: – propertyType – isSingular – isReadOnly – isKey

Method Types

Creating and freeing a DBExpression

- initForEntity:fromDescription:
- initForEntity:fromName:usingType:
- copyFromZone:
- free

Setting the entity and description

- setEntity:andDescription:

Archiving

- read:
- write:

Instance Methods

copyFromZone:

– **copyFromZone:**(NXZone *)*zone*

Creates and returns a copy of the receiving DBExpression. The new object is created in the given zone.

free

– **free**

Frees the DBExpression.

initForEntity:fromDescription:

– **initForEntity:**(id <DBEntities>)*anEntity*
  fromDescription:(const unsigned char *)*descriptionFormat*, ...

A designated initializer for the DBExpression class, this initializes a freshly allocated DBExpression by setting its entity to *anEntity* and setting its description as specified by the other arguments. The description is in the style of a **printf** statement: *descriptionFormat* is a quoted string that establishes the format of the description, the following arguments supply the description with values. The arguments are separated by commas. See the class description above for the rules governing the format of the description string.

If the description refers to a single, unmanipulated property, then the DBExpression will be "simple"—the property that the DBExpression represents will be the property referred to in the description. If the description manipulates one or more existing properties, then the object is "derived," and a new property object is created to describe the manipulation. The data type of a derived DBExpression is a string, and it's given a unique name.

Returns **self**, or **nil** if either of the arguments is **nil**.

See also: – **initForEntity:fromName:usingType:**

initForEntity:fromName:usingType:

– **initForEntity:**(id <DBEntities>)*anEntity*
  fromName:(const char *)*aPropertyName*
  usingType:(const char *)*aType*

A designated initializer for the DBExpression class, this initializes a freshly allocated DBExpression by setting its entity to *anEntity*, and creating a property object (owned by the DBExpression) that points to the property named by *aPropertyName*. The data type of the new property is set to *aType*, so that data retieved by this expression will be coerced to the indicated type.

Returns **self**, or **nil** if *anEntity* is **nil** or if the named property doesn't exist in the entity.

See also: – **initForEntity:fromDescription:**

read:

– **read:**(NXTypedStream *)*stream*

Reads the DBExpression from the typed stream *stream*. Returns **self**.

setEntity:andDescription:

– **setEntity:**(id <DBEntities>)*anEntity*
andDescription:(const unsigned char *)*descriptionFormat*, ...

Replaces the DBExpression's entity and description with those provided by the arguments. See the class description for more information on the format of the description string.

See also: – **initForEntity:fromDescription:**

write:

– **write:**(NXTypedStream *)*stream*

Writes the DBExpression to the typed stream *stream*. Returns **self**.

DBFetchGroup

Inherits From: Object

Declared In: dbkit/DBFetchGroup.h

Class Description

A DBFetchGroup routes information from a DBRecordList to the various user interface objects that display its contents. It also routes flow in the reverse direction, when the user edits the displays. A DBFetchGroup belongs to a DBModule; each DBModule has at least one DBFetchGroup. A DBFetchGroup contains a set of DBAssociations; each maps one database property to be fetched (a DBExpression) to an element of the application program, usually an element of the user interface, such as a TextField, a DBImageView, or a row or column within a DBTableView.

If your application relies on the Database Kit's standard facilities, you will not need to make explicit use of DBFetchGroup. In Interface Builder, you need only drag an instance of DBModule off the palette and make connections between it and elements of your user interface. At run time, the necessary DBFetchGroups and their various DBAssociations will be created for you automatically when the nib module is loaded into the running application.

In a DBModule, its prime (and perhaps only) fetch group is called its *root fetch group*. The module may also require one or more subordinate fetch groups. Whenever the expression being fetched traverses a one-to-many relationship, the DBModule requires separate DBRecordLists, each with its own DBFetchGroup. The fetch groups are in a hierarchy that corresponds to the data being fetched. For example, suppose your application has a scrollable display of customers; for each customer there is a list of orders; for each order there's a list of items in the order. As the user selects a customer, the order display must be updated to show that customer's orders. As the user selects an order, the item display must be updated to show that order's line items. The synchronization is managed by a set of three DBFetchGroups, each with its own DBRecordList. The root DBFetchGroup manages data for the customer display. Subordinate to it, a second DBFetchGroup keeps the order display in step with the currently selected customer. And subordinate to that, a third DBFetchGroup keeps the line-item display in step with the currently selected order.

Whenever there's a fetch, the DBFetchGroup takes care of updating the display to reflect the data newly arrived in the record list. Similarly, when the user edits a control, the DBFetchGroup updates the record list, and then notifies any other elements that may be displaying the same property. The first fetch of a DBFetchGroup causes a **setProperties:ofSource**: message to be sent to its DBRecordList.

The DBFetchGroup also manages a second kind of user-interface state: the current record and the current selection (which may be one record or several). The notion of "current record" exists because controls can display one value at a time, although a record list can contain many records. The current record is the one displayed in a TextField or a DBImageView. The fetch group remembers which record in the record list is the current record. The designation of a current record can be changed by the user or under program control.

Note: The DBFetchGroup's current record and selected record list are independent of the cursor of a DBRecordSteam or DBRecordList.

Multiple Selection

In an object that can display a list of values, such as an NXBrowser or a DBTableView, the user can make a multiple selection. Shift-click selects additional records without deselecting those already selected. They don't have to be contiguous. But when there is a multiple selection, no record is the current record, and subordinate displays keyed to the current record are cleared.

The DBFetchGroup relies on objects in the user interface (such as the DBTableView) to represent multiple selection to the user. The DBFetchGroup will make use of multiple-selection information (as in **deleteCurrentSelection**), but does not manage it. If your application needs to set a multiple selection, it should send the appropriate DBTableView one of its selection-setting messages. Then, to keep the DBFetchGroup synchronized with change in selection at the DBTableView, it must send the following messages:

```
[[theTableView dataSource] tableViewDidChangeSelection:theTableView];
```

Instance Variables

None declared in this class.

Method Types

Initializing	– initEntity:
	– setName:

Reporting current context	– name – module – entity – recordList – currentRecord – recordCount
Controlling current selection	– setAutoSelect: – doesAutoSelect – setCurrentRecord: – clearCurrentRecord – selectedRowAfter: – redisplayEverything
Manipulating contents	– deleteCurrentSelection – insertNewRecordAt: – fetchContentsOf:usingQualifier:
Dealing with changes	– hasUnsavedChanges – validateCurrentRecord – saveChanges – discardChanges
Using associations	– addExpression: – makeAssociationFrom:to: – takeValueFromAssociation: – addAssociation: – removeAssociation:
Using a delegate	– delegate – setDelegate:

Instance Methods

addAssociation:

– **addAssociation:***newAssociation*

Adds an association to the list of associations that govern the DBFetchGroup's selection of rows. The argument *newAssociation* is a DBAssociation object. Returns **self**.

addExpression:

– **addExpression:***newExpression*

Adds the DBExpression *anExpression* to the list of expressions that the DBFetchGroup will fetch from the database. These expressions are passed to the DBRecordList that the fetch group uses to get data into and out of the database. Returns **self**.

clearCurrentRecord

– **clearCurrentRecord**

Deselects the currently selected record (or records), so that there is no selected record. DBAssociations that may have been involved in the formerly selected records are notified of the change. Returns **self**. However, if there is no permission to change the rows of the DBFetchGroup's DBRecordList, the method has no effect and returns **nil**.

currentRecord

– (unsigned int)**currentRecord**

Returns the position (index number) of the current record in the DBFetchGroup's DBRecordList.

delegate

– **delegate**

Returns the DBFetchGroup's delegate.

See also: – **setDelegate**

deleteCurrentSelection

– **deleteCurrentSelection**

Deletes the currently selected row (or rows) from the DBFetchGroup's DBRecordList. Following the deletion, no rows are selected. All DBAssociations are notified of the change.

Returns **self**. However, if no rows were selected, or there is no permission to change the rows of the DBFetchGroup's DBRecordList, the method has no effect and returns **nil**.

discardChanges

– **discardChanges**

Terminates any editing changes currently in progress for this DBFetchGroup and recursively for any of its subordinate DBFetchGroups. All the DBAssociations involved are notified so that they can update the display accordingly. Returns **self**.

doesAutoSelect

– (BOOL)**doesAutoSelect**

Returns YES if autoselection is in effect. When this flag has been set to YES, following each fetch through the DBFetchGroup, the first retrieved record is selected; following a delete, the first remaining record after the first deleted record is selected. When the flag is NO, following fetch or delete, no record is selected.

entity

– **entity**

Returns the DBEntity to which the DBFetchGroup belongs.

fetchContentsOf:usingQualifier:

– **fetchContentsOf:***aSource* **usingQualifier:***aQualifier*

Replaces the content of the current DBRecordList by records fetched from the database. Any editing in progress for this fetch group is terminated and changes are lost. The argument *aSource* may be nil, in which case all records in the DBFetchGroup's entity are fetched. If *aSource* is a DBValue containing NULL, the effect is to clear the DBRecordList without fetching any new records.

Alternatively, *aSource* may be a DBValue that specifies a relationship. For example, suppose the relationship joins the entity called Department to the entity called Employees, containing the employees belonging to each department. The DBValue may contain a specific value for the property "Department Number" and also the entity to which it is joined (Employees). Records will be fetched for all employees in the indicated department, using the key value of Department Number as a foreign key that qualifies the selection of records from Employees.

The argument *aQualifier* is a DBQualifier that further restricts the records that will be fetched.

If the parent DBModule's delegate responds to **fetchGroupWillFetch:**, it is notified. Similarly, after the fetch, if the DBModule's delegate responds to **fetchGroupDidFetch**:, it is a notified. Provided the fetch is successful, the various DBAssociations are notified that the contents of their views has changed, so they can redraw themselves. The current record index is set to 0 (the index of the first record). Returns **self**.

hasUnsavedChanges

– (BOOL)**hasUnsavedChanges**

Returns YES if there are unsaved changes in this DBFetchGroups's DBRecordList, or in any of its subordinate DBRecordLists, and NO otherwise.

initEntity:

– **initEntity:***anEntity*

Initializes an instance of DBFetchGroup. The fetch group thus initialized will coordinate fetches for the owning DBModule from the DBEntity named *anEntity.* Returns **self**.

insertNewRecordAt:

– (BOOL)**insertNewRecordAt:**(unsigned int)*index*

Instructs the DBFetchGroup's DBRecordList to insert a new record at the position indicated by *index*. When *index* is negative, the method appends the new record (that is, inserts it at the end of the DBRecordList instance.

Returns YES if the DBRecordList is able to comply, and NO otherwise. A NO return may arise if the application has no authorization to modify rows, if no records have been fetched, or if for any reason the DBRecordList returns NO.

If the DBFetchGroup has appointed a delegate and the delegate implements the method **fetchGroup:didInsertRecordAt:**, the method **insertNewRecordAt:** notifies the delegate. The delegate may then fill in default values in the new record.

makeAssociationFrom:to:

– **makeAssociationFrom:***anExpr* **to:***aView*

Creates a new instance of DBAssociation for the destination DBFetchGroup. The new association will link the DBExpression *anExpr* (an expression to be fetched) with the user interface object *aView* where the data is displayed. Returns the new DBAssociation.

module

– **module**

Returns the DBModule instance to which the receiving DBFetchGroup belongs.

name

– (const char *)**name**

Returns the name of the DBFetchGroup. Fetch groups that are created automatically are given names that match the names assigned in the model. Fetch groups that were created by the application and initialized (for example, by **initEntity:**) remain unnamed until explicitly named by **setName:**.

See also: – **setName:**

recordCount

– (unsigned int)**recordCount**

Returns the number of records in the DBFetchGroup's DBRecordList.

recordList

– **recordList**

Returns the DBRecordList instance that the receiving DBFetchGroup serves.

redisplayEverything

– **redisplayEverything**

Causes redisplay of all the fields governed by the DBFetchGroup's DBAssociations. (The redisplay is prompted by sending all the DBAssociations a notification that the contents changed, and they respond in the same way as for any other change to their contents.) As a side effect, this method checks the value of the current record index, and, if it is out of range, sets it to the index of the last record. Returns **self**.

removeAssociation:

– **removeAssociation:***anAssociation*

Removes the indicated association from the DBFetchGroup's list of associations. Returns **self**.

saveChanges

– **saveChanges**

Saves changes made to any of the records governed by the receiving DBFetchGroup and any subordinate DBFetchGroups. Before saving, the method terminates any editing that may have been in progress in the affected DBFetchGroups. After saving, notifies the DBModule's delegate that the save took place. Returns **self**.

selectedRowAfter:

– (unsigned int)**selectedRowAfter:**(unsigned int)*previousRow*

Returns the index of the first selected row that is located after the row specified by *previousRow*. (Ordinarily, there is one selected row, also known as the current row. But under some conditions the user may select multiple rows. In that case, the return is the index of the first of them.)

If no row is selected, or the only selected rows occur earlier than *previousRow*, returns DB_NoIndex (which other methods interpret to mean "after the last record").

setAutoSelect:

– **setAutoSelect:***flag*

Enables or disables autoselection, according to whether *flag* is YES or NO. When autoselection is enabled, following each fetch through the DBFetchGroup, the first retrieved record is selected; following a delete, the first remaining record after the first deleted record is selected. When *flag* is NO, following fetch or delete, no record is selected.

setCurrentRecord:

– **setCurrentRecord:**(unsigned int)*newIndex*

Sets the index of the current record to *newIndex*. However, if the proposed value is less than the index of the first record, sets it to the first record; if the proposed value is greater than the last record, sets it the last record. If executing this method changes the current record index, the DBFetchGroup's DBAssociations are notified that the selection changed (and can update the display accordingly). Returns **self**.

setDelegate:

– **setDelegate:***anObject*

Makes *anObject* the DBFetchGroup's delegate. Returns **self**.

See also: – **delegate**

setName:

– **setName:**(const char *)*aName*

Sets the name of the DBFetchGroup. This method is invoked automatically when the fetch group is created, and your application will need to call it explicitly only if you explicitly create a new fetch group. Returns **self**.

See also: – **name**

takeValueFromAssociation:

– **takeValueFromAssociation:***anAssociation*

Takes a value from the part of the display governed by *anAssociation*, and inserts it in the corresponding position in the DBFetchGroup's DBRecordList. The method then updates the display of other displayed fields that are governed by other DBAssociations belonging to the same DBFetchGroup. Returns **self**.

validateCurrentRecord

– (BOOL)**validateCurrentRecord**

Returns YES if changes that have been proposed for the current record are valid (or if there is no current record).

The validation is done in two stages. If there is a TextField editor for the field that changed, it reviews the changes first. If the TextField editor says NO, that's the return. If there is no text field editor, or the editor raises no objection to the change, the task of validation is passed to the DBModule's delegate. (Each DBFetchGroup is owned by a DBModule.) Whatever the delegate returns becomes the return for this method.

Methods Implemented by the Delegate

fetchGroup:didInsertRecordAt:

– **fetchGroup:***fetchGroup* **didInsertRecordAt:**(int)*index*

Notification that the DBFetchGroup *fetchGroup* has inserted a record in its DBRecordList at the position indicated by *index*.

fetchGroup:willDeleteRecordAt:

– **fetchGroup:***fetchGroup* **willDeleteRecordAt:**(int)*index*

Invoked when the DBFetchGroup *fetchGroup* is about to delete the record at *index* from the DBRecordList. The notification is sent by the DBFetchGroup method **deleteCurrentSelection**. The notification gives the delegate a chance to note the fact (for example, to adjust its count of records, or to record information about the deleted record). It doesn't matter what this method returns, since the calling method ignores the result. The behavior of **fetchGroup:willDeleteRecordAt:** is simply a notification, without an opportunity to intercede. But it's sent in advance of the actual deletion so that the delegate method can—if desired—take a look at the record before it's gone.

fetchGroup:willFailForReason:

– (DBFailureResponse)**fetchGroup:***fetchGroup*
    willFailForReason:(DBFailureCode)*code*

Invoked when a failure is reported from the DBRecordList owned by *fetchGroup*. The reason for failure is encoded as one of the following DBFailureCodes:

DB_ReasonUnknown = 0
DB_RecordBusy
DB_RecordStreamNotReady
DB_RecordHasChanged
DB_RecordLimitReached
DB_NoRecordKey
DB_RecordKeyNotUnique
DB_NoAdaptor
DB_AdaptorError
DB_TransactionError

The failure response that is returned must be one of the following constants, declared as type DBFailureResponse in the header file **dbkit/enums.h**:

DB_NotHandled	Displays a default attention panel but takes no other action
DB_Abort	Terminates the operation that encountered the error in its present state, and displays an attention panel
DB_Continue	Ignores the problem; permits the action to continue if possible.

If the delegate does not implement this method, the effect is the same as returning DB_NotHandled.

fetchGroup:willValidateRecordAt:

– (BOOL)**fetchGroup:***fetchGroup* **willValidateRecordAt:**(int)*index*

Notification that the DBFetchGroup *fetchGroup*, while preparing to save its DBRecordList, has reached the point at which it would be appropriate to insert a validity check on the record indicated by *index*. If you implement this method in the DBModule's delegate, you can insert any checks you like. These might include checks for internal consistency between fields, or even checks that require a separate query to the database (for example, "Is this person already in the database?" or "Is data for 'Salary' consistent with 'Salary Range' for this person's job title?")

Notice that validation for a single field ("Is this a valid phone number?" or "Is this in a valid format for a telephone number?") should be handled when a field editor notices that the user has changed a field's display. See the DBModule delegate method **textWillChange**.

If your implementation of **fetchGroup:willValidateRecordAt:** returns YES (or if your delegate doesn't respond to that method), the record is treated as valid. If it returns NO, the record is treated as invalid, the attempt to save records fails, and the user is notified by an attention panel.

fetchGroupDidFetch:

– **fetchGroupDidFetch:***fetchGroup*

Invoked when *fetchGroup* has completed a fetch from the database.

fetchGroupDidSave:

– **fetchGroupDidSave:***fetchGroup*

Invoked when *fetchGroup* has completed a save to the database.

fetchGroupWillChange:

– **fetchGroupWillChange:***fetchGroup*

Invoked when *fetchGroup* is about to record change based on input from the user interface.

fetchGroupWillFetch:

– **fetchGroupWillFetch:***fetchGroup*

Invoked when *fetchGroup* is about to fetch data from the database.

fetchGroupWillSave:

– (BOOL)**fetchGroupWillSave:***fetchGroup*

Invoked when *fetchGroup* is about to save the contents of the fetch group to the database.

DBFormatter

Inherits From: Object

Declared In: dbkit/DBFormatter.h

Class Description

DBFormatter is an abstract superclass; each of its subclasses provides a mechanism that formats and displays data in a DBTableView. The Database Kit provides three DBFormatter subclasses:

- DBImageFormatter scales, aligns, and displays images.
- DBTextFormatter displays uneditable text.
- DBEditableFormatter displays editable text.

The central method in a DBFormatter is **drawFieldAt::inside:inView:withAttributes::usePositions::**. This method defines the way in which a DBFormatter formats and displays data. It's invoked automatically by the DBTableView when it wants to display a value. The default implementation of this method does nothing; each subclass must implement it in a meaningful way.

Instance Variables

id **value**;

value	The value to be formatted

Method Types

Getting and displaying a value	– getValueAt::withAttributes::usePositions:: – drawFieldAt::inside:inView:withAttributes:: usePositions::
Batching format requests	– beginBatching: – resetBatching: – endBatching

Instance Methods

beginBatching:

– **beginBatching:**(id <DBTableVectors>)*attrs*

Tells the DBFormatter that a formatting session is about to begin. You never invoke this method directly; it's invoked automatically by the DBTableView just before it sends the first in a series of **drawFieldAt::...** messages. The end of the formatting session is signalled by the **endBatching** message and it's restarted through **resetBatching:**.

The default implementation of **beginBatching:** does nothing. You can reimplement this method in a subclass to perform pre-formatting initialization. The return value is ignored. The argument to this method (and to **resetBatching:**) is currently unused (it's always **nil**).

drawFieldAt::inside:inView:withAttributes::usePositions::

– **drawFieldAt:**(unsigned int)*row*
:(unsigned int)*column*
inside:(NXRect *)*frame*
inView:*view*
withAttributes:(id <DBTableVectors>)*rowAttrs*
:(id <DBTableVectors>)*columnAttrs*
usePositions:(BOOL)*useRow*
:(BOOL)*useColumn*

Retrieves a value from the data source, formats it, and displays it. The DBFormatter implementation of this actually does nothing and returns **self**; it's up to the subclasses to implement this method in meaningful ways.

Typically, an implementation follows these steps:

5. The value is retrieved. This is done by forwarding the method's arguments to **getValueAt::...**, thus:

```
[self getValueAt:row :column
        withAttributes:rowAttrs :columnAttrs
        usePositions:useRow :useColumn];
```

6. The value that's set by **getValueAt::...** (keep in mind that the method sets the **value** instance variable) is formatted for display.
7. The formatted value is displayed inside *frame*, which is given in *view*'s coordinate system. Note well that the focus will be locked on *view* before this message is sent—you don't have to lock focus yourself.

endBatching

– **endBatching**

Notifies the DBFormatter that a formatting session is over. See the **beginBatching:** method for more information.

See also: – **beginBatching:**, – **resetBatching:**

getValueAt::withAttributes::usePositions::

– **getValueAt:**(unsigned int) *row*
  :(unsigned int) *column*
  withAttributes:(id <DBTableVectors>) *rowAttrs*
  :(id <DBTableVectors>) *columnAttrs*
  usePositions:(BOOL) *useRowPos*
  :(BOOL) *useColumnPos*

Retrieves a value from the data source, places it in the DBFormatter's **value** instance variable, and then returns the variable. You never invoke this method from your application; however, if you create a subclass of DBFormatter, you'll need to invoke it from the implementation of **drawFieldAt::...**, as explained in the description of that method. You shouldn't need to reimplement this method in a subclass.

resetBatching:

– **resetBatching:**(id <DBTableVectors>)*attrs*

Tells the DBFormatter to restart a formatting session. See the **beginBatching:** method for more information.

See also: – **beginBatching:**, – **endBatching**

DBImageFormatter

Inherits From: DBFormatter : Object

Declared In: dbkit/DBImageFormatter.h

Class Description

DBImageFormatter is one of three subclasses of DBFormatter; the others are DBTextFormatter and DBEditableFormatter (which deal with text rather than images). See the description of the superclass, DBFormatter.

Instance Variables

id **defaultImage**;

defaultImage	Used when the source to be formatted contains no image

Method Types

Initializing	– init – free
Default	– setDefaultImage:anImage – defaultImage
Drawing	– drawFieldAt::inside: inView:withAttributes:: usePositions::
Archiving	– write: – read:

Instance Methods

defaultImage

– **defaultImage**

Returns the default image. This is the image that **drawFieldAt:...** will substitute if asked to draw a field that does not contain an image.

drawFieldAt::inside:inView:withAttributes::usePositions::

– **drawFieldAt:**(unsigned int) *row*
:(unsigned int) *column*
inside:(NXRect *)*frame*
inView:*view*
withAttributes:(id <DBTableVectors>) *rowAttrs*
:(id <DBTableVectors>) *columnAttrs*
usePositions:*useRowPos*
:(BOOL)*useColumnPos*

Displays an image in one field of data. You never invoke this method directly; it's invoked automatically by the DBTableView that's using this DBEditableFormatter when a field needs to be displayed.

The displayed image is centered vertically; its horizontal alignment is controlled by *rowAttrs* or *columnAttrs*; it may be centered, left aligned, or right aligned. The image is clipped to the frame.

Returns **self**.

See also: – **getValueAt::withAttributes::usePositions::** (DBFormatter), – **setAlignment** (DBVectors protocol)

free

– **free**

Frees the DBImageFormatter instance.

init

– **init**

Initializes the DBImageFormatter instance. In the course of initializing, an initial value is set for the default image (to be displayed when a field where an image was expected in fact has none). Returns **self**.

read:

– **read:**(NXTypedStream *) *stream*

Restores the values of the object's instance variables from the archive *stream*, including its font and delegate. Returns *self.*

setDefaultImage:

– **setDefaultImage:***anImage*

Makes *anImage* the image that **drawFieldAt:...** will substitute when asked to draw a field that doesn't contain an image. If you haven't explicitly set a default image, the default established when the DBImageFormatter is initialized is a gray rectangle. Returns **self**.

write:

– **write:**(NXTypedStream *) *stream*

Writes the DBTextFormatter's instance variables to *stream*, including its font and its delegate.

DBImageView

Inherits From: Control : View : Responder : Object

Declared In: dbkit/DBImageView.h

Class Description

A DBImageView displays a single NXImage object bordered by one of four types of frame. Providing editing is enabled, the user can drag a new image into a DBImageView's frame (using the Application Kit's image-dragging mechanism).

The Database Kit permits a DBImageView object to be connected to any database field whose data is of type object and class NXImage.

Instance Variables

None declared in this class.

Method Types

Internals	– initFrame: – drawSelf::
Accessing the image	– image – setImage:
Accessing the border	– setStyle: – style
Editing	– isEditable – setEditable:

Instance Methods

drawSelf::

– **drawSelf:**(const NXRect *)*rects* **:**(int)*rectCount*

Draws the DBImageView. You never invoke this method yourself, it's invoked automatically by the Application Kit's display mechanism. Returns **self**.

See also: – **drawSelf::** (View; Application Kit)

image

– **image**

Returns the image view's NXImage object.

initFrame:

– **initFrame:**(const NXRect *)*frameRect*

Initializes the image view with the given frame. Returns **self**.

isEditable

– (BOOL)**isEditable**

Returns YES if the image can be replaced or deleted.

See also: – **setEditable:**

setEditable:

– **setEditable:**(BOOL)*flag*

Makes the DBImageView editable or not, as *flag* is YES or NO. When an image view is editable, it still must be deleted or replaced as a whole; "editable" doesn't involve fiddling with bits.

See also: – **isEditable**

setImage:

– **setImage:***newImage*

Sets the image view's NXImage to *newImage*. Returns **self**.

setStyle:

– **setStyle:**(int)*newStyle*

Sets the style in which the image's border is drawn. The argument *newStyle* must be one of the following:

DB_ImageNoFrame = 0
DB_ImagePhoto
DB_ImageGrayBezel
DB_ImageGroove

See also: – style:

style

– (int)**style**

Returns the current border style, as one of the possible styles listed as arguments of **setStyle:**.

DBModule

Inherits From: Object

Declared In: dbkit/DBModule.h

Class Description

The DBModule class provides the connection between the Database Kit's user interface layer and its access layer. It does this by letting you associate a set of interface objects with a set of DBRecordLists. The methods defined by DBModule control the flow of data between the interface objects and the DBRecordLists. The class also defines a handful of convenience methods that control transactions between a DBModule's "main" DBRecordList (the DBRecordList association with the *root fetch group*, as explained below) and the external database.

It's strongly recommended that you use Interface Builder to create and instantiate DBModule objects. (For this, you need the Database Kit palette, described in the section "Database Palette for Interface Builder" in this chapter's introduction.) Through Interface Builder you can denote the record lists that a DBModule will represent and specify the connections between these record lists and the objects in your application's interface.

Because of Interface Builder's intercession, you don't need to know much about the DBModule class. However, you may want to use DBModules to inspect or modify data as it's shuffled between a database and your application's user interface. For this, you need to know a little bit about how DBModules are built.

Record Lists, Fetch Groups, and Associations

When it's initialized (through **initDatabase:entity:** method), a DBModule automatically creates two objects: a DBRecordList, as described by the arguments of the initialization method, and an instance of DBFetchGroup, called the *root fetch group.* An instance of DBFetchGroup represents a single DBRecordList and associates it with one or more interface objects; the root fetch group is the object that corresponds to the DBModule's (initial) DBRecordList. If the DBRecordList contains only one-to-one relationships, then the root fetch group is sufficient for the DBModule. However, if there are one-to-many relationships in the DBRecordList, additional DBFetchGroups must be created and added to the DBModule, one for each such relationship. (If you use Interface Builder, the additional DBFetchGroups, if needed, are created and added automatically.)

DBFetchGroups are important not only for the utility that they bring to DBModule, but also because it's through the DBFetchGroup that you can get to a DBModule's DBRecordList objects (which opens the door to the classes in the Database Kit's acces layer). You can retrieve a DBModule's list of DBFetchGroups through its **getFetchGroups:** method.

As stated above, a DBFetchGroup contains only one DBRecordList, but can associate that DBRecordList with any number of user interface objects. Each such association (in other words, each association between an interface object and a DBRecordList) is represented by a DBAssociation object. It's the DBAssociation's task to take data from the DBRecordList, permute it (if necessary), and send it to the interface object for display. It must also perform the opposite function, updating the data in the DBRecordList as the user manipulates the data in the interface. If you're using the standard interface objects supplied by the Database Kit and the Application Kit to display data, then you never need to be aware of the DBAssociations in your application. However, if you want to use a custom interface object—an instance of a class of your own design—then that object must implement the DBCustomAssociation informal protocol. You can retrieve the DBAssociation for a particular interface object through DBModule's **associationForObject:** method.

Instance Variables

id **database**;
id **delegate**;

database	The DBDatabase object through which the module is connected to the database
delegate	The object that receives notification messages

Method Types

Initializing a DBModule	– initDatabase:entity:
Querying the DBModule	– database – entity

Accessing fetch groups and associations	
	– getFetchGroups: – rootFetchGroup – fetchGroupNamed: – addFetchGroup: – associationForObject: – editingAssociation
Performing transactions	– fetchContentsOf:usingQualifier: – fetchAllRecords: – saveChanges: – discardChanges: – deleteRecord: – appendNewRecord: – insertNewRecord:
Browsing the record list	– nextRecord: – previousRecord:
Interface methods	– takeValueFrom: – textDidEnd:endChar: – textWillChange: – textWillEnd:
Accessing the delegate	– setDelegate – delegate:

Instance Methods

addFetchGroup:

– **addFetchGroup:***aFetchGroup*

Adds the given DBFetchGroup object to the list of fetch groups that the DBModule manages. Returns **self**.

appendNewRecord:

– **appendNewRecord:***sender*

Creates a new record and adds it to the end of the root fetch group's DBRecordList. This is a convenience method that's implemented by sending an **insertNewRecordAt:** message to the root fetch group. Returns **self** if the record was successfully appended; otherwise returns **nil**.

See also: – **insertNewRecordAt:** (DBFetchGroup)

associationForObject:

– **associationForObject:***anObject*

Returns the DBAssociation object that's associated with the given user interface object.

database

– **database**

Returns the DBDatabase object for which the DBModule was created.

See also: – **initDatabase:entity:**

delegate

– **delegate**

Returns the DBModule's delegate.

See also: – **setDelegate:**

deleteRecord:

– **deleteRecord:***sender*

Deletes the currently selected records by sending **deleteCurrentSelection** to the root fetch group and returns **self**.

See also: – **deleteCurrentSelection** (DBFetchGroup)

discardChanges:

– **discardChanges:***sender*

Terminates any editing changes currently in progress for the DBModule's fetch groups. The user interface object and the corresponding instance of DBRecordList are cleared in response to this message. All the DBAssociations involved are notified so that they can update the display accordingly. The method is implemented by sending a **discardChange**s message to the DBModule's root fetch group. Returns **self**.

editingAssociation

– **editingAssociation**

Returns the DBAssociation that is currently involved in editing (the one that contains the text insertion cursor). If none of the DBAssociation objects is involved in editing, returns **nil**.

entity

– **entity**

Returns the DBEntity corresponding to this DBModule.

See also: – **initDatabase:entity:**

fetchAllRecords:

– **fetchAllRecords:***sender*

Fetches records into the root fetch group. This method is implemented by invoking **fetchContentsOf:usingQualifier:** with *aSource* and *aQualifier* both **nil**. Returns **self**, unless the fetch fails. The fetch will fail if the connection to the database is closed and cannot be reopened, or if any of the fetch groups has unsaved changes that may not be discarded.

fetchContentsOf:usingQualifier:

– **fetchContentsOf:***aSource* **usingQualifier:***aQualifier*

Replaces the records in the current DBRecordList with records fetched from the database. Any editing in progress for this fetch group is terminated.

The argument *aSource* may be a DBEntity; it may also be a DBValue that specifies a relationship. When it specifies a relationship, the DBValue object contains both the key value of a source entity and the target entity to which it is joined; such an object responds YES to an **isEntity** message. For example, if the DBValue is the value "10" for the attribute "Department," the effect is to use "Department = 10" as a key that defines the set of records to be fetched. If *aSource* is **nil**, the DBModule's DBEntity is assumed.

The argument *aQualifier* is a DBQualifier that further restricts the records that will be fetched. If *aQualifier* is nil, there is no further qualification and all records are returned.

If the parent DBModule's delegate responds to **fetchGroupWillFetch:**, it is notified. Similarly, after the fetch, if the DBModule's delegate responds to **fetchGroupDidFetch**:, it is a notified, giving it a change to set up null values for the DBRecordList. The various

DBAssociations are notified that the contents of their views has changed, so they can redraw themselves. The current record index is set to 0 (the index of the first record).

Returns **self** when the fetch is successful, and **nil** otherwise. A **nil** return may arise if the root fetch group has unsaved changes that may not be discarded.

See also: – **fetchContentsOf:usingQualifier:** (DBFetchGroup), – **isEntity** (DBTypes protocol)

fetchGroupNamed:

– **fetchGroupNamed:**(const char *)*aName*

Returns the DBFetchGroup whose name matches *aName* (as declared in the model file or set through the DBFetchGroup method s**etName:**). If *aName* is **nil**, the method returns the root fetch group. Returns **nil** if the name isn't found.

getFetchGroups:

– **getFetchGroups:**(List *)*aList*

Fills *aList* with the DBModule's DBFetchGroup objects. Returns *aList.*

initDatabase:entity:

– **initDatabase:***aDatabase* **entity:***anEntity*

Initializes an instance of DBModule for the given database and entity, and creates and adds the object's root fetch group. Returns **self**.

insertNewRecord:

– **insertNewRecord:***sender*

Creates a new record and inserts it into the root fetch group's DBRecordList. This is done by sending an **insertNewRecordAt:** message to the root fetch group, passing the index of the current record as the argument. Returns **self** if the record was successfully inserted; otherwise returns **nil**.

See also: – **insertNewRecordAt:** (DBFetchGroup)

nextRecord:

– **nextRecord:***sender*

Advances the currently selected record in the root fetch group to the next record in the list. If there is no currently selected record, does nothing. Returns **self**.

previousRecord:

– **previousRecord:***sender*

Moves the current selection back to the previous record. However, if there is no currently selected record, does nothing. Returns **self**.

rootFetchGroup

– **rootFetchGroup**

Returns the module's one required DBFetchGroup (the first in the list of fetch groups).

saveChanges:

– **saveChanges:***sender*

Causes all changes made within the module to be saved to the database, by saving all the module's fetch groups. Returns **self**, but **nil** if any error occurred.

Instructs the root DBFetchGroup to save the changes that the user has introduced by editing the module's data display. Returns **self** if the changes were successfully saved (or if there were no changes to save).

If the database supports transactions and no other transaction is in progress, the **saveChanges:** method signals the start of a new transaction before starting the save, and commits the transaction if the save is completed successfully. Thus all changes within the module are saved as a single transaction (see the DBDatabase methods **beginTransaction** and **commitTransaction**).

If for any reason the save could not be carried out, **saveChanges:** returns **nil**, and leaves the database unchanged. There are several reasons a save might be unsuccessful. Before starting the save, the fetch groups may run a validation check. The method also notifies the DBModule's delegate by sending it a **moduleWillSave** message, giving the delegate a chance to interpose its own checks. When the save has been carried out, the method again notifies the delegate, this time by sending it a **moduleDidSave** message. The delegate may still object at this point; if it does, the save is rolled back.

setDelegate:

– **setDelegate:** *anObject*

Makes *anObject* the delegate of the DBModule instance. Returns **self**.

takeValueFrom:

– **takeValueFrom:***sender*

Notifies the DBModule that the user modified one of the displays (DBImageView, NXBrowser). The DBModule finds the corresponding DBAssociations and through them their DBFetchGroups and causes the object's new value to be read into the appropriate part of the DBRecordList. Returns **self**; however, if *sender* has no association linking it to the module's DBRecordList, returns **nil**.

textDidEnd:endChar:

– **textDidEnd:***textObject* **endChar:**(unsigned short)*whyEnd*

Called by a DBEditableTextFormatter object when it has relinquished first responder status. The argument *whyEnd* identifies the character (Tab, Shift-Tab, or Return) that caused the sender to cease being first responder. A return of YES permits the change to proceed; a return of NO prevents the change and selects the entire text field. Your application will not normally need to use this method explicitly.

textWillChange:

– (BOOL)**textWillChange:***textObject*

Called by a DBEditableTextFormatter object when the user first makes a change to an editable field in the display. A return of YES permits editing to proceed. Your application will not normally need to use this method explicitly.

textWillEnd:

– (BOOL)**textWillEnd:***textObject*

Called by a DBEditableTextFormatter object when it is about to relinquish first responder status. A return of YES permits the change to proceed; a return of NO prevents the change and selects the entire text field. Your application will not normally need to use this method explicitly.

Methods Implemented by the Delegate

moduleDidSave:

– **moduleDidSave:***module*

Called when *module* has completed a save to the database.

moduleWillLoseChanges:

– (BOOL)**moduleWillLoseChanges:***module*

Called when *module* is about to discard changes received from the user interface.

moduleWillSave:

– (BOOL)**moduleWillSave:***module*

Called when *module* is about to save its data to the database.

DBQualifier

Inherits From: Object

Conforms To: DBExpressionValues

Declared In: dbkit/DBQualifier.h

Class Description

A DBQualifier object creates a predicate statement, expressed in the database's query language, that's applied as records are fetched from the database. Records that don't pass the predicate, or *description*, aren't selected for the fetch. The predicate that's created by a description is usually one or more expressions in which the value for a property is compared to a constant value, or to the value for another property.

Creating a Description

A DBQualifier's description is created through the **initForEntity:fromDescription:** or **setEntity:andDescription:** methods. You can add to an existing description through the **addDescription:** method. Each of these methods takes a **printf**-style format-and-values list as its final argument: The first element (the format) is a quoted string that establishes the format of the description, the following elements supply the description with values. Neighboring elements are separated by a comma.

Strings, numbers, and objects can be represented in the format string through the following substitution symbols:

Format symbol	Expected value
%s	A constant string (**const char** *).
%p	A (**const char** *) that names a property of the object's entity.
%d	An **int**.
%f	A **double** or **float**.
%@	An object that conforms to the DBExpressionValues protocol, or a property object created by the Database Kit. (The former includes DBQualifier, allowing you to created a nested qualification.)
%%	No value—this passes a single '%' literally.

The rest of the format string should comprise valid query-language operators and symbols, the names of properties, and whitespace. The adaptor applies the description as a predicate, so you needn't define it as such yourself—for example, if you're creating a DBQualifier description in SQL, a "WHERE" is automatically appended to your description by the adaptor.

Applying a DBQualifier

Once you've created a DBQualifier, there are two ways to apply it:

- If you're using a DBRecordStream or DBRecordList, you can qualify a fetch by passing a DBQualifier object as the argument to the **fetchUsingQualifier:** method.
- If you're using a DBBinder, you can set the qualifier that's used in subsequent selects through **setQualifier:** or **initForDatabase:withProperties:andQualifier:**. (DBBinder separates the select and fetch operations; the qualification is actually placed on the select.)

As an example, let's say you want to retrieve records from the "grocers" database, but you only want those grocers that have a hat size greater than 12 and an IQ less than 95. You could create a DBQualifier and apply it thus:

```
/* The grocers entity is assumed to exist. */
id hatProp = [grocers propertyNamed:"hatsize"];
id iqProp = [grocers propertyNamed:"iq"];
float minHat = 12.0;
int maxIQ = 95;
```

```
/* Create the qualifier. */
DBQualifier *bigButEmpty =
   [[DBQualifier alloc] initForEntity:"grocers"
               fromDescription:"%@ > %d AND %@ < 95",
               hatProp, minHat, iqProp, maxIQ];

/* Apply it to a fetch (assume that the DBRecordList exists). */
[aRecList fetchUsingQualfier:bigButEmpty];
```

Using the convenience of the "%p" substitution, the same description could have been created without the use of property objects:

```
... fromDescription:"%p > %d AND %p < %d",
        "grocers.hatsize", minHat, "grocers.iq", maxIQ];
```

Instance Variables

None declared in this class.

Adopted Protocols

DBExpressionValues	– expressionValue – isDeferredExpression

Method Types

Initializing and freeing	+ initialize – initForEntity: – initForEntity:fromDescription: – copyFromZone: – free
Modifying	– addDescription: – setEntity:andDescription: – setName: – empty
Querying	– name – entity – isEmpty
Archiving	– read: – write:

Class Methods

initialize

+ **initialize**

Initializes the DBQualifier class. This is invoked automatically; you should never invoke it directly.

Instance Methods

addDescription:

– **addDescription:**(const unsigned char *)*descriptionFormat*, ...

Appends the string that's created by the arguments to the DBQualifier's current description. The arguments are in the style of a **printf** statement; see the class description above for the rules governing the format of the description string. Returns **self**.

See also: – **initForEntity:fromDescription:**, – **setEntity:andDescription:**

copyFromZone:

– **copyFromZone:**(NXZone*)*z*

Creates a copy of the DBQualifier, allocating space for it from zone *z*. Returns the copy.

empty

– (BOOL)**empty**

Deletes the DBQualifier's description. Returns YES.

See also: – **isEmpty**

entity

– (id <DBEntities>)**entity**

Returns the entity object to which this DBQualifier can be applied, as set through **setEntity:andDescription:** or one of the **initForEntity:** methods.

See also: – **initForEntity:fromDescription:**, – **setEntity:andDescription:**

free

– **free**

Frees the DBQualifier.

initForEntity:

– **initForEntity:**(id <DBEntities>)*anEntity*

The designated initializer for the DBQualifier class, this initializes a freshly allocated DBQualifier by setting its entity to the argument, but leaving its description empty. Returns **self**.

See also: – **initForEntity:fromDescription:**, – **setEntity:andDescription:**

initForEntity:fromDescription:

– **initForEntity:**(id <DBEntities>)*anEntity*
  fromDescription:(const unsigned char *)*descriptionFormat*, ...

Initializes a freshly allocated DBQualifier by setting its entity to *anEntity* and setting its description as specified by the other arguments, in the style of a **printf** statement: *descriptionFormat* is a quoted string that establishes the format of the description, the following arguments supply the description with values. Neighboring arguments are separated by a comma. See the class description above for the rules governing the format of the description string.

See also: – **initForEntity:**, – **setEntity:andDescription:**

isEmpty

– (BOOL)**isEmpty**

Returns YES if the DBQualifier's description is empty (if it hasn't been set or if the object has received an **empty** message). If the DBQualifier has a description, this returns NO.

See also: – **empty**

name

– (const char *)**name**

Returns the name of the DBQualifier, as set through **setName:**. The ability to name a DBQualifier is provided as a convenience, and to support interface objects. The name isn't used by the mechanism that accesses the database—in other words, a name isn't as important for a DBQualifier's as it is for a property or entity.

See also: – **setName:**

read:

– **read:**(NXTypedStream *)*stream*

Reads the DBQualifier from the typed stream *stream*. Returns **self**.

setEntity:andDescription:

– **setEntity:**(id <DBEntities>)*anEntity*
andDescription:(const unsigned char *)*descriptionFormat, ...*

Sets the DBQualifier's entity and description as given by the arguments. See the **addDescription:** method and the class description, above, for more information on the description format. Returns **self**.

See also: – **addDescription:**, – **initForEntity:fromDescription:**

setName:

– (BOOL)**setName:**(const char *)*aName*

Sets the name of the DBQualifier to *aName*. The name isn't essential, as discussed in the **name** method description. Returns YES.

See also: – **name**

write:

– **write:**(NXTypedStream *)*stream*

Writes the DBQualifier to the typed stream *stream*. Returns **self**.

DBRecordList

Inherits From: DBRecordStream : Object

Conforms To: DBContainers
DBCursorPositioning

Declared In: dbkit/DBRecordList.h

Class Description

The DBRecordList class supports buffered access to records in a database. A DBRecordList object fetches groups of records from a database and presents them as an array that can be accessed using the methods declared in the DBCursorPositioning protocol. A DBRecordList object permits modifications, deletions, and insertions to the individual records which can then be saved to the database as a group. This batch approach to record operations distinguishes DBRecordList from its superclass, DBRecordStream. Note, however, that this increased functionality comes at the cost of increased memory usage.

Setting Up a DBRecordList

You prepare a DBRecordList to fetch records in the same way you would a DBRecordStream. (See the DBRecordStream class specification for details.) Additionally, using the **setRetrieveMode:** method, you can specify whether the fetch will be done synchronously or asynchronously. By default, a DBRecordList retrieves records synchronously, meaning that it won't respond to further messages until it retrieves all records selected by a given query. If you specify the asynchronous mode, the DBRecordList creates a separate Mach thread to fetch the records. The DBRecordList itself is immediately ready to respond to further messages. As the separate thread fetches records, it passes them back to the DBRecordList, which adds them to its list.

There are actually two asynchronous modes, identified by the constants DB_BackgroundStrategy and DB_BackgroundNoBlockingStrategy. These modes differ only in the way the DBRecordList behaves when asked to access a record that hasn't yet returned from the database. For example, if a DBRecordList using the DB_BackgroundStrategy receives a **setLast** message before all records have been retrieved, the **setLast** method will block until it can access the last record. If the DBRecordList were using the DB_BackgroundNoBlockingStrategy, the **setLast** method would return **nil** immediately, indicating a failure to access the last record.

Accessing and Modifying Data

All of DBRecordStream's methods for accessing and modifying records (for example, **deleteRecord**, **isModified**, and **getValue:forProperty:**) work with DBRecordList objects. However, since a DBRecordList can contain multiple records, it also declares methods that take an additional argument, a record index (**deleteRecordAt:**, **isModifiedAt:**, and **getValue:forProperty:at:**).

Methods that access records but don't specify an index act on the record at the present position of the cursor. The cursor can be reported or set by methods declared in the DBCursorPositioning protocol.

Note: The internal cursor maintained by a DBRecordList is independent of the DBFetchGroup's current row or current selection (which depend on actions in the user interface).

Saving Changes

As with a DBRecordStream object, a DBRecordList object attempts to save additions, changes, and deletions when it receives a **saveModifications** message. If an error occurs during the save operation, the DBRecordList sends its delegate a **recordStream:willFailForReason:** message (see the DBRecordStream class description for more information). At the same time, the DBRecordList's cursor is set to point to the row that is failing. Any rows that fail will be "dirty" after the **saveModifications** has completed. This combination of events lets you go back and fix failures, and then resubmit.

Instance Variables

None declared in this class.

Adopted Protocols

DBContainers	– addObject:forBinder:
	– count
	– empty
	– freeObjects
	– objectAt:forBinder:
	– prepareForBinder:

DBCursorPositioning	– currentPosition – setFirst – setLast – setNext – setPrevious – setTo:

Method Types

Initializing and freeing	– init – free – clear
Setting the retrieval mode	– setRetrieveMode: – currentRetrieveMode
Fetching data from the database	– fetchUsingQualifier: – fetchUsingQualifier:empty: – fetchRecordForRecordKey: – recordLimit – setRecordLimit:
Accessing data	– getValue:forProperty: – getValue:forProperty:at: – getRecordKeyValue: – getRecordKeyValue:at:
Modifying data	– setValue:forProperty: – setValue:forProperty:at: – insertRecordAt: – appendRecord – newRecord – isNewRecord – isNewRecordAt: – deleteRecord – deleteRecordAt: – isModified – isModifiedAt: – isModifiedForProperty:at:
Using record indexes	– positionForRecordKey: – moveRecordAt:to: – swapRecordAt:withRecordAt:
Saving data	– saveModifications

Instance Methods

appendRecord

– **appendRecord**

Adds an empty record at the end of the record list by invoking DBRecordList's **insertRecordAt:** method. Returns the value returned by **insertRecordAt:**.

See also: – **insertRecordAt:**, – **newRecord**, – **deleteRecord**, – **deleteRecordAt:**

clear

– **clear**

Resets the DBRecordList. The DBRecordList's record data, list of properties, and list of key properties are emptied. Its **database** instance variable is set to **nil**, but its delegate remains unchanged. Its status is set to DB_NotReady. Returns **self**.

See also: – **empty** (DBRecordStream)

currentRetrieveMode

– (DBRecordListRetrieveMode)**currentRetrieveMode**

Returns the DBRecordList's retrieve mode, which can be DB_SynchronousStrategy, DB_BackgroundStrategy, or DB_BackgroundNoBlockingStrategy. See the class description above for more information.

See also: – **setRetrieveMode:**

deleteRecord

– **deleteRecord**

Deletes the current record. Returns **nil** if there's no current record; otherwise, returns **self**.

See also: – **deleteRecordAt:**

deleteRecordAt:

– **deleteRecordAt:**(unsigned)*index*

Deletes the record at position *index*. Returns **nil** if there's no record at *index*; otherwise, returns **self**.

See also: – **deleteRecord**, – **currentPosition** (DBCursorPositioning)

fetchRecordForRecordKey:

– **fetchRecordForRecordKey:**(DBValue *)*aValue*

Fetches the record identified by the record key stored in *aValue*. Typically, this method is used to find data in DBRecordLists containing related information. For example, suppose one DBRecordList contains employee data and another contains department data. The department data for a specific employee can be found by first getting the value of the department number from the employee record (see **getRecordKeyValue:at:**) and then using it as the argument to **fetchRecordForRecordKey:** in a message to the DBRecordList containing department information.

Returns **nil** if no record has the supplied key value or if an error occurs; otherwise, returns **self**.

See also: – **fetchUsingQualifier:**, – **fetchUsingQualifier:empty:**

fetchUsingQualifier:

– **fetchUsingQualifier:**(DBQualifier *)*aQualifier*

Invoking this method is equivalent to invoking – **fetchUsingQualifier:empty:** with YES as the argument to **empty:**. See – **fetchUsingQualifier:empty:**, below.

fetchUsingQualifier:empty:

– **fetchUsingQualifier:**(DBQualifier *)*aQualifier* **empty:***emptyFirst*

Loads the DBRecordList with records from the database. Before invoking this method, use **setProperties:ofSource:** to specify the source and properties of the data to be retrieved. The scope of the retrieved records is controlled by *aQualifier*. For example, assuming the data source is an SQL database, *aQualifier* could be an object that represents the expression "where name = 'Holbein'". If *aQualifier* is **nil**, all records are retrieved.

If *emptyFirst* is YES, before loading new data, the method first empties the DBRecordList and its list of properties. Setting *emptyFirst* to NO leaves records already fetched in the DBRecordList, and append to them the unique records retrieved by the current fetch. In that case, the effect of successive invocations with different qualifiers builds in the DBRecordList the union of the sets returned by the various qualifiers.

Each fetch can be done synchronously or asynchronously, depending on the fetch mode in effect at the time the fetch is begun (see the class description above for details). If you specify an invalid fetch mode, **fetchUsingQualifier:empty:** raises a DB_UNIMPLEMENTED_ERROR exception.

A synchronous fetch is subject to a limit on the total number of records in the DBRecordList, set by **setRecordLimit:**. If the number of qualifying records would exceed that limit, the DBRecordList receives that number, and the delegate is sent a **recordStream:willFailForReason:** message with the argument DB_RecordLimitReached.

Returns **nil** if the data can't be selected (for example, if the DBDatabase isn't connected to the database) or if the qualifier and DBRecordList refer to different entities in the database; otherwise, returns **self**. After **fetchUsingQualifier:empty:** returns, the DBRecordList's current record is set to the first record in the list.

See also: – **cancelFetch**, – **fetchUsingQualifier:**, – **setProperties:ofSource:**

free

– **free**

Releases the storage for the DBRecordList.

getRecordKeyValue:

– **getRecordKeyValue:**(DBValue *)*aValue*

Places the value of the current record's key property (or properties) into *aValue*.

Returns **nil** if the DBRecordList has status DB_NotReady or if there is no current record; otherwise, returns *aValue*.

See also: – **getRecordKeyValue:at:**

getRecordKeyValue:at:

– **getRecordKeyValue:**(DBValue *)*aValue* **at:**(unsigned)*index*

Places the value of the key property (or properties) for the record at *index* into *aValue*.

This method is especially useful when data must be exchanged between DBRecordLists. For example, suppose one DBRecordList supplies employee information and another supplies department information to the user interface of an application. A user can change an employee's department by selecting from a list of department names. After a department name is selected, you can use **getRecordKeyValue:** to determine the corresponding record's key value so that you can set the department identification in the employee's record.

Returns **nil** if the DBRecordList has status DB_NotReady or if there is no record at *index*; otherwise, returns *aValue*.

See also: – **getRecordKeyValue:**

getValue:forProperty:

– **getValue:**(DBValue *)*aValue* **forProperty:***aProperty*

Places the value for the property *aProperty* of the current record into the DBValue object *aValue* and returns *aValue*.

See also: – **setValue:forProperty:at:**, – **setValue:forProperty**,
– **getValue:forProperty:at:**

getValue:forProperty:at:

– **getValue:**(DBValue *)*aValue*
forProperty:*aProperty*
at:(unsigned)*index*

Places the value for the property *aProperty* of the record at position *index* into *aValue* and returns *aValue*. *aProperty* is an object that conforms to the DBProperties protocol. Such an object is returned by DBDatabase's **propertyNamed:** method. The argument *index* identifies the record within the DBRecordList and has the range from 0 to the value returned by the **count** method.

See also: – **setValue:forProperty:at:**, – **setValue:forProperty**,
– **getValue:forProperty:**

init

– **init**

Initializes a newly allocated DBRecordList. The DBRecordList's **delegate** instance variable is set to **nil**, its retrieve mode is set to DB_SynchronousStrategy, and its cursor (its current record) is set to DB_NoIndex. Returns **self**.

This method is the designated initializer for DBRecordList.

insertRecordAt:

– **insertRecordAt:**(unsigned)*index*

Adds a new, empty record to the record list at *index*. The newly inserted record becomes the current record.

Returns **nil** if the DBRecordList has a DB_NotReady status or if an error prevents the insertion of the record. Otherwise, returns **self**.

See also: – **appendRecord**, – **deleteRecord**, – **deleteRecordAt:**

isModified

– (BOOL)**isModified**

Returns YES if any record in the DBrecordList has been modified, added, or deleted; NO otherwise.

See also: – **isModifiedAt:**, – **isModifiedForProperty:at:**

isModifiedAt:

– (BOOL)**isModifiedAt:**(unsigned int)*index*

Returns YES if the record at *index* is new or has been modified; NO otherwise.

See also: – **isModified**, – **isModifiedAt:for:**

isModifiedForProperty:at:

– (BOOL)**isModifiedForProperty:***aProperty* **at:**(unsigned int)*index*

Returns YES if *aProperty* in the record at *index* has been modified since the record was added to the DBRecordList or fetched from the database; NO otherwise.

See also: – **isModified**, – **isModifiedAt:**

isNewRecord

– (BOOL)**isNewRecord**

Returns YES if the current record is new; that is, it the result of the DBRecordList receiving an **appendRecord**, **insertRecordAt:**, or **newRecord** message.

See also: – **isNewRecordAt:**, – **isModified**

isNewRecordAt:

– (BOOL)**isNewRecordAt:**(unsigned int)*index*

Returns YES if the record at *index* is new; that is, if it was produced by the DBRecordList's receiving an **appendRecord**, **insertRecordAt:**, or **newRecord** message.

See also: – **isNewRecord**, – **isModified**

moveRecordAt:to:

– **moveRecordAt:**(unsigned int)*sourceIndex* **to:**(unsigned int)*destinationIndex*

Moves the record at *sourceIndex* to *destinationIndex*. Returns **nil** if there is no record at *sourceIndex* or if an error prevents the insertion of the record are *destinationIndex*; otherwise, returns **self**.

newRecord

– **newRecord**

Creates a new, empty record by invoking DBRecordList's **insertRecordAt:** method and passing the index of the current row as the argument. Before this operation can take place, the DBRecordList attempts to save modifications of the current record to the database. If these changes can't be saved, **newRecord** returns **nil**, and no new record is created. Otherwise, **newRecord** returns **self**, and the new record becomes the current record.

See also: – **saveModifications**

positionForRecordKey:

– (unsigned int)**positionForRecordKey:**(DBValue *)*aValue*

Searches the records in the DBRecordList for the first record whose key value matches *aValue*. Returns DB_NoIndex if no such record is found; otherwise, returns the index of the matching record.

recordLimit

– (unsigned int)**recordLimit**

Returns the maximum number of records that a fetch can deliver to a DBRecordList (as set by **setRecordLimit:**). If no limit has been set, returns DB_NoIndex.

saveModifications

– (unsigned int)**saveModifications**

Saves to the database any changes (additions, deletions, or modifications) that have been made to the list of records. If the database supports transactions and there's no transaction in progress, this save operation is nested within a new transaction, called a *local transaction*. If there is already a transaction in progress for the RecordList's database, the modification is attempted within that transaction context, without generating a new transaction.

The possible return values from **saveModifications** are as follows:

Value	Reason
0	The save operation was successful.
1	The save completed but not all records were saved. This happens if errors are encountered but the delegate requests that the save proceed anyway.
DB_NoIndex	Either the DBRecordList isn't ready (its status is DB_NotReady or DB_NoRecordKey), or one or more records in the database have changed since they were fetched and the delegate hasn't forced the modifications to be saved. (See **recordStream:willFailForReason:** (DBRecordStream))

If a local transaction can't be committed due to errors, a DB_TRANSACTION_ERROR exception is raised.

If the attempt to save modifications fails, the DBRecordList's delegate is notified by sending it a **recordStream:willFailForReason:** message, and the DBRecordStream's internal cursor is set to the first of the first of the records that should have been saved but weren't.

See also: – **areTransactionsEnabled** (DBDatabase), – **beginTransaction** (DBDatabase)

setRecordLimit:

– **setRecordLimit:**(unsigned int)*count*

Makes *count* the maximum number of records that can be retrieved during a fetch. If a fetch is attempted with a qualifier that would fetch more than this number of records, the method returns the maximum number permitted but sends a **recordStream:willFailForReason:** message to the delegate with the argument DB_RecordLimitReached. Returns **self**.

setRetrieveMode:

– **setRetrieveMode:**(DBRecordListRetrieveMode)*aMode*

Sets the DBRecordList's retrieve mode, which can be DB_SynchronousStrategy, DB_BackgroundStrategy, or DB_BackgroundNoBlockingStrategy. See the class description above for more information.

See also: – **currentRetrieveMode:**

setValue:forProperty:

– **setValue:**(DBValue *)*aValue* **forProperty:***aProperty*

Sets the value for *aProperty* in the current record to that contained in *aValu*e. Returns a nonzero value if successful; otherwise, returns **nil**.

See also: – **getValue:forProperty:**, – **setValue:forProperty:at:**

setValue:forProperty:at:

– **setValue:**(DBValue *)*aValue*
forProperty:*aProperty*
at:(unsigned int)*index*

Sets the value for *aProperty* in the record at *index* to that contained in *aValu*e. Returns a nonzero value if successful; otherwise, returns **nil**.

See also: – **getValue:forProperty:**, – **setValue:forProperty**

swapRecordAt:withRecordAt:

– **swapRecordAt:**(unsigned int)*anIndex* **withRecordAt:**(unsigned int)*anotherIndex*

Transposes the locations of two records. Both arguments must be valid positions in the DBRecordList's sequence of records. Returns **self**, but if an argument is invalid, returns **nil**.

DBRecordStream

Inherits From: Object

Declared In: dbkit/DBRecordStream.h

Class Description

The DBRecordStream class defines an object that gives stream-based access to records in a database. Once a fetch has been made, a DBRecordStream allows sequential access to the returned records, from first to last. The position in the stream is referred to as the cursor or current record (but note that this cursor is unrelated to the current record or current selection in the user interface or the DBFetchGroup). The position in the stream can only be changed by advancing it by 1 (by the **setNext** method), and can't be set back. You can't access the records in random order. (To get random access, use DBRecordList, a subclass of DBRecordStream.) A DBRecordStream allows the addition of records, also one at a time.

Setting Up a DBRecordStream

You create a new DBRecordStream object in the usual way, by sending **alloc** and **init** messages. Before you can use a DBRecordStream to access records in a database, you must specify the source of the data (say, the "authors" table of an SQL database) and the properties (for example, name, address, and telephone number) that are to be fetched from that source. The **setProperties:ofSource:** method lets you do both.

```
id database, authors, recordStream, propertyList;

database = [DBDatabase findDatabaseNamed:"pubs" connect:YES];
authors = [database entityNamed:"authors"];
recordStream = [[DBRecordList alloc] init];
propertyList = [[List alloc] init];

[authors getProperties:propertyList];
[recordStream setProperties:propertyList ofSource:authors];
```

To allow modification of records in the database, a DBRecordStream must know the *key property* (or properties) for the source. A key property uniquely identifies individual records within the source. For example, within a table of employee data, the employee's identification number uniquely identifies the records. Typically, the model created by

DBModeler identifies the key properties of the data sources, but you can set them directly using **setKeyProperties:**.

Optionally, you can specify that the records be returned in sorted order. Sending an **addRetrieveOrder:for:** message to the DBRecordStream associates a sorting order with a property. These messages are additive; for example:

```
id lastName, firstName;

firstName = [authors propertyNamed:"au_fname"];
lastName = [authors propertyNamed:"au_lname"];
[recordStream addRetrieveOrder:DB_AscendingOrder for:lastName];
[recordStream addRetrieveOrder:DB_AscendingOrder for:firstName];
```

The records will be retrieved in alphabetical order according to the authors' last names. For authors having identical last names, the retrieval order will be determined by first names.

Fetching Data

A DBRecordStream accesses data in the database when it is sent a **fetchUsingQualifier:** message.

```
[recordStream fetchUsingQualifier:nil];
```

If the qualifier argument is **nil**, all records within the source will be made available through the DBRecordStream. If you supply a qualifier, only the set of records meeting its restrictions (for example, "au_lname = 'Smith'") will be made available.

Accessing Data in the DBRecordStream

After receiving a **fetchUsingQualifier:** message, the DBRecordStream can be queried for record data. The first record returned by the fetch operation is available immediately; the second and subsequent records can be accessed by sending the DBRecordStream **setNext** messages.

You access the data within a record indirectly, through DBValue objects. The **getValue:forProperty:** method causes the DBRecordStream to set a DBValue object's value equal to a specified property in the current record:

```
id authors, state, recordStream, value;

state = [authors propertyNamed:"state"];
value = [[DBValue alloc] init];

[recordStream getValue:value forProperty:state];
printf("state: %s\n", [value stringValue]);
```

Modifying Records

The data in the DBRecordStream's current record can be modified using the **setValue:forProperty:** method. The current record can be deleted by invoking **deleteRecord**.

To add a new record to the DBRecordStream, you first create an empty record by sending a **newRecord** message. The DBRecordStream responds by using its current set of properties (as returned by **getProperties:**) to create an empty record. Once the empty record has been created, you can set the values for its properties as you would any record.

These modifications, deletions, and additions only affect the current record in the DBRecordStream. To reflect these changes in the database itself, you must send the DBRecordStream a **saveModifications** message. If the database being accessed supports transactions, they should always be enabled before saving modifications. In general, it's both safer for the integrity of the data involved and much more efficient to do this.

Emptying, initing, or fetching records into the DBRecordStream (or DBRecordList) resets it to an "unmodified" state. After that, modifications are tracked until the DBRecordList is refilled or it receives a **saveModifications** message.

Responding to Notification that a Modification Will Fail

A DBRecordStream (or its subclass DBRecordList) notifies its delegate of the impending failure of an operation that would modify, delete, or add records to the database. The delegate receives a **recordStream:willFailForReason:** message. It can then take action to review the condition that caused the failure. In some circumstances, it can refuse to accept the failure.

Saving a record (or a set of records) happens in two stages. First the records are verified. Then they are written out to the database. If a failure occurs during the verification stage, the application can choose to abort the transaction. Having the delegate return YES to the notification **recordStream:willFailForReason:** means that the delegate assents to the failure, and permits the entire save to fail. (This failure doesn't, of itself, abort the transaction of which the save is part.) Alternatively, the application can pretend that the verification succeeded and let the save proceed.

If a failure occurs during the writing stage, here again the delegate can either return YES (thereby assenting to the failure and aborting the operation), or it can return NO (thereby skipping the particular record for which writing failed but going ahead with writing the others). If you choose to have the delegate return NO, you may be left with a situation in which the record's "modified" flag is set and so is the "modified" flag for its DBRecordStream or DBRecordList, *but the offending record is nevertheless unsaved*, and the transaction will nevertheless continue, commit, and return success.

Warning: Before having the delegate return NO to **recordStream:willFailForReason:**, you should be very sure this is what you want it to do! Returning NO permits what looks like successful completion of a save, despite the fact that some of the application's data still differs from the data in the database.

For failures denoted by the failure codes DB_NoRecordKey or DB_RecordStreamNotReady, there isn't much you can do to keep going. In those situations, the method fails regardless of what the delegate returns.

Instance Variables

id **delegate;**
id **source**;
id **properties**;
id **database**;

delegate	The object that responds to notification messages
source	The database entity from which records are to be retrieved
properties	The list of properties of records to be retrieved
database	The DBDatabase object that owns the record stream

Method Types

Initializing and freeing	– init – free
Setting up a DBRecordStream	– addRetrieveOrder:for: – setProperties:ofSource: – getProperties: – setKeyProperties: – getKeyProperties:
Fetching data	– fetchUsingQualifier: – cancelFetch – currentRetrieveStatus
Accessing data	– getValue:forProperty: – getRecordKeyValue: – setNext

Modifying data	– setValue:forProperty: – newRecord – isNewRecord – deleteRecord – isModified – isReadOnly
Saving modifications	– saveModifications
Resetting a DBRecordStream	– clear
Assigning Delegates	– delegate – setDelegate: – binderDelegate – setBinderDelegate:

Instance Methods

addRetrieveOrder:for:

– **addRetrieveOrder:**(DBRetrieveOrder)*anOrder* **for:**(id <DBProperties>)*aProperty*

Associates a retrieval order with the property *aProperty*. The permissible values of *anOrder* are:

Constant	**Meaning**
DB_NoOrder	Remove ordering associated with *aProperty*
DB_AscendingOrder	Sort records in ascending order of the values in *aProperty*
DB_DescendingOrder	Sort records in descending order of values in *aProperty*

You can specify sort orders for multiple properties by sending multiple **addRetrieveOrder:for:** messages; the sorts will be nested. For example, assume you specify an ascending order for a property associated with employee names and a descending order for a property associated with employee salaries. Records will be retrieved in alphabetical order based on the employee's last name and, for employees having the same last name, will be ordered in descending numerical order based on salaries.

If an **addRetrieveOrder:for:** message hasn't been sent to a DBRecordStream object, it retrieves records in ascending order of the first property in its property list.

Returns a **nil** if an error occurs; otherwise, returns **self**.

See also: – **getProperties:**

binderDelegate

– **binderDelegate**

Returns the delegate used by the DBRecordStream's DBBinder objects.

See also: – **setBinderDelegate:**

cancelFetch

– **cancelFetch**

Terminates the current fetch operation and causes a **fetchDone:** message to be sent to the DBRecordStream's DBDatabase object. Returns **self**.

See also: – **fetchUsingQualifier:**, – **fetchDone:** (DBDatabase)

clear

– **clear**

Resets the DBRecordStream. The DBRecordStream's record data, list of properties, and list of key properties are emptied. Its **database** instance variable is set to **nil**, but its delegate remains unchanged. Its status is set to DB_NotReady. Returns **self**.

See also: – **currentRetrieveStatus**, – **free**

currentRetrieveStatus

– (DBRecordRetrieveStatus)**currentRetrieveStatus**

Returns the DBRecordStream's status, which can be:

Constant	Meaning
DB_NotReady	Not ready to fetch or insert data
DB_Ready	Ready to fetch or insert data
DB_FetchInProgress	Fetch in progress; more records are available
DB_FetchCompleted	Fetch finished; no more records remain

delegate

– **delegate**

Returns the DBRecordStream's delegate or **nil** if no delegate has be set.

See also: – **setDelegate:**, – **recordStream:willFailForReason:** (delegate method)

deleteRecord

– **deleteRecord**

Deletes the current record in the DBRecordStream and causes the DBRecordStream to access the next record in sequence, if any.

Returns **nil** if the deletion can't be accomplished; otherwise, returns **self**. If the deletion fails, the DBRecordStream will attempt to notify its delegate of the reason, and the cursor remains unchanged (pointing to the record that should have been deleted but wasn't).

See also: – **recordStream:willFailForReason:** (delegate method)

fetchUsingQualifier:

– **fetchUsingQualifier:**(DBQualifier *)*aQualifier*

Selects data from the database and makes it available to the DBRecordStream. The scope of records retrieved from the database is controlled by *aQualifier*. For example, assuming the data source is an SQL database, *aQualifier* could be an object that represents the expression "where name = 'Holbein'". If *aQualifier* is **nil**, all records in *aSource* are selected. The argument *aQualifier* and the current property list must refer to the same entity; otherwise an error occurs.

In case of error, this method makes the DBRecordStream's list of properties empty, and returns **nil**. Otherwise, returns **self**.

See also: – **cancelFetch**, – **setProperties:ofSource:**

free

– **free**

Releases the storage for the DBRecordStream.

getKeyProperties:

– (List *)**getKeyProperties:**(List *)*keyList*

Fills *keyList* with objects that represent the key properties of the DBRecordStream. Each of these objects conforms to the DBProperties protocol. Returns the newly filled List object.

See also: – **setKeyProperties:**

getProperties:

– (List *)**getProperties:**(List *)*propertyList*

Places the DBRecordStream's property list in *propertyList* and returns *propertyList*.

See also: – **setProperties:ofSource:**

getRecordKeyValue:

– **getRecordKeyValue:**(DBValue *)*aValue*

Places the value of the current record's key property (or properties) in *aValue*.

This method is especially useful when data must be exchanged between DBRecordStreams. For example, suppose one DBRecordStream supplies employee information and another supplies department information to the user interface of an application. A user can change an employee's department by selecting from a list of department names. After a department name is selected, you can use **getRecordKeyValue:** to determine the corresponding record's key value so that you can set the department identification in the employee's record.

Returns **nil** if the DBRecordStream has status DB_NotReady; otherwise, returns *aValue*.

getValue:forProperty:

– **getValue:**(DBValue *)*aValue* **forProperty:***aProperty*

Places the value for *aProperty* into *aValue*. This method is the only means of retrieving record data stored in the DBRecordStream.

When *aProperty* is a relationship, the method sets *aValue* so that it includes the key value of the relationship's source property and the entity that is the relationship's target. (In that case, sending *aValue* the DBValues message **isEntity** would get the response YES.) The fact that the value object identifies the target entity is exploited by the method **setProperties:ofSource:**.

If the status of the DBRecordStream is DB_NotReady, this method return **nil**. Otherwise, it returns the DBValue object.

See also: – **setValueFor:from:**, – **propertyNamed:** (DBDatabase), – **isEntity** (DBValues protocol), – **setProperties:ofSource:**

init

– init

Initializes and returns a newly allocated DBRecordStream. The DBRecordStream's **delegate** instance variable is set to **nil** and its retrieve status is set to DB_NotReady.

This method is the designated initializer for DBRecordStream.

isModified

– (BOOL)**isModified**

Returns YES if the current record has been modified since it was added to the DBRecordStream or fetched from the database; NO otherwise.

See also: – **isNewRecord**

isNewRecord

– (BOOL)**isNewRecord**

Returns YES if the current record is new; that is, it the result of the DBRecordStream receiving a **newRecord** message.

See also: – **newRecord**, – **isModified**

isReadOnly

– (BOOL)**isReadOnly**

Returns YES if the records in the DBRecordStream can only be read, not modified. If a DBRecordStream's key properties haven't been set, **isReadOnly** will return YES.

See also: – **setKeyProperties:**, – **getKeyProperties:**

newRecord

– newRecord

Creates a new, empty record. Before this operation can take place, the DBRecordStream attempts to save modifications of the current record to the database. If these changes can't be saved, **newRecord** returns **nil**, no new record is created, and the cursor is not advanced. Otherwise, **newRecord** returns **self**, and the cursor is advanced to make the new record the current record.

See also: – **saveModifications**

saveModifications

– (unsigned int)**saveModifications**

Saves the new or modified record to the database. If the database supports transactions and there's no transaction in progress, this save operation is nested within a new transaction.

If there is no transaction in progress, a new transaction is created for this operation. If the modifications can be made to the database, this transaction is committed. An error during this commit process raises a DB_TRANSACTION_ERROR exception.

Returns these values:

Value	Reason
1	The save operation was successful.
0	There were no modifications to save.
DB_NoIndex	Either the DBRecordStream isn't ready (its status is DB_NotReady or DB_NoRecordKey), or the record in the database has changed since it was fetched and the delegate hasn't forced the modification to be saved. (See **recordStream:willFailForReason:**)

If the attempt to save modifications fails, the delegate is notified by sending it a **recordStream:willFailForReason:** message, and the DBRecordStream's internal cursor is not advanced to the next record.

See also: – **areTransactionsEnabled** (DBDatabase), – **beginTransaction** (DBDatabase)

setBinderDelegate:

– **setBinderDelegate:***newDelegate*

Sets the delegate for the DBRecordStream's DBBinder objects. This delegate can intercede in operations that would add or modify the database. See the DBBinder class specification for more information.

See also: – **binderDelegate**

setDelegate:

– **setDelegate:***anObject*

Sets the DBRecordStream's delegate. Returns **self**.

See also: – **delegate**, – **recordStream:willFailForReason:** (delegate method)

setKeyProperties:

– (List *)**setKeyProperties:**(List *)*propertyList*

Sets the DBRecordStream's list of key properties to *propertyList*. Each of the objects in *propertyList* must conform to the DBProperties protocol. Typically, key properties are identified in the database model using DBModeler, so you rarely invoke this method.

Returns **nil** if any property in *propertyList* is not a property of the DBRecordStream's source; otherwise, returns the property list.

See also: – **getKeyProperties:**

setNext

– **setNext**

Advances the DBRecordStream's internal cursor by 1, so that it points to the next record in the group of records made available by a fetch operation.

Returns **self** if successful and **nil** if not. A **nil** return can mean that there are no further records to return or that the DBRecordStream was unable to save modifications to the current record.

See also: – **saveModifications**

setProperties:ofSource:

– (List *)**setProperties:**(List *)*propertyList* **ofSource:***aSource*

Sets the properties that will be fetched or stored by a DBRecordStream, or its subclass, a DBRecordList. The properties transferred will be those contained in *propertyList*. The argument *aSource* specifies the entity that contains the properties. If *aSource* is **nil**, the entity for the first property in *propertyList* is used.

The argument *aSource* can also be a DBValue object representing the value of a relationship. In that case, it contains the key value of a source property and the entity of the relationship's target. For example, suppose your application has two record lists, one containing orders (called **orderRL**) and another containing line items (called **lineItemRL**). They are joined by a relationship in which a key value from **orderRL** serves as a foreign key to **lineItemRL**.

The following code fragment prepares to fetch or insert records by using **value** to hold both a value from **orderRL** and the "line item" entity to which the relationship joins it. When **value** is suppied as the argument of **ofSource:**, the effect is to specify both the property to be fetched and the qualifier that selects records from **lineItemRL**.

```
[orderRL getValue:value forProperty:lineItems];
[lineItemRL setProperties:propList ofSource:value];
/* Fetch or insert records here */
```

The application should send a **setProperties:ofSource:** message before doing anything with a DBRecordStream or DBRecordList. Once the list of properties has been set, the application can send **fetchUsingQualifier:** messages, based on the list of properties that has been set. To a DBRecordList, the application can also send **fetchUsingQualifier:empty:**, or can make multiple inserts or multiple deletes. (After once calling **setProperties:ofSource:**, you shouldn't call it again until you really need to establish a new property list, since each use discards any prior data without saving.)

Returns **nil** if the properties in *propertyList* don't share the same entity or if some other error occurs; otherwise, returns **self**.

See also: – **getProperties:**, – **getValue:forProperty:**, – **isEntity** (DBValues protocol)

setValue:forProperty:

– **setValue:**(DBValue *)*aValue* **forProperty:***aProperty*

Sets the value for *aProperty* in the current record to that contained in *aValue*. Returns a nonzero value if successful; otherwise, returns **nil**.

See also: – **getValue:forProperty:**

Methods Implemented by the Delegate

recordStream:willFailForReason:

– (BOOL)**recordStream:***sender* **willFailForReason:**(DBFailureCode) *aCode*

Responds to a message informing the delegate that a modification couldn't be saved to the database. In general, returning YES to this message acknowledges the failure and permits the operation to be aborted, thereby aborting the local transaction of which it is part.

Note: If the local transaction is nested within another transaction, it is the application's responsibility to either rollback or commit the outer transaction.

Returning NO skips the specific record involved but permits the operation to continues the processing of others records (if any).

The *aCode* argument identifies the reason for the failure and can have the following values:

Constant	**Meaning**
DB_RecordHasChanged	The record in the database has changed since it was fetched by the DBRecordStream. Saving the modification would overwrite someone else's changes. Returning YES to this message acknowledges the failure and permits the operation to be aborted. Returning NO skips the record and continues with the others.
DB_RecordKeyNotUnique	More than one record in the database corresponds to the record in the DBRecordStream that is being updated or deleted. Returning YES to this message acknowledges the failure and permits the operation to be aborted. Returning NO permits a *delete* to proceed with the other records, but can't help an update, since update is never permitted with an ambiguous key.
DB_RecordStreamNotReady	The DBRecordStream isn't ready for this operation (its status is DB_NotReady). The boolean return value of the message is ignored.
DB_NoRecordKey	The modification couldn't be saved because no property (or combination of properties) within the record was identified as the record key. The boolean return value of the message is ignored.
DB_AdaptorError	The modification couldn't be saved because of some sort of error reported by the adaptor. Returning YES to this message acknowledges the failure and permits the operation to be aborted. Returning NO skips the record and continues with the others.

See also: – **saveModifications**, – **setDelegate:**, – **delegate**

recordStreamPrepareCurrentRecordForModification:

– (BOOL)**recordStreamPrepareCurrentRecordForModification:***aRecordStream*

Notifies the delegate of a proposed modification to the current record, verifies that the record is unique, and permits modification to proceed only if the return is YES.

If implemented, this delegate method provides an alternative to the standard check that a DBRecordStream performs before deleting or modifying a record. (The DBRecordStream or its subclass normally verifies that a record still exists, and that it is unique. It invokes a "confirming select" on the DBDatabase using the key value, and then compares all properties to see that none has changed. The select is usually a locking select.) This delegate method replaces that mechanism, making the delegate responsible for verification and locking. If the method returns YES, the record is considered to be verified, and modification proceeds. If the method returns NO, the record is not modified, which may cause the entire sequence containing **saveModifications:** to fail, depending on the transaction model being used.

This method should not call any of the methods implemented by DBRecordStream or DBRecordList other than **getValue:forProperty:**

DBTableVector

Inherits From: Object

Conforms To: DBTableVectors

Declared In: dbkit/DBTableVector.h

Class Description

There's a DBTableVector to represent each of the fields (that is, each of the static rows or columns) in a DBTableView. The DBFormatter for each row or column consults the corresponding DBTableVector for the value of various parameters that affect the display.

Instance Variables

id **identifier**
id **formatter**
id **titleFont**;
NXCoord **minSize**
NXCoord **maxSize**
NXCoord **currentSize**
char ***title**;

identifier	The vector's identifying attribute
formatter	The vector's DBFormatter
titleFont	The font for the vector's title
minSize	The vector's minimum height or width
maxSize	The vector's maximum height or width
currentSize	The vectors current height ot width
title	The vector's title

Adopted Protocols

DBTableVectors	– formatter – setFormatter: – identifier – setIdentifier: – isEditable – setEditable: – isResizable – setResizable: – isAutosizable – setAutosizable: – size – sizeTo: – minSize – setMinSize: – maxSize – setMaxSize: – title – setTitle: – titleFont – setTitleFont: – titleAlignment – setTitleAlignment: – contentAlignment – setContentAlignment:

Method Types

Creating the object	– initIdentifier: – free

Instance Methods

free

– **free**

Frees the space that the DBTableVector was allocated. Returns **self**.

initIdentifier:

– **initIdentifier:***newIdentifier*

Initializes a new instance of DBTableVector for the property identified by *newIdentifier*. Returns **self**.

DBTableView

Inherits From: ScrollView : View : Responder : Object

Declared In: dbkit/DBTableView.h

Class Description

DBTableView is a class that displays data in a table. It's similar to the Matrix class, but with two important differences: First, the data resides not in the DBTableView instance but in an external data source (usually a DBRecordList). Second, the table's rows and columns can be individually resized and repositioned by the user.

A DBTableView object consists of up to three different views: A row title view, a column title view, and a content view. The content view can be made scrollable, horizontally, vertically, or both. The row and column title views display title information; the titles automatically scroll with their contents. Either or both the title views may be hidden.

Rows and Columns

Although the appearance of the DBTableView is completely configurable, the usual arrangement is to have a fixed number of properties (fields) arranged as columns. Columns are therefore said to be the table's *static* axis. The rows, representing records, vary dynamically with the data source or with the qualifier used to select records. In that case, rows are said to be the table's *dynamic* axis. Usually such a DBTableView has column titles but no row titles. (If you ask for titles on a dynamic axis, the display shows consecutive integers, reporting the record's position in the data source.)

When a new DBTableView is initialized, it has no rows and no columns, and neither rows nor columns are static. Sending it the first **addColumn:withTitle:** message both adds a column and makes columns static rather than dynamic. Similarly, sending it an **addRow:...** message would do the same thing for rows. A few applications may want to have both rows and columns static. In the common case (that is, static columns, dynamic rows), you call **addColumn:...** for each column, and then hook up a data source to provide the data. The rows will then be determined lazily at display time through the data source's **getValueFor:at:into:** method. Like a very lazy browser, the DBTableView doesn't cache data.

There are two ways to refer to a static vector: by its row or column number, or by the property that it represents. Most of the methods that manipulate specific rows or columns refer to them by row number or column number. These numbers are like indexes to an array: if the user or the application moves a vectors to a new position, or deletes or inserts a vector, the row or column numbers change accordingly.

Formatting

To format the display of its content view, a DBTableView uses subclasses of the abstract superclass DBFormatter (see the specifications of DBFormatter, DBTextFormatter, DBEditableFormatter, and DBImageFormatter). A formatter is responsible for taking the data from a particular row/column intersection within the DBTableView's grid and displaying it in a particular rectangle on the screen. That row/column intersection is in some ways like a Cell within a Matrix object, but there are important differences. Whereas a Cell actually stores its data, a formatter does not; a DBTableView must always refer to its data source to get the values it displays.

Although a formatter displays the field at a single row/column intersection, its formatting rule applies to any of the fields having the same property. That is, in the usual case (with static columns), it applies to all the fields in a particular column. When rows are static, it applies to all the fields in a particular row. Since the formatter can apply either to a row or to a column, it is said to apply to a *vector*—that is, to one axis of the table (be it row or column). The DBVectors protocol provides methods for specifying the format of fields within a vector.

Response to User Action

Although DBTableView is not a subclass of Control, it does implement the target/action paradigm, so that the target to be notified and the action to be performed can be selected in Interface Builder's Conection Inspector. Whenever the user double clicks, or selects a new row or column, whether by mouse action or by pressing the arrow keys, notification is sent to the delegate.

Instance Variables

id **delegate**
id **dataSource**
id **rowLayout**
id **columnLayout**
id **rowHeading**
id **columnHeading**
id **rowsClip**
id **columnsClip**
id **gridView**
id **rowSel**
id **columnSel**
id **cornerView**
id **target**
SEL **action**
SEL **doubleAction**

delegate	The object notified of a double click or change of selection
dataSource	The DBAssociation linking this view to its data
rowLayout	Row layout information
columnLayout	Column layout information
rowHeading	Heading of the selected row
columnHeading	Heading of the selected column
rowsClip	Clip view for the row headings
columnsClip	Clip view for the column headings
gridView	The actual data view
rowSel	The list of selected rows
columnSel	The list of selected columns
cornerView	View in the upper left corner of the DBTableView
target	The object that receives target/action messages
action	Selector of the action of a target/action message
doubleAction	Selector of the action of a double-click message

Method Types

Initializing and freeing	– initFrame: – free
Setting up the DBTableView	– setDataSource: – dataSource
Setting and reporting formatting	
	– formatterAt:: – dynamicRows – dynamicColumns – isRowHeadingVisible – isColumnHeadingVisible – setIntercell: – getIntercell: – setGridVisible: – isGridVisible – acceptArrowKeys: – doesAcceptArrowKeys – allowVectorReordering: – doesAllowVectorReordering – allowVectorResizing: – doesAllowVectorResizing
Notifying the DBTableView of change	
	– reloadData: – layoutChanged: – rowsChangedFrom:to: – columnsChangedFrom:to:

Handling rows and columns	– columnCount – rowCount – columnList – rowList – rowAt: – columnAt: – addColumn:at: – addColumn:withTitle: – addColumn:withFormatter:andTitle:at: – removeColumnAt: – moveColumnFrom:to: – addRow:at: – addRow:withTitle: – addRow:withFormatter:andTitle:at: – removeRowAt: – moveRowFrom:to:
Editing support	– editFieldAt:: – setEditable: – isEditable – endEditing
Handling the selection	– setMode: – mode – allowEmptySel: – doesAllowEmptySel – selectedRowCount – selectedColumnCount – selectedRow – selectedColumn – isRowSelected: – isColumnSelected: – deselectAll: – selectAll: – setRowSelectionOn::to: – setColumnSelectionOn::to: – selectRow:byExtension: – selectColumn:byExtension: – deselectRow: – deselectColumn: – selectedRowAfter: – selectedColumnAfter: – sendAction:to:forSelectedRows: – sendAction:to:forSelectedColumns:

Setting DBTableView components	– rowHeading
	– setRowHeading:
	– setRowHeadingVisible:
	– columnHeading
	– setColumnHeading:
	– setColumnHeadingVisible:
Adjusting the view	– drawSelf::
	– scrollClip:to:
	– isHorizScrollerVisible
	– setHorizScrollerRequired:
	– isVertScrollerVisible
	– setVertScrollerRequired:
	– tile
	– sizeTo::
	– scrollRowToVisible:
	– scrollColumnToVisible:
	– acceptsFirstResponder
Transmitting action	– setAction:
	– action
	– setDoubleAction:
	– doubleAction
	– setTarget:
	– target
Archiving	– read:
	– write:
	– finishUnarchiving
Appointing a delegate	– setDelegate:
	– delegate

Instance Methods

acceptArrowKeys:

– **acceptArrowKeys:**(BOOL)*flag*

Enables or disables the arrow keys for keystrokes the user makes within the DBTableView, as *flag* is YES or NO. The default when a DBTableView is initialized is YES. Returns **self**.

When at least one row is selected, ↑ moves the selection to the row below the highest selected row, and ↓ to the row above it (if necessary, scrolling to make the newly selected row visible); the horizontal arrows do nothing. Similarly, when at least one column is selected, ← moves the selection to the column to the left of the leftmost selected column, and → to the column to the right of it (if necessary, scrolling to make the newly selected column visible); the vertical arrows do nothing. In either case, arrows don't wrap around; if the selection is the first or last vector, pressing the arrow that points to the edge does nothing.

See also: – **doesAcceptArrowKeys**

acceptsFirstResponder

– (BOOL)**acceptsFirstResponder**

Returns YES if the DBTableView accepts the role of first responder for its Window.

action

– (SEL)**action**

Returns the selector for the action method that will be sent to the DBTableView's target when a target/action event occurs in the DBTableView. Usually, this is the action you selected in Interface Builder's Connections Inspector.

addColumn:at:

– **addColumn:***identifier* **at:**(unsigned int)*aPosition*

Inserts a new static column into the DBTableView. The data for the new column will come from the DBRecordList's attribute identified by *identifier*. The new column will be inserted so that it precedes the column whose column-number (before the insertion) was *aPosition*. No title is assigned to the new column; its formatting will be handled by a default formatter. Return **self**.

addColumn:withFormatter:andTitle:at:

– **addColumn:***identifier*
  withFormatter:*formatter*
  andTitle:(const char *)*title*
  at:(unsigned int)*aPosition*

Inserts a new static column into the DBTableView. The data for the new column will come from the DBRecordList's attribute identified by *identifier*. Text for the new column's title will be taken from *title*. The column's formatting will be handled by *formatter*. The new column will be inserted so that it precedes the column whose column-number (before the insertion) was *aPosition*.

addColumn:withTitle:

– **addColumn:***identifier* **withTitle:**(const char *)*title*

Appends a new static column following the last existing column in the DBTableView. The data for the new column will come from the DBRecordList's attribute identified by *identifier.* Text for the new column's title will be taken from *title*. The new column has its own default DBTextFormatter. Returns **self**.

addRow:at:

– **addRow:***identifier* **at:**(unsigned int)*aPosition*

Inserts a new static row into the DBTableView. The data for the new row will come from the DBRecordList's attribute identified by *identifier.* The new row will be inserted so that it precedes the row whose row-number (before the insertion) was *aPosition.* No title is assigned to the new row; its formatting will be handled by a default formatter. Returns **self**.

addRow:withFormatter:andTitle:at:

– **addRow:***identifier*
  withFormatter:*formatter*
  andTitle:(const char *)*title*
  at:(unsigned int)*aPosition*

Inserts a new static row into the DBTableView. The data for the new row will come from the DBRecordList's attribute identified by *identifier.* Text for the new row's title will be taken from *title*. The row's formatting will be handled by *formatter.* The new row will be inserted so that it precedes the row whose row-number (before the insertion) was *aPosition.* Returns **self**.

addRow:withTitle:

– **addRow:***identifier* **withTitle:**(const char *)*title*

Appends a new static row following the last existing row in the DBTableView. The data for the new row will come from the DBRecordList's attribute identified by *identifier.* Text for the new row's title will be taken from *title*. The new row gets it its own DBTextFormatter. If the DBTableView previously had no rows, adding a row makes rows static. Returns **self**.

allowEmptySel:

– **allowEmptySel:**(BOOL)*flag*

Permits the user to deselect a vector (with shift-click) when that would leave nothing selected (or prohibits it, when *flag* is NO). The default is NO. Returns **self**.

See also: – **doesAllowEmptySel**

allowVectorReordering:

– **allowVectorReordering:**(BOOL)*flag*

Permits the user to drag a static vector to a new position within the DBTableView (or prohibits it, when *flag* is NO). The default is YES. To drag a vector, the user must click in the vector's title area (to select it) and then drag; it isn't possible to drag an untitled vector. The new ordering of vectors depends on the ordering of their midpoints. That is, if column B is to the right of column A, to reverse their positions the user must drag B until its midpoint is to the left of A's midpoint. Returns **self**.

See also: – **doesAllowVectorReordering**

allowVectorResizing:

– **allowVectorResizing:**(BOOL)*flag*

Permits the user to drag the edges of a static vector so as to change its height or width (or prohibits it, when *flag* is NO). To resize a vector, the user must start to drag from a position over the title's edge. In that position, the cursor changes to a double arrow (like this ↔ for a column, or the corresponding vertical form for a row). It isn't possible to resize an untitled vector. Returns **self**.

See also: – **doesAllowVectorResizing**

columnAt:

– (id <DBTableVectors>)**columnAt:**(unsigned int)*aPosition*

Returns the object that controls the formatting of the (static) column identified by *aPosition*.

columnCount

– (unsigned int)**columnCount**

For a DBTableView with static columns, returns the number of columns. For a table view whose columns are dynamic, returns the number of columns in the data source.

columnHeading

– **columnHeading**

Returns the view that contains the DBTable's column headings.

columnList

– **columnList**

Returns a list of the identifiers of successive columns in the order that they currently appear in the DBTableView. (If columns aren't static, returns **nil**.)

columnsChangedFrom:to:

– **columnsChangedFrom:**(unsigned int)*startColumn* **to:**(unsigned int)*endColumn*

Notification that the data source has changed the values in a block of consecutive columns, so their display should be redrawn. The first of the changed columns is identified by *startColumn*, the last by *endColumn*. Returns **self**.

dataSource

– **dataSource**

Returns an object that identifies the source from which the DBTableView is getting the data it's displaying. The returned object is a private subclass of DBAssociation; sending it a **fetchGroup** message will return the fetch group that is fetching the data.

delegate

– **delegate**

Returns the DBTableView's delegate. The delegate receives notification of a double click within the DBTableView, or any of the actions that cause a change in the row or column selected.

deselectAll:

– **deselectAll:***sender*

If empty selection is permitted, deselects all selected vectors and their row or column headings. If empty selection is not permitted, deselects all but the first. Notifies the deleegate by sending it a **tableViewDidChangeSelection:** message, and sends an action message to the DBTableViews's target. Returns **self**.

See also: – **allowEmptySel**

deselectColumn:

– **deselectColumn:**(unsigned int)*column*

Deselects the indicated column. However, if this is the only selected column and an empty selection is not allowed, does nothing. Returns **self**.

deselectRow:

– **deselectRow:**(unsigned int)*row*

Deselects the indicated row. However, if this is the only selected row and an empty selection is not allowed, does nothing. Returns **self**.

doesAcceptArrowKeys

– (BOOL)**doesAcceptArrowKeys**

Returns YES if arrow keys are enabled while the DBTableView is first responder.

See also: – **acceptArrowKeys**

doesAllowEmptySel

- (BOOL)**doesAllowEmptySel**

Returns YES if the DBTableView permits the user to deselect a vector (with Shift-click) when that would leave nothing selected. The default is NO.

See also: – **allowEmptySel**

doesAllowVectorReordering

– (BOOL)**doesAllowVectorReordering**

Returns YES if the DBTableView permits the user to drag a static vector (row or column) to a new position. The default is YES.

See also: – **allowVectorReordering**

doesAllowVectorResizing

– (BOOL)**doesAllowVectorResizing**

Returns YES if the DBTableView permits the user to resize a static vector (row or column). The default is YES.

See also: – **allowVectorResizing**

doubleAction

– (SEL)**doubleAction**

Returns the selector for the action to be taken when the user double clicks within the DBTableView. (Usually, the action is interpreted as a request to edit a particular row/column intersection within the table.)

drawSelf::

– **drawSelf:**(const NXRect *)*rects* **:**(int)*count*

Invoked by various methods during scrolling or dragging to redraw the DBTableView. Your application shouldn't need to call this method directly. The argument *rects* is a list of pointers to the coordinates of rectangles in which the DBTableView is visible, while *count* is the number of such rectangles. Returns **self**.

dynamicColumns

– (BOOL)**dynamicColumns**

Returns YES if the DBTableView's columns are dynamic: that is, if the number of available columns is determined by the number of records available (in contrast to the static number of attributes).

dynamicRows

– (BOOL)**dynamicRows**

Returns YES if the DBTableView's rows are dynamic: that is, if the number of available rows is determined by the number of records available (in contrast to the static number of attributes).

editFieldAt::

– **editFieldAt:**(unsigned int)*row* **:**(unsigned int)*column*

Selects the entry at the indicated row and column, and invokes an editor. This achieves programmatically the effect the user would produce by double-clicking a field within the DBTableView's content view.

Editing a field permits the user to change the text displayed there. When the user signals completion (by pressing Enter, or by clicking outside the field being edited), the editor may invoke methods to validate the revised field, and, if it is acceptable, copy its value to the table view's data source. Returns **self**.

endEditing

– **endEditing**

Invoked automatically to redraw the field that has been edited at the conclusion of editing. Returns **self**.

finishUnarchiving

– **finishUnarchiving**

Invoked as the last step in reading a DBTableView from an archive, to position the table view within its frame, layout its rows and columns and their headings (if appropriate), and initialize the selection of rows and columns. You shouldn't need to invoke this explicitly, since it is done automatically as part of the process of reading from an archive. Returns **self**.

formatterAt::

– **formatterAt:**(unsigned int)*row* **:**(unsigned int)*column*

Returns the formatter responsible for the field at the intersection of the indicatated row and column of the display. In a typical display, one axis (usually columns) is static and the other (usually rows) is dynamic. In that case, the same formatter applies throughout a given static position, and the dynamic index is immaterial. If there is no formatter explicitly assigned to the specified field, the method returns a default formatter for the type of data (text or image).

You may want to override this method in order to apply different formatting rules.

free

– **free**

Frees the storage used by a DBTableView instance (by freeing the table view's various internal components before invoking the superclass's **free** method). Returns **nil**.

getIntercell:

– **getIntercell:**(NXSize *)*theSize*

Reports the number of pixels of spacing between adjacent cells, by setting *theSize* with the two values, for horizontal and vertical separation. The default is 2, 2. Returns **self**.

initFrame:

– **initFrame:**(const NXRect *)*newFrame*

Initializes a DBTableView instance within the frame boundaries specified by *newFrame*. The new view has no rows or columns, and both axes are considered dynamic. Initially, there is no title; there are column headings but not row headings; vertical scrollbars but not horizontal ones. Reordering and resizing are enabled (but this has no effect until rows or columns become static). The arrow keys are enabled. Returns **self**.

isColumnHeadingVisible

– (BOOL)**isColumnHeadingVisible**

Returns YES if the column-heading view (containing the headings for all columns) is visible.

isColumnSelected:

– (BOOL)**isColumnSelected:**(unsigned int)*column*

Returns YES if the indicated column is selected.

isEditable

– (BOOL)**isEditable**

Returns YES if the DBTableView is editable.

See also: – **setEditable**

isGridVisible

– (BOOL)**isGridVisible**

Returns YES if the DBTableView's grid lines are visible.

See also: – **setGridVisible**

isHorizScrollerVisible

– (BOOL)**isHorizScrollerVisible**

Returns YES if the horizontal scroller is visible. The default is NO.

See also: – **setHorizScrollerRequired**

isRowHeadingVisible

– (BOOL)**isRowHeadingVisible**

Returns YES if the row-heading view (containing the headings for all rows) is visible.

isRowSelected:

– (BOOL)**isRowSelected:**(unsigned int)*row*

Returns YES if the indicated row is selected.

isVertScrollerVisible

– (BOOL)**isVertScrollerVisible**

Returns YES if the vertical scroller is visible. The default is YES.

See also: – **setVertScrollerRequired**

layoutChanged:

– **layoutChanged:***sender*

Invoked when there is any change in the number, position, width, height, titling, or format of the DBTableView's content, to update all of these. Returns **self**.

mode

– (int)**mode**

Returns the selection mode.

See also: – **setMode**

moveColumnFrom:to:

– (BOOL)**moveColumnFrom:**(unsigned int)*oldPos* **to:**(unsigned int)*newPos*

Changes the position of one of the static columns. The column to move is identified by *oldPos*, its position before the move. Its new position will be *newPos*. That is, in the new sequence, it will precede the column that used to be at *newPos*. The method also makes the corresponding change in the column headings. Returns YES if the move is permitted, NO otherwise. It is never permissible to move a dynamic column.

See also: – **allowVectorReordering:**, – **doesAllowVectorReordering**

moveRowFrom:to:

– (BOOL)**moveRowFrom:**(unsigned int)*oldPos* **to:**(unsigned int)*newPos*

Changes the position of one of the static rows. The row to move is identified by *oldPos*, its position before the move. Its new position will be *newPos*. That is, in the new sequence, it will precede the row that used to be at *newPos*. The method also makes the corresponding change in the row headings. Returns YES if the move is permitted, NO otherwise. It is never permissible to move a dynamic row.

See also: – **allowVectorReordering:**, – **doesAllowVectorReordering**

read:

– **read:**(NXTypedStream *)*stream*

Unarchives a DBTableView object from the archive identified by *stream*.

reloadData:

– **reloadData:***sender*

Rechecks the layout and redraws the display. Returns **self**.

removeColumnAt:

– **removeColumnAt:**(unsigned int)*columnPosition*

Deletes a static column (and its heading) from the display. Returns **self**.

removeRowAt:

– **removeRowAt:**(unsigned int)*rowPosition*

Deletes a static row (and its heading) from the display. Returns **self**.

rowAt:

– (id <DBTableVectors>)**rowAt:**(unsigned int)*aPosition*

Returns the object that controls the formatting of the static row whose row number is *aPosition*.

rowCount

– (unsigned int)**rowCount**

For a DBTableView with static rows, returns the number of rows. For a table view whose rows are dynamic, returns the number of rows in the data source.

rowHeading

– **rowHeading**

Returns the view that contains the DBTableView's row headings.

rowList

– **rowList**

Returns a list of the identifiers of successive static rows in the order that they currently appear in the DBTableView. (If rows aren't static, returns **nil**.)

rowsChangedFrom:to:

– **rowsChangedFrom:**(unsigned int)*startRow* **to:**(unsigned int)*endRow*

Notification that the data source has change the values in a block of rows, so their display should be redrawn. The first of the changed rows is identified by *startRow*, and the last by *endRow*. Returns **self**.

scrollClip:to:

– **scrollClip:***aClip* **to:**(const NXPoint *)*newOrigin*

Changes the portion of the content of the clip view *aClip* that is visible. The change makes the position *newOrigin* (in the content view's coordinates) appear at the clip view's origin (that is, its lower left corner). This message is usually sent automatically, in response to scrolling in the view aClip. It is used to coordinate the scrolling of the content view and the two heading views with a table view, or when the arrow keys make the selected portion of the view outside the clip view. Returns **self**.

scrollColumnToVisible:

– **scrollColumnToVisible:**(unsigned int)*column*

Scrolls the content view and column headings horizontally so that the requested column is visible. Returns **self**.

scrollRowToVisible:

– **scrollRowToVisible:**(unsigned int)*row*

Scrolls the content view and row headings vertically so that the requested row is visible. Returns **self**.

selectAll:

– **selectAll:***sender*

Provided the DBTableView is in list mode (permitting multiple selection), selects all rows and columns and their headings. Notifies the delegate by sending it a **tableViewDidChangeSelection:** message. Returns **self**.

selectColumn:byExtension:

– **selectColumn:**(unsigned int)*column* **byExtension:**(BOOL)*flag*

Selects the column (and its heading) identified by *column*. When *flag* is YES and the DBTableView's mode permits multiple selection, includes *column* in the set of selected columns. Otherwise, this method deselects other columns. Returns **self**.

selectedColumn

– (int)**selectedColumn**

Returns the column number of the selected column. Column numbers are successive integers starting at 0, for the columns actually displayed, in their current left-to-right order in the display. Returns –1 of no column is selected.

selectedColumnAfter:

– (unsigned int)**selectedColumnAfter:**(unsigned int)*aColumn*

Returns the column number of the first selected column that is further to the right than *aColumn*. If *aColumn* is DB_NoIndex and there is at least one selected column, returns the first selected column. If no column is selected, or there is no selected column to the right of *aColumn*, returns DB_NoIndex.

selectedColumnCount

– (unsigned int)**selectedColumnCount**

Returns the number of selected columns.

selectedRow

– (int)**selectedRow**

Returns the row number of the selected row. Row numbers are successive integers starting at 0, for the rows actually displayed, in their current top-to-bottom order in the display. Returns –1 if no row is selected.

selectRow:byExtension:

– **selectRow:**(unsigned int)*row* **byExtension:**(BOOL)*flag*

Selects the row (and its heading) identified by *row*. When *flag* is YES and the DBTableView's mode permits multiple selection, includes *row* in the set of selected rows. Otherwise, this method deselects other rows. Returns **self**.

selectedRowAfter:

– (unsigned int)**selectedRowAfter:**(unsigned int)*aRow*

Returns the row number of the first selected row that is further down than *aRow*. If *aRow* is DB_NoIndex and there is at least one selected row, returns the first selected row. If no row is selected, or there is no selected row lower than *aColumn*, returns DB_NoIndex.

selectedRowCount

– (unsigned int)**selectedRowCount**

Returns the number of selected rows.

sendAction:to:forSelectedColumns:

– **sendAction:**(SEL)*anAction*
  to:*anObject*
  forSelectedColumns:(BOOL)*flag*

Sends the message *anAction* to the object *anObject* once for each column (when flag is NO) or once for each selected column (when flag is YES). Returns **self**.

sendAction:to:forSelectedRows:

– **sendAction:**(SEL)*anAction*
  to:*anObject*
  forSelectedRows:(BOOL)*flag*

Sends the message *anAction* to the object *anObject* once for each row (when flag is NO) or once for each selected row (when flag is YES). Returns **self**.

setAction:

– **setAction:**(SEL)*aSelector*

Sets the action method that will be sent to the DBTableView's target when a target/action event occurs in the DBTableView.

See also: – **action**

setColumnHeading:

– **setColumnHeading:***newColumnHeading*

Sets the view that contains the DBTable's column headings.

See also: – **columnHeading**

setColumnHeadingVisible:

– **setColumnHeadingVisible:**(BOOL)*flag*

Causes the DBTableView to include a heading view across the top of the columns (when *flag* is YES), or to omit it (when *flag* is NO). This in turn causes the DBTableView to recompute its layout and redisplay in response to the change,

setColumnSelectionOn::to:

– **setColumnSelectionOn:**(unsigned int)*start*
:(unsigned int)*end*
to:(BOOL)*flag*

Selects (when *flag* is YES) or deselects (when *flag* is NO) the block of columns from *start* to *end*, inclusive. Returns **self**.

setDataSource:

– **setDataSource:***aSource*

Makes *aSource* the data source from which the DBTableView gets its values, and redisplays the table. Returns **self**.

setDelegate:

– **setDelegate:***delegate*

Makes *delegate* the DBTableView's delegate. Returns **self**.

See also: – **delegate**

setDoubleAction:

– **setDoubleAction:**(SEL)*aSelector*

Sets the action method that will be sent to the DBTableView's target when there's a double-click in the DBTableView. Returns **self**.

setEditable:

– **setEditable:**(BOOL)*flag*

Permits or prohibits editing (as *flag* is YES or NO). The default is YES. Returns **self**.

See also: – **isEditable**

setGridVisible:

– **setGridVisible:**(BOOL)*flag*

Makes grid lines between adjacent rows and columns of the content view visible or not (as *flag* is YES or NO). The space the gridlines use is in addition to the intercell spacing. (Row and column headings always have a separating line, regardless of whether there's a grid in the content view.) Returns **self**.

See also: – **isGridVisible**, – **setIntercell:**

setHorizScrollerRequired:

– **setHorizScrollerRequired:**(BOOL)*flag*

Includes or omits a horizontal scroller along the lower edge of the DBTableView, as *flag* is YES or NO. Including a scroller takes space away from the area otherwise available for the content display. When a scroller is included, it contains a slider and scroll buttons when the total width of the columns exceeds the width of the display; at other times it's blank. Returns **self**.

See also: – **isHorizScrollerVisible**

setIntercell:

– **setIntercell:**(const NXSize *)*aSize*

Sets the number of pixels that separate adjacent rows and columns. The argument *aSize* specifies two values, for horizontal and vertical separation. When gridlines are used, the space they use is in addition to the intercell spacing. Returns **self**.

setMode:

– **setMode:**(int)*newMode*

Sets the DBTableView's selection mode. The possible values are member of the enumeration set DBSelectionType, to wit:

DB_LISTMODE	Shift-clicking a vector adds it to the current selection if it is not already selected, or removes it if it is. (Deselecting a vector may not be permitted if it is the only selected vector and empty selection is not permitted.)
DB_RADIOMODE	Selecting a vector automatically deselects the previous selection.
DB_NOSELECT	Selecting a vector is not permitted.

setRowHeading:

– **setRowHeading:***newRowHeading*

Sets the view that contains the DBTable's row headings.

See also: – **rowHeading**

setRowHeadingVisible:

– **setRowHeadingVisible:**(BOOL)*flag*

Causes the DBTableView to include a heading view down the left side of the rows (when *flag* is YES), or to omit it (when *flag* is NO). Changing the row heading in turn causes the DBTableView to recompute its layout and redisplay in response to the change.

setRowSelectionOn::to:

– **setRowSelectionOn:**(unsigned int)*start*
:(unsigned int)*end*
to:(BOOL)*flag*

Selects (when *flag* is YES) or deselects (when *flag* is NO) the block of rows from *start* to *end*, inclusive. Returns **self**.

setTarget:

– **setTarget:***anObject*

Makes *anObject* the target of a target/action message sent in response to an event within the DBTableView. Returns **self**.

setVertScrollerRequired:

– **setVertScrollerRequired:**(BOOL)*flag*

Includes or omits a vertical scroller along the left edge of the DBTableView, as *flag* is YES or NO. Including a scroller takes space away from the area otherwise available for the content display. When a scroller is included, it contains a slider and scroll buttons while when the total width of the columns exceeds the width of the display; at other times it's blank. Returns **self**.

See also: – **isVertScrollerVisible**

sizeTo::

– **sizeTo:**(NXCoord)*width* **:**(NXCoord)*height*

Resets the overall size of the DBTableView, and then recomputes its layout and redisplays it.

target

– **target**

Returns the object that is the target for a target/action event in the DBTableView.

tile

– **tile**

Places the DBTableView's three component views (content, column heading, and row heading—or as many of them as have been made visible) within the DBTableView's frame. Returns **self**.

write:

– **write:**(NXTypedStream *)*stream*

Archives the DBTableView object by writing it to the NXTypedStream identified by *stream*. Returns **self**.

Methods Implemented by the Delegate

tableView:movedColumnFrom:to:

– **tableView:***sender* **movedColumnFrom:**(unsigned int)*old* **to:**(unsigned int)*new*

Invoked when the user changes the position of a static column. By implementing this method, the delegate can take corresponding action of its own; for example, it might recompute a sort of the displayed record reflecting the changed sequence of columns. Returns **self**.

tableView:movedRowFrom:to:

– **tableView:***sender* **movedRowFrom:**(unsigned int)*old* **to:**(unsigned int)*new*

Invoked when the user changes the position of a static rows. By implementing this method, the delegate can take corresponding action of its own. Returns **self**.

tableViewDidChangeSelection:

– **tableViewDidChangeSelection:***aTableView*

Invoked when the user has changed the selection. The delegate may wish to respond by making corresponding changes to another display that is synchronized with the TableView that sent the message. Returns **self**.

tableViewWillChangeSelection:

– (BOOL)**tableViewWillChangeSelection:***aTableView*

Invoked when the user has taken action to change the selection. By implementing this method, the delegate has a chance to interpose some test of its own. Returning YES permits the change in selection to proceed.

DBTextFormatter

Inherits From:	DBFormatter : Object
Declared In:	dbkit/DBTextFormatter.h

Class Description

DBTextFormatter is one of three subclasses of DBFormatter; the others are DBEditableFormatter and DBImageFormatter. For read-only character-based display of numeric or character information, DBTextFormatter is faster than DBEditableTextFormatter. See the description of the superclass, DBFormatter.

Instance Variables

id **font**;
BOOL **batching**;

font	The current font for displaying text
batching	YES if the same formats apply to a batch of records

Method Types

Initializing	– init – free
Manipulating font	– font – setFont:
Batching format requests	– beginBatching: – resetBatching: – endBatching
Archiving	– write: – read:

Instance Methods

beginBatching:

– **beginBatching:**(id <DBTableVectors>)*attrs*

Notifies the DBTextFormatter that a formatting session is about to begin. You never invoke this method directly; it's invoked by the DBTableView that's using this object as a formatter. The end of a formatting session is signalled by **endBatching**.

See also: – **endBatching**, – **resetBatching:**

endBatching

– **endBatching**

Notifies the DBTextFormatter that a formatting session is over. You never invoke this method directly; it's invoked by the DBTableView that's using this object as a formatter. The beginning of a formatting session is signalled by **beginBatching**:.

See also: – **beginBatching:**, – **resetBatching:**

font

– **font**

Returns the DBTextFormatter's Font object.

free

– **free**

Frees the DBTextFormatter instance.

init

– **init**

Initializes the DBTextFormatter instance. In the course of initializing, the display font is set to the system default font at 12 point and batching is turned off. Returns **self**.

read:

– **read:**(NXTypedStream *)*stream*

Reads the DBTextFormatter from *stream*. Returns **self**.

resetBatching:

– **resetBatching:**(id <DBTableVectors>) *attrs*

Same as **beginBatching:**, but has no effect if batching is already in effect. Returns **self**.

setFont:

– **setFont:***aFont*

Sets the current font to the Font object *aFont*. Returns **self**.

write:

– **write:**(NXTypedStream *)*stream*

Archives the DBTextFormatter to *stream*. Returns **self**.

DBValue

Inherits From: Object

Conforms To: DBExpressionValues

Declared In: dbkit/DBValue.h

Class Description

The DBValue class provides objects that can embody different types of data. DBValue objects are used throughout the Database Kit to retrieve and modify arbitrarily typed values.

A DBValue object consists of two parts: a value and a type. The value and type are set at the same time, through methods such as **setIntValue:** and **setStringValue:**; the value is passed as the argument, the type is set as indicated by the method's name. Once this information has been set, you can retrieve the DBValue's value through methods such as **intValue** and **stringValue**. The value is converted, if possible, to the requested return type. You can retrieve a DBValue's type—the type that was named by the method that set the value—as a DBTypes-conforming object through the **valueType** method.

The type of a DBValue object can be one of the following:

- An object
- A string
- An integer
- A single-precision floating-point number
- A double-precision floating point number
- NULL

The type conversion mentioned above applies only to strings, numeric values, and NULL; you can't convert an object to or from the other data types.

The primary use the Database Kit makes of DBValue objects is to store the values that are contained in a record. The objects are necessary because you can't examine or set a record's values directly: You have to get a record value (indexed by property) into a DBValue object, examine and/or modify the DBValue, and set the DBValue back into the record. Getting and setting record values is typically done through the DBRecordList (or DBRecordStream) methods **getValue:forProperty:** and **setValue:ForProperty:**.

The following example demonstrates how to use a DBRecordList and a DBValue to modify the record that the DBRecordList is currently pointing to:

```
/* Create a DBValue to retrieve and modify a record value. */
DBValue *age = [[DBValue alloc] init];

/* Retrieve the value of a property from a DBRecordList. */
/* (aRecordList and aProperty are assumed to exist. */
[aRecordList getValue:age forProperty:ageProperty];

/* Modify the value and write it back to the record. */
[birthRight setFloatValue:[age intValue]+1.0];
[aRecordList setValue:age forProperty:aProperty];
```

DBBinder also defines a method, **valueForProperty:**, that returns a DBValue that contains the value of the current record for a particular property. However, unlike with a DBRecordList, you can modify the DBValue returned by this method and so modify the record directly.

DBValues are also used to store the values of a record's key properties, and to store the value that's embodied in a DBAssociation.

Instance Variables

None declared in this class.

Adopted Protocols

DBExpressionValues	– expressionValue – isDeferredExpression

Method Types

Creating and Freeing	+ initialize – init – free
Setting values	– setDoubleValue: – setFloatValue: – setIntValue: – setObjectValue: – setObjectValueNoCopy: – setStringValue: – setStringValueNoCopy: – setValueFrom: – setNull
Reporting values	– valueType – isEqual: – doubleValue – floatValue – intValue – objectValue – stringValue – isNull
Archiving	– read: – write:

Class Methods

initialize

+ initialize

Prepares the class for use. You normally don't need to invoke this method; however, if you're creating a subclass that implements an **initialize** method, you should certainly send **initialize** to **super** as part of the implementation. Returns **self**.

Instance Methods

doubleValue

– (double)**doubleValue**

Returns the DBValue's value converted to a double-precision floating-point number. If the conversion can't be performed, a DB_COERCION_ERROR exception is raised.

floatValue

– (float)**floatValue**

Returns the DBValue's value converted to a single-precision floating-point number. If the conversion can't be performed, a DB_COERCION_ERROR exception is raised.

free

– **free**

Frees the DBValue.

init

– **init**

The designated initializer for the DBValue class, **init** initializes a newly allocated DBValue object.

intValue

– (int)**intValue**

Returns the DBValue's value converted to an integer. If the conversion can't be performed, a DB_COERCION_ERROR exception is raised.

isEqual:

– (BOOL)**isEqual:**(DBValue *)*anotherValue*

Compares the DBValue with *anotherValue* and returns YES or NO as their values are or aren't equivalent. The two objects' types needn't be the same; the method will convert the argument's value to that of the receiving DBValue, if necessary, and then perform the comparison. A DB_COERCION_ERROR exception is raised if the conversion isn't supported.

isNull

– (BOOL)**isNull**

Returns YES if the DBValue's value hasn't been set, or if it's been set to the null value appropriate for its type.

objectValue

– **objectValue**

Returns the DBValue's value. The value must be an object, otherwise a DB_COERCION_ERROR exception is raised.

read:

– **read:**(NXTypedStream *)*stream*

Reads the DBValue from the typed stream *stream*. Returns **self**.

setDoubleValue:

– **setDoubleValue:**(double)*aDouble*

Sets the DBValue's value to *aDouble* and declares its type to be a double. Returns **self**.

setFloatValue:

– **setFloatValue:**(float)*aFloat*

Sets the DBValue's value to *aFloat* and declares its type to be a float. Returns **self**.

setIntValue:

– **setIntValue:**(int)*anInt*

Sets the DBValue's value to *anInt* and declares its type to be an integer. Returns **self**.

setNull

– **setNull**

Sets the DBValue's value and type to NULL. Returns **self**.

setObjectValue:

– **setObjectValue:**(id)*anObject*

Sets the DBValue's value to a copy of *anObject* and declares its type to be an object. Returns **self**.

setObjectValueNoCopy:

– **setObjectValueNoCopy:**(id)*anObject*

Sets the DBValue's value to *anObject* and declares its type to be an object. Returns **self**.

setStringValue:

– **setStringValue:**(const char *)*aString*

Sets the DBValue's value to a copy of *aString* and declares its type to be a string. Returns **self**.

setStringValueNoCopy:

– **setStringValueNoCopy:**(const char *)*aString*

Sets the DBValue's value to point to *aString* and declares its type to be a string. Returns **self**.

setValueFrom:

– **setValueFrom:**(DBValue *)*aValue*

Sets the DBValue's value and type to those of *aValue*. Returns **self**.

stringValue

– (const char *)**stringValue**

Returns the DBValue's value converted to a string. If the conversion can't be performed, a DB_COERCION_ERROR exception is raised.

valueType

– (id <DBTypes>)**valueType**

Returns a private, DBTypes-conforming object that stores the DBValue's type. To get a string that represents the Objective C data type from this object, you would send it an **objcType** message. The following table gives DBTypes string representations of the DBValue types:

DBValue type	DBTypes representation
object	"@"
string	"*"
integer	"i"
float	"f"
double	"d"
NULL	NULL

write:

– **write:**(NXTypedStream *)*stream*

Writes the DBValue object to the typed stream *stream*. Returns **self**.

Protocols

DBContainers

Adopted By: DBRecordList

Declared In: dbkit/containers.h

Protocol Description

When a DBBinder fetches a record from a database, it creates a record object to store the data and stores the record object in a container. The DBContainers protocol allows an object to be used as just such a container. See the DBBinder class description for more information on how containers are used.

The DBContainers protocol declares a set of mandatory methods as well as two optional methods, **binder:didAcceptObject:** and **binder:didRejectObject:**. These two are notification methods that are invoked by the DBBinder when objects from the container are used in database-modification operations.

Note: The DBBinder class implements DBContainers as a category of List (declared in the header file **dbkit/DBBinder.h**). This permits a DBBinder to use a List object as a container.

Method Types

Mandatory methods	– addObject:forBinder: – count – empty – freeObjects – objectAt:forBinder: – prepareForBinder:
Optional methods	– binder:didAcceptObject: – binder:didRejectObject:

Instance Methods

addObject:forBinder:

– **addObject:***anObject* **forBinder:**(DBBinder *)*aBinder*

Adds the record object *anObject* to the container. If the addition is successful, this returns **self**, otherwise it returns **nil**. This method is invoked automatically—once per record—by the DBBinder that owns the container as it fetches records from the database.

binder:didAcceptObject:

– **binder:**(DBBinder *)*aBinder* **didAcceptObject:***anObject*

This method is automatically invoked by *aBinder* (the DBBinder that owns the container) after each successful insert, update, or delete operation; *anObject* is the record object that was operated on. This is an optional method that a DBContainers-adopting class can implement to create specialized behavior; if the method isn't implemented, then it isn't invoked. The implementation mustn't change the contents of the container. The return value is ignored.

binder:didRejectObject:

– **binder:**(DBBinder *)*aBinder* **didRejectObject:***anObject*

This method is automatically invoked by *aBinder* (the DBBinder that owns the container) after each unsuccessful insert, update, or delete operation; *anObject* is the record object that was operated on. This is an optional method that a DBContainers-adopting class can implement to create specialized behavior; if the method isn't implemented, then it isn't invoked. The implementation mustn't change the contents of the container. The return value is ignored.

count

– (unsigned int)**count**

Returns the number of objects in the container.

empty

– **empty**

Removes the container's contents, but doesn't free them.

freeObjects

– **freeObjects**

Frees the container's contents.

objectAt:forBinder:

– **objectAt:**(unsigned)*index* **forBinder:**(DBBinder *)*aBinder*

Returns the object at the *index*'th place in the container. Returns **nil** if *index* is out of bounds.

prepareForBinder:

– (unsigned int)**prepareForBinder:**(DBBinder *)*aBinder*

Prepares the container for a data operation. For example, if the container is lazy—if it compacts, sorts, or otherwise keeps itself up-to-date only on demand—then this is the place for it to dust itself off. Returns the number of objects in the container.

DBCursorPositioning

Adopted By:	DBRecordList DBBinder
Declared In:	dbkit/cursors.h

Protocol Description

The DBCursorPositioning protocol lets an object be used as a cursor (or pointer) into a list of records, as contained by a DBRecordList or a DBBinder's container. You should need to adopt this protocol in a custom class only if you're creating your own container for a DBBinder (in the manner of DBRecordList). And in that case, you should only access records through methods defined by your container. In other words, if you position the cursor by sending your object one of the DBCursorPositioning messages, you shouldn't then try to retrieve record values through DBBinder's **valueForProperty:** method.

Method Types

Setting the position	– setFirst – setLast – setNext – setPrevious – setTo:
Querying the position	– currentPosition

Instance Methods

currentPosition

– (long)**currentPosition**

Returns the index of the record to which the cursor is currently pointing.

setFirst

– **setFirst**

Sets the cursor to point to the first record in the container and returns that record. Returns **nil** if the container holds no records.

setLast

– **setLast**

Sets the cursor to point to the last record in the container and returns that record. Returns **nil** if the container holds no records.

setNext

– **setNext**

Sets the cursor to point to the next record in the container and returns that record. Returns **nil** and doesn't move the cursor if it's currently pointing to the last record.

setPrevious

– **setPrevious**

Sets the cursor to point to the previous record in the container and returns that record. Returns **nil** and doesn't move the cursor if it's currently pointing to the first record.

setTo:

– **setTo:**(long int)*index*

Sets the cursor to point to the *index*'th record in the container and returns that record. Returns **nil** and doesn't move the cursor if *index* is out of bounds.

DBCustomAssociation

(informal protocol)

Category Of: Object

Declared In: dbkit/DBAssociation.h

Category Description

Where an application uses a custom subclass of DBAssociation to record the link between a data source (such as a DBRecordList or the contents of a DBBinder), the object in the user interface that displays the associated data should implement methods from this informal protocol. They correspond to instance methods in DBAssociation.

Method Types

Access to the associated value	– association:setValue: – association:getValue:
Notifications to the associated display	– associationContentsDidChange: – associationSelectionDidChange: – associationCurrentRecordDidDelete:

Instance Methods

association:getValue:

– **association:***association* **getValue:**(DBValue *)*value*

Gets the value of the associated destination, and copies it to *value*. Returns **self**.

See also: – **getValue:** (DBAssociation class)

association:setValue:

– **association:***association* **setValue:**(DBValue *)*value*

Causes the destination to display *value*. Returns **self**.

See also: – **setValue:** (DBAssociation class)

associationContentsDidChange:

– **associationContentsDidChange:***association*

Notification that there has been a change to the data values in a portion of the DBFetchGroup's DBRecordList, necessitating a corresponding change in the user interface object.

associationCurrentRecordDidDelete:

– **associationCurrentRecordDidDelete:***association*

Notification that the current record has been deleted from the DBFetchGroup's DBRecordList, necessitating a corresponding change in the user interface object.

associationSelectionDidChange:

– **associationSelectionDidChange:***association*

Notification that there has been some sort of change in the current record of the DBFetchGroup. The change could be to change the selection to a different row, or to add a selection, or to deselect an existing section so that no row is selected. Usually the change is produced by something the user did.

DBEntities

Adopted By: no NeXTSTEP classes

Incorporates: DBTypes

Declared In: dbkit/entities.h

Protocol Description

The DBEntities protocol lets an object represent a database *entity*. An entity comprises a list of data categories, or *properties*. As data is read from a database for a particular entity, an "instance" of the entity (a *record*) is created and filled with data, one datum per property.

It's tempting to speak of an entity as a database table. They're similar. You can think of a table as the corporealization of an entity. Put another way, an entity describes how a table organizes its data into columns (properties). However, you should keep in mind that an entity doesn't contain data (nor do the properties within the entity). Furthermore, neither entities nor properties are "placeholders" for data. Entities and properties neither store nor make room for data, they simply provide a description of the type and location of data so some other object (a record) can be created to adequately store this data.

Typically, an application doesn't create entity objects directly, but, instead, reads them from a database model file. This is performed by creating a DBDatabase object and connecting it to the file (through methods described in the DBDatabase class specification). You can retrieve, in a List, the entity objects that the DBDatabase read from the model file by sending the DBDatabase a **getEntities:** message. Alternatively, you can retrieve a single entity object by name through **entityNamed:**. Both of these methods return private DBEntities-conforming objects that are created and owned by the Database Kit.

Entity object are used as arguments in a handful of important methods. Most notable of these, you typically use an entity as the source in an invocation of DBRecordList's **setProperties:ofSource:**. In addition, an entity is required by the DBQualifier and DBExpression initialization methods.

The DBEntities protocol incorporates the DBTypes protocol. It does this for one reason: the type of Objective C data described by a property that represents a relationship is a DBEntities object. Thus, if the **isEntity** message returns YES when sent to the value returned by sending **propertyType** to a property, then that property is a relationship. This is demonstrated in the following example:

```
/* Get the properties from an entity.  Check for relationships. */
int counter;
List *propList = [[List alloc] init];
id prop;

[anEntity getProperties:propList];
for (counter = 0; counter < [aList count]; counter++)
{
   prop=[aList objectAt:counter];
   if ([[prop propertyType] isEntity])
      printf("Property named %s is a relationship.\n", [prop name]);
}
```

Warning: You should never send the DBTypes messages **objcClassName** or **databaseType** to the private entity objects that are returned by the aforementioned DBDatabase methods. The private entity class implements these DBTypes methods to raise DB_UNIMPLEMENTED_ERROR exceptions.

It isn't anticipated that you should need to create your own class that adopts the DBEntities protocol. The entity objects returned by **getEntities:** and **entityNamed:** should be adequate for most applications.

Method Types

Querying the object	– name – database – getProperties: – propertyNamed:
Comparing the object	– matchesEntity:

Instance Methods

database

– (DBDatabase *)**database**

Returns the DBDatabase object that created the entity.

getProperties:

– **getProperties:**(List *)*aList*

Returns, in *aList*, a list of the entity's properties. Each object in the list conforms to the DBProperties protocol.

matchesEntity:

– (BOOL)**matchesEntity:**(id <DBEntities>)*anEntity*

Returns YES or NO if the receiving entity and *anEntity* were created from the same model file entity.

name

– (const char *)**name**

Returns the entity's name. This is the same name as given to the entity in the model file from which it was read.

propertyNamed:

– **propertyNamed:**(const char *)*aName*

Returns the property named *aName*. If the entity has no such property, **nil** is returned.

DBExpressionValues

Adopted By: DBExpression
DBQualifier
DBValue

Declared In: dbkit/expressionValues.h

Protocol Description

The DBExpressionValues protocol allows an object to be used in a query-language statement. Its principal method, **expressionValue**, returns a string that gives an object's representation as it should appear in such a statement.

A second method, **isDeferredExpression**, returns a boolean that indicates whether the invocation of **expressionValue** should be deferred until the "last possible moment." This is useful for classes, such as DBExpression, that concatenate values stored in separate objects. As the larger expression is being built, the DBExpression asks each of the value-holding objects whether it is deferred. If the values aren't deferred, it can send an **expressionValue** message as soon as the value-holding object is added. But if any is deferred, it should delay until all the objects are in place, and then send an **expressionValue** message to each of them.

Instance Methods

expressionValue

– (const char *)**expressionValue**

Returns the value of an expression object as a string that represents the expression in the query language.

isDeferredExpression

– (BOOL)**isDeferredExpression**

Returns YES if evaluation of the expression should be deferred (for example, until related expressions are ready).

DBFormatConversion
(informal protocol)

Category Of: Object

Declared In: dbkit/customType.h

Category Description

This category is the companion of the category DBFormatInitialization. The two provide part of the mechanism the Database Kit uses to transfer Objective C objects between the database and the application. DBFormatConversion provides a method that specifies the format of the data contained in a buffer that the adaptor will use while transferring data from the application to the database. You'll need explicit use of these methods only if your application uses formats other than those already supported in the Database Kit. (The kit supports any object in the archive format appropriate to its class, as well as NXData using RTF format, or NXImage using TIFF or EPS format.)

Instance Methods

writeBuffer:ofLength:usingFormat:

– **writeBuffer:**(void **)*bufferPtr*
ofLength:(unsigned *)*lengthPtr*
usingFormat:(const char *)*aFormatName*;

If your application creates a custom class that's associated with a property and your class implements this method, this method will be invoked automaticaily when the Database Kit tries to store the object into the database.

The pointer **bufferPtr* may point either to an existing buffer or to NULL. If it points to an existing buffer, **lengthPtr* points to the buffer's length. But if **bufferPtr* points to NULL, the method should allocate space for a new buffer as needed, and should write the length it allocates into the location that **lengthPtr* points to.

The argument *aFormatName* is a string containing the name of the format in which the data is written. The Database Kit defines the following names for formats:

- "EPS"
- "RTF"
- "TIFF"

Alternatively, the string may be the name of any type your application recognizes, as declared in DBModeler's Attribute Inspector for data of type Object.

DBFormatInitialization
(informal protocol)

Category Of: Object

Declared In: dbkit/types.h

Category Description

This category is the companion of the category DBFormatConversion. The two provide part of the mechanism the Database Kit uses to transfer Objective C objects between the database and the application. DBFormatInitialization provides a method that specifies the format of the data contained in a buffer that the adaptor uses while reading data from the database. You'll need explicit use of these methods only if your application uses formats other than those already supported in the Database Kit. (The kit supports any object in the archive format appropriate to its class, as well as NXData using RTF format, or NXImage using TIFF or EPS format.)

Instance Methods

initFromBuffer:ofLength:withFormat:

– **initFromBuffer:**(void *)*buffer*
  ofLength:(unsigned)*length*
  withFormat:(const char *)*aFormatName*

If your application creates a custom class that's associated with a property and your class implements this method, this method will be invoked automatically when the Database Kit tries to read data from the database for delivery as an instance of your class.

The argument *buffer* is an already allocated buffer, and *length* describes the buffer's length.

The argument *aFormatName* is a string containing the name of the format in which the data is written. The Database Kit defines the following names for formats:

- "EPS"
- "RTF"
- "TIFF"

Alternatively, the string may be the name of any type your application recognizes, as declared in DBModeler's Attribute Inspector for data of type Object.

DBFormatterValidation

(informal protocol)

Category Of: Object

Declared In: dbkit/tableProtocols.h

Category Description

This informal protocol is one of the mechanisms the Database Kit uses to place objects into the database. If a class is associated with a property and it implements this method, this method will be called when the kit tries to store the object into the database.

Method Types

Notifications by identifiers	– formatterDidChangeValueFor::to:sender: – formatterWillChangeValueFor::sender: – formatterWillChangeValueFor::to:sender:
Notification by position	– formatterDidChangeValueFor:at:to:sender: – formatterWillChangeValueFor:at:sender: – formatterWillChangeValueFor:at:to:sender:

Instance Methods

formatterDidChangeValueFor::sender:

– **formatterDidChangeValueFor:***rowIdentifier*
:*columnIdentifer*
sender:*sender*

Notification that may be sent when the formatter has changed the value in a field. The field that changed is identified by its *rowIdentifier* and its *columnIdentifier* (for the situation in which both rows and columns are static).

The argument *sender* is the sender of the message (usually a formatter). Returns **self**.

formatterDidChangeValueFor::to:sender:

– **formatterDidChangeValueFor:***rowIdentifier*
  :*columnIdentifer*
  to:*aValue*
  sender:*sender*

Notification that may be sent when the formatter has changed the value in a field. The field that changed is identified by its *rowIdentifier* and its *columnIdentifier* (for the situation in which both rows and columns are static).

The argument *aValue* is the object that contains the new value. The argument *sender* is the sender of the message (usually a formatter). Returns **self**.

formatterDidChangeValueFor:at:sender:

– **formatterDidChangeValueFor:***identifier*
  at:(unsigned int)*position*
  sender:*sender*

Notification that may be sent when the formatter has changed the value in a field. The field that changed is identified by its *identifier* (usually associated with a column, but could be the identifier of a row if rows are static) and its *position* (usually a row number, but could be a column number if columns are dynamic).

The argument *sender* is the sender of the message (usually a formatter). Returns **self**.

formatterDidChangeValueFor:at:to:sender:

– **formatterDidChangeValueFor:***identifier*
  at:(unsigned int)*position*
  to:*aValue*
  sender:*sender*

Notification that may be sent when the formatter has changed the value in a field. The field that changed is identified by its *identifier* (usually associated with a column, but could be the identifier of a row if rows are static) and its *position* (usually a row number, but could be a column number if columns are dynamic).

The argument *aValue* is the object that contains the new value. The argument *sender* is the sender of the message (usually a formatter). Returns **self**.

formatterWillChangeValueFor::to:sender:

– (BOOL)**formatterWillChangeValueFor:***rowIdentifier*
:*columnIdentifier*
to:*aValue*
sender:*sender*

Notification that may be sent when the formatter is about to change the value in a field. The field in which the proposed change will take place is identified by its *rowIdentifier* and its *columnIdentifier* (for the situation in which both rows and columns are static).

The argument *aValue* is the object that contains the proposed new value. The argument *sender* is the sender of the message (usually a formatter). Returning YES permits the change to be recorded in the record list (and thus ultimately in the database).

formatterWillChangeValueFor:at:to:sender:

– (BOOL)**formatterWillChangeValueFor:***identifier*
at:(unsigned int)*position*
to:*aValue*
sender:*sender*

Notification that may be sent when the formatter is about to change the value in a field. The field in which the proposed change will take place is identified by its *identifier* (usually associated with a column, but could be the identifier of a row if rows are static) and its *position* (usually a row number, but could be a column number if columns are dynamic).

The argument *aValue* is the object that contains the proposed new value. The argument *sender* is the sender of the message (usually a formatter). Returning YES permits the change to be recorded in the record list (and thus ultimately in the database).

DBFormatterViewEditing

Adopted By: no NeXTSTEP classes

Declared In: dbkit/DBEditableFormatter.h

Protocol Description

The method in this protocol provides a means by which a view containing a field that is being edited can receive a message from the object doing the editing (for example, an instance of DBEditableFormatter).

Instance Methods

formatterDidEndEditing:endChar:

– (BOOL)**formatterDidEndEditing:***sender* **endChar:**(unsigned short)*whyEnd*

Invoked by an editor when the user completes editing of an editable field by pressing one of the keys that moves to another field (Return, Tab, or Shift-Tab). The field that was being edited is redrawn, and the cursor is moved to the next field, depending on which character was *whyEnd*: NX_RETURN, NX_TAB, or NX_BACKTAB. Returns YES, unless invoked while no field was being edited.

DBProperties

Adopted By: DBExpression

Declared In: dbkit/properties.h

Protocol Description

An object that conforms to the DBProperties protocol represents a named category of information in an entity (an object that conforms to the DBEntities protocol). Put less formally, a property represents a column in a database table. For example, a table that contains information about a physician's patients might contain the columns "name", "address", and "blood type". The "name" column would be represented as a single property object; similarly, "address" would be a separate property.

While a property object represents a column, it doesn't contain the data that's in the column—data is contained in a table's rows, or *records*. A records is said to have a value *for* a property: A record from the physician's patients table would have a value *for* the blood type property.

A property object describes a column, primarily, through three elements, an entity, a name, and a data type:

- The entity is the object to which the property belongs—a property can only belong to one entity at a time.
- Within an entity, a property has a unique name such that if two property objects belong to the same entity and have the same name, then they're representing the same category.
- A property's data type establishes the type of data that's held by a record for that property—all values for that property must be of the same type. The type is embodied in a private object that conforms to the DBTypes protocol; the object can be retrieved through the **propertyType** method.

To retrieve a list of properties contained in a particular entity object, you send the entity a **getProperties:** message. You can find a particular property by name by sending the entity a **propertyNamed:** message. The DBProperties that these methods return are created privately by the Database Kit when the entity is read from a model file. You would typically use these properties to initialize a DBBinder, DBRecordList, or DBRecordStream object. Properties are also needed by methods defined by these classes as "value indices" into records. For example, the DBBinder method **valueForProperty:** returns the DBValue object that's stored in the current record for the given property. Put more naturally, the method returns the value in a particular column.

The DBExpression class adopts the DBProperties protocols. The DBExpression objects that you create and the properties returned by the DBEntities methods described above should suffice for most applications—you shouldn't need to create your own class that adopts the DBProperties protocol.

Method Types

Identifying a property	– name – setName: – entity
Querying a property	– propertyType – isSingular – isReadOnly – isKey – matchesProperty:

Instance Methods

entity

– (id <DBEntities>)**entity**

Returns the entity to which the property belongs.

isKey

– (BOOL)**isKey**

Returns YES if the property can be used as a *key property* for its entity. A key property is one that can distinguish the records in the entity; in other words, the value of each record for the key property must be unique.

isReadOnly

– (BOOL)**isReadOnly**

Returns YES if the data categorized by the property is read-only; in other words, if it can't be written back to the database.

isSingular

– (BOOL)**isSingular**

Returns YES if the property represents an attribute or a one-to-one relationship. Otherwise—to wit, if it's a one-to-many relationship—it returns NO.

matchesProperty:

– (BOOL)**matchesProperty:** (id <DBProperties>)*aProperty*

Returns YES if the receiving property and *aProperty* identify the same thing—if they're in the same entity and have the same name. Otherwise returns NO.

name

– (const char *)**name**

Returns the property's name. For a property read from a model file, this is the name given it by the DBModeler application. To name a DBExpression object, use the **setName:** method.

propertyType

– (id <DBTypes>) **propertyType**

Returns a DBTypes-conforming object that encapsulates the property's data type. All the values that the property categorizes are of this type.

setName:

– (BOOL)**setName:**(const char *)*aName*

Sets the property's name to a copy of *aName*. This method is designed to be used to name DBProperties objects that you create yourself (as explained in the class description, above, such objects will almost certainly be DBExpressions). You shouldn't alter the name of a property that was created for you from a model file. Returns YES if the name was set as requested, otherwise return NO.

DBTableDataSources

(informal protocol)

Category Of:	Object
Declared In:	dbkit/tableProtocols.h

Category Description

The DBTableDataSource protocol provides methods used by the DBTableView and its formatters to determine what should be displayed to the user. The object designated as the DBTableView's data source must be prepared to report how many rows of data are available, to supply values for a given row and column, and to accept modified values for a given row and column.

Method Types

Reporting table size	– rowCount – columnCount
Getting/setting data	– getValueFor:at:into: – getValueFor::into: – setValueFor:at:from: – setValueFor::from:

Instance Methods

columnCount

– (unsigned int)**columnCount**

Returns the number of columns in the data table from which values are being displayed.

getValueFor::into:

– **getValueFor:***rowIdentifier*
 :*columnIdentifier*
 into:*aValue*

Copies the value of an attribute from the data source (for example, a DBRecordList) into the object *aValue*. The arguments *rowIdentifier* and *columnIdentifier* are properties (so this method of extracting a value does not depend on position either in the data source or in the display). Returns **self**.

See also: – **getValueFor:at:into:**

getValueFor:at:into:

– **getValueFor:***identifier*
 at:(unsigned int)*aPosition*
 into:*aValue*

Copies the value of an attribute from a position in the data source (for example, a DBRecordList) into the object *aValue*. The argument *identifier* describes the desired attributed in terms used by the source, rather than those used by the display, which may differ. (See the discussion of *identifier* in the DBTableVectors protocol.) The argument *aPosition* is an index in the source table. Returns **self**.

See also: – **getValueFor::into:**

rowCount

– (unsigned int)**rowCount**

Returns the number of rows in the data table from which values are being displayed.

setValueFor::from:

– **setValueFor:***rowIdentifier*
 :*columnIdentifier*
 from:*aValue*

Sets an attribute in the data source (for example, a DBRecordList) so that its value becomes *aValue*. The arguments *rowIdentifier* and *columnIdentifier* are properties (so this method of setting a value does not depend on position either in the data source or in the display). Returns **self**.

See also: – **setValueFor:at:from:**

setValueFor:at:from:

– **setValueFor:***identifier*
 at:(unsigned int)*aPosition*
 from:*aValue*

Sets an attribute at a position in the data source (for example, a DBRecordList) so that its value becomes *aValue*. The argument *identifier* describes the target attributed in terms used by the source, rather than those used by the display, which may differ. (See the discussion of *identifier* in the DBTableVectors protocol.) Copies the value of the object *aValue* into *aPosition*, an index in the source table. Returns **self**.

See also: – **setValueFor::from:**

DBTableVectors

Adopted By: DBTableVector

Declared In: dbkit/tableProtocols.h

Protocol Description

Methods in the DBTableVectors protocol are used to specify the formatting of cells within a DBTableView. In general, a format applies throughout a *vector* (that is, one of the table's rows or columns). When a DBTableView is structured so that attributes are shown as static columns while records are dynamically arranged on successive rows, there is usually a separate format for each static column, but a single row format that applies to all rows.

An *identifier* identifies an attribute (that is, a field) as it is known to the data source from which data is being taken. (The data source is an association to a fetch group for DBRecordList or DBRecordStream. Fields in the associated data source may be at different positions or have different names from those used in the display.)

A *formatter* is the DBFormatter object responsible for formatting the display.

Method Types

Controlling/reporting formatter	– formatter – setFormatter:
Controlling/reporting data link	– identifier – setIdentifier:
Controlling/reporting editing	– isEditable – setEditable:

Controlling/reporting size	– isResizable – setResizable: – isAutosizable – setAutosizable: – size – sizeTo: – minSize – setMinSize: – maxSize – setMaxSize:
Controlling/reporting title	– title – setTitle: – titleFont – setTitleFont: – titleAlignment – setTitleAlignment:
Controlling/reporting content alignment	– contentAlignment – setContentAlignment:

Instance Methods

contentAlignment

– (int)**contentAlignment**

Returns the horizontal alignment of the row or column's content. The return value can be one of three constants: NX_LEFTALIGNED, NX_CENTERED, or NX_RIGHTALIGNED.

formatter

– **formatter**

Returns the formatter responsible for displaying items.

identifier

– **identifier**

Returns the property of the data source from which the displayed data is taken.

isAutosizable

– (BOOL)**isAutosizable**

Returns YES if the row or column is autosizable (that is, it resizes itself in response to a change in the DBTableView's content view).

isEditable

– (BOOL)**isEditable**

Returns YES if the displayed row or column is editable.

isResizable

– (BOOL)**isResizable**

Returns YES if the row or column is resizable (that is, it permits the user to change its width in the display).

maxSize

– (NXCoord)**maxSize**

Returns a vector's greatest permissible size (the width or a column or the height of a row).

minSize

– (NXCoord)**minSize**

Returns a vector's least permissible size (the width or a column or the height of a row).

setAutosizable:

– **setAutosizable:**(BOOL)*flag*

Permits or prohibits autosizing of the row or column, as the value of *flag* is YES or NO.

setContentAlignment:

– **setContentAlignment:**(int)*align*

Sets the horizontal alignment of the row or column's content. The argument *align* can be one of three constants: NX_LEFTALIGNED, NX_CENTERED, or NX_RIGHTALIGNED.

setEditable:

– **setEditable:**(BOOL)*flag*

Permits or prohibits editing of the row or column, as the value of *flag* is YES or NO.

setFormatter:

– **setFormatter:***newFormatter*

Makes *newFormatter* the object responsible for displaying an item in this vector (row or column). Returns **self**.

setIdentifier:

– **setIdentifier:***aDataAttribute*

Sets the attribute of the data source from which the displayed data is taken.

setMaxSize:

– **setMaxSize:**(NXCoord)*newMaxSize*

Sets a vector's greatest permissible size (the width or a column or the height of a row)

setMinSize:

– **setMinSize:**(NXCoord)*newMinSize*

Sets a vector's least permissible size (the width or a column or the height of a row).

setResizable:

– **setResizable:**(BOOL)*flag*

Permits or prohibits resizing the row or column, as *flag* is YES or NO.

setTitle:

– **setTitle:**(const char *)*title*

Sets the title of the row or column to *title*.

setTitleAlignment:

– **setTitleAlignment:**(int)*align*

Sets the horizontal alignment of the row or column's title. The argument *align* can be one of three constants: NX_LEFTALIGNED, NX_CENTERED, or NX_RIGHTALIGNED.

setTitleFont:

– **setTitleFont:***fontObj*

Sets the font used to draw the row or column's title to *fontObj*.

size

– (NXCoord)**size**

Returns the width and height of the display cell.

sizeTo:

– (NXCoord)**sizeTo:**(NXCoord)*newSize*

Sets the width and height of the display cell to the values in *newSize*. Returns **self**.

title

– (const char *)**title**

Returns the title of the row or column.

titleAlignment

– (int)**titleAlignment**

Returns the horizontal alignment of the row or column's title. The return value can be one of three constants: NX_LEFTALIGNED, NX_CENTERED, or NX_RIGHTALIGNED.

titleFont

– titleFont

Returns (as a Font object) the font for the row or column's title.

DBTransactions

Adopted By: no NeXTSTEP classes

Declared In: dbkit/transactions.h

Protocol Description

This protocol defines the three methods that are required of an adaptor that supports transaction processing.

Method Types

Basic transaction commands	– beginTransaction – commitTransaction – rollbackTransaction

Instance Methods

beginTransaction

– (BOOL)**beginTransaction**

The adaptor tells the database to start a transaction. Returns YES to indicate success, NO otherwise, based on the response from the database.

commitTransaction

– (BOOL)**commitTransaction**

The adaptor tells the database to commit the current transaction. Returns YES to indicate success, NO otherwise, based on the response from the database.

rollbackTransaction

– (BOOL)**rollbackTransaction**

The adaptor tells the database to roll back the current transaction. Returns YES to indicate success, NO otherwise, based on the response from the database.

DBTypes

Adopted By: no NeXTSTEP classes

Declared In: dbkit/types.h

Protocol Description

The methods in the DBTypes protocol return information about the type of data that's held or described by the object upon which they are invoked (principally, DBProperties and DBValue objects, as explained below). This information doesn't necessarily correspond to an actual value—a DBTypes object may not even embody a "real" value, and the protocol makes no provision for storing values—it simply provides a means for abstractly describing a data type.

The protocol's two primary methods are **objcType** and **databaseType**; they return strings that represent, respectively, an Objective C data type, and a data type as given in the actual database. The Database Kit uses the following convention in representing Objective C data types as strings:

Objective C type	DBTypes representation
id	"@"
char *	"*"
int	"i"
float	"f"
double	"d"

The value returned by **databaseType**, on the other hand, is completely adaptor-dependent. In addition, not all objects have a database type. For example, a relationship that's read from a database model file isn't represented in the actual database, and so will have no database type.

None of the public Database Kit classes implements the DBTypes protocol. However, the kit automatically creates private DBTypes-conforming objects which it uses to store the data types of properties and DBValues. The DBProperties method **propertyType** returns such a private DBTypes object, as does DBValue's **valueType** method.

Method Types

Querying for type	– objcType – databaseType – objcClassName
Comparing types	– isEntity – matchesType:

Instance Methods

databaseType

– (const char *)**databaseType**

Returns a string that represents the object's data type as it resides in the database from which it was read (or to which it will be written).

isEntity

– (BOOL)**isEntity**

Returns YES if the object's data type is an **id** that conforms to the DBEntities protocol, otherwise returns NO. This method is intended to be used to determine if a property is a relationship. The data type of a relationship is an entity; thus if this method returns YES when invoked upon a DBProperties object, that property is a relationship.

matchesType:

– (BOOL)**matchesType:**(id <DBTypes>)*anObject*

Returns YES if the object's data type matches that of *anObject*, otherwise returns NO.

objcClassName

– (const char *)**objcClassName**

If the object's type is an **id**, this returns the name of the **id**'s class. If the type isn't an **id**, this returns **nil**.

objcType

– (const char *)**objcType**

Returns a string that represents the object's Objective C data type. The strings that are used by the Database Kit to represent the standard Objective C types are listed in the class description, above.

Types and Constants

Defined Types

DBExceptions

DECLARED IN dbkit/exceptions.h

SYNOPSIS

```
typedef enum _DBAccessErrors {
        DB_UnimplementedException = DB_ERROR_BASE,
        DB_CoercionException,
        DB_FormatException,
        DB_CursorException,
        DB_CommitException
} DBExceptions;
```

DESCRIPTION Exceptions raised during a database access.

DBFailureCode

DECLARED IN dbkit/enums.h

SYNOPSIS

```
typedef enum {
        DB_ReasonUnknown,
        DB_RecordBusy,
        DB_RecordStreamNotReady,
        DB_RecordHasChanged,
        DB_RecordLimitReached,
        DB_NoRecordKey,
        DB_RecordKeyNotUnique,
        DB_NoAdaptor,
        DB_AdaptorError,
        DB_TransactionError
} DBFailureCode;
```

DESCRIPTION Error codes returned by an adaptor.

DBFailureResponse

DECLARED IN dbkit/enums.h

SYNOPSIS

```
typedef enum {
        DB_NotHandled,
        DB_Abort,
        DB_Continue
} DBFailureResponse;
```

DESCRIPTION Possible returns from methods that respond to a failure notification.

DBImageStyle

DECLARED IN dbkit/DBImageView.h

SYNOPSIS

```
typedef enum {
        DB_ImageNoFrame,
        DB_ImagePhoto,
        DB_ImageGrayBezel,
        DB_ImageGroove
} DBImageStyle;
```

DESCRIPTION Style of frame to surround an image.

DBRecordListRetrieveMode

DECLARED IN dbkit/enums.h

SYNOPSIS

```
typedef enum _DBRecordListMode {
        DB_SynchronousStrategy,
        DB_BackgroundStrategy,
        DB_BackgroundNoBlockingStrategy,
} DBRecordListRetrieveMode;
```

DESCRIPTION Access strategy used by a DBRecordList.

DBRecordRetrieveStatus

DECLARED IN dbkit/enums.h

SYNOPSIS

```
typedef enum _DBRecordRetrievalStatus {
        DB_NotReady,
        DB_Ready,
        DB_FetchLimitReached,
        DB_FetchInProgress,
        DB_FetchCompleted
} DBRecordRetrieveStatus;
```

DESCRIPTION Status of a DBRecordStream or a DBRecordList.

DBRetrieveOrder

DECLARED IN dbkit/enums.h

SYNOPSIS

```
typedef enum {
        DB_NoOrder,
        DB_AscendingOrder,
        DB_DescendingOrder
} DBRetrieveOrder;
```

DESCRIPTION Order in which retrieved records are sorted.

DBSelectionMode

DECLARED IN dbkit/DBTableView.h

SYNOPSIS

```
typedef enum {
        DB_RADIOMODE,
        DB_LISTMODE,
        DB_NOSELECT
} DBSelectionMode
```

DESCRIPTION Modes in which the user may select rows or columns in a DBTableView.

DB_RADIOMODE	Selecting a row or column deselects those previously selected.
DB_LISTMODE	Selecting a previously unselected row or column adds it to the selection already made; selecting a previously selected row or column deselects.
DB_NOSELECT	No selection is permitted.

Symbolic Constants

Error Code Base Value

DECLARED IN dbkit/exceptions.h

SYNOPSIS DB_ERROR_BASE

DESCRIPTION Constant added to Database Kit error codes.

Format Types

DECLARED IN dbkit/customType.h

SYNOPSIS

Name	Value
DBFormat_EPS	"EPS"
DBFormat_RTF	"RTF"
DBFormat_TIFF	"TIFF"

DESCRIPTION Type of the source image to be displayed or transferred.

No Index Indicator

DECLARED IN dbkit/enums.h

SYNOPSIS DB_NoIndex

DESCRIPTION No selected position in an indexed array (such as DBTableView).

Null Values

DECLARED IN dbkit/DBValue.h

SYNOPSIS

Name	Value
DB_NullDouble	(NAN)
DB_NullFloat	(NAN)
DB_NullInt	((int)0x7ffffffe)

DESCRIPTION Null returns of appropriate type.

Record Limit Default

DECLARED IN dbkit/DBFetchGroup.h

SYNOPSIS DB_DEFAULT_RECORD_LIMIT 1000

DESCRIPTION Maximum number of records that a DBFetchGroup will fetch unless explicitly set by the DBRecordList method **setRecordLimit:**.

5 *Display PostScript*

5 *Display PostScript*

Library: libNeXT_s.a

Header File Directory: /NextDeveloper/Headers/dpsclient

Import: dpsclient/dpsclient.h

Introduction

This chapter describes the NeXTSTEP implementation of the Display PostScript® Client Library, and NeXTSTEP's additions to the catalog of PostScript operators. The Client Library and PostScript operators are mainly documented by Adobe Systems, Inc. (see "Suggested Readings" at the end of Volume 2). Documented here are only those elements that are unique to or different in the NeXTSTEP implementation.

The chapter is divided into four sections:

- "Operators" describes the PostScript operators that are unique to NeXTSTEP, or that have different effects from the same operators as implemented by Adobe. You can use these operators as you would any of the standard operators provided by Adobe.
- "Single Operator Functions" lists the C functions that correspond to the NeXTSTEP operators. These functions fulfill the guarantee that for every operator there will be a C-language function interface. The list of functions given in this section are offered without description (for which you must refer to the similarly named operator in the "Operators" section).

- "Client Library Functions" describes the NeXTSTEP-specific functions that provide an interface to the Display PostScript system.
- "Types and Constants" describes the defined types and symbolic constants used in NeXTSTEP's implementation of the Display PostScript Client Library.

PostScript Operators

This section contains descriptions of the PostScript operators that are either unique to NeXTSTEP or that have different or additional effects in the NeXTSTEP implementation of the Display PostScript system. The standard PostScript operators are documented by Adobe Systems Inc. (see “Suggested Reading” at the end of Volume 2).

The PostScript operators can be used only in PostScript language code. However, every operator has a C function interface associated with it, allowing you to execute the operator from a program or application written in C or Objective C. The functions that correspond to the NeXTSTEP-unique operators described here are given in the “Single-Operator Functions” section of this chapter.

Some operators shouldn’t be used in applications that use the Application Kit. In addition, some standard operators are unimplemented in NeXTSTEP. Both categories of operators are marked with a warning in the descriptions in this section.

adjustcursor

dx dy **adjustcursor** –

Moves the cursor location by (*dx*, *dy*) from its current location. *dx* and *dy* are given in the current coordinate system. If the current device isn't a window, the **invalidid** error is executed.

ERRORS **invalidid**, **stackunderflow**, **typecheck**

SEE ALSO **currentmouse, setmouse**

alphaimage

pixelswide pixelshigh bits/sample matrix $datasrc_0$ *[...*$datasrc_n$*] multiproc ncolors* **alphaimage** –

Renders an image whose samples include an alpha component. (Most programmers should use **NXImageBitmap()** instead of **alphaimage**.) This operator is similar to the standard **colorimage** operator (as documented by Adobe Systems). However, note the following:

- When supplying the data components, alpha is always given last—either as the last data source ($datasrc_n$) if the data is given in separate vectors, or as the last element in a set of interleaved data.
- The *ncolors* operand doesn't account for alpha—the value of *ncolors* is the number of color components only.

ERRORS **invalidid**, **limitcheck**, **rangecheck**, **stackunderflow**, **typecheck**, **undefined**, **undefinedresult**

basetocurrent

bx by **basetocurrent** *cx cy*

Converts (*bx*, *by*) from the current window's base coordinate system to its current coordinate system. If the current device isn't a window, the **invalidid** error is executed.

ERRORS **invalidid**, **stackunderflow**, **typecheck**

SEE ALSO **basetoscreen, currenttobase, currenttoscreen, screentobase, screentocurrent**

basetoscreen

bx by **basetoscreen** *sx sy*

Converts (*bx*, *by*) from the current window's base coordinate system to the screen coordinate system. If the current device isn't a window, the **invalidid** error is executed.

ERRORS **invalidid**, **stackunderflow**, **typecheck**

SEE ALSO **basetocurrent, currenttobase, currenttoscreen, screentobase, screentocurrent**

buttondown

– **buttondown** *isdown*

Returns *true* if the left or only mouse button is currently down; otherwise it returns *false*.

Note: To test whether the mouse button is still down from a mouse-down event, use **stilldown** instead of **buttondown**; **buttondown** will return *true* even if the mouse button has been released and pressed again since the original mouse-down event.

ERRORS none

SEE ALSO **currentmouse, rightbuttondown, rightstilldown, stilldown**

cleartrackingrect

trectnum gstate **cleartrackingrect** –

Clears the tracking rectangle identified by *trectnum*, as set by **settrackingrect**, in the device referred to by *gstate* (or the current graphics state if *gstate* is **null**). If no such rectangle exists, the **invalidid** error is executed.

ERRORS **invalidid**, **stackunderflow**, **typecheck**

SEE ALSO **settrackingrect**

composite

src_x src_y *width height srcgstate* $dest_x$ $dest_y$ *op* **composite** –

Performs the compositing operation specified by *op* between pairs of pixels in two images, a source and a destination. The source pixels are in the window device referred to by the *srcgstate* graphics state, and the destination pixels are in the current window. If *srcgstate* is **null**, the current graphics state is assumed. If either graphics state doesn't refer to a window device, the **invalidid** error is executed.

The rectangle specified by src_x, src_y, *width*, and *height* defines the source image. The outline of the rectangle may cross pixel boundaries due to fractional coordinates, scaling, or rotated axes. The pixels included in the source are all those that the outline of the rectangle encloses or enters.

The destination image has the same size, shape, and orientation as the source; $dest_x$ and $dest_y$ give destination's location image compared to the source. (Even if the two graphic states have different orientations, the images will not; **composite** will not rotate images.)

Both images are clipped to the frame rectangles of their respective windows. The destination image is further clipped to the clipping path of the current graphics state. The result of a composite operation replaces the destination image.

op specifies the compositing operation. The choices for *op* and the result of each operation are given in the following illustration.

ERRORS **invalidid**, **rangecheck**, **stackunderflow**, **typecheck**

SEE ALSO **compositerect, setalpha, setgray, sethsbcolor, setrgbcolor**

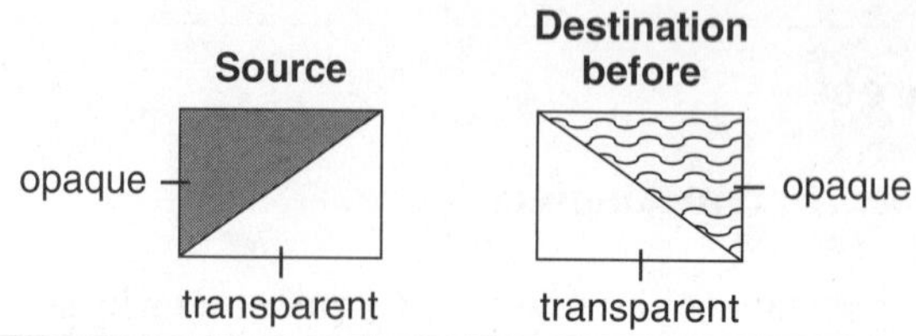

Operation	Destination after	
Copy	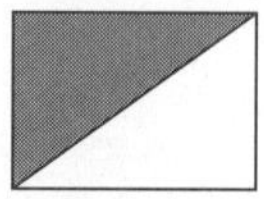	Source image.
Clear	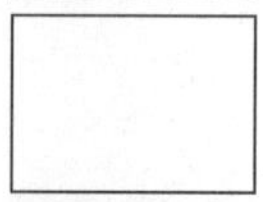	Transparent.
PlusD	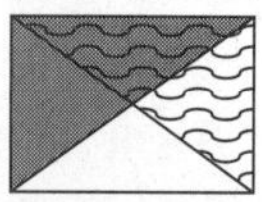	Sum of source and destination images, with color values approaching 0 as a limit.
PlusL	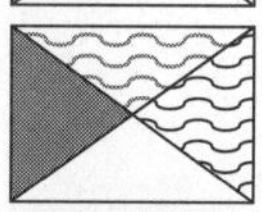	Sum of source and destination images, with color values approaching 1 as a limit. (PlusL is not implemented for the MegaPixel Display.)
Sover	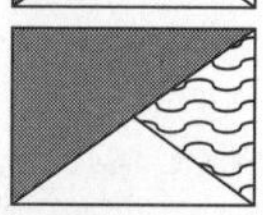	Source image wherever source image is opaque, and destination image elsewhere.
Dover	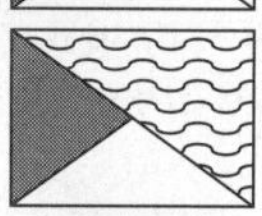	Destination image wherever destination image is opaque, and source image elsewhere.
Sin		Source image wherever both images are opaque, and transparent elsewhere.
Din	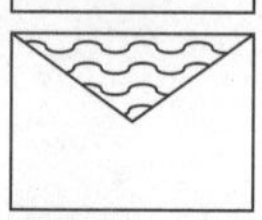	Destination image wherever both images are opaque, and transparent elsewhere.
Sout	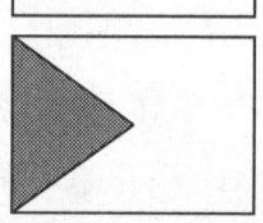	Source image wherever source image is opaque but destination image is transparent, and transparent elsewhere.
Dout	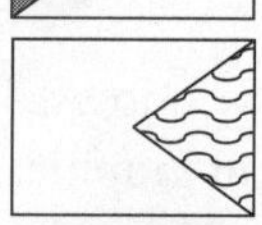	Destination image wherever destination image is opaque but source image is transparent, and transparent elsewhere.
Satop	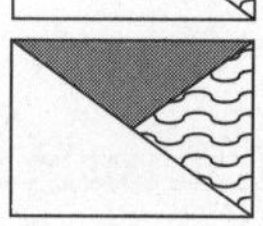	Source image wherever both images are opaque, destination image wherever destination image is opaque but source image is transparent, and transparent elsewhere.

Figure 5-1. Compositing Operations

compositerect

$dest_x$ $dest_y$ width height op **compositerect** –

In general, this operator is the same as the **composite** operator except that there's no real source image. The destination is in the current graphics state; $dest_x$, $dest_y$, *width*, and *height* describe the destination image in that graphics state's current coordinate system. The effect on the destination is as if there were a source image filled with the color and coverage specified by the graphics state's current color parameter. *op* has the same meaning as the *op* operand of the **composite** operator; however, one additional operation, Highlight, is allowed.

On the MegaPixel Display, Highlight turns every white pixel in the destination rectangle to light gray and every light gray pixel to white, regardless of the pixel's coverage value. Repeating the same operation reverses the effect. (Highlight may act differently on other devices. For example, on displays that assign just one bit per pixel, it would invert every pixel.)

Note: The Highlight operation doesn't change the value of a pixel's coverage component. To ensure that the pixel's color and coverage combination remains valid, Highlight operations should be temporary and should be reversed before any further compositing.

For **compositerect**, the pixels included in the destination are those that the outline of the specified rectangle encloses or enters. The destination image is clipped to the frame rectangle and clipping path of the window in the current graphics state.

If the current graphics state doesn't refer to a window device, the **invalidid** error is executed.

ERRORS **invalidid**, **rangecheck**, **stackunderflow**, **typecheck**

SEE ALSO **composite**, **setalpha**, **setgray**, **sethsbcolor**, **setrgbcolor**

copypage

Warning: This standard PostScript operator has no effect in the NeXTSTEP implementation of the Display PostScript system.

countframebuffers

– **countframebuffers** *count*

Returns the number of frame buffers that the Window Server is actually using.

ERRORS **stackoverflow**

SEE ALSO **framebuffer**

countscreenlist

context **countscreenlist** *count*

Returns the number of windows in the screen list that were created by the PostScript context specified by *context*. This is in contrast with **countwindowlist**, which returns the number of windows created by the context without regard to their inclusion in the screen list.

If *context* is 0, all windows in the screen list are counted, without regard to the context that created them.

ERRORS **invalidid, rangecheck, stackunderflow, typecheck**

SEE ALSO **countwindowlist, screenlist, windowlist**

countwindowlist

context **countwindowlist** *count*

Returns the number of windows that were created by the PostScript context specified by *context*. This is in contrast with **countscreenlist**, which returns the number of windows in the screen list that were created by the PostScript context specified by *context*.

If *context* is 0, all windows are counted, without regard to the context that created them.

ERRORS **stackunderflow, typecheck**

SEE ALSO **countscreenlist, screenlist, windowlist**

currentactiveapp

– **currentactiveapp** *context*

Warning: Don't use this operator if you're using the Application Kit.

Returns the active application's context. This operator is used by the window packages to assist with wait cursor operation.

ERRORS **stackoverflow**

SEE ALSO **setactiveapp**

currentalpha

– **currentalpha** *coverage*

Returns the coverage parameter of the current graphics state.

ERRORS none

SEE ALSO **composite, setalpha**

currentdefaultdepthlimit

– **currentdefaultdepthlimit** *depth*

Warning: Don't use this operator if you're using the Application Kit. Use Window's **defaultDepthLimit** class method instead.

Returns the current context's default depth limit. This value determines a new window's depth limit.

ERRORS **stackoverflow**

SEE ALSO **setdefaultdepthlimit**, **setwindowdepthlimit**, **currentwindowdepthlimit**, **currentwindowdepth**

currentdeviceinfo

window **currentdeviceinfo** *min max iscolor*

Returns device-related information about the current state of *window. min* and *max* are the smallest and largest number of bits per sample, respectively, and *iscolor* is a boolean value indicating whether the device is a color device.

ERRORS **invalidid**, **stackunderflow**, **typecheck**

currenteventmask

window **currenteventmask** *mask*

Warning: Don't use this operator if you're using the Application Kit. Use Window's **eventMask** method instead.

Returns the current Window Server-level event mask for the specified window.

ERRORS **invalidid**, **stackunderflow**, **typecheck**

SEE ALSO **seteventmask**

currentframebuffertransfer

fbnum **currentframebuffertransfer** *redproc greenproc blueproc grayproc*

Returns the current transfer functions in effect for the framebuffer indexed by *fbnum. fbnum* ranges from 0 to (**countframebuffers** – 1).

ERRORS **invalidid**, **stackunderflow**, **typecheck**

SEE ALSO **setframebuffertransfer, countframebuffers, framebuffer**

currentmouse

window **currentmouse** *x y*

Warning: Don't use this operator if you're using the Application Kit. Use Window's **getMouseLocation:** instead.

Returns the current x and y coordinates of the mouse location in the base coordinate system of the specified window. If the mouse isn't inside the specified window, these coordinates may be outside the coordinate range defined for the window. If *window* is 0, the current mouse position is returned relative to the screen coordinate system.

ERRORS **invalidid**, **stackunderflow**, **typecheck**

SEE ALSO **basetocurrent**, **basetoscreen**, **buttondown**, **rightbuttondown**, **rightstilldown**, **setmouse**, **stilldown**

currentowner

window **currentowner** *context*

Returns a number identifying the PostScript context that currently owns the specified window. By default, this is the PostScript context that created the window.

ERRORS **invalidid**, **stackunderflow**, **typecheck**

SEE ALSO **setowner**, **termwindow**, **window**

currentshowpageprocedure

window **currentshowpageprocedure** *proc*

Returns the PostScript procedure that's executed when the **showpage** operator is executed while the specified window is the current device.

ERRORS **invalidid**, **stackunderflow**, **typecheck**

SEE ALSO **setshowpageprocedure**

currentrusage

– **currentrusage** *ctime utime stime msgsend msgrcv nsignals nvcsw nivcsw*

Returns information about the current time of day and about resource usage by the Window Server, as provided by the UNIX system call **getrusage()**. The items returned, and their types, are as follows:

Name	Type	Value
ctime	float	Current time in seconds, modulo 10000
utime	float	User time for the Server process in seconds
stime	float	System time for the Server process in seconds
msgsend	int	Messages sent by the Server to clients
msgrcv	int	Message received by the Server from clients
nsignals	int	Number of signals received by the Server process
nvcsw	int	Number of voluntary context switches
nivcsw	int	Number of involuntary context switches

currenttobase

cx cy **currenttobase** *bx by*

Converts (*cx*,*cy*) from the current coordinate system of the current window to its base coordinate system. If the current device isn't a window, the **invalidid** error is executed.

ERRORS **invalidid**, **stackunderflow**, **typecheck**

SEE ALSO **basetocurrent**, **basetoscreen**, **currenttoscreen**, **screentobase**, **screentocurrent**

currenttoscreen

cx cy **currenttoscreen** *sx sy*

Converts (*cx*, *cy*) from the current coordinate system of the current window to the screen coordinate system. If the current device isn't a window, the **invalidid** error is executed.

ERRORS **invalidid, stackunderflow, typecheck**

SEE ALSO **basetocurrent, basetoscreen, currenttobase, screentobase, screentocurrent**

currentuser

– **currentuser** *uid gid*

Returns the user id (*uid*) and the group id (*gid*) of the user currently logged in on the console of the machine that's running the Window Server.

ERRORS **stackoverflow**

currentwaitcursorenabled

context **currentwaitcursorenabled** *isenabled*

Returns the state of *context*'s wait cursor flag. If *context* is 0, returns the state of the global wait cursor flag.

ERRORS **invalidid, stackunderflow, typecheck**

SEE ALSO **setwaitcursorenabled**

currentwindow

– **currentwindow** *window*

Returns the window number of the current window. Executes the **invalidid** error if the current device isn't a window.

ERRORS **invalidid**

SEE ALSO **windowdeviceround**

currentwindowalpha

window **currentwindowalpha** *alpha*

Returns an integer indicating whether the Window Server is currently storing alpha values for the specified window. Possible *alpha* values are:

–2 Window is opaque; alpha values are explicitly allocated.
0 Alpha values are stored explicitly
2 Window is opaque; no explicit alpha

ERRORS **invalidid**, **stackunderflow**, **typecheck**

currentwindowbounds

window **currentwindowbounds** *x y width height*

Warning: Don't use this operator if you're using the Application Kit. Use Window's **getFrame:** or Application's **getScreenSize:** method instead.

Returns the location and size of the window in screen coordinates. Pass 0 for *window* to get the size of the entire workspace (the smallest rectangle that encloses all active screens).

x and *y* will be in the range $[-2^{15}, 2^{15}-1]$; *width* and *height* will be in the range [0, 10000].

ERRORS **invalidid**, **stackunderflow**, **typecheck**

SEE ALSO **movewindow**, **placewindow**

currentwindowdepth

window **currentwindowdepth** *depth*

Warning: Don’t use this operator if you’re using the Application Kit.

Returns *window*’s current depth. The **invalidid** error is executed if *window* doesn't exist.

ERRORS **invalidid**, **stackunderflow**, **typecheck**

SEE ALSO **setwindowdepthlimit**, **currentwindowdepthlimit**, **setdefaultdepthlimit**, **currentdefaultdepthlimit**

currentwindowdepthlimit

window **currentwindowdepthlimit** *depth*

Warning: Don’t use this operator if you’re using the Application Kit. Use Window’s **depthLimit** method instead.

Returns the window’s current depth limit, the maximum depth to which the window can be promoted. Unless altered by the **setwindowdepthlimit** operator, a window’s depth limit is equal to its context’s default depth limit. The **invalidid** error is executed if *window* doesn’t exist.

ERRORS **invalidid**, **stackunderflow**, **typecheck**

SEE ALSO **setwindowdepthlimit**, **currentwindowdepth**, **setdefaultdepthlimit**, **currentdefaultdepthlimit**

currentwindowdict

window **currentwindowdict** *dict*

Warning: Don't use this operator if you're using the Application Kit.

Returns the specified window's dictionary.

ERRORS **invalidid**, **stackunderflow**, **typecheck**

SEE ALSO **setwindowdict**

currentwindowlevel

window **currentwindowlevel** *level*

Returns *window*'s tier. Executes the **invalidid** error if *window* doesn't exist.

ERRORS **invalidid**, **stackunderflow**, **typecheck**

SEE ALSO **setwindowlevel**

currentwriteblock

– **currentwriteblock** *doesblock*

Returns whether the Window Server delays sending data to a client application whenever the Server's output buffer fills. **currentwriteblock** assumes the current context. If *doesblock* is *true*, the Server waits until the buffer can accept more data. If *doesblock* is *false*, the Server discards data that can't be accepted immediately.

ERRORS none

SEE ALSO **setwriteblock**

dissolve

src_x src_y width height srcgstate $dest_x$ $dest_y$ delta **dissolve** –

The effect of this operation is a blending of a source and a destination image. The first seven arguments choose source and destination pixels as they do for **composite**. The exact fraction of the blend is specified by *delta*, which is a floating-point number between 0.0 and 1.0; the resulting image is:

delta *source + (1– *delta*)*destination

If *srcgstate* is null, the current graphics state is assumed. If *srcgstate* or the current graphics state does not refer to a window device, this operator executes the **invalidid** error.

ERRORS **invalidid**, **stackunderflow**, **typecheck**

SEE ALSO **composite**

dumpwindow

dumplevel window **dumpwindow** –

Warning: Don't use this operator if you're using the Application Kit.

Prints information about *window* to the standard output file. Only *dumplevel* 0 is implemented. The information printed is the position and number of bytes of backing storage for the window.

ERRORS **invalidid**, **rangecheck**, **stackunderflow**, **typecheck**

SEE ALSO **dumpwindows**

dumpwindows

dumplevel context **dumpwindows** –

Warning: Don't use this operator if you're using the Application Kit.

Prints information about all windows owned by *context* to the standard output file. If *context* is 0, it prints information about all windows. Only *dumplevel* 0 is implemented.

ERRORS **invalidid**, **rangecheck**, **stackunderflow**, **typecheck**

SEE ALSO **dumpwindow**

erasepage

– **erasepage** –

Warning: This standard operator is different in the NeXTSTEP implementation.

Erases the entire window to opaque white.

ERRORS **invalidid**

SEE ALSO **copypage**, **showpage**

findwindow

x y place otherwindow **findwindow** *x' y' window found*

findwindow starts from a given position in the screen list, as explained below, and searches for the first window below that position that contains the point (*x*, *y*). The *x* and *y* values are given in screen coordinates.

The starting position is determined by *place* and *otherwindow*. *place* can be **Above** or **Below**, and *otherwindow* is the window number of a window in the screen list. If you specify **Above 0**, **findwindow** checks all windows in the screen list.

If a window containing the point is found, **findwindow** returns *true*, along with the window number and the corresponding location in the base coordinate system of the window. Otherwise, it returns *false*, and the values of *x'*, *y'*, and *window* are undefined.

ERRORS **rangecheck**, **stackunderflow**, **typecheck**

---

flushgraphics

– **flushgraphics** –

Warning: Don't use this operator if you're using the Application Kit. Use Window's **flushWindow** method instead.

Flushes to the screen all drawing done in the current buffered window. If the current window is retained or nonretained, **flushgraphics** has no effect.

ERRORS **invalidid**, **stackunderflow**, **typecheck**

---

framebuffer

index string **framebuffer** *name slot unit romid x y width height maxdepth*

Provides information on the active frame buffer specified by *index*, where *index* ranges from 0 to **countframebuffers**–1. *string* must be large enough to hold the resulting name of the frame buffer. *slot* is the NeXTbus™ slot the frame buffer is physically occupying. If a board supports multiple frame buffers, *unit* uniquely identifies the frame buffer within a slot. The ROM product code is returned in *romid*. The bottom left corner of the frame buffer is returned in *x* and *y* (relative to the screen coordinate system). The size of the frame buffer in pixels is returned in *width* and *height*. *maxdepth* is the maximum depth displayable on this frame buffer (for example, NX_TwentyFourBitRGB).

The **limitcheck** error is executed if *string* isn't large enough to hold *name*. The **rangecheck** error is executed if *index* is out of bounds.

ERRORS **limitcheck**, **rangecheck**, **stackunderflow**, **typecheck**

SEE ALSO **countframebuffers**

frontwindow

– **frontwindow** *window*

Warning: Don't use this operator if you're using the Application Kit.

Returns the window number of the frontmost window on the screen. If there aren't any windows on the screen, **frontwindow** returns 0.

ERRORS none

SEE ALSO **orderwindow**

hidecursor

– **hidecursor** –

Removes the cursor from the screen. It remains in effect until balanced by a call to **showcursor**.

ERRORS none

SEE ALSO **obscurecursor**, **showcursor**

hideinstance

x y width height **hideinstance** –

In the current window, **hideinstance** removes any instance drawing from the rectangle specified by *x*, *y*, *width*, and *height*. *x*, *y*, *width*, and *height* are given in the window's current coordinate system.

ERRORS **invalidid**, **stackunderflow**, **typecheck**

SEE ALSO **newinstance**, **setinstance**

image

dict **image** –

Allows a window's graphics state object to be used as a source of sample data. *dict* must be an image dictionary in which only those keys listed in the following table are significant:

Key	Type	Value or Meaning
ImageType	integer	(*Required*) Must be 2.
XOrigin	real	(*Required*) X origin of the source rectangle in user space coordinates as specified by the transformation in the **DataSource** entry.
YOrigin	real	(*Required*) Y origin of the same.
Width	real	(*Required*) Width of the same.
Height	real	(*Required*) Height of the same.
ImageMatrix	array	(*Required*) The transformation matrix.
DataSource	gstate	(*Required*) A graphics state object that contains the device that will be used as the source of sample data. This device will also be used to determine the pixel representation for the source, and the color space to be used by the image.
Interpolate	boolean	(*Optional*) Request for image interpolation.
UnpaintedPath	(various)	(*Return value*) If some of the pixels in the source weren't available (because of clipping), then the **UnpaintedPath** entry contains a userpath in the current (destination) user space that encloses the area that couldn't be filled.
PixelCopy	boolean	(*Optional*) If *true*, indicates that the source pixels should be copied directly, without going through the normal color conversion, transfer function, or halftoning. The bits per pixel of the source must match the bits per pixel of the destination, otherwise a **typecheck** error will occur. If *false* or not present, the pixels will be imaged in the usual way.

ERRORS **invalidid**, **rangecheck**, **stackunderflow**, **typecheck**

SEE ALSO **alphaimage**

---

initgraphics

– **initgraphics** –

Warning: This standard operator has additional effects in the NeXTSTEP implementation of the Display PostScript system.

In addition to the effects documented by Adobe, this operator sets the coverage parameter in the current window's graphics state to 1 (opaque) and turns off instance drawing

ERRORS none

SEE ALSO **hideinstance**, **newinstance**, **setalpha**, **setinstance**

---

machportdevice

width height bbox matrix hostname portname pixelencoding **machportdevice** –

Sets up a PostScript device that can provide a generic rendering service for device-control programs requiring page bitmaps from PostScript documents. For each rendered page, **machportdevice** sends a Mach message containing the page bitmap to a port that has been registered with the name server on the network.

width and *height* are integers that determine the number of device pixels for the page.

bbox is an array of integers that defines the rectangle (by giving its lower left and upper right corners) that encompasses the imageable area. The array takes the form

[*lowerLeftX lowerLeftY upperRightX upperRightY*]

For the common case where the entire raster is imageable, *bbox* may be expressed as an empty array. If *bbox* isn't in the correct form, or if any portion of the rectangle it expresses falls outside [0 0 *width height*], a **rangecheck** results. The bitmap data is stored in x-axis major indexing order. The device coordinate of the lower left corner of the first pixel is

(0,0), the coordinate of the next pixel is (1,0) and so on for the entire scanline. Scanlines are long-word aligned.

matrix is the default transformation matrix for the device.

hostname and *portname* are strings that together identify the port that will receive the Mach messages. If *hostname* is empty, the local host is assumed. If it's "*", the port is searched for on all available hosts. If (in any case) the port can't be found, a **rangecheck** results.

pixelencoding is a dictionary describing the format for the image data rendered by the Window Server. It should contain these entries:

Key	Type	Value
samplesPerPixel	integer	Must be 1.
bitsPerSample	integer	Must be 1 or 2.
colorSpace	integer	Color space specification (see below).
isPlanar	boolean	*true* if sample values are stored in separate arrays (currently must be *false*).
defaultHalftone	dictionary	Passed to **sethalftone** during device creation to set up device default halftone.
initialTransfer	procedure	Passed to **settransfer** during device creation to set up the initial transfer function for device.
jobTag	integer	Allows **machportdevice** to tag rendering jobs. This value is included in the **jobTag** field of all printpage messages generated by this device.

The value of **colorSpace** should be one of the following values, predefined in **nextdict**:

Name	Value	Description
NX_OneIsBlackColorSpace	0	Monochromatic, high sample value is black.
NX_OneIsWhiteColorSpace	1	Monochromatic, high sample value is white.
NX_RgbColorSpace	2	RGB, (1,1,1) is white.
NX_CmykColorSpace	5	CMYK, (0,0,0,0) is white.

Only the following combinations of **colorSpace** and **bitsPerSample** are supported:

colorSpace	bitsPerSample
NX_OneIsBlackColorSpace	1
NX_OneIsWhiteColorSpace	2

These read-only pixel-encoding dictionaries are predefined in **nextdict**:

Name	**Description**
NeXTLaser-300	NeXT Laser Printer at 300 dpi resolution
NeXTLaser-400	NeXT Laser Printer at 400 dpi resolution
NeXTMegaPixelDisplay	MegaPixel Display's 2 bits-per-pixel gray

The pagebuffer data is passed out-of-line, appearing in the receiving application's address space. (If the receiver is on the same host, the received pagebuffer references the same physical memory as the Window Server's pagebuffer, and is mapped copy-on-write.) The application should use **vm_deallocate()** to release the pagebuffer memory when it's no longer needed. The receiver must acknowledge receipt of the data by sending a simple **msg_header_t** (with **msg_id** == NX_PRINTPAGEMSGID) back to the **remote_port** passed in the print message. The Window Server will not continue executing the page description until acknowledgement is received.

If more than one copy of the page is needed (through either the **copypage** or **#copies** mechanism) each copy is sent as a separate message. In this case the same pagebuffer will be sent in multiple messages. The **letter**, **legal**, and **note** page types are gracefully ignored.

Messaging errors cause the **invalidaccess** error to be executed.

EXAMPLES This example sets up a 400 dpi 8.5 by 11 inch page on a raster with upper left origin (as with the NeXT 400 dpi Laser Printer) and sends its print page messages to the port named "nlp-123" on the local host:

```
/dpi 400 def
/width dpi 8.5 mul cvi def
/height dpi 11 mul cvi def

width height     % page bitmap dimensions in pixels
[]               % use it all
[dpi 72 div 0 0 dpi -72 div 0 height] % device transform
() (nlp-123)     % host (local) & port
NeXTLaser-400    % pixel-encoding description
machportdevice
This example sets up an 8 by 10 inch page on the same 8.5 by 11 inch
page.  It specifies a 400 dpi raster with 1/4 inch horizontal margins
and 1/2 inch vertical margins:
/dpi 400 def
/width dpi 8.5 mul cvi def
/height dpi 11 mul cvi def
/topdots dpi .5 mul cvi def
/leftdots dpi .25 mul cvi def
```

```
width height         % page bitmap dimensions in pixels
[
    leftdots
    topdots
    width leftdots sub
    height topdots sub
]                    % imageable area of bounding box
[
    dpi 72 div
    0
    0
    dpi -72 div
    leftdots
    height topdots sub
]                    % device transform
() (nlp-123)         % host (local) & port
NeXTLaser-400        % pixel-encoding description
machportdevice
```

Note that in this example, the user space origin is at the lower left corner of the imageable area (*leftdots*, *height-topdots*) in the device raster coordinate system. Usually, the imageable area is meant to correspond with the ultimate destination of the bits. For example, a printer may have a constant-sized pagebuffer with a fixed orientation in the paper path, but be able to accept various sizes of paper. In this case, the page bitmap size will always be fixed, but the imageable area and default device transformation can be adjusted to make the user space origin appear at the lower left corner of each printed page.

ERRORS **invalidaccess**, **limitcheck**, **rangecheck**, **stackunderflow**, **typecheck**

---

movewindow

x y window **movewindow** –

Warning: Don't use this operator if you're using the Application Kit. Use Window's **moveTo::** method instead.

Moves the lower left corner of the specified window to the screen coordinates (*x*, *y*). No portion of the repositioned window can have an x or y coordinate with an absolute value greater than 16000. The operands can be integer, real, or radix numbers; however, they are converted to integers in the Window Server by rounding toward 0.

The window need not be the frontmost window. This operator doesn't change *window*'s ordering in the screen list.

ERRORS **invalidid**, **rangecheck**, **stackunderflow**, **typecheck**

SEE ALSO **currentwindowbounds**, **placewindow**

---

newinstance

– **newinstance** –

Removes any instance drawing from the current window.

ERRORS **invalidid**

SEE ALSO **hideinstance**, **setinstance**

---

nextrelease

– **nextrelease** *string*

Returns version information about this release of NeXTSTEP.

ERRORS **stackoverflow**

SEE ALSO **osname**, **ostype**

NextStepEncoding

– **NextStepEncoding** *array*

Pushes the NextStepEncoding vector on the operand stack. This is a 256-element array, indexed by character codes, whose values are the character names for those codes.

ERRORS **stackoverflow**

obscurecursor

– **obscurecursor** –

Removes the cursor image from the screen until the next time the mouse is moved. It's usually called in response to typing by the user, so the cursor won't be in the way. If the cursor has already been removed due to an **obscurecursor** call, **obscurecursor** has no effect.

ERRORS none

SEE ALSO **hidecursor**, **revealcursor**

orderwindow

place otherwindow window **orderwindow** –

Warning: Don't use this operator if you're using the Application Kit. Use Window's **orderWindow:relativeTo:** instead.

Orders *window* in the screen list as indicated by *place* and *otherwindow*. *place* can be **Above**, **Below**, or **Out**:

- If *place* is **Above** or **Below**, the window is placed in the screen list immediately above or below the window specified by *otherwindow*.
- If *place* is **Above** or **Below** and *otherwindow* is 0, the window is placed above or below all windows in its tier.
- If *place* is **Above** or **Below**, *otherwindow* must be a window in the screen list; otherwise, the **invalidid** error is executed.
- If *place* is **Out**, *otherwindow* is ignored, and the window is removed from the screen list, so it won't appear anywhere on the screen. Windows that aren't in the screen list don't receive user events.

Note: **orderwindow** doesn't change which window is the current window.

ERRORS **invalidid**, **rangecheck**, **stackunderflow**, **typecheck**

SEE ALSO **frontwindow**

osname

– **osname** *string*

Returns a string identifying the operating system of the Window Server's current operating environment. **osname** is defined in the **statusdict** dictionary, a dictionary that defines operators specific to a particular implementation of the PostScript language. **osname** can be executed as follows:

```
statusdict /osname get exec
```

ERRORS none

SEE ALSO **nextrelease**, **ostype**

ostype

– **ostype** *int*

Returns a number identifying the operating system of the Window Server's current operating environment. **ostype** is defined in the **statusdict** dictionary, a dictionary that defines operators specific to a particular implementation of the PostScript language. **ostype** can be executed as follows:

```
statusdict /ostype get exec
```

ERRORS none

SEE ALSO **nextrelease**, **osname**

placewindow

x y width height window **placewindow** –

Warning: Don't use this operator if you're using the Application Kit. Use Window's **placeWindow:** method instead.

Repositions and resizes the specified window, effectively allowing it to be resized from any corner or point. *x*, *y*, *width*, and *height* are given in the screen coordinate system. No portion of the repositioned window can have an x or y coordinate with an absolute value greater than 16000; *width* and *height* must be in the range from 0 to 10000. The four operands can be integer or real numbers; however, they are converted to integers in the Window Server by rounding toward 0.

placewindow places the lower left corner of the window at (*x*, *y*) and resizes it to have a width of *width* and a height of *height*. The pixels that are in the intersection of the old and new positions of the window survive unchanged (see Figure 5-2). Any other areas of the newly positioned window are filled with the window's exposure color (see **setexposurecolor**).

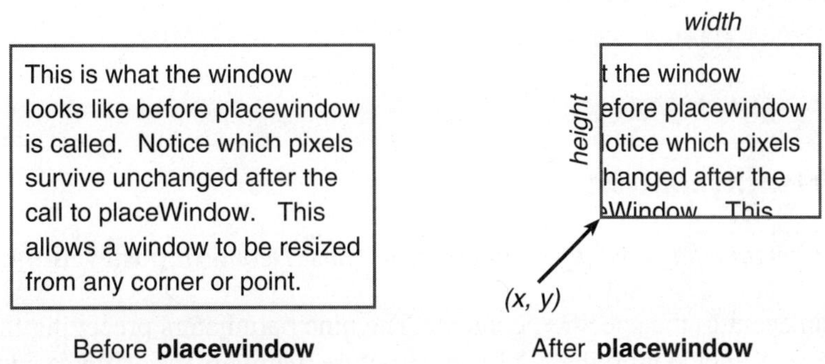

Figure 5-2. placewindow

After moving or resizing a window with **placewindow**, you must execute the **initmatrix** and **initclip** operators to reestablish the window's default transformation matrix and default clipping path.

ERRORS **invalidid**, **rangecheck**, **stackunderflow**, **typecheck**

SEE ALSO **currentwindowbounds**, **movewindow**, **setexposurecolor**

playsound

soundname priority **playsound** –

Plays the sound *soundname*. The Window Server searches for a standard soundfile of the name

soundname.**snd**

The search progresses through the following directories in the order given, stopping when the sound is located.

~/Library/Sounds
/LocalLibrary/Sounds
/NextLibrary/Sounds

No error occurs if the soundfile isn't found: The operator has no effect.

The soundfile's playback is assigned the priority level *priority.* The playback interrupts any currently playing sound of the same or lower priority level.

ERRORS **stackunderflow**, **typecheck**

posteventbycontext

type x y time flags window subtype misc0 misc1 context **posteventbycontext** *success*

Posts an event to the specified context. The nine parameters preceding the context parameter coincide with the NXEvent structure members (see "Types and Constants" for the definition of the NXEvent structure). The *x* and *y* coordinate arguments are passed directly to the receiving context without undergoing any transformations. *window* is the Window Server's global window number. Returns *true* if the event was successfully posted to *context*, and *false* otherwise.

You use this operator to post an application-defined event to your own application. Use Mach messaging to communicate between applications.

ERRORS **stackunderflow**, **typecheck**

readimage

x y width height $proc_0$ [... $proc_{n-1}$] *string bool* **readimage** –

Reads the pixels that make up the rectangular image described by *x*, *y*, *width*, and *height* in the current window. (Most programmers should use **NXReadBitmap()** instead of this operator.)

Usually the image is the rectangle that has a lower left corner of (*x*, *y*) in the current coordinate system and a width and height of *width* and *height*. If the axes have been rotated so that the sides of the rectangle are no longer aligned with the edges of the screen, the image is the smallest screen-aligned rectangle enclosing the given rectangle.

You typically call **sizeimage** before **readimage** (sending it the same *x*, *y*, *width*, and *height* values you'll use for **readimage**) to find out *ncolors*, the number of color components that **readimage** must read. *bool* is a boolean value that determines whether **readimage** reads the alpha component in addition to the color component(s) for each pixel. The total number of components to be read for each pixel, together with the *multiproc* value returned by **sizeimage**, determine *n*, the number of procedures that **readimage** requires. If *multiproc* is *false*, *n* equals 1. Otherwise, *n* equals the number of color components plus the alpha component, if present.

readimage executes the procedures in order, 0 through *n–1,* as many times as needed. For each execution, it pushes on the operand stack a substring of *string* containing the data from as many scanlines as possible. The length of the substring is a multiple of

width * *bits/sample* * (*samples/proc*) / 8

rounded up to the nearest integer. (The *width* and *bits/sample* values are provided by the **sizeimage** operator. *samples* is the number of color components plus 1 for the alpha component, if present.)

The samples are ordered and packed as they are for the **image**, **colorimage**, or **alphaimage** operator. For example, the alpha component is last and, if necessary, extra bits fill up the last character of every scanline. Note that the contents of *string* are valid only for the duration of one call to one procedure because the same string is reused on each procedure call. The **rangecheck** error is executed if *string* isn't long enough for one scanline.

ERRORS **rangecheck**, **stackunderflow**, **typecheck**

SEE ALSO **alphaimage**, **sizeimage**

revealcursor

– **revealcursor** –

Redisplays the cursor that was hidden by a call to **obscurecursor**, assuming that the cursor hasn't already been revealed by mouse movement. If the cursor hasn't been removed from the screen by a call to **obscurecursor**, **revealcursor** has no effect.

ERRORS none

SEE ALSO **obscurecursor**

rightbuttondown

– **rightbuttondown** *isdown*

Returns *true* if the right mouse button is currently down; otherwise it returns *false*.

Note: To test whether the right mouse button is still down from a mouse-down event, use **rightstilldown** instead of **rightbuttondown**; **rightbuttondown** will return *true* even if the mouse button has been released and pressed again since the original mouse-down event.

ERRORS none

SEE ALSO **buttondown**, **currentmouse**, **rightstilldown**, **stilldown**

rightstilldown

eventnum **rightstilldown** *stilldown*

Returns *true* if the right mouse button is still down from the mouse-down event specified by *eventnum*; otherwise it returns *false*. *eventnum* should be the number stored in the **data** component of the event record for an event of type **Rmousedown**.

ERRORS **stackunderflow**, **typecheck**

SEE ALSO **buttondown**, **currentmouse**, **rightbuttondown**, **stilldown**

screenlist

array context **screenlist** *subarray*

Fills the array with the window numbers of all windows in the screen list that are owned by the PostScript context specified by *context*. It returns the subarray containing those window numbers, in order from front to back. If *array* isn't large enough to hold them all, this operator will return the frontmost windows that fit in the array.

If *context* is 0, all windows in the screen list are returned.

EXAMPLE This example yields an array containing the window numbers of all windows in the screen list that are owned by the current PostScript context:

```
currentcontext
countscreenlist              % find out how many windows
array                        % create array to hold them
currentcontext screenlist    % fill it in
```

ERRORS **invalidaccess**, **invalidid**, **rangecheck**, **stackunderflow**, **typecheck**

SEE ALSO **countscreenlist**, **countwindowlist**, **windowlist**

screentobase

sx sy **screentobase** *bx by*

Converts (*sx*, *sy*) from the screen coordinate system to the current window's base coordinate system. If the current device isn't a window, the **invalidid** error is executed.

ERRORS **invalidid**, **stackunderflow**, **typecheck**

SEE ALSO **basetocurrent**, **basetoscreen**, **currenttobase**, **currenttoscreen**, **screentocurrent**

screentocurrent

sx sy **screentocurrent** *cx* cy

Converts (*sx*,*sy*) from the screen coordinate system to the current coordinate system of the current window. If the current device isn't a window, the **invalidid** error is executed.

ERRORS **invalidid**, **stackunderflow**, **typecheck**

SEE ALSO **basetocurrent**, **basetoscreen**, **currenttobase**, **currenttoscreen**, **screentobase**

setactiveapp

context **setactiveapp** –

Warning: Don't use this operator if you're using the Application Kit.

Records the active application's main (usually only) context. **setactiveapp** is used by the window packages to assist with wait cursor operation.

ERRORS **invalidid**, **stackunderflow**, **typecheck**

SEE ALSO **currentactiveapp**

setalpha

coverage **setalpha** –

Sets the coverage parameter in the current window's graphics state to *coverage*. *coverage* must be a number between 0 and 1, with 0 corresponding to transparent, 1 corresponding to opaque, and intermediate values corresponding to partial coverage. This establishes how much background shows through for purposes of compositing.

ERRORS **stackunderflow**, **typecheck**, **undefined**

SEE ALSO **composite**, **currentalpha**, **setgray**, **sethsbcolor**, **setrgbcolor**

setautofill

flag window **setautofill** –

Applies only to nonretained windows; sets the autofill property of *window* to the value of *flag*. If *true*, newly exposed areas of the window or areas created by **placewindow** will automatically be filled with the window's exposure color. If *false*, these areas will not change (typically they will continue to contain the image of the last window in that area). If the current device is not a window, this operator executes the **invalidid** error.

ERRORS **invalidid**, **stackunderflow**, **typecheck**

SEE ALSO **placewindow**, **setexposurecolor**, **setsendexposed**

setcursor

x y mx my **setcursor** –

Sets the cursor image and hot spot. Rather than executing this operator directly, you'd normally use a NXCursor object to define and manage cursors.

A cursor image is derived from a 16-pixel-square image in a window that's generally placed off-screen. The *x* and *y* operands specify the upper left corner of the image in the window's current coordinate system. The *mx* and *my* operands specify the relative offset (in units of the current coordinate system) from (*x*, *y*) to the *hot spot*, the point in the cursor that coincides with the mouse location. Assuming the current coordinate system is the base coordinate system, *mx* must be an integer from 0 to 16, and *my* must be an integer from 0 to –16. After **setcursor** is executed, the image in the window is no longer needed.

The cursor is placed on the screen using Sover compositing. The cursor's opaque areas (alpha = 1) completely cover the background, while its transparent areas (alpha < 1) allow the background to show through to a greater extent depending on the alpha values present in the cursor image.

Note: To make the off-screen window transparent, you can use **compositerect** with **Clear**.

The **rangecheck** error is executed if the image doesn't lie entirely within the specified window or if the point (*mx*, *my*) isn't inside the image. If the current device isn't a window, the **invalidid** error is executed.

ERRORS **invalidid**, **rangecheck**, **stackunderflow**, **typecheck**

SEE ALSO **hidecursor**, **obscurecursor**, **setmouse**

---

setdefaultdepthlimit

depth **setdefaultdepthlimit** –

Warning: Don't use this operator if you're using the Application Kit.

Sets the current context's default depth limit to *depth*. The Window Server assigns each new context a default depth limit equal to the maximum depth supported by the system. When a new window is created, its depth limit is set to its context's default depth limit.

These depths are defined in **nextdict**:

Depth	Meaning
NX_TwoBitGray	1 spp, 2bps, 2bpp, planar
NX_EightBitGray	1 spp, 8bps, 8bpp, planar
NX_TwelveBitRGB	3 spp, 4bps, 16bpp, interleaved
NX_TwentyFourBitRGB	3 spp, 8bps, 32bpp, interleaved

where *spp* is the number of samples per pixel; *bps* is the number of bits per sample; and *bpp* is the number of bits per pixel, also known as the window's depth. (The samples-per-pixel value excludes the alpha sample, if present.) *planar* and *interleaved* refer to how the sample data is configured. If a separate data channel is used for each sample, the configuration is *planar*. If data for all samples is stored in a single data channel, the configuration is *interleaved*.

When an alpha sample is present, the number of bits per pixel doubles for planar configurations (4 for NX_TwoBitGray and 16 for NX_EightBitGray). Interleaved configurations already account for an alpha sample whether or not it's present; thus, the number of bits per pixel for NX_TwelveBitRGB and NX_TwentyFourBitRGB depths remains unchanged.

The constant NX_DefaultDepth is also available. If *depth* is NX_DefaultDepth, the context's default depth limit is set to the Window Server's maximum visible depth, which is determined by which screens are active.

The **rangecheck** error is executed if *depth* is invalid.

ERRORS **rangecheck**, **stackunderflow**, **typecheck**

SEE ALSO **currentdefaultdepthlimit**, **setwindowdepthlimit**, **currentwindowdepthlimit**, **currentwindowdepth**

---

seteventmask

mask window **seteventmask** –

Warning: Don't use this operator if you're using the Application Kit. Use Window's **setEventMask:** method instead.

Sets the Server-level event mask for the specified window to *mask*. For windows created by the window packages, this mask may allow additional event types beyond those requested by the application. The following operand names are defined for *mask*:

Mask Operand	Event Type Allowed
Lmousedownmask	Mouse-down, left or only mouse button
Lmouseupmask	Mouse-up, left or only mouse button
Rmousedownmask	Mouse-down, right mouse button
Rmouseupmask	Mouse-up, right mouse button
Mousemovedmask	Mouse-moved
Lmousedraggedmask	Mouse-dragged, left or only mouse button
Rmousedraggedmask	Mouse-dragged, right mouse button
Mouseenteredmask	Mouse-entered
Mouseexitedmask	Mouse-exited
Keydownmask	Key-down
Keyupmask	Key-up
Flagschangedmask	Flags-changed
Kitdefinedmask	Kit-defined
Sysdefinedmask	System-defined
Appdefinedmask	Application-defined
Allevents	All event types

ERRORS **invalidid**, **stackunderflow**, **typecheck**

SEE ALSO **currenteventmask**

---

setexposurecolor

– **setexposurecolor** –

Applies to nonretained windows only; sets the exposure color to the color specified by the current color parameter in the current graphics state. The exposure color (white by default) determines the color of newly exposed areas of the window and of new areas created by **placewindow**. The alpha value of these areas is always 1 (opaque). If the current device is not a window, this operator executes the **invalidid** error.

ERRORS **invalidid**, **stackunderflow**, **typecheck**

SEE ALSO **placewindow**, **setautofill**, **setsendexposed**

setflushexposures

flag **setflushexposures** –

Warning: Don't use this operator if you're using the Application Kit.

Sets whether window-exposed and screen-changed subevents are flushed to clients. If *flag* is *false*, no window-exposed or screen-changed events are flushed to the client until **setflushexposures** is executed with *flag* equal to *true*. By default, window-exposed and screen-changed events are flushed to clients.

ERRORS **invalidid**, **stackunderflow**, **typecheck**

setframebuffertransfer

redproc greenproc blueproc grayproc fbnum **setframebuffertransfer** –

Warning: This operator should only be used for the development of screen-calibration products.

Sets the framebuffer transfer functions in effect for the framebuffer indexed by *fbnum*. *fbnum* ranges from 0 to **countframebuffers**–1. The framebuffer transfer describes the relationship between the framebuffer values of the display, and the voltage produced to drive the monitor.

The initial four operands define the transfer procedures: Monochrome devices use *grayproc* (but see the Note below), color devices use the others. The procedures must be allocated in shared virtual memory. In addition, the Window Server assumes that the framebuffer values are directly proportional to screen brightness. This is important for the accuracy of dithering, compositing, and similar calculations.

The default transfer for NeXT Color Displays is

```
{ 1 2.2 div exp } bind dup dup {}
```

Note: **setframebuffertransfer** is unsupported on the current generation of NeXT monochrome displays.

It's possible to make framebuffer transfer functions persist beyond the lifetime of the Window Server by storing a property in the NetInfo screens database. In the local NetInfo domain, **/localconfig/screens** holds the configuration information for the screens known to the Window Server (MegaPixel, NeXTdimension, and so on). These specify the layout and activation state of the screen. The NetInfo **defaultTransfer** property can contain a string of PostScript code suitable for execution by the **setframebuffertransfer** operator (without the *fbnum* parameter). For example, the following represents the NetInfo configuration for a NeXTdimension screen with a default gamma of 2.0:

```
localhost:1#  niutil -read  . /localconfig/screens/NeXTdimension
    name: NeXTdimension
    slot: 2
    unit: 0
    defaultTransfer: {1 2.0 div exp } dup dup dup
    bounds: 0 1120 0 832
    active: 1
    _writers: *
```

The **defaultTransfer** property is used to configure the screen each time the Window Server starts up. This allows monitor calibration products to save their settings so the next time the Window Server starts up, the new values will be used. Note that in some cases, the NetInfo configuration state for a monitor will not have **active** equal to 1, although the monitor is being used by the Window Server. If there are no active screens (screens that are explicitly marked as being active), the Window Server uses a suitable default, however, the other NetInfo properties for that screen are ignored. Thus, you must be sure that the screen for which you are adding a **defaultTransfer** value has **active** set to 1.

ERRORS **invalidid**, **stackunderflow**, **typecheck**

SEE ALSO **setframebuffertransfer**, **countframebuffers**, **framebuffer**

---

setinstance

flag **setinstance** –

Sets the instance-drawing mode in the current graphics state on (if *flag* is *true*) or off (if *flag* is *false*).

ERRORS **stackunderflow**, **typecheck**

SEE ALSO **hideinstance**, **newinstance**

setmouse

x y **setmouse** –

Moves the mouse location (and, correspondingly, the cursor) to (*x*, *y*), given in the current coordinate system. If the current device isn't a window, the **invalidid** error is executed.

ERRORS **invalidid**, **stackunderflow**, **typecheck**

SEE ALSO **adjustcursor**, **basetocurrent**, **currentmouse**, **screentocurrent**

setowner

context window **setowner** –

Sets the owning PostScript context of *window* to *context*. The window is terminated automatically when *context* is terminated.

ERRORS **invalidid**, **stackunderflow**, **typecheck**

SEE ALSO **currentowner**, **termwindow**, **window**

setsendexposed

flag window **setsendexposed** –

Warning: Don't use this operator if you're using the Application Kit.

Controls whether the Window Server generates a window-exposed subevent (of the kit-defined event) for *window* under the following circumstances:

- Nonretained window: When an area of the window is exposed, or a new area is created by **placewindow**
- Retained or buffered window: When an area of the window that had instance drawing in it is exposed

By default, window-exposed subevents are generated under these circumstances. In any case, the window-exposed subevent isn't flushed to the application until the Window Server receives another event.

ERRORS **invalidid**, **stackunderflow**, **typecheck**

SEE ALSO **setflushexposures**, **placewindow**, **setautofill**, **setexposurecolor**

---

setshowpageprocedure

proc window **setshowpageprocedure** –

Warning: Don't use this operator if you're using the Application Kit.

Sets the PostScript procedure that's executed, for the specified window, when the **showpage** procedure is executed. *proc* must be allocated in shared virtual memory.

ERRORS **invalidid**, **stackunderflow**, **typecheck**

SEE ALSO **currentshowpageprocedure**

---

settrackingrect

x y width height leftbool rightbool insidebool userdata trectnum gstate
settrackingrect –

or

x y width height optionarray trectnum gstate **settrackingrect** –

Important: The **settrackingrect** operator boasts two form, distinguished by the number and contents of the operands that are passed. The operator itself looks at its operands to determine how to proceed. The common portion of the two forms is described immediately below. Attention is then paid to the features that set the forms apart.

Sets a tracking rectangle in the window referred to by *gstate* to the rectangle specified by *x*, *y*, *width*, and *height* (in the coordinate system of that graphics state). If *gstate* is **null**, the window referred to by the current graphics state is used. *trectnum* is an arbitrary integer that can be any number except 0. It's used to identify tracking rectangles; no two tracking rectangles can share the same *trectnum* value. Any number of tracking rectangles may be set in a single window.

The tracking rectangle will remain in effect until **cleartrackingrect** is called, or until another tracking rectangle with the same *trectnum* is set.

Form 1

x y width height leftbool rightbool insidebool userdata trectnum gstate
settrackingrect –

In this form, the application receives mouse-exited and mouse-entered events as the cursor leaves and reenters the visible portion of the tracking rectangle. In the event record for a mouse-exited or mouse-entered event, the **data** component will contain *trectnum* along with the event number of the last mouse-down event.

userdata is an arbitrary integer that you assign to the tracking rectangle. Since several tracking rectangles can share the same *userdata* value, you can use *userdata* to identify an object in your application that will be notified when a mouse-entered or mouse-exited event occurs in any of the tracking rectangles.

You can specify that mouse-entered and mouse-exited events be generated only if certain mouse buttons are down. If *leftbool* is *true*, the events will be generated only when the left mouse button is down; likewise for *rightbool* and the right mouse button. If both *leftbool* and *rightbool* are *true*, the events will be generated only if both mouse buttons are down. If both *leftbool* and *rightbool* are *false*, the position of the mouse buttons isn't taken into account in generating mouse-entered and mouse-exited events.

settrackingrect causes the Window Server to repeatedly compare the current cursor position to the previous one to see whether the cursor has moved from inside the tracking rectangle to outside it or vice versa. *insidebool* tells **settrackingrect** whether to consider the initial cursor position to be inside or outside the tracking rectangle:

- If *insidebool* is *true* and the cursor is initially outside the tracking rectangle, a mouse-exited event is generated.
- If *insidebool* is *false* and the cursor is initially inside the tracking rectangle, a mouse-entered event is generated.

Form 2

x y width height optionarray trectnum gstate **settrackingrect** –

In this form, **settrackingrect** sets special event-gathering attributes of a rectangle (events are *not* generated when the boundary is crossed).

optionarray contains key-value pairs that define the attributes that you're interested in. An empty option array is meaningless and will raise a **rangecheck** error. The following keys are currently defined:

Key	Type	Meaning
Pressure	bool	Treat non-zero pressure values as a mouse-down (*false* by default)
Coalesce	bool	Coalesce mouse motion events (*true* by default)

EXAMPLE This example turns pressure on and coalescing off (thereby switching the default values):

```
0 0 10 10 [/Pressure true /Coalesce false] 1 null settrackingrect
```

ERRORS **invalidid**, **rangecheck**, **stackunderflow**, **typecheck**

SEE ALSO **cleartrackingrect**

---

setwaitcursorenabled

bool context **setwaitcursorenabled** –

Allows applications to enable and disable wait cursor operation in the specified context. If *context* is 0, **setwaitcursorenabled** sets the global wait cursor flag, which overrides all per-context settings. If the global flag is set to *false*, the wait cursor is disabled for all contexts.

ERRORS **invalidid**, **stackunderflow**, **typecheck**

SEE ALSO **currentwaitcursorenabled**

setwindowdepthlimit

depth window **setwindowdepthlimit** –

Warning: Don't use this operator if you're using the Application Kit. Use Window's **setDepthLimit:** method instead.

Sets the depth limit of *window* to *depth*. These depths are defined in **nextdict**:

Depth	Meaning
NX_TwoBitGray	1 spp, 2bps, 2bpp, planar
NX_EightBitGray	1 spp, 8bps, 8bpp, planar
NX_TwelveBitRGB	3 spp, 4bps, 16bpp, interleaved
NX_TwentyFourBitRGB	3 spp, 8bps, 32bpp, interleaved

where *spp* is the number of samples per pixel; *bps* is the number of bits per sample; and *bpp* is the number of bits per pixel, also know as the window's depth. (The samples-per-pixel value excludes the alpha sample, if present.) *planar* and *interleaved* refer to how the sample data is configured. If a separate data channel is used for each sample, the configuration is *planar.* If data for all samples is stored in a single data channel, the configuration is *interleaved.*

When an alpha sample is present, the number of bits per pixel doubles for planar configurations (4 for NX_TwoBitGray and 16 for NX_EightBitGray). Interleaved configurations already account for an alpha sample whether or not it's present; thus, the number of bits per pixel for NX_TwelveBitRGB and NX_TwentyFourBitRGB depths remains unchanged.

Another constant, NX_DefaultDepth, is defined as the default depth limit in the Window Server's current context. If *depth* is NX_DefaultDepth, then the window's depth limit is set to the context's default depth limit. If the resulting depth is lower than the window's current depth, the window's data is dithered down to this depth, which may result in the loss of graphic information.

The **rangecheck** error is executed if *depth* is invalid. The **invalidid** error is executed if *window* doesn't exist.

ERRORS **invalidid**, **rangecheck**, **stackunderflow**, **typecheck**

SEE ALSO **currentwindowdepthlimit**, **setdefaultdepthlimit**, **currentdefaultdepthlimit**, **currentwindowdepth**

setwindowdict

dict window **setwindowdict** –

Warning: Don't use this operator if you're using the Application Kit.

Sets the dictionary for *window* to *dict*.

ERRORS **invalidid**, **stackunderflow**, **typecheck**

SEE ALSO **currentwindowdict**

setwindowlevel

level window **setwindowlevel** –

Sets the window's tier to that specified by *level*. Window tiers constrain the action of the **orderwindow** operator; see **orderwindow** for more information.

You rarely use this operator. To make a panel float above other windows, use the Panel class's **setFloatingPanel:** method.

Attempting to change the level of **workspaceWindow** executes the **invalidaccess** error. (**workspaceWindow** is a PostScript name whose value is the window number of the workspace window.)

ERRORS **invalidaccess**, **invalidid**, **rangecheck**, **stackunderflow**, **typecheck**

SEE ALSO **currentwindowlevel**, **orderwindow**

setwindowtype

type window **setwindowtype** –

Warning: Don't use this operator if you're using the Application Kit. Use Window's **setBackingType:** method instead.

Sets the window's buffering type to that specified. Currently, the only allowable type conversions are from Buffered to Retained and from Retained to Buffered. All other possibilities execute the **limitcheck** error.

ERRORS **invalidaccess**, **invalidid**, **limitcheck**, **stackunderflow**, **typecheck**

SEE ALSO **window**

setwriteblock

bool **setwriteblock** –

Sets how the Window Server responds when its output buffer to a client application fills. If *bool* is *true*, the Server defers sending data (event records, error messages, and so on) to that application until there's once again room in the output buffer. In this way, no output data is lost—this is the Server's default behavior. If *bool* is *false*, the Server ignores the state of the output buffer: If the buffer fills and there's more data to be sent, the new data is lost. **setwriteblock** operates on the current context.

Most programmers won't need to use this operator. If you do use it, make sure that you disable the Window Server's default behavior only during the execution of your own PostScript code. If it's disabled while Application Kit code is being executed, errors will result.

ERRORS **stackoverflow**, **typecheck**

SEE ALSO **currentwriteblock**

showcursor

– **showcursor** –

Restores the cursor to the screen if it's been hidden with **hidecursor**, unless an outer nested **hidecursor** is still in effect (because it hasn't yet been balanced by a **showcursor**). For example:

```
% cursor is showing initially
. . .
hidecursor      % hides the cursor
. . .
    hidecursor  % cursor stays hidden
    . . .
    showcursor  % cursor still hidden due to first hidecursor
. . .
showcursor      % displays the cursor
```

ERRORS none

SEE ALSO **hidecursor**

showpage

– **showpage** –

Warning: This standard operator is different in the NeXTSTEP implementation of the Display PostScript system.

This has no effect if the current device is a window; otherwise, it functions as documented by Adobe.

ERRORS none

SEE ALSO **copypage**, **erasepage**

sizeimage

x y width height matrix **sizeimage** *pixelswide pixelshigh bits/sample matrix multiproc ncolors*

Returns various parameters required by the **readimage** operator when reading the image contained in the rectangle given by *x*, *y*, *width*, and *height* in the current window. (See **readimage** for more information.)

pixelswide and *pixelshigh* are the width and height of the image in pixels. The operand *matrix* is filled with the transformation matrix from user space to the image coordinate system and pushed back on the operand stack.

The other results of this operator describe the window device and are dependent on the window's depth. Each pixel has *ncolors* color components plus one alpha component; the value of each component is described by *bits/sample* bits. If *multiproc* is *true*, **readimage** will need multiple procedures to read the values of the image's pixels. Here are the values that **sizeimage** returns for windows of various depths:

Window Depth	*ncolors*	*bits/sample*	*multiproc*
NX_TwoBitGray	1	2	*true*
NX_EightBitGray	1	8	*true*
NX_TwelveBitRGB	3	4	*false*
NX_TwentyFourBitRGB	3	8	*false*

ERRORS **stackunderflow**, **typecheck**

SEE ALSO **alphaimage**, **readimage**

stilldown

eventnum **stilldown** *stilldown*

Returns *true* if the left or only mouse button is still down from the mouse-down event specified by *eventnum*; otherwise it returns *false*. *eventnum* should be the number stored in the **data** component of the event record for an event of type **Lmousedown**.

ERRORS **stackunderflow**, **typecheck**

SEE ALSO **buttondown**, **currentmouse**, **rightbuttondown**, **rightstilldown**

termwindow

window **termwindow** –

Warning: Don't use this operator if you're using the Application Kit. Use Window's **close** method instead.

Marks *window* for destruction. If the window is in the screen list, it's removed from the screen list and the screen. The given window number will no longer be valid; any attempt to use it will execute the **invalidid** error. The window will actually be destroyed and its storage reclaimed only after the last reference to it from a graphics state is removed. This can be done by resetting the device in the graphics state to another window or to the null device.

Note: After you use the **termwindow** operator, if the terminated window had been the current window, you should use the **nulldevice** operator to remove references to it.

ERRORS **invalidid**, **stackunderflow**, **typecheck**

SEE ALSO **window**, **windowdevice**, **windowdeviceround**

window

x y width height type **window** *window*

Warning: Don't use this operator if you're using the Application Kit. Create a Window object instead.

Creates a window that has a lower left corner of (*x*, *y*) and the indicated width and height. *x*, *y*, *width*, and *height* are given in the screen coordinate system. No portion of a window can have an x or y coordinate with an absolute value greater than 16000; *width* and *height* must be in the range from 0 to 10000. Exceeding these limits executes the **rangecheck** error. The four operands can be integer or real numbers; however, they are converted to integers in the Window Server by rounding toward 0. This operator returns the new window's window number, a nonzero integer that's used to refer to the window.

type specifies the window's buffering type as **Buffered**, **Retained**, or **Nonretained**.

The new window won't be in the screen list; you can put it there with the **orderwindow** operator. Windows that aren't in the screen list don't appear on the screen and don't receive user events.

The **window** operator also does the following:

- Sets the origin of the window's base coordinate system to the lower left corner of the window
- Sets the window's clipping path to the outer edge of the window
- Fills the window with opaque white and sets the window's exposure color to white

Note: This operator does not make the new window the current window; to do that, use **windowdeviceround** or **windowdevice**.

ERRORS **invalidid**, **rangecheck**, **stackunderflow**, **typecheck**

SEE ALSO **setexposurecolor**, **termwindow**, **windowdeviceround**

---

windowdevice

window **windowdevice** –

Sets the current device of the current graphics state to the given window device. It also sets the origin of the window's default matrix to the lower left corner of the window. One unit in the user coordinate system is made equal to 1/72 of an inch. The clipping path is reset to a rectangle surrounding the window. Other elements of the graphics state remain unchanged. This matrix becomes the default matrix for the window: **initmatrix** will reestablish this matrix.

windowdevice is rarely used in NeXTSTEP since the coordinate system it establishes isn't aligned with the pixels on the screen. Use the related operator **windowdeviceround** to create a coordinate system that is aligned.

Don't use this operator lightly, as it creates a new matrix and clipping path. It's significantly more expensive than a **setgstate** operator.

ERRORS **invalidid**, **stackunderflow**, **typecheck**

SEE ALSO **windowdeviceround**

windowdeviceround

window **windowdeviceround** –

Sets the current device of the current graphics state to the given window device. It also sets the origin of the window's default matrix to the lower left corner of the window. One unit in the user coordinate system is made equal to the width of one pixel, approximately 1/92 inch. The clipping path is reset to a rectangle surrounding the window. Other elements of the graphics state remain unchanged. This matrix becomes the default matrix for the window: **initmatrix** will reestablish this matrix.

Don't use this operator lightly, as it creates a new matrix and clipping path. It's significantly more expensive than a **setgstate** operator.

ERRORS **invalidid**, **stackunderflow**, **typecheck**

SEE ALSO windowdevice

windowlist

array context **windowlist** *subarray*

Fills the array with the window numbers of all windows that are owned by the PostScript context specified by *context*. It returns the subarray containing those window numbers, in order from front to back. If *array* isn't large enough to hold them all, this operator returns the frontmost windows that fit in the array.

EXAMPLE This example yields an array containing the window numbers of all windows that are owned by the current PostScript context:

```
currentcontext
countwindowlist                % find out how many windows
array                          % create array to hold them
currentcontext windowlist      % fill it in
```

ERRORS **stackunderflow**, **typecheck**

SEE ALSO **countscreenlist**, **countwindowlist**, **screenlist**

Single-Operator Functions

The Display PostScript system provides a C function for each operator in the PostScript language, allowing you to execute individual PostScript operators from your application. Adobe Systems Inc. provides the primary documentation for these operators and for **pswrap**, the utility that creates a C function for one or more PostScript operators.

NeXT has added several operators and their corresponding single-operator functions to the basic Display PostScript system. The operators are described in the section "PostScript Operators," and the functions are listed (without description) in this section.

Operands and Arguments

Some of the C functions listed in this section take arguments that match the operands of their corresponding PostScript operators. Some functions also take pointers that return values by reference, corresponding to results returned on the operand stack by the PostScript operators. Where an argument corresponds to an operand, the argument takes the operand's name as given in the "PostScript Operators" section. If an operator takes or returns an array of values, the corresponding C function will take an extra argument that gives the size of the array.

Other C functions have no arguments (or an insufficient number of arguments) where the corresponding PostScript operators expect operands or leave results on the operand stack. These functions assume that they'll be called with the appropriate objects already on the operand stack, and they'll leave any PostScript objects they generate on the operand stack instead of returning them.

To support the functions that use the operand stack rather than arguments, the Display PostScript system has several additional functions for putting values on and getting values off the stack:

Function	Effect
PSsendint() PSsendfloat() PSsendboolean() PSsendstring()	Puts one value of the specified type on the operand stack
PSgetint() PSgetfloat() PSgetboolean() PSgetstring()	Gets one value from the stack
PSsendintarray() PSsendfloatarray() PSsendchararray()	Puts an array of values on the stack
PSgetintarray() PSgetfloatarray() PSgetchararray()	Gets an array of values from the stack

Argument Data Types

In addition to the standard C types, the functions listed here use **boolean** and **userobject** as argument data types. A **boolean** variable is an **int** having either a zero or a nonzero value. The zero value is equivalent to the PostScript value *false*, and the nonzero value is equivalent to the PostScript value *true*. The **userobject** type is an **int** that refers to the value returned by **DPSDefineUserObject()**. The appearance of these types in the function listings is simply to assist in understanding—you can't use these types directly in your code.

Functions that require a graphics state **userobject** argument can use the constant NXNullObject to refer to the current graphics state.

Return Values

All the functions listed here return **void**—a single-operator function's return value is never significant.

PS and DPS Functions

For each operator, there are actually two C functions: One that takes a context argument and another that assumes the current PostScript context. The functions that take a context argument have a "DPS" prefix; those that assume the current context have a "PS" prefix. For example, the **adjustcursor** operator is represented by these functions:

DPSadjustcursor(DPSContext *context*, float *x*, float *y*)
PSadjustcursor(float *dx*, float *dy*)

Only the single-operator functions prefixed with "PS" are listed here.

PSadjustcursor(float *dx*, float *dy*)

PSalphaimage(void)

PSbasetocurrent(float *bx*, float *by*, float **cx*, float **cy*)

PSbasetoscreen(float *bx*, float *by*, float **sx*, float **sy*)

PSbuttondown(boolean **isdown*)

PScleartrackingrect(int *trectnum*, userobject *gstate*)

PScomposite(float src_x, float src_y, float *width*, float *height*, userobject *srcgstate*, float $dest_x$, float $dest_y$, int *op*)

The value passed as *op* should be one of the following:

NX_CLEAR
NX_COPY
NX_SOVER
NX_DOVER
NX_XOR
NX_SIN
NX_DIN
NX_SOUT
NX_DOUT
NX_SATOP
NX_DATOP
NX_PLUSD
NX_PLUSL

PScompositerect(float $dest_x$, float $dest_y$, float *width*, float *height*, int *op*)

The value passed as *op* should be one of the constants listed under **PScomposite()**, plus NX_HIGHLIGHT.

PScountframebuffers(int **count*)

PScountscreenlist(int *context*, int **count*)

PScountwindowlist(int *context*, int **count*)

PScurrentactiveapp(int **context*)
Warning: Don't use this function if you're using the Application Kit.

PScurrentalpha(float **coverage*)

PScurrentdefaultdepthlimit(int **depth*)
Warning: Don't use this function if you're using the Application Kit.

PScurrentdeviceinfo(userobject *window*, int **min*, int **max*, int **iscolor*)

PScurrenteventmask(userobject *window*, int **mask*)
Warning: Don't use this function if you're using the Application Kit.

PScurrentframebuffertransfer(void)

PScurrentmouse(userobject *window*, float **x*, float **y*)
Warning: Don't use this function if you're using the Application Kit.

PScurrentowner(userobject *window*, int **context*)

PScurrentshowpageprocedure(void)

PScurrentrusage(float **ctime*, float **utime*, float **stime*, int **msgsend*, int **msgrcv*, int **nsignals*, int **nvcsw*, int **nivcsw*)

PScurrenttobase(float *cx*, float *cy*, float **bx*, float **by*)

PScurrenttoscreen(float *cx*, float *cx*, float **sx*, float **sy*)

PScurrentuser(int **uiId*, int **gid*)

PScurrentwaitcursorenabled(boolean **isenabled*)

PScurrentwindow(userobject **window*)

PScurrentwindowalpha(userobject *window*, int **alpha*)

PScurrentwindowbounds(userobject *window*, float **x*, float **y*, float **width*, float **height*)
Warning: Don't use this function if you're using the Application Kit.

PScurrentwindowdepth(userobject *window*, int **depth*)
Warning: Don't use this function if you're using the Application Kit.

PScurrentwindowdepthlimit(userobject *window*, int **depth*)
Warning: Don't use this function if you're using the Application Kit.

PScurrentwindowdict(userobject *window*)
Warning: Don't use this function if you're using the Application Kit.

PScurrentwindowlevel(userobject *window*, int **level*)

PScurrentwriteblock(bool **doesblock*)

PSdissolve(float src_x, float src_y, float *sourceWidth*, float *width*, userobject *srcgstate*, float $dest_x$, float $dest_y$, float *delta*)

PSdumpwindow(int *dumplevel*, userobject *window*)
Warning: Don't use this function if you're using the Application Kit.

PSdumpwindows(int *dumplevel*, userobject *context*)
Warning: Don't use this function if you're using the Application Kit.

PSfindwindow(float *x*, float *y*, int *place*, userobject *otherwindow*, float **x'*, float **y'*, userobject **window*, boolean **found*)

The value passed as *place* should be one of the following:

NX_ABOVE
NX_BELOW

PSflushgraphics(void)
Warning: Don't use this function if you're using the Application Kit.

PSframebuffer(int *index*, int *stringlen*, char *string*[], int **slot*, int **unit*, int **romid*, int **x*, int **y*, int **width*, int **height*, int **maxdepth*)

PSfrontwindow(int **window*)
Warning: Don't use this function if you're using the Application Kit.

PShidecursor(void)

PShideinstance(float *x*, float *y*, float *width*, float *height*)

PSmachportdevice(int *width*, int *height*, const int *bbox*[], int *bboxSize*, const float *matrix*[], const char **hostname*, const char **portname*, const char **pixelencoding*)

PSmovewindow(float *x*, float *y*, userobject *window*)
Warning: Don't use this function if you're using the Application Kit.

PSnewinstance(void)

PSnextrelease(int *size*, char *string*[])

PSobscurecursor(void)

PSorderwindow(int *place*, userobject *otherwindow*, int *window*)
Warning: Don't use this function if you're using the Application Kit.

The value passed as *place* should be one of the following:

NX_ABOVE
NX_BELOW
NX_OUT

PSosname(int *size*, char *string*[])

PSostype(int **type*)

PSplacewindow(float *x*, float *y*, float *width*, float *height*, userobject *window*)[†]
Warning: Don't use this function if you're using the Application Kit.

PSplaysound(const char **soundname*, int *priority*)

PSposteventbycontext(int *type*, float *x*, float *y*, int *time*, int *flags*, int *window*, int *subtype*, int *misc0*, int *misc1*, int *context*, boolean **success*)

PSreadimage(void)

PSrevealcursor(void)

PSrightbuttondown(int **isdown*)

PSrightstilldown(int *eventnum*, boolean **stilldown*)

PSscreenlist(int *context*, int *count*, int *array*[])

PSscreentobase(float *sx*, float *sy*, float **bx*, float **by*)

PSscreentocurrent(float *sx*, float *sy*, float **cx*, float **cy*)

PSsetactiveapp(int *context*)
Warning: Don't use this function if you're using the Application Kit.

PSsetalpha(float *coverage*)

PSsetautofill(boolean *flag*, userobject *window*)

PSsetcursor(float *x*, float *y*, float *mx*, float *my*)

PSsetdefaultdepthlimit(int *depth*)
Warning: Don't use this function if you're using the Application Kit.

PSseteventmask(int *mask*, userobject *window*)
Warning: Don't use this function if you're using the Application Kit.

See the constants listed under "Event Type Masks" in the section "Types and Constants" for a list of *mask* values.

PSsetexposurecolor(void)

PSsetflushexposures(boolean *flag*)
Warning: Don't use this function if you're using the Application Kit.

PSsetframebuffertransfer(void)

PSsetinstance(boolean *flag*)

PSsetmouse(float *x*, float *y*)

PSsetowner(userobject *context*, userobject *window*)

PSsetsendexposed(boolean *flag*, userobject *window*)†
Warning: Don't use this function if you're using the Application Kit.

PSsetshowpageprocedure(int *window*)
Warning: Don't use this function if you're using the Application Kit.

PSsettrackingrect(float *x*, float *y*, float *width*, float *height*, boolean *leftbool*, boolean *rightbool*, boolean *insidebool*, int *userdata*, int *trectnum*, userobject *gstate*)

Note: Only the Form 1 version of the **settrackingrect** operator is offered as a C function.

PSsetwaitcursorenabled(boolean *flag*)

PSsetwindowdepthlimit(int *depth*, userobject *window*)
Warning: Don't use this function if you're using the Application Kit.

PSsetwindowdict(userobject *window*)
Warning: Don't use this function if you're using the Application Kit.

PSsetwindowlevel(int *level*, userobject *window*)

PSsetwindowtype(int *type*, userobject *window*)
Warning: Don't use this function if you're using the Application Kit

PSsetwriteblock(int *flag*)

PSshowcursor(void)

PSsizeimage(float *x*, float *y*, float *width*, float *height*, int **pixelswide*, int **pixelshigh*, int **bits/sample*, float *matrix*[], boolean **multiproc*, int **ncolors*)

PSstilldown(int *eventnum*, boolean **stilldown*)

PStermwindow(userobject *window*)
Warning: Don't use this function if you're using the Application Kit.

PSwindow(float *x*, float *y*, float *width*, float *height*, int *type*, int **window*)
Warning: Don't use this function if you're using the Application Kit.

PSwindowdevice(userobject *window*)

PSwindowdeviceround(userobject *window*)

PSwindowlist(int *context*, int *count*, int *subarray*[])

Client Library Functions

The Display PostScript Client Library comprises functions (and function-like macros) that gain access to the Display PostScript system. The library is system-dependent; the functions described in this section comprise that part of NeXTSTEP's implementation of the Client Library that varies from the specification provided by Adobe Systems Inc., as described in their *Display PostScript System Reference Manual.*

DPSAddFD(), DPSRemoveFD()

SUMMARY Monitor a file descriptor

DECLARED IN dpsclient/dpsNeXT.h

SYNOPSIS void **DPSAddFD(**int *fd*, DPSFDProc *handler*, void **userData*, int *priority*)
void **DPSRemoveFD(**int *fd*)

DESCRIPTION **DPSAddFD()** registers the function *handler* to be called each time your application asks for an event or peeks at the event queue. The function is called provided the following are true:

- The file descriptor *fd* must be valid and open; typically *fd* is generated through a call to **open()**. There needn't be any data waiting to be read on *fd*.
- *priority*, an integer from 0 to 30, must be equal to or greater than the application's current priority threshold. See **DPSAddTimedEntry()** for a further explanation.

DPSFDProc, *handler*'s defined type, takes the form

```
void *handler(int fd, void *userData)
```

where *fd* is the file descriptor that prompted the function call and *userData* is the same pointer that was passed as the third argument to **DPSAddFD()**. The *userData* pointer is provided as a convenience, allowing you to pass arbitrary data to *handler*.

DPSRemoveFD() removes the specified file descriptor from the list of those that the application will check.

Typically, **DPSAddFD()** is used to listen to a socket or pipe; it's rarely used to monitor a common file.

SEE ALSO **DPSAddPort()**, **DPSAddTimedEntry()**

DPSAddNotifyPortProc(), DPSRemoveNotifyPortProc()

SUMMARY Set the handler function for the notify port

DECLARED IN dpsclient/dpsNeXT.h

SYNOPSIS void **DPSAddNotifyPortProc**(DPSPortProc *handler*, void **userData*)
void **DPSRemoveNotifyPortProc**(DPSPortProc *handler*)

DESCRIPTION **DPSAddNotifyPortProc()** registers *handler* as the function that's called when a message arrives on the notify port, the unique port, created through the **task_notify()** Mach function, on which notifications (such as port death) are sent. You don't need to create the notify port yourself; **DPSAddNotifyPortProc()** creates it for you if it doesn't already exist.

DPSPortProc, *handler*'s defined type, takes the form

```
void *handler(msg_header_t *msg, void *userData)
```

where *msg* is a pointer to the message that was received at the port and *userData* is the same pointer that was passed as the second argument to **DPSAddNotifyPortProc()**. The *userData* pointer is provided as a convenience, allowing you to pass arbitrary data to *handler.*

The notify port can have only one handler at a time; adding a handler removes the current one. You can remove the port's handler without specifying a new one with the **DPSRemoveNotifyPortProc()** function. The function's argument must match the notify port's current handler.

SEE ALSO **DPSAddPort(), DPSAddTimedEntry()**

DPSAddPort(), DPSRemovePort()

SUMMARY Monitor a Mach port

DECLARED IN dpsclient/dpsNeXT.h

SYNOPSIS void **DPSAddPort**(port_t *port*, DPSPortProc *handler*, int *maxMsgSize*, void **userData*, int *priority*)
void **DPSRemovePort**(port_t *port*)

DESCRIPTION **DPSAddPort()** registers the function *handler* to be called each time your application asks for an event or peeks at the event queue. The function is called provided the following are true:

- The Mach port *port* must be valid and it must hold a message waiting to be read.
- *priority*, an integer from 0 to 30, must be equal to or greater than the application's current priority threshold. See **DPSAddTimedEntry()** for a further explanation.

DPSPortProc, *handler*'s defined type, takes the form

```
void *handler(msg_header_t *msg, void *userData)
```

where *msg* is a pointer to the message that was received at the port and *userData* is the same pointer that was passed as the fourth argument to **DPSAddPort()**. The *userData* pointer is provided as a convenience, allowing you to pass arbitrary data to *handler*.

If, within *handler*, you want to call **msg_receive()** to receive further messages at the port, you must first call **DPSRemovePort()** to remove the port from the system's port set. (This is because your application can't receive messages from a port that's in a port set.) After your application is finished receiving messages directly from the port, it can call **DPSAddPort()** to have the system continue to monitor the port.

The contents of the message buffer *msg*, as received by *handler*, are invalid after the function returns. If you need to save any of the information that you find.

The *maxMsgSize* argument is an integer that gives the size, in bytes, of the largest message you expect to receive.

DPSRemovePort() removes the specified Mach port from the list of those that the application will check.

SEE ALSO **DPSAddFD()**, **DPSAddTimedEntry()**

DPSAddTimedEntry(), DPSRemoveTimedEntry()

SUMMARY Create a timed entry

DECLARED IN dpsclient/dpsNeXT.h

SYNOPSIS DPSTimedEntry **DPSAddTimedEntry**(double *period*, DPSTimedEntryProc *handler*, void **userData*, int *priority*)
void **DPSRemoveTimedEntry**(DPSTimedEntry *tag*)

DESCRIPTION **DPSAddTimedEntry()** registers *handler* as a "timed entry," a function that's called repeatedly at a given time interval. *period* determines the number of seconds between calls to the timed entry. Whenever an application based on the Application Kit attempts to retrieve events from the event queue, it also checks (depending on *priority*) to determine whether any timed entries are due to be called. *userData* is a pointer that you can use to pass some data to the timed entry.

The function registered as *handler* has the form:

```
void *handler(DPSTimedEntry tag, double now, char *userData)
```

where *teNumber* is the timed entry identifier returned by **DPSAddTimedEntry()**, *now* is the number of seconds since some arbitrary point in the past, and *userData* is the pointer **DPSAddTimedEntry()** received when this timed entry was installed.

An application's priority threshold can be set explicitly as an integer from 0 to 31 through a call to **DSPGetEvent()** or **DPSPeekEvent()**. It's against this threshold that *priority* is measured (note that *priority* can be no greater than 30—the additional threshold level, 31, is provided to disallow all inter-event function calls). However, if you're using the Application Kit, you should access the event queue through Application class methods such as **getNextEvent:**. Although some of these methods let you set the priority threshold explicity, you typically invoke the methods that set it automatically. Such methods use only three priority levels:

Constant	Meaning
NX_BASETHRESHOLD	Normal execution
NX_RUNMODALTHRESHOLD	An attention panel is being run
NX_MODALRESPTHRESHOLD	A modal event loop is being run

When applicable, you should use these constants as the value for *priority*. For example, if you want *handler* to be called during normal execution, but not if an attention panel or a modal loop is running, then you would set *priority* to NX_BASETHRESHOLD.

DPSRemoveTimedEntry() removes a previously registered timed entry.

RETURN **DPSAddTimedEntry()** returns a number identifying the timed entry or –1 to indicate an error.

DPSAsynchronousWaitContext()

SUMMARY Procede asynchronously while PostScript code is executed

DECLARED IN dpsclient/dpsNeXT.h

SYNOPSIS void **DPSAsynchronousWaitContext**(DPSContext *context*, DPSPingProc *handler*, void **userData*)

DESCRIPTION This function is similar to the more familiar **DPSWaitContext()** functions, except that rather than wait for all PostScript code to execute, it returns immediately, allowing your application to procede while the PostScript code is executed in the background. The DPSPingProc function *handler* is called (with *context* and *userData* as its two arguments) when all the PostScript code has been executed. The DPSPingProc function takes the form

```
void *handler(DPSContext context, void *userData);
```

Warning: Be careful when you use this function; you mustn't send more PostScript code while waiting for the handler to be called. In general, it's best to not make any demands on the Application Kit or the Client Library if you're waiting for an asynchronous handler to return.

DPSCreateContext(), DPSCreateContextWithTimeoutFromZone(), DPSCreateNonsecureContext(), DPSCreateStreamContext()

SUMMARY Create a PostScript execution context

DECLARED IN dpsclient/dpsNeXT.h

SYNOPSIS DPSContext **DPSCreateContext**(const char **hostName*, const char **serverName*, DPSTextProc *textProc*, DPSErrorProc *errorProc*)

DPSContext **DPSCreateContextWithTimeoutFromZone**(const char **hostName*, const char **serverName*, DPSTextProc *textProc*, DPSErrorProc *errorProc*, int *timeout*, NXZone **zone*)

DPSContext **DPSCreateNonsecureContext**(const char **hostName*, const char **serverName*, DPSTextProc *textProc*, DPSErrorProc *errorProc*, int *timeout*, NXZone **zone*)

DPSContext **DPSCreateStreamContext**(NXStream **stream*, int *debugging*, DPSProgramEncoding *progEnc*, DPSNameEncoding *nameEnc*, DPSErrorProc *errorProc*)

DESCRIPTION **DPSCreateContext**() establishes a connection with the Window Server and creates a PostScript execution context in it. The new context becomes the current context. The first argument, *hostName*, identifies the machine that's running the Window Server; the second argument, *serverName*, identifies the Window Server that's running on that machine. With these two arguments and the help of the Mach network server **nmserver**, the Mach port for the Window Server can be identified. If *hostName* is NULL, the network server on the local machine is queried for the Window Server's port. If *serverName* is NULL, a default name for the Window Server is used.

The last two arguments, *textProc* and *errorProc*, refer to call-back functions (defined in the Client Library specification) that handle text returned from the Window Server and errors generated on either side of the connection.

For an application that's based on the Application Kit, you could create an additional context by making this call:

```
DPSContext  c;

c = DPSCreateContext(NXGetDefaultValue([NXApp appName], "NXHost"),
                     NXGetDefaultValue([NXApp appName], "NXPSName"),
                     NULL,
                     NULL);
```

This example queries the application's default values for the indentity of the host machine and the Window Server. By doing this, the new context is created in the correct Window Server even if that Server is not on the same machine as the application process.

The context that **DPSCreateContext()** creates allocates memory from the default allocation zone. Also, when there's difficulty creating the context, **DPSCreateContext()** waits up to 60 seconds before raising an exception. If you want to change either of these parameters, use **DPSCreateContextWithTimeoutFromZone()**. Its two additional arguments let you specify the zone for the context to use when allocating context-specific data and a timeout value in milliseconds.

DPSCreateNonsecureContext() creates a "nonsecure" context in which you can use PostScript operators that are normally disallowed. The most significant of these are operators that let you write files.

DPSCreateStreamContext() is similar to **DPSCreateContext()**, except that the new context is actually a connection from the client application to a stream. This connection becomes the current context. PostScript code that the application generates is sent to the stream rather than to the Window Server. The first argument, *stream*, is a pointer to an NXStream structure, as created by **NXOpenFile()** or **NXMapFile()**. The *debugging* argument is intended for debugging purposes but is not currently implemented. *progEnc* and *nameEnc* specify the type of program and user-name encodings to be used for output to the stream. The last argument, *errorProc*, identifies the procedure that's called when errors are generated.

Few programmers will need to call either of these functions directly: The Application Kit manages contexts for programs based on the Kit. For example, when an application is launched, its Application object calls **DPSCreateContext()** to create a context in the Window Server. Similarly, to print a View the Kit calls **DPSCreateStreamContext()** to temporarily redirect PostScript code from the View to a stream.

RETURN Each of these functions returns the newly created DPSContext structure.

EXCEPTIONS **DPSCreateContext()** and **DPSCreateContextWithTimeoutFromZone()** raise a dps_err_outOfMemory exception if they encounter difficulty allocating ports or other resources for the new context. They raise a dps_err_cantConnect exception if they can't return a context within the timeout period.

DPSCreateContextWithTimeoutFromZone() → See DPSCreateContext()

DPSCreateNonsecureContext() → See DPSCreateContext()

DPSCreateStreamContext() → See DPSCreateContext()

DPSDefineUserObject(), DPSUndefineUserObject()

SUMMARY Create a user object

DECLARED IN dpsclient/dpsNeXT.h

SYNOPSIS int **DPSDefineUserObject**(int *index*)
void **DPSUndefineUserObject**(int *index*)

DESCRIPTION **DPSDefineUserObject()** associates *index* with the PostScript object that's on the top of the operand stack, thereby creating a user object (as defined by the PostScript language). If *index* is 0, the object is assigned the next available index number. The function returns the new index, which can then be passed to a **pswrap**-generated function that takes a user object.

Warning: To avoid coming into conflict with user objects defined by the Client Library or Application Kit, use **DPSDefineUserObject()** rather than the PostScript operator **defineuserobject** or the single-operator functions **DPSdefineuserobject()** and **PSdefineuserobject()**.

DPSUndefineUserObject() removes the association between *index* and the PostScript object it refers to, thus destroying the user object. By destroying a user object that's no longer needed, you can let the garbage collector reclaim the previously associated PostScript object.

RETURN **DPSDefineUserObject()**, if successful in assigning an index, returns the index that the object was assigned. If unsuccessful, it returns 0.

DPSDiscardEvents() → See DPSGetEvent()

DPSDoUserPath(), DPSDoUserPathWithMatrix()

SUMMARY Send an encoded PostScript path to the Window Server

DECLARED IN dpsclient/dpsNeXT.h

SYNOPSIS void **DPSDoUserPath**(void **coords*, int *numCoords*, DPSNumberFormat *numType*, unsigned char **ops*, int *numOps*, void **bbox*, int *action*)
void **DPSDoUserPathWithMatrix**(void **coords*, int *numCoords*, DPSNumberFormat *numType*, unsigned char **ops*, int *numOps*, void **bbox*, int *action*, float *matrix*[6])

DESCRIPTION **DPSDoUserPath()** and **DPSDoUserPathWithMatrix()** send an encoded user path to the Window Server and then execute, upon that path, the operator specified by *action*. The use of these functions, rather than the analogous step-by-step path construction, is encouraged; rendering an encoded path is much more efficient than executing the individual PostScript operators that would otherwise be needed.

An encoded user path consists of an array of coordinate values, a sequence of PostScript operators, and a bounding box specification. The values in the coordinate array are used as operands to the operators; the operands are distributed to the operators in the order that they're given. The resulting path must fit within the bounding box.

The coordinates, operators, and bounding box are given by the functions' first five arguments:

- The array of coordinate values is given by *coords*.
- *numCoords* is the number of elements in *coords*.
- *numType* specifies the data type of the coordinates, as described below. All the values in *coords* must be of the same type.
- *ops* is the sequence of PostScript operators, represented by constants as listed below.
- The bounding box is defined by the four coordinate values that you pass as an array in the *bbox* argument. These are passed as operands to the **setbbox** operator. (If you don't supply a **setbbox** as part of the *ops* sequence, one is inserted for you.)

The following integer constants represent the data types that you can pass as the *numType* argument:

Constant	Meaning
dps_float	single-precision floating-point number
dps_long	32-bit integer
dps_short	8-bit integer

You can also specify 16- and 32-bit fixed-point real numbers. For 16-bit fixed-point numbers, use **dps_short** plus the number of bits in the fractional portion. For 32-bit fixed-point numbers, use **dps_long** plus the number of bits in the fractional portion.

These constants are provided for *ops*:

dps_setbbox
dps_moveto
dps_rmoveto
dps_lineto
dps_rlineto
dps_curveto
dps_rcurveto
dps_arc
dps_arcn
dps_arct
dps_closepath
dps_ucache

Once the user path has been constructed, the operator specified by *action* is executed. The value of *action* is an index into Display PostScript's encoded system names; the following constants, provided as a convenience, represent the most commonly used actions:

dps_uappend
dps_ufill
dps_ueofill
dps_ustroke
dps_ustrokepath
dps_inufill
dps_inueofill
dps_inustroke
dps_def
dps_put

DPSDoUserPathWithMatrix()'s *matrix* argument represents the transformation matrix operand used by the **ustroke**, **inustroke**, and **ustrokepath** operators. If *matrix* is NULL, the argument is ignored.

The following program fragment demonstrates the use of **DPSDoUserPath()** as it creates and strokes a user path (an isosceles triangle) within a bounding rectangle whose lower left corner is located at (0, 0) and whose width and height are 200.

```
short   coords[6] = {0, 0, 200, 0, 100, 200};
char    ops[4] = {dps_moveto, dps_lineto,dps_lineto,
                   dps_closepath};
short   bbox[4] = {0, 0, 200, 200};

DPSDoUserPath(coords, 6, dps_short, ops, 4, bbox, dps_ustroke);
```

DPSDoUserPathWithMatrix() → See DPSDoUserPath()

DPSFlush(), DPSSendEOF()

SUMMARY Send PostScript data to the Window Server

DECLARED IN dpsclient/dpsNeXT.h

SYNOPSIS void **DPSFlush**()
void **DPSSendEOF**(DPSContext *context*)

DESCRIPTION **DPSFlush**() flushes the application's output buffer, forcing any buffered PostScript code or data to the Window Server.

DPSSendEOF() sends a PostScript end-of-file marker to the given context. The connection to the context isn't closed or disturbed in any way by this function.

DPSGetEvent(), DPSPeekEvent(), DPSDiscardEvents()

SUMMARY Access events from the Window Server

DECLARED IN dpsclient/dpsNeXT.h

SYNOPSIS int **DPSGetEvent**(DPSContext *context*, NXEvent **anEvent*, int *mask*, double *timeout*, int *threshold*)

int **DPSPeekEvent**(DPSContext *context*, NXEvent **anEvent*, int *mask*, double *timeout*, int *threshold*)

void **DPSDiscardEvents**(DPSContext *context*, int *mask*)

DESCRIPTION **DPSGetEvent()** and **DPSPeekEvent()** are macros that access event records in an application's event queue. These routines are provided primarily for programs that don't use the Application Kit. An application based on the Kit should use the corresponding Application class methods (such as **getNextEvent:** and **peekNextEvent:into:**) or the function **NXGetOrPeekEvent()** so that it can be journaled. **DPSDiscardEvents()** removes all event records of a specified type from the queue.

DPSGetEvent() and **DPSPeekEvent()** differ only in how they treat the accessed event record. **DPSGetEvent()** removes the record from the queue after making its data available to the application; **DPSPeekEvent()** leaves the record in the queue.

DPSGetEvent() and **DPSPeekEvent()** take the same parameters. The first, *context*, represents a PostScript execution context within the Window Server. Virtually all applications have only one execution context, which can be returned using **DPSGetCurrentContext()**. Applications having more than one execution context can use the constant DPS_ALLCONTEXTS to access events from all contexts belonging to them.

The second argument, *anEvent*, is a pointer to an event record. If **DPSGetEvent()** or **DPSPeekEvent()** is successful in accessing an event record, the record's data is copied into the storage referred to by *anEvent*.

mask determines the types of events sought. See the section "Types and Constants" for a list of the constants that represent the event type masks. To check for more than one type of event, you combine individual constants using the bitwise OR operator.

If an event matching the event mask isn't available in the queue, **DPSGetEvent()** or **DPSPeekEvent()** waits until one arrives or until *timeout* seconds have elapsed, whichever occurs first. The value of *timeout* can be in the range of 0.0 to NX_FOREVER. If *timeout* is 0.0, the routine returns an event only if one is waiting in the queue when the routine asks for it. If *timeout* is NX_ FOREVER, the routine waits until an appropriate event arrives before returning.

The last argument, *threshold*, is an integer in the range 0 through 31 that determines which other services may be provided during a call to **DPSGetEvent()** or **DPSPeekEvent()**.

Requests for services are registered by the functions **DPSAddTimedEntry()**, **DPSAddPort()**, and **DPSAddFD()**. Each of these functions takes an argument specifying a priority level. If this level is equal to or greater than *threshold*, the service is provided before **DPSGetEvent()** or **DPSPeekEvent()** returns.

DPSDiscardEvents()'s two parameters, *context* and *mask*, are the same as those for **DPSGetEvent()** and **DPSPeekEvent()**. **DPSDiscardEvents()** removes from the application's event queue those records whose event types match *mask* and whose context matches *context*.

RETURN **DPSGetEvent()** and **DPSPeekEvent()** return 1 if they are successful in accessing an event record and 0 if they aren't.

SEE ALSO **DPSAddFD()**, **DPSAddPort()**, **DPSAddTimedEntry()**, **DPSPostEvent()**, **NXGetOrPeekEvent()**

DPSInterruptContext()

Warning: This function is unimplemented in the NeXTSTEP version of the Client Library.

DPSNameFromTypeAndIndex()

SUMMARY Access the system and user name tables

DECLARED IN dpsclient/dpsNeXT.h

SYNOPSIS const char ***DPSNameFromTypeAndIndex**(short *type*, int *index*)

DESCRIPTION **DPSNameFromTypeAndIndex()** returns the text associated with *index* from the system or user name table. If *type* is –1, the text is returned from the system name table; if *type* is 0, it's returned from the user name table.

The name tables are used primarily by the Client Library and **pswrap**; few programmers will access them directly.

RETURN This function returns a read-only character string.

DPSPeekEvent() → See DPSGetEvent()

DPSPostEvent()

SUMMARY Create an event

DECLARED IN dpsclient/dpsNeXT.h

SYNOPSIS int **DPSPostEvent(**NXEvent **anEvent*, int *atStart***)**

DESCRIPTION **DPSPostEvent()** lets you add an event record to your application's event queue without involving the Window Server. *anEvent* is a pointer to the event record to be added. *atStart* specifies where the new record will be placed in relation to any other records in the queue. If *atStart* is TRUE, the event is posted in front of all others and so will be the next one your application receives. If *atStart* is FALSE, the event is posted behind all others and so won't be returned until events that precede it are processed.

You can free, reuse, or otherwise mangle *anEvent* after you've posted it without fear of corrupting the posted record. **DPSEvent()** copies the record it receives and posts the copy.

Note that event records you post using **DPSPostEvent()** aren't filtered by an event filter function set with **DPSSetEventFunc()**.

RETURN **DPSPostEvent()** returns 0 if successful in posting the event record; it returns –1 if unsuccessful in posting the record because the event queue is full.

SEE ALSO **DPSSetEventFunc()**

DPSPrintError(), DPSPrintErrorToStream()

SUMMARY Print error messages

DECLARED IN dpsclient/dpsNeXT.h

SYNOPSIS

void **DPSPrintError**(FILE **fp*, const DPSBinObjSeq *error*)
void **DPSPrintErrorToStream**(NXStream **stream*, const DPSBinObjSeq *error*)

DESCRIPTION **DPSPrintError**() and **DPSPrintErrorToStream**() format and print error messages received from a PostScript execution context in the Window Server. The error message is extracted from the binary object sequence *error*. **DPSPrintError**() prints the error message to the file identified by *fp*; **DPSPrintErrorToStream**() prints the error message to *stream*.

You rarely need to call these functions directly. However, if you reset the error handler for a PostScript execution context, the new handler you install could use one of these functions to process errors that it receives.

DPSPrintErrorToStream() → See DPSPrintError()

DPSRemoveFD() → See DPSAddFD()

DPSRemovePort() → See DPSAddPort()

DPSRemoveTimedEntry() → See DPSAddTimedEntry()

DPSResetContext()

Warning: This function is unimplemented in the NeXTSTEP version of the Client Library.

DPSSendEOF() → See DPSFlush()

DPSSetDeadKeysEnabled()

SUMMARY Allow dead key processing for a context's events

DECLARED IN dpsclient/dpsNeXT.h

SYNOPSIS void **DPSSetDeadKeysEnabled**(DPSContext *context*, int *flag*)

DESCRIPTION **DPSSetDeadKeysEnabled**() turns dead key processing on or off for *context*. If flag is 0, dead key processing is turned off; otherwise, it's turned on (the default).

Dead key processing is a technique for extending the range of characters that can be entered from the keyboard. In NeXTSTEP, it provides one way for users to enter accented characters. For example, a user can type Alternate-e followed by the letter "e" to produce the letter "é ". The first keyboard input, Alternate-e, seems to have no efect—it's the "dead key ". However, it signals Client Library routines that it and the following character should be analyzed as a pair. If, within NeXTSTEP, the pair of characters has been associated with a third character, a keyboard event record representing the third character is placed in the application's event queue, and the first two event records are discarded. If there is no such association between the two characters, the two event records are added to the event queue.

See the *NeXT User's Reference* manual for a listing of the keys that produce accent characters.

DPSSetEventFunc()

SUMMARY Set the function that filters events

DECLARED IN dpsclient/dpsNeXT.h

SYNOPSIS DPSEventFilterFunc **DPSSetEventFunc**(DPSContext *context*, DPSEventFilterFunc *func*)

DESCRIPTION **DPSSetEventFunc()** establishes the function *func* as the function to be called when an event record is returned from the PostScript context *context* in the Window Server. The registered function is called before the event record is put in the event queue. If the registered function returns 0, the record is discarded. If the registered function returns 1, the record is passed on for further processing.

Only event records coming from the Window Server are filtered by the registered function. Records that you post to the event queue using **DPSPostEvent()** aren't affected.

A DPSEventFilterFunc function takes the following form:

```
int *func(NXEvent *anEvent)
```

RETURN **DPSSetEventFunc()** returns a pointer to the previously registered event function. This lets you chain together the current and previous event functions.

SEE ALSO **DPSPostEvent()**

DPSSetTracking()

SUMMARY Coalesce mouse events

DECLARED IN dpsclient/dpsNeXT.h

SYNOPSIS int **DPSSetTracking**(int *flag*)

DESCRIPTION **DPSSetTracking()** turns mouse event-coalescing on or off for the current context. If *flag* is 0, coalescing is turned off; otherwise, it's turned on (the default).

Event coalescing is an optimization that's useful when tracking the mouse. When the mouse is moved, numerous events flow into the event queue. To reduce the number of events awaiting removal by the application, adjacent mouse-moved events are replaced by the most recent event of the contiguous group. The same is done for left and right mouse-dragged events, with the addition that a mouse-up event replaces mouse-dragged events that come before it in the queue.

RETURN **DPSSetTracking()** returns the previous state of the event-coalescing switch.

DPSStartWaitCursorTimer()

SUMMARY Initiate a count down for the wait cursor

DECLARED IN dpsclient/dpsNeXT.h

SYNOPSIS void **DPSStartWaitCursorTimer**()

DESCRIPTION **DPSStartWaitCursorTimer**() triggers the mechanism that displays a wait cursor when an application is busy and can't respond to user input. In most cases, wait cursor support is automatic: You'll only need to call this function if your application starts a time-consuming operation that's not initiated by a user-generated event.

Client Library routines and the Window Server cooperate to display the wait cursor whenever more than a preset amount of time elapses between the time an application takes an event record from the event queue and the time the application is again ready to consume events. However, when an application starts an operation that isn't initiated by an event—such as one caused by receiving a Mach message or by processing data from a file (see **DPSAddPort**() and **DPSAddFD**())—the wait cursor mechanism is bypassed. To ensure proper wait cursor behavior in these cases, call **DPSStartWaitCursorTimer**() before beginning the time-consuming operation.

SEE ALSO **DPSAddFD(), DPSAddPort(), setwaitcursorenabled**

DPSSynchronizeContext()

SUMMARY Synchronize a context with your application

DECLARED IN dpsclient/dpsNeXT.h

SYNOPSIS int **DPSSynchronizeContext**(DPSContext *context*, int *flag*)

DESCRIPTION **DPSSynchronizeContext**() causes **DPSWaitContext**() to be called after each **pswrap** function is called, thus synchronizing the PostScript context with your application.

DPSTraceContext(), DPSTraceEvents()

SUMMARY Trace data and events

DECLARED IN dpsclient/dpsNeXT.h

SYNOPSIS int **DPSTraceContext**(DPSContext *context*, int *flag*)
void **DPSTraceEvents**(DPSContext *context*, int *flag*)

DESCRIPTION **DPSTraceContext**() and **DPSTraceEvents**() control the tracing of data and events between a PostScript execution context (or contexts) in the Window Server and an application process.

The first argument for both functions, *context*, specifies the context to be traced. An application's single context can be returned with **DPSGetCurrentContext**(). Applications having more than one execution context can use the constant DPS_ALLCONTEXTS to trace all contexts belonging to them.

The second argument, *flag*, determines whether tracing is enabled.

When data tracing is enabled (**DPSTraceContext**()), a copy of the PostScript code generated by an application and the values returned to it by the Window Server is sent to UNIX standard error. Values returned to the application are marked by the prepended string:

```
% value returned ==>
```

When event tracing is enabled (**DPSTraceEvents**()), information about each event that the application receives is sent to UNIX standard error. For example, for a left mouse-down event the listing might look like this:

```
Receiving: LMouseDown at: 343.0,69.0 time: 1271899
              flags: 0x0 win: 6 ctxt: 76128 data: 1111,1
```

The listing displays the fields of the event record: type, location, time, flags, local window number, PostScript execution context, and data. The contents of the data field listing depends on the event type; for instance, in the preceding example the event number and the click count were displayed.

For applications based on the Application Kit, there are two preferable methods for turning on data tracing: You can use the NXShowPS command-line switch when you launch an application from Terminal. Alternatively, when you run the application under GDB, you can use the **showps** and **shownops** commands to control tracing output. Similarly, there are more convenient ways to turn on event tracing: You can use the **NXTraceEvents** command-line switch when you launch an application from Terminal. Alternatively, when you run the application under GDB, you can use the **traceevents** and **tracenoevents** commands to control event-tracing output.

Only one tracing context can be created for the supplied *context*. If you attempt to create additional tracing contexts for a context that's already being traced, no new context is created and **DPSTraceContext**() returns –1.

RETURN **DPSTraceContext**() returns 0 if successful in creating a tracing context, or –1 if not.

DPSTraceEvents() → See DPSTraceContext()

DPSUndefineUserObject() → See DPSDefineUserObject()

NX_EVENTCODEMASK()

SUMMARY Generate an event mask for an event type

DECLARED IN dpsclient/event.h

SYNOPSIS int **NX_EVENTCODEMASK**(int *type*)

DESCRIPTION This handy utility macro returns an event mask that corresponds to the given (single) event type.

Types and Constants

The types and constants given in this section are used by the Display PostScript language. The scope and significance of a particular item depends on the file in which it's declared:

- **dpsclient.h** defines types and constants that are common to all implementations of the Display PostScript language.
- **dpsfriends.h** defines types and constants that may vary in different implementations of the language. Documented here are only those elements that, as implemented in NeXTSTEP, are different from the implementation supplied by Adobe.
- **dpsNeXT.h** defines types and constants that are unique to the NeXTSTEP implementation of the Display PostScript language.

Defined Types

DPSContextRec

DECLARED IN dpsclient/dpsfriends.h

SYNOPSIS

```
typedef struct _t_DPSContextRec {
        char *priv;
        DPSSpace space;
        DPSProgramEncoding programEncoding;
        DPSNameEncoding nameEncoding;
        struct _t_DPSProcsRec const * procs;
        void (*textProc)();
        void (*errorProc)();
        DPSResults resultTable;
        unsigned int resultTableLength;
        struct _t_DPSContextRec *chainParent, *chainChild;
        DPSContextType type;
} DPSContextRec, *DPSContext;
```

DESCRIPTION The **DPSContextRec** structure represents a Display PostScript context.

DPSContextType

DECLARED IN dpsclient/dpsfriends.h

SYNOPSIS

```
typedef enum {
        dps_machServer,
        dps_fdServer,
        dps_stream
} DPSContextType;
```

DESCRIPTION These represent the context types supported by NeXT's version of Display PostScript, as used in the **type** field of a **DPSContextRec** structure.

DPSErrorCode

DECLARED IN dpsclient/dpsclient.h

SYNOPSIS typedef enum _DPSErrorCode {
    dps_err_ps = DPS_ERROR_BASE,
    dps_err_nameTooLong,
    dps_err_resultTagCheck,
    dps_err_resultTypeCheck,
    dps_err_invalidContext,
    dps_err_select = DPS_NEXT_ERROR_BASE,
    dps_err_connectionClosed,
    dps_err_read,
    dps_err_write,
    dps_err_invalidFD,
    dps_err_invalidTE,
    dps_err_invalidPort,
    dps_err_outOfMemory,
    dps_err_cantConnect
} **DPSErrorCode**;

DESCRIPTION Error codes passed to a **DPSErrorProc()** function.

DPSEventFilterFunc

DECLARED IN dpsclient/dpsNeXT.h

SYNOPSIS typedef int (***DPSEventFilterFunc**)(NXEvent **ev*);

DESCRIPTION Call-back function used to filter events.

DPSFDProc

DECLARED IN dpsclient/dpsNeXT.h

SYNOPSIS typedef void (***DPSFDProc**)(int *fd*, void **userData*);

DESCRIPTION Call-back function used when a file descriptor is registered through **DPSAddFD**().

DPSNumberFormat

DECLARED IN dpsclient/dpsNeXT.h

SYNOPSIS

```
typedef enum _DPSNumberFormat {
#ifdef __BIG_ENDIAN__
        dps_float = 48,
        dps_long = 0,
        dps_short = 32
#else
        dps_float = 48+128,
        dps_long = 0+128,
        dps_short = 32+128
} DPSNumberFormat;
```

DESCRIPTION These constants are used by the **DPSDoUserPath()** function to describe the type of numbers that are being passed.

DPSPingProc

DECLARED IN dpsclient/dpsNeXT.h

SYNOPSIS typedef void (***DPSPingProc**)
(DPSContext *ctxt*,
void **userData*);

DESCRIPTION Call-back function used by **DPSAsynchronousWaitContext**().

DPSPortProc

DECLARED IN dpsclient/dpsNeXT.h

SYNOPSIS typedef void (***DPSPortProc**)
(msg_header_t **msg*,
void **userData*);

DESCRIPTION Call-back function used when a port is registered through **DPSAddPort()**.

DPSTimedEntry

DECLARED IN dpsclient/dpsNeXT.h

SYNOPSIS typedef struct __DPSTimedEntry ***DPSTimedEntry**;

DESCRIPTION The return type for **DPSAddTimedEntry**().

DPSTimedEntryProc

DECLARED IN dpsclient/dpsNeXT.h

SYNOPSIS typedef void (***DPSTimedEntryProc**)
(DPSTimedEntry *timedEntry*,
double *now*,
void **userData*);

DESCRIPTION Call-back function used when a timed entry is registered through **DPSAddTimedEntry**().

DPSUserPathAction

DECLARED IN dpsclient/dpsNeXT.h

SYNOPSIS

```
typedef enum _DPSUserPathAction {
    dps_uappend,
    dps_ufill,
    dps_ueofill,
    dps_ustroke,
    dps_ustrokepath,
    dps_inufill,
    dps_inueofill,
    dps_inustroke,
    dps_def,
    dps_put
} DPSUserPathAction;
```

DESCRIPTION These constants are convenient representations of some of the PostScript operator indices, suitable for enrollment in the action array passed to **DPSDoUserPath**().

DPSUserPathOp

DECLARED IN dpsclient/dpsNeXT.h

SYNOPSIS

```
typedef enum _DPSUserPathOp {
        dps_setbbox,
        dps_moveto,
        dps_rmoveto,
        dps_lineto,
        dps_rlineto,
        dps_curveto,
        dps_rcurveto,
        dps_arc,
        dps_arcn,
        dps_arct,
        dps_closepath,
        dps_ucache
} DPSUserPathOp;
```

DESCRIPTION These constants represent the PostScript operators that can be passed in **DPSDoUserPath()**'s operator array.

NXCoord

DECLARED IN dpsclient/event.h

SYNOPSIS typedef float **NXCoord**

DESCRIPTION Used to represent a single coordinate in a Cartesian coordinate system.

NXEvent

DECLARED IN dpsclient/event.h

SYNOPSIS

```
typedef struct _NXEvent {
    int type;
    NXPoint location;
    long time;
    int flags;
    unsigned int window;
    NXEventData data;
    DPSContext ctxt;
} NXEvent, *NXEventPtr;
```

DESCRIPTION Represents a single event; this structure is also known as the *event record*. The fields are:

type	The type of event (see "Event Types," below)
location	The event's location in the base coordinate system of its window
time	The time of the event (in hardware-dependent units) since system startup
flags	Mouse-button and modifier-key flags (see "Event Flags," below)
window	The window number of the window associated with the event
data	Additional type-specific data (see "NXEventData," below)
ctxt	The PostScript context of the event

NXEventData

DECLARED IN dpsclient/event.h

SYNOPSIS

```
typedef union {
        struct {
                short eventNum;
                int click;
                unsigned char pressure;
        } mouse;
        struct {
                short repeat;
                unsigned short charSet;
                unsigned short charCode;
                unsigned short keyCode;
                short keyData;
        } key;
        struct {
                short eventNum;
                int trackingNum;
                int userData;
        } tracking;
        struct {
                short subtype;
                union {
                        float F[2];
                        long L[2];
                        short S[4];
                        char C[8];
                } misc;
        } compound;
} NXEventData;
```

DESCRIPTION This structure supplies type-specific information for an event. It's a union of four structures, where the type of the event determines which structure is pertinent:

- **mouse** is used for mouse events.
- **key** is used for keyboard events.
- **tracking** is for tracking-rectangle events.
- **compound** is for system-, kit-, and application-defined events.

NXPoint

DECLARED IN dpsclient/event.h

SYNOPSIS

```
typedef struct _NXPoint {
        NXCoord x;
        NXCoord y;
} NXPoint;
```

DESCRIPTION Represents a point in a Cartesian coordinate system.

NXSize

DECLARED IN dpsclient/event.h

SYNOPSIS

```
typedef struct _NXSize {
        NXCoord width;
        NXCoord height;
} NXSize;
```

DESCRIPTION Represents a two-dimensional size.

Symbolic Constants

All Contexts

DECLARED IN dpsclient/dpsNeXT.h

SYNOPSIS DPS_ALLCONTEXTS

DESCRIPTION This constant represents all extant contexts.

Alpha Constants

DECLARED IN dpsclient/dpsNeXT.h

SYNOPSIS NX_DATA
NX_ONES

DESCRIPTION These constants represent alpha values.

Character Set Values

DECLARED IN dpsclient/event.h

SYNOPSIS NX_ASCIISET
NX_SYMBOLSET
NX_DINGBATSSET

DESCRIPTION These constants represent the values that may occur in the **data.key.charSet** field of an NXEvent structure.

Compositing Operations

DECLARED IN dpsclient/dpsNeXT.h

SYNOPSIS
NX_CLEAR
NX_COPY
NX_SOVER
NX_SIN
NX_SOUT
NX_SATOP
NX_DOVER
NX_DIN
NX_DOUT
NX_DATOP
NX_XOR
NX_PLUSD
NX_HIGHLIGHT
NX_PLUSL

DESCRIPTION These represent the compositing operations used by **PScomposite()** and the NXImage class.

Error Code Bases

DECLARED IN dpsclient/dpsclient.h

SYNOPSIS
DPS_ERROR_BASE
DPS_NEXT_ERROR_BASE

DESCRIPTION These constants represent the lowest values for Display PostScript error codes.

Event Types

DECLARED IN dpsclient/event.h

SYNOPSIS

Type	Meaning
NX_NULLEVENT	A non-event
NX_LMOUSEDOWN	Left mouse-down
NX_LMOUSEUP	Left mouse-up
NX_LMOUSEDRAGGED	left mouse-dragged
NX_MOUSEDOWN	Same as NX_LMOUSEDOWN
NX_MOUSEUP	Same as NX_LMOUSEUP
NX_MOUSEDRAGGED	Same as NX_LMOUSEDRAGGED
NX_RMOUSEDOWN	Right mouse-down
NX_RMOUSEUP	Right mouse-up
NX_RMOUSEDRAGGED	Right mouse-dragged
NX_MOUSEMOVED	Mouse-moved
NX_MOUSEENTERED	Mouse-entered
NX_MOUSEEXITED	Mouse-exited
NX_KEYDOWN	Key-down
NX_KEYUP	Key-up event
NX_FLAGSCHANGED	Flags-changed
NX_KITDEFINED	Application Kit-defined
NX_SYSDEFINED	System-defined
NX_APPDEFINED	Application-defined
NX_TIMER	Timer used for tracking
NX_CURSORUPDATE	Cursor tracking
NX_JOURNALEVENT	Event used by journaling
NX_FIRSTEVENT	The smallest-valued event constant
NX_LASTEVENT	The greatest-valued event constant
NX_ALLEVENTS	A value that includes all event types

DESCRIPTION These constants represent event types. They're passed as the **type** field of the NXEvent structure that's created when an event occurs.

Event Type Masks

DECLARED IN dpsclient/event.h

SYNOPSIS
NX_NULLEVENTMASK
NX_LMOUSEDOWNMASK
NX_LMOUSEUPMASK
NX_RMOUSEDOWNMASK
NX_RMOUSEUPMASK
NX_MOUSEMOVEDMASK
NX_LMOUSEDRAGGEDMASK
NX_RMOUSEDRAGGEDMASK
NX_MOUSEENTEREDMASK
NX_MOUSEEXITEDMASK
NX_KEYDOWNMASK
NX_KEYUPMASK
NX_FLAGSCHANGEDMASK
NX_KITDEFINEDMASK
NX_APPDEFINEDMASK
NX_SYSDEFINEDMASK
NX_TIMERMASK
NX_CURSORUPDATEMASK
NX_MOUSEDOWNMASK
NX_MOUSEUPMASK
NX_MOUSEDRAGGEDMASK
NX_JOURNALEVENTMASK

DESCRIPTION These masks correspond to the event types defined immediately above. They let you query the **type** field of an NXEvent structure for the existence of a particular event type.

Forever

DECLARED IN dpsclient/dpsNeXT.h

SYNOPSIS NX_FOREVER

DESCRIPTION A long, long time. Typically used as the timeout argument to **DPSGetEvent()**.

Keyboard State Flags Masks

DECLARED IN dpsclient/event.h

SYNOPSIS

Type	Meaning
NX_ALPHASHIFTMASK	Shift lock
NX_SHIFTMASK	Shift key
NX_CONTROLMASK	Control key
NX_ALTERNATEMASK	Alt key
NX_COMMANDMASK	Command key
NX_NUMERICPADMASK	Number pad key
NX_HELPMASK	Help key
NX_NEXTCTRLKEYMASK	Control key
NX_NEXTLSHIFTKEYMASK	Left shift key
NX_NEXTRSHIFTKEYMASK	Right shift key
NX_NEXTLCMDKEYMASK	Left command key
NX_NEXTRCMDKEYMASK	Right command key
NX_NEXTLALTKEYMASK	Left alt key
NX_NEXTRALTKEYMASK	Right alt key

DESCRIPTION These masks correspond to keyboard states that might be included in an NXEvent structure's **flags** mask. The masks are grouped as device-independent (NX_ALPHASHIFTMASK through NX_HELPMASK) and device-dependent (all others).

Miscellaneous Event Flags Masks

DECLARED IN dpsclient/event.h

SYNOPSIS

Type	Meaning
NX_STYLUSPROXIMITYMASK	Stylus is in proximity (for tablets)
NX_NONCOALSESCEDMASK	Event coalescing disabled

DESCRIPTION These masks correspond to miscellaneous states that might be included in an NXEvent structure's **flags** mask.

Window Backing Types

DECLARED IN dpsclient/dpsNeXT.h

SYNOPSIS NX_RETAINED
NX_NONRETAINED
NX_BUFFERED

DESCRIPTION These represent the three backing types provided by window devices (and used by the Application Kit's Window objects).

Window Screen List Placement

DECLARED IN dpsclient/dpsNeXT.h

SYNOPSIS NX_ABOVE
NX_BELOW
NX_OUT

DESCRIPTION These represent the placement of a window device in the screen list.

6 *Distributed Objects*

6 *Distributed Objects*

Library: libsys_s.a

Header File Directory: /NextDeveloper/Headers/remote

Introduction

The Distributed Objects system provides a relatively simple way for applications to communicate with one another by allowing them to share Objective C objects, even amongst applications running on different machines across a network. They are useful for implementing client-server and cooperative applications. The Distributed Objects system subsumes the network aspects of typical remote procedure call (RPC) programming, and allow an application to send messages to remote objects using ordinary Objective C syntax.

The Distributed Objects system takes the form of two classes, NXConnection and NXProxy. NXConnection objects are primarily bookkeepers that manage resources passed between applications. NXProxy objects are local objects that represent remote objects. When a remote object is passed to your application, it is passed in the form of a proxy that stands in for the remote object; messages to the proxy are forwarded to the remote object, so for most intents and purposes the proxy can be treated as though it were the object itself. Note that direct access to instance variables of the remote object isn't available through the proxy.

Terminology

In this document, the terms "server" and "client" are used loosely. Whenever an object in an application is returned to a remote application, the object effectively becomes a server, capable of responding to remote messages. For this document, "client" refers to the object originating a remote message, and "server" refers the remote object responding to the message. For example, if a database server sends a remote message to a database client, from the perspective of the Distributed Objects system the database server is the client of the message.

Making an Object Available

The Distributed Objects system allows an application to send a message to an object that exists in another application. The message may include most data types (including objects) as arguments, and it may return most data types, again including objects. Clearly, no messages can be sent to a remote application until the local application has gotten a proxy to some object in the remote application. Therefore, in order to bootstrap the communication process, one or more objects must be made available by name using the Network Name Server. Such an object is known as a *root object*, and is available to any application that knows the registered name of the object. While it is possible to have multiple objects available by name, it is also common to have just one, and to get additional proxies to remote objects in response to messages (to both the root object and objects returned by the root object).

Here is a simple example that shows how to make an instance of the MyServer class available to other applications:

```
id myServer = [[MyServer alloc] init];
id myConnection = [NXConnection registerRoot: myServer
        withName:"exampleServer"];

[myConnection run];
```

The first line creates **myServer**, the object that is to be made available to other applications. The next line registers **myServer** as a root object, available to any application that asks for the object named "exampleServer". This method returns an NXConnection object that will dispatch messages sent from remote objects and track resources (such as objects) vended to connecting applications. The last line tells the connection object to begin its process of waiting for messages and dispatching them to the proper receivers. The **run** method shown doesn't return, but there are variations that run the connection concurrently in another thread or pseudo-concurrently from the DPS client routines that dispatch events.

Establishing a Connection

In the example above, an instance of MyServer is made available under the name "exampleServer". Another application can get a proxy to the object like this:

```
id server = [NXConnection connectToName:"exampleServer"];
```

When this message is sent, a connection to the application that registered the MyServer object is established. The returned object, **server**, is a proxy to the remote MyServer object. Because **server** forwards messages across the connection to the MyServer object, it can generally be treated as though it were that object.

Connections may also be formed automatically when proxies are passed between applications. For example, imagine that two client objects (call them client A and client B) have connected to a server object. If client B sends its **id** to the server, the server gets a proxy to client B. If client A then asks the server to return client B, the server does this by returning client B, which is actually its proxy. However, client A doesn't receive a proxy to the server's proxy. Instead, a new connection is established between client A and client B, and client A receives its own direct proxy (over the new connection) to client B.

Sending Data Between Applications

The Distributed Objects system can use most data types as message arguments or return values. Here are some examples:

```
[server aSimpleMessage];             // no parameters
[server useAnInteger: 12];           // simple scalars
[server useAnIntByReference: &i];    // sending a pointer
[server useAString:"hello"];         // sending a string
[server useAnId: self];              // send an arbitrary local object
[server useAnotherId: server];       // send back the shared object!
```

In both the **useAnIntByReference:** and **useAString:** methods, a pointer is automatically dereferenced on the client side, and the resulting data is sent to the server. On the server side, space for the data is allocated, and a pointer to the local data is received. The server's allocated copy of the data is local in scope and will be freed by the system when the server's method returns.

In the **useAnId:** method, the server is passed an **id** to a local object, and the server receives a proxy to that object. In the **useAnotherId:** method, the server is passed the client's proxy to the server. The Distributed Objects system makes sure that the correct object is returned; in this case the server receives the local **id** for itself rather than a proxy.

The Distributed Objects system allows callbacks in the midst of a method implementation. For example, the server can send a message back to the client in the midst of its **useAnId:** implementation. Such a callback doesn't deadlock, and can be useful, but its ramifications must be carefully considered. Methods in the client can be invoked by the server before the client's invocation of the **useAnId:** method returns.

Structures

The Distributed Objects system can utilize structures for both message arguments and as return values, but there are some important limitations. The following example demonstrates that complex structures can be passed as arguments in remote messages:

```
typedef struct {
    char aChar;
    int anInt;
    unsigned int bitfield:3;
    enum { red, green, blue } color;
    id anObject;
    char *aString;
    int array[2];
} exampleStruct;
exampleStruct e = {'a',9,5,green,nil,"Hello",{42,17}};

[server useStructByValue:e];
[server useStructByReference:&e];
```

In general, a structure to be used as a parameter for a remote message can't contain pointers. Pointers are only valid in one address space, so the Distributed Objects system would have to reconstruct the pointer's data on the remote end. The system can't know how deep to recurse when dereferencing pointers, so it implements the simple case and doesn't dereference pointers to most types, with two exceptions. Structures can contain pointers to objects (**id**s) and pointers to character strings. At the time a remote message is sent, these pointers must point to valid data or they must be null pointers, since the system may need to send the pointer's data across the connection in order to yield a valid pointer on the remote side.

Structures can be passed both by value and by reference. In the current implementation, however, structures can only be returned by reference. In other words, a remote method can't return a structure, but it can return a pointer to a structure. If a method returns a structure by reference, memory for the structure is allocated on the caller's side, and the caller is responsible for freeing this memory.

Pointers to Data

The Distributed Objects system can send data by reference as well as by value. Pointers used in remote messages must point to valid data or be null, since they may need to be dereferenced. By default, when you send most data types by reference, the data is copied across the connection so the server can receive a valid local pointer. The data then may or may not be modified, and is copied back across the connection so the client gets any modifications to the data. Needless copying of data is not efficient, so the Distributed Objects system adds three new Objective C keywords to determine how data passed by reference should be copied. The keywords are **in**, **out**, and **inout**. **In** arguments are copied from the client to the server, but not copied back. **Out** arguments are not sent the server, but are copied back to the client, presumably because the server filled in a value. **Inout** arguments are copied in both directions. By default, **const** pointer arguments are treated as **in** parameters, and all other pointer arguments are treated as **inout**. Here are some example definitions showing directionality of arguments:

```
- sendAnInt: (in int *)p;
- receiveAnInt: (out int *)p;
- sendAndReceiveAnInt: (inout int *)p;
```

The system can't tell whether a pointer points to a single data item or to an array; it assumes all **char** pointers point to null-terminated strings and that all other pointers point to single data elements. If you have arrays that must be passed by reference, you might consider encapsulating the data in a custom object or using a subclass of NXData.

Memory Allocation

When you send **in** or **inout** pointer parameters to the server, the system must allocate space for the data on the server side (so that it can supply a pointer valid in the server's address space). This memory is owned by the system and is local to the scope of the server's method; it is freed automatically when the server's method returns.

The Distributed Objects system can allocate client memory for string and structure parameters. To return strings or structures in this manner, you must pass a pointer to a **char** pointer or a pointer to a structure, so that the system can allocate the memory and make the pointer point to it. If the system allocates memory to return data to the client, the client is responsible for freeing this memory. You must be careful about returning data in this manner, because you receive a pointer to an allocated copy of the data if you send the message to a remote object (through a proxy) but you receive a pointer to the data itself (as with ordinary Objective C) if you send the message to a local object. Here is an example that gets a string by sending a **char** pointer by reference, and then frees the string only if it sent the message to a remote object:

```
char *cp;
[anObject getString:&cp];
printf("The string is %s",cp);
if ([anObject isProxy]) free(cp);
```

The Distributed Objects system also allocates memory in the client's address space in order to return a pointer to a structure as a method return value. Again, the client is responsible for freeing this memory.

Types That Don't Work

The Distributed Objects system can't send the following data types:

- Unions—The Distributed Objects system can't distinguish how to correctly encode the data to send it to the server.
- void *—This is a generic pointer, and the system can't correctly dereference it and encode the data.
- Pointers in structures, other than those of type **char *** and **id**.

In addition, remote methods can't return data of type **double** or **struct** (though pointers to structures work). These limitations may be lifted in future implementations.

Sharing Objects

The most important data type that the Distributed Objects system can use in messages, both as arguments and as return values, is **id**. Objects are usually passed around as proxies, which forward messages to their corresponding real objects and thus appear to be those objects.

Proxies (instances of the NXProxy class) are created automatically when an object is returned to a remote application. To give a client access to a remote object, two proxies are created, one on the server side and one on the client side. The proxy on the server side is known as a local proxy because it tracks a local resource (an object in the proxy's application). A local proxy is used for reference counting by the server's NXConnection object, and to send incoming messages to its corresponding real object. Local proxies are generally hidden from view in the Distributed Objects implementation, and most of their functionings are uninteresting to application developers. More interesting to developers are remote proxies, the objects returned to the client that can generally be treated as though they were the remote objects themselves. These objects receive messages from the client directed to the real object and forward the messages across the connection.

Consider the following code in which a client needs to access a server's list of Widget objects:

```
List *aList;
Widget *aWidget;
aList = [server widgetList];
aWidget = [aList objectAt:0];
```

In the third line, the server returns its list of widgets to the client. The List object exists in the server application, and the client gets a proxy to that List object, which is assigned to **aList**. In the fourth line, the client sends a message to **aList**, and the message is forwarded by the proxy to the actual List object in the server. The List implementation in the server returns the first Widget object in the list. Again, the Widget object is local to the server, so the client receives a proxy to the Widget.

The example above demonstrates that it is very easy to have proxies created. This is an important feature of the Distributed Objects system, but it has performance ramifications that must be considered. Consider the common case where a method in the server returns **self**. The system assumes that you actually intend to return a usable object to the client, so it will return a proxy for the server to the client. If the client's connection doesn't already have a proxy to the server, one will be created. This may or may not be what you intend. It makes most sense to return some non-object type (like **int**) from methods that will be called remotely, unless the object is really intended to be used. (Returning objects isn't horribly expensive, however, and an object is represented by only one proxy on a given connection, even if it is returned many times.)

Reference Counting

With the Distributed Objects system, it is possible for an object to be shared by several applications. Since an object may be in use by many applications, a reference counting scheme may be necessary to insure that an object in use doesn't go away simply because a single application is done with it and frees it. The NXReference protocol is declared to allow objects to implement reference counting. Both the NXConnection and NXProxy classes conform to this protocol in order to know to what extent references are being held. You may wish to make your shared objects conform to this protocol; NXConnection will check if your object conforms to the NXReference protocol before it gives away references to it. If your object conforms to the protocol, a reference is added to the object the first time the object is seen on a connection. Note that a reference is *not* added every time an object is vended, only the first time it is seen on each connection. This works well if the object arrives only once per client application. In other cases, you can add a reference to an object every additional time you receive it, and eliminate the reference (by sending it the free message) every time you are finished with the object.

Object Copies vs. Proxies

While it is often desirable to share an object through the use of proxies, you may occasionally want to pass a copy of an object rather than a proxy. For example, if you have an object that doesn't change over time, it may be more efficient to pass the object by copy rather than as a proxy; messages to the local copy will require much less overhead than remote messages over a connection. As another example, if an object will be sent many messages before it changes, it may be most efficient to send a copy of the object and send the messages to the copy. This is because sending one large remote message is often more efficient than sending many small remote messages; the overhead of the messaging process is typically much higher than the cost of data transmission.

A new keyword, **bycopy**, has been added to the Objective C language to indicate that an object passed as a method parameter ought to be copied rather than passed as a proxy. (The default, without the **bycopy** keyword, is to pass the object as a proxy.)

In the following method declarations, the first method copies the widget across the connection; messages to the copy of the widget will be fast, but changes to the original object will not be reflected in the copy (and vice versa). In the second method, a proxy to widget is given out. The message overhead for remote messages is higher than for messages to a local object, but the widget is truly shared by the applications.

```
- useCopiedWidget: (bycopy in id) widget;
- useSharedWidget: widget;
```

To copy an object over a connection, the receiving application must have a copy of the object's class implementation. This is necessary because the object must be instantiated on the receiving side. Also, an object that is to be copied over a connection must conform to the NXTransport protocol; this protocol defines how an object encodes and decodes itself across a connection. The protocol is as follows:

```
@protocol NXTransport
- encodeUsing:(id <NXEncoding>)portal;
- decodeUsing:(id <NXDecoding>)portal;
- encodeRemotelyFor:(NXConnection *)connection
    freeAfterEncoding:(BOOL *)flagp isBycopy:(BOOL)isBycopy;
@end
```

When an object is to encode itself, it is sent an **encodeUsing:** message where the *portal* argument is an object that conforms to the NXEncoding protocol and thus knows how to encode various data types across a connection. To create the copy of the object on the receiving side, the object is allocated and a **decodeUsing:** message is sent to it. The newly allocated object is *not* initialized, so the **decodeUsing:** implementation generally should invoke the object's designated initializer method. You may occasionally want to substitute another object instead of using the instance that the Distributed Objects system allocated. If you return the substitute object instead of **self**, the substitute object will be used and the system will free the initially allocated memory.

As an example of copying objects, consider the List class, which implements the NXTransport protocol to copy a List object across the connection. The objects in the list are not copied, so the list copy will contain proxies to the objects the real list contains. This behavior may be necessary, because the contents of the list might not conform to the NXTransport protocol and therefore might not be able to be copied. However, if you know the list will only contain objects that conform to the protocol, it may be reasonable to use a list that can be copied, together with its contents, across a connection. The following subclass of List demonstrates exactly this, and shows how a newly allocated object is initialized in the **decodeUsing:** method:

```
@implementation FullCopyList
- encodeUsing:(id <NXEncoding>)portal {
    int i, n = [self count];
    [portal encodeData:&n ofType:"i"];
    for (i = 0; i < n; i++)
        [portal encodeObjectBycopy:[self objectAt:i]];
    return self;
}

- decodeUsing:(id <NXDecoding>)portal {
    int i, n;
    [portal decodeData:&n ofType:"i"];
    [self initCount:n];
    for (i = 0; i < n; i++)
        [self addObject:[portal decodeObject]];
    return self;
}
@end
```

Determining the Object to Encode

When an object is to be vended to a remote application, the **encodeRemotelyFor:freeAfterEncoding:isBycopy:** method determines what object gets encoded. The default behavior of this method, inherited from the Object class, is to return a local proxy to the object; when the local proxy is encoded, it's received as a remote proxy to the object. However, if this method returns **self**, the NXTransport methods for the object are invoked to copy the object over the connection. The implementation of this method should generally test the value of the **isBycopy** parameter to determine what object to encode:

```
- encodeRemotelyFor:(NXConnection *)connection
    freeAfterEncoding:(BOOL *)flagp
    isBycopy:(BOOL)isBycopy
{
    if (isBycopy) return self;    // encode the object, copying it

    // otherwise, super's behavior is to encode a proxy
    return [super encodeRemotelyFor:connection
                freeAfterEncoding:flagp
                isBycopy:isBycopy];
}
```

Moving an Object Between Applications

It is occasionally useful to move an object from one application to another, and the **encodeRemotelyFor:freeAfterEncoding:isBycopy:** method shown above allows you to do this by setting a flag indicating that the original object is to be freed after encoding and then specifying that the object is to be encoded by copying it across the connection. Note, however, that when you move an object you must be very careful that other applications do not have problems due to the original object getting freed. The following example demonstrates an object that will move every time a reference is given to a remote application.

```
- encodeRemotelyFor:(NXConnection *)connection
    freeAfterEncoding:(BOOL *)flagp
    isBycopy:(BOOL)isBycopy
{
    *flagp = YES;
    return self;
}
```

Asynchronous Messages

By default, remote messages are performed synchronously; execution of the client code doesn't continue until the method in the server returns and the Distributed Objects system sends a reply back to the client (containing the return value if there is one). However, a new keyword for method return values, **oneway**, has been added to the Objective C language to specify asynchronous messages. When a client sends an asynchronous message to the server, the method returns to the client immediately. **Oneway** messages implicitly return **void** since the client doesn't wait for a return value from the server. If a method doesn't need to return data and the client doesn't need to stay synchronized to the server, there can be several advantages to **oneway**, asynchronous messages. Because the client continues processing rather than waiting for the server, overall throughput may increase. Less obviously, **oneway** messages can provide the client with a measure of control over when the client is willing to receive messages back from the server. The server may send a message (like a callback) back to the client anytime the client's connection is running or the client awaits a reply from the server. Occasionally it's unacceptable to receive a callback from the server in the middle of a method implementation (an example might be where the callback is used to clean up and free objects in the client); in such a case you can use **oneway** messages to help insure that the connection is not running and the client won't receive messages until it's ready to do so.

Robust Usage

Although the Distributed Objects system greatly simplifies the sharing of objects, applications that communicate with other applications (distributed applications) are inherently more complex than stand-alone applications. Issues regarding application deaths, communication problems, security, exception handling, and resource allocation must be considered. This section discusses some of the considerations for writing robust distributed applications.

Application Deaths

Distributed applications generally need to know when cooperating applications die. For example, a server application should know when a client application dies (due to an application crash, a system crash, a signal, or other reason) so it can deallocate resources held on the client's behalf, and also avoid sending messages to a client that no longer exists. The Mach operating system tracks all resources held by a process, including the Mach ports used by the Distributed Objects system to send remote messages. The operating system notifies the Distributed Objects system of port deaths when an application dies. The Distributed Objects system, in turn, allows any number of objects to register for notification of the invalidation of the NXConnection object that is used to communicate over its port.

An object must do two things to be notified of the death of a cooperating application:

- It must register for notification of invalidation of the connection to the application.
- It must conform to the NXSenderIsInvalid protocol and take appropriate action when the connection is invalidated.

If the application has no Application object, it must spawn a separate thread to disburse port death notifications. This can be done as follows:

```
[NXPort worryAboutPortInvalidation];
```

Note that in this case, **senderIsInvalid:** messages will be sent from the resultant separate thread, so the receiving object should be thread-safe.

Typically, a new connection is created to vend the first object from one application to another. When your application gets an object in this manner, it should use the returned proxy to get the connection over which the object is accessed, and register for invalidation notification to know when the object becomes inaccessible. The following code gets the proxy for a remote server object and registers for notification of when the server goes away:

```
server = [NXConnection connectToName:REGISTERED_NAME onHost:"*"];
if (server)
{
    NXConnection *myConnection = [server connectionForProxy];
    [myConnection registerForInvalidationNotification:self];
    [myConnection setDelegate:self];
}
```

In this example, the client also registered itself as the connection's delegate. In this way, the client can be informed (using the **connection:didConnect:** delegate method) when new connections are automatically created that share **myConnection**'s input port. New, direct connections are formed when proxies are handed between applications. (This eliminates the inefficiency of sending a message over a connection to a proxy that would then forward the message over another connection to the real object.) When a new connection is formed in this manner, the client then has a dependency on the application from which it received the new object, so it should similarly register for invalidation notification on the new connection and it should set the delegate of the new connection appropriately.

If an object registered for a connection's invalidation notification, it receives a **senderIsInvalid:** message from the NXConnection object when the connection is broken (when the connection receives a port death notification indicating an application death, typically). Proper behavior in response to such a notification is nontrivial. The application can examine the NXConnection's list of remote objects (by the **remoteObjects** method) to determine what objects, presumably in use by the application, are no longer accessible. There is no single solution to dealing with application deaths, but a robust architecture is generally one that enables associating a resource to a connection and allows the application to deal with the implications of a broken connection with a cooperating application.

Exceptions

The Distributed Objects system returns exceptions that are raised by method implementations. In other words, if a client sends a message to an object in the server and the implementation in the server raises an exception (see **NX_RAISE**), the exception is forwarded to the client. Also, the Distributed Objects system can raise exceptions in response to communication problems. For this reason, messages to remote objects should generally be bracketed by **NX_DURING...NX_ENDHANDLER** constructs. Keep in mind that control isn't returned to a method that doesn't catch an exception that gets raised; for programs using the Application Kit, unhandled exceptions are caught by the Application object's **run** method, which simply continues the event loop.

Memory Leaks

For local messages, returning a pointer to data involves no memory allocation. However, for remote messages, the system must allocate memory to return data, which increases the opportunity to "leak" memory (in other words, to have allocated memory that has no pointer references, is essentially forgotten and will never be freed). Your application architecture should avoid sending data that needs to be allocated on the client side, or should make it as apparent as possible when data is coming from a remote source. There may still be situations where it isn't immediately obvious whether the recipient of a message is a remote object or not; in this case, if you receive a pointer to data you should check whether the object was a proxy, and if so, take responsibility for freeing the data when you are done. See "Memory Allocation" earlier in this chapter for an example.

Using Protocols for Efficiency

A message sent to a remote object through a proxy may require two round-trip messages. The first round trip is a request to the real object for its *method signature*, which specifies the types the method requires as arguments. This enables the proxy to encode the data that it has been passed and forward it to the real object. Note that a method signature is not cached; without the use of protocols, it will need to be fetched for every message. The second message (also a round-trip, unless it's a **oneway** message) is used to send the actual message including its encoded arguments, and to return the result.

You can eliminate the need for the first round-trip message by specifying to the proxy the protocol that the corresponding real object conforms to. It's generally known in advance what messages a client will send to a server; the protocol could be as small as a single message a client uses to query the server or as large as every message the server responds to. When a protocol is specified, the proxy knows the types of the arguments for every message you anticipate sending to the server, and the initial (and somewhat expensive) round-trip message is avoided. If the client sends a message to the server that isn't in the protocol, nothing untoward happens, but an additional round-trip to retrieve the method signature is required. Here is an example of setting the protocol that a client will use to send messages to a server object:

```
@protocol serverMethods
- (int)addClient:(id <clientMethods>)remoteClient;
- getRecordForName:(char *)name
@end

server = [NXConnection connectToName:REGISTERED_NAME onHost:"*"];
if (server)
    [server setProtocolForProxy:@protocol(serverMethods)];
```

Restricting Messages

A key feature of proxies is that they forward any message, including arguments, to the real, remote object. If you return a server object to a remote client, the client can send any message that the server responds to. In fact, the proxy returned to the client will forward any message, whether the server responds to it or not. For security considerations, you might limit the implementation of an object that is to be given out to only methods that the object is willing to receive from remote clients. This is often not practical, however.

An alternative is to group the methods that an object is willing to receive from remote clients into a protocol. You can then use an NXProtocolChecker object (from the Mach Kit) to enforce the protocol. The NXProtocolChecker object forwards all messages in its assigned protocol, but raises an exception for other messages. When an object returns itself as a result of a message forwarded through a protocol checker, the checker substitutes its own **id** for the real object to prevent the sender from receiving an **id** that can receive unchecked messages.

Security

When you register an object with the Network Name Server, it is available to any application that knows the object's name. Because an application must know the object's name, a modicum of security is provided; however, if security is an issue you should not make sensitive objects (or objects capable of providing sensitive objects) available through the Network Name Server. One possible solution is to register only a security validation object with the Network Name Server. This object could require clients to identify themselves as known secure objects before vending sensitive objects.

Multithreaded Applications

The Distributed Objects system is thread-safe. This means that with the proper precautions, the Distributed Objects system can be used to write a multithreaded server. Perhaps more important to application writers is that you can write a server that runs in the main application thread but responds to messages coming from clients running in different threads. This is useful because many parts of the system are not thread-safe and therefore cannot be invoked by clients outside the main thread, but non-thread-safe tasks can be performed on the client's behalf by a server in the main thread. See the discussion of C threads in *NeXTSTEP Operating System Software* for information about which parts of the system are thread-safe.

Relationship to Speaker/Listener

The Speaker and Listener classes in the Application Kit provide a subset of the functionality of the Distributed Objects system. The Distributed Objects system provides a more flexible and dynamic way of communicating between applications. Speaker and Listener are still used by applications to communicate with the Workspace Manager, and will continue to be provided in the near future for backwards compatibility. Nevertheless, the Distributed Objects system is a superior system and should be regarded as a move towards obsoleting the Speaker and Listener classes.

Classes

NXConnection

Inherits From: NXInvalidationNotifier (Mach Kit) : Object

Conforms To: NXSenderIsInvalid
NXReference (NXInvalidationNotifier)

Declared In: remote/NXConnection.h

Class Description

The NXConnection class is used to establish a connection that allows objects in one process to send messages to objects in another process, and it defines instances that manage the local side of such a connection.

To establish a connection, some object must first be registered with the Network Name Server using **registerRoot:withName:**. This creates an NXConnection and makes the given root object available (through **connectToName:**) to any application that knows the registered name.

NXConnection objects can also be automatically created by the system. When a proxy is vended to an application, the application doesn't receive a proxy to the proxy. Instead, a new connection is formed if necessary, and the application receives a proxy to the original object. The delegate method **connection:didConnect:** is used to inform the application of the automatic creation of new connections.

An NXConnection maintains a table containing an NXProxy object for every local object that has been vended. It also maintains a table of remote NXProxy objects; these proxies are used to send messages to real objects that exist in other applications. A local NXProxy is created automatically by an NXConnection when a local object is vended to another application. Similarly, a remote NXProxy is created automatically when a remote object is vended to the NXConnection; this remote proxy forwards the messages it receives to its corresponding real object, with the effect that it generally appears to be the real object to the local application.

Running a Connection

When a connection is created, it is able to originate messages, and it sends these messages out to a port known as its *out-port* (available though the **outPort** method). Having sent a message, the connection will generally need to receive a reply message, which comes in over the connection's *in-port*. While it awaits this reply, the connection may dispatch messages in response to other messages that appeared on its in-port. However, once the desired reply is found, the connection will return its thread of control back to the caller, and the connection won't be able to receive unsolicited messages. In order to wait on unsolicited messages, a connection must be run, a process that involves waiting for messages on its in-port. The connection's thread is unavailable for other tasks while it runs. For this reason, there are a variety of run methods that allow a connection to run concurrently from the event loop, in its own thread, or for a limited period of time. The run methods are:

– run
– runWithTimeout:
– runInNewThread
– runFromAppKit
– runFromAppKitWithPriority:

A connection can receive remote messages from connections running in other threads or processes, and it will queue up these messages and dispatch them locally from its own thread. However, you cannot run a connection in one thread and send outgoing two-way messages over that connection from another thread; the process of running the connection has the connection's thread waiting on the in-port, so this port is not available for a return message for the caller's thread.

Instance Variables

id **delegate**

delegate	The connection's delegate

Adopted Protocols

NXSenderIsInvalid	– senderIsInvalid:

Method Types

Establishing a connection	+ connectToName: + connectToName:fromZone: + connectToName:onHost: + connectToName:onHost:fromZone: + connectToPort: + connectToPort:fromZone: + connectToPort:withInPort: + connectToPort:withInPort:fromZone:
Ascertaining connections	+ connections:
Registering an object	+ registerRoot: + registerRoot:fromZone: + registerRoot:withName: + registerRoot:withName:fromZone:
Eliminating references	+ removeObject:
Invalidation	+ unregisterForInvalidationNotification:
Statistics	+ messagesReceived
Timeouts	+ setDefaultTimeout: + defaultTimeout – setInTimeout: – setOutTimeout: – inTimeout – outTimeout
Zone usage	+ setDefaultZone: – defaultZone
Assigning a delegate	– setDelegate: – delegate
Returning port objects	– inPort – outPort
Getting and setting the root object	– rootObject – setRoot:
Imported and exported objects	– remoteObjects – localObjects
Returning a proxy	– getLocal: – newRemote:withProtocol:

Running a connection — run
– runWithTimeout:
– runInNewThread
– runFromAppKit
– runFromAppKitWithPriority:

Freeing an NXConnection instance
– free

Class Methods

connections:

+ **connections:**(List *) *aList*

Adds all the application's NXConnections to the supplied list *aList* (but doesn't delete its prior contents). A reference is added to every connection in the list. Returns *aList*.

connectToName:

+ (NXProxy *)**connectToName:**(const char *)*rootName*

Returns an NXProxy to the object registered with the Network Name Server as *rootName*. This method is a cover for **connectToName:onHost:fromZone:** with a null host-name and using the NXConnection class's default zone.

connectToName:fromZone:

+ (NXProxy *)**connectToName:**(const char *)*rootName* **fromZone:**(NXZone *)*zone*

Returns an NXProxy to the object registered with the Network Name Server as *rootName*. This method is a cover for **connectToName:onHost:fromZone:** with a null host-name and using the specified zone *zone*.

connectToName:onHost:

+ (NXProxy *)**connectToName:**(const char *)*rootName*
onHost:(const char *)*hostName*

Returns an NXProxy to the object registered with the Network Name Server as *rootName*. This method is similar to **connectToName:onHost:fromZone:** using the NXConnection class's default zone.

connectToName:onHost:fromZone:

+ (NXProxy *)**connectToName:**(const char *)*rootName*
 onHost:(const char *)*hostName*
 fromZone:(NXZone *)*zone*

Returns an NXProxy to the object registered with the Network Name Server as *rootName*, or **nil** if no connection can be established. Functionally, this method can be thought to return that root object. If *hostName* is explicitly specified, this method queries the Network Name Server on *hostName* for the object registered under *rootName*. If *hostName* is NULL, this method queries the Network Name Server on the local host. If *hostName* is "*", this method will query the Network Name Server on each machine on the subnet until it finds an object registered under *rootName*. Note that querying each machine on a subnet can take a bit of time, so if the host is known, it should be specified.

In addition to creating and returning an NXProxy, this method creates an NXConnection. If this connection will be used to receive remote messages (as is the common case), you will need to run it by sending it a variation of the **run** message. A connection that isn't run will dispatch incoming messages only while it awaits a callback in response to a locally initiated message, so unsolicited remote messages will not be handled in a timely manner. To get the connection of the returned proxy (in order to run it), use NXProxy's **connectionForProxy** method.

If *zone* is specified, the objects associated with the new connection will be allocated from that zone; if *zone* is NULL they will be allocated from the NXConnection class's default zone.

See also: + **registerRoot:withName:**, – **runFromAppKit**, – **connectionForProxy** (NXProxy)

connectToPort:

+ (NXProxy *)**connectToPort:**(NXPort *)*aPort*

Returns an NXProxy to the root object for the connection identified with the port *aPort*, or **nil** if no connection can be established. This method is a cover for **connectToPort:fromZone:** using the NXConnection class's default zone.

connectToPort:fromZone:

+ (NXProxy *)**connectToPort:**(NXPort *)*aPort* **fromZone:**(NXZone *) *zone*

Returns an NXProxy to the root object for the connection identified with the port *aPort*, or **nil** if no connection can be established. You can use this method to establish a connection based on a port you are vended. In other words, you can use this method to establish a connection based on another connection's out-port that is handed to your application.

If *zone* is specified, the objects associated with the new connection will be allocated from that zone; if *zone* is NULL they will be allocated from the NXConnection class's default zone.

See also: + **connectToName:onHost:**, – **outPort**, + **connectToPort:withInPort:**

connectToPort:withInPort:

+ (NXProxy *)**connectToPort:**(NXPort *)*aPort* **withInPort:**(NXPort *)*inPort*

Returns an NXProxy to the root object for the connection identified with the port *aPort*, or **nil** if no connection can be established. This method is a cover for **connectToPort:withInPort:fromZone:** using the NXConnection class's default zone.

connectToPort:withInPort:fromZone:

+ (NXProxy *)**connectToPort:**(NXPort *)*aPort*
    withInPort:(NXPort *)*inPort*
    fromZone:(NXZone *)*zone*

Returns an NXProxy to the root object for the connection identified with the port *aPort*, or **nil** if no connection can be established. The supplied port *inPort* will be used to receive incoming messages.

If *zone* is specified, the objects associated with the new connection will be allocated from that zone; if *zone* is NULL they will be allocated from the NXConnection class's default zone.

See also: + **connectToName:onHost:**, + **connectToPort:**

defaultTimeout

+ (int)**defaultTimeout**

Returns the default connection timeout interval in milliseconds. The interval is 15000 milliseconds unless set to some other value by **setDefaultTimeout:**. A connection will initially use the default timeout interval for both its input and output ports; however, these values can be changed for any port using the **setInTimeout:** or **setOutTimeout:** method.

defaultZone

+ (NXZone *)**defaultZone**

Returns the default zone for all connections. If a zone isn't specified when a connection is created, memory (and objects) associated with the connection will be allocated from this zone. The default zone is initially set to **NXDefaultMallocZone()**, but can be set to another zone using **setDefaultZone:**.

messagesReceived

+ (int)**messagesReceived**

Returns the number of messages received by all connections in the application. This value can be helpful when you attempt to optimize an application's performance by minimizing remote messages.

registerRoot:

+ **registerRoot:***anObject*

Establishes *anObject* as a root object, creating a new NXConnection if necessary. This method is a cover for **registerRoot:fromZone:** using the NXConnection class's default zone.

registerRoot:fromZone:

+ **registerRoot:***anObject* **fromZone:**(NXZone *)*zone*

Establishes *anObject* as a root object, creating a new NXConnection if necessary. *anObject* isn't advertised by the Network Name Server, though you can allow other objects to access it by vending its in-port to private clients, who can then connect to that port using **connectToPort:**. Returns *anObject*'s NXConnection, which must then receive a variant of the **run** message to receive unsolicited remote messages and forward them to *anObject*.

If *zone* is specified, the objects associated with the new connection will be allocated from that zone; if *zone* is NULL they will be allocated from the NXConnection class's default zone.

See also: + **registerRoot:withName:**, – **runFromAppKit**, – **inPort**

registerRoot:withName:

+ **registerRoot:***anObject* **withName:**(const char *)*name*

Establishes *anObject* as a root object, creating a new NXConnection if necessary. This method is a cover for **registerRoot:withName:fromZone:** using the NXConnection class's default zone.

registerRoot:withName:fromZone:

+ **registerRoot:***anObject*
  withName:(const char *)*name*
  fromZone:(NXZone *)*zone*

Establishes *anObject* as a root object, creating a new NXConnection if necessary. *anObject* is advertised by the Network Name Server with the name *name*. Returns *anObject*'s NXConnection, which must then receive a variant of the **run** message to pass remote messages to **anObject**.

If *zone* is specified, the objects associated with *anObject*'s connection will be allocated from that zone; if *zone* is NULL they will be allocated from the NXConnection class's default zone.

See also: – **runFromAppKit**

removeObject:

+ **removeObject:***anObject*

Removes all proxies to *anObject*. If *anObject* has been vended to clients, the clients hold proxies for it which ought to be removed before *anObject* is destroyed. You will therefore probably need to invoke **removeObject:** in *anObject*'s **free** method to avoid dangling references and memory leaks. Returns **self**.

setDefaultTimeout:

+ **setDefaultTimeout:**(int)*interval*

Sets the default connection time interval to *interval*. A connection initially uses this interval for both its input and output ports; however, these values can be changed for any port using the **setInTimeout:** or **setOutTimeout:** method.

See also: + **defaultTimeout**

setDefaultZone:

+ **setDefaultZone:**(NXZone *)*zone*

Sets the default zone for all connections. If a zone isn't specified when a connection is created, memory (and objects) associated with the connection will be allocated from this zone. The default zone is initially set to **NXDefaultMallocZone()**.

See also: + **defaultZone**

unregisterForInvalidationNotification:

+ **unregisterForInvalidationNotification:***anObject*

Unregisters *anObject* so it won't be notified of the invalidation of any of its connections.

See also: – **unregisterForInvalidationNotification:** (NXInvalidationNotifier), – **registerForInvalidationNotification:** (NXInvalidationNotifier)

Instance Methods

delegate

– **delegate**

Returns the connection's delegate.

free

– **free**

Removes a reference to the connection. If outstanding references remain, the NXConnection isn't actually freed and this method returns **self**. If no references remain, this method frees the NXConnection and the proxies it maintains and returns **nil**.

getLocal:

– **getLocal:***anObject*

Returns the local NXProxy for *anObject*, or **nil** if *anObject* isn't represented by a local proxy on the receiving NXConnection. Vending *anObject*'s local proxy is essentially the same as vending *anObject* itself except that by vending the local proxy you determine the connection over which *anObject* is referenced.

inPort

– (NXPort *)**inPort**

Returns the connection's in-port, the NXPort used by the connection to receive incoming messages.

inTimeout

– (int)**inTimeout**

Returns the timeout interval (in milliseconds) for incoming messages. A value of –1 means the connection will wait forever for incoming messages.

See also: – **setInTimeout:**, – **outTimeout**

localObjects

– (List *)**localObjects**

Creates and returns a List of the proxies to local objects vended by the connection. The proxies belong to the connection and should not be altered, but the returned List should be freed by the sender of this message.

newRemote:withProtocol:

– **newRemote:**(unsigned int)*anObject* **withProtocol:**(Protocol *)*proto*

Creates and returns a remote proxy for the local object identified by *anObject*. This proxy can then be given to other objects to vend *anObject* over the receiving connection. *anObject* is the **id** of the local object, though you must cast it to an unsigned integer to satisfy the implementation. *proto*, if non-NULL, is used to specify the protocol that *anObject* responds to; performance is increased if the protocol is specified because a round-trip message to fetch argument types (for encoding purposes) is obviated.

outPort

– (NXPort *)**outPort**

Returns the connection's out-port, the NXPort object used to identify the remote port (and connection) that the receiving connection communicates with. This NXPort can be used to create a new connection by **connectToPort:**.

outTimeout

– (int)**outTimeout**

Returns the timeout interval (in milliseconds) for outgoing messages. A value of –1 means outgoing messages will never time out.

See also: – **setOutTimeout:**, – **inTimeout**

remoteObjects

– (List *)**remoteObjects**

Creates and returns a List of the proxies to remote objects maintained by the receiving connection. The proxies belong to the connection and should not be altered, but the returned List should be freed by the sender of this message. If the connection becomes invalid, objects in the application will no longer be able to send remote messages to the objects in this List.

See also: – **localObjects**

rootObject

– **rootObject**

Returns the connection's root object, which is the object returned (by way of a proxy) to other applications when they connect to the NXConnection.

See also: + **registerRoot:withName:**, – **setRoot**

run

– **run**

Runs the connection by waiting for messages and dispatching them. This method runs in the same thread that it was invoked from, and it doesn't return until the connection is invalidated. If the connection becomes invalid, this method returns **self**. This method is a cover for **runWithTimeout:** with an argument of –1.

See also: – **runFromAppKit**, – **runInNewThread**, – **runWithTimeout:**

runFromAppKit

– **runFromAppKit**

Runs the connection by waiting for messages and dispatching them. This method adds the connection's port to those that the DPS client library monitors for messages, at a priority of NX_RUNMODALTHRESHOLD. When a message arrives over the connection, it will be handled between events. The connection isn't really run concurrent to the application, but the effect is close enough to concurrency for most uses.

This method is typically the best way to run a connection that will dispatch messages to objects that use the Application Kit or Window Server, since these objects cannot be messaged from multiple threads. (Note, however, that the connection run from the DPS client library can communicate with connections running in separate threads.)

This method immediately returns **self**.

See also: – **run**, – **runFromAppKitWithPriority:**, – **runInNewThread**, – **runWithTimeout:**

runFromAppKitWithPriority:

– **runFromAppKitWithPriority:**(int)*priority*

Runs the connection by waiting for messages and dispatching them. This method adds the connection's port to those that the DPS client library monitors for messages, at a priority of *priority*. Otherwise this method is identical to **runFromAppKit**.

runInNewThread

– **runInNewThread**

Runs the connection by waiting for messages and dispatching them. This method forks a new thread that invokes the **run** method; it then immediately returns **self**. All messages sent to this connection are dispatched by the new thread. Because the Window Server and Application Kit aren't thread-safe, you shouldn't send messages to a connection in a separate thread that call upon them. If you need some concurrency in a connection that will invoke the Window Server or Application Kit, you should use **runFromAppKit**.

See also: – **runFromAppKit**, – **run**, – **runWithTimeout:**

runWithTimeout:

– **runWithTimeout:**(int)*timeout*

Runs the connection by waiting for messages and dispatching them. This method runs for *timeout* milliseconds or until the connection is invalidated before returning **self**. If *timeout* is (-1) the connection will run forever or until it is invalidated, whichever occurs first.

See also: – **runFromAppKit**, – **runInNewThread**, – **run**

senderIsInvalid:

– **senderIsInvalid:***sender*

Responds to a message that the connection's port has died. This method invalidates the connection, invalidates the proxies to remote objects (which can no longer be accessed), and sends a **free** message to all the local objects vended by the connection that conform to the NXReference protocol, thereby giving up the connection's references to these objects. *sender* is an instance of a private port management class; your code shouldn't send messages to it.

setDelegate:

– **setDelegate:***anObject*

Sets the connection's delegate. Returns **self**.

setInTimeout:

– **setInTimeout:**(int)*timeout*

Sets the connection's timeout for incoming messages to *timeout* milliseconds. This is the amount of time the connection will wait for return parameters, return values, callbacks, and the like. If a message isn't received before the timeout, an exception will be raised. Setting *timeout* to –1 results in an infinite timeout interval. Returns **self**.

See also: + **setDefaultTimeout:**, – **setOutTimeout:**

setOutTimeout:

– **setOutTimeout:**(int)*timeout*

Sets the connection's timeout for outgoing messages to *timeout* milliseconds. This is the amount of time the connection will wait for a message send to succeed. If an outgoing message can't be sent before the timeout, an exception will be raised. Setting *timeout* to –1 results in an infinite timeout interval, and setting it to 0 has the effect that a message will be delivered only if the receiver's port has room. Returns **self**.

See also: + **setDefaultTimeout**, – **setInTimeout**

setRoot:

– **setRoot:***anObject*

Sets the connection's root object to *anObject*. This method should be invoked only for a connection that doesn't have a root object.

See also: – **rootObject**

Methods Implemented By The Delegate

connection:didConnect:

– **connection:**(NXConnection *)*conn* **didConnect:**(NXConnection *)*newConn*

Notifies *conn*'s delegate that a new connection has been established using *conn*'s input port. *newConn* is the NXConnection object that was just created. This method must return the NXConnection object that should be used, which is typically *newConn*; if another connection is returned, the application is responsible for freeing *newConn*.

NXProxy

Inherits From: none (*NXProxy is a root class.*)

Conforms To: NXReference (Mach Kit)
NXTransport

Declared In: remote/NXProxy.h

Class Description

The NXProxy class defines objects that are used to stand in for real objects (descendants of the Object class), where the real objects may exist within another process, even across a network. To the application, the NXProxy appears to be the real object, though the real object may not be directly accessible. The real object is known as the proxy's *correspondent*, indicating both that the objects are counterparts and that the real object is required to respond to messages sent to the proxy.

The NXProxy class defines very few methods, because proxies respond to very few messages directly. Instead, when an NXProxy receives a message that it doesn't respond to, it encodes the message, including the arguments, and forwards it to its remote correspondent (the "real" object). The actual communication details involved in forwarding the message are taken care of by an NXConnection object. The message is then acted upon by the real object, and any return values and parameters are encoded and sent back to the proxy.

An application never instantiates NXProxy objects directly; they are created for your application when you are given a reference to an object that doesn't exist in your address space. The proxies vended to your application are reference-counted, so only a single NXProxy per connection is instantiated for any real object. When you're done with a remote object, you should typically send it a **free** message to eliminate its remote proxy locally and its local proxy remotely. This will decrement the reference-count on the proxy, and free it if there are no outstanding references. The **free** message will also be forwarded to the proxy's correspondent, which will free it (or dereference it if the object conforms to the NXReference protocol). An application alternatively might free the proxy's NXConnection, which will free all the connection's resources, including all its proxies.

The methods defined in this class are the ones that the NXProxy class directly responds to. Unless otherwise noted, none of these methods are forwarded to the proxy's correspondent.

Instance Variables

None declared in this class.

Adopted Protocols

NXReference	– addReference – free – references
NXTransport	– encodeRemotelyFor: freeAfterEncoding:isBycopy: – encodeUsing: – decodeUsing:

Method Types

Returning the proxy's connection	– connectionForProxy
Freeing an NXProxy instance	– freeProxy
Determining if an object is a proxy	– isProxy
Specifying a protocol	– setProtocolForProxy:

Instance Methods

connectionForProxy

– **connectionForProxy**

Returns the local NXConnection instance used by the receiving NXProxy. A client might send messages to the returned NXConnection to be notified of invalidations (such as port deaths), or to instruct it to begin receiving messages with a variant of the **run** message.

See also: – **registerForInvalidationNotification** (NXInvalidationNotifier in Mach Kit), – **runFromAppKit** (NXConnection)

free

– **free**

Decrements the reference count on the proxy. If there are remaining references to the proxy, the **free** message isn't forwarded across the connection and this method returns **self**. If there are no remaining references, the proxy forwards the **free** message to its corresponding object, invokes the **freeProxy** method to free the proxy locally, and returns **nil**.

freeProxy

– **freeProxy**

Frees the receiving NXProxy instance. You generally shouldn't send this message; it isn't forwarded across the connection, so remote NXConnection objects may still have references to the freed NXProxy and it won't get removed from remote hashtables. If you want to free the local proxy and eliminate outstanding references, the real object should obey the NXReference protocol; then when you send the object a **free** message, the proper dereferencing (and perhaps freeing) will occur both locally and remotely.

isProxy

– (BOOL)**isProxy**

Returns YES to indicate that the receiver is an NXProxy rather than a normal object. This method is also implemented in a category of the Object class (where it returns NO), so you can send this message to any object to determine whether it is a real object or a proxy.

setProtocolForProxy:

– **setProtocolForProxy:**(Protocol *)*proto*

Formally establishes the messages and arguments that the proxy will forward to its corresponding object. It's a good idea to send this message to an NXProxy immediately after it is vended to your application.

If you don't send this message to a proxy (and therefore a protocol isn't established), at run-time the proxy doesn't know a message's argument types, and can't immediately encode the arguments. It must then send a remote message to its corresponding object to get the argument types. This round trip increases the cost of the message. You should therefore send the **setProtocolForProxy:** message to the proxy to cache the argument types, alleviating the need for the initial round trip.

If you send a message that isn't in the established protocol, the round trip to establish the argument types will still be performed. You must take care that the argument types in the given protocol *proto* accurately reflect the argument types of the methods in the proxy's corresponding object; otherwise the arguments will not be correctly encoded. Returns **self**.

Object Additions

Category Of: Object

Declared In: remote/transport.h

Category Description

The Distributed Objects system adds two methods, **isProxy** and **encodeRemotelyFor:freeAfterEncoding:isBycopy:**, to the root Object class. These methods allow all normal objects to be remotely accessed and allow objects to be differentiated from proxies acting in their stead. Only these two method are described here. See Chapter 1, "Root Class," for a general description of the Object class and the methods it defines.

Instance Methods

encodeRemotelyFor:freeAfterEncoding:isBycopy:

– **encodeRemotelyFor:**(NXConnection *)*connection*
freeAfterEncoding:(BOOL *)*flagp*
isBycopy:(BOOL)*isBycopy*

Encodes a proxy for the receiving object over the supplied connection to ensure that all objects are capable of being remotely accessed.

This method is responsible for returning the object that must be encoded to send the receiver over *connection*. The default implementation returns a local proxy to the receiver which, when encoded, yields a remote proxy that forwards all messages to the original object.

You can override this method to change how an object is transported. If you return another object (like **self**), that object will be encoded instead. The returned object must conform to the **NXTransport** protocol. You may wish to test the *isBycopy* flag and return **self** only if the object (rather than a proxy) is to be copied across the connection. If you want the receiving object to be freed after it is encoded, you can set the boolean pointed to by *flagp* to YES.

isProxy

– (BOOL)**isProxy**

Returns NO to indicate that the receiver is a normal object and not a proxy. This method is also implemented by the NXProxy class (where it returns YES), so you can send this message to any object to determine whether it is a real object or a proxy.

Protocols

NXDecoding

Adopted By: a private class

Declared In: remote/transport.h

Protocol Description

An object that implements the NXDecoding protocol is passed as the *portal* argument for the **decodeUsing:** message of the NXTransport protocol. The object implementing the **decodeUsing:** method should send the *portal* object messages from the NXDecoding protocol to decode the data required to instantiate a local copy of the encoded object.

Every method in the NXDecoding protocol corresponds to a method in the NXEncoding protocol, and is used to receive data encoded at the other end of a connection in order to move objects that adopt the NXTransport protocol. See the Distributed Objects introduction for more information.

Instance Methods

decodeBytes:count:

– **decodeBytes:**(void *)*buffer* **count:**(int)*count*

Decodes data (of size *count* bytes) into *buffer.*

decodeData:ofType:

– **decodeData:**(void *)*data* **ofType:**(const char *)*type*

Decodes a data structure, whose fields are indicated by the character string *type*, into the buffer indicated by *data*. *type* is specified with the following format characters:

Format Character	Data Type
c	char
s	short
i	int
f	float
d	double
@	id
*	char *
%	NXAtom
:	SEL
!	int; corresponding data won't be read or written
{<type>}	struct
[<count><type>]	array

decodeMachPort:

– **decodeMachPort:**(port_t *)*portPointer*

Decodes a Mach port and returns it in the variable indicated by *portPointer.*

decodeObject

– **decodeObject**

Decodes and returns an object. The object could have been encoded with either **encodeObject:** or **encodeObjectBycopy:**.

decodeVM:count:

– **decodeVM:**(void **)*bufferPointer* **count:**(int *)*count*

Decodes memory, returning the buffer in the variable indicated by *bufferPointer* and the size in the variable pointed to by *count.*

NXEncoding

Adopted By: a private class

Declared In: remote/transport.h

Protocol Description

An object that implements the NXEncoding protocol is passed as the *portal* argument for the **encodeUsing:** message to distribute an object that adopts the NXTransport protocol. The object implementing the **encodeUsing:** method should send the *portal* object messages from the NXEncoding protocol to encode the data required to instantiate a copy of the object on the other end of the connection.

Every method in the NXEncoding protocol has a corresponding method in the NXDecoding protocol that will be used to receive encoded data. See the Distributed Objects introduction for more information.

Instance Methods

encodeBytes:count:

– **encodeBytes:**(const void *)*buffer* **count:**(int)*count*

Encodes the buffer (of size *count* bytes) indicated by *buffer*.

encodeData:ofType:

– **encodeData:**(void *)*data* **ofType:**(const char *)*type*

Encodes the data structure pointed to by *data*, whose fields are indicated by the character string *type*, consisting of the following values:

Format Character	Data Type
c	char
s	short
i	int
f	float
d	double
@	id
*	char *
%	NXAtom
:	SEL
!	int; corresponding data won't be read or written
{<type>}	struct
[<count><type>]	array

encodeMachPort:

– **encodeMachPort:**(port_t)*port*

Encodes the Mach port *port*.

encodeObject:

– **encodeObject:***anObject*

Usually encodes a proxy to *anObject*. The object to be encoded is determined by sending *anObject* an **encodeRemotelyFor:freeAfterEncoding:isBycopy:** message, which will, by default, return a proxy to *anObject*.

encodeObjectBycopy:

– **encodeObjectBycopy:***anObject*

Usually encodes *anObject*, so that a copy will be instantiated on the other end of the connection; the object to be encoded is determined by sending *anObject* an **encodeRemotelyFor:freeAfterEncoding:isBycopy:** message. *anObject* must conform to the NXTransport protocol.

encodeVM:count:

– **encodeVM:**(const void *)*bytes* **count:**(int)*count*

Encodes memory (of *count* bytes) that was allocated with **vm_allocate**().

NXTransport

Adopted By: List (common classes)
NXData (Mach Kit)
NXPort (Mach Kit)
NXProxy class (Distributed Objects)

Declared In: remote/transport.h

Protocol Description

The NXTransport protocol allows objects to be copied over a Distributed Objects connection. This protocol consists of three methods:

```
- encodeRemotelyFor:freeAfterEncoding:isBycopy:
- encodeUsing:
- decodeUsing:
```

When an object must be vended over a connection, the **encodeRemotelyFor:freeAfterEncoding:isBycopy:** method is invoked to determine what object is sent. The Object class implements a version of this method that returns an NXProxy; thus all objects may be sent over a connection in virtual form through the use of a proxy. Classes can override this method to specify another object (that conforms to the NXTransport protocol) to be sent over the connection. By sending a real object over the connection rather than a proxy, some applications can save the overhead of remote messaging (though if the object changes, keeping copies synchronized is an issue).

When an object is to be encoded, it is sent an **encodeUsing:** message. The *portal* argument for this message is an object that implements the NXEncoding protocol and thus knows how to encode various data types. The object to be encoded should send data to *portal* that allows a copy of itself to be decoded.

In order to create the copy of the object on the receiving side, the object is allocated and a **decodeUsing:** message is sent to it. The newly allocated object is not initialized, so the **decodeUsing:** implementation generally should invoke the object's designated initializer method.

Instance Methods

decodeUsing:

– **decodeUsing:**(id <NXDecoding>)*portal*

A newly allocated instance is sent this message in order to initialize itself when an object has been sent by copy over a connection. The instance is not initialized, so it should generally invoke the object's designated initializer. You must send messages (from the NXDecoding protocol) to the *portal* object to fetch any data that was encoded; these messages may be sent before or after initializing the new instance.

This method generally returns **self** to indicate that **self** is the object that is to be used as the local copy of the sent object. If it returns another object, that object is used as the local copy, and the instance that received this message is freed.

See also: – **encodeUsing:**

encodeRemotelyFor:freeAfterEncoding:isBycopy:

– **encodeRemotelyFor:**(NXConnection *)*connection*
freeAfterEncoding:(BOOL *)*flagp*
isBycopy:(BOOL)*isBycopy*

This method is responsible for returning the object that must be encoded to send the receiver over *connection*. The default implementation inherited from the Object class returns a local proxy to the receiver which, when encoded, yields a remote proxy that forwards all messages to the original object.

You can override this method to change how an object is transported. If you return another object (like **self**), that object will be encoded instead. The returned object must conform to the **NXTransport** protocol. You may wish to test the *isBycopy* flag and return **self** only if the object (rather than a proxy) is to be copied across the connection. If you want the receiving object to be freed after it is encoded, you can set the boolean pointed to by *flagp* to YES.

A typical implementation of this method simply ensures that the object or a proxy gets encoded, based on the value of *isBycopy*:

```
- encodeRemotelyFor:(NXConnection *)connection
    freeAfterEncoding:(BOOL *)flagp isBycopy:(BOOL)isBycopy
{
    if (isBycopy) return self;
    return [super encodeRemotelyFor:connection
        freeAfterEncoding:flagp isBycopy:isBycopy];
}
```

encodeUsing:

– **encodeUsing:**(id <NXEncoding>)*portal*

This method must send enough data to *portal* (an object that conforms to the NXEncoding protocol) that a copy of the object can be created on the other side of a connection using the **decodeUsing:** method. See the introduction to Distributed Objects for an example implementation of this method.

Types and Constants

Defined Types

NXRemoteException

DECLARED IN remote/NXProxy.h

SYNOPSIS

```
typedef enum {
        NX_REMOTE_EXCEPTION_BASE,
        NX_couldntSendException,
        NX_couldntReceiveException,
        NX_couldntDecodeArgumentsException,
        NX_unknownMethodException,
        NX_objectInaccessibleException,
        NX_objectNotAvailableException,
        NX_remoteInternalException,
        NX_multithreadedRecursionDeadlockException,
        NX_destinationInvalid,
        NX_originatorInvalid,
        NX_sendTimedOut,
        NX_receiveTimedOut,
        NX_REMOTE_LAST_EXCEPTION
} NXRemoteException
```

DESCRIPTION These are the exceptions that the Distributed Objects system might raise as a result of a remote message gone awry.

Symbolic Constants

Timeout Constants

DECLARED IN remote/NXConnection.h

SYNOPSIS NX_CONNECTION_DEFAULT_TIMEOUT

DESCRIPTION This is the default timeout for a connection (currently, 15 seconds).

7 *Indexing Kit*

7 *Indexing Kit*

Library: libIndexing_s.a

Header File Directories: /NextDeveloper/Headers/btree
/NextDeveloper/Headers/indexing
/NextDeveloper/Headers/store

Introduction

The Indexing Kit is a set of programmatic tools for managing data, especially the large amounts of data characteristic of information-intensive applications. Much as the Application Kit provides a framework for a graphical interface, the Indexing Kit provides a framework for data management.

The Indexing Kit supplies facilities for building custom databases and for searching the UNIX file system. Key benefits include guaranteed data integrity, excellent performance, thread-safe operation, tight integration with the NeXTSTEP programming environment, and the ability to efficiently store and retrieve Objective C objects and unstructured data like text, sound, and images.

The Indexing Kit consists of:

- A transaction-oriented foundation for storing and retrieving persistent data, using virtual memory mapping for efficient random access to parts of a file without reading or writing the entire file. Transactions guarantee data integrity on persistent storage media, and are also used to manage concurrent access to shared data.

- Fast sequential and associative access to stored data. Associative access is untyped, in that the programmer defines the data types of keys and their ordering by means of a comparison function or a format string.

- A simple data management capability based on the Objective C run-time system. Records can be moved efficiently between working memory and the storage substrate in the form of Objective C objects. Multiple indexes can be built over programmer-defined attributes, so that records can be ordered and retrieved by the values of their indexed attributes.

- A general query processing facility, including a declarative query language and its interpreter. Queries can be applied to individual objects, to collections of objects, or to the attribute/value lists produced by Indexing Kit's customizable text processing tools.

- High-level file system searching facilities based on the supporting layers described above, including fast literal searching of file contents.

Architecture of the Indexing Kit

The Indexing kit has four layers, corresponding to the areas of functionality described above (the query and text processing tools are part of the data management layer, but are described apart from it). Classes at each layer rely on the services provided by the lower layers. There are a total of seventeen classes and eighteen protocols in the Indexing Kit.

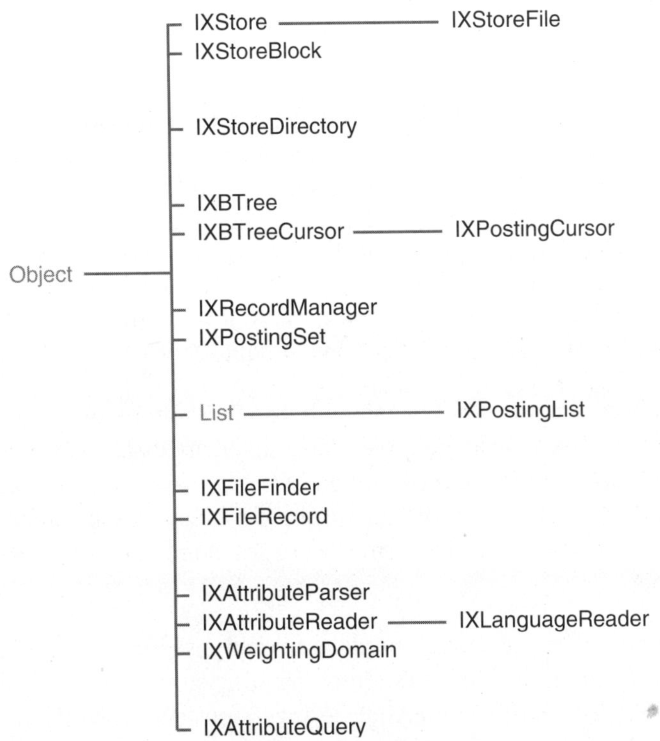

Figure 7-1. The Indexing Kit Inheritance Hierarchy

Storage Management

The foundation of the Indexing Kit consists primarily of the IXStore and IXStoreFile classes, along with IXStoreBlock. There are two protocols at this layer: IXBlockAndStoreAccess and IXNameAndFileAccess.

IXStore is a fast, transaction-oriented, compacting storage allocator, providing efficient storage management within a single address space. IXStoreFile is a file-based subclass of IXStore. IXStoreBlock is a convenience class for creating objects that refer to individual blocks of storage within an IXStore.

An IXStore is an array of resizable blocks of untyped storage. Each block is identified by an integer *handle*. Classes in the layers above the storage management layer add data typing and specialized identification and retrieval mechanisms to this basic model.

IXStore defines a transaction model that permits thread-safe, shared access to data and allows changes to data to be reversed. These features guarantee data integrity in the context of shared access or in the event of program or system interruption. They can be used to build databases and other structured collections of data.

The IXBlockAndStoreAccess and IXNameAndFileAccess protocols, along with the IXStoreDirectory class from the associative access layer, are used to create store clients. A *store client* is an object that manages data in an IXStore. A store client is a persistent object; since its data resides in the store, its run-time representation can be freed and later reconstituted from that same data. The primary classes at the higher layers of the Indexing Kit are store clients.

For detailed information on the storage model and on transaction management, see the IXStore class specification. For information on creating store clients, see the IXBlockAndStoreAccess and IXNameAndFileAccess protocol specifications and the IXStoreDirectory class specification.

Associative Access

The classes of the Indexing Kit's associative access layer are IXBTree, IXBTreeCursor, IXStoreDirectory, IXPostingCursor, and IXPostingSet. Protocols defined at this layer are IXCursorPositioning, IXComparatorSetting, IXComparisonSetting, IXPostingExchange, and IXPostingOperations.

IXBTree and IXBTreeCursor add a flexible associative retrieval model to IXStore. Untyped blocks of storage, called *values*, are identified by keys of an arbitrary type, and are logically arranged in an ordered key space. This allows the values to be identified by such things as strings or floating-point numbers, or even complex structures. The programmer using an IXBTree defines its key space with methods declared in the IXComparatorSetting and IXComparisonSetting protocols, providing either a function that compares keys, or a comparison format that describes the keys.

Access to an IXBTree's key space is provided by the IXBTreeCursor class. An IXBTreeCursor is an object that can move within an IXBTree's key space and access the value stored at its current position. Multiple IXBTreeCursors can be used concurrently in the same IXBTree, providing for shared access to the data.

An IXStoreDirectory uses an IXBTree to provide a naming scheme for store clients within a single IXStore. See the description of the storage management layer and the IXStoreDirectory class specification for more information.

IXPostingCursor, a subclass of IXBTreeCursor, maintains attribute inversions, in which the value of a specified attribute of a collection of data items is used as a key in a secondary IXBTree. The value stored under each key in the secondary IXBTree is a set of *postings*, which are weighted references to data items in the collection. The posting set for a particular key contains references to all data items in the collection whose attribute is equal to that key.

An IXPostingSet holds a set of postings in working storage. Its primary use is for combining sets of postings: an IXPostingSet can perform a set union, intersection, or difference with another IXPostingSet (or any object conforming to the IXPostingExchange protocol, described below). This allows records to be selected from a collection according to more than one criterion.

For example, an IXPostingSet might be initialized from an IXPostingCursor for the "department" attribute of a collection of employees. The set would hold references to all employee records in the collection that belonged to the department defined by the IXPostingCursor's key position, for example, "accounting." To find all employees in that department with a given income, the set could then be refined by intersection with an IXPostingSet derived from an inversion on the income attribute.

The IXPostingExchange protocol declares methods for trading sets of postings, and the IXPostingOperations protocol declares methods for retrieving information about postings and for adding postings to or removing postings from a set.

For detailed information on key spaces and cursoring, see the IXKeyCursoring protocol specification. For information on working with postings, see the IXPostingCursor and IXPostingSet class specifications and the IXPostingOperations protocol specification.

Data Management

The data management classes are IXRecordManager and IXPostingList. The data management protocols are IXRecordReading, IXRecordWriting, IXRecordDiscarding, IXBlobWriting, IXRecordTranscription, IXTransientAccess, and IXTransientMessaging.

IXRecordManager maintains a repository of Objective C objects that represent individual records, and builds and maintains indexes on those records. Each index is based on one attribute of the objects in the repository. An attribute is defined by a name and a selector; the attribute's value for a given object is the value returned by the designated message for that object. An attribute's scope is necessarily restricted to those objects that respond to the designated message, and may optionally be restricted further to the instances of a designated class or any of its subclasses. A text parser may be attached to a text valued attribute to invert the component *lexemes* (words or phrases that are to be treated as individual terms), rather than the entire piece of text. When objects are added to the IXRecordManager, they are automatically added to any attribute indexes that apply.

As a structured storage facility, IXRecordManager provides a fast and space-efficient serializing mechanism based on Objective C run-time information for objects conforming to the appropriate Indexing Kit protocols (by default, however, it uses the standard **read:** and **write:** archiving messages, so that it can store objects that don't conform to those protocols). When referring to the serializing mechanism, objects are said to be *passivated* and *activated* rather than archived and unarchived. Since objects may contain references to data whose length can't be determined from the run-time information, IXRecordManager sends a notification message to an object being passivated or activated, allowing the object to store or retrieve any data that needs special handling. IXRecordManager also provides direct access to the instance variables and method return values of passivated objects, eliminating the need to explicitly activate objects in order to query their content or state.

Records can be retrieved through an attribute index with an IXPostingCursor. The IXPostingCursor is simply positioned at the desired key, and the postings for that key are then used to activate the objects. IXPostingSets can be used to retrieve records based on compound criteria.

IXPostingList, a subclass of List, performs lazy instantiation of retrieved objects. An IXPostingList can be initialized with a set of postings retrieved from an index, and thereafter behaves as a List, returning an object corresponding to the posting at a particular position in the List on demand. This frees the programmer from having to explicitly activate a set of retrieved objects one at a time.

For more information on data management, see the IXRecordManager class specification. For more information on object passivation and activation in the Indexing Kit, see the IXRecordTranscription, IXRecordReading, IXRecordWriting, and IXRecordDiscarding protocol specifications.

File System Searching

There are two classes and two protocols in the file system searching layer. The classes are IXFileFinder and IXFileRecord, and the protocols are IXFileFinderConfiguration and IXFileFinderQueryAndUpdate.

IXFileFinder extends the capabilities of IXRecordManager to the UNIX file system, treating files in a subtree of the file system as records. The archive actually contains IXFileRecord objects, which are used as proxies for the files.

An IXFileFinder can automatically update its indexes in a background thread, and supports concurrent querying by multiple programmer-supplied threads, as well. It can be configured to ignore specific files or types of files, and has options for ignoring file systems mounted within its subtree of the file system and for traversing symbolic links.

IXFileFinder supports the Indexing Kit's query language, allowing for searches by whole or partial word in specific attributes. Searches can be made using literal strings and regular expressions. A full suite of arithmetic, relational, and other operators are also available.

For information on using IXFileFinder, see the IXFileFinderQueryAndUpdate protocol specification and "The Indexing Kit Query Language" in the "Other Features" section.

Text Parsing

The Indexing Kit's text parsing system is made of four classes and two protocols. The classes are named IXAttributeParser, IXAttributeReader, IXLanguageReader, and IXWeightingDomain. The protocols are IXAttributeReading and IXLexemeGeneration.

The text parsing system builds attribute/value lists from unstructured text. An IXAttributeParser uses a list of one or more IXAttributeReaders to break the text into individual lexemes, which it can then count and classify. The lexemes are assigned weights based on their frequency of occurrence for a given attribute. Lexemes can be weighted absolutely, by frequency, or by peculiarity. Peculiarity weighting uses an IXWeightingDomain, which holds lexeme counts and rankings for a reference domain, usually a large collection of text, such as the collected works of William Shakespeare. Lexemes that are common in the reference domain will have a lower peculiarity than lexemes that are rare in the domain.

The process of decomposing a text stream into its constituent lexemes can be customized by creating a subclass of IXLanguageReader, itself a subclass of IXAttributeReader. Language-specific readers are provided for all languages supported by NeXT. Custom readers can be written to analyze specific languages or types of text, to reduce related terms to a common form, and to recognize multi-word lexemes.

For more information on text parsing, see the IXAttributeParser class description and "Attribute Reader Format" in the "Other Features" section.

Query Processing

The query processing system is made of one class, IXAttributeQuery, and the Indexing Kit's query language. IXAttributeQueries accept query expressions formulated in the query language. It evaluates these against an IXRecordManager or IXFileFinder to return an IXPostingList containing those objects which match the query.

For more information on text parsing, see the IXAttributeQuery class description and "The Indexing Kit Query Language" in the "Other Features" section.

Classes

IXAttributeParser

Inherits From: Object

Declared In: indexing/IXAttributeParser.h

Class Description

An IXAttributeParser breaks text streams down into lists of lexemes occurring in the text. A *lexeme* is a word or phrase that should be treated as a single term. Though not directly accessible, the lists are used by other classes in the Indexing Kit to build indexes for the text, or to resolve queries against the text.

An IXAttributeParser uses a number of IXAttributeReaders to divide a text stream into individual lexemes, each associated with a specific attribute, like Title, Author, or Abstract, and collects the lexemes into a histogram for each attribute. The parser can weight the lexemes for a given attribute in several ways: by the number of occurrences within the attribute, by the relative frequency of occurrence within the attribute, or by peculiarity within the attribute relative to a reference domain. A lexeme's peculiarity is the square root of the ratio of its frequency within the attribute to its frequency within the reference domain; for example, the word "computer" has a much lower peculiarity with respect to the domain of computer science literature than to that of archaeological literature because it occurs much more frequently in the former.

An IXAttributeParser parses any of three text formats: Attribute Reader Format (ARF), RTF, or ASCII text (it prefers them in that order). A parser determines a file's or stream's format by examining the type argument to a **parse...** or **analyze...** method. If that type is ARF, RTF, or ASCII, the parser can simply start processing the text. If not, the parser will examine the first few bytes of the text to see if it is, indeed, in one of the parsable formats; for example, if it finds "{\rtf" at the beginning of a stream, it assumes that the stream contains RTF. Failing this, the parser will attempt to convert the text into one of the parsable formats using the filtering services provided by the Application Kit. If the text can't be converted into a parsable format using the filtering services, the parser simply treats the file or stream as though it were ASCII, checking first for nonprintable characters; if there is a significant number of them on the first page (more than 1 in 16), the file or stream isn't parsed at all. For example, if told to parse a WordPerfect document, the parser would attempt to convert the document from WordPerfect format to one of the three parsable formats. If the document couldn't be converted, it would be parsed as ASCII, control words, formatting commands, and all (unless the document contained enough nonprintable characters that it would be regarded as unprintable by the parser).

To attempt conversion of a file of type *mytype*, the parser will call the Application Kit function **NXCreateTypedFileName()** to generate a typed file-name pasteboard type. Thus, the filter must declare this as its input type in a services file in order to be visible to the parser. If no filter is found by this approach, and the file is readable, then the parser will attempt conversion a second time using the function **NXCreateTypedFileContents()** to generate a typed file contents pasteboard type.

When a parser isn't supplied for a class or method that needs one (for example, an IXFileFinder), a default parser is created, along with a default reader for the current user's preferred language, as set in the Preferences application. NeXT ships language-specific IXLanguageReaders for all supported user languages in **/NextLibrary/Readers**. These IXLanguageReaders are dynamically loaded into an application when needed. Your code can get a reader for a specific language by sending the IXLanguageReader class object a **readerForLanguage:** message. If the language is specified as "Default", the reader for current user's preferred language is loaded. If a reader for the requested language can't be found, the English reader is used by default.

Instance Variables

None declared in this class.

Method Types

Initializing an instance	– init
Managing readers	– setAttributeReaders: – getAttributeReaders:
Managing text stream types	– understandsType: – addSourceType: – removeSourceType:
Managing parse options	– setMinimumWeight: – minimumWeight – setPercentPassed: – percentPassed – setWeightingDomain: – weightingDomain – setWeightingType: – weightingType

Parsing text	– parseFile:ofType: – parseStream:ofType: – analyzeFile:ofType: – analyzeStream:ofType: – reset

Instance Methods

addSourceType:

– **addSourceType:**(const char *)*aType*

Records the Pasteboard type or file extension *aType* as one of the types for which the IXAttributeParser will respond YES when sent an **understandsType:** message, and which the IXAttributeParser will attempt to parse. If an IXAttributeParser has had no source types added, or has had all source types removed with **removeSourceType:**, it acts as though it understands any type, and will parse any file or stream. Returns **self**.

See also: – **removeSourceType:**, – **understandsType:**, – **analyzeFile:ofType:**, – **analyzeStream:ofType:**, – **parseFile:ofType:**, – **parseStream:ofType:**, Pasteboard class of the Application Kit

analyzeFile:ofType:

– (NXStream *)**analyzeFile:**(const char *)*filename* **ofType:**(const char *)*aType*

Parses the contents of *filename*, and returns the contents of *filename* in Attribute Reader Format as produced by the IXAttributeParser's IXAttributeReaders. If the IXAttributeParser doesn't understand the type *aType*, this method returns NULL. Otherwise, *aType* is used to determine whether the contents of *filename* are in a parsable format (one of ARF, RTF, or ASCII), or if not, to locate a filter service that can convert the contents of *filename*. Files that can't be converted into a parsable format are parsed as though they contained ASCII text, unless they contain a significant amount of nonprintable text (for example, control characters), in which case the file is assumed to be binary, and not parsed.

See also: – **analyzeStream:ofType:**, – **parseFile:ofType:**, – **parseStream:ofType:**, – **understandsType:**, – **addSourceType:**, Attribute Reader Format ("Other Features" section), Pasteboard class of the Application Kit

analyzeStream:ofType:

– (NXStream *)**analyzeStream:**(NXStream *)*stream* **ofType:**(const char *)*aType*

Parses *stream*, and returns the contents of *stream* in Attribute Reader Format as read by the IXAttributeParser's IXAttributeReaders. If the IXAttributeParser doesn't understand the pasteboard type *aType*, this method returns NULL. Otherwise, *aType* is used to determine whether *stream* is in a parsable format (one of ARF, RTF, or ASCII), or if not, to locate a filter service that can convert the contents of *stream*. Streams that can't be converted into a parsable format are parsed as though they contained ASCII text, unless a significant amount of the text is nonprintable, in which case the stream isn't parsed.

See also: – **analyzeFile:ofType:**, – **parseStream:ofType:**, – **parseFile:ofType:**, – **understandsType:**, – **addSourceType:**, Attribute Reader Format (Other Features section), Pasteboard class of the Application Kit

getAttributeReaders:

– **getAttributeReaders:**(List *)*aList*

Empties *aList*, fills it with the IXAttributeReaders used by the IXAttributeParser, and returns it by reference. The sender of this message may free the List, but not its contents. Returns **self**.

See also: – **setAttributeReaders:**

init

– **init**

Initializes a newly created IXAttributeParser, setting the percent passed to 100 and the weighting type to IX_NoWeighting. Returns **self**.

See also: – **setPercentPassed:**, – **setWeightingType:**

minimumWeight

– (unsigned int)**minimumWeight**

Returns the minimum weight required for a lexeme to be included in the attribute/value list.

See also: – **setMinimumWeight**:, – **percentPassed**

parseFile:ofType:

– **parseFile:**(const char *)*filename* **ofType:**(const char *)*aType*

Parses the contents of *filename*, and returns **self**. If the IXAttributeParser doesn't understand the type *aType*, this method returns **nil**. Otherwise, *aType* is used to determine whether the contents of *filename* are in a parsable format (one of ARF, RTF, or ASCII), or if not, to locate a filter service that can convert the contents of *filename*. Files that can't be converted into a parsable format are parsed as though they contained ASCII text, unless a significant amount of the text is nonprintable, in which case the stream isn't parsed.

See also: – **parseStream:ofType:**, – **analyzeFile:ofType:**, – **analyzeStream:ofType:**, – **understandsType:**, – **addSourceType:**, Pasteboard class of the Application Kit

parseStream:ofType:

– **parseStream:**(NXStream *)*stream* **ofType:**(const char *)*aType*

Parses *stream*, and returns **self**. If the IXAttributeParser doesn't understand the type *aType*, this method returns **nil**. Otherwise, *aType* is used to determine whether *stream* is in a parsable format (one of ARF, RTF, or ASCII), or if not, to locate a filter service that can convert the contents of *stream*. Streams that can't be converted into a parsable format are parsed as though they contained ASCII text, unless a significant amount of the text is nonprintable, in which case the stream isn't parsed.

See also: – **parseFile:ofType:**, – **analyzeStream:ofType:**, – **analyzeFile:ofType:**, – **understandsType:**, – **addSourceType:**, Pasteboard class of the Application Kit

percentPassed

– (unsigned int)**percentPassed**

Returns the percentage of the lexemes for each attribute that will be included in the result of a parse. Any lexeme whose weight puts it at this percentile or higher will be included.

See also: – **setPercentPassed:**, – **minimumWeight**

removeSourceType:

– **removeSourceType:**(const char *)*aType*

Removes the pasteboard type or file extension *aType* from the IXAttributeParser's list of understood types. The IXAttributeParser will respond NO to subsequent

understandsType: messages with *aType* as the argument, and won't parse files or streams of that type. Returns **self**.

See also: – **addSourceType:**, – **understandsType:**, Pasteboard class of the Application Kit

reset

– **reset**

Clears the state built up by parsing a file or stream, preparing the IXAttributeParser to analyze a different file or stream. It is possible to combine multiple streams or files by parsing them in sequence without resetting the IXAttributeParser, in which case the results accumulate in the attribute/value list. Returns **self**.

See also: – **analyzeFile:ofType:**, – **analyzeStream:ofType:**, – **parseFile:ofType:**, – **parseStream:ofType:**

setAttributeReaders:

– **setAttributeReaders:**(List *)*aList*

Establishes the objects in *aList* as the IXAttributeReaders used by the IXAttributeParser, and frees any of the previous set of IXAttributeReaders that the IXAttributeParser will no longer use. The List must contain instances of IXAttributeReader or a subclass. Readers will be used on a stream of text in the order they appear in the List. Returns **self**.

See also: – **getAttributeReaders:**

setMinimumWeight:

– **setMinimumWeight:**(unsigned int)*anInt*

Sets the minimum weight required for inclusion in the parse result. For example, setting the minimum weight to 10 causes all lexemes with weight less than 10 to be dropped from the result of a parse. Returns **self**.

The IXAttributeParser uses only one of minimum weight or percent passed. If the minimum weight is set, the percent passed is reset to 100; if the percent passed is set, the minimum weight is reset to 0.

See also: – **minimumWeight**, – **setPercentPassed:**

setPercentPassed:

– **setPercentPassed:**(unsigned int)*anInt*

Sets the percentage of lexemes for a given attribute that will be included in the result of a parse. Any lexeme whose weight puts it at this percentile or higher will be included. For example, setting this value to 25 would include the top quarter of the lexemes in the search result; if there were 2000 lexemes, the 500 heaviest lexemes by weight would be included.

The IXAttributeParser uses only one of minimum weight or percent passed. If the minimum weight is set, the percent passed is reset to 100; if the percent passed is set, the minimum weight is reset to 0.

Returns **self**.

See also: – **percentPassed**, – **setMinimumWeight:**

setWeightingDomain:

– **setWeightingDomain:**(IXWeightingDomain *)*aDomain*

Sets the weighting domain used by the IXAttributeParser to *aDomain*, and returns **self**. The weighting domain is used to assign peculiarity weights to lexemes for a given attribute; the frequency of the lexeme within the attribute is divided by the frequency of the lexeme in the domain to give the lexeme's peculiarity, and the result is normalized by taking its square root. This is only done when the IXAttributeParser's weighting type is IX_PeculiarityWeighting.

See also: – **weightingDomain**, – **setWeightingType:**

setWeightingType:

– **setWeightingType:**(IXWeightingType)*anInt*

Sets the weighting type used by the IXAttributeParser to *anInt* and returns **self**. The weighting type is used to determine how to calculate lexeme weights, and may be one of the following values:

IX_NoWeighting
IX_AbsoluteWeighting
IX_FrequencyWeighting
IX_PeculiarityWeighting

IX_NoWeighting means that all lexemes are assigned a weight of 0. With IX_AbsoluteWeighting, each lexeme is assigned a weight equal to the number of times it occurs within the attribute. IX_FrequencyWeighting results in each lexeme being weighted by relative frequency of occurrence: the number of times it occurs in the attribute divided by the total number of lexemes in the attribute. IX_PeculiarityWeighting uses a weighting domain to calculate a frequency relative to some large body of text; the final weight of a lexeme is calculated by taking the square root of its frequency in the attribute divided by its frequency in the domain. IX_PeculiarityWeighting is useful for lowering the significance of lexemes that are common in a particular set of texts.

See also: – **weightingType**, – **setWeightingDomain:**

understandsType:

– (BOOL)**understandsType:**(const char *)*aType*

Returns YES if the IXAttributeParser will parse files of the pasteboard type or file extension *aType*, NO if not. If no types have been added with **addSourceType:**, or if all types added have been removed with **removeSourceType:**, this method always returns YES.

See also: – **addSourceType:**, – **removeSourceType:**, Pasteboard class of the Application Kit

weightingDomain

– (IXWeightingDomain *)**weightingDomain**

Returns the weighting domain used by the IXAttributeParser, or **nil** if there is none.

See also: – **setWeightingDomain:**, – **setWeightingType**:

weightingType

– (IXWeightingType)**weightingType**

Returns the weighting type used by the IXAttributeParser. See **setWeightingType:** for a list of the possible values and their meanings.

See also: – **setWeightingType:**, – **setWeightingDomain:**

IXAttributeQuery

Inherits From: Object

Declared In: indexing/IXAttributeQuery.h

Class Description

IXAttributeQuery is an interpreter for the Indexing Kit's query language. An IXAttributeQuery is initialized with a single query expression, which it can evaluate against a "context" object: an IXRecordManager, an IXFileRecord, or an IXAttributeParser. When it evaluates the query, it returns an IXPostingList containing the objects selected by the query expression, or **nil** if no objects were selected. See "The Indexing Kit Query Language" in the "Other Features" section of this chapter for more information on query evaluation.

When a query is evaluated against a context that acts as a container (for example, an IXRecordManager), the resulting IXPostingList contains the objects selected from the container by the query expression. When a query is evaluated against an immediate context (for example, an IXAttributeParser or IXFileRecord), the resulting IXPostingList contains only the context. Evaluating a query against a single object is useful when a yes/no answer is desired, especially with an IXAttributeParser loaded from a stream of text.

Instance Variables

unsigned char ***queryString**;
id **attributeParser**;
id **queryContext**;

queryString	The query language expression to be evaluated.
attributeParser	The IXAttributeParser used to parse portions of the query.
queryContext	The object against which the query expression is evaluated.

Method Types

Initializing	– initQueryString:andAttributeParser:
Accessing attributes	– attributeNames – attributeParser
Retrieving the query expression	– queryString
Evaluating the query	– evaluateFor:

Instance Methods

attributeNames

– (char *)**attributeNames**

Returns a newline-separated list of the attribute names found in the query string. This can be used to compare the attributes named in the query against those in an IXRecordManager, for example. The sender of this message is responsible for freeing the string returned.

See also: – **initQueryString:andAttributeParser:**, – **attributeNames** (IXRecordManager)

attributeParser

– (IXAttributeParser *)**attributeParser**

Returns the IXAttributeParser used for **parse()** operators in the query string.

See also: – **initQueryString:andAttributeParser:**

evaluateFor:

– (IXPostingList *)**evaluateFor:***anObject*

Evaluates the query string against information in *anObject*. *anObject* must be an instance of IXAttributeParser, IXFileRecord, or IXRecordManager. Returns the results of the query in an IXPostingList, or **nil** if there is no match. The sender of this message is responsible for freeing both the IXPostingList and the objects it contains.

If *anObject* is an IXAttributePaser or IXFileRecord and it matches the query, it will be the only object in the IXPostingList; its handle and weight will be 0, and the IXPostingList's source will be **nil**. If *anObject* is an IXRecordManager that contains records that match the query, the IXPostingList will be contain postings for those records, and the IXPostingList's source will be the IXRecordManager.

initQueryString:andAttributeParser:

– **initQueryString:**(const char *)*aString*
  andAttributeParser:(IXAttributeParser *)*aParser*

Initializes the receiver, a newly allocated IXAttributeQuery, compiling *aString* as its query and using *aParser* as the IXAttributeParser for any **parse**() operators in *aString*. *aString* must be a legal expression in the Indexing Kit query language, as documented in "The Indexing Kit Query Language." *aParser* may be **nil**; in this case a default instance of IXAttributeParser will be created by the IXAttributeQuery when a **parse**() operator is encountered. Returns **self** if *aString* is a well formed query, or **nil** if a compilation error is encountered.

aParser and its IXAttributeReaders should be configured in the same manner as the IXAttributeParser and IXAttributeReaders used to generate attribute values for the context. For example, if an IXRecordManager contains a parsed attribute named Text, then any IXAttributeQuery used to query the Text attribute of that IXRecordManager should be initialized with a parsing configuration similar to the Text attribute's parsing configuration. Once an IXAttributeQuery is initialized, its parser shouldn't be sent any messages until after the IXAttributeQuery is freed; the parser may be safely freed or reused at that time.

See also: – **queryString**, – **attributeParser**, – **evaluateFor:**,
– **setParser:forAttributeNamed:** (IXRecordManager)

queryString

– (const char *)**queryString**

Returns the IXAttributeQuery's query string.

See also: – **initQueryString:andAttributeParser:**

IXAttributeReader

Inherits From: Object

Conforms To: IXAttributeReading

Declared In: indexing/IXAttributeReader.h

Class Description

An IXAttributeReader breaks a stream of text into lexemes, emitting a format suitable for consumption by an IXAttributeParser. Lexemes are the lexical components of the text, and are usually words, though they may be phrases, numbers, formulas, or even binary encoded graphics or sound bites.

An IXAttributeReader accepts text in one of three formats: Attribute Reader Format (ARF), RTF, or ASCII. Processed lexemes and unrecognized text, if any, are both output in ARF. This allows multiple attribute readers to process a single stream in series, so that different parts of the stream are handled by different readers. For more information on ARF, see "Attribute Reader Format" in the "Other Features" section of this chapter.

An IXAttributeReader can perform any of four predefined operations while analyzing a stream of text. It can fold case, reducing uppercase characters to their lowercase equivalents; it can unique the lexemes, emitting numerical backward references instead of fully formed lexemes when duplicates are encountered; it can fold plurals, reducing plural terms to their singular form; and it can perform stemming, reducing terms to their stems (for example, "write," "writing," and "written" would all be reduced to "write"). The first two of these operations are fully implemented by IXAttributeReader. The other two are declared as abstract methods for language-specific subclasses.

Instance Variables

```
NXHashTable *stopWords;
const char *punctuation;
unsigned char *charMapping;
struct {
        unsigned caseFolding:1;
        unsigned pluralFolding:1;
        unsigned stemsReduced:1;
        unsigned lexemeUniquing:1;
} booleanOptions;
```

stopWords	Words removed from output.
punctuation	Characters that delimit words.
charMapping	Character mapping table.
booleanOptions.caseFolding	YES if uppercase letters are converted to lowercase.
booleanOptions.pluralFolding	YES if plurals are converted to singular form.
booleanOptions.stemsReduced	YES if derivative terms are reduced to their stems.
booleanOptions.lexemeUniquing	YES if lexemes are uniqued for more compact output.

Adopted Protocols

IXAttributeReading	– analyzeStream:

Method Types

Altering lexemes	– foldPlural:inLength: – reduceStem:inLength:

Setting reader options

- – setCaseFolded:
- – isCaseFolded
- – setPluralsFolded:
- – arePluralsFolded
- – setStemsReduced:
- – areStemsReduced
- – setPunctuation:
- – punctuation
- – setStopWords:
- – stopWords

Instance Methods

arePluralsFolded

– (BOOL)**arePluralsFolded**

Returns YES if the IXAttributeReader reduces plurals to their singular forms when reading text, NO otherwise. For example, if plurals are folded, then "boxes" will be folded to "box" and "children" to "child." The default is NO.

IXAttributeReader itself doesn't fold plurals; a subclass must override **foldPlural:inLength:** to provide this functionality. This method simply reports the value of a flag. To implement plural folding, simply override the **foldPlural:inLength:** method.

See also: – **setPluralsFolded:**, – **foldPlural:inLength:**

areStemsReduced

– (BOOL)**areStemsReduced**

Returns YES if the IXAttributeReader reduces derivatives to their stems, NO otherwise. For example, if stems are reduced, "forest", "deforest", "reforest", "deforestation", "forestry", and "unforested" will all be reduced to "forest." The default is NO.

IXAttributeReader itself doesn't reduce stems; a subclass must override **reduceStem:inLength:** to provide this functionality. This method simply reports the value of a flag.

See also: – **setStemsReduced:**, – **reduceStem:inLength:**

foldPlural:inLength:

– (unsigned int)**foldPlural:**(char *)*aString* **inLength:**(unsigned int)*aLength*

Does nothing and returns the length of *aString*. Overridden by subclasses to perform language-specific plural-to-singular form conversion.

Subclass implementations should convert *aString* from a plural to a singular form in a language specific manner. *aLength* is the length of the string buffer, not the string itself. If *aString* is altered, its new length should be the return value of this method.

See also: – **setPluralsFolded:**

isCaseFolded

– (BOOL)**isCaseFolded**

Returns YES if the IXAttributeReader converts text to lowercase when reading, NO otherwise. The default is YES.

See also: – **setCaseFolded:**

punctuation

– (char *)**punctuation**

Returns a string containing the characters used by the IXAttributeReader to separate lexemes. The sender of this message is responsible for freeing the string.

See also: – **setPunctuation:**

reduceStem:inLength:

– (unsigned int)**reduceStem:**(char *)*aString* **inLength:**(unsigned int)*aLength*

Does nothing and returns the length of *aString*. Overridden by subclasses to perform language-specific stem reduction.

Subclass implementations should reduce *aString* to its stem in a language specific manner. *aLength* is the length of the string buffer, not the string itself. If *aString* is altered, its new length should be the return value of this method.

See also: – **areStemsReduced**, – **setStemsReduced:**

setCaseFolded:

– **setCaseFolded:**(BOOL)*flag*

If *flag* is YES, the IXAttributeReader converts text to lowercase when reading. If *flag* is NO, it doesn't affect the case of text. The default is YES. Returns **self**.

See also: – **isCaseFolded**

setPluralsFolded:

– **setPluralsFolded:**(BOOL)*flag*

If *flag* is YES, the IXAttributeReader reduces all plurals to singular form when it reads text. If *flag* is NO, it doesn't alter plural forms. The default is YES. Returns **self**.

IXAttributeReader itself doesn't fold plurals; a subclass must override **foldPlural: inLength:** to provide this functionality. This method simply sets the value of a flag.

See also: – **arePluralsFolded**, – **foldPlural:inLength:**

setPunctuation:

– **setPunctuation:**(const char *)*aString*

Sets the punctuation string to *aString*. The punctuation string defines the characters that the IXAttributeReader uses to separate lexemes. Returns **self**.

The ASCII null character (0) is always a punctuation character. The default is the set of characters for which **NXIsAlNum()** returns 0 (false), except underscore.

See also: – **punctuation**, **NXIsAlNum()** (Common Classes and Functions)

setStemsReduced:

– **setStemsReduced:**(BOOL)*flag*

If *flag* is YES, the IXAttributeReader reduces words to common stems when it reads text. If *flag* is NO, it doesn't reduce stems. The default is YES. Returns **self**.

The IXAttributeReader class itself doesn't reduce stems; a subclass must override **reduceStem:inLength:** to provide this functionality. This method simply sets the value of a flag.

See also: – **areStemsReduced**, – **reduceStem:inLength:**

setStopWords:

– **setStopWords:**(const char *)*stopWords*

Sets the IXAttributeReader's stop word list using the newline-separated words in *stopWords*. An IXAttributeReader deletes stop words from the stream of lexemes it produces. The default is to use no stop words.

See also: – **stopWords:**

stopWords

– (char *)**stopWords**

Returns a string containing a newline-separated list of the stop words used by the IXAttributeReader. An IXAttributeReader deletes stop words from the lexemes it emits. The sender of this message is responsible for freeing the string.

See also: – **setStopWords:**

IXBTree

Inherits From: Object

Conforms To: IXBlockAndStoreAccess
IXNameAndFileAccess
IXComparatorSetting
IXComparisonSetting

Declared In: btree/IXBTree.h

Class Description

An IXBTree provides ordered associative storage and retrieval of untyped data. It identifies and orders data items, called *values*, by key using a comparator function or key format description. A companion class, IXBTreeCursor, is used to actually manipulate the contents of the IXBTree.

An IXBTree can be used with a memory-based IXStore, or with an IXStoreFile. File-based IXBTrees can be used to build persistent dictionaries and databases. As examples, the IXStoreDirectory class makes use of an IXBTree to provide names for other store clients, and the IXRecordManager uses multiple IXBTrees to provide a data management facility that uses Objective C objects as records.

Setting Up an IXBTree

An IXBTree can either be initialized as a new client of an IXStore or opened from existing data in an IXStore. In either case, since IXBTree is a store client (as described in the IXBlockAndStoreAccess protocol specification) the IXBTree must use an IXStore to hold its contents. The protocol methods **initInStore:** and **initWithName:inFile:** can be used to initialize a new IXBTree in an IXStore. To open an IXBTree from previously created data, use the protocol methods **initFromBlock:inStore:** or **initFromName:inFile:forWriting**.

After the IXBTree has been initialized, it must have its comparator function or key format description set with the **setComparator:context:** or **setComparisonFormat:** messages. A comparator function takes as arguments two pieces of arbitrary data and their lengths, and returns an integer indicating their ordering relative to one another. A key format description is a character string in the Objective C standard type encoding that describes the contents of the keys; the legal type codes are listed in the IXComparisonSetting protocol specification. IXBTrees compare keys as strings by default. See the **IXCompareBytes()** and **IXFormatComparator()** function descriptions for examples and for more information on key comparison.

Getting Data into and out of an IXBTree

As stated above, IXBTree simply provides the capacity for associative storage. An IXBTreeCursor is needed to take advantage of that capacity. An IXBTreeCursor is like a pointer into the IXBTree: it can move to specific positions within the key space and perform operations on the values stored at those locations, independent of other cursors. The IXCursorPositioning protocol specification describes basic cursoring techniques, and the IXBTreeCursor class specification describes additional methods unique to IXBTreeCursor.

Multiple IXBTreeCursors may independently access a single IXBTree. The actions of one cursor don't affect any of the other cursors in the IXBTree, except to the extent that they modify the contents of the IXBTree. It is both safe and meaningful to remove a record that another IXBTreeCursor has just located, as long as the code using the other IXBTreeCursor anticipates this possibility, as described below. IXBTree has a mutex lock which may be used to prevent collisions between cursors operating from different threads.

In the case of one cursor removing a value that another cursor has just located, the second cursor will have received an indication from a key-locating method (for example, **setKey:andLength:**) that it has found a key. When it tries to access the value associated with that key, however, the key may no longer exist. The cursor will detect the deletion and slide forward to the next available key if asked to read the value (see the IXCursorPositioning protocol specification), or will raise an exception if asked to remove or write the value. If your code allows multiple cursors to be concurrently active on a single IXBTree, it must anticipate this behavior by handling the exceptions that may be raised, and by comparing the key against the expected value after invoking **getKey:andLength:**. Alternatively, your code may group key location and value manipulation operations by locking the IXBTree's mutex with **IXLockBTreeMutex()** and **IXUnLockBTreeMutex()** around the pair, or by some alternative mechanism, like a condition, applied at a higher point in the application.

Working with an IXBTree's Store

Since IXBTree is a store client, as defined in the IXBlockAndStoreAccess protocol specification, the transaction model of IXStore applies to changes made to the contents of an IXBTree. In particular, the IXBTree's store must be sent **commitTransaction** messages to make changes to the IXBTree take effect (and be flushed to disk for a file-based store). If an IXBTree is used on a strictly read-only basis, transaction management can be ignored.

Instance Variables

struct mutex **mutexLock**;

mutexLock	Used to manage concurrent access in multithreaded applications.

Adopted Protocols

IXBlockAndStoreAccess	– initInStore: – initFromBlock:inStore: – freeFromStore + freeFromBlock:andStore: – getBlock:andStore:
IXNameAndFileAccess	– initWithName:inFile: – initFromName:inFile:forWriting: – freeFromStore + freeFromName:andFile: – getName:andFile:
IXComparatorSetting	– setComparator:andContext: – getComparator:andContext:
IXComparisonSetting	– setComparisonFormat: – comparisonFormat

Method Types

Accessing IXBTree information	– count – keyLimit
Affecting IXBTree contents	– empty – compact
Optimizing performance	– optimizeForTime – optimizeForSpace

Instance Methods

compact

– **compact**

Compacts the contents of the IXBTree so that it consumes as little space as possible (the average amount of reduction is about 25%). This method may move significant amounts of data, so it can take some time to complete. Key insertion will become slower for a while after this method is invoked, because data has to be moved around again to make room. Key search may become substantially faster however, since less data is paged from disk when searching. Compaction is useful when occasional updates to an IXBTree are followed by lots of reading. Returns **self**.

Note: This method does nothing in NeXTSTEP Release 3, but should be fully implemented in a later update of the Indexing Kit. Your code may invoke this method freely in anticipation of its being implemented.

See also: – **optimizeForTime**, – **optimizeForSpace**

count

– (unsigned int)**count**

Returns the number of key/value pairs stored in the IXBTree.

empty

– **empty**

Removes all key/value pairs from the IXBTree, and reduces its storage allocation to the smallest possible size (128 bytes). Returns **self**.

keyLimit

– (unsigned int)**keyLimit**

Returns the maximum allowable length of keys kept in the IXBTree. An IXBTreeCursor positions itself with a key and the length of the key. That length should never be greater than the key limit. If it is, the IX_TooLargeError exception is raised.

optimizeForSpace

– optimizeForSpace

Causes the IXBTree to move its contents around when inserting keys, so that the total amount of storage allocated is kept as small as possible. This will result in slower insertion times, but faster seek times. Your code should send this message when the IXBTree will be used mostly for reading.

Once optimization is enabled, it can't be disabled; however, the type of optimization may be switched at any time between space (fast seek times) and time (fast insertions). Also, an IXBTree doesn't record its optimization type in its IXStore, so optimization must be re-enabled whenever an IXBTree is reconstituted.

See also: **– optimizeForTime**, **– compact**

optimizeForTime

– optimizeForTime

Causes the IXBTree to avoid moving its contents around when inserting keys, so that insertions happen as fast as possible. This can result in more unused storage space and slower seek times. Your code should send an IXBTree this message when it will be making a lot of insertions.

Once optimization is enabled, it can't be disabled; however, the type of optimization may be switched at any time between space (fast seek times) and time (fast insertions). Also, an IXBTree doesn't record its optimization type in its IXStore, so optimization must be re-enabled whenever an IXBTree is reconstituted.

See also: **– optimizeForSpace**, **– compact**

IXBTreeCursor

Inherits From: Object

Conforms To: IXCursorPositioning

Declared In: btree/IXBTreeCursor.h

Class Description

An IXBTreeCursor provides access to the keys and values stored in an IXBTree. It's essentially a pointer into the IXBTree's key space, and may be positioned by key to perform operations on the value stored at a given location. See the IXCursorPositioning protocol specification for information on cursoring or on manipulating keys and values.

An IXBTreeCursor works with a single IXBTree, but several IXBTreeCursors may access the same IXBTree and be positioned independently without conflict. See the IXBTree class specification for more information on concurrent access with multiple IXBTreeCursors.

Using Hints to Speed Key Search

In addition to the basic cursoring methods described in the IXCursorPositioning protocol specification, IXBTreeCursor supports hinting. Hints essentially allow the IXBTreeCursor to find keys by absolute position. This can speed key search dramatically as long as the IXBTree is relatively static. If a lot of insertions and removals are performed, however, the use of hints will probably slow down key search; hints will frequently fail to identify the physical locations of their keys because those keys will have moved, and key search will incur the cost of hint failure in addition to the cost of searching.

Instance Variables

struct BTree ***btree**;
void ***keyBuffer**;
unsigned int **bufferSize**;
unsigned int **keyLength**;
unsigned int **keyLimit**;
unsigned int **traceHint**;
unsigned int **cursorVersion**;
unsigned int **cursorDepth**;
NXZone ***cursorZone**;
struct BTreeTraceRecord ***cursorTrace**;
struct {...} **cursorStatus**;

btree	The IXBTree accessed by the IXBTreeCursor.
keyBuffer	The internal key buffer.
bufferSize	The size in bytes of the internal key buffer.
keyLength	The length of the key in the internal key buffer.
keyLimit	The maximum length in bytes of a key.
traceHint	The current hint value.
cursorVersion	Used to synchronize the activity of multiple cursors.
cursorDepth	The number of levels in the tree.
cursorZone	The memory allocation zone in which the cursor resides.
cursorTrace	The cache of the trace path followed by last key search.
cursorStatus	For internal use by the IXBTreeCursor.

Adopted Protocols

IXCursorPositioning
- – setFirst
- – setLast
- – setNext
- – setPrevious
- – setKey:andLength:
- – getKey:andLength:
- – isMatch

Method Types

Initializing an IXBTreeCursor	– initWithBTree:
Accessing the IXBTree	– btree
Positioning with hints	– setKey:andLength:withHint: – getKey:andLength:withHint:
Accessing IXBTree data	– writeValue:andLength: – writeRange:andLength:atOffset: – readValue: – readRange:ofLength:atOffset: – removeValue

Instance Methods

btree

– (IXBTree *)**btree**

Returns the IXBTree that the IXBTreeCursor accesses. This is useful if your code didn't initialize the IXBTreeCursor, since it allows your code to reconfigure the IXBTree, or empty or free it.

See also: – **initWithBTree:**

getKey:andLength:withHint:

– (BOOL)**getKey:**(void **)*aKey*
andLength:(unsigned int *)*aLength*
withHint:(unsigned int *)*aHint*

Returns by reference the key defining the IXBTreeCursor's position in its IXBTree, along with the key's length, and a hint that your code can use to speed up a subsequent key search for the same key using **setKey:andLength:withHint:**. The hint is guaranteed to remain useful as long as no insertions or removals are performed; however, the more the IXBTree changes, the less useful the hint becomes.

If the IXBTreeCursor is at a key, this method returns YES. If the IXBTreeCursor is between two keys or before the first one, this method advances it to the next key and returns YES. If the IXBTreeCursor is beyond the last key, this method returns NO, and the contents of *aKey*, *aLength*, and *aHint* are undefined.

The contents of *aKey* aren't guaranteed to remain valid across subsequent messages to the IXBTreeCursor, since it may relocate its key buffer. Your code should copy its contents if it needs to save them. Your code should *not* write into the buffer pointed to by *aKey;* doing so may corrupt your application's memory, causing errors or a crash.

See also: – **getKey:andLength:** (IXCursorPositioning protocol), – **setKey:andLength:withHint:**

initWithBTree:

– **initWithBTree:**(IXBTree *)*aBTree*

Initializes the IXBTreeCursor to work with *aBTree*. It will use that IXBTree's comparator or comparison format to position itself at keys. This is the designated initializer for IXBTreeCursors. Returns **self**.

See also: – **btree**

readRange:ofLength:atOffset:

– (unsigned int)**readRange:**(void **)*aRange*
ofLength:(unsigned int)*aLength*
atOffset:(unsigned int)*anOffset*

Copies a portion of the value in the IXBTree at the IXBTreeCursor's position, and returns the length actually read (which may be less than the length requested). If there is no key/value pair at the IXBTreeCursor's position, the IX_NotFoundError exception is raised.

If **aRange* is NULL, then up to *aLength* bytes will be allocated from the IXBTreeCursor's zone, and the data will be copied into that buffer. Your code is responsible for freeing the memory allocated. If a non-NULL value is provided in **aRange*, then it is assumed to be the address of a valid buffer, and up to *aLength* bytes will be copied into it starting from *anOffset* within the IXBTree's value.

Important: Using the address of an uninitialized pointer variable as *aRange* is incorrect, and will result in data being copied into a random location in the application's address space. Your code should always allocate memory for the pointer variable or set it to NULL before passing its address to this method.

See also: – **readValue:**, – **writeValue:andLength:**, – **writeRange:atOffset:forLength:**, – **openRange:ofLength:atOffset:forWriting:**, – **removeValue**

readValue:

– (unsigned int)**readValue:**(void **)*aValue*

Copies the value in the IXBTree at the IXBTreeCursor's position, and returns the length of the value. If there is no key/value pair at the IXBTreeCursor's position, the IXBTreeCursor moves to the next higher position if possible. If the IXBTreeCursor is at the end of the key space, IX_NotFoundError is raised.

If **aValue* is NULL, then a buffer will be allocated from the IXBTreeCursor's zone, and the data will be copied into that buffer. Your code is responsible for freeing the memory allocated. If a non-NULL value is provided in **aValue*, then it is assumed to be the address of a valid buffer, and the value stored in the IXBTree will be copied into it. Your code is responsible for making sure the buffer is large enough to hold the value. This is useful for fixed-length values, or values with a known maximum length.

Important: Using the address of an uninitialized pointer variable as *aValue* is incorrect, and will result in data being copied into a random location in the application's address space. Your code should always allocate memory for the pointer variable or set it to NULL before passing its address to this method.

This method may be used to determine the size of the buffer needed: invoke it first with NULL as *aValue* to get the buffer length without copying the data, then a second time with the length to copy the data. This is an efficient usage pattern, unless multiple cursors are active, in which case, it will be very inefficient if the tree is modified by another cursor between the two invocations.

See also: – **writeValue:**, – **removeValue**, – **readRange:atOffset:forLength:**, – **writeRange:atOffset:forLength:**

removeValue

– **removeValue**

Removes the key and the associated value at the IXBTreeCursor's position. This method raises IX_NotFoundError if there is no key at the IXBTreeCursor's position. Returns **self**.

See also: – **readValue:**, – **writeValue:**, – **readRange:atOffset:forLength:**, – **writeRange:atOffset:forLength:**

setKey:andLength:withHint:

– (BOOL)**setKey:**(void *)*aKey*
andLength:(unsigned int)*aLength*
withHint:(unsigned int)*aHint*

Positions the IXBTreeCursor at *aKey* if *aKey* is stored in the IXBTree; otherwise, positions the IXBTreeCursor where *aKey* would be (which may be between two keys, or off either end of the key space). *aLength* is the length of *aKey*. Returns YES if *aKey* is in the IXBTree (that is, if the IXBTreeCursor finds the key), and NO if it's not.

This method uses a hint as returned by **getKey:andLength:withHint:** to find *aKey* quickly. A hint is like a bookmark; it defines a physical position in the IXBTree, so the IXBTreeCursor can just go there and check if *aKey* is still there. If the IXBTree has been modified, *aKey* may no longer reside at the position indicated by *aHint;* in that case a key search is performed. Using hints can actually slow down key search in highly dynamic IXBTrees; use them for reading static or read-only IXBTrees.

See also: – **getKey:andLength:withHint:**,
– **getKey:andLength:** (IXCursorPositioning protocol),
– **setKey:andLength:** (IXCursorPositioning protocol)

writeRange:atOffset:forLength:

– **writeRange:**(void *)*aRange*
atOffset:(unsigned int)*anOffset*
forLength:(unsigned int)*aLength*

Writes *aRange* over a portion of the value in the IXBTree at the IXBTreeCursor's position. Data starting at *anOffset* within the IXBTree's value is overwritten for *aLength* bytes. If the range would extend past the end of the value, the value is enlarged to hold the new amount. Returns **self**.

If there is no key/value pair at the IXBTreeCursor's position, this method raises IX_NotFoundError.

See also: – **readRange:atOffset:forLength:**, – **readValue:**, – **writeValue:andLength:**, – **removeValue**

writeValue:andLength:

– (BOOL)**writeValue:**(void *)*aValue* **andLength:**(unsigned int)*aLength*

Writes *aLength* bytes from *aValue* as the value in the IXBTree at the IXBTreeCursor's position, possibly overwriting a previously stored value. Returns YES if the write resulted in an insertion, and NO if the write overwrote a previously stored value.

Overwriting completely replaces a value; the previous value is removed and replaced with a new one. If the IXBTreeCursor is not positioned at a key/value pair, a new pair will be inserted with the key last used to position the IXBTreeCursor (with **setKey:andLength:** or **setKey:andLength:withHint:**). For example, inserting a completely new value into the IXBTree involves positioning the IXBTreeCursor, checking that the positioning method returns NO (that is, that it didn't find an existing value), and simply using **writeValue:andLength:** to insert the new value with the key just set.

See also: – **readValue:**, – **removeValue**, – **readRange:atOffset:forLength:**, – **writeRange:atOffset:forLength:**

IXFileFinder

Inherits From: Object

Conforms To: IXBlockAndStoreAccess
IXNameAndFileAccess
IXFileFinderConfiguration
IXFileFinderQueryAndUpdate
NXReference (Mach Kit)

Declared In: indexing/IXFileFinder.h

Class Description

IXFileFinder answers queries against file attributes over a file system subtree, and can maintain indexes to improve query performance. IXFileFinder manipulates instances of the IXFileRecord class as proxies for the actual files; queries return IXPostingLists containing IXFileRecords representing the selected files. When used with an IXStore or IXStoreFile, IXFileFinder uses a private instance of the IXRecordManager class to store and index the IXFileRecords; this permits the efficient resolution of many queries without requiring the file system subtree to be scanned every time a query is performed.

IXFileFinder is completely thread-safe; it supports multiple asynchronous queries by programmer-supplied threads without conflict, and also provides an asynchronous index updating mechanism managed by a single, private background thread.

The functionality of IXFileFinder is primarily described in its two protocol specifications, IXFileFinderConfiguration and IXFileFinderQueryAndUpdate, which anticipate its use with NeXTSTEP's Distributed Object facility. This class specification documents only the initialization methods.

Instance Variables

```
unsigned int references;
List *attributeParsers;
id recordManager;
NXHashTable *ignoredNames;
NXHashTable *ignoredTypes;
char *rootPath;
unsigned int commitDelay;
struct {
    unsigned int crossesDeviceChanges:1;
    unsigned int followsSymbolicLinks:1;
    unsigned int generatesDescriptions:1;
    unsigned int updatesAutomatically:1;
    unsigned int scansForModifiedFiles:1;
    unsigned int removesAutomatically:1;
} booleanOptions;
```

references	The reference count.
attributeParsers	A List of IXAttributeParsers used to parse files.
recordManager	The object that manages the file records.
ignoredNames	The names of files that are ignored by the IXFileFinder.
ignoredTypes	The types of files that are ignored by the IXFileFinder.
rootPath	The root directory of the IXFileFinder. This is considered the base of the subtree for which queries can be made.
commitDelay	The delay in seconds between consecutive transaction commitments during index update.
booleanOptions.crossesDeviceChanges	YES if the IXFileFinder addresses files on physical devices other than the one its primary directory is on. NO by default.
booleanOptions.followsSymbolicLinks	YES if the IXFileFinder follows symbolic links. NO by default.
booleanOptions.generatesDescriptions	YES if the IXFileFinder automatically generates descriptions for IXFileRecords from the file contents. NO by default.

booleanOptions.updatesAutomatically

YES if the IXFileFinder automatically queues out-of-date files for indexing when a query is performed. YES by default.

booleanOptions.scansForModifiedFiles

YES if the IXFileFinder scans for modified files when a query is performed. YES by default.

booleanOptions.removesAutomatically

YES if the IXFileFinder scans for deleted files when updating, removing their proxies from the index. YES by default.

Adopted Protocols

IXBlockAndStoreAccess	– initInStore: – initFromBlock:inStore: + freeFromBlock:inStore: – freeFromStore – getBlock:andStore:
IXNameAndFileAccess	– initWithName:inFile: – initFromName:inFile:forWriting: + freeFromName:inFile: – freeFromStore – getName:andFile:
IXFileFinderConfiguration	– setAttributeParsers: – getAttributeParsers: – setCrossesDeviceChanges: – crossesDeviceChanges – setFollowsSymbolicLinks: – followsSymbolicLinks – setGeneratesDescriptions: – generatesDescriptions – setIgnoredNames: – ignoredNames – setIgnoredTypes: – ignoredTypes – setScansForModifiedFiles: – scansForModifiedFiles – setUpdatesAutomatically: – updatesAutomatically

IXFileFinderQueryAndUpdate	– rootPath – recordManager – performQuery:atPath:forSender: – stopQueryForSender: – updateIndexAtPath: – isUpdating – suspendUpdating – resumeUpdating – clean – reset
NXReference	– references – addReference – free

Method Types

Initializing an IXFileFinder	– initInStore:atPath: – initFromBlock:inStore:atPath: – initWithName:inFile:atPath: – initWithName:inFile:forWriting:atPath:

Instance Methods

initFromBlock:inStore:

– **initFromBlock:**(unsigned int)*aHandle* **inStore:**(IXStore *)*aStore*

Initializes a newly allocated IXFileFinder as **initFromBlock:inStore:atPath:** with a *path* argument of NULL. This method is useful for opening an IXFileFinder whose root directory hasn't changed, which is usually the case.

See also: – **initFromBlock:inStore:atPath:**

initFromBlock:inStore:atPath:

– **initFromBlock:**(unsigned int)*aHandle*
  inStore:(IXStore *)*aStore*
  atPath:(const char *)*path*

Initializes a newly allocated IXFileFinder by opening it from data stored in the block of *aStore* identified by *aHandle*. This data should have been created by a previous instance of IXFileFinder. The IXFileFinder's root path is reset to *path*; it will search for files within the subtree rooted at that directory. *path* may be an absolute or relative pathname. If *path* is NULL, the root path remains unchanged from its previous value. The root path may not be changed after initialization. Returns **self**.

This is the designated initializer for opening a pre-existing IXFileFinder with the IXBlockAndStoreAccess protocol.

See also: – **initInStore:atPath:**, – **initWithName:inFile:atPath:**, IXBlockAndStoreAccess protocol

initFromName:inFile:forWriting:

– **initFromName:**(const char *)*aName*
  inFile:(const char *)*filename*
  forWriting:(BOOL)*flag*

Initializes a newly allocated IXFileFinder as **initFromName:inFile:forWriting:atPath:** with a *path* argument of NULL. This method is useful for opening an IXFileFinder whose root directory hasn't changed, which is usually the case.

See also: – **initFromName:inFile:forWriting:atPath:**

initFromName:inFile:forWriting:atPath:

– **initFromName:**(const char *)*aName*
  inFile:(const char *)*filename*
  forWriting:(BOOL)*flag*
  atPath:(const char *)*path*

Initializes a newly allocated IXFileFinder by opening it from data stored under *aName* in *filename* by a previous instance. The IXFileFinder's root path is reset to *path*; it will search for files within the subtree rooted at that directory. *path* can be an absolute or relative pathname, or it can be NULL, in which case the IXFileFinder's root path remains unchanged. The root path may not subsequently be changed unless the IXFileFinder is freed and then reopened. If *flag* is YES, *filename* is opened for reading and writing, and the IXFileFinder is initialized to build and update its index; if *flag* is NO, *filename* is opened for reading only. Returns **self** if successful, or **nil** if *flag* is YES and *filename* can't be written or created.

An IXFileFinder opened for reading only *can* be modified; however, the changes occur only in memory, and are never written to disk. This can be useful for keeping an index up-to-date until the application terminates, without affecting the original file.

This is the designated initializer for opening a pre-existing IXFileFinder with the IXNameAndFileAccess protocol. Note that the underlying IXStoreFile is opened by the IXFileFinder when this method is used, and that it will be closed when the IXFileFinder is freed.

See also: – **initWithName:inFile:atPath:**, IXNameAndFileAccess protocol

initInStore:

– **initInStore:**(IXStore *)*aStore*

Initializes a newly allocated IXFileFinder as **initInStore:atPath:** with a path argument of NULL.

See also: – **initInStore:atPath:**

initInStore:atPath:

– **initInStore:**(IXStore *)*aStore* **atPath:**(const char *)*path*

Initializes a newly allocated IXFileFinder in *aStore*, to search for files in the subtree rooted at the directory named *path*. *path* is considered the root path for the IXFileFinder, and can be an absolute or relative pathname. If *path* is NULL, the program's working directory is used. The root path may not be changed after initialization. If *aStore* is **nil**, then the IXFileFinder won't attempt to maintain indexes on file attributes using IXRecordManager. This doesn't affect query semantics in any way; an IXFileFinder initialized without an IXStore will return the same query results as an IXFileFinder initialized with an IXStore. The presence or absence of an IXStore merely affects query performance. Returns **self**.

This is the designated initializer for creating new IXFileFinders with the IXBlockAndStoreAccess protocol.

See also: – **initFromBlock:inStore:atPath:**, – **initWithName:inFile:atPath:**, – **initWithName:inFile:forWriting:atPath:**, IXBlockAndStoreAccess protocol

initWithName:inFile:

– **initWithName:**(const char *)*aName* **inFile:**(const char *)*filename*

Initializes a newly allocated IXFileFinder as **initWithName:inFile:atPath:**, with a *path* argument of NULL.

See also: – **initWithName:inFile:atPath:**

initWithName:inFile:atPath:

– **initWithName:**(const char *)*aName*
  inFile:(const char *)*filename*
  atPath:(const char *)*path*

Initializes the IXFileFinder as a store file client named *aName* in the store file *filename*. If *filename* doesn't exist, it's created. The IXFileFinder will search for files in the subtree rooted at the directory named *path*, which is considered the root path for the IXFileFinder. *path* can be an absolute or relative pathname If *path* is NULL, the current working directory will be used. The root path may not be changed after initialization. *filename* is opened for writing and reading, so that indexes can be created, updated, and cleaned. Returns **self**.

This is the designated initializer for creating new IXFileFinders with the IXNameAndFileAccess protocol.

See also: – **initInStore:atPath:**, – **initFromBlock:inStore:atPath:**, – **initWithName:inFile:forWriting:atPath:**, IXNameAndFileAccess protocol

IXFileRecord

Inherits From: Object

Conforms To: NXTransport

Declared In: indexing/IXFileRecord.h

Class Description

An IXFileRecord represents a single file in a file system, and is used primarily by instances of IXFileFinder. Queries against an IXFileFinder return sets of IXFileRecords representing the selected files; the IXFileFinder may also store IXFileRecords in an IXRecordManager to improve query performance. An IXFileRecord records the file's name, type, and other information which may be useful to display to a user after performing a query; the file's name may also be used to access the file itself.

Instance Variables

unsigned int **filedate**;
IXFileFinder ***fileFinder**;
char ***filename**;
char ***filetype**;
char ***description**;
struct stat ***statBuffer**;

filedate	The date that the file was last modified.
fileFinder	The IXFileFinder using this IXFileRecord.
filename	The name of the file.
filetype	The type of the file (for example, "ps" or "man"). This is often the same as its extension, though it need not be.
description	A description of the file.
statBuffer	The UNIX stat buffer for the file.

Adopted Protocols

NXTransport	– encodeRemotelyFor:freeAfterEncoding:isBycopy: – encodeUsing: – decodeUsing:

Method Types

Initializing a new instance	– initWithFileFinder:
Getting the file finder	– fileFinder
Accessing file attributes	– setFilename: – filename – setFiletype: – filetype – setDescription: – description – setFiledate: – filedate
Accessing UNIX file information	– statBuffer

Instance Methods

description

– (const char *)**description**

Returns the description of the file, or NULL if one hasn't been set.

See also: – **setDescription:**

filedate

– (unsigned int)**filedate**

Returns the time that the file was last modified as the number of seconds since January 1, 1970, or 0 if one hasn't been set.

See also: – **setFiledate:**

fileFinder

– (IXFileFinder *)**fileFinder**

Returns the IXFileFinder that created and stores the receiving IXFileRecord.

See also: – **initWithFileFinder:**

filename

– (const char *)**filename**

Returns the file's name relative to the root path of the IXFileRecord's IXFileFinder, or NULL if one hasn't been set.

See also: – **setFilename:**

filetype

– (const char *)**filetype**

Returns the file's type, or NULL if one hasn't been set. A file's type is used by the IXFileFinder to convert it to a parsable format, and is also a queryable attribute of the file. File types are such things as "rtf" for Rich Text Format, "eps" for PostScript and Encapsulated PostScript, or "man" for UNIX manual pages. A file's type string is often the same as its extension, though it need not be (as is the case for "man").

See also: – **setFiletype:**

initWithFileFinder:

– **initWithFileFinder:**(IXFileFinder *)*aFileFinder*

Initializes the IXFileRecord to work with *aFileFinder* and returns **self**. This establishes a root path for the IXFileRecord.

See also: – **fileFinder**

setDescription:

– **setDescription:**(const char *)*aDescription*

Sets the description of the file to *aDescription*. This method is usually invoked from the **fileFinder:willAddFile:** delegate method, which is sent by IXFileFinder when the IXFileRecord is created. Returns **self**.

See also: – **description**, – **generatesDescriptions** (IXFileFinderConfiguration protocol), – **fileFinder:willAddFile:** (IXFileFinderQueryAndUpdate protocol)

setFiledate:

– **setFiledate:**(unsigned int)*aDate*

Records the time the file was last modified as *aDate*, expressed in seconds since January 1, 1970. Returns **self**.

See also: – **filedate**

setFilename:

– **setFilename:**(const char *)*aName*

Records the file's name as *aName*. *aName* should be the path of the file relative to the IXFileFinder's root path. Returns **self**.

See also: – **filename**

setFiletype:

– **setFiletype:**(const char *)*aType*

Records the file's type as *aType*. A file's type is used by the IXFileFinder to convert it to a parsable format, and is a queryable attribute. Returns **self**.

See also: – **filetype**

statBuffer

– (const struct stat *)**statBuffer**

Returns the file's UNIX status information: its creation date, permissions, whether it's a directory or special file, and so on. Returns NULL if the status information isn't available.

Your code can use this information to determine whether to display specific information about this file (for example, if the user doesn't have read permission, that file's name could be listed in dimmed text, or perhaps not listed at all).

The stat buffer is generally available only in the **fileFinder:willAddFile:** method for the sender of an update request. **fileFinder:willAddFile:** is invoked by IXFileFinder when the IXFileRecord is created.

See also: **stat**(2) UNIX manual page,
– **fileFinder:willAddFile:** (IXFileFinderQueryAndUpdate protocol)

IXLanguageReader

Inherits From: IXAttributeReader : Object

Conforms To: IXAttributeReading (IXAttributeReader)

Declared In: indexing/IXLanguageReader.h

Class Description

The IXLanguageReader class is used to locate and load language-specific IXAttributeReaders supplied by NeXT. These readers are shipped in **/NextLibrary/Readers**, and are named for their target languages; for example, **English.reader**. If an Indexing Kit object needs a reader, it uses this class to get a reader for the user's preferred language (as set in the Preferences application). Your code can use this class to obtain a reader for a specific language.

IXLanguageReader is also used as an abstract superclass for language-specific readers. Subclasses of IXLanguageReader that perform language-specific processing can be dynamically loaded from a reader file. If you plan to create a loadable reader for a language not supported by NeXT, it should be a subclass of IXLanguageReader; contact NeXT Technical Support for further instructions on doing this. If you plan to create a reader for something other than a natural language, create a subclass of IXAttributeReader.

Instance Variables

None declared in this class.

Method Types

Getting language information	+ installedLanguages + classForLanguage:
Getting objects associated with languages	+ readerForLanguage: + domainForLanguage:
Getting the target language	+ targetLanguage – targetLanguage
Disabling dynamic loading	+ disableLoading

Class Methods

classForLanguage:

+ (Class)**classForLanguage:**(const char *)*aLanguage*

Returns the subclass of IXLanguageReader whose instances read text in *aLanguage*. Only those readers found in **/NextLibrary/Readers** are considered.

disableLoading

+ **disableLoading**

Disables dynamic loading of IXLanguageReader subclasses for the application.

domainForLanguage:

+ **domainForLanguage:**(const char *)*aLanguage*

Returns an IXWeightingDomain specific to *aLanguage*, or **nil** if one can't be found. Only those readers found in **/NextLibrary/Readers** are considered. If *aLanguage* is "Default" the user's default language (as chosen by the user with the Preferences application) is used.

installedLanguages

+ (char *)**installedLanguages**

Returns a string containing a newline-separated list of the languages for which readers are available. The sender of this message is responsible for freeing the string. Only the languages for readers found in **/NextLibrary/Readers** are returned.

readerForLanguage:

+ **readerForLanguage:**(const char *)*aLanguage*

Returns an IXLanguageReader which reads text in *aLanguage*. If a reader specific to *aLanguage* can't be found, returns a reader for English, or a generic IXAttributeReader if the English reader is unavailable. If *aLanguage* is "Default" the user's default language (as chosen by the user with the Preferences application) is used.

targetLanguage

+ (NXAtom)**targetLanguage**

Returns the name of the language that the receiving IXLanguageReader subclass reads, or NULL if the receiving class is IXLanguageReader.

See also: – **targetLanguage**

Instance Methods

targetLanguage

– (NXAtom)**targetLanguage**

Returns the name of the language that the IXLanguageReader reads.

See also: + **targetLanguage**

IXPostingCursor

Inherits From: IXBTreeCursor : Object

Conforms To: IXPostingExchange
IXPostingOperations
IXCursorPositioning (IXBTreeCursor)

Declared In: btree/IXPostingCursor.h

Class Description

IXPostingCursor is a subclass of IXBTreeCursor that treats the values in its IXBTree as sets of postings, which are weighted references to data. This class is primarily intended for maintaining inversions for databases. An IXPostingCursor can be positioned in an IXBTree to find a set of postings, and from there the postings can be manipulated: each posting in the set can be examined, postings can be added to or removed from the set of postings, or the set can be completely emptied. An IXPostingCursor can exchange its postings with any object that conforms to the IXPostingExchange protocol, including instances of IXPostingList and IXPostingSet.

IXPostingCursor is very efficient in the storage of postings. Weights are stored only when needed; if all of the postings for a given key have zero weight, then only the handles are stored. An IXPostingCursor with unweighted postings consumes half the storage of an IXPostingCursor with weighted postings. Similarly, until 32-bit quantities are needed for handles or weights, they're stored as 16-bit quantities on a per-key basis, and promoted as needed. In addition, IXPostingCursor uses the range-oriented methods of IXBTreeCursor to read or write as little data as possible when manipulating posting sets.

For more information on basic cursoring techniques, see the IXCursorPositioning protocol specification. For more information on manipulating postings, see the IXPostingExchange and IXPostingOperations protocol specifications.

Instance Variables

None declared in this class.

Adopted Protocols

IXPostingExchange	– setCount:andPostings: – getCount:andPostings:
IXPostingOperations	– addHandle:withWeight: – removeHandle: – count – empty – setFirstHandle – setNextHandle – setHandle: – getHandle:andWeight:

Instance Methods

None declared in this class.

IXPostingList

Inherits From: List : Object

Conforms To: IXPostingExchange
NXTransport

Declared In: indexing/IXPostingList.h

Class Description

IXPostingList is a subclass of List tailored for use with objects, or *records*, stored in an archiving object, called the *source*. (Generally the source is an IXRecordManager, which can use a different form of archiving from the standard **read:** and **write:** methods—the processes of archiving and unarchiving are referred to as *passivation* and *activation* in this case.) Records are activated on demand, and their persistent identifiers are accessible as postings. IXPostingList can exchange postings with instances the IXPostingCursor and IXPostingSet classes, or any other object that conforms to the IXPostingExchange protocol.

Initially, an IXPostingList stores persistent record identifiers in the form of postings (see "Associative Access" in the chapter introduction). The records themselves reside in a store managed by some other object, called the source. A source is any object that conforms to the IXRecordReading protocol. When the IXPostingList is asked for an object, it has the source activate the object, returns the objects's **id**, and caches the **id** in case it's needed again. This cache of **id**s remains aligned with the postings: if the postings are replaced, or moved around by insertion or deletion, the **id**s are replaced, or moved around with them. Objects can also be added or replaced directly, as with a List; objects added or replaced without postings are assigned null handles and weights.

Note: If your code needs to iterate over all of the objects in a large IXPostingList, be sure to start with the last object in the list. An IXPostingList dynamically grows its cache of **id**s; asking for the last object first will cause space to be immediately allocated for all of the **id**s. This avoids cache resizing as the objects are requested.

A common use for an IXPostingList is iterating over the records described by a set of postings; the simple function listed below prints out descriptions for records stored in an IXRecordManager. It also shows how an IXPostingList can gets its postings directly from another object, in this case an IXPostingCursor.

```
int printRecords(IXRecordManager *aSource,
    const char *anAttribute, void *aKey, unsigned aLength)
{
    IXPostingList   *theList;
    IXPostingCursor *aCursor;
    int              i, count;

    count = 0;
    // get a cursor on the attribute and position it
    aCursor = [aSource cursorForAttributeNamed:anAttribute];
    if ([aCursor setKey:aKey andLength:aLength])
    {
        // load a posting list from the cursor
        if (theList = [[IXPostingList alloc]
            initWithSource:aSource andPostingsIn:aCursor])
        {
            // get space for all the object ids right away.
            count = [theList count];
            [theList objectAt:count - 1];

            // print out the description of each activated record.
            for (i = 0; i < count; i++)
                printf("%s\n", [[theList objectAt:i] description];
        }
    }

    [aCursor free];
    [[theList freeObjects] free];
    return count;
}
```

Instance Variables

unsigned int **maxPointers**;
id <IXRecordReading> **recordSource**;
struct IXPosting ***postingList**;

maxPointers	The number of slots allocated for object **id**s.
recordSource	The object which stores the records kept in the IXPostingList.
postingList	The handle/weight pairs in the IXPostingList.

Adopted Protocols

IXPostingExchange	– setCount:andPostings: – getCount:andPostings:
NXTransport	– encodeRemotelyFor:freeAfterEncoding:isBycopy: – encodeUsing: – decodeUsing:

Method Types

Initializing an IXPostingList	– initWithSource: – initWithSource:andPostingsIn:
Retrieving the source	– source
Manipulating objects by handle	– addHandle:withWeight: – insertHandle:withWeight:at: – replaceHandleAt:with:weight:
Manipulating objects by **id**	– addObject:withWeight: – insertObject:withWeight:at: – replaceObjectAt:with:weight:
Manipulating objects by index	– indexForHandle: – handleOfObjectAt: – weightOfObjectAt:
Sorting the contents	– sortByWeightAscending: – sortBySelector:ascending:

Instance Methods

addHandle:withWeight:

– **addHandle:**(unsigned int)*aHandle* **withWeight:**(unsigned int)*aWeight*

Inserts *aHandle* with *aWeight* at the end of the IXPostingList. The object identified in the IXPostingList's source by *aHandle* can be retrieved by **id** with **objectAt:**. Returns **self**.

See also: – **insertHandle:at:withWeight:**, – **addObject:withWeight:**, – **insertObject:withWeight:at:**, – **handleOfObjectAt:**, – **weightOfObjectAt:**

addObject:withWeight:

– **addObject:***anObject* **withWeight:**(unsigned int)*aWeight*

Inserts *anObject* with *aWeight* at the end of the IXPostingList, and returns **self**. *anObject* is added to the IXPostingList with no handle; **addHandle:withWeight:** should be used instead of this method whenever possible, in order to store a valid handle for every record.

Note: This method currently allows **nil** to be added to the list. This isn't recommended, and may be disallowed in a future release.

See also: – **insertHandle:at:withWeight:**, – **handleOfObjectAt:**, – **weightOfObjectAt:**

getCount:andPostings:

– **getCount:**(unsigned int *)*count* **andPostings:**(IXPosting **)*thePostings*

Returns by reference the number of postings, and a copy of the postings sorted by handle. The sender of this message is responsible for freeing the postings when they are no longer needed. Returns **self**.

Since objects can be added to an IXPostingList by **id** instead of by handle, or inserted in any order, an IXPostingList's set of postings may not conform to the requirements imposed by the IXPostingExchange protocol (that is, sorted by handle and containing no null handles). In a future release, IXPostingList may sort its postings by handle and remove null handles when returning the postings with this method.

See also: – **setCount:andPostings:**

handleOfObjectAt:

– (unsigned int)**handleOfObjectAt:**(unsigned int)*index*

Returns the handle of the posting at *index* if there is a posting there and it has a valid handle. If *index* is greater than or equal to the number of postings in the list, or if the object was entered into the list by **id** instead of by handle, this method returns 0.

See also: – **weightOfObjectAt:**, – **objectAt:** (List), – **addHandle:withWeight:**, – **addObject:withWeight:**

indexForHandle:

– (unsigned int)**indexForHandle:**(unsigned int)*handle*

Returns the position in the IXPostingList of the posting identified by *handle*, or NX_NOT_IN_LIST if that posting isn't in the IXPostingList.

See also: – **handleOfObjectAt:**, – **indexOf:** (List)

initWithSource:

– **initWithSource:**(id <IXRecordReading>)*aSource*

Initializes the receiver, a newly allocated IXPostingList, with *aSource* providing record activation. *aSource* should be an object that conforms to the IXRecordReading protocol, for example, an IXRecordManager. The IXPostingList initially contains no postings. Returns **self**.

See also: – **initWithSource:andPostingsIn:**, – **source**

initWithSource:andPostingsIn:

– **initWithSource:**(id <IXRecordReading>)*aSource*
andPostingsIn:(id <IXPostingExchange>)*anObject*

Initializes the receiver, a newly allocated IXPostingList, with *aSource* providing record activation, and *anObject* providing an initial set of postings (this will usually be an IXPostingCursor or IXPostingSet). *anObject* should have the same source as the IXPostingList of this message. This is the designated initializer for the IXPostingList class. Returns **self**.

See also: – **initWithSource:**, – **source**, – **setCount:andPostings:**, IXRecordReading protocol

insertHandle:withWeight:at:

– **insertHandle:**(unsigned int)*aHandle*
withWeight:(unsigned int)*aWeight*
at:(unsigned int)*index*

Inserts *aHandle* with *aWeight* at position *index* in the IXPostingList, moving existing postings down one slot, if necessary. If *index* is equal to the number of postings in the IXPostingList, *aHandle* is added at the end. The insertion fails, and this method returns **nil**, if *index* is greater than the number of postings in the list or if *aHandle* is 0.

If the insertion is successful, returns **self**; if not, returns **nil**.

See also: – **insertObject:withWeight:at:**, – **addHandle:withWeight:**, – **addObject:withWeight:**, – **handleOfObjectAt:**, – **weightOfObjectAt:**

insertObject:withWeight:at:

– **insertObject:***anObject*
withWeight:(unsigned int)*aWeight*
at:(unsigned int)*index*

Inserts *anObject* with *aWeight* at position *index* in the IXPostingList, moving existing objects down one slot, if necessary. If *index* is equal to the number of postings in the IXPostingList, *anObject* is added at the end. The insertion fails, and this method returns **nil**, if *index* is greater than the number of postings in the IXPostingList. *anObject* is inserted into the list with no handle; **insertHandle:withWeight:at:** should be used instead of this method whenever possible, in order to store a valid handle for every record.

If the insertion is successful, returns **self**; if not, returns **nil**.

See also: – **insertObject:withWeight:at:**, – **addHandle:withWeight:**, – **addObject:withWeight:**, – **handleOfObjectAt:**, – **weightOfObjectAt:**

replaceHandleAt:with:weight:

– **replaceHandleAt:**(unsigned int)*index*
with:(unsigned int)*aHandle*
weight:(unsigned int)*aWeight*

Replaces the posting at *index* with a posting made from *aHandle* and *aWeight*. The replacement fails, and this method returns **nil**, if *index* is greater than or equal to the number of postings in the IXPostingList or if *aHandle* is 0.

If the replacement is successful, returns **self**; if not, returns **nil**.

See also: – **replaceObjectAt:with:weight:**

replaceObjectAt:with:weight:

– **replaceObjectAt:**(unsigned int)*index*
with:*anObject*
weight:(unsigned int)*aWeight*

Replaces the object and its posting at *index* with *anObject* and a posting with a handle of 0 and weight of *aWeight*. The replacement fails, and this method returns **nil**, if *index* is greater than or equal to the number of postings in the IXPostingList, or if *anObject* is **nil**. *anObject* is inserted with no handle; your code should use **replaceHandleAt:with:weight:** whenever possible, in order to store a valid handle for every posting.

If the replacement is successful, returns **self**; if not, returns **nil**.

See also: – **replaceHandleAt:with:weight:**

sortBySelector:ascending:

– **sortBySelector:**(SEL)*aSelector* **ascending:**(BOOL)*flag*

Sorts the contents of the IXPostingList by constructing a key from the value each record returns when *aSelector* is sent to it. If *flag* is YES, the sort is ascending (ABCD...), if *flag* is NO, the sort is descending (ZXYW...). Returns **self**.

The sort ordering used is determined by the return type of *aSelector*. The IXPostingList determines which of the standard Indexing Kit comparator functions to use, and applies the appropriate function to the result of each message send. However, unlike the keys of an IXBTree, the data being compared doesn't have to be inline (serialized); the return value of *aSelector* can be a pointer type, and the IXPostingList will construct a proper key for it.

See the IXComparisonSetting protocol specification for more information on legal comparison values.

See also: – **sortByWeightAscending:**, **IXCompareBytes()** (C Functions)

sortByWeightAscending:

– **sortByWeightAscending:**(BOOL)*flag*

Sorts the contents of the IXPostingList based on the weight of each record. If *flag* is YES, the sort is from low weight to high, if *flag* is NO, the sort is from high weight to low.

See also: – **sortBySelector:ascending:**

source

– (id <IXRecordReading>)**source**

Returns the object which provides storage for the records referenced by the IXPostingList.

See also: – **initWithSource:**, – **initWithSource:andPostings:**, IXRecordReading protocol

weightOfObjectAt:

– (unsigned int)**weightOfObjectAt:**(unsigned int)*index*

Returns the weight of the posting at *index*, or 0 if *index* is greater than or equal to the number of postings in the IXPostingList.

See also: – **handleOfObjectAt:**, – **addHandle:withWeight:**

IXPostingSet

Inherits From: Object

Conforms To: IXPostingExchange
IXPostingOperations

Declared In: btree/IXPostingSet.h

Class Description

An IXPostingSet stores sets of postings in memory. An IXPostingSet can be loaded from any object that conforms to the IXPostingExchange protocol such as IXPostingCursor, IXPostingList, or another IXPostingSet; it can also forms set unions, intersections, and differences with the postings stored in such an object. IXPostingSet is particularly well suited to building up query results for databases.

The following example shows how an IXPostingSet might be used to find all of the records in an IXRecordManager whose value for some string valued attribute matches some prefix:

```
IXPostingSet *matchPrefix(IXRecordManager *aSource,
    const char *attributeName, const char *thePrefix)
{
    IXPostingSet     *theSet;
    IXPostingCursor *aCursor;
    char             *theKey;
    unsigned         keyLength;
    unsigned         theLength;

    // get a cursor for the attribute
    aCursor = [aSource cursorForAttributeNamed:attributeName];
    if (aCursor == nil) return nil;

    // create an empty posting set
    theSet = [[IXPostingSet alloc] initCount:0 andPostings:NULL];
```

```
    // iterate over the keys while there's a match
    theLength = strlen(thePrefix);
    [aCursor setKey:thePrefix andLength:theLength];
    while ([aCursor getKey:(void **)&theKey andLength:&keyLength])
    {
        // check for key out of bounds
        if (keyLength < theLength || bcmp(theKey, thePrefix,
                theLength) break;

        // add the postings for this key to the set and move cursor
        [theSet formUnionWithPostingsIn:aCursor];
        [aCursor setNext];
    }

    [aCursor free];

    // free set if empty
    return [theSet count] ? theSet : [theSet free];
}
```

Instance Variables

unsigned int **thisElement**;
unsigned int **numElements**;
unsigned int **maxElements**;
IXPosting ***postings**;

thisElement	The position of the selected posting.
numElements	The number of postings in the set.
maxElements	The maximum allowable number of postings in the set.
postings	The postings.

Adopted Protocols

IXPostingExchange	– setCount:andPostings: – getCount:andPostings:
IXPostingOperations	– addHandle:withWeight: – removeHandle: – count – empty – setFirstHandle – setNextHandle – setHandle: – getHandle:andWeight:

Method Types

Initializing instances	– initCount:andPostings: – initWithPostingsIn:
Setting the postings	– setCount:andPostings:byCopy:
Accessing postings by position	– setPosition:
Performing set operations	– formUnionWithPostingsIn: – formIntersectionWithPostingsIn: – subtractPostingsIn:

Instance Methods

formIntersectionWithPostingsIn:

– **formIntersectionWithPostingsIn:**(id <IXPostingExchange>)*anObject*

Combines the postings in the IXPostingSet with those in *anObject*, so that on return the IXPostingSet will contain only those postings that were in both objects; that is, it performs a logical AND on the two sets of postings. If each set has a posting with the same handle, but different weights, the weights are averaged. *anObject* is unaffected by this method. Returns **self**.

See also: – **formUnionWithPostingsIn:**, – **subtractPostingsIn:**

formUnionWithPostingsIn:

– **formUnionWithPostingsIn:**(id <IXPostingExchange>)*anObject*

Combines the postings in the IXPostingSet with those in *anObject*, so that on return the IXPostingSet will contain all postings that were in either object (duplicates are reduced to a single posting); that is, it performs a logical OR on the two sets of postings. If each set has a posting with the same handle, the weights are averaged. *anObject* is unaffected by this method. Returns **self**.

See also: – **formIntersectionWithPostingsIn:**, – **subtractPostingsIn:**

initCount:andPostings:

– **initCount:**(unsigned int)*count* **andPostings:**(const IXPosting *)*postings*

Initializes the IXPostingSet with *count* postings, copied from *postings*. This is the designated initializer for IXPostingSet objects.

See also: – **initWithPostingsIn:**, – **setCount:andPostings:byCopy:**

initWithPostingsIn:

– **initWithPostingsIn:**(id <IXPostingExchange>)*anObject*

Initializes the IXPostingSet with the postings in *anObject*. *anObject* should conform to the IXPostingExchange protocol. Returns **self**.

See also: – **initCount:andPostings:**

setCount:andPostings:byCopy:

– **setCount:**(unsigned int)*count*
  andPostings:(const IXPosting *)*postings*
  byCopy:(BOOL)*flag*

Sets the count and postings in the IXPostingSet, replacing and deallocating any previous contents. If *flag* is YES, a copy of *postings* is made and set to be the IXPostingSet's postings; if *flag* is NO, then the IXPostingSet assumes responsibility for the set of postings, and will free them when they are replaced or when the IXPostingSet is freed. Returns **self**.

See also: – **initCount:andPostings:**

setPosition:

– (unsigned int)**setPosition:**(unsigned int)*index*

Selects a posting by position in the posting set, and returns that posting's handle. Your code can use this method to quickly access a handle based on its position.

See also: – **setHandle:** (IXPostingSetOperations protocol)

subtractPostingsIn:

– **subtractPostingsIn:**(id <IXPostingExchange>)*anObject*

Removes from the IXPostingSet those postings that are also in *anObject;* that is, it performs a logical AND NOT between the two sets of postings. *anObject* is unaffected by this method. Returns **self**.

See also: – **formUnionWithPostingsIn:**, – **formIntersectionWithPostingsPostingsIn:**

IXRecordManager

Inherits From: Object

Conforms To: IXBlockAndStoreAccess
IXNameAndFileAccess
IXBlobWriting
IXRecordDiscarding
IXRecordWriting
IXTransientAccess
IXTransientMessaging

Declared In: indexing/IXRecordManager.h

Class Description

IXRecordManager is a record manager based on the Objective C run-time system; it stores objects in an IXStore, and maintains indexes on programmer-defined attributes. Attributes are defined in terms of the return values of messages sent to the stored objects. The stored objects can be retrieved by persistent identifiers, by their attribute values, or by posing a question with IXAttributeQuery, a class that defines a declarative query language for IXRecordManager and other Indexing Kit classes.

Storing Records

IXRecordManager archives, or *passivates*, an object by writing its data into an IXBTree record. Two archiving mechanisms are provided: Objective C archiving, as performed by the standard **read:** and **write:** methods, and serialization, a very fast transcription mechanism that writes or reads an object's instance variables directly into or out of storage. An object will be serialized instead of archived if it conforms to the IXRecordTranscription protocol. For the purpose of serialization, a data type can be serialized if its length can be unambiguously determined from its type declaration and its physical representation; this includes all scalar ANSI C data types, pointers to character strings (which are assumed to be null-terminated), and fixed length arrays of the preceding kinds of data types.

Before serializing an object that conforms to the IXRecordTranscription protocol, IXRecordManager sends it a **source:willWriteRecord:** message, giving the object an opportunity to prepare itself for passivation, or to request the IXRecordManager to write its unserializable data as *blobs*. The process of archiving blobs is described in the IXBlobWriting protocol specification. When a record is deserialized, or *activated*, the IXRecordManager sends **source:didReadRecord:** to it.

The IXRecordManager interface allows a record to be added, discarded, removed, or replaced by another record. When a record is discarded, IXRecordManager treats it as though it didn't exist until it's either reclaimed or removed. See the IXRecordDiscarding protocol specification for more information on discarding and reclaiming records.

Indexing Records

IXRecordManager allows attributes to be defined by name and method, such as "EmployeeName" with the method given by **@selector(empName)**. The value of an attribute for a given record is the value returned when the attribute's message is sent to that record. If a record doesn't respond to the message, then the attribute isn't defined for that record. By default, an attribute is defined for every record that responds to its message; its scope may be further restricted to those records which are instances of a specific class or subclasses of that class.

Here's an example of setting up an attribute for employees by full name (with a method **empName** that returns a character string), and restricting it to instances of MyEmployeeRecord and its subclasses:

```
[recordManager addAttributeNamed:"EmployeeName"
    forSelector:@selector(empName)];
[recordManager setTargetClass:[MyEmployeeRecord class]
    forAttributeNamed:"EmployeeName"];
```

IXRecordManager maintains an index for each of its attributes; the index is an inversion of the attribute's value over all of the records for which it's defined. An attribute index is an IXBTree managed by an IXPostingCursor; IXRecordManager determines the comparator for the IXBTree by examining the return type of the attribute's selector. The default comparator can be overridden (as would be necessary for methods that returned structures or unions) with the **setComparator:andContext:forAttributeNamed:** or **setComparisonFormat:andContext:forAttributeNamed:** methods. In the example given above, the default comparator would be IXCompareStrings, since **empName** is defined as returning a string. For more information on comparators, see the IXComparatorSetting and IXComparisonSetting protocol specifications.

The IXAttributeParser class can be used to index string-valued attributes under each of the separate *lexemes* (words or other useful units of text) in a string, instead of using the entire string as the value. The **setParser:forAttributeNamed:** message assigns a parser that will break the selector's return value into its constituent words. If the attribute in the example above were based on a method that returns a text string containing unstructured, miscellaneous notes, then assigning a parser might be appropriate. Using the default parser configuration for English, an employee record with the note "Has three kids named Bobby, Judy and Sam" would be recorded in the index under the values "Has," "three," "kid," "named," "Bobby," "Judy," and "Sam." Note that "and," being considered a noise word in English, isn't included, and that the plural "kids" was reduced to "kid." See the IXAttributeParser and IXAttributeReader class specifications for more information on parsers.

Retrieving Records

References to records are stored as postings in the attribute indexes. A *posting* is a reference identifier plus its weight (a measure of its frequency or importance in the index). Any index can be examined through an IXPostingCursor returned by **cursorForAttributeNamed:**. A new copy of the cursor is returned for each invocation of this method, so the sender should free each copy when it's no longer needed. The basic cursoring techniques described in the IXCursorPositioning protocol specification can be used to locate references to all of the records having a given value for the attribute, or to iterate over the set of existing values for the attribute. As described in the IXPostingSet class specification, an IXPostingSet can be used to retrieve sets of postings directly from the IXPostingCursor, and can combine those sets in various ways. References to records for a range of attribute values can be collected using one IXPostingCursor and one IXPostingSet. See the IXPostingSet class specification for an example.

IXPostingSets built against different attributes can be combined to resolve multi-attribute queries. For example, all employees with a last name of "Draper" and a salary of at least $60,000 could be found by collecting the appropriate postings from the EmployeeName and Salary attributes into two separate IXPostingSets, and intersecting the results. Another Indexing Kit class, IXAttributeQuery, resolves declarative queries expressed in a functional language against instances of IXRecordManager and other classes using these techniques.

Instance Variables

None declared in this class.

Adopted Protocols

IXBlobWriting	– setValue:andLength:ofBlob:forRecord: – getValue:andLength:ofBlob:forRecord:
IXBlockAndStoreAccess	– initWithStore: – initFromBlock:andStore: – freeFromStore + freeFromBlock:andStore: – getBlock:andStore:
IXNameAndFileAccess	– initWithName: – initFromName:inFile: – freeFromStore + freeFromName:inFile: – getName:andFile:
IXRecordDiscarding	– discardRecord: – reclaimRecord: – clean
IXRecordWriting	– addRecord: – removeRecord: – replaceRecord:with: – empty – count – readRecord:fromZone:
IXTransientAccess	– getOpaqueValue:ofIvar:forRecord: – getIntValue:ofIvar:forRecord: – getFloatValue:ofIvar:forRecord: – getDoubleValue:ofIvar:forRecord: – getStringValue:ofIvar:forRecord: – getStringValue:inLength:ofIvar:forRecord: – getObjectValue:ofIvar:forRecord:
IXTransientMessaging	– getOpaqueValue:ofMessage:forRecord: – getIntValue:ofMessage:forRecord: – getFloatValue:ofMessage:forRecord: – getDoubleValue:ofMessage:forRecord: – getStringValue:ofMessage:forRecord: – getStringValue:inMessage:ofIvar:forRecord: – getObjectValue:ofMessage:forRecord:

Method Types

Adding and removing attributes	– addAttributeNamed:forSelector: – hasAttributeNamed: – removeAttributeNamed:
Key comparison	– setComparisonFormat:forAttributeNamed: – comparisonFormatForAttributeNamed: – setComparator:andContext:forAttributeNamed: – getComparator:andContext:forAttributeNamed:
Setting attribute targets	– setTargetClass:forAttributeNamed: – getTargetName:andVersion:forAttributeNamed:
Accessing attributes	– cursorForAttributeNamed:
Getting attribute information	– selectorForAttributeNamed: – attributeNames
Accessing classes	– classNames – attributeNamesForClass: – recordsForClass:
Retrieving discarded records	– discards
Setting attribute descriptions	– setDescription:forAttributeNamed: – getDescription:forAttributeNamed:
Setting parsers	– setParser:forAttributeNamed: – parserForAttributeNamed:

Instance Methods

addAttributeNamed:forSelector:

– **addAttributeNamed:**(const char *)*aName* **forSelector:**(SEL)*aSelector*

Creates an attribute for records that respond to *aSelector*, associates it with name *aName*, and builds an index for that attribute. Note that records already passivated by the IXRecordManager that respond to *aSelector* are *not* added to the new index automatically. This may change in a future release. If an attribute already exists with name *aName*, returns **nil**; otherwise returns non-**nil**.

See also: – **removeAttributeNamed:**, – **selectorForAttributeNamed:**

attributeNames

– (char *)**attributeNames**

Returns a newline-separated list of the names of all attributes in the IXRecordManager. The sender of this message is responsible for freeing the string returned.

See also: – **addAttributeNamed:forSelector:**

attributeNamesForClass:

– (char *)**attributeNamesForClass:***aClass*

Returns a newline-separated list of the names of all of the attributes maintained by the IXRecordManager that are defined for instances of *aClass*. This includes all of the attributes whose selectors are recognized by instances of *aClass*, and whose target class is *aClass* or one of its superclasses. The sender of this message is responsible for freeing the string returned.

See also: – **setTargetClass:forAttributeNamed:**

classNames

– (char *)**classNames**

Returns a newline-separated list of the names of all the classes which have instances stored in the IXRecordManager. The sender of this message is responsible for freeing the string returned.

comparisonFormatForAttributeNamed:

– (const char *)**comparisonFormatForAttributeNamed:**(const char *)*aName*

Returns a string defining the comparison format of keys in the index named *aName*, or NULL if one hasn't been set. This is a string encoding the Objective C data types that comprise the key; for example, "[3i]" describes an array of 3 integers. An IXBTree uses this format to determine how to compare keys. For more information on comparison formats, see the IXComparisonSetting protocol specification.

See also: – **setComparisonFormat:forAttributeNamed:**, – **getComparator:andContext:forAttributeNamed:**

cursorForAttributeNamed:

– (IXPostingCursor *)**cursorForAttributeNamed:**(const char *)*aName*

Returns an IXPostingCursor that addresses the index for the attribute named *aName*. This cursor can be used to find references to records having a given value for the attribute. For more information on using cursors, see the IXCursorPositioning protocol specification, and the IXPostingCursor class specification.

This method returns a copy of a private cursor each time it's invoked, so your code should free the copy when it's no longer needed.

discards

– (IXPostingList *)**discards**

Returns an IXPostingList containing all records that have been discarded (by sending **discardRecord:** to the IXRecordManager). This IXPostingList can be used to reclaim the discarded records with **reclaimRecord:**. See the IXRecordDiscarding protocol specification for more information.

If the IXRecordManager is asked to read a discarded record (with the IXRecordReading protocol's **readRecord:FromZone:** method), the result will be **nil**; for most purposes the record no longer exists. However, discarded records will still have references in the IXRecordManager's attribute indexes. If your code doesn't deal gracefully with **nil** records, you can filter posting sets before using them by subtracting the discards from them.

getComparator:andContext:forAttributeNamed:

– **getComparator:**(IXComparator **)*aComparator*
    andContext:(const void **)*aContext*
    forAttributeNamed:(const char *)*aName*

Returns by reference the function used to compare attribute values, and the context associated with that function, for the attribute named *aName*. If the attribute has a comparison format set instead, the comparator and context will be NULL. A comparator function takes two data items and returns an answer indicating whether the first is less than, equal to, or greater than the second. The context is arbitrary data for use by that function. Returns **self**.

For more information on comparators, see the IXComparatorSetting protocol specification and the IXBTree class specification.

See also: – **setComparator:andContext:forAttributeNamed:**, – **comparisonFormat:forAttributeNamed:**

getDescription:forAttributeNamed:

– **getDescription:**(char **)*aDescription* **forAttributeNamed:**(const char *)*aName*

Returns by reference the description for the attribute named *aName*. The description can be used to record extra information pertaining to the attribute. Returns **self**.

See also: – **setDescription:forAttributeNamed:**, – **addAttributeNamed:forSelector:**

getTargetName:andVersion:forAttributeNamed:

– **getTargetName:**(const char **)*aName*
  andVersion:(unsigned int *)*targetVersion*
  forAttributeNamed:(const char *)*aName*

Returns by reference the name and version of the class that the attribute named *aName* is defined for, or NULL and 0 if none has been set. If an attribute has a target class set, it will be defined only for records of that class or a subclass. Returns **self**.

See also: – **setTargetClass:forAttributeNamed:**

hasAttributeNamed:

– (BOOL)**hasAttributeNamed:**(const char *)*aName*

Returns YES if the IXRecordManager has an attribute named *aName*, NO if it doesn't.

parserForAttributeNamed:

– (IXAttributeParser *)**parserForAttributeNamed:**(const char *)*aName*

Returns the parser, if any, assigned to the attribute named *aName*. The parser will break the return value of the attribute's selector into separate words when the attribute is evaluated.

See also: – **setParser:forAttributeNamed:**

recordsForClass:

– (IXPostingList *)**recordsForClass:***aClass*

Returns an IXPostingList containing all of the records in the IXRecordManager which are instances of *aClass* or a subclass of *aClass*.

removeAttributeNamed:

– **removeAttributeNamed:**(const char *)*aName*

Removes the attribute named *aName* from the IXRecordManager. Records referenced by the attribute's index aren't affected. Returns **self**.

See also: – **addAttributeNamed:forSelector:**

selectorForAttributeNamed:

– (SEL)**selectorForAttributeNamed:**(const char *)*aName*

Returns the selector for the message that defines the attribute named *aName*. Unless the attribute is restricted to a specific class, this message is sent to any record that responds to it in order to evaluate the attribute. Otherwise it's only sent to records of the attribute's target class (or a subclass of the target class).

See also: – **addAttributeNamed:forSelector:**

setComparator:andContext:forAttributeNamed:

– **setComparator:**(IXComparator *)*aComparator*
  andContext:(const void *)*aContext*
  forAttributeNamed:(const char *)*aName*

Sets the function used to compare attribute values, and the context associated with that function, for the attribute named *aName*. A comparator function should accept two data items and return an answer indicating whether the first is less than, equal to, or greater than the second. The context is arbitrary data for use by that function. Returns **self**.

For more information on comparators, see the IXComparatorSetting protocol specification and the IXBTree class specification.

See also: – **getComparator:andContext:forAttributeNamed:**,
– **setComparisonFormat:forAttributeNamed:**

setComparisonFormat:forAttributeNamed:

– **setComparisonFormat:**(const char *)*aFormat*
  forAttributeNamed:(const char *)*aName*

Installs a string defining the comparison format of keys in the index named *aName*. This is a string encoding the Objective C data types that comprise the key; for example, "[3i]" describes an array of 3 integers (although the length is currently ignored). An IXBTree uses this format to determine how to compare keys. For more information on comparison formats, see the IXComparisonSetting protocol specification.

See also: – **comparisonFormat:forAttributeNamed:**,
– **setComparator:andContext:forAttributeNamed:**

setDescription:forAttributeNamed:

– **setDescription:**(const char *)*aDescription*
forAttributeNamed:(const char *)*aName*

Sets the description for the attribute named *aName* to *aDescription*. The description can be used to record extra information pertaining to the attribute. Returns **self**.

See also: – **getDescription:forAttributeNamed:**

setParser:forAttributeNamed:

– **setParser:**(IXAttributeParser *)*aParser* **forAttributeNamed:**(const char *)*aName*

Assigns the parser *aParser* to the attribute named *aName*. The parser will break the return value of the attribute's selector into separate words when the attribute is evaluated. Returns **self**.

See also: – **parserForAttributeNamed:**

setTargetClass:forAttributeNamed:

– **setTargetClass:***aClass* **forAttributeNamed:**(const char *)*aName*

Sets the target class for the attribute named *aName* to *aClass*. The attribute will be defined only for instances of class *aClass* or any of its subclasses. Your code should set the target class before any records have been added to the IXRecordManager; otherwise, the index for the named attribute may collect references to instances of other classes before the restriction is imposed. This behavior may change in a future release, so that records that aren't of *aClass* are removed from the index when the target class is set. Returns **self**.

See also: – **getTargetName:andVersion:forAttributeNamed:**

IXStore

Inherits From: Object

Declared In: store/IXStore.h

Class Description

IXStore is a transaction based, compacting storage allocator designed for data-intensive applications. Its main features include compaction and relocatability of storage, for reducing and optimizing memory usage; transaction management, for making compound operations atomic and for ensuring data integrity; and concurrency control, for ensuring safe access to shared storage.

An IXStore manages a single memory-based heap. Blocks of storage managed by the IXStore are addressed indirectly by the client, through unsigned integers called *handles*. To gain access to the contents of a block, the client must open the block for reading or writing. An IXStore opens a block by resolving the block's handle into a pointer. While a block is open, client code is free to address its contents through the pointer, and can safely assume that the block won't move. When a block is closed, however, the IXStore is free to move it in order to compact storage; pointers cached by the client may therefore become invalid.

The contents of an IXStore are relocatable to and from other instances of IXStore and its subclasses. Since block handles are indirect reference to data, it's possible to retrieve the contents of an IXStore as a single unit and to store that unit in another IXStore without invalidating handle-based referential data structures residing in the IXStore, like linked lists or trees. This makes it easy to copy complex structures, or to quickly save them to a file.

IXStore implements transactions, allowing several operations to be grouped together in such a way that either all of them take effect, or none of them does. This helps to ensure semantic integrity by making compound operations atomic, and provides a convenient way to undo a series of changes. The use of transactions also ensures data integrity against process and system crashes when used with a persistent storage medium; for example, IXStoreFile, a subclass of IXStore, keeps its storage in a UNIX file. This means that if a system loses power, the IXStoreFile's contents can be recovered intact on power up, in the state they were in after the last transaction that actually finished. For more details on persistence, see the IXStoreFile class specification.

IXStore is thread-safe. All methods perform the locking needed to ensure the integrity of shared data structures when the IXStore is addressed by different Mach threads. Clients of an IXStore need only synchronize higher-level operations to ensure semantic integrity (see the IXBTree class specification for an example of this).

It's possible for two or more instances of IXStore to share the same contents; these instances are called *store contexts*. IXStore mediates access to the blocks among multiple contexts through transactions. No block may be accessed by more than one context at a time, and an open block becomes available again only when the transaction that opened it aborts, or when the last outstanding transaction on the context that opened it is committed. A block opened only for reading, however, becomes available as soon as it's closed. When a context tries to open a block that's already been opened by another context, an exception is raised. This supports the use of deadlock avoidance strategies by the client.

Using Transactions

To start a transaction, send **startTransaction** to the IXStore. This defines a checkpoint your code can go back to if it has to undo changes. Transactions aren't enabled by default; the first time one is started, the IXStore permanently enables transactions. Your code can check whether transactions have been enabled with **areTransactionsEnabled**. You may want to do this if your code is invoked by higher level methods that determine the transaction management policy for the application. For example, IXBTree uses **areTransactionsEnabled** to determine whether or not to invoke **startTransaction** before responding to an **empty** message.

Using transactions makes updates slower, since blocks must be copied when they're opened for writing. On the other hand, in the case of an IXStoreFile, it's nearly certain that the storage will be unrecoverable following a crash if your code doesn't use transactions. Always use IXStore without transactions, unless you need undo capability, since its contents are always destroyed by a crash. Always use IXStoreFile with transactions, except for data that can be easily reconstructed, such as an index.

Once you've started a transaction, your code can open blocks and make changes to them, or even start another transaction inside the previous one. The **nestingLevel** method tells how many transactions are pending on the context. This is important if a transaction has already been started by a method that invokes yours, so that yours doesn't finish a transaction that the invoking method is still working on. The nesting level also determines when blocks are made available to other contexts. Modified blocks are made available when the nesting level becomes 0—that is, when the last transaction is committed, or when the transaction that opened them is aborted. Unmodified blocks are made available when they're closed.

At any point in a transaction, your code can send **abortTransaction** to the IXStore. This undoes everything you've done up to that point in the current transaction: created blocks are destroyed, freed blocks are recovered, block resizes are undone, and any changes made to blocks opened after the corresponding **startTransaction** message are undone and those blocks are closed. Also, any blocks opened in that transaction are made available to other contexts.

When your code is ready to commit its changes, it sends **commitTransaction** to the IXStore. This closes all blocks opened since the last **startTransaction**, and makes sure all changes are recorded. Changes aren't flushed immediately, however, if the transaction is nested within another one. This means that changes committed by nested transactions can be undone by their parents. If the **commitTransaction** results in a nesting level of 0, then all pending changes are physically flushed, making them permanent, and all blocks that had been opened by the committing context are made available to other contexts.

One restriction on transaction nesting is that changes to a block are associated with the transaction that opened the block. That is, within a nested transaction, changes made to any block opened by an outer transaction are associated with the outer transaction, not the nested transaction. The changes aren't undone when the inner transaction is aborted; the outer transaction must be aborted to undo the changes. Changes made to any block opened by the nested transaction, however, are associated with the nested transaction, not the outer transaction, and can be undone by aborting either transaction.

Note that if your code makes changes outside any transaction while transactions are enabled, an enclosing transaction is started automatically. The next invocation of **startTransaction**, if any, before an intervening abort or commit, simply picks up this enclosing transaction, and reports a nesting level of 1. Thus, if nesting isn't needed, your code can simply enable transactions initially with a pair of **startTransaction/commitTransaction** messages, and thereafter use only **commitTransaction** to mark transaction boundaries, leaving transactions implicitly begin with the first modification following each commit.

When using an IXStoreFile without transactions, try to cluster your updates into small windows of activity, and invoke **commitTransaction** at the close of each window to flush them immediately, as this will minimize the probability of damage in the event of a system crash or power loss. Also note that any modifications that haven't been committed are aborted when an IXStore is freed.

Instance Variables

unsigned int **changeCount**;
unsigned int **nestingLevel**;
unsigned int **queueForward**;
unsigned int **queueReverse**;
struct StoreBroker ***storeBroker**;

changeCount	The number of the changes made to the IXStore's contents since the IXStore was created.
nestingLevel	The number of the current nested transaction.
queueForward	For internal use by the IXStore.
queueReverse	For internal use by the IXStore.
storeBroker	For internal use by the IXStore.

Method Types

Initializing, copying, and freeing instances	
	– init – copy – free
Creating, copying, and freeing blocks	
	– createBlock:ofSize: – copyBlock:atOffset:forLength: – freeBlock:
Opening and closing blocks	– openBlock:atOffset:forLength: – readBlock:atOffset:forLength: – closeBlock:
Managing block sizes	– resizeBlock:toSize: – sizeOfBlock:
Using transactions	– startTransaction – abortTransaction – commitTransaction – areTransactionsEnabled – nestingLevel – changeCount

Accessing the contents	– getContents:andLength: – setContents:andLength:
Reducing memory consumption	– compact

Instance Methods

abortTransaction

– **abortTransaction**

Reverts the IXStore to the state it was in before the last time it received a **startTransaction** message, if transactions are enabled. Discards all changes made to blocks that were opened by the current transaction (even if they've been closed), closes those blocks if necessary, and makes them available to other contexts. Any blocks created by the current transaction are destroyed, any blocks freed are reclaimed, and any blocks resized are restored to their previous size. The current transaction is terminated, and the transaction in effect, if any, when the current transaction was started is made the current transaction. If the nesting level is 1 (that is, no transaction is pending), the state reverts to the last time a **commitTransaction** was received. Returns **self**.

Blocks opened by an enclosing transaction are *not* affected, even if their contents have been changed since the receipt of the last **startTransaction** message. If transactions aren't enabled, only the block creations and freeings performed since the last **commitTransaction** message are reverted; changes made to the contents of blocks aren't undone. Even if your code never uses **startTransaction**, it should periodically send **commitTransaction** to establish a checkpoint for **abortTransaction**.

This method increases the change count of the IXStore, indicating that a change in state has occurred which may have closed blocks.

See also: – **commitTransaction**, – **startTransaction**, – **nestingLevel**, – **changeCount**, – **closeBlock:**

areTransactionsEnabled

– (BOOL)**areTransactionsEnabled**

Returns YES if transactions are enabled for the IXStore (that is, if the IXStore was ever sent a **startTransaction** message). Otherwise, it returns NO. You should use this method if you're not sure whether or not to send **startTransaction** messages, or when invoked by higher-level code that establishes the transaction management policy.

The transaction management policy is a property of the contents of an IXStore. If your code copies the contents of an IXStore that has transactions enabled into an IXStore that doesn't, transactions will be enabled for the receiving IXStore.

See also: – **startTransaction**, – **nestingLevel**

changeCount

– (unsigned int)**changeCount**

Returns the number of **commitTransaction** and **abortTransaction** messages received by the IXStore since it was created. That is, this number indicates the number of changes made to the IXStore's contents since the run-time object was initialized.

This method is useful for determining if cached pointers to the contents of opened blocks are still valid, so the overhead of the block opening methods can be avoided. For example, if an object needs to repeatedly access the same block within a transaction, it can cache the pointer to the block's contents when it opens the block, along with the change count. From then on, whenever the object needs to access the block, it can check the IXStore's change count; if the change count hasn't increased, then no commits or transactions have occurred since the block was opened, which means that the cached pointer is still valid, and the object can use the pointer safely without having to open the block again—unless, of course, the object itself has since closed the block. (The use of this method by IXBTreeCursor accounts for a 40% performance improvement on sequential key reads when all pages are in memory.)

See also: – **nestingLevel**, – **abortTransaction**, – **commitTransaction**

closeBlock:

– **closeBlock:**(unsigned int)*aHandle*

Closes the block identified by *aHandle*. This allows the IXStore to relocate the block if needed. Changes to the block don't take effect until the transaction that opened it is committed; similarly, changes aren't undone until the transaction that opened the block is aborted. Open blocks are automatically closed when the transaction that opened them is either committed or aborted. Returns **self**.

Note: Closing a block that was opened for writing does *not* make it available to other contexts; the transaction in which the block was opened must be aborted, or pending transactions committed until the nesting level is 0, for it to become available again. Blocks opened for reading become available when closed, since there are no changes to protect.

See also: – **openBlock:atOffset:forLength:**, – **readBlock:atOffset:forLength:**, – **startTransaction**, – **commitTransaction**, – **abortTransaction**

commitTransaction

– **commitTransaction**

Commits all changes made to blocks opened since the last **startTransaction**, closes the blocks. If the nesting level becomes 0, makes the blocks available to other contexts. Any creations, freeings or resizes performed since the **startTransaction** are also committed. The current transaction is terminated, and the enclosing transaction, if any, becomes the current transaction. Returns **self**.

Your code may use this message even if transactions aren't enabled; the reversal of block-level operations (creating and freeing) is supported even in the absence of transactions. **commitTransaction** commits all such changes made since the last **commitTransaction**, and **abortTransaction** cancels all such changes made since the last **commitTransaction**. If transactions aren't enabled, this method closes *all* open blocks, making them available to other contexts, and commits *all* outstanding creates and frees.

This method increases the change count of the IXStore, indicating that a change in state has occurred which may have closed blocks.

See also: – **abortTransaction**, – **startTransaction**, – **changeCount**, – **closeBlock:**

compact

– **compact**

Compacts the contents of the IXStore so that they consume as little storage as possible. This method moves blocks around physically within the IXStore, and so may take some time to complete. The amount of storage consumed may be reduced by as much as 50%. Returns **self**.

If this method is invoked while transactions are pending, the actual compaction will be postponed until there are no transactions outstanding. When used with IXStoreFile, this method actually reduces the size of the file. Compaction also may occur automatically. This won't occur unless the IXStore consumes at least 16 MB of storage, and may not occur until much more storage is actually consumed.

copy

– **copy**

Creates and returns a new store context, which addresses the same storage as the original. Changes made by either context will affect the shared storage, and will be reflected in both contexts.

If you want to create a completely independent duplicate of an IXStore, you can use **getContents:andLength:** and **setContents:andLength:** as follows:

```
IXStore      *aStore, *twinStore;
vm_address_t theStorage;
vm_size_t    theLength;

[aStore compact]; // Makes the transfer more efficient.
[aStore getContents:&theStorage andLength:&theLength];
twinStore = [[IXStore alloc] init];
[twinStore setContents:theStorage andLength:theLength];
```

This technique is also effective for saving the contents of an IXStore into an IXStoreFile.

See also: – **getContents:andLength:**, – **setContents:andLength:**

copyBlock:atOffset:forLength:

– (unsigned int)**copyBlock:**(unsigned int)*aHandle*
atOffset:(unsigned int)*anOffset*
forLength:(unsigned int)*aLength*

Returns a handle to a new block whose contents are identical to the region of the block identified by *aHandle* specified by *anOffset* and *aLength*.

If there is no block identified by *aHandle*, IX_NotFoundError is raised. If the block has been opened by another context, IX_LockedError is raised. See the class description for more information on when a block becomes available to other contexts.

See also: – **openBlock:atOffset:forLength:**, – **readBlock:atOffset:forLength:**, – **abortTransaction**, – **commitTransaction**, – **closeBlock:**

createBlock:ofSize:

– **createBlock:**(unsigned int *)*aHandle* **ofSize:**(unsigned int)*size*

Creates a new block of *size* bytes and returns its handle by reference in *aHandle*. The new block is guaranteed to be zeroed. If you create a block of size **vm_page_size** or more, it's guaranteed to be page-aligned (**vm_page_size** is declared in the header file **mach/mach_init.h**). It isn't possible to create a block of size 0. Returns **self**.

free

– **free**

Frees the IXStore. The storage substrate is also freed if there are no other store contexts addressing it. Returns **nil**.

See also: – **freeBlock:**

freeBlock:

– **freeBlock:**(unsigned int)*aHandle*

Removes and frees the block identified by *aHandle*. Returns **self**.

If there is no block identified by *aHandle*, IX_NotFoundError is raised. If the block has been opened by another context, IX_LockedError is raised. See the class description for more information on when a block becomes available to other contexts.

See also: – **free**, – **abortTransaction**, – **commitTransaction**, – **closeBlock:**

getContents:andLength:

– **getContents:**(vm_address_t *)*theContents* **andLength:**(vm_size_t *)*aLength*

Returns by reference the address and length of a copy of the IXStore's contents. *theContents* is a copy-on-write image of the original (**vm_address_t** is declared in the header file **mach/mach_types.h**). Returns **self**.

Your code can use this method along with **setContents:andLength:** to create an independent copy of an IXStore (see the **copy** method description for an example). Be sure to compact the IXStore before invoking this method, so that the amount of memory copied is as small as possible. These methods also provide an efficient means of saving the contents of an IXStore into an IXStoreFile.

getContents:andLength: must not be invoked when transactions are pending; if it is, IX_ArgumentError is raised. Your code should also not invoke this method while any blocks are open outside the scope of a transaction (since they may have been changed).

See also: – **setContents:andLength:**, – **copy**

init

– **init**

Initializes a new IXStore with zero capacity and transactions not enabled. This is the designated initializer for the IXStore class. Returns **self**.

nestingLevel

– (unsigned int)**nestingLevel**

Returns the number of the transactions pending against the IXStore. If transactions aren't enabled, this method always returns 0.

See also: – **abortTransaction**, – **commitTransaction**, – **areTransactionsEnabled**, – **startTransaction**

openBlock:atOffset:forLength:

– (void *)**openBlock:**(unsigned int)*aHandle*
atOffset:(unsigned int)*anOffset*
forLength:(unsigned int)*aLength*

Returns a pointer to a region of the block identified by *aHandle*, beginning at *anOffset* and of *aLength* bytes, after opening it for writing. If your code writes outside of the opened area, your data may become corrupt, and neither **abortTransaction** nor **commitTransaction** will restore data damaged in this manner.

If there is no block identified by *aHandle*, IX_NotFoundError is raised. If the block has been opened by another context, IX_LockedError is raised. See the class description for more information on when a block becomes available to other contexts.

See also: – **readBlock:atOffset:forLength:**, – **freeBlock:**, – **abortTransaction**, – **commitTransaction**, – **closeBlock:**

readBlock:atOffset:forLength:

– (void *)**readBlock:**(unsigned int)*aHandle*
atOffset:(unsigned int)*anOffset*
forLength:(unsigned int)*aLength*

Returns a pointer to a region in the block identified by *aHandle*, beginning at *anOffset* and of *aLength* bytes, after opening it for reading. It's assumed that your code won't alter the block. If your code does alter the block, your data may become corrupt, and neither **abortTransaction** nor **commitTransaction** will restore data damaged in this manner.

If there is no block identified by *aHandle*, IX_NotFoundError is raised. If the block has been opened by another context, IX_LockedError is raised. See the class description for more information on when a block becomes available to other contexts.

See also: – **openBlock:atOffset:forLength:**, – **freeBlock:**, – **abortTransaction**, – **commitTransaction**, – **closeBlock:**

resizeBlock:toSize:

– **resizeBlock:**(unsigned int)*aHandle* **toSize:**(unsigned int)*aSize*

Resizes the block identified by *aHandle* to *aSize*. Returns **self**.

If there is no block identified by *aHandle*, IX_NotFoundError is raised. If the block has been opened by another context, IX_LockedError is raised. See the class description for more information on when a block becomes available to other contexts.

See also: – **sizeOfBlock:**, – **openBlock:atOffset:forLength:**, – **readBlock:atOffset:forLength**, – **abortTransaction**, – **commitTransaction**, – **closeBlock:**

setContents:andLength:

– **setContents:**(vm_address_t)*someContents* **andLength:**(vm_size_t)*aLength*

Replaces the contents of the IXStore with the contents specified by *someContents* and *aLength*. The original contents of the IXStore are lost. *someContents* should be a virtual memory image retrieved by **getContents:andLength:** (**vm_address_t** is declared in the header file **mach/mach_types.h**). The IXStore assumes responsibility for freeing the virtual memory image, and may simply use it directly. Contents copied in this manner between instances of IXStore are shared as copy-on-write data. Returns **self**.

Your code can use this method along with **getContents:andLength:** to create an independent copy of an IXStore (see the **copy** method description for an example). These methods also provide an efficient means of saving the contents of an IXStore into an IXStoreFile.

setContents:andLength: must not be invoked when transactions are pending; if it is, IX_ArgumentError is raised.

See also: – **getContents:andLength:**

sizeOfBlock:

– (unsigned int)**sizeOfBlock:**(unsigned int)*aHandle*

Returns the size, in bytes, of the block identified by *aHandle*.

If there is no block identified by *aHandle*, IX_NotFoundError is raised. If the block has been opened by another context, IX_LockedError is raised. See the class description for more information on when a block becomes available to other contexts.

See also: – **resizeBlock:toSize:**, – **openBlock:atOffset:forLength:**, – **readBlock:atOffset:forLength**, – **abortTransaction**, – **commitTransaction**, – **closeBlock:**

startTransaction

– (unsigned int)**startTransaction**

Begins a new transaction, which will be aborted or committed before all other outstanding transactions on the receiving context. If transactions aren't enabled for the IXStore, they're permanently enabled. Returns a number identifying the new transaction, and indicating the number of transactions outstanding, including the new one. This is the same value returned by the **nestingLevel** method. For example, if the nesting level is 0 and the IXStore receives **startTransaction** three times, the invocations of the method will return, in order, 1, 2, 3.

See also: – **abortTransaction**, – **commitTransaction**, – **areTransactionsEnabled**, – **nestingLevel**

IXStoreBlock

Inherits From:	Object
Conforms To:	IXBlockAndStoreAccess NXReference
Declared In:	store/IXStoreBlock.h

Class Description

An IXStoreBlock manages a single block within an IXStore, supporting access methods similar to those of IXStore and permitting multiple references to the same block. It also implements methods for archiving and unarchiving an object in its block of storage. You can use this class as a convenient means of manipulating blocks of storage without needing to know the **id** of the associated IXStore, and for storing NeXTSTEP objects in an IXStore.

This class is intended primarily as a means of associating a name with a block in an IXStoreDirectory. To associate names with large numbers of nonobject values, use an IXBTree. To archive large numbers of objects, use IXRecordManager.

Instance Variables

IXStore ***store**;
unsigned int **handle**;
unsigned int **blockSize**;

store	The IXStore that the block resides in.
handle	The block handle.
blockSize	The size of the block.

Adopted Protocols

IXBlockAndStoreAccess	– initInStore: – initFromBlock:inStore: – freeFromStore + freeFromBlock:andStore: – getBlock:andStore:
NXReference	– addReference – free – references

Method Types

Accessing the block's contents	– openAtOffset:forLength: – readAtOffset:forLength: – copyAtOffset:forLength: – close
Managing the block size	– resizeTo: – size
Archiving an object in an IXStoreBlock	– readObject – writeObject:

Instance Methods

close

– **close**

Closes the block of storage managed by the IXStoreBlock. To destroy the block of storage, send a **freeFromBlock:andStore:** message to the IXStoreBlock (this will also free the IXStoreBlock). Returns the IXStore containing the block.

This method doesn't affect transactions in any way. If you want to make the block available to other contexts, you should send **commitTransaction** to the IXStore.

copyAtOffset:forLength:

– (unsigned int)**copyAtOffset:**(unsigned int)*anOffset*
forLength:(unsigned int)*aLength*

Copies a portion of the IXStoreBlock's block, creating a new block. The copy is made from the section of the block beginning at *anOffset* within the block, of *aLength* bytes. Returns the handle of the copy.

See also: – **copyBlock:atOffset:forLength:** (IXStore)

openAtOffset:forLength:

– (void *)**openAtOffset:**(unsigned int)*anOffset* **forLength:**(unsigned int)*aLength*

Returns a pointer to the portion of the IXStoreBlock's block specfied by *anOffset*, of *aLength* bytes, after having the IXStore open it for writing. If your code writes outside of the specified area, the IXStore's contents may be corrupted.

See also: – **readAtOffset:forLength:**, – **openBlock:atOffset:forLength:** (IXStore), – **readBlock:atOffset:forLength:** (IXStore)

readAtOffset:forLength:

– (void *)**readAtOffset:**(unsigned int)*anOffset* **forLength:**(unsigned int)*aLength*

Returns a pointer to the portion of the IXStoreBlock's block specfied by *anOffset*, of *aLength* bytes, after having the IXStore open it for reading. If you write to the block, the IXStore's contents may be corrupted

See also: – **openAtOffset:forLength:**, – **openBlock:atOffset:forLength:** (IXStore), – **readBlock:atOffset:forLength:** (IXStore)

readObject

– **readObject**

Unarchives and returns the object that was previously archived in the IXStoreBlock's block. The archived object must implement the **read:** method in order to be unarchived.

See also: – **writeObject:**, – **read:** (Object), – **write:** (Object)

resizeTo:

– **resizeTo:**(unsigned int)*size*

Resizes the IXStoreBlock's block to be size bytes long, and returns **self**. The block can only be resized when it's not open.

See also: – **size**, – **resizeBlock:ToSize:** (IXStore), – **sizeOfBlock:** (IXStore)

size

– (unsigned int)**size**

Returns the size of the IXStoreBlock's block, in bytes.

See also: – **resizeToSize:**, – **sizeOfBlock:** (IXStore), – **resizeBlock:ToSize:** (IXStore)

writeObject:

– **writeObject:**(unsigned int)*anObject*

Archives *anObject* into the IXStoreBlock's block. *anObject* must implement the **write:** method in order to be archived. The block is resized to fit the archived object if necessary. Returns **self**.

See also: – **readObject**, – **write:** (Object), – **read:** (Object)

IXStoreDirectory

Inherits From: Object

Conforms To: IXBlockAndStoreAccess
IXNameAndFileAccess

Declared In: btree/IXStoreDirectory.h

Class Description

An IXStoreDirectory provides access to store clients by name instead of by block handle. You can use this facility for more convenient access to objects within a single IXStore. It's particularly useful in implementing the IXNameAndFileAccess protocol, which is used to support a conventional store file organization. See the IXNameAndFileAccess protocol specification for more information on the conventional store file organization. This class specification also assumes that you know about store clients, which are described in the IXBlockAndStoreAccess protocol specification.

Instance Variables

None declared in this class.

Adopted Protocols

IXBlockAndStoreAccess	– initInStore: – initFromBlock:inStore: – freeFromStore + freeFromBlock:andStore: – getBlock:andStore:
IXNameAndFileAccess	– initWithName:inFile: – initFromName:inFile:forWriting: – freeFromStore + freeFromName:andFile: – getName:andFile:

Method Types

Adding entries or objects	– addEntryNamed:ofClass: – addEntryNamed:ofClass:atBlock: – addEntryNamed:forObject:
Removing entries	– freeEntryNamed: – removeName: – empty – reset
Getting entries	– hasEntryNamed: – getBlock:ofEntryNamed: – getClass:ofEntryNamed: – openEntryNamed: – entries

Instance Methods

addEntryNamed:forObject:

– **addEntryNamed:**(const char *)*aName* **forObject:***anObject*

Associates *anObject* with *aName*. *anObject* must conform to the IXBlockAndStoreAccess protocol, and must be a client of the same IXStore as the IXStoreDirectory. Returns the newly created instance, or **nil** if an entry already exists with the specified name.

Use this method to associate a name with an existing and instantiated store client. If you want to associate a name with a store client that has already been created, but isn't currently instantiated (that is, its data exists in the IXStore, but there's no run-time object accessing it), use **addEntryNamed:ofClass:atBlock:**. If you want to immediately create a new store client and associate a name with it, use **addEntryNamed:ofClass:**.

If *aName* is NULL or empty, *anObject* doesn't respond to **getBlock:andStore:**, or *anObject* isn't a client of the same IXStore as the IXStoreDirectory, IX_ArgumentError is raised.

See also: – **addEntryNamed:ofClass:atBlock:**, – **openEntryNamed:**

addEntryNamed:ofClass:

– **addEntryNamed:**(const char *)*aName* **ofClass:***aClass*

Creates an instance of class *aClass*, initializes it by sending **initInStore:** (an IXBlockAndStoreAccess protocol method), and associates it with *aName*. Returns the newly created instance.

If an entry already exists for *aName*, IX_DuplicateError is raised. If *aName* is NULL or empty, or if instances of *aClass* don't respond to **initInStore:**, IX_ArgumentError is raised.

See also: – **addEntryNamed:ofClass:atBlock:**, – **openEntryNamed:**, – **initInStore:** (IXBlockAndStoreAccess protocol)

addEntryNamed:ofClass:atBlock:

– **addEntryNamed:**(const char *)*aName*
  ofClass:*aClass*
  atBlock:(IXBlockHandle)*aHandle*

Creates an instance of class *aClass*, reconstitutes it from the block at *aHandle* by sending **initFromBlock:inStore:** (an IXBlockAndStoreAccess protocol method), and associates it with *aName*. If *aHandle* is 0, this method is equivalent to **addEntryNamed:ofClass:**, and creates a new instance of *aClass*. Returns the reconstituted or created instance.

Use this method to associate a name with the data for a previously created store client. The stored data should have been created by a previous instance of *aClass*.

If an entry already exists for *aName*, IX_DuplicateError is raised. If *aName* is NULL or empty, or if instances of *aClass* don't respond to **initFromBlock:inStore:**, IX_ArgumentError is raised.

See also: – **addEntryNamed:forObject:**, – **addEntryNamed:ofClass:**, – **openEntryNamed:**, – **initFromBlock:inStore:** (IXBlockAndStoreAccess protocol)

empty

– **empty**

Removes all entries from the directory, instantiating the store clients, and freeing them from the store. Returns **self**.

See also: – **freeEntryNamed:**, – **freeFromBlock:inStore:** (IXBlockAndStoreAccess protocol)

entries

– (const char **)**entries**

Creates and returns a NULL-terminated list of the names of all currently defined entries. The sender of this message responsible for freeing the list, but not the strings in the list, which are NXAtoms.

If space for the array of entries can't be allocated, IX_MemoryError is raised.

freeEntryNamed:

– **freeEntryNamed:**(const char *)*aName*

Removes the named entry from the directory by sending **freeFromBlock:inStore** to the named entry's class object. Returns **self**.

See also: – **empty**, – **freeFromBlock:inStore:** (IXBlockAndStoreAccess protocol)

getClass:ofEntryNamed:

– **getClass:**(id *)*aClass* **ofEntryNamed:**(const char *)*aName*

Returns by reference the class object for the entry named *aName*, or **nil** if there is no such entry. Returns **self**.

hasEntryNamed:

– (BOOL)**hasEntryNamed:**(const char *)*aName*

Returns YES if there is an entry named *aName*, NO otherwise.

openEntryNamed:

– **openEntryNamed:**(const char *)*aName*

Creates and initializes (with **initFromBlock:inStore:**) an instance of the object previously entered as *aName*, or **nil** if there is no such entry. It's possible to create multiple instances from the same entry; your code should avoid doing this, as the separate objects may corrupt the data they share in the IXStore if they try to change it.

See also: – **addEntryNamed:ofClass:**, – **addEntryNamed:ofClass:atBlock:**, – **initFromBlock:inStore:** (IXBlockAndStoreAccess protocol)

removeName:

– **removeName:**(const char *)*aName*

Removes *aName* as an entry in the IXStoreDirectory, but doesn't remove the store client. That is, the client can still be recovered by handle. Returns **self**.

See also: – **reset**, – **initFromBlock:inStore:** (IXBlockAndStoreAccess protocol)

reset

– **reset**

Removes all entries in the IXStoreDirectory, but doesn't remove the store clients. That is, the clients can still be recovered by handle. Returns **self**.

See also: – **removeName:**, – **initFromBlock:inStore:** (IXBlockAndStoreAccess protocol)

IXStoreFile

Inherits From: IXStore : Object

Declared In: store/IXStoreFile.h

Class Description

IXStoreFile is a subclass of IXStore that keeps its storage in a file. Since a file can outlive processes, IXStoreFile can store persistent data. IXStoreFile also guarantees the integrity of stored data against process and system crashes when protected by transactions, provided that the physical media remains intact.

IXStoreFile can open files for reading and writing, or for reading only, and it locks them with the **flock()** UNIX system call for exclusive or shared access, accordingly. This locking is advisory only, but effectively prevents cache conflict between instances residing in separate processes on the same host. Note, however, that the advisory locks aren't visible over the network, due to limitations of **flock()**; responsibility for managing cache conflicts when sharing files over the network falls to the program using the IXStoreFile. The suggested approach is to build a server with NeXTSTEP Distributed Objects that mediates access to files among client processes.

To support the use of preconfigured files, an IXStoreFile opened for reading only may be modified freely by the process using it; all modified pages are reflected only in the address space of that process. The modifications are never written to the file, and are discarded when the IXStoreFile is freed.

IXStoreFile is extremely efficient with respect to paging. When pages would be forced from memory by the virtual memory system, IXStoreFile writes them directly back to the storage file instead of allowing them to go through the swap file. The transaction management architecture takes advantage of this, ensuring the minimum number of page faults per transaction.

Instance Variables

```
int descriptor;
const char *filename;
struct {
        unsigned int needsClose:1;
        unsigned int isCreating:1;
} fileStatus;
```

descriptor	The file descriptor for the storage file.
filename	The name of the storage file.
fileStatus.needsClose	True if the storage file was opened by this IXStoreFile.
fileStatus.isCreating	True if the storage file was created by this IXStoreFile.

Method Types

Initializing and freeing instances	– init – initWithFile: – initFromFile:forWriting: – free
Limiting the file mapping size	– setSizeLimit: – sizeLimit
Getting file information	– descriptor – filename

Instance Methods

descriptor

– (int)**descriptor**

Returns the file descriptor for the IXStoreFile's storage file.

See also: – **filename**

filename

– (const char *)**filename**

Returns the name of the IXStoreFile's storage file.

See also: – **descriptor**

free

– **free**

Unlocks and closes the storage file and frees the IXStoreFile. The file isn't removed from the file system, even if it was a temporary file created by the **init** method. Returns **nil**.

This method aborts any pending modifications. Your code should always send **commitTransaction** until the transaction nesting level is 0 before closing an IXStoreFile in order to save any outstanding changes.

See also: – **init**, – **commitTransaction** (IXStore), – **abortTransaction** (IXStore)

init

– **init**

Initializes the IXStoreFile with a temporary file (created in **/tmp**) that's opened for writing. Returns **self**.

See also: – **initWithFile:**, – **initFromFile:forWriting:**

initFromFile:forWriting:

– **initFromFile:**(const char *)*filename* **forWriting:**(BOOL)*flag*

Initializes the IXStoreFile from the previously created *filename*. *filename* must have been previously created by the **initWithFile:** method. If *flag* is YES, then *filename* is opened for reading and writing, and locked for exclusive access. If *flag* is NO, then *filename* is opened for reading only, and locked for shared access. If *filename* is opened for reading only, any changes made to the IXStoreFile will be reflected only memory, and will never be flushed to disk. This is the designated initializer for IXStoreFile objects that use an existing storage file. Returns **self**.

See also: – **initWithFile:**

initWithFile:

– **initWithFile:**(const char *)*filename*

Initializes the IXStoreFile with *filename* as its storage file. *filename* is created and opened for reading and writing, and locked for exclusive access. This the designated initializer for the IXStoreFile class. Returns **self**.

See also: – **init**, – **initFromFile:forWriting:**

setSizeLimit:

– **setSizeLimit:**(vm_size_t)*aLimit*

Limits the amount of virtual address space consumed by file mapping to *aLimit*. If *aLimit* is zero, the size limit is removed. The size limit determines how much of the file the IXStoreFile will try to cache in main memory. Given enough memory, the higher the size limit, the better the performance. If your code will be operating on a machine with little memory, you should set the limit to a relatively small number; for example, 128KB on an 8-megabyte machine. Returns **self**.

See also: – **sizeLimit**

sizeLimit

– (vm_size_t)**sizeLimit**

Returns the maximum amount of virtual address space consumed by file mapping. The size limit determines how much of the file the IXStoreFile will try to cache in main memory. Given enough memory, the higher the size limit, the better the performance.

See also: – **setSizeLimit:**

IXWeightingDomain

Inherits From: Object

Declared In: indexing/IXWeightingDomain.h

Class Description

An IXWeightingDomain represents word count, rank, and frequency information for a body of text. It can be used to convert word counts between several different formats, and to discover information about specific words, or tokens, in the body of text. An IXWeightingDomain doesn't store the body of text whose statistics it represents, and doesn't maintain any sort of record of what the body of text is. It is simply a summary of the word frequency information, to be used as needed.

IXAttributeParser uses IXWeightingDomain to compute word peculiarities when parsing text. The peculiarity of a word in a text sample is its frequency in the sample divided by its frequency in the IXWeightingDomain (in this case called the *reference domain*), normalized by taking the square root. The result is a measure of the frequency of the word in the sample relative to the reference domain. Words that are common in the reference domain receive lesser significance than they would have had, and words that are rare in the reference domain receive greater significance. The effect is to bias the weights with a filter that reduces domain-specific "noise words."

Instance Variables

unsigned int **beenRanked**;
unsigned int **totalTokens**;
unsigned int **uniqueTokens**;
unsigned int **indexCount**;
unsigned int **totalLength**;
void ***tokenArray**;
unsigned int ***tokenIndex**;

beenRanked	YES if tokens have been ranked.
totalTokens	The number of tokens in the sample.
uniqueTokens	The number of unique tokens in the sample.
indexCount	The number of entries in the token index.
totalLength	The total of all the token lengths.
tokenArray	Array of tokens with rank and count.
tokenIndex	Array of offsets into **tokenArray**.

Method Types

Initializing instances	– initFromDomain: – initFromHistogram: – initFromWFTable:
Saving domain information	– writeDomain: – writeHistogram: – writeWFTable:
Counting tokens	– totalTokens – uniqueTokens
Retrieving information about tokens	– countForToken:ofLength: – rankForToken:ofLength: – frequencyOfToken:ofLength: – peculiarityOfToken:ofLength:andFrequency:

Instance Methods

countForToken:ofLength:

– (unsigned int)**countForToken:**(void *)*aToken* **ofLength:**(unsigned int)*aLength*

Returns the number of times *aToken* occurs in the body of text represented by the IXWeightingDomain. *aLength* must be the length, in bytes, of *aToken*.

See also: – **rankForToken:ofLength:**, – **frequencyOfToken:ofLength:**, – **peculiarityOfToken:ofLength:andFrequency:**

frequencyOfToken:ofLength:

– (float)**frequencyOfToken:**(void *)*aToken* **ofLength:**(unsigned int)*aLength*

Returns the frequency of occurrence for *aToken* in the body of text represented by the IXWeightingDomain. *aLength* must be the length, in bytes, of *aToken*. The frequency is equal to the number of times *aToken* occurs divided by the total number of tokens in the IXWeightingDomain.

See also: – **peculiarityOfToken:ofLength:andFrequency:**, – **countForToken:ofLength:**, – **rankForToken:ofLength:**

initFromDomain:

– **initFromDomain:**(NXStream *)*stream*

Initializes a newly allocated IXWeightingDomain from *stream*, which should contain data in domain format as created by the **writeDomain:** method.

See also: – **initFromHistogram:**, – **initFromWFTable:**, – **writeDomain:**

initFromHistogram:

– **initFromHistogram:**(NXStream *)*stream*

Initializes the IXWeightingDomain from *stream*, which should contain data in histogram format as created by the **writeHistogram:** method.

See also: – **initFromDomain:**, – **initFromWFTable:**, – **writeHistogram:**

initFromWFTable:

– **initFromWFTable:**(NXStream *)*stream*

Initializes the IXWeightingDomain from *stream*, which should contain data in the NeXTSTEP Release 2 WFTable format.

See also: – **initFromDomain:**, – **initFromHistogram:**, – **writeWFTable:**

peculiarityOfToken:ofLength:andFrequency:

– (float)**peculiarityOfToken:**(void *)*aToken*
ofLength:(unsigned int)*aLength*
andFrequency:(float)*aFrequency*

Returns the peculiarity of *aToken* occurring in some domain with frequency *aFrequency*, relative to the body of text represented by the reference domain. *aLength* must be the length, in bytes, of *aToken*. The peculiarity is equal to the square root of *aFrequency* divided by the frequency of the token within the reference domain.

See also: – **frequencyOfToken:ofLength:**, – **countForToken:ofLength:**, – **rankForToken:ofLength:**

rankForToken:ofLength:

– (unsigned int)**rankForToken:**(void *)*aToken* **ofLength:**(unsigned int)*aLength*

Returns the rank of *aToken* in the IXWeightingDomain; the rank is the token's position in an ordering of the set of unique tokens by count. *aLength* must be the length, in bytes, of *aToken*. The token with the highest count has a rank of 1; the token with the lowest count has a rank equal to the number of unique tokens.

See also: – **countForToken:ofLength:**, – **frequencyOfToken:ofLength:**, – **peculiarityOfToken:ofLength:andFrequency:**

totalTokens

– (unsigned int)**totalTokens**

Returns the total number of tokens in the IXWeightingDomain; that is, the sum of the number of occurrences each token, over the set of unique tokens.

See also: – **uniqueTokens**

uniqueTokens

– (unsigned int)**uniqueTokens**

Returns the number of unique tokens in the IXWeightingDomain.

See also: – **totalTokens**

writeDomain:

– **writeDomain:**(NXStream *)*stream*

Writes the IXWeightingDomain to *stream* in domain format.

See also: – **writeHistogram:**, – **writeWFTable:**, – **initFromDomain:**

writeHistogram:

– **writeHistogram:**(NXStream *)*stream*

Writes the IXWeightingDomain to *stream* in histogram format.

See also: – **writeDomain:**, – **writeWFTable:**, – **initFromHistogram:**

writeWFTable:

– **writeWFTable:**(NXStream *)*stream*

Writes the IXWeightingDomain to *stream* in NeXTSTEP Release 2 WFTable format.

See also: – **writeDomain:**, – **writeHistogram:**, – **initFromWFTable:**

Protocols

IXAttributeReading

Adopted By: IXAttributeReader

Declared In: indexing/IXAttributeReader.h

Protocol Description

IXAttributeReading defines a single method that lexically analyzes a stream of text for consumption by a parser, such as an IXAttributeParser. Objects that conform to this protocol are called *attribute readers*, and are used to reduce source text into discrete lexemes associated with textual attributes, which may be collected into histograms by the parser.

An attribute reader must be able to read ASCII, RTF, and an extension of RTF called Attribute Reader Format (ARF). The reader must return from its **analyzeStream:** method a stream of text in ARF. Attribute Reader Format is described under "Attribute Reader Format" in the "Other Features" section, later in this chapter.

Instance Methods

analyzeStream:

– (NXStream *)**analyzeStream:**(NXStream *)*stream*

Scans *stream* for lexemes, returning a stream which contains the results of the lexical analysis in Attribute Reader Format. Several objects that implement this protocol may be chained together, each one further analyzing the output of its predecessor.

IXBlobWriting

Adopted By: IXRecordManager

Declared In: indexing/protocols.h

Protocol Description

The IXBlobWriting protocol defines a mechanism for storing and retrieving amorphous data items, called *blobs*, that aren't susceptible to structural serialization due to unknown length or complexity. Some examples of blobs are compressed sounds, serialized graph structures, and relocatable code modules.

During the writing or reading of an object that conforms to the IXRecordTranscription protocol, the transcriber sends the object a notification message defined by that protocol (**source:willWriteRecord:** or **source:didReadRecord:**, respectively); if the transcriber conforms to this protocol, the object may request that the transcriber write or read blobs.

The methods defined by this protocol identify blobs by name and record handle. This provides a means of maintaining property lists on behalf of transcribed records. Since this protocol provides no way of iterating over the property names or of getting a list of all blob names for an object, users should store their own such lists in a well known blob if the list membership can't be determined statically.

Instance Methods

getValue:andLength:ofBlob:forRecord:

– (BOOL)**getValue:**(void **)*aValue*
    andLength:(unsigned int *)*aLength*
    ofBlob:(const char *)*blobName*
    forRecord:(unsigned int)*aHandle*

Returns by reference the value and length of *blobName* for the record identified by *aHandle*. Returns YES if the blob is successfully retrieved, NO if it isn't.

setValue:andLength:ofBlob:forRecord:

– (BOOL)**setValue:**(const void *)*aValue*
andLength:(unsigned int)*aLength*
ofBlob:(const char *)*blobName*
forRecord:(unsigned int)*aHandle*

Stores the value and length of a blob for the record identified by *aHandle*, associating it with the name *blobName*. Returns YES if the blob is successfully stored, NO if it wasn't.

If *aLength* is 0, the blob won't be stored, and this method will return NO.

IXBlockAndStoreAccess

Adopted By: IXBTree
IXFileFinder
IXRecordManager
IXStoreBlock
IXStoreDirectory

Declared In: store/protocols.h

Protocol Description

The IXBlockAndStoreAccess protocol defines methods for initializing and freeing store clients. A *store client* is any object that keeps data in an IXStore. You use this protocol both to create new store client instances, and to initialize store client instances from data previously stored in an IXStore. IXBlockAndStoreAccess defines methods based directly on IXStore; that is, store clients are identified by the IXStore's integer block handles. A related protocol, IXNameAndFileAccess, defines methods for accessing store clients by name instead of by handles.

A store client is different from most Objective C objects in that it uses data which can outlive it, but which is considered an integral part of the store client itself. Unlike objects unarchived from an Interface Builder nib file, which have no connection to that file, a store client remains connected to its store, and can both read and write data in it. This gives store clients a limited form of persistence.

A store client instance can be initialized from scratch in an IXStore, or it can be initialized from previously created data in that same IXStore; the second type of initialization is called *reconstituting* or *opening* a store client. When a store client instance is freed, only its run-time data is destroyed; the data in the store remains intact, ready to be used by a later store client instance. A store client can also completely destroy itself by removing its data from the store and freeing itself.

When a new store client is initialized, it's given an IXStore in which to keep its persistent data. One of the first things it does is create a block in that IXStore. This "boot block" can contain the handles of other blocks, making it a single point of entry for reconstituting the store client from that pre-existing data. The boot block is identified with the store client's persistent image, in that a later instance can use that single block to retrieve all of the data created by the original instance.

Temporary Store Clients

In addition to the methods in this protocol, you may find it convenient to implement a simple **init** method that initializes a store client for temporary use by creating an IXStore private to that instance, and which that instance will free when it receives a **free** message. In such a case, of course, the store client will essentially be like most other objects; its storage won't be persistent, but will be freed when it is.

Closing a Store

Before a store is closed (that is, before the IXStore object is sent a **free** message), all of the store clients should be properly cleaned up and freed. This involves freeing the store clients, sending either **abortTransaction** or **commitTransaction** if needed to the IXStore until all transactions are completed, and finally, freeing the IXStore object.

It's important to complete all transactions before freeing the store, since a store client may actually be working with an IXStoreFile. If the store is actually an IXStoreFile, changes made since the store file was opened aren't flushed when the IXStoreFile is freed; pending transactions have to be explicitly completed beforehand, or they're all effectively aborted.

Method Types

Initializing and freeing a client	– initInStore: – initFromBlock:inStore: – freeFromStore + freeFromBlock:andStore:
Retrieving the block and store	– getBlock:andStore:

Class Methods

freeFromBlock:andStore:

+ **freeFromBlock:**(unsigned int)*aHandle* **andStore:**(IXStore *)*aStore*

Removes from *aStore* the client whose boot block is identified by *aHandle*, along with all storage that client had created. Normally, your code would have to instantiate a client for the data in the block identified by *aHandle* and send it a **freeFromStore** message. This method provides a convenient way to remove an object from an IXStore without your code having to allocate and initialize it. Returns **self**.

One way to implement this method is to create an instance of the client class, reconstitute it from *aHandle*, and free it. Here's a simple example, without any error handling:

```
+ freeFromBlock:(unsigned int)aHandle andStore:(IXStore *)aStore
{
    [[[self alloc] initFromBlock:aHandle inStore:aStore]
        freeFromStore];
    return self;
}
```

Classes whose instances normally perform a lot of time-consuming initialization should implement a lightweight initialization method, which prepares the instance only to access its storage for efficient removal from its IXStore.

If your store client class only creates a single block in its IXStore, you can implement this method by simply freeing that block:

```
+ freeFromBlock:(unsigned int)aHandle andStore:(IXStore *)aStore
{
    [aStore freeBlock:aHandle];
    return self;
}
```

See also: – **freeFromStore**

Instance Methods

freeFromStore

– **freeFromStore**

Removes the receiver's storage from its IXStore and frees the run-time object. A store client's **free** method simply frees the run-time object without affecting any data in the IXStore. Returns **nil**.

See also: + **freeFromBlock:andStore:**, – **free** (Object)

getBlock:andStore:

– **getBlock:**(unsigned int *)*aHandle* **andStore:**(IXStore **)*aStore*

Returns by reference the handle of the receiver's boot block, and its IXStore. Also returns **self**.

Since a store client needs to record its boot block handle and its IXStore to function properly, implementing this method is simply a matter of putting those values into *aHandle* and *aStore*.

initFromBlock:inStore:

– **initFromBlock:**(unsigned int)*aHandle* **inStore:**(IXStore *)*aStore*

Initializes the receiver using existing data from the boot block identified by *aHandle* in *aStore*. That block should have been created by a previous invocation of the **initInStore:** method on the original instance of the store client. The receiver isn't required to be of the same class as the original creator of the store data, but it must be able to make sense of that data. Returns **self** if successful, or **nil** if the receiver can't be initialized (for example, if *aHandle* doesn't exist in *aStore*).

To implement this method, simply access the data in *aHandle* to set up a usable state for the client instance. This may involve opening other blocks whose handles are stored in the boot block.

Note: While a store client instance exists, it's considered to own its data in the IXStore. Your code should never use this method a second time with a specific boot block unless it's known for certain that any previous instance using that data has been freed (or that both instances will be using the storage for read-only access). If a second store client is initialized from the same block as an active client, the data associated with it will probably be corrupted, since there is no means provided in the Indexing Kit for synchronizing changes made by the two instances.

See also: – **initInStore:**

initInStore:

– **initInStore:**(IXStore *)*aStore*

Initializes the receiver, creating a new boot block in *store*. After initialization, the boot block can be used to hold the receiver's data. That block's handle can be retrieved with **getBlock:andStore:**. Returns **self** if successful, or **nil** if the receiver can't initialize itself.

To implement this method, simply create a block in *aStore*, record its handle as the boot block, and store whatever initialization values your client may need there. If your client needs to use several blocks within *aStore*, it can also create those, and store their handles in its boot block. This allows a later instance to retrieve those blocks when it receives an **initFromBlock:andStore:** message.

See also: – **initFromBlock:inStore:**

IXComparatorSetting

Adopted By: IXBTree

Declared In: btree/protocols.h

Protocol Description

The IXComparatorSetting protocol is implemented by objects that compare data elements of unknown type using a comparison function provided by the client. This gives the object great flexibility in handling an open set of data types. A comparator function as used by this protocol is of type (IXComparator *), which has the form:

typedef int **IXComparator**(const void **data1*, unsigned short *length1*,
  const void **data2*, unsigned short *length2*, const void **context*);

where *data1* is a pointer to any block of *length1* bytes, *data2* is a pointer to a block of *length2* bytes, and *context* is a pointer to blind data which may be used by the comparator function (for an example of this, see **IXFormatComparator()** in the "Functions" section, later in this chapter). The comparator function returns a number less than 0 if *data1* is considered less then *data2*, greater than 0 if *data1* is considered greater than *data2*, and equal to zero if *data1* and *data2* are considered equal.

There are several standard comparator functions defined by the Indexing Kit. See the "Functions" section for the full listing.

Comparator functions are intended to compare serial arrays of data, particularly keys in an associative store (like an IXBTree or a hash table). A key is always serialized when placed in a store; the resulting representation doesn't contain pointers. A comparator function like **IXCompareStrings()** doesn't expect to receive arrays of character pointers; rather, it expects *data1* and *data2* to be serial arrays containing strings separated by embedded nulls.

Instance Methods

getComparator:andContext:

– **getComparator:**(IXComparator **)*aComparator*
andContext:(const void **)*aContext*

Returns by reference the function used to compare data elements, and the context associated with the function. *aContext* is blind data that the object passes to the comparator function as the *context* argument. Returns **self**.

setComparator:andContext:

– **setComparator:**(IXComparator *)*aComparator*
andContext:(const void *)*aContext*

Sets the function used to compare data elements, and the context associated with the function. *aContext* is blind data that the object passes to its comparator function as the *context* argument whenever it calls that function. Returns **self**.

IXComparisonSetting

Adopted By: IXBTree

Declared In: btree/protocols.h

Protocol Description

The IXComparisonSetting protocol is implemented by objects that compare data elements of unknown type using a comparison format that encodes the types of the data elements. The comparison format is a string containing an Objective C type encoding.

An object implementing this protocol compares two arrays of Objective C scalar values: signed and unsigned short and long integers, signed and unsigned bytes (characters), and single- and double-precision floating-point numbers. Based on the comparison format, an object implementing this protocol iteratively compares the elements of the two arrays until it finds an element that isn't equal to its counterpart in the other array, or until it exhausts the elements of one or both arrays. If the two arrays are otherwise equal, the shorter one is considered the lesser of the two.

Comparison Format Interpretation

A comparison format is simply a string containing an Objective C type encoding for the arrays to be compared. For example, to compare data items as arrays of long integers, the comparison format would be "[5I]" (the number specified in the array is currently ignored).

There are two classes and one function in the Indexing Kit that interpret comparison formats: IXRecordManager, IXPostingList and **IXFormatComparator()**. A given comparison format may be interpreted differently by all three, due to differences in the physical representation of the data. The following table summarizes the general interpretation policy as implemented by **IXFormatComparator()**:

Code	Meaning
c	A **char**
i	An **int**
s	A **short int**
l	A **long int**
C	An **unsigned char**
I	An **unsigned int**
S	An **unsigned short int**
L	An **unsigned long int**
f	A **float**
d	A **double**
*	A character string (**char ***, null-terminated)
@	treated as an **unsigned long int**
#	treated as an **unsigned long int**
:	treated as an character string
^*type*	A pointer to valid *type*
[	ignored (count is stripped)
]	ignored if balanced by start of array

IXFormatComparator() doesn't follow pointers, since the data is assumed to be serialized. Also, since **IXFormatComparator()** uses the other comparator functions to perform its comparisons, only the first valid component is used, except that the following pairs are legal:

Format String	Comparator used
"I*"	**IXCompareUnsignedAndStrings()**
"L*"	**IXCompareUnsignedAndStrings()**
"*I" or "*L"	**IXCompareStringAndUnsigneds()**

IXRecordManager derives comparison formats automatically from the return types of its attributes' selectors. Pointers are followed, and class references ("@") are treated as name ("*") followed by version ("I"), and **IXCompareStringAndUnsigneds()** is used.

IXPostingList also derives comparison formats from the return types of the selectors used to sort its contents. Pointers are followed to arbitrary depth.

Instance Methods

comparisonFormat

– (const char *)**comparisonFormat**

Returns a character string containing an Objective C type encoding describing data elements compared by the receiver.

setComparisonFormat:

– **setComparisonFormat:**(const char *)*format*

Records a character string containing an Objective C type encoding describing data elements compared by the receiver. Returns **self**.

IXCursorPositioning

Adopted By: IXBTreeCursor

Declared In: btree/protocols.h

Protocol Description

The IXCursorPositioning protocol defines methods for locating an item in a key space. A *key space* is an ordered set of all possible keys of a particular type. An example of an integer key space is the natural ordering of integers; one key space of type **char *** is the lexical ordering of all ASCII strings; another key space of type **char *** is the case insensitive lexical ordering of all ASCII strings. The range of a key space may be restricted by a maximum key length.

Key spaces are generally used to store values, each key being associated with exactly one value. Consider a key space that associates string-valued keys with personnel records. Say the key contains the last name of the employee, followed by a comma, followed by the first name. Using an IXBTreeCursor, the record for an employee named Jane Draper could be found as follows:

```
IXBTreeCursor *cursor;
BOOL           found;
char          *aKey = "Draper,Jane";

// the null terminator is included in the length by convention
found = [cursor·setKey:(void *)aKey andLength:1+strlen(aKey)];
```

setKey:andLength: returns YES if the cursor successfully locates a value for the given key. The cursor will remain positioned at that key following the operation, and subsequent messages to the cursor may either access that value, or move the cursor to another position. For example, telling the cursor to write a value in the example above would overwrite Jane Draper's record, and telling the cursor to remove the value would remove her record from the key space. Telling the cursor to move to the next key in the key space would cause it to access a different employee's record. The cursor is therefore like an agent in the key space; it can move about and operate on the values associated with keys.

If the **setKey:andLength:** in the preceding example returned NO, it would indicate that there was no record associated with the key "Draper,Jane"; the cursor would nevertheless be positioned at that key. This may be between two existing records, before the first record, or after the last existing record. Subsequent messages to the cursor may cause it to slide forward to the next key with an associated record.

Sliding and Insertion

A cursor at a position with no key can't access a value there. If the cursor is asked to access a value anyway, it has two options: try to find a value, or indicate that it can't access one. Where it makes sense, a cursor should try to find a value by sliding forward in the key space to the next actual key. When this isn't possible or desirable, the cursor should indicate that it can't find or access a value, by raising the IX_NotFoundError exception.

Suppose the IXBTreeCursor above is asked to look for Anne Draper instead of Jane, and that there is no record for Anne Draper; also, there are no records whose keys would fall between Anne Draper and Jane Draper. The IXBTreeCursor will position itself *before* Jane's key and return NO:

```
aKey = "Draper,Anne";

found = [cursor setKey:(void *)aKey andLength:1+strlen(aKey)];
```

In this case, **found** will be NO, indicating that there is no key with the value "Draper,Anne". If the IXBTreeCursor is asked to read the value of either the key or the personnel record, the key will slide forward to Jane's record and return that data. For example, on determining that there is no record with the key "Draper,Anne", the program could send **getKey:andLength:** to find out where the cursor actually landed. In this case, the cursor will move forward to Jane Draper's record, and return the key "Draper,Jane", along with its length. This lets the program know that the cursor landed before Jane's record (and incidentally finds the record the program was actually interested in).

If the IXBTreeCursor is asked to write a value at a location where there is none, the value and the key are added to the key space. Since the cursor is where it should be for the key being added, it can simply create a key and store the record under the key. There will then be an entry in the IXBTree for Anne Draper. This is exactly how an insertion is performed with a cursor: set the key position with **setKey:andLength:**, and if the return value is NO, a write message immediately following will insert the value provided under the key.

If the IXBTreeCursor is asked to write inside or to remove the record at a location where there is no key, there's a problem. Since there is no record, and since writing into part of a record or removing it would change data that the programmer probably doesn't want altered (namely, the record for the next actual key), the IXBTreeCursor will indicate that there is no value to write into by raising IX_NotFoundError.

Iteration and Partial Lookup

A cursor can be explicitly told to slide forward with the **setNext** method, which returns YES if there is a next key and the cursor has moved there, and NO if the cursor was already at the last key and has moved past it. By sending a **setFirst** message to a cursor, which positions it at the first key (if there is one), and then many **setNext** messages, it's possible to iterate over the entire set of keys and values stored in the key space. The same can be done in reverse order with **setLast** and **setPrevious**.

Cursor sliding and iteration can be used together to perform partial lookups, where the goal is to find all records whose keys lie within a certain range; for example, finding all employees whose last name is Draper. This can be done by positioning the cursor at the lowest valued key, and moving it forward until the key becomes greater than the greatest valued desired. For example, to find all employees whose last name is Draper:

```
BOOL  found;
char *aKey, *lastName;
int   aLength;

/*
 * Tell the cursor to find the first record whose key starts with
 * "Draper,".  Notice the comma at the end; this is to make sure
 * the last name is matched exactly.
 */
aKey = lastName = "Draper,";
found = [cursor setKey:(void *)aKey andLength:1+strlen(aKey)];

/*
 * This forces the cursor to move to a real key if it didn't hit
 * one, which is probably the case.
 */
[cursor getKey:&(void *)aKey andLength:&aLength];

/*
 * While the key contains the last name we're looking for,
 * keep processing.  If the range were integers from 10-100,
 * aKey would be an int *, *aKey would be set to 10 for
 * the setKey:andLength: method above, and this test
 * would be (*aKey <= 100).
 */
while (strncmp(aKey, lastName, strlen(lastName)) > 0) {
    processRecordAtCursor(cursor); // process the record
    found = [cursor setNext];      // go to the next one
    if (found == NO) break;        // at end of key space
}
```

Method Types

Absolute positioning	– setKey:andLength: – getKey:andLength:
Relative positioning	– setFirst – setNext – setLast – setPrevious
Checking positioning success	– isMatch

Instance Methods

getKey:andLength:

– (BOOL)**getKey:**(void **)*aKey* **andLength:**(unsigned int *)*aLength*

Returns by reference the key defining the cursor's position in its key space, along with the key's length.

If the cursor is at a key which has a value associated with it, this method returns YES. If the cursor is between two values or before the first one, this method advances the cursor to the key for the next value, returns that key by reference, and returns YES. If the cursor is beyond the last key, this method returns NO, and the contents of *aKey* and *aLength* aren't set.

aKey isn't guaranteed to remain the same after subsequent messages to the cursor, since the cursor reallocate its buffer or may slide as a side effect of a message. Your code should copy their contents if it needs to save them. Your code should *not* write into *aKey*; doing so will corrupt the cursor.

See also: – setKey:andLength:, – isMatch

isMatch

– (BOOL)**isMatch**

Returns YES if the cursor is on a key with an associated value, NO if the cursor is between two values or past either end of the set of values.

If the cursor isn't on a key with a value, then trying to get a key or read a value can cause the cursor to move forward to the next key with a value before reading the key or value, or raise IX_ArgumentError if the cursor can't move (because it's at the end of the key space). Any attempt to write into or remove a nonexistent value will raise IX_ArgumentError.

See also: – setKey:andLength:, – getKey:andLength:

setFirst

– (BOOL)**setFirst**

If there is at least one value associated with a key, this method positions the cursor at the first element's key and returns YES. Otherwise it returns NO, and any attempt to remove or read a value at the cursor's position will raise IX_ArgumentError.

See also: – **setNext**, – **setLast**, – **setPrevious**

setKey:andLength:

– (BOOL)**setKey:**(void *)*aKey* **andLength:**(unsigned int)*aLength*

Sets the current position of the cursor to that specified by *aKey* and *aLength*. If a value is associated with *aKey*, returns YES. Otherwise returns NO. If there is no value with a key before *aKey*, this method positions the cursor before the first value. If there is no value with a key after *aKey*, this method positions the cursor beyond the last values.

If this method returns NO, then any attempt to write into or remove a value at the cursor's position will raise IX_ArgumentError, and any attempt to read a key or value will cause the cursor to move to the key for the next value before reading the key or value, or raise IX_ArgumentError if the cursor can't move (because it's at the end of the key space).

See also: – **getKey:andLength:**, – **isMatch**

setLast

– (BOOL)**setLast**

If there is at least one value associated with a key, this method positions the cursor at the last element's key and returns YES. Otherwise it returns NO, and any attempt to remove or read a value at the cursor's position will raise IX_ArgumentError.

See also: – **setPrevious**, – **setFirst**, – **setNext**

setNext

– (BOOL)**setNext**

Sets the cursor's position to the next key with an associated value. Returns YES if there is a next element, and NO if the cursor is already positioned at the end of the key space. If this method returns NO, then any attempt to remove or read a value at the cursor's position will raise IX_ArgumentError.

See also: – **setFirst**, – **setLast**, – **setPrevious**

setPrevious

– (BOOL)**setPrevious**

Sets the cursor's position to the previous key with an associated value. Returns YES if there is a previous element, and NO if the cursor was positioned at the beginning of the key space and has moved to a position before the first key. If this method returns NO, then any attempt to read a value will cause the cursor to move to the next key with a value, or raise IX_ArgumentError if the cursor can't move (because it's at the end of the key space).

See also: – **setLast**, – **setFirst**, – **setNext**

IXFileFinderConfiguration

Adopted By: IXFileFinder

Declared In: indexing/IXFileFinder.h

Protocol Description

The IXFileFinderConfiguration protocol defines methods for controlling how an IXFileFinder builds and updates its index, and how it treats various files and properties of the file system. This information is kept in the file finder's store, so your code doesn't have to re-establish a configuration each time it uses the file finder.

Method Types

Managing attribute parsers	– setAttributeParsers: – getAttributeParsers:
Generating descriptions	– setGeneratesDescriptions: – generatesDescriptions
Enabling automatic updating	– setUpdatesAutomatically: – updatesAutomatically
Setting file system options	– setCrossesDeviceChanges: – crossesDeviceChanges – setFollowsSymbolicLinks: – followsSymbolicLinks – setScansForModifiedFiles: – scansForModifiedFiles
Ignoring files	– setIgnoredTypes: – ignoredTypes – setIgnoredNames: – ignoredNames

Instance Methods

crossesDeviceChanges

– (BOOL)**crossesDeviceChanges**

Returns YES if the file finder indexes files stored on physical devices other than the device that the primary directory (the file finder's root path) is on, NO if it doesn't. For example, if the user has a hard disk mounted in the file finder's primary directory, this method will return YES if the file finder indexes and searches files on that disk. The default is NO.

See also: – **setCrossesDeviceChanges:**

followsSymbolicLinks

– (BOOL)**followsSymbolicLinks**

Returns YES if the file finder follows symbolic links when building or updating indexes, NO if it ignores them. The default is NO.

See also: – **setFollowsSymbolicLinks:**

generatesDescriptions

– (BOOL)**generatesDescriptions**

Returns YES if the file finder generates descriptions for the files it indexes based on their contents, NO if it doesn't.

See also: – **setGeneratesDescriptions:**

getAttributeParsers:

– **getAttributeParsers:**(List *)*aList*

Empties *aList* and fills it with the IXAttributeParsers used by the IXFileFinder. These are the objects the file finder uses to parse files when building or updating indexes. The sender of this message is responsible for creating and freeing the List, but shouldn't free the objects put in the List. Returns **self**.

See also: – **setAttributeParsers:**

ignoredNames

– (char *)**ignoredNames**

Returns a string containing a newline-separated list of names of files that the file finder ignores when building or updating indexes, or performing queries. The file names are relative to the file finder's root path. The sender is responsible for freeing the string returned by this method.

See also: – **setIgnoredNames:**, – **ignoredTypes**

ignoredTypes

– (char *)**ignoredTypes**

Returns a string containing a newline-separated list of extensions of files that the file finder ignores when building or updating indexes, or performing queries. A file type is determined by the file finder on the basis of its extension or a brief examination of its contents. The sender is responsible for freeing the string returned by this method.

See also: – **setIgnoredTypes:**, – **ignoredNames**

scansForModifiedFiles:

– (BOOL)**scansForModifiedFiles:**

Returns YES if the file finder scans files in the background, checking their modification times against those recorded in its index, and updating the index for files that have been modified. Returns NO if the file finder doesn't perform this background scanning.

See also: – **setScansForModifiedFiles:**

setAttributeParsers:

– **setAttributeParsers:**(List *)*aList*

Replaces the IXAttributeParsers used by the file finder with those in *aList* and frees any of the previous set of IXAttributeParsers that the file finder will no longer use. These are the objects the file finder uses to parse files when building or updating indexes. Returns **self**.

See also: – **getAttributeParsers:**

setCrossesDeviceChanges:

– **setCrossesDeviceChanges:**(BOOL)*flag*

If *flag* is YES, the file finder will index files on physical devices other than the one its primary directory is on. If *flag* is NO, it will ignore other devices. The default is NO. Returns **self**.

See also: – **crossesDeviceChanges**

setFollowsSymbolicLinks:

– **setFollowsSymbolicLinks:**(BOOL)*flag*

If *flag* is YES, the file finder will follow symbolic links when building or updating indexes. If *flag* is NO, the file finder will ignore symbolic links. The default is NO. Returns **self**.

See also: – **followsSymbolicLinks**

setGeneratesDescriptions:

– **setGeneratesDescriptions:**(BOOL)*flag*

If *flag* is YES, the file finder will generate descriptions for the files it indexes based on their contents. If *flag* is NO, it won't generate descriptions.

See also: – **generatesDescriptions**

setIgnoredNames:

– **setIgnoredNames:**(const char *)*names*

Replaces the file finder's set of ignored file names with those in *names*. *names* should be a string containing a newline-separated list of names of files to ignore. Returns **self**.

Each file name should be the name alone, with no path before it. Any files in the file finder's subtree of the file system with that name will be ignored.

See also: – **ignoredFilenames**, – **setIgnoredTypes:**

setIgnoredTypes:

– **setIgnoredTypes:**(const char *)*types*

Replaces the file finder's set of ignored file types with those in *types*. *types* should be a string containing a newline-separated list of file extensions for the types of files to ignore. Returns **self**.

See also: – **ignoredTypes**, – **setIgnoredNames:**

setScansForModifiedFiles:

– **setScansForModifiedFiles:**(BOOL)*flag*

If *flag* is YES, the file finder will scan files in the background, checking their modification times against those recorded in its index, and updating the index for files that have been modified. If *flag* is NO, the file finder won't perform this background scanning.

See also: – **scansForModifiedFiles**

setUpdatesAutomatically:

– **setUpdatesAutomatically:**(BOOL)*flag*

If *flag* is YES, then the file finder records out of date index references whenever a query is performed, and updates its index in the background based on that information. If *flag* is NO, no index checking or background updating is done. The default is YES. Returns **self**.

See also: – **updatesAutomatically**, IXFileFinderQueryAndUpdate protocol

updatesAutomatically

– (BOOL)**updatesAutomatically**

Returns YES if the file finder checks its index whenever a query is performed, and updates it in the background, NO otherwise. The default is YES.

See also: – **setUpdatesAutomatically:**, IXFileFinderQueryAndUpdate protocol

IXFileFinderQueryAndUpdate

Adopted By: IXFileFinder

Declared In: indexing/IXFileFinder.h

Protocol Description

The IXFileFinderQueryAndUpdate protocol defines much of the real functionality of the IXFileFinder class. All of the querying and index building methods are in this protocol. There are also a few methods for getting miscellaneous information about the IXFileFinder.

Sending a Query or an Update Request

The methods for performing a query or updating the file finder's index—**performQuery:atPath:forSender:**, and **updateIndex:atPath:forSender:**—specify an object to be passed as the sender of the message. The file finder can then send messages back to the sender while processing the query or update request.

When a file finder receives a **performQuery:atPath:forSender:** message, it immediately returns a list of all the files in its index that match the supplied query. In addition, if the file finder uses an index and the index is out of date, it checks all of its out of date files in the background to see if they match the query. If the sender of a query responds to **fileFinder:didFindFile:** or **fileFinder:didFindFile:**, then it will receive those messages for out of date files found after the query message has returned. This guarantees that all files in the file finder's directory get checked for every query. To stop receiving these messages after a query has begun, send the file finder a **stopQueryForSender:** message.

When a file finder receives an **updateIndex:atPath:forSender:** message, it checks whether the sender responds to **fileFinder:willAddFile:**. If so, then every time a new file record would be added to the index or changed, it sends that message back to the sender of the update message. The sender can then alter or replace the file record and return it to the file finder. The record returned by the sender is added to the index instead of the original file record.

The sender can be specified as **nil**, in which case no per-file messages will be sent. Passing **nil** as the sender for a query will produce incomplete results if the index is at all out of date.

Method Types

Getting the target directory	– rootPath
Getting the record manager	– recordManager
Performing queries	– performQuery:atPath:forSender: – stopQueryForSender:
Updating indexes	– updateIndexAtPath:forSender: – isUpdating – suspendUpdating – resumeUpdating – clean – reset

Instance Methods

clean

– **clean**

Removes all inaccurate or out of date information from the file finder's index, leaving the index in an incomplete, but otherwise accurate, state. Returns **self**.

See also: – **reset**

isUpdating

– (BOOL)**isUpdating**

Returns YES if the file finder is updating its index in the background. That is, if each time it performs a query, it records those files that are out of date with respect to its index, and updates them in the background.

See also: – **suspendUpdating,** – **resumeUpdating,** – **updateIndexAtPath:forSender:**, – **setUpdatesAutomatically:** (IXFileFinderConfiguration)

performQuery:atPath:forSender:

– (IXPostingList *)**performQuery:**(const char *)*aQuery*
atPath:(const char *)*path*
forSender:*sender*

Performs a query within the file finder's directory for all files within the subdirectory named *path* relative to the file finder's root path. *aQuery* is a string defining a request in the file finder's query language (described under "The Indexing Kit Query Language" in the "Other Features" section of this chapter). If there's an index, it's checked first, and results matching *aQuery* for all valid index entries are returned. If there is no index, or if there are any files that are out of date with respect to the index, the file finder continues its search directly on those files in the background, sending **fileFinder:didFindFile:** or **fileFinder:didFindList:** messages to *sender* as it finds additional files that match *aQuery*. If *sender* is **nil** or doesn't respond to **fileFinder:didFindFile:**, then no background searching is done.

This method returns an IXPostingList containing the immediate results of the query (the file records that were retrieved directly from the index). It contains a set of IXFileRecords containing basic information about the files: their names, types, modification dates, and so on.

See also: – **stopQueryForSender:**, – **fileFinder:didFindFile:** ("Methods Implemented by the Sender of a Query or Update")

recordManager

– **recordManager**

Returns the record manager (usually of class IXRecordManager) used by the file finder to maintain its index.

reset

– **reset**

Removes all information from the file finder's index, but doesn't remove the indexes themselves. This is useful if for rebuilding a file finder's index from scratch: to do so, send this message followed by an **updateIndex:atPath:forSender:** message. Returns **self**.

See also: – **clean**

resumeUpdating

– **resumeUpdating**

Resumes automatic background updating of the file finder's index after a **suspendUpdating** message. If automatic updating hasn't been suspended, this method has no effect. Returns **self**.

See also: – **suspendUpdating**, – **updateIndexAtPath:forSender:**, – **isUpdating**, – **setUpdatesAutomatically:** (IXFileFinderConfiguration)

rootPath

– (const char *)**rootPath**

Returns the full pathname of file finder's primary directory—the top level directory that the indexes are built over. This directory is set when the file finder is initialized, and can't be changed.

stopQueryForSender:

– **stopQueryForSender:***sender*

Stops background searching for the query last requested by *sender*. This is useful if *sender* doesn't want to receive any more **fileFinder:didFindFile:** messages after performing a query (for example, if it was looking for a specific file and found it). This message doesn't need to be sent if the sender passed to **performQuery:atPath:forSender:** doesn't respond to **fileFinder:didFindFile:**, or if the sender was passed as **nil**. Returns **self**.

See also: – **performQuery:atPath:usingIndexes:**, – **fileFinder:didFindFile:** ("Methods Implemented by the Sender of a Query or Update")

suspendUpdating

– **suspendUpdating**

Suspends automatic background updating, if it's being done. Automatic updating may be reestablished with **resumeUpdating**. Returns **self**.

See also: – **resumeUpdating**, – **updateIndexAtPath:forSender:**, – **isUpdating**, – **setUpdatesAutomatically:** (IXFileFinderConfiguration), – **updatesAutomatically** (IXFileFinderConfiguration)

updateIndexAtPath:forSender:

– **updateIndexAtPath:**(const char *)*path* **forSender:***sender*

Updates information in the file finder's index for all files in the subdirectory of the file finder's primary directory named *path* relative to the file finder's root path. If *sender* responds to **fileFinder:willAddFile:**, then during the update the file finder will send that message for every file it discovers that isn't in its index. This operation may take some time. Returns **self**.

See also: – **suspendUpdating**, – **resumeUpdating**, – **isUpdating**, – **fileFinder:willAddFile:** ("Methods Implemented by the Sender of a Query or Update")

Methods Implemented by the Sender of a Query or Update

fileFinder:didFindFile:

– **fileFinder:**(IXFileFinder *)*aFinder* **didFindFile:**(IXFileRecord *)*aRecord*

Sent during a background search by the file finder to the sender of a **performQuery:atPath:forSender:** message when it finds a file matching the sender's query. Returns **self**.

aRecord can be used to access information about the file that matched the query, which can be displayed to the user or processed.

See also: – **performQuery:atPath:forSender:**, – **fileFinder:didFindList:**

fileFinder:didFindList:

– **fileFinder:**(IXFileFinder *)*aFinder* **didFindList:**(IXPostingList *)*aList*

Sent during a background search by the file finder to the sender of a **performQuery:atPath:forSender:** message when it finds a set of files matching the sender's query. Returns **self**.

aList contains IXFileRecord objects, which can be used to access information about the files that matched the query, which can be displayed to the user or processed.

See also: – **performQuery:atPath:forSender:**, – **fileFinder:didFindFile:**

fileFinder:willAddFile:

– **fileFinder:**(IXFileFinder *)*aFinder* **willAddFile:**(IXFileRecord *)*aRecord*

Sent by the file finder to the sender of an **updateIndexAtPath:forSender:** message before it adds *aRecord* to its indexes. The file finder will add the record returned by this method (which should be an IXFileRecord or subclass). The receiver may alter, replace, or even free *aRecord*, and return the record as the receiver wants it added, or **nil** if the receiver doesn't want it added. If it turns out that no changes need to be made, your implementation of this method should simply return *aRecord*.

See also: – **updateIndexAtPath:forSender:**

IXLexemeExtraction

Adopted By: no NeXTSTEP classes

Declared In: indexing/IXAttributeReader.h

Protocol Description

IXLexemeExtraction defines methods implemented by *readers*, which are objects that lexically analyze a stream of text for consumption by a *parser*, such as an IXAttributeParser. IXAttributeReader subclasses that conform to this protocol are called custom readers, as they implement this protocol to customize certain aspects of lexical analysis.

Method Types

Lexing a stream	– getLexeme:inLength:fromStream:
Manipulating a word/lexeme	– foldCase:inLength:

Instance Methods

foldCase:inLength:

– (unsigned int)**foldCase:**(char *)*aString* **inLength:**(unsigned int)*aLength*

Changes all characters in *aString* to be lowercase, according to the rules of the language being read. *aLength* is the length of the string buffer in which *aString* resides, not the length of the string, which is null-terminated. Returns the length of the changed string.

getLexeme:inLength:fromStream:

– (unsigned int)**getLexeme:**(char *)*aString*
inLength:(unsigned int)*aLength*
fromStream:(NXStream *)*stream*

Extracts a lexeme from *stream*, putting it into *aString*. *aLength* is the length of the string buffer into which the receiver may place the lexeme. This method should return the actual length of the string put into the buffer.

This method may be implemented by subclasses of IXAttributeReader that need more control over lexeme recognition than IXAttributeReader's simple delimiter map strategy can provide. This includes readers that need to recognize phrases or idioms (like "joie de vivre") and readers that handle text in non-phonetic alphabets or in streams that contain special escape sequences. For example, the IXJapaneseReader class developed by Canon uses this method to override the default lexeme recognition, in order to detect embedded escape sequences that denote shifts among the three different Kanji character encodings.

IXNameAndFileAccess

Adopted By: IXBTree
IXFileFinder
IXRecordManager
IXStoreDirectory

Incorporates: IXBlockAndStoreAccess

Declared In: store/protocols.h

Protocol Description

The IXNameAndFileAccess protocol defines methods for initializing and freeing store file clients by name instead of by block handle. A store file client is an object that keeps data in a store file (see below). You use this protocol both to create new objects in a store file, and to initialize objects from data previously stored in a store file. For general information on store clients, see the IXBlockAndStoreAccess protocol specification.

Store Files

Files with a ".store" extension are assumed by convention to contain an IXStoreDirectory at block handle 1. You can take advantage of this convention when implementing IXNameAndFileAccess for your class by accessing the contents of the store file through its IXStoreDirectory.

Note: Although the term "store file" can refer to any file created by an IXStoreFile, the term "storage file" is preferred. "Store file," in this protocol specification, refers specifically to a storage file obeying the above convention; that is, a storage file having an IXStoreDirectory at block handle 1 (the ".store" extension merely advertises this fact, and is entirely optional).

A store file can be created by allocating an IXStoreDirectory and sending it **initWithName:inFile:** (with the file name ending in ".store" if desired). This method will create the file if needed, get a block handle for the IXStoreDirectory, and make sure that the handle is 1 before proceeding. If the handle isn't 1, the **initWithName:inFile:** method will free the IXStoreDirectory and return **nil**. Your code can also explicitly create an IXStoreFile and immediately allocate an IXStoreDirectory and send it an **initInStore:** message. An IXStore guarantees that the first block ever allocated from it will have a handle of 1, so you can safely use this technique to manually create a store file.

To open a store file, initialize an IXStoreFile on it with the **initFromFile:forWriting:** method, and then create an IXStoreDirectory and send it an **initFromBlock:andStore:** message with 1 as the block handle and the **id** of the IXStoreFile as the store. You can then use the IXStoreDirectory to access entries in the store file by name, either having it reconstitute its entries, or getting the boot blocks for those entries and sending **initFromBlock:inStore:** messages to instances of the store file clients.

The IXStoreDirectory at block 1 is intended as a root directory for implementing this protocol. Your store file clients shouldn't use it to store named private clients, as this clutters the name space of the root directory. Any clients belonging to a store file client should be accessed only through that client's boot block, and referenced by handle. If your client needs to store other clients by name, it should create a private IXStoreDirectory and record the handle in its own boot block.

Temporary Store File Clients

In addition to the methods in this protocol, you may find it convenient to implement a simple **init** method that initializes the store file client for temporary use by creating an IXStoreFile or IXStore private to that instance. The temporary instance is then responsible for freeing the run-time store and removing any storage file from the file system when it receives a **free** message. In such a case, of course, the store file client will essentially be a regular (nonpersistent) object.

Closing a Store File

Before a store file is closed (that is, before the IXStoreFile object is sent a **free** message), all of the store file clients should be properly cleaned up and freed. This involves freeing the store file clients, sending either **abortTransaction** or **commitTransaction** to the IXStoreFile until all transactions are completed, and finally, freeing the IXStoreFile object (which closes the file). Changes made since the store file was opened aren't flushed when the IXStoreFile is freed; pending transactions have to be explicitly completed beforehand, or they're all effectively aborted.

Method Types

Initializing and freeing a client	– initWithName:inFile:
	– initFromName:inFile:forWriting:
	– freeFromStore
	+ freeFromName:inFile:
Retrieving the block and store	– getName:andFile:

Class Methods

freeFromName:inFile:

+ **freeFromName:**(const char *)*aName* **inFile:**(const char *)*filename*

Removes from *filename* the storage for the named client. Normally, your code would have to instantiate a client for the data stored under *aName* in *filename*, and send that client a **freeFromStore** message. This method provides a convenient way to remove an object from a storage file without allocating and initializing it yourself. Returns **self**.

One way to implement this method is to create an IXStoreDirectory, and have it free the entry with **freeEntryNamed:** (which in turn sends **freeFromBlock:andStore:** to the client's class object). Here's a simple example, without any error handling:

```
+ freeFromName:(const char *)aName andFile:(const char *)filename
{
    IXStoreFile      *theStore;
    IXStoreDirectory *theDirectory;

    theStore = [[IXStoreFile alloc] initFromFile:filename]
                forWriting:YES];
    theDirectory = [[IXStoreDirectory alloc] initFromBlock:1
                    inStore:theStore];
    [theDirectory freeEntryNamed:aName];
    [theDirectory free];
    [[theStore commitTransaction] free];
    return self;
}
```

Notice that **commitTransaction** must be sent to the IXStoreFile before freeing it, or the removal won't take effect.

See also: – **freeFromStore**, – **freeEntryNamed:** (IXStoreDirectory)

Instance Methods

freeFromStore

– **freeFromStore**

Removes the client's data from its IXStoreFile's store file and frees the run-time object. A store file client's **free** method simply frees the run-time object without affecting any data in the store file. Returns **nil**.

See also: + **freeFromName:inFile:**, – **free** (Object)

getName:andFile:

– **getName:**(const char **)*aName* **andFile:**(const char **)*filename*

Returns by reference the name of the client and of the store file in which it keeps its data. Also returns **self**.

A store file client must record at least its name (preferably in an instance variable). The file name can be retrieved from the IXStoreFile by sending it a **filename** message. If this is done, the implementation of this method can simply put those values into *aName* and *filename*.

initFromName:inFile:forWriting:

– **initFromName:**(const char *)*aName*
  inFile:(const char *)*filename*
  forWriting:(BOOL)*flag*

Initializes the receiver from data previously stored in *filename* under entry *aName*. That data should have been created by a previous invocation of the **initWithName:inFile:** method on the original instance of the store file client. If *flag* is YES, *filename* is opened for reading and writing. If *flag* is NO, *filename* is opened for reading only; changes can be made to the store file's data, but they won't be flushed out to disk. The receiver isn't required to be of the same class as the original creator of the store data, but it must be able to make sense of it. Returns **self** if successful, or **nil** if the receiver can't be initialized (for example, if *aName* doesn't exist in *filename*, or if *filename* itself doesn't exist).

One way to implement this method is to create an IXStoreDirectory, have it get the block for the entry named *aName*, and initialize from that block. Here's a simple example, without any error handling:

```
- initFromName:(const char *)aName
    inFile:(const char *)filename
    forWriting:(BOOL)flag
{
    IXStoreFile       *theStore;
    IXStoreDirectory *theDirectory;
    unsigned int       bootBlock;

    theStore = [[IXStoreFile alloc] initFromFile:filename
                forWriting:flag];
    theDirectory = [[IXStoreDirectory alloc] initFromBlock:1
                    inStore:theStore];
    [theDirectory getBlock:&bootBlock ofEntryNamed:aName];
```

```
    /*
     * Take advantage of the IXBlockAndStoreAccess protocol.
     */
    [self initFromBlock:bootBlock andStore:theStore];
    [theDirectory free];
    /* Don't free theStore. */
    return self;
}
```

Notice that the IXStoreFile has to be created and retained separately from the IXStoreDirectory, which is freed. This implementation also assumes that the client conforms to the IXBlockAndStoreAccess protocol.

Note: While a store file client instance exists, it's considered to own its data in the store file. Your code should never use this method a second time with a specific name unless it's known for certain that any previous instance using that data has been freed (or that both instances will be using the storage for read-only access). If a second store file client is initialized from the same name as an active client, the data associated with it will probably be corrupted, since there is no means provided for synchronizing changes made by the two instances.

See also: – **initWithName:inFile:**

initWithName:inFile:

– **initWithName:**(const char *)*aName* **inFile:**(const char *)*filename*

Initializes the receiver to create and keep its data in *filename* (creating the file if necessary) under the name *aName*. Returns **self**, or **nil** if the receiver can't initialize itself (for example, if a store file client named *aName* already exists, or if *filename* couldn't be created).

Here's a simple example implementation, without any error handling:

```
- initWithName:(const char *)name inFile:(const char *)aFile
{
    IXStoreFile       *theStore;
    IXStoreDirectory *theDirectory;
    IXBTree           *theEntry;

    theStore = [[IXStoreFile alloc] initFromFile:aFile
                forWriting:YES];  // Have to write to initialize
```

```
    /*
     * If the file doesn't exist, create a new one.
     */
     if (nil == theStore) {
         theStore = [[IXStoreFile alloc] initWithFile:aFile];
         if (nil == theStore) return [self free];
     }

     theDirectory = [IXStoreDirectory alloc];
     [theDirectory initFromBlock:1 inStore:theStore]

    /*
     * If the file was created, there won't be anything in the store,
     * so create a new one; it's guaranteed to have block 1.
     * (This isn't the best way to check that the store file is new.)
     */
     if (nil == theDirectory) {
         theDirectory = [[IXStoreDirectory alloc]
                             initInStore:theStore];
     }

    /*
     * Take advantage of the IXBlockAndStoreAccess protocol.
     */
     [self initInStore:theStore];

    /*
     * entryName is an instance variable.  All store file clients
     * should cache their name and at least the id of the IXStoreFile.
     */
     entryName = NXCopyStringBufferFromZone(name, NXZoneFromPtr(self));
     [theDirectory addEntryNamed:aName forObject:self];
     [theDirectory free];
     [theStore commitTransaction];  // Don't free the store file.
     return self;
}
```

See also: **– initFromName:inFile:forWriting:**

IXPostingExchange

Adopted By: IXPostingCursor
IXPostingList
IXPostingSet

Declared In: btree/protocols.h

Protocol Description

The IXPostingExchange protocol allows Indexing Kit classes to exchange their postings with one another. A *posting* is an optionally weighted opaque reference. A posting set is an array of postings ordered by handle, with no duplicates.

Instance Methods

getCount:andPostings:

– **getCount:**(unsigned int *)*count* **andPostings:**(IXPosting **)*thePostings*

Returns by reference the number of postings, and a copy of the postings sorted by handle. The sender of this message is responsible for freeing the postings when they are no longer needed. Returns **self**.

setCount:andPostings:

– **setCount:**(unsigned int)*count* **andPostings:**(IXPosting *)*postings*

Sets the number of postings to *count*, and installs a copy of the contents of *postings* into the receiver. The sender of this message is responsible for freeing the postings when they are no longer needed. (Note: IXPostingCursor frees its postings.) Returns **self**.

IXPostingOperations

Adopted By:	IXPostingCursor IXPostingSet
Declared In:	btree/protocols.h

Protocol Description

The IXPostingOperations protocol defines methods for manipulating postings. See the IXPostingExchange protocol specification for a description of the term "posting."

The IXPostingOperations protocol requires the implementor to logically order its postings by handle, eliminating duplicates, and to maintain a cursor on this ordering which defines a current selection. This protocol defines methods for the selection of postings by position or by handle, and for iteration over the entire set of postings.

Method Types

Manipulating postings by handle	
	– addHandle:withWeight: – removeHandle:
Getting the number of postings	– count
Emptying a posting set	– empty
Traversing a posting set	– setHandle: – getHandle:andWeight: – setFirstHandle – setNextHandle

Instance Methods

addHandle:withWeight:

– **addHandle:**(unsigned int)*aHandle* **withWeight:**(unsigned int)*aWeight*

Adds a posting consisting of *aHandle* and *aWeight* to the set. If *aHandle* is already present, assigns the posting a new weight by averaging *aWeight* and the existing weight. (Note: if *aHandle* is already present, IXPostingCursor overwrites the existing weight with *aWeight*). Returns **self**.

See also: **– removeHandle:**, **– getHandle:andWeight:**

count

– (unsigned int)**count**

Returns the number of postings in the set.

empty

– empty

Removes all postings from the set. Returns **self**.

See also: **– removeHandle:**

getHandle:andWeight:

– (unsigned int)**getHandle:**(unsigned int *)*aHandle*
    andWeight:(unsigned int *)*aWeight*

Returns by reference the handle and weight of the selected posting. Explicitly returns the handle, or 0 if the current selection is undefined.

See also: **– setHandle:**

removeHandle:

– **removeHandle:**(unsigned int)*aHandle*

If a posting with handle *aHandle* exists, removes that posting. Returns **self**.

See also: **– addHandle:withWeight:**, **– getHandle:andWeight:**

setFirstHandle

– (unsigned int)**setFirstHandle**

Selects the first posting, and returns that posting's handle, or 0 if the set is empty.

See also: – **setNextHandle**, – **setHandle:**

setHandle:

– (unsigned int)**setHandle:**(unsigned int)*aHandle*

Selects the posting with handle *aHandle*, and returns that posting's handle. If the value returned isn't *aHandle*, that posting wasn't found, and the next higher-numbered posting is selected.

Note: For both IXPostingSet and IXPostingCursor, this is an efficient operation, with a cost on the order of $O\log_2(n)$, where n is the number of postings.

See also: – **getHandle:andWeight:**

setNextHandle

– (unsigned int)**setNextHandle**

Selects the next posting. Returns the handle for that posting, or 0 if there are no more postings.

See also: – **setFirstHandle**, – **setHandle:**

IXRecordDiscarding

Adopted By: IXRecordManager

Declared In: indexing/protocols.h

Protocol Description

The IXRecordDiscarding protocol defines methods for marking records for deletion, for reclaiming deleted records and for cleaning their repository. Discarded records are treated as though they don't exist—they can't be read, for example. They will either be physically removed when the repository is cleaned, or explicitly reclaimed by the caller. This protocol is designed to support lazy index maintenance; references to discarded records may safely be allowed to remain in the inversions until the repository is cleaned. It also supports a form of disaster recovery when add and discard operations are used instead of replacement.

Method Types

Discarding records	– discardRecord: – reclaimRecord:
Removing discarded records	– clean

Instance Methods

clean

– clean

Removes all discarded records from the receiver. Those records will no longer be reclaimable. Returns **self**.

See also: – **discardRecord:**, – **reclaimRecord:**, – **empty** (IXRecordWriting)

discardRecord:

– **discardRecord:**(unsigned int)*aHandle*

Discards the record identified by *aHandle*, so that the record can't be read, removed or replaced. **reclaimRecord:** retrieves discarded records, and **clean** removes all discarded records. Returns **self**.

See also: – **reclaimRecord:**, – **clean**, – **removeRecord:** (IXRecordWriting)

reclaimRecord:

– **reclaimRecord:**(unsigned int)*aHandle*

Reclaims a record previously discarded with **discardRecord:**. *aHandle* is the identifier of the discarded record. A discarded record must be reclaimed in order to access it or remove it completely from the archive (although **clean** removes all discarded records at once). Returns **self**.

See also: – **discardRecord:**, – **clean**

IXRecordReading

Adopted By: IXRecordManager

Declared In: indexing/protocols.h

Protocol Description

The IXRecordReading protocol defines methods for retrieving objects by an abstract identifier, or *handle*. The implementor of this protocol is called an *object repository.* The stored objects are called *records*. IXRecordManager uses this protocol, along with IXRecordTranscription and IXBlobWriting, to retrieve stored objects.

Instance Methods

count

– (unsigned int)**count**

Returns the number of records in the receiver.

readRecord:fromZone:

– **readRecord:**(unsigned int)*aHandle* **fromZone:**(NXZone *)*zone*

Reads and returns the record identified by *aHandle*. The record is allocated from *zone*; its class is instantiated if necessary. Returns **nil** if the record doesn't exist or can't be read.

If the record conforms to the IXRecordTranscription protocol, the implementor of this message sends **source:didReadRecord:** and **finishReading** to the instantiated record.

IXRecordTranscription

Adopted By: no NeXTSTEP classes

Declared In: indexing/protocols.h

Protocol Description

The IXRecordTranscription protocol is used by objects that archive other objects with the IXRecordWriting and IXRecordReading protocols to notify objects that they've been archived or unarchived by transcription. *Transcription* is an efficient means of archiving in which an object's instance variables are written or read directly into or out of an archive. Transcription avoids the overhead of the standard archiving mechanism (the **write:** and **read:** methods), but removes control of the archiving process from the object being archived.

Since transcription isn't done by the object being archived, that object can't choose what data to archive and what data not to archive; the transcriber simply writes all of the instance variables that it can. However, there may be data that the transcriber doesn't archive that should be archived with the object. If an object conforms to this protocol, the transcriber can notify it that it's being written or read, and the object can then ask the transcriber to store or retrieve any data that the transcriber would not.

There are two kinds of data that can't be transcribed: data that aren't stored as instance variables (for example, the contents of a file or an entry in the defaults database), which the transcriber never knows about; and untyped data (anything referred to by a pointer to **void**), whose length the transcriber can't determine. These data are called blobs, and if the transcriber provides a way to store these for the object (such as by conforming to the IXBlobWriting protocol), the object being transcribed can ask the transcriber to store or retrieve its blobs by name.

Instance Methods

finishReading

– **finishReading**

Informs the receiver that it has been fully read into memory by a transcriber. This allows the receiver to replace the unarchived object with a new object if necessary. A **finishReading** message is sent to every object after it has been unarchived by a transcriber and sent a **source:didReadRecord:** message. This method normally returns **self**.

Important: The method description for **finishUnarchiving** in the Object class specification states that that method should return **nil** if no substitution is desired. This isn't the case with this method. The return value must be **self** if no substitution is desired; returning **nil** will cause **nil** to be substituted for the object.

The **finishReading** message gives the application an opportunity to test an unarchived and initialized object to see whether it's usable, and, if not, to replace it with another object that is. This method should return **nil** if the unarchived instance (self) is OK; otherwise, it should free the receiver and return another object to take its place.

See also: – **finishUnarchiving** (Object)

source:didReadRecord:

– **source:***aTranscriber* **didReadRecord:**(unsigned int)*aHandle*

Informs the receiver that it has been read into memory by *aTranscriber*, so it can perform any needed reinitialization. If *aTranscriber* provides a way to retrieve blobs, the receiver can ask it to do so, for example with the **getValue:andLength:ofBlob:forRecord:** method from the IXBlobWriting protocol. This method normally returns **self**, but the receiver may return a substitute, in which case the receiver is freed.

See also: – **getValue:andLength:ofBlob:forRecord:** (IXBlobWriting)

source:willWriteRecord:

– **source:***aTranscriber* **willWriteRecord:**(unsigned int)*aHandle*

Informs the receiver that it's about to be archived by *aTranscriber*. If *aTranscriber* provides a way to store blobs, the receiver can ask it to do so, for example with the **setValue:andLength:ofBlob:forRecord:** method from the IXBlobWriting protocol. This method normally returns **self**, but the receiver may return a substitute to be archived in its place, in which case the receiver is freed.

See also: – **setValue:andLength:ofBlob:forRecord:** (IXBlobWriting)

IXRecordWriting

Adopted By: IXRecordManager

Incorporates: IXRecordReading

Declared In: indexing/protocols.h

Protocol Description

The IXRecordWriting protocol defines methods for storing Objective C objects in an object acting as an repository. The stored objects are called *records*, and are identified by unsigned integers called *handles*. IXRecordManager implements this protocol, along with IXRecordTranscription and IXBlobWriting, in order to store objects.

Method Types

Manipulating records by handle	– addRecord: – replaceRecord:with: – removeRecord:
Emptying a record repository	– empty

Instance Methods

addRecord:

– (unsigned int)**addRecord:***anObject*

Adds *anObject* as a record to the repository, and returns the handle assigned to that record.

See also: – **removeRecord:**, – **replaceRecord:with:**

empty

– **empty**

Removes all records from the repository. Returns **self**.

See also: – **removeRecord:**, – **clean** (IXRecordDiscarding)

removeRecord:

– **removeRecord:**(unsigned int)*aHandle*

Removes the record identified by *aHandle* from the repository. The record is physically destroyed; use **discardRecord:** from the IXRecordDiscarding protocol if your code may need to retrieve the record again later. Returns **self**, or **nil** if the record doesn't exist.

See also: – **discardRecord:** (IXRecordDiscarding), – **empty**, – **addRecord:**

replaceRecord:with:

– **replaceRecord:**(unsigned int)*aHandle* **with:***anObject*

Overwrites the record identified by *aHandle* by storing *anObject* at that handle. *aHandle* will then refer to *anObject*; the original record is physically destroyed. Returns **nil** if the record identified by *aHandle* doesn't exist, or if *anObject* is **nil**. Otherwise returns **self**.

See also: – **addRecord:**

IXTransientAccess

Adopted By: IXRecordManager

Declared In: indexing/protocols.h

Protocol Description

The IXTransientAccess protocol defines a set of methods for retrieving the values of the instance variables of records stored in a repository. It's useful for getting these values without explicitly instantiating the stored records. All of the methods perform type casting, if necessary; for example, it's meaningful to request the integer value of a floating-point instance variable.

Instance Methods

getDoubleValue:ofIvar:forRecord:

– (BOOL)**getDoubleValue:**(double *)*aValue*
ofIvar:(const char *)*ivarName*
forRecord:(unsigned int)*aHandle*

Returns by reference the value of the instance variable *ivarName* from the record identified by *aHandle*. The value of *ivarName* is returned as a double-precision floating-point number. Returns YES if the value is successfully retrieved, NO otherwise.

getFloatValue:ofIvar:forRecord:

– (BOOL)**getFloatValue:**(float *)*aValue*
ofIvar:(const char *)*ivarName*
forRecord:(unsigned int)*aHandle*

Returns by reference the value of the instance variable *ivarName* from the record identified by *aHandle*. The value of *ivarName* is returned as a single-precision floating-point number. Returns YES if the value is successfully retrieved, NO otherwise.

getIntValue:ofIvar:forRecord:

– (BOOL)**getIntValue:**(int *)*aValue*
ofIvar:(const char *)*ivarName*
forRecord:(unsigned int)*aHandle*

Returns by reference the value of the instance variable *ivarName* from the record identified by *aHandle*. The value of *ivarName* is returned as an integer. Returns YES if the value is successfully retrieved, NO otherwise.

getObjectValue:ofIvar:forRecord:

– (BOOL)**getObjectValue:**(Object **)*aValue*
ofIvar:(const char *)*ivarName*
forRecord:(unsigned int)*aHandle*

Returns by reference the value of the instance variable *ivarName* from the record identified by *aHandle*. The value of *ivarName* is returned as an Objective C object. Returns YES if the value is successfully retrieved, NO otherwise.

getOpaqueValue:ofIvar:forRecord:

– (BOOL)**getOpaqueValue:**(NXData **)*aValue*
ofIvar:(const char *)*ivarName*
forRecord:(unsigned int)*aHandle*

Returns by reference the value of the instance variable *ivarName* from the record identified by *aHandle*. The value of *ivarName* is returned as an instance of class NXData. Returns YES if the value is successfully retrieved, NO otherwise.

getStringValue:ofIvar:forRecord:

– (BOOL)**getStringValue:**(char **)*aValue*
ofIvar:(const char *)*ivarName*
forRecord:(unsigned int)*aHandle*

Returns by reference the value of the instance variable *ivarName* from the record identified by *aHandle*. The value of *ivarName* is returned as a string. Returns YES if the value is successfully retrieved, NO otherwise. The sender is responsible for freeing the string.

getStringValue:inLength:ofIvar:forRecord:

– (BOOL)**getStringValue:**(char **)*aValue*
inLength:(unsigned int)*aLength*
ofIvar:(const char *)*ivarName*
forRecord:(unsigned int)*aHandle*

Returns by reference the value of the instance variable *ivarName* from the record identified by *aHandle*. The value of *ivarName* is returned by copy as a string in the supplied buffer, truncated if needed to fit within *length* bytes (including the terminating null character). Returns YES if the value is successfully retrieved, NO otherwise.

IXTransientMessaging

Adopted By: IXRecordManager

Declared In: indexing/protocols.h

Protocol Description

The IXTransientMessaging protocol defines a set of methods for retrieving the return values of methods from records stored in a repository (the methods must take no arguments). It's useful for getting these values without your code having to explicitly instantiate the stored records. All of the methods perform type casting, if necessary; for example, it's meaningful to request the string value of a floating point return value.

Since the records addressed by these methods are actually activated and messaged, you should be wary of any side effects that may be triggered. The implementor of this protocol frees the unarchived record without re-archiving it, so changes to the state of the unarchived record won't be retained.

Instance Methods

getDoubleValue:ofMessage:forRecord:

– (BOOL)**getDoubleValue:**(double *)*aValue*
  ofMessage:(SEL)*aSelector*
  forRecord:(unsigned int)*aHandle*

Returns by reference the value that *aSelector* returns when sent to the record identified by *aHandle*. The return value of *aSelector* is interpreted as a double-precision floating-point number. Returns YES if the value is successfully retrieved, NO otherwise.

getFloatValue:ofMessage:forRecord:

– (BOOL)**getFloatValue:**(float *)*aValue*
ofMessage:(SEL)*aSelector*
forRecord:(unsigned int)*aHandle*

Returns by reference the value that *aSelector* returns when sent to the record identified by *aHandle*. The return value of *aSelector* is interpreted as a double precision floating point number. Returns YES if the value is successfully retrieved, NO otherwise.

getIntValue:ofMessage:forRecord:

– (BOOL)**getIntValue:**(int *)*aValue*
ofMessage:(SEL)*aSelector*
forRecord:(unsigned int)*aHandle*

Returns by reference the value that *aSelector* returns when sent to the record identified by *aHandle*. The return value of *aSelector* is interpreted as an integer. Returns YES if the value is successfully retrieved, NO otherwise.

getObjectValue:ofMessage:forRecord:

– (BOOL)**getObjectValue:**(Object **)*aValue*
ofMessage:(SEL)*aSelector*
forRecord:(unsigned int)*aHandle*

Returns by reference the value that *aSelector* returns when sent to the record identified by *aHandle*. The return value of *aSelector* is interpreted as an Objective C object. Returns YES if the value is successfully retrieved, NO otherwise.

getOpaqueValue:ofMessage:forRecord:

– (BOOL)**getOpaqueValue:**(NXData **)*aValue*
ofMessage:(SEL)*aSelector*
forRecord:(unsigned int)*aHandle*

Returns by reference the value that *aSelector* returns when sent to the record identified by *aHandle*. The return value of *aSelector* is interpreted as an instance of class NXData. Returns YES if the value is successfully retrieved, NO otherwise.

getStringValue:ofMessage:forRecord:

– (BOOL)**getStringValue:**(char **)*aValue*
ofMessage:(SEL)*aSelector*
forRecord:(unsigned int)*aHandle*

Returns by reference the value that *aSelector* returns when sent to the record identified by *aHandle*. The return value of *aSelector* is interpreted as a string. Returns YES if the value is successfully retrieved, NO otherwise. The sender is responsible for freeing the string.

getStringValue:inLength:ofMessage:forRecord:

– (BOOL)**getStringValue:**(char **)*aValue*
inLength:(unsigned int)*aLength*
ofMessage:(SEL)*aSelector*
forRecord:(unsigned int)*aHandle*

Returns by reference the value that *aSelector* returns when sent to the record identified by *aHandle*. The return value of *aSelector* is returned by copy as a string in the supplied buffer, of length up to *aLength*. Returns YES if the value is successfully retrieved, NO otherwise.

Functions

These functions and macros are for use with several Indexing Kit classes. Comparator functions form the bulk of functions in the Indexing Kit. There are also functions for archiving objects to IXStore blocks, and for locking IXBTree mutexes to perform thread-safe operations with multiple IXBTreeCursors.

IXCompareBytes(), IXCompareUnsignedBytes(), IXCompareShorts(), IXCompareUnsignedShorts(), IXCompareLongs(), IXCompareUnsignedLongs(), IXCompareFloats(), IXCompareDoubles()

SUMMARY Compare two data items as arrays of numbers and return their ordering.

DECLARED IN btree/protocols.h

SYNOPSIS

int **IXCompareBytes**(const void **data1*, unsigned short *length1*, const void **data2*, unsigned short *length2*, const void **context*)

int **IXCompareUnsignedBytes**(const void **data1*, unsigned short *length1*, const void **data2*, unsigned short *length2*, const void **context*)

int **IXCompareShorts**(const void **data1*, unsigned short *length1*, const void **data2*, unsigned short *length2*, const void **context*)

int **IXCompareUnsignedShorts**(const void **data1*, unsigned short *length1*, const void **data2*, unsigned short *length2*, const void **context*)

int **IXCompareLongs**(const void **data1*, unsigned short *length1*, const void **data2*, unsigned short *length2*, const void **context*)

int **IXCompareUnsignedLongs**(const void **data1*, unsigned short *length1*, const void **data2*, unsigned short *length2*, const void **context*)

int **IXCompareFloats**(const void **data1*, unsigned short *length1*, const void **data2*, unsigned short *length2*, const void **context*)

int **IXCompareDoubles**(const void **data1*, unsigned short *length1*, const void **data2*, unsigned short *length2*, const void **context*)

DESCRIPTION Each of these functions compares two arrays of arbitrary data, *data1* and *data2* (of *length1* and *length2* bytes respectively), and returns an integer indicating their ordering. The arrays are compared as though they contained elements of the type indicated by the function name; for example, **IXCompareUnsignedLongs**() compares *data1* and *data2* as arrays of items of type **unsigned long int**. All of these functions return an integer less than, equal to, or greater than 0, according to whether *data1* is less than, equal to, or greater than *data2*.

The data in the arrays is compared serially until one element isn't equal to the other, or until either *length1* or *length2* bytes have been exhausted in the corresponding array. If two arrays are otherwise equal, the shorter is considered the lesser in value.

All of these functions match the IXComparator function type, which has the form:

typedef int **IXComparator**(const void **data1*, unsigned short *length1*,
const void **data2*, unsigned short *length2*, const void **context*);

Where *data1* is an array of *length1* bytes, *data2* is an array of *length2* bytes; *context* is a pointer to arbitrary data for use by the function. Only **IXFormatComparator()** (see below) makes use of a *context* argument (for that function it's called *format*). You are free to write functions matching this type definition that use *context* in any way you choose.

RETURN These functions return an integer less than 0 if *data1* is considered less than *data2*, 0 if they are considered equal, or an integer greater than 0 if *data1* is considered greater than *data2*.

SEE ALSO **IXCompareBytes()**, IXBTree class, IXComparatorSetting protocol

---

IXCompareShort(), IXCompareUnsignedShort(), IXCompareLong(), IXCompareUnsignedLong(), IXCompareFloat(), IXCompareDouble()

SUMMARY Compare two data items as numbers and return their ordering.

DECLARED IN btree/protocols.h

SYNOPSIS int **IXCompareShort**(const void **data1*, unsigned short *length1*, const void **data2*, unsigned short *length2*, const void **context*)

int **IXCompareUnsignedShort**(const void **data1*, unsigned short *length1*, const void **data2*, unsigned short *length2*, const void **context*)

int **IXCompareLong**(const void **data1*, unsigned short *length1*, const void **data2*, unsigned short *length2*, const void **context*)

int **IXCompareUnsignedLong**(const void **data1*, unsigned short *length1*, const void **data2*, unsigned short *length2*, const void **context*)

int **IXCompareFloat**(const void **data1*, unsigned short *length1*, const void **data2*, unsigned short *length2*, const void **context*)

int **IXCompareDouble**(const void **data1*, unsigned short *length1*, const void **data2*, unsigned short *length2*, const void **context*)

DESCRIPTION Each of these functions compares two data items, pointed to by *data1* and *data2*, as elements of the type indicated by the function name, and returns an integer indicating their ordering (*length1*, *length2* and *context* are ignored). The items are compared by pointer dereference; for example, **IXCompareFloat()** compares the values pointed to by *data1* and *data2* as type **float**. All of these functions return an integer less than, equal to, or greater than 0, depending on whether *data1* is less than, equal to, or greater than *data2*.

For more information on comparator functions, see the **IXCompareBytes()** function description.

RETURN These functions return an integer less than 0 if *data1* is considered less than *data2*, 0 if they are considered equal, or an integer greater than 0 if *data1* is considered greater than *data2*.

SEE ALSO **IXCompareBytes()**, IXBTree class, IXComparatorSetting protocol

---

IXCompareStringAndUnsigneds(), IXCompareUnsignedAndStrings()

SUMMARY Compare two data items as a combinations of strings and numbers and return their ordering.

DECLARED IN btree/protocols.h

SYNOPSIS int **IXCompareStringAndUnsigneds**(const void **data1*, unsigned short *length1*, const void **data2*, unsigned short *length2*, const void **context*)

int **IXCompareUnsignedAndStrings**(const void **data1*, unsigned short *length1*, const void **data2*, unsigned short *length2*, const void **context*)

DESCRIPTION These functions combine the comparisons of **IXCompareStrings()** and **IXCompareUnsignedLongs()**.

IXCompareStringAndUnsigned() compares *data1* and *data2* as strings until the first null character is encountered. If the strings are equal up to and including the null character, the remainders are compared in the manner of **IXCompareUnsignedLongs()**. Each length argument must be the length in bytes of the string, plus 1 for the terminating null character, plus the length in bytes of the array of unsigned integers following the string.

IXCompareUnsignedAndStrings() compares the first part of *data1* and *data2* as a single unsigned long integer. If those are equal, the remainders are compared in the manner of **IXCompareStrings**(). Each length argument must be the length in bytes of an unsigned long integer, plus the length in bytes of the string, plus 1 for the terminating null character.

For more information on comparator functions, see the **IXCompareBytes**() function description.

RETURN These functions return an integer less than 0 if *data1* is considered less than *data2*, 0 if they are considered equal, or an integer greater than 0 if *data1* is considered greater than *data2*.

SEE ALSO **IXCompareBytes**(), IXBTree class, IXComparatorSetting protocol

---

IXCompareStrings(), IXCompareMonocaseStrings()

SUMMARY Compare two sets of data as strings and return their ordering.

DECLARED IN btree/protocols.h

SYNOPSIS int **IXCompareStrings**(const void **data1*, unsigned short *length1*, const void **data2*, unsigned short *length2*, const void **context*)
int **IXCompareMonocaseStrings**(const void **data1*, unsigned short *length1*, const void **data2*, unsigned short *length2*, const void **context*)

DESCRIPTION These functions compare serial arrays of strings in the NeXTSTEP character encoding. They accept either single null-terminated strings along with their lengths, or arrays of characters forming consecutive null-terminated strings (for example, "This is a string\0And this is another\0") along with the total length. Only the length argument is used to determine the length of a string; a null character is treated as any other character for comparison purposes. Both of these functions return an integer less than, equal to, or greater than 0, depending on whether *data1* is less than, equal to, or greater than *data2*.

The data in the arrays is compared serially until one element isn't equal to the other, or until either *length1* or *length2* bytes have been exhausted in the corresponding array. If two arrays are otherwise equal, the shorter is considered the lesser in value.

IXCompareStrings() distinguishes between uppercase and lowercase when comparing strings. **IXCompareMonocaseStrings()** disregards case distinctions in its comparison.

For more information on comparator functions, see the **IXCompareBytes()** function description.

RETURN These functions return an integer less than 0 if *data1* is considered less than *data2*, 0 if they are considered equal, or an integer greater than 0 if *data1* is considered greater than *data2*.

SEE ALSO **IXCompareBytes()**, IXBTree class, IXComparatorSetting protocol

---

IXFormatComparator()

SUMMARY Compare two arrays of data based on a type encoding and return their ordering.

DECLARED IN btree/protocols.h

SYNOPSIS int **IXFormatComparator**(const void **data1*, unsigned short *length1*, const void **data2*, unsigned short *length2*, void **format*)

DESCRIPTION **IXFormatComparator()** compares two arrays of data, determining the data type from an Objective C type encoding supplied in *format*. For example, supplying "l" as the format indicates that *data1* and *data2* are arrays of long integers. **IXFormatComparator()** uses the other standard comparison functions as needed on the data arrays until their ordering is decided.

IXFormatComparator() currently uses only the first type declared in the format string, except for the compound formats corresponding to **IXCompareStringAndUnsigneds()** and **IXCompareUnsignedAndStrings()**, which it recognizes. Any array lengths in the format string are ignored; the actual lengths are determined from the *length1* and *length2* arguments passed to the function. If a comparison function can't be determined from the format string, **IXCompareStrings()** is used. NeXT reserves the right to interpret more than the first type declaration in future releases, as well as structure declarations, bit fields and unions.

For more information on comparator functions, see the **IXCompareBytes()** function description. For more information on comparison formats, see the IXComparisonSetting protocol specification.

RETURN **IXFormatComparator**() returns an integer less than 0 if *data1* is considered less than *data2*, 0 if they are considered equal, or an integer greater than 0 if *data1* is considered greater than *data2*.

SEE ALSO **IXCompareBytes**(), IXBTree class, IXComparisonSetting protocol

---

IXLockBTreeMutex(), IXUnlockBTreeMutex()

SUMMARY Lock and unlock an IXBTree for thread-safe access

DECLARED IN btree/IXBTree.h

SYNOPSIS void **IXLockBTreeMutex**(IXBTree **aBTree*)
void **IXUnlockBTreeMutex**(IXBTree **aBTree*)

DESCRIPTION These macros expand to calls to **mutex_lock()** or **mutex_unlock()** on the mutex lock instance variable of their IXBTree. They should be used to guarantee that the IXBTree isn't accessed simultaneously by two Mach threads.

SEE ALSO **mutex_lock()** (*NeXTSTEP Operating System Software*), **mutex_unlock()** (*NeXTSTEP Operating System Software*), IXBTree class

---

IXWriteRootObjectToStore(), IXReadObjectFromStore()

SUMMARY Archive or unarchive an object to or from an IXStore

DECLARED IN store/IXStoreBlock.h

SYNOPSIS unsigned int **IXWriteRootObjectToStore**(IXStore **aStore*, unsigned int *aHandle*, id *anObject*)
id **IXReadObjectFromStore**(IXStore **aStore*, unsigned int *aHandle*, NXZone **aZone*)

DESCRIPTION **IXWriteRootObjectToStore()** archives *anObject* into the IXStore block identified by *aStore* and *aHandle*. This involves creating a memory stream, archiving the object into that stream, resizing the block to accommodate the resulting stream length, and then copying the contents of the stream into the block. Any object that implements the **write:** method using the standard archiving functions (including **NXWriteObjectReference()**) can be archived in this way. **IXReadObjectFromStore()** unarchives an object from the IXStore block identified by *aStore* and *aHandle*, allocating the unarchived object from *aZone*. For further information on object archiving, see the description for the **NXReadObject()** function in the Application Kit documentation.

RETURN **IXWriteRootObjectToStore()** returns *aHandle*. **IXReadObjectFromStore()** returns the **id** of the unarchived object.

SEE ALSO **NXWriteRootObject()** (Application Kit Function), **NXReadObject()** (Application Kit Function), IXStoreBlock class.

Types and Constants

Defined Types

IXComparator

DECLARED IN btree/protocols.h

SYNOPSIS

typedef int **IXComparator**
(const void **data1*,
unsigned short *length1*,
const void **data2*,
unsigned short *length2*,
const void **context*);

DESCRIPTION The standard comparator function type. Used by IXBTree and other classes to check the functions they use to perform key comparisons.

IXPosting

DECLARED IN btree/protocols.h

SYNOPSIS

typedef struct IXPosting {
unsigned **handle**;
unsigned **weight**;
} **IXPosting**;

DESCRIPTION Used by classes such as IXPostingCursor to store a weighted reference. **handle** is the identifier, and **weight** is a value associated with the posting; though it's usually a rank of weight or importance, it can also be used to store other information, such as a hint.

IXStoreErrorType

SYNOPSIS

```
typedef enum IXStoreErrorType {
    IX_NoError = IX_STOREUSERERRORBASE,
    IX_InternalError,
    IX_ArgumentError,
    IX_QueryEvalError,
    IX_QueryTypeError,
    IX_QueryAttrError,
    IX_QueryImplError,
    IX_QueryYaccError,
    IX_MemoryError,
    IX_LockedError,
    IX_MachineError,
    IX_VersionError,
    IX_DamagedError,
    IX_DuplicateError,
    IX_NotFoundError,
    IX_TooLargeError,
    IX_UnixErrorBase = IX_STOREUNIXERRBASE,
    IX_MachErrorBase = IX_STOREMACHERRBASE,
} IXStoreErrorType;
```

DESCRIPTION Used to specify exception codes in the Indexing Kit. Where an exception can occur in a method, the method description details the meaning of the exception codes as they relate to that method. Here are their general meanings:

IX_NoError	No error
IX_InternalError	An error in the Indexing Kit's implementation
IX_ArgumentError	An invalid argument was passed to a routine
IX_QueryEvalError	A query was ill-formed or couldn't be evaluated
IX_QueryTypeError	A query contained an invalid type binding
IX_QueryAttrError	A query contained an invalid attribute reference
IX_QueryImplError	An error or missing feature in query evaluation
IX_QueryYaccError	A query was grammatically incorrect
IX_MemoryError	Insufficient memory available
IX_LockedError	The requested file or block handle is locked
IX_MachineError	The target store has an incompatible format
IX_VersionError	The target store is of an incompatible version
IX_DamagedError	The target store is damaged
IX_DuplicateError	An entry with the same identifier already exists

IX_NotFoundError	The entry couldn't be found
IX_TooLargeError	A value was too large, usually an IXBTree key
IX_UnixErrorBase	Unix **errno** added to this base value
IX_MachErrorBase	Mach **kern_return** added to this base value

---

IXWeightingType

DECLARED IN indexing/IXAttributeParser.h

SYNOPSIS

typedef enum {
    IX_NoWeighting = 0,
    IX_AbsoluteWeighting,
    IX_FrequencyWeighting,
    IX_PeculiarityWeighting
} **IXWeightingType**;

DESCRIPTION Used to define weighting strategies for IXAttributeParser. IX_NoWeighting means all tokens have a weight of 0. IX_AbsoluteWeighting means the weight of each token is its count in the sample. IX_FrequencyWeighting gives the weight of a token by dividing its count in the sample by the total number of tokens in the sample. IX_PeculiarityWeighting is frequency weighting with regard to some reference domain; a token's weight is the square root of its frequency within its sample divided by its frequency within the larger domain. IX_PeculiarityWeighting is used to filter out domain specific noise; for example, the word "computer" in a set of documentation about computers isn't very relevant to a search, because it's assumed to occur quite often, but the word "grill" would probably be very unusual for such a topic.

Symbolic Constants

IXStore Constants

DECLARED IN store/protocols.h

SYNOPSIS IX_ALLBLOCKS

DESCRIPTION Used as a convenience value for freeing or closing all blocks in an IXStore or IXStoreFile; for example, sending **closeBlock:** with IX_ALLBLOCKS as the argument will result in all blocks opened by the receiving IXStore being closed.

Note: This is currently unimplemented; using IX_ALLBLOCKS does nothing at this time.

Indexing Kit Error Base Constants

SYNOPSIS IX_STOREUSERERRBASE
IX_STOREMACHERRBASE
IX_STOREUNIXERRBASE

DESCRIPTION Used as base values for the defined type IXStoreErrorType.

Global Variables

IXStore Pasteboard Type

DECLARED IN store/protocols.h

SYNOPSIS NXAtom **IXStorePboardType**;

DESCRIPTION IXStorePboardType is the Pasteboard type for the entire contents of an IXStore, as used by IXStore's **getContents:andLength:** and **setContents:andLength:** methods.

Indexing Pasteboard Types

DECLARED IN indexing/IXAttributeParser.h

SYNOPSIS NXAtom **IXAttributeReaderPboardType**;
NXAtom **IXFileDescriptionPboardType**;

DESCRIPTION IXAttributeReaderPboardType indicates text in Attribute Reader Format. IXFileDescriptionPboardType indicates a file's description as generated by an IXFileFinder; a file description is usually generated by a filter service.

Other Features

Attribute Reader Format

The Indexing Kit's Attribute Reader Format (ARF) is a simple extension of Microsoft's Rich Text Format (RTF) designed to support content analysis. For more information on how ARF is generated or used by the Indexing Kit, see the IXAttributeReader and IXAttributeParser class specifications, and the IXAttributeReading protocol specification.

This document assumes that you are at least briefly familiar with the Rich Text Format specification. Specifically, it assumes that you know what control groups and control words are, and how they are delimited.

Attributes

The content of most texts can be analyzed in terms of various attributes, like author, title, date of publication, bibliography list, and so on. ARF supports the declaration of arbitrary attributes, and the association of those attributes with individual lexemes, for the purpose of describing an analysis of textual content. For example, one might select all articles arriving on a news wire that have the word "wilderness" in their titles.

An attribute is declared by an RTF control group starting with the control word **\zd** followed by the name of the attribute. For example:

```
{\zd Title}
```

A type may be declared for the attribute by the control word **\zt** followed by an Objective C type encoding. If no type is specified, "*" (string) is assumed by default. The following RTF control group declares an unsigned integer-valued attribute representing the year of publication:

```
{\zd YearOfPublication\ztI}
```

Note: Currently, "*" (string) is the only supported type for attributes.

As an attribute reader declares attributes, it numbers them sequentially, beginning with 1. An attribute's sequence number may be used later to refer to that attribute in a lexeme declaration (described below). For example, of the attributes declared so far, Title would be number 1 and YearOfPublication would be number 2. A pre-defined attribute, Default, is pre-assigned the number 0, and is associated with every lexeme that has no explicit association.

Lexemes

A lexeme is a unit of content extracted from a text, and associated with an attribute by a lexical analyzer, such as an IXAttributeReader. Lexemes are declared by an RTF control group starting with the control word **\z**; the value of the lexeme immediately follows. The attribute association, if any, is indicated by the control word **\za**, which takes the attribute number as a numeric parameter. If no attribute is specified, the Default attribute is assumed. For example, the word "excursions" could be declared as a lexeme in the Title attribute, and "summer" as a lexeme in the Default attribute, as follows:

```
{\z excursions\za1}
{\z summer}
```

A lexeme may contain multiple words to represent a phrase or an idiom. For example:

```
{\z joie de vivre}
{\z tongue in cheek}
```

A weight for the lexeme may also be specified by the **\zw** control word. The weight is interpreted as a count of the number of occurrences of the lexeme. Normally, this control word is omitted, since weights are usually computed automatically by the parser. It may be useful, however, on occasion, to explicitly specify the count of a particular lexeme in an attribute. For example, this fragment gives this occurrence of the lexeme "camping" in the Title attribute a count of 100:

```
{\z camping\za1\zw100}
```

Finally, a cookie, introduced by the **\zc** control word, may accompany the lexeme. The cookie is an ASCII string encoding a value opaque to the parser. This is typically used to identify entities within a source, such as cells in a spreadsheet, or footnotes in a document. Here's a sample lexeme declaration with a cookie whose value is "ae00fc24":

```
{\z bike\zcae00fc24}
```

References

Lexemes can be numbered in the same manner as attributes, as they are encountered, beginning with 1. The control word **\zr**, which takes a lexeme number as a numeric parameter, may be substituted for the lexeme with that number. This provides great space savings when processing large amounts of text. For example, if the "excursions" lexeme declared earlier were the 37th lexeme, then the following fragment would indicate another occurrence of that lexeme, resulting in a compression ratio of more than 3 to 1:

```
\zr37
```

The Indexing Kit Query Language

The Indexing Kit defines a declarative query language for selecting objects from an *evaluation context* (an object about which the query is made, or about whose contents the query is made). A query language expression is an assertion; the objects selected by a query are those objects in the evaluation context that satisfy the assertion. An assertion consists of *predicates* combined by logical operators to form logical expressions.

The query language is attribute-based. Objects have *attributes* defined by the programmer; an attribute has a name, a type, and a selector. The value of an attribute for a given object is the value returned when the message for the attribute's selector is sent to that object. The predicates in a query expression are formulated in terms of these attributes. For example, in a set of students, one attribute might be the student's age, another might be his or her home state, and another his or her grade point average. Some informal predicates based on these attributes are:

- Age is greater than 20.
- Grade point average is 4.0.
- Home state is Michigan.

Combining these predicates with logical operators to form logical expressions gives:

- Age is greater than 20 *and* grade point average is 4.0.
- Age is over 20 *or* home state is Michigan.
- Home state is Michigan and grade point average is *not* 4.0.
- Age is greater than 20 *and* home state is Michigan, and grade point average is *not* 4.0.

A *query expression* is evaluated against an evaluation context, resulting in an object or a set of objects from the evaluation context that satisfy the query expression. During query evaluation, the attribute names in the expression are bound to the attributes of each object in turn, and the truth of the assertion is checked. The object currently under consideration is bound to the special symbol **self**, much like in an Objective C method.

Predicates can be built with boolean, arithmetic, and relational operators, as well as with search operators that look for values within other values or within sets of values. The elements of the query language that are used to build and combine predicates are described in the following sections.

Symbols

The Indexing Kit's query language defines four kinds of symbols: literals, operators, attributes, and the special symbol **self**. Symbols are delimited by white space, as well as by the parentheses associated with operators. A *literal* is a scalar value, like a number or a string. The boolean literals are **yes**, **true**, **no**, and **false**. Numbers can simply be written in integer or floating-point form: 0, –1, 27.35. Strings are indicated by balanced pairs of quotation marks (single or double), or with the **quote**() operator (described below). To include a closing delimiter in a string, precede it with a backslash. For example:

```
"This is a string with a \" quotation mark in it"
'This is \'too'
 quote(This string contains an embedded \) parenthesis)
```

Other escape sequences allowed in strings are: '\n' (newline), '\r' (carriage return), '\t' (tab), '\f' (form feed), '\b' (space), and '\\' (backslash itself).

Operators denote actions that are performed during the compilation or evaluation of a query, like adding two numbers or parsing a string. Operators are formed with a name and a pair of parentheses, much like functions in C. A fixed set of operators is defined by the query language; there is no way to define a new operator or function.

Attributes are references to properties of objects in the evaluation context. An attribute has a name and a type, and is bound to values during query evaluation, as the query is applied in turn to each object in the evaluation context. Attribute names are any otherwise non-reserved symbols; that is, any alphanumeric string that isn't an operator name or the special symbol **self**. By convention, they usually begin with a capital letter. Content, Age, and Publisher are examples of legal attribute names. Content is a special attribute, described in the section "Predefined Attributes."

self is an unbound object reference; it's bound during query evaluation, as the query is applied to each object in the evaluation context. Its presence is usually implicit in a predicate, but can be made explicit for special purposes, as described below.

Types

There are three scalar types in the query language: boolean, number, and string. There are also three compound types: vector, object, and regular expression. Each of the symbols in a query expression has a type, or produces a value of some type when evaluated. The types of operands may determine the behavior of operators.

The scalar types are coercible; type coercion is implicit, and occurs automatically when necessary. Numbers become strings, as generated by **printf()**, or become boolean values in the manner of C: 0 is **false**, any other value is **true**. Strings are interpreted as numbers by **scanf()**, or coerced to 0 if **scanf()** fails. When a string is coerced to a boolean value, it first becomes a number; the number is then coerced to its boolean equivalent. Boolean **false** is coerced to the number 0 or the string "no"; boolean **true** is coerced to the number 1 or the string "yes". Scalar values are referred to as *atoms* throughout the remainder of this section.

A *vector* is a weighted collection of atoms. Vectors occur most frequently as attribute values, since an attribute's value can be generated by an attribute parser from a text string. A vector can be viewed as a position in a space whose axes comprise the set of all possible values for the underlying scalar type. For example, if a vector holds strings representing words in the English language, then the vector represents a position in the space of English words; this type of vector is called a *signature* when used to describe a document's content.

The purpose of a query is to select objects from the evaluation context that satisfy the query expression. The only objects directly accessible from within the query expression are **self**, and the surrogate objects generated by the **parse()** operator (described below).

A *regular expression* is a pattern generated from a string. A comparison between a string and a regular expression is more powerful than a comparison between a string and another string. A regular expression isn't so much a type as a data structure compiled from a string for purposes of comparison.

Operators

Operators take one or more arguments and produce a single result of a specific type. The operators of the Indexing Kit's query language fall into six categories: transform, projection, boolean, relational, arithmetic, and search. Their behavior often depends on the types of their arguments, which must be enclosed in parentheses and delimited by white space.

The *transform operators* take a single argument and produce a single result derived from the argument. **quote()**, as mentioned above, forms a string from the text in its parentheses. **regex()** and **shell()** both transform the text between their parentheses into regular expressions. **regex()** builds regular expressions from Berkeley regular expression strings, and **shell()** builds regular expressions from Bourne shell expansion notation. For example, the following two expressions result in the same regular expression:

```
regex(term.*)
shell(term*)
```

The last transform operator is **parse()**; it parses the text between its parentheses to create a a surrogate object with attribute values derived from the text. A *surrogate* is a vehicle for attribute values supplied by the query expression; it isn't a member of the evaluation context's set of objects, but since it returns attribute values to query language operators, treats it as such. This operator uses an instance of IXAttributeParser to parse its argument.

There's only one *projection operator*, **project()**. **project()** takes two or more arguments. The last is an object; the others are attributes, which the operator extracts from the object, returning the projected attributes. The result is bound if the source was bound, and unbound otherwise. For example, in the query fragments below, the first **project()** operator produces the bound attributes Name and Age, since **parse()** always produces a surrogate object; the second **project()** produces the same attributes, but unbound, since **self** is an unbound object reference.

```
project(Name Age parse(Jane Draper, 24, Boston, MA))
project(Name Age self)
```

The *boolean operators* perform logical operations on boolean atoms or on vectors, coercing the second argument to a boolean value if it's a number or string. The **or()** and **and()** operators, when given boolean arguments, perform logical OR and AND, respectively. For example, **or(true false)** is **true** while **and(true false)** is **false**. The **not()** operator is a shorthand for applying **and()** to the first argument and the logical negation of the second argument. That is, **not(***a b***)** is equivalent to **and(***a* **not(***b***))**, where *a* and *b* are any boolean values. **not()** can be applied to a single boolean value; the result is the logical negation of that value.

When boolean operators are applied to vectors, they perform set operations. The set operation **and()** results in the set intersection of its two arguments—only those elements that are in both vectors are included in the result. The set operation **or()** results in the set union of its arguments—any element in either set is included in the result. Finally, set **not()** performs a set subtraction—only those elements of the first argument that aren't in the second are included in the result.

Unary forms of the set **or()** and set **and()** operators are also available. Their evaluation is deferred, however, to the enclosing operator, which provides additional context. Thus, **and()** with one argument effectively means, "all of these arguments," while **or()** with one argument means "any one or more of these arguments." They're essentially implicit arguments to the enclosing operator, proscribing search semantics, and can be used in this fashion only with the search operators, described below.

For example, in the following query fragments, the first expression selects objects whose Employee attribute contains any of the words in the parsed text; the second selects objects whose Employee attribute contains all of the words in the parsed text. (**whole()** is one of the search operators.)

```
whole(Employee or(parse(Jane Draper, 24, Boston, MA)))
whole(Employee and(parse(Jane Draper, 24, Boston, MA)))
```

The *relational operators* are **gt()**, **ge()**, **eq()**, **ne()**, **lt()**, and **le()**: greater than, greater than or equal to, equal, not equal, less than, and less than or equal to, respectively. These operators perform the expected comparisons with numbers and booleans, and lexical comparisons on strings, so that, for example, "graze" is less than "style." **add()**, **sub()**, **mul()**, **div()**, and **neg()** are the *arithmetic operators*: add, subtract, multiply, divide, and negate, respectively. All of these, except for **neg()**, require two arguments; **neg()** allows only one. All of these operators take atoms or vectors as their arguments, casting the second argument to have the same type as the first; for example, adding a number and a boolean will add the number with the boolean cast as a number.

The example predicates given earlier can be expressed in the query language using the relational and set operators. Naming the attributes Age, GPA, and HomeState, we have:

```
gt(Age 20)
eq(GPA 4.0)
eq(HomeState "Michigan")
and(gt(Age 20), eq(GPA 4.0))
or(gt(Age 20), eq(HomeState "Michigan")
not(eq(HomeState "Michigan"), eq(GPA 4.0))
not(and(gt(Age 20), eq(HomeState "Michigan")), eq(GPA 4.0))
```

The last group of operators, the *search operators*, provide a general and powerful way to search for strings within a string-valued attribute for the current object. They can be used with either one or two arguments. Used with two arguments, they require the first to be a string, a surrogate object, or an attribute (specified by an attribute name, the **project()** operator, or **self**), and the second to be an atom or vector (either literal or produced by the evaluation of a bound surrogate object or attribute), or a regular expression. Used with one argument, a search operator implicitly uses **self** as a first argument, so that the single argument is effectively the second. The three search operators are **whole()**, **prefix()**, and **within()**. Each specifies a different way in which strings must match. **whole()** indicates that full-term matches are desired: the desired string will only match one in the attribute if they match exactly from beginning to end. **prefix()** indicates that the requested value need only match the beginning part of the attribute's value. **within()** requests a substring search: a value can match any portion of the attribute's value.

Here are some examples of search expressions:

```
prefix(HomeState "Mi")
whole(HomeState regex(Mi.*))
whole(HomeState shell(Mi*))
```

The expressions above all search for objects whose HomeState begins with "Mi"—this can be used to find abbreviations of state names as well as full names. It will match values like "Michigan" and "Mississippi," but it will also match any word beginning with "Mi," like "Misery." For this particular example, a more careful search would be better:

```
or(eq(HomeState "Michigan"), eq(HomeState "Mi"))
or(whole(HomeState parse("Michigan")), whole(HomeState parse("Mi"))
```

These two examples explicitly check for the full name of the state, or for its abbreviation. The first example has the weakness of being case-sensitive; the abbreviation must be exactly "Mi" to match. The second example, by using the **parse()** operator, takes advantage of case folding (which is done by default, but can be turned off), so that "Mi", "MI", and "mi" will all match.

```
whole(parse(small dog))
whole(self and(parse(small dog)))
whole(Pets parse(small dog))
whole(project(Pets self) and(parse(small dog)))
```

The first two expressions above are equivalent. They search for objects containing the words "small" and "dog" (both words must be present, but might be in any attribute). The second pair are equivalent to the first, except that they match only the words in the Pets attribute. Note that "project(Pets self)" is equivalent to simply writing "Pets".

```
whole(or(parse(small dog)))
whole(Pets or(parse(small dog)))
```

The expressions above search for objects containing the words "small" or "dog" (only one need be present). The second expression restricts its search to the Pets attribute.

```
prefix(parse(small dog))
prefix(or(parse(small dog)))
within(parse(small dog))
within(or(parse(small dog)))
```

The first two expressions above search for objects containing words beginning with "small" and "dog"—for example, "smallpox" or "doggerel." The first example finds objects that have at least one match for each word, while the second finds objects that have at least one match for either word. The second pair of expressions search for objects containing the sequences "small" or "dog" as substrings of words—words like "smallish," "dismally," "endogen," or "underdog." The first example of the pair finds objects that have at least one match for each word, while the second finds objects that have at least one match for either.

```
whole("The beasts of the Mohave desert, the Russian steppes,
   and the Serengeti plain" Location)
```

The example above illustrates a different kind of search, in which objects whose Location attribute is a substring of the string on the left (such as "Russian steppes"). This is useful for finding objects related to a particular fragment of text.

Evaluation

Formally, a *query* is a logical expression consisting of predicates combined with set operators. Predicates consist of search, relational, or binary boolean expressions, with one of the arguments usually being an unbound attribute or surrogate object. The arguments can all be bound, but this results in an expression that is either always true or always false, and will select either all of the objects in the evaluation context, or none of them. For example, **gt**(5 3) is always true, so this query will simply select all objects in the context against which the query is evaluated.

Attributes can be specified in a predicate wherever an atom or vector would be allowed; in particular, they're allowed as arguments to boolean, relational, and arithmetic operators. Attributes are required with the search operators if they're not to evaluate as always true or always false.

Predefined Attributes

The query language implicitly defines one attribute, Default. Values of an object that can't be bound to any other attribute are bound to Default. This generally applies only to parsed text, for which Default indicates the body of the text. Parsing can generate many attributes based on keywords, such as Title, Author, PublicationDate, and so on. None of these is guaranteed to be generated for a body of text, so Default covers the general case.

If a query expression is evaluated by an IXFileFinder, the expression can also use the Content attribute. Content is defined as the entire unparsed contents of a file, and can be used for literal substring search with an IXFileFinder. Here are some examples of its use:

```
eq(Content "small dog")
whole(Content "small dog")
```

The expressions above are equivalent, and search for files whose contents are exactly "small dog".

```
prefix(Content "small dog")
within(Content "small dog")
```

The expressions above search for the literal phrase "small dog" at the beginning of the file and anywhere in the file, respectively.

The IXFileRecord class also defines a set of attributes, which can be specified in a query against an IXFileFinder or against a single IXFileRecord. The Content attribute isn't available in queries evaluated against an IXFileRecord, as that class doesn't have any way of actually reading the file's contents. Here are the attributes defined for IXFileRecords:

Attribute Name	Description
FileName	The file's relative pathname (string)
FileType	The file's type (string); for example, "rtf"
FileDevice	The file's logical device number (number)
FileInode	The file's inode number (number)
FileMode	The file's permissions (number)
FileCount	The number of hard links to the file (number)
FileOwner	The file owner's user id (number)
FileGroup	The file group's group id (number)
FileSize	The file's physical size, in bytes (number)
AccessTime	The time the file was last accessed (number)
ModifyTime	The time the file's contents were last changed (number)
ChangeTime	The time the file's status was last changed (number)
UnixType	The UNIX type of the file (number)

Values for the UnixType attribute can be:

Value	UNIX File Type
0	Normal UNIX file
1	A directory
2	A block device file
3	A character device file
4	A symbolic link
5	A socket

8 *Interface Builder*

8 *Interface Builder*

Library: None, this API is defined by the Interface Builder application

Header File Directory: /NextDeveloper/Headers/apps

Import: apps/InterfaceBuilder.h

Introduction

This chapter describes the application programming interface that lets you build custom palettes, inspectors, and editors for Interface Builder.

Interface Builder gives you direct access to the majority of the objects defined in NeXTSTEP. Adding a Text object or a DBTableView object to your application—objects that represent years of programming and testing effort—is as easy as dragging the object from Interface Builder's Palette window into your application's window. By creating a custom palette containing objects of your own design, you and other developers can manipulate these objects as easily as you do the ones in Interface Builder's standard palettes.

Using the facilities described in this chapter, you can easily create a palette that contains one or more objects of your own design. These objects can be of various types:

Type	**Instantiation**
View objects	Can be dragged into one of the application's standard windows.
MenuCell objects	Can be dragged into one of the application's menus.
Window objects	Can be dragged into the workspace.
Other non-View objects	Can be dragged into Interface Builder's File window.

The API described here also lets you provide inspectors for any custom object. There are four kinds of inspectors: Attributes, Connections, Size, and Help. The most common inspector to implement is the Attributes inspector, which lets the user set the custom object's unique features. For example, if you define a custom button object that sends a message repeatedly when it is pressed, the Attributes inspector could let the user set the repeat rate. Objects with special connection requirements (like those in the Database Kit) can provide their own Connection inspectors. The Size and Help inspectors are rarely overridden since they are appropriate for most types of objects.

If you need to provide the user with a more sophisticated system for interacting with your custom objects, you can implement an *editor* using the API described in this chapter. Whereas an inspector borrows one of Interface Builder's windows for its display, an editor provides its own window. The size of this window is not constrained as is the inspector window. Since each object can have its own editor, there can be multiple editor windows on the screen at once, making "copy and paste" and "drag and drop" interactions possible between editor windows. If the edited object contains other objects, the editor can open subeditors to let the user interact with the contained objects.

The DBModule object available from the Database Kit palette (in **/NextDeveloper/Palettes/DatabaseKit.palette**) provides an example of the use of an editor. If you drag a DBModule object into the File window and then double-click it, the editor opens its window.

To provide a better context for the discussion of the programming interface that makes custom palettes, inspectors, and editors possible, the next section gives a broad overview of Interface Builder's design.

Interface Builder's Design

You use Interface Builder to assemble and interconnect your application's objects. You start the process by creating a new document (or, more likely, by modifying the default document provided by Project Builder). When you save the document, it's represented by a file package having a name ending in ".nib". What's in this document or the nib file that represents it?

An Interface Builder document contains:

- An object hierarchy
- References to custom classes
- Connection information

Within Interface Builder, these components are managed by a *document object*. This object is of a private class, but can be queried and updated through the methods declared in the IBDocuments protocol.

The Object Hierarchy

A document object stores and maintains an object hierarchy. At the top of the hierarchy is the File's owner object—the object that's represented in the top-left portion of the File window. This is actually a proxy object, since the actual object that owns the interface will exist outside of the nib file. When a user adds an object to the interface project, it becomes part of the document by being attached to some other object—the *parent* object—in the object hierarchy. (In this hierarchy, a parent object may have many children, but each child can have only one parent object.) An object must be part of this hierarchy for it to be archived in the nib file.

Interface Builder declares and implements several methods as a category of Object (see the Object Additions specification) so that it can query any object in the hierarchy for crucial information. For example, each object can identify its various inspectors and its editor since it inherits these methods:

getInspectorClassName
getConnectInspectorClassName
getSizeInspectorClassName
getHelpInspectorClassName
getEditorClassName

When you define a class for a custom palette object, you can override any of these methods to provide your own inspector or editor.

Class References

Often, the object you want instantiated when your application runs is not available to Interface Builder either from its own library of objects or from any palette that has been dynamically loaded. For these cases, Interface Builder provides a proxy object such as the CustomView object in the Basic Views palette. When you drag a CustomView into your application, you are in fact adding this proxy object to the document's object hierarchy. When the resulting nib file is loaded within a running application, the proxy object is unarchived and queried to determine the identity of the class that the proxy represents. Then, an instance of this custom class is created (through the facilities of the **alloc** and **init** messages), and the proxy is freed.

Note that this distinction between objects that are unarchived and objects that are represented by proxies has important consequences. An objects that's unarchived can receive can receive **awake** and **finishUnarchiving** messages, but won't receive an **init** message. On the other hand, an object that's represented by a proxy object in the nib file will only receive an **init** message—it won't receive an **awake** or **finishUnarchiving** message.

Connection Information

An Interface Builder document also contains information about how objects within the object hierarchy are interconnected. This connection information is embodied in objects that conform to the IBConnectors protocol. Each connector object stores information about a connection between one source object and one destination object. Interface Builder's Connections inspector is the interface to a document's connector objects. Each time you connect a source object with a destination object, you are creating another connection object.

When you save the document, connector objects are archived in the nib file along with the objects they interconnect. When an application loads the nib file, the objects from the object hierarchy are unarchived, proxy objects are replaced with the appropriate instances, and connection objects are unarchived. Interface Builder then sends each connection object an **establishConnection** message, giving it an opportunity to connect its source and destination as it deems appropriate. For example, the standard connection object that Interface Builder provides (again, of an unspecified class) stores the identity of the source object's outlet variable and the destination object's action method, if any. So, when such a connector object receives an **establishConnection** message, it sets the source object's outlet to the destination object and—if the source object's outlet is named "target"—it sets the source's action to the destination's action method.

In most cases, Interface Builder's standard connection objects will be sufficient for your needs. However, you can create a Connection inspector and connection objects of your own, and through the methods declared in the IBDocuments protocol, you can have these connection objects archived in the nib file. Also, note that since connection objects are archived in the nib file, and since they all receive an **establishConnection** message when the nib file is loaded, they provide a convenient mechanism for storing any sort of information, not just connection information.

Interface Builder's Programming Interface

The API that Interface Builder defines is organized as two class definitions, several protocols, and several methods that are added, through the use of categories, to the definitions of the Object and View classes. The function of these components is summarized in the following tables.

Classes

Interface Builder uses these two class definitions as links to your custom palette and to inspectors. It's through the methods defined in these classes that Interface Builder locates and loads the user-interface objects that appear in the custom palette and in the inspector for a custom object.

IBPalette	This class is provided as the owner of palette's interface. If you custom palette includes only View objects, there's no reason to subclass IBPalette. If the objects that appear in the palette represent MenuCells, Windows, or other non-View objects, you'll have to create a subclass of IBPalette to associate the images in the Palette window with the real objects you intend to have instantiated.
IBInspector	This is the abstract superclass for inspectors. Your inspector provides Interface Builder with the controls to be loaded into the Inspector panel when the user attempts to inspect the custom object. The inspector also interprets the user's actions on these controls as commands to modify the custom object's state.

Protocols

These protocols define the ways your dynamically loaded palette module can communicate with Interface Builder (the IB and IBDocuments protocols) and the ways Interface Builder can communicate with objects in your module (the remaining protocols).

IB	This protocol gives you access to global information: the object that represents the active document, whether Interface Builder is in test mode, the source and destination objects of a connection, and so on.
IBDocuments	This protocol defines the programming interface to a document object in Interface Builder. Through this interface, you can add and remove objects from the document's object hierarchy, add or remove a connector object, and set the active editor.
IBInspectors	This protocol declares the methods that all inspector objects must have: **ok:**, **revert:**, and **wantsButtons**.
IBEditors	This protocol declares the methods through which Interface Builder can interact with an editor object. Interface Builder invokes these methods to make the editor's selected object visible; to copy, paste or delete the selection; and to open an close subeditors, among other things.
IBDocumentControllers	This protocol declares the notification methods Interface Builder can use to inform an object in your module about the state of the document—that it has been loaded or that it's about to be saved. You use the IB protocol to register an object as a document controller.
IBSelectionOwners	Editor objects conform to this protocol, which declares methods for counting the number of objects in the selection and for filling a List object with the objects in the selection.
IBConnectors	This protocol declares the methods that connector objects must implement. These include methods for identifying the source and destination of a connection and for establishing the connection between these objects.

Other Programming Interfaces

Through the use of categories, Interface Builder adds methods to the Object and View classes.

Object Additions	Interface Builder uses these methods to discover the various inspectors for the selected object. Default inspectors and editors are provided for all objects.
View Additions	These methods let custom View objects control how they are resized and redrawn.

Creating a Custom Palette

The process of creating a custom palette is most easily explained by example. See Chapter 18, "Creating a Custom Palette" in the *NeXTSTEP Development Tools and Techniques* manual for such an example. (This information is also available on-line in **/NextLibrary/Documentation/NextDev/DevTools/Part2_Techniques/18_CustomPalette**.)

Classes

IBInspector

Inherits From: Object

Conforms To: IBInspectors

Declared In: apps/InterfaceBuilder.h

Class Description

The IBInspector class defines the interface between an inspector for a loadable module and the Interface Builder application. When you build a new inspector for Interface Builder, you create a subclass of IBInspector.

The inspector you define must load its interface (that is, the nib file containing the interface), and it must override the inherited **ok:**, **revert:**, and **wantsButtons:** methods. The nib file is generally loaded as part of the inspector's **init** method. The **wantsButtons:** method controls whether the inspector displays OK and Revert button. (As with Interface Builder's standard inspectors, most custom inspectors won't need these buttons—instead, the user's actions in the Inspector panel are registered immediately by the inspected object.) The **ok:** and **revert:** methods control the synchronization of the Inspector panel's state with that of the inspected object. Interface Builder sends the inspector a **revert:** message to make the inspector reflect the current state of the inspected object. The **ok:** message should cause the inspector to set the state of the inspected object to that displayed in the Inspector panel.

An inspector should send itself a **touch:** message when the user begins modifying the data it displays. This message displays a broken "X" in the panel's close box and enables the inspector's OK and Revert buttons, if present. (See **textDidChange:** for alternate way to achieve this result.)

Instance Variables

id **object**;
id **window**;
id **driver**;
id **okButton**;
id **revertButton**;

object	The object that's being inspected.
window	The Panel that contains the inspector's user interface
okButton	The Inspector panel's OK button, if present.
revertButton	The Inspector panel's Revert button, if present.

Adopted Protocols

IBInspectors	– ok: – revert: – wantsButtons

Method Types

Accessing objects	– object – window
Managing changes	– touch: – textDidChange:

Instance Methods

object

– object

Returns the object that's being inspected in Interface Builder.

textDidChange:

– textDidChange:*sender*

Sends the IBInspector a **touch:** message on behalf of some Text object in the Inspector panel.

By making your inspector object the delegate of any Text object in the Inspector panel, the panel will be updated appropriately as the user alters the panel's contents.

See also: – touch:

touch:

– **touch:***sender*

Changes the image in the Inspector panel's close box to a broken "X" to indicate that the contents have been edited. Also, enables the buttons that allow the user to commit or abandon changes.

See also: – **textDidChange:**

window

– **window**

Returns the Window object that contains the user interface for the inspector.

IBPalette

Inherits From: Object

Declared In: apps/InterfaceBuilder.h

Class Description

The IBPalette class defines Interface Builder's link to a dynamically loaded palette. Interface Builder uses the facilities of this class to load a custom palette's interface and executable code.

Each loadable palette must contain a subclass of IBPalette, and this class must be identified in the palette's **palette.table** file. Interface Builder creates an instance of this subclass when it loads the palette. It then sends this object an **originalWindow** message to access the window that contains the objects to be loaded into the Palettes window.

If a palette contains non-View objects (MenuCells, Windows, or objects that will be deposited in the File window), the subclass must implement the **finishInstantiate** method to associate each View object that's displayed in the File window with the non-View object that should be created when the user instantiates the object by dragging it from the palette.

For example, consider a custom palette that provides an AddressBook object that manages people's names and addresses. This object, a subclass of Object, is to be dragged into the File window. Further, image that the subclass of IBPalette for this custom palette, AddressBookPalette, has two outlets: **addressBookObject** and **addressBookView**. When the palette was created, these outlets were connected to the AddressBook object and to a View object that will represent it in the Palette window. Within AddressBookPalette class implementation file, the **finishInstantiate** method would look like this:

```
- finishInstantiate
{
    [self associateObject:addressBookObject
        type:IBObjectPboardType with:addressBookView];
    return self;
}
```

Notice that the subclass establishes an association by sending itself an **associateObject:type:with:** message. IBPalette implements this method. The second argument controls where the palette image may be deposited:

Type	**Usage**
IBObjectPboardType	For objects that the user must deposit in the File window
IBMenuCellPboardType	For MenuCells without submenus; must be deposited in a menu
IBMenuPboardType	For MenuCells that have submenus; must be deposited in a menu
IBWindowPboardType	For Windows and Panels; must be deposited in the workspace

Instance Variables

id **paletteDocument**;
id **originalWindow**;
id **paletteView**;
id **draggedView**;

paletteDocument	An object conforming to the IBDocuments protocol that represents the dynamically loaded palette.
originalWindow	The window containing the interface objects that will be loaded into Interface Builder's Palettes window.
paletteView	private
draggedView	private

Method Types

Associating Views and Objects	– associateObject:type:with:
Initializing the palette	– finishInstantiate
Accessing related objects	– paletteDocument – originalWindow – findImageNamed:

Instance Methods

associateObject:type:with:

– **associateObject:***anObject*
  type:(NXAtom)*type*
  with:*aView*

Establishes an association between a View in a palette (*aView*) and the object that should be instantiated when the user drags the View from the palette (*anObject*). The *type* argument controls where the palette object may be deposited. (See the "Class Description" above for more information.

If your custom palette provides non-View objects, override IBPalette's **finishInstantiate** method with an implementation that sends **associateObject:type:with:** messages to associate each View object in the palette with the non-View object that it represents.

findImageNamed:

– **findImageNamed:**(const char *)*name*

Returns the NXImage instance associated with *name*. If no such image can be found, this method returns **nil**.

Use this method to refer to images in your custom palette. This method first tries to find the image by invoking NXImage's version of **findImageNamed:**. If that's unsuccessful, it uses the facilities of the NXBundle class to check the "**.palette**" directory for this resource. See **getPath:forResource:ofType:** for a description of NXBundle's search path.

See also: – **findImageNamed:**(NXImage class of the Application Kit), – **getPath:forResource:ofType:** (NXBundle common class)

finishInstantiate

– **finishInstantiate**

Implement to complete the initialization of your IBPalette object. Interface Builder sends a **finishInstantiate** message to the IBPalette object after it has been unarchived from the palette file. A typical use of this method is to associate a View object within the custom palette with a non-View object that is meant to represent it in the Palette window. See "Class Description," above, for more information.

See also: – **associateObject:type:with:**

originalWindow

– originalWindow

Returns the Window that contains the View objects to be loaded into Interface Builder's Palette window. When it loads a custom palette, Interface Builder sends the IBPalette subclass an **originalWindow** message. In your custom palette, you must connect the **originalWindow** outlet of your subclass of IBPalette to the Window that contains the Views that represent your palette objects.

paletteDocument

– paletteDocument

Returns an object that represents the dynamically loaded palette. This object is of unspecified class; however, it conforms to the IBDocuments protocol.

Object Additions

Category Of: Object

Declared In: apps/InterfaceBuilder.h

Category Description

Interface Builder adds these methods to the definition of the Object class so that any palette object can be queried for its various inspectors, for its editor, and for an image to represent the object when it's instantiated in the File window.

The inspector methods below return the class name for the object that will own the Inspector panel's display. Interface Builder caches this information so that when the user attempts to inspect an object, Interface Builder knows what type of inspector to instantiate (if it hasn't yet been instantiated). The inspector object provides the interface that Interface Builder displays in the Inspector panel.

Interface Builder supplies default implementations of these methods; you only override them if your custom palette object requires it. For example, if you create a TextField palette object that validates its input, you would probably provide an Attributes inspector that lets the user specify the acceptable input values. Thus, you would override the **getInspectorName** method to return the class name for the Attributes inspector object. However, you would probably not have to override the other inspector methods since the standard inspectors would be satisfactory.

Override the **getEditorClassName** method to return the class name of the editor to use for this object. The editor is invoked when the user double-clicks the object. View objects inherit Interface Builder's standard View editor.

You only need to override the **getIBImage** method if you want a special image to represent your custom palette object when it's dragged into the File window. If you don't supply such an image, Interface Builder will use the standard sphere image.

Instance Methods

getConnectInspectorClassName

– (const char *)**getConnectInspectorClassName**

Returns the class name of the receiver's Connection inspector. Interface Builder uses this information to instantiate the inspector object for the currently selected object. You should rarely need to override the standard Connection inspector.

getEditorClassName

– (const char *)**getEditorClassName**

Returns the class name of the receiver's editor. Interface Builder uses this information to instantiate the editor object for the currently selected object.

getHelpInspectorClassName

– (const char *)**getHelpInspectorClassName**

Returns the class name of the receiver's Help inspector. Interface Builder uses this information to instantiate the help inspector object for the currently selected object. You should rarely need to override the standard Help inspector.

getIBImage

– (NXImage *)**getIBImage**

Returns the image that's displayed in the File window when an instance of this class is created. By default, Interface Builder provides an image of a sphere. If you want to provide a different image, implement this method in your custom class.

getInspectorClassName

– (const char *)**getInspectorClassName**

Returns the class name of the receiver's Attributes inspector. Interface Builder uses this information to instantiate the help inspector object for the currently selected object.

getSizeInspectorClassName

– (const char *)**getSizeInspectorClassName**

Returns the class name of the receiver's size inspector. Interface Builder uses this information to instantiate the size inspector object for the currently selected object.

View Additions

Category Of: View

Declared In: apps/InterfaceBuilder.h

Category Description

Interface Builder adds these two methods to the definition of the View class so that a View that's dragged from the Palette window can control its size and make other adjustments as a consequence of resizing. As the user begins to drag one of the View's control points, Interface Builder sends it a **getMinSize:MaxSize:from:** message. When the user releases the mouse button, the View receives a **placeView:** message.

Instance Methods

getMinSize:maxSize:from:

– **getMinSize:**(NXSize *)*minSize* **maxSize:**(NXSize *)*maxSize* **from:**(int)*where*

Implement this method to control the minimum and maximum dimensions of your View. Place the dimensions you choose in the structures referred to by *minSize* and *maxSize*.

The *where* argument specifies which control point the user is dragging to resize the object. It can have these values:

IB_BOTTOMLEFT
IB_MIDDLELEFT
IB_TOPLEFT
IB_MIDDLETOP
IB_TOPRIGHT
IB_MIDDLERIGHT
IB_BOTTOMRIGHT
IB_MIDDLEBOTTOM

You can use the *where* argument to determine how the View will resize. For example, a Box determines which control point it being dragged and then lets the user shrink its size from that point only to the degree that no subview (Button, TextField) would be obscured.

placeView:

– **placeView:**(NXRect *)*frameRect*

Notifies a View of a change in its frame size. Interface Builder's implementation of this method is to send a **setFrame:** message to the receiver, using *frameRect* as the argument.

You can implement this method, for example, to resize the View's subviews. In your implementation, you should also send a **setFrame:** message to **self** to set the View's new size.

Protocols

IB

Adopted By: no NeXTSTEP classes

Declared In: apps/InterfaceBuilder.h

Protocol Description

Interface Builder's subclass of the Application class conforms to this protocol. Thus, objects in your custom palette can interact with Interface Builder's main module by sending messages (corresponding to the methods in this protocol) to NXApp. For example, if your editor window wants to cause Interface Builder to remove the connection lines from the screen, it would send this message:

```
[NXApp stopConnecting];
```

Method Types

Accessing the document	– activeDocument
Accessing the selection owner	– selectionOwner
Managing connections	– connectSource – connectDestination – isConnecting – stopConnecting – displayConnectionBetween:and:
Querying the mode	– isTestingInterface
Registering controllers	– registerDocumentController: – unregisterDocumentController:

Instance Methods

activeDocument

– activeDocument

Returns the active document, as represented by an object that conforms to the IBDocuments protocol. (For the user, the active document is represented by the active File window.)

connectDestination

– **connectDestination**

Returns the object that's the destination of the connection; that is, the object to which the user has dragged a connection line.

See also: – **connectSource**

connectSource

– **connectSource**

Returns the object that's the source of the connection; that is, the object from which the user dragged a connection line.

See also: – **connectDestination**

displayConnectionBetween:and:

– **displayConnectionBetween:***source* **and:***destination*

Causes Interface Builder to draw connection lines between *source* and *destination*. For example, when the user clicks an entry in the Connections list in the Connections inspector, Interface Builder uses this method to display the corresponding connection.

The act of displaying a connection between these two objects doesn't require that a connection really exist, and doesn't create a connection. It's the Connection inspector's responsibility to establish the programmatic connection. This method simply draws lines between two objects and attempts to make both objects visible.

See also: – **stopConnecting**

isConnecting

– (BOOL)**isConnecting**

Returns YES if connection lines are being displayed in Interface Builder. You can use this information to control how your object is drawn during the connection process. For example, when you drag a connection line from a button, the button's black border and text are redrawn in gray.

See also: – **stopConnecting**

isTestingInterface

– (BOOL)**isTestingInterface**

Returns YES if Interface Builder is in Test mode.

registerDocumentController:

– **registerDocumentController:***aController*

Adds *aController* to the list of objects to be notified when Interface Builder documents are opened or saved. See the IBDocumentControllers protocol for a description of the notification messages. Controllers should be registered as the palette is loaded, perhaps as part of the IBPalette object's **finishInstantiate** method.

See also: – **unregisterDocumentController:**

selectionOwner

– **selectionOwner**

Returns the editor of the currently selected object or **nil** if no object is selected.

stopConnecting

– **stopConnecting**

Causes Interface Builder to remove any connection lines from the screen. Interface Builder uses this method to remove connection lines when the user drags a window.

See also: – **isConnecting**

unregisterDocumentController:

– **unregisterDocumentController:***aController*

Removes *aController* from the list of objects to be notified when Interface Builder documents are opened or saved.

See also: – **registerDocumentController:**

IBConnectors

Adopted By: no NeXTSTEP classes

Declared In: apps/InterfaceBuilder.h

Protocol Description

This protocol declares Interface Builder's link to a connector object. Connectors are designed to store information about connections between objects in a nib document. For example, the private class that Interface Builder uses to store information about outlet connections conforms to this protocol and adds a method to store the name of the outlet. Connector objects are archived in the nib file.

When an application begins executing and it loads a nib file, the connector objects in the nib file are unarchived and are sent the **establishConnection** message. It is at this point that the connector can establish its type of connection between the source and destination. For example, Interface Builder's outlet connector sets the named outlet to point to the destination object.

Since connector objects are guaranteed to be archived in the nib file and are guaranteed to receive an **establishConnection** message at run time, they provide a mechanism for you to store other application-specific information in a nib file.

Your Connection inspector must set the source and destination in each of its connectors (for example, with **setSource:** and **setDestination:** methods). This protocol doesn't include methods to set these outlets, only to query them.

Instance Methods

destination

– destination

Implement to return the object that is the destination of the connection.

See also: **– source**

establishConnection

– **establishConnection**

Implement to connect the source and destination objects. Interface Builder sends this message to each connector object after all objects have been unarchived from the nib file.

free

– **free**

Implement to release the storage for the connector object.

nibInstantiate

– **nibInstantiate**

Implement to verify the identities of the connector's source and destination objects.

Interface Builder sends a **nibInstantiate** message to a connector object to give it an opportunity to verify that its **source** and **destination** instance variables point to the intended objects. For example, consider the case in which a user puts a CustomView in a window and then reassigns the CustomView's class to MyView. The MyView class has a **textfield** outlet that the user connects to a neighboring TextField object. This action causes Interface Builder to create a connector object and set its destination to the TextField and its source to the CustomView. (The source can't be set to the MyView object since that class doesn't exist in InterfaceBuilder—that's why the CustomView was used in the first place.)

When the resulting nib file is loaded in the finished application, the connector object is unarchived and sent a **nibInstantiate** message. It's at this point that the connector must reset its **source** instance variable from the CustomView object to the MyView object.

The Application Kit, in a category of Object, provides a default implementation of this method. This implementation returns **self**. (Please note that the method isn't publically declared, a problem that will be remedied in a later release.) Consequently, all objects can respond to a **nibInstantiate** message. Your connector, therefore, should minimally implement this method to send **nibInstantiate** messages to its source and destination objects. For example, assuming the outlets are named *theSource* and *theDestination*, the implementation is:

```
- nibInstantiate
{
    theSource = [theSource nibInstantiate];
    theDestination = [theDestination nibInstantiate];
    return self;
}
```

This will allow the source and destination objects to return the **id**s of the intended objects.

read:

– **read:**(NXTypedStream *)*stream*

Implement to unarchive the connector object from *stream*. The connector should read in its instance variables and do any other initialization it requires.

See also: – **write**

renewObject:to:

– **renewObject:***old* **to:***new*

Implement to update a connector by replacing its old source or destination object (*old*) with a new object (*new*). This is used by Interface Builder, for example, when a user drags a Button object into a Matrix of ButtonCells. Assuming that the Button was connected, the connection information must be updated to reflect that fact that the Button has been replaced by a ButtonCell. Interface Builder updates this information by sending the appropriate connector object a **renewObject:to:** message with the Button as *old* and the ButtonCell as *new*.

source

– **source**

Implement to return the object that is the source of the connection.

See also: – **destination**

write:

– **write:**(NXTypedStream *)*stream*

Implement to archive the connector object to *stream*.

See also: – **read**

IBDocumentControllers

Adopted By: no NeXTSTEP classes

Declared In: apps/InterfaceBuilder.h

Protocol Description

This is the protocol that Interface Builder uses to communicate with objects that have been registered as document controllers. (See **registerDocumentController:** in the IB protocol specification.) A document controller could, for example, use these notification messages to ensure that if a nib file containing an older version of a custom palette object is loaded, it will be saved with the new version of the object.

Instance Methods

didOpenDocument:

– **didOpenDocument:***theDocument*

Notifies the controller that *theDocument* has been opened.

didSaveDocument:

– **didSaveDocument:***theDocument*

Notifies the controller that *theDocument* has been saved.

willSaveDocument:

– **willSaveDocument:***theDocument*

Notifies the controller that the user is attempting to save *theDocument*.

IBDocuments

Adopted By: no NeXTSTEP classes

Declared In: apps/InterfaceBuilder.h

Protocol Description

This is the protocol to use to communicate with Interface Builder's document object. The document object is private to Interface Builder but may be accessed by sending Interface Builder's subclass of Application an **activeDocument** message:

```
theActiveDoc = [NXApp activeDocument];
```

The document object maintains the components of a document:

- The object hierarchy
- The list of connectors
- The active editor

It also mediates in copy and paste operations and controls the redisplay of objects in Interface Builder.

Through the document object, you keep Interface Builder informed of changes to the data structure that you want archived in the nib file. For example, if your custom editor allows the user to add an object by dragging it into the editor's window, you must inform Interface Builder of this addition by sending the document object an **attachObject:to:** message. Interface Builder won't archive an object in the nib file unless it has been added to the object hierarchy. (Note: A paste operation, which uses the **pasteType:fromPasteboard:parent:** method, automatically updates the hierarchy.)

Method Types

Managing the document	– touch – getDocumentPathIn:
Managing the object hierarchy	– attachObject:to: – attachObjects:to: – deleteObject: – deleteObjects: – copyObject:type:inPasteboard: – copyObjects:type:inPasteboard: – pasteType:fromPasteboard:parent: – objectIsMember: – getObjects: – getParentForObject:
Setting object names	– setName:for: – getNameIn:for:
Managing connectors	– addConnector: – removeConnector: – listConnectors:forSource: – listConnectors:forDestination: – listConnectors:forSource:filterClass: – listConnectors:forDestination:filterClass:
Managing editors	– setSelectionFrom: – editorDidClose:for: – getEditor:for: – openEditorFor:
Updating the display	– redrawObject:

Instance Methods

addConnector:

– **addConnector:***aConnector*

Adds a connector object to the list maintained by Interface Builder. (See the IBConnectors protocol for more information.) This is the message a custom connection inspector sends Interface Builder's document object to register a connection.

See also: – **addConnector:**

attachObject:to:

– **attachObject:***anObject* **to:***parent*

Adds *anObject* to the document's object hierarchy by attaching it to *parent*. This method (and the related method **attachObjects:to:**) lets you keep the document's object hierarchy informed of changes in the objects under the control of your custom editor.

See also: – **attachObjects:to:**

attachObjects:to:

– **attachObjects:**(List *)*objectList* **to:***parent*

Adds the objects in *objectList* to the document's object hierarchy by attaching them to *parent*. This method (and the related method **attachObject:to:**) lets you keep the document's object hierarchy informed of changes in the objects under the control of your custom editor.

See also: – **attachObject:to:**

copyObject:type:inPasteboard:

– **copyObject:***anObject*
  type:(NXAtom)*type*
  inPasteboard:(Pasteboard *)*aPasteboard*

Copies *anObject* to the specified pasteboard. The *type* argument can be one of the following:

IBObjectPboardType
IBCellPboardType
IBMenuPboardType
IBMenuCellPboardType
IBViewPboardType
IBWindowPboardType

An editor should send the document object a **copyObject:type:inPasteboard:** or **copyObjects:type:inPasteboard:** message as part of its implementation of its **copySelection** method.

See also: – **copyObjects:type:inPasteboard:**

copyObjects:type:inPasteboard:

– **copyObjects:**(List *)*objectList*
  type:(NXAtom)*type*
  inPasteboard:(Pasteboard *)*aPasteboard*

Copies the objects in *objectList* to the specified pasteboard. The *type* argument can be one of the following:

IBObjectPboardType
IBCellPboardType
IBMenuPboardType
IBMenuCellPboardType
IBViewPboardType
IBWindowPboardType

An editor should send the document object a **copyObject:type:inPasteboard:** or **copyObjects:type:inPasteboard:** message as part of its implementation of its **copySelection** method.

See also: – **copyObject:type:inPasteboard**:

deleteObject:

– **deleteObject:***anObject*

Removes *anObject* from the document's object hierarchy. An editor should send the document object a **deleteObject:** or **deleteObjects:** message as part of its implementation of the **deleteSelection** method. This will keep the document's accounting of the objects in the nib document in agreement with the actual state of the document.

See also: – **deleteObjects:**

deleteObjects:

– **deleteObjects:**(List *)*objectList*

Removes the objects in *objectList* from the document's object hierarchy. An editor should send the document object a **deleteObject:** or **deleteObjects:** message as part of its implementation of the **deleteSelection** method. This will keep the document's accounting of the objects in the nib document in agreement with the actual state of the document.

See also: – **deleteObject:**

editorDidClose:for:

– **editorDidClose:***anEditor* **for:***anObject*

Informs the document object that *anEditor* is no longer active. By sending this message to the document object when you close an editor, you keep Interface Builder's record of the active editor up to date. Interface Builder itself invokes this method whenever an editor is closed because of a user action, such as the closing of a window.

getDocumentPathIn:

– **getDocumentPathIn:**(char *)*buffer*

Places the document's path in *buffer*. This is the path displayed as the title of Interface Builder's File window. Make sure that *buffer* is sufficiently larger to hold the path. Returns the document object.

getEditor:for:

– **getEditor:**(BOOL)*createIt* **for:***anObject*

Returns the editor object for *anObject*. If *createIt* is YES and the editor hasn't been instantiated, it will be instantiated and returned. If *createIt* is NO, the editor is returned only if it has already been instantiated. If *createIt* is NO and the editor hasn't been instantiated, this method returns **nil**.

getNameIn:for:

– **getNameIn:**(char *)*buffer* **for:***anObject*

Places the name associated with *anObject* in *buffer*. Make sure the buffer you pass in is sufficiently large to accommodate the name. Returns the document object.

See also: – **setName:for:**

getObjects:

– **getObjects:**(List *)*objectList*

Places the objects from the document's object hierarchy into *objectList*. The object's are not arranged in any particular order.

getParentForObject:

– **getParentForObject:***anObject*

Returns the object above *anObject* in the document's object hierarchy. The top object is the File's owner. Returns **nil** if *anObject* is the File's owner.

listConnectors:forDestination:

– **listConnectors:**(List *)*aList* **forDestination:***aDestination*

Places in *aList* all connector objects whose destinations are *aDestination*. Returns *aList*.

Since a given object can be the destination of multiple connections, the connection information is returned as a list of objects. Each object in the list conforms to the IBConnectors protocol and contains the information for one connection.

aList is a List object that you provide. When you're done with *aList*, free it but don't free the connection objects within it since they're managed by Interface Builder.

See also: – **listConnectors:forDestination:filterClass:**, – **listConnectors:forSource:**

listConnectors:forDestination:filterClass:

– **listConnectors:**(List *)*aList*
  forDestination:*aDestination*
  filterClass:*aClass*

Places in *aList* the connector objects of class *aClass* whose destinations are *aDestination*. Returns *aList*.

Since a given object can be the destination of multiple connections, the connection information is returned as a list of objects. Each object in the list conforms to the IBConnectors protocol and contains the information for one connection.

aList is a List object that you provide. When you're done with *aList*, free it but don't free the connection objects within it since they're managed by Interface Builder.

See also: – **listConnectors:forDestination:**, – **listConnectors:forSource:**

listConnectors:forSource:

– **listConnectors:**(List *)*aList* **forSource:***aSource*

Places in *aList* all connector objects whose sources are *aSource*. Returns *aList*.

Since a given source can have multiple connections, the connection information is returned as a list of objects. Each object in the list conforms to the IBConnectors protocol and contains the connection information for one connection.

aList is a List object that you provide. When you're done with *aList*, free it but don't free the connection objects within it since they're managed by Interface Builder.

See also: – **listConnectors:forSource:filterClass:**, – **listConnectors:forDestination:**

listConnectors:forSource:filterClass:

– **listConnectors:**(List *)*aList*
forSource:*aSource*
filterClass:*aClass*

Places in *aList* the connector objects of class *aClass* whose sources are *aSource*. Returns *aList*.

Since a given source can have multiple connections, the connection information is returned as a list of objects. Each object in the list conforms to the IBConnectors protocol and contains the connection information for one connection.

aList is a List object that you provide. When you're done with *aList*, free it but don't free the connection objects within it since they're managed by Interface Builder.

See also: – **listConnectors:forSource:**, – **listConnectors:forDestination:**

objectIsMember:

– (BOOL)**objectIsMember:***anObject*

Returns YES if *anObject* is a part of the document's object hierarchy; NO otherwise. You might send an **objectIsMember:** message to the document object before attempting to open a subeditor for *anObject*.

openEditorFor:

– (BOOL)**openEditorFor:***anObject*

Opens the editor object for *anObject*. This method ensures that editors for all the objects above *anObject* in the object hierarchy are open before opening *anObject*'s editor.

pasteType:fromPasteboard:parent:

– (List *)**pasteType:**(NXAtom)*type*
fromPasteboard:(Pasteboard *)*thePasteboard*
parent:*theParent*

Alerts the document object that one or more objects were pasted. Returns a List containing the **id**s of the objects that were pasted. The pasteboard and the type being pasted are identified by *thePasteboard* and *type*.

An editor uses this method to keep Interface Builder's document object up to date. The implementation of this method invokes **attachObjects:to:** and **touch** for you. The List object that's returned lets you add the objects to your data structures. It is your responsibility to free the returned List.

redrawObject:

– **redrawObject:***anObject*

Redraws the selected object by opening its editor—and the editor for its parent object, and so on up the object hierarchy—and sending each editor a **resetObject:** message.

removeConnector:

– **removeConnector:***aConnector*

Removes *aConnector* from the list of connectors maintained by Interface Builder. (See the IBConnectors protocol for more information on connectors.) This is the message a custom connection inspector sends Interface Builder's document object to break a connection.

Interface Builder doesn't free *aConnector*; it's your responsibility to do so.

See also: – **addConnector:**

setName:for:

– (BOOL)**setName:**(const char *)*name* **for:***anObject*

Sets the name associated with the *anObject*. For objects in the File window, this is the name displayed below the object's image. Except for objects in the File window, setting an object's name is generally not needed.

See also: – **getNameIn:for:**

setSelectionFrom:

– **setSelectionFrom:***anEditor*

Registers *anEditor* as the editor that owns the selection.

When you activate an editor or change the selection, make sure you send this message to the document object. This keeps Interface Builder informed of the selection's owner. In this way, when the user switches from one window to another, or from one document to another, Interface Builder can inform the proper editor to display its selection. Also, Interface Builder uses the selection information to determine which inspector to display in its Inspector panel.

touch

– **touch**

Marks the document as edited by causing the File window's close box to display a broken "X". Returns the document object.

IBEditors

Adopted By: no NeXTSTEP classes

Incorporates: IBSelectionOwners

Declared In: apps/InterfaceBuilder.h

Protocol Description

This protocol, and the IBSelectionOwners protocol that it incorporates, define the required programmatic interface to an editor object in Interface Builder. When a user double-clicks a custom object, Interface Builder instantiates the object's editor (using **initWith: inDocument:**). (Interface Builder would have previously determined the editor's class by sending the custom object a **getEditorClassName** message. See the Object Additions specification for more information.) The editor presents its window, allowing the user to make alterations to the displayed data.

For example, assume that a custom palette provides an AddressBook object. Once instantiated in the File window, the AddressBook object can be double-clicked to activate the editor. The editor presents the user with a window that permits the entry of names and addresses. As data is entered, the editor can update the AddressBook object with the new information.

Besides letting users edit an object's state, an editor intercedes in copy and paste operations. When the user chooses the Cut or Copy command, Interface Builder sends a **deleteSelection** or **copySelection** message to the editor. The editor takes the appropriate action and then alerts Interface Builder's document object that the cut or copy operation has occurred. This keeps the document object up-to-date with the actual state of the document.

When a paste operation is attempted, Interface Builder sends the active editor an **acceptsTypeFrom:** message to determine if it will accept any of the types on the pasteboard. If the editor refuses the offered types, Interface Builder sends the same message to the next higher editor in the object hierarchy, and so on until it reaches the top. This explains why, if a paste operation is attempted when a Button object is on the pasteboard and the Pop-up list editor is open, nothing is pasted in the selected PopUpList; instead, the Button is pasted in the window that contains the PopUpList. The PopUpList refused the pasteboard type, but the View editor accepted it.

If the editor accepts one of the offered types, the editor receives a **pasteInSelection** message. The editor then replaces the selection with the pasted data and alerts Interface Builder of the change by sending the document object a **pasteType:fromPasteboard:parent:** message.

Editors also control the opening and closing of subeditors. Imagine that an AddressBook object can contain not only addresses, but other AddressBooks. For example, an AddressBook for a university could contain AddressBooks for each department of the university. When the AddressBook for the Spanish department is double-clicked, a subeditor must be opened to allow the editing of this nested AddressBook.

Method Types

Initializing	– initWith:inDocument:
Identifying objects	– document – editedObject – window
Displaying objects	– resetObject:
Managing the selection	– wantsSelection – selectObjects: – makeSelectionVisible:
Copying and pasting objects	– copySelection – deleteSelection – pasteInSelection – acceptsTypeFrom:
Opening and closing editors	– close – openSubeditorFor: – closeSubeditors
Activating the editor	– orderFront – activate

Instance Methods

acceptsTypeFrom:

– (NXAtom)**acceptsTypeFrom:**(const NXAtom *)*typeList*

Implement to return the pasteboard types your editor accepts. *typeList* is an array of character pointers holding the type names, with the last pointer being NULL. Each of the pointers is of the type NXAtom, meaning that the type name is a unique string. If your editor doesn't accept any of the supplied types, it should return NULL.

For example, if an editor only accepts the type IBObjectPboardType, it could implement this method in this way:

```
- (NXAtom)acceptsTypeFrom:(const NXAtom *)typeList
{
    int i = 0;
    if (!typeList) return NULL;
    while (typeList[i]) {
        if (IBObjectPboardType == typeList[i])
            return IBObjectPboardType;
        i++;
    }
    return NULL;
}
```

activate

– (BOOL)**activate**

Implement to activate the editor. Typically, an editor activates itself by making its window key, displaying its selection, and advising the document object that it owns the selection:

```
- (BOOL)activate
{
    [window makeKeyAndOrderFront:self];
    [self makeSelectionVisible:YES];
    [document setSelectionFrom:self];
    return YES;
}
```

Your implementation of this method should return YES if the editor activates itself and NO otherwise.

When a user double-clicks an object controlled by an editor, the editor receives an **orderFront** and then an **activate** message.

See also: – **orderFront**

close

– **close**

Implement to close the editor and free its resources. This method can be invoked for a number of reasons. For example, Interface Builder invokes this method when the user closes the document. Or, your editor might send itself a **close** message when the user closes the editor's window.

As part of the implementation of this method, send an **editorDidClose:for:** message to the active document to inform IB that this editor has closed:

```
[[NXApp activeDocument] editorDidClose:self for:editedObject];
```

See also: – **editorDidClose:for:** (IBDocuments protocol)

closeSubeditors

– **closeSubeditors**

Implement to close all subeditors.

See also: – **openSubeditorFor:**

copySelection

– (BOOL)**copySelection**

Implement to copy the selected object(s) to the pasteboard. When the user chooses the Cut or Copy commands in Interface Builder, the editor that owns the selection receives a **copySelection** message.

In your implementation of this method, you should send the document object a **copyObject:type:inPasteboard:** or a **copyObjects:type:inPasteboard:** message, as declared in the IBDocuments protocol. Return YES if the selection was copied to the pasteboard; NO otherwise.

See also: – **deleteSelection**

deleteSelection

– (BOOL)**deleteSelection**

Implement to delete the selected object(s). This method is invoked when the user deletes the selection by using the Delete key or as part of the Cut command (after the selection has been copied using the **copySelection** method).

In your implementation of this method, you should send the document object a **deleteObject:** or a **deleteObjects:** message, as declared in the IBDocuments protocol. Return YES if the selection was deleted; NO otherwise.

See also: – **copySelection**

document

– **document**

Implement this method to return the currently active document, as would be returned by sending an **activeDocument** message to NXApp.

editedObject

– **editedObject**

Implement to return the object that's being edited. This is generally the object that the user double-clicked to open the editor.

initWith:inDocument:

– **initWith:***anObject* **inDocument:***aDocument*

Implement this method to initialize a newly allocated editor. *anObject* is the object that is being edited (for example, the object that the user has double-clicked). *aDocument* is the currently active document, as would be returned by sending an **activeDocument** message to NXApp. Typically, an editor object caches the document object in one of its instance variables, since editors must frequently communicate with the document object.

makeSelectionVisible:

– **makeSelectionVisible:**(BOOL)*flag*

Implement to add or remove the selection markings from the current selection. An editor receives a **makeSelectionVisible:** message whenever Interface Builder wants to ensure that the selection is properly marked. For example, when a window becomes key, the editor that owns the selection in the window receives a **makeSelectionVisible:**YES message. When the window loses its key window status, the editor that owns the selection receives a **makeSelectionVisible:**NO message.

openSubeditorFor:

– **openSubeditorFor:***anObject*

Implement to open the subeditor for *anObject*. An editor receives this message when the user double-clicks within the editor's selection. For the return value of this method, the editor should return **nil** if there is no subeditor; otherwise, it should return the **id** of the subeditor.

orderFront

– **orderFront**

Implement to bring the editor's window to the front. When a user double-clicks an object, the controlling editor receives an **orderFront** and then an **activate** message.

See also: – **activate**

pasteInSelection

– (BOOL)**pasteInSelection**

Implement to paste the object(s) from the pasteboard into the current selection. When the user chooses the Paste command in Interface Builder, the editor that owns the selection receives a **pasteInSelection** message. The implementation of the corresponding method should invoke the document object's **pasteType:fromPasteboard:parent:** method.

This method should return YES if the paste operation was successful; NO otherwise.

See also: – **pasteType:fromPasteboard:parent:** (IBDocuments protocol)

resetObject:

– **resetObject:***anObject*

This method should redraw *anObject*. When the document object receives a **redrawObject:** message, it makes sure that the editor for that object—and for each of its parent objects—is open. It then sends **resetObject:** messages to each of the editors in this object hierarchy.

selectObjects:

– **selectObjects:**(List *)*objectList*

Implement to draw the objects in *objectList* in a way that indicates that they are selected.

wantsSelection

– (BOOL)**wantsSelection**

Implement to return YES if the editor is willing to become the selection owner; NO if not.

window

– **window**

Implement to return the editor window.

IBInspectors

Adopted By: IBInspector

Declared In: apps/InterfaceBuilder.h

Protocol Description

The IBInspectors protocol declares the three methods that all inspectors in Interface Builder must implement: **ok:**, **revert:**, and **wantsButtons:**. Since you invariably create an inspector by creating a subclass of IBInspector—a class that adopts the IBInspectors protocol—your inspector will inherit default implementations of these methods, which you can override.

Instance Methods

ok:

– **ok:***sender*

Implement in your subclass of IBInspector to commit the changes that the user makes in the Inspector panel. The OK button in the Inspector panel—if present—sends an **ok:** message when the user clicks it.

Your implementation of this method must send the same message to **super**:

```
ok:sender
{
    /* your code to commit changes */
    [super ok:sender];
    return self;
}
```

The message to super replaces the broken "X" in the panel's close box with the standard "X", indicating that the changes have been committed.

See also: – **revert:**, – **touch:** (IBInspector class)

revert:

– **revert:**sender

Implement in your subclass of IBInspector to load data into the inspector's display. Interface Builder sends this message to the inspector object whenever the inspector's display might need to be updated, for example, when the user opens the Inspector panel and the selected object in Interface Builder is of the type associated with this inspector object. The Revert button in the Inspector panel—if present—also sends a **revert:** message when the user clicks it.

Your subclass must implement this method, and it must send the same message to **super** as part of its implementation:

```
revert:sender
{
    /* your code to inspect selected object */
    [super revert:sender];
    return self;
}
```

This message to **super** replaces the broken "X" in the panel's close box with the standard "X", indicating that the changes have been discarded.

See also: – **ok:**, – **touch:** (IBInspector class)

wantsButtons

– (BOOL)**wantsButtons**

Returns a boolean value indicating whether the inspector object requires Interface Builder to display the OK and Revert buttons in the Inspector panel.

See also: – **wantsButtons** (IBInspector class)

IBSelectionOwners

Adopted By: no NeXTSTEP classes

Declared In: apps/InterfaceBuilder.h

Protocol Description

All editors must conform to this protocol. By implementing this protocol, an editor advertises its selection to other objects in Interface Builder. (The *selection* is that object or objects that would be copied if the user chose the Copy command.)

For example, Interface Builder invokes an editor's **selectionCount** and **getSelectionInto:** methods to determine how to update the Inspector panel. If the selection count is more than one, the Inspector panel displays the message "Multiple Selection". If there is only one object in the selection, Interface Builder invokes the editor's **getSelectionInto:** method to access the object and then determines the appropriate inspector to display in the Inspector panel.

Instance Methods

getSelectionInto:

– **getSelectionInto:**(List *)*objectList*

Implement this method to place the currently selected objects into *objectList*. If the editor doesn't have a selection, it should simply make sure *objectList* is empty.

See also: – **selectionCount**

redrawSelection

– **redrawSelection**

Implement this method to redraw the objects in the selection.

selectionCount

– (unsigned int)**selectionCount**

Implement to return the number of objects in your editor's selection.

See also: – **getSelectionInto:**

Types and Constants

Symbolic Constants

Control Point Constants

DECLARED IN apps/InterfaceBuilder.h

SYNOPSIS

IB_BOTTOMLEFT
IB_MIDDLELEFT
IB_TOPLEFT
IB_MIDDLETOP
IB_TOPRIGHT
IB_MIDDLERIGHT
IB_BOTTOMRIGHT
IB_MIDDLEBOTTOM

DESCRIPTION These constants identify the control points that appear around a selected View object in a application that's under construction. See the description of the **getMinSize:MaxSize:from:** method in the View Additions specification for more information.

Global Variables

Pasteboard Types

DECLARED IN apps/InterfaceBuilder.h

SYNOPSIS NXAtom **IBObjectPboardType**;
NXAtom **IBCellPboardType**;
NXAtom **IBMenuPboardType**;
NXAtom **IBMenuCellPboardType**;
NXAtom **IBViewPboardType**;
NXAtom **IBWindowPboardType**;

DESCRIPTION These global variables identify some additional pasteboard types used by Interface Builder. See the IBPalette class specification for information on the use of these types.

9 *Mach Kit*

9 *Mach Kit*

Library: libNeXT_s.a

Header File Directory: /NextDeveloper/Headers/machkit

Introduction

The Mach Kit provides an object-oriented interface to some of the features of the Mach operating system. At this time, it is most useful to applications that make use of the Distributed Objects system, since these applications rely upon Mach's message sending abilities to transport objects, ports, and data between processes. The Mach Kit may also be useful for drivers and multithreaded applications. The Mach Kit provides several classes and protocols, listed below.

Mach Kit Classes

NXProtocolChecker	Defines objects that restrict the messages that other objects can receive.
NXPort	Defines an object corresponding to a mach port.
NXNetNameServer	Provides an interface to the Network Name Server to allow public access to ports.
NXInvalidationNotifier	Defines objects that notify others when they are no longer fully functional.
NXData	Provides an object-oriented interface to data, allowing data to be transferred between applications as an object.
NXSpinLock, NXConditionLock, NXLock, NXRecursiveLock	Define various kinds of locks that can be useful for protecting critical sections of code in drivers and multithreaded applications

Mach Kit Protocols

NXLock	A protocol for objects that protect resources with locks.
NXReference	A protocol to allow reference counting of shared objects.
NXSenderIsInvalid	A protocol for objects that need to be informed when other objects become unusable.

Classes

NXConditionLock

Inherits From: Object

Conforms To: NXLock

Declared In: machkit/NXLock.h

Class Description

NXConditionLock is a type of lock with which a state can be used. The user of the lock can request that the lock be acquired when it enters a particular state, and can reset the state when releasing the lock. The meaning of this state is defined by the user of the lock. NXConditionLock is well suited to synchronizing different modules, such as a producer-consumer problem where a producer and consumer must share data but the consumer should sleep until a condition is met (such as, until data is available).

NXConditionLock class provides two ways of locking its objects (**lock** and **lockUntil:**) and two ways of unlocking (**unlock** and **unlockWith:**). Any combination of locking method and unlocking method is legal. Following is an example of how the producer-consumer problem might be handled using condition locks. The producer need not wait for a condition, but must wait for the lock to be made available so it can safely create shared data. Example producer code follows:

```
id condLock;        // uses currentState to guard access to data

/* create the lock only once, and set initial state */
condLock = [[NXConditionLock alloc] initWith:NO_DATA];

while (/*stuff to process*/) {
    [condLock lock];
    /* Manipulate global data, change state if needed. */
    [condLock unlockWith:DATA_AVAILABLE];
}
```

A consumer can then lock until the producer has data available and the producer is out of locked critical sections:

```
for(;;) {
    [condLock lockWhen:DATA_AVAILABLE];
    /* Manipulate global data... */
    [condLock unlockWith:NO_DATA];
}
```

An NXConditionLock doesn't busy-wait, so it can be used to lock time-consuming operations without degrading system performance.

The NXConditionLock, NXLock, NXRecursiveLock, and NXSpinLock classes all implement the NXLock protocol with various features and performance characteristics; see the other class descriptions for more information.

Instance Variables

None declared in this class.

Method Types

Initializing an instance	– init – initWith:
Get the condition of the lock	– condition
Acquire or release the lock	– lock – lockWhen: – unlock – unlockWith:

Instance Methods

condition

– (int)**condition**

Returns the lock's current condition. This condition can be set with the **initWith:** or **unlockWith:** methods.

init

– **init**

Initializes a newly allocated NXConditionLock instance and sets its condition to 0.

initWith:

– **initWith:**(int)*condition*

Initializes a newly allocated NXConditionLock instance and sets its condition to *condition*. This message should not be sent to an instance that has already been initialized.

lock

– **lock**

Waits until the lock isn't in use, then grabs the lock. The lock can subsequently be released with either **unlock** or **unlockWith:**.

lockWhen:

– **lockWhen:**(int)*condition*

Waits until the lock isn't in use and the lock's condition matches *condition*, then grabs the lock. The lock's condition can be set by **initWith:** or **unlockWith:**. The lock can subsequently be released with either **unlock** or **unlockWith:**.

unlock

– **unlock**

Releases the lock but doesn't change its condition.

See also: – **unlockWith:**

unlockWith:

– **unlockWith:**(int)*condition*

Sets the lock's condition to *condition* and releases the lock.

See also: – **unlock**

NXData

Inherits From: Object

Conforms To: NXTransport (Distributed Objects)

Declared In: machkit/NXData.h

Class Description

NXData is an object-oriented wrapper for data. It's especially useful in Distributed Objects applications because of its conformance to the NXTransport protocol, allowing NXData objects to be copied or moved between applications. NXData can be used to wrap data of any size; it allocates small amounts of memory from its own zone using a malloc-related function, and allocates page-aligned data from the virtual memory system for requests of a page or larger. NXData can also be used to wrap preexisting data, regardless of how the data was allocated.

If data is to be moved between applications (rather than copied), you may find it necessary to override the **encodeRemotelyFor:...** method in a subclass of NXData to ensure that data is properly deallocated after it is passed across a connection; see the Distributed Objects introduction for more information on moving objects between applications.

Instance Variables

None declared in this class.

Adopted Protocols

NXTransport	– encodeRemotelyFor:freeAfterEncoding:isBycopy: – encodeUsing: – decodeUsing:

Method Types

Initializing and freeing instances	
	– initWithSize:
	– initWithData:size:dealloc:
	– free
Getting the object's data	– data
Getting the data's size	– size
Copying the object	– copyFromZone:

Instance Methods

copyFromZone:

– **copyFromZone:**(NXZone *)*zone*

Returns a newly allocated NXData instance containing a copy of the receiver's data. The new object's data will be deallocated when the new object gets freed.

data

– (void *)**data**

Returns a pointer to the data contained in the object.

encodeRemotelyFor: freeAfterEncoding:isBycopy:

– **encodeRemotelyFor:** (NXConnection *)*conn*
freeAfterEncoding:(BOOL *)*flagPointer*
isBycopy:(BOOL)*isBycopy*

Returns **self** to indicate that a copy of the NXData object (and not a proxy to it) is to be copied across a connection any time the object is vended to a remote object. The data for the remote copy will be freed when the copy is freed. If you want the local NXData to be freed after being sent across the connection, you will need to override this method to set the boolean indicated by *flagPointer* to YES.

free

– **free**

Deallocates the receiver's storage, including the data if it was initialized to do so, and returns **nil**.

See also: – **initWithData:size:dealloc:**, – **initWithSize:**

initWithData:size:dealloc:

– **initWithData:**(void *)*data*
 size:(unsigned int)*size*
 dealloc:(BOOL)*flag*

Initializes the receiver, a new NXData object, with *data*, which must be at most *size* bytes long. If *flag* is YES, then *data* will be deallocated when the NXData object is freed. *data* could have been allocated with **vm_allocate()** or a **malloc()** variant. Returns **self**.

See also: – **initWithSize:**, – **free**

initWithSize:

– **initWithSize:**(unsigned int)*size*

Initializes the receiver, a new NXData object, so that it can contain at most *size* bytes of data. The memory will be allocated directly from the virtual memory system if it is one page or greater in size (though applications shouldn't care where the memory came from); otherwise the data will be allocated from the object's zone. The data will be freed when the NXData object is freed. Returns **self**.

See also: – **initWithData:size:dealloc:**, – **free**

size

– (unsigned int)**size**

Returns the size of the data that the object holds.

NXInvalidationNotifier

Inherits From: Object

Conforms To: NXReference

Declared In: machkit/NXInvalidationNotifier.h

Class Description

The NXInvalidationNotifier class is an abstract class that defines reference-counted objects that notify other objects when they become invalid. An NXInvalidationNotifier becomes invalid when no more references to it are held (all references have been given up by sending the object a **free** message). An NXInvalidationNotifier could also become invalid for other reasons; for example, an NXConnection object (which is a subclass of NXInvalidationNotifier) becomes invalid when its connection is broken. An invalid object usually exists for a short time after becoming invalid so it can clean up, but it shouldn't be treated as though it were fully usable.

Examples of NXInvalidationNotifier subclasses include NXConnection and NXPort.

Instance Variables

unsigned int **refcount**;
BOOL **isValid**;
NXLock ***listGate**;
List ***funeralList**;

refcount	The object's reference count
isValid	YES if the object is valid
listGate	A lock to protect data structures
funeralList	A list of objects to be notified upon invalidation

Adopted Protocols

NXReference	– addReference – free – references

Method Types

Initializing a new object	– init
Really freeing an object	– deallocate
Getting and setting validity	– invalidate – isValid
Registering for notification	– registerForInvalidationNotification: – unregisterForInvalidationNotification:

Instance Methods

deallocate

– deallocate

Deallocates the object's storage, freeing the object regardless of its reference count. A subclass of NXInvalidationNotifier should generally invoke this method from within its implementation of **free** when no more references are held to ensure normal freeing behavior.

See also: **– free**

free

– free

Decrements the reference count of the object, marking the object invalid, sending invalidation notifications, and returning **nil** if no more references to the object are held. If references are still held, this method returns **self**. Unlike the **free** method for most classes, this method *never* deallocates the object's storage. (In other words, it never actually frees the object.) This means that the object still exists to receive messages after it becomes invalid due to freeing, which can be useful for objects that need to do some final housekeeping when no more references are held. Generally a subclass of NXInvalidationNotifier should implement a version of **free** that deallocates itself when no more references are held, with the result that **free** will properly deallocate the object as expected at the appropriate time. For example:

```
- free
{
    id ret = [super free];
    if (ret) return self;
    // No more references held, do the required cleanup
    return [super deallocate];
}
```

See also: **– deallocate**, **– invalidate**

init

– init

Initializes the receiver, a newly allocated NXInvalidationNotifier instance. Returns **self**.

invalidate

– invalidate

Marks the object as invalid, which means that though the object exists, it's not completely functional and might not exist for long. Once an object becomes invalid, there is no way provided to make the object valid again, and it would be difficult to implement in a subclass in a thread-safe manner. This method sends a **senderIsInvalid:** message to every object that registered for invalidation notification, frees the **funeralList** (but not the objects in it), and returns **self**.

See also: **– registerForInvalidationNotification:**

isValid

– (BOOL)**isValid**

Returns YES if the object is valid. Generally, invalid objects should be sent only messages that allow other objects to clean up and eliminate their use of the object.

registerForInvalidationNotification:

– **registerForInvalidationNotification:**(id <NXSenderIsInvalid>)*anObject*

Registers *anObject* so that it will receive a **senderIsInvalid:** message when the receiver becomes invalid. An object might become invalid because it is about to be freed, because a Distributed Objects connection is broken, or for some other application-specific reason. Returns **self**.

See also: – **invalidate**, – **unregisterForInvalidationNotification:**

unregisterForInvalidationNotification:

– **unregisterForInvalidationNotification:**(id <NXSenderIsInvalid>)*anObject*

Removes *anObject* from the list of objects that are notified when the receiver becomes invalid; thus *anObject* won't be notified. Returns **self**.

See also: – **registerForInvalidationNotification:**

NXLock

Inherits From: Object

Conforms To: NXLock

Declared In: machkit/NXLock.h

Class Description

An NXLock is used to protect regions of code that can consume long periods of time, such as disk I/O or heavy computations. A lock is created once and is subsequently used to protect one or more regions of code. If a region of code is in use, an NXLock waits using the **condition_wait()** function, so the thread doesn't busy-wait. The following example shows the use of an NXLock:

```
NXLock *theLock = [[NXLock alloc] init];        // done once!
/* ... other code */
[theLock lock];
/* ... possibly a long time of fussing with global data... */
[theLock unlock];
```

The NXConditionLock, NXLock, NXRecursiveLock, and NXSpinLock classes all implement the NXLock protocol with various features and performance characteristics; see the other class descriptions for more information.

Instance Variables

None declared in this class.

Method Types

Acquire or release a lock	– lock – unlock

Instance Methods

lock

– lock

Waits until the lock isn't in use, using **condition_wait()** if necessary, then grabs the lock.

unlock

– unlock

Releases the lock, using **condition_signal()** to signal the next party that the lock is available.

NXNetNameServer

Inherits From: Object

Declared In: machkit/NXNetNameServer.h

Class Description

This class provides an object-oriented interface to the Network Name Server. It can be useful for making NXPort objects (which correspond to Mach ports) available over the network, and for accessing those ports from other applications.

Instance Variables

None declared in this class.

Method Types

Making a port available	+ checkInPort:withName:
Removing a port	+ checkOutPort:withName:
Getting ports	+ lookUpPortWithName: + lookUpPortWithName:onHost:

Class Methods

checkInPort:withName:

+ **checkInPort:**(NXPort *)*port* **withName:**(const char *)*aName*

Makes the NXPort object *port* available with the name *aName*. Returns **self** if the port is successfully checked in, **nil** otherwise.

checkOutPortWithName:

+ **checkOutPortWithName:**(const char *)*name*

Removes the port identified by *name* from the Network Name Server; the port can be removed only by the application that checked it in. Returns **self** if the port is successfully removed, **nil** otherwise.

lookUpPortWithName:

+ (NXPort *)**lookUpPortWithName:**(const char *)*name*

Returns an NXPort object for the port registered (via the Network Name Server) on the local machine under the name *name*, or **nil** upon failure.

lookUpPortWithName:onHost:

+ (NXPort *)**lookUpPortWithName:**(const char *)*name*
    onHost:(const char *)*hostName*

Returns an NXPort object for the port registered (via the Network Name Server) on host *hostName* under the name *name*, or **nil** upon failure. If *hostName* is "*" the search will be conducted for each host on the subnet, although this might take a bit of time.

NXPort

Inherits From: NXInvalidationNotifier : Object

Conforms To: NXReference (through NXInvalidationNotifier)
NXTransport (Distributed Objects)

Declared In: machkit/NXPort.h

Class Description

The NXPort class provides an object-oriented interface to Mach ports. NXPort objects are used by the Distributed Objects system whenever a Mach port is needed.

Instance Variables

port_t **machPort**;

machPort	The Mach port managed by the NXPort

Adopted Protocols

NXReference	– addReference – free – references
NXTransport	– encodeRemotelyFor:freeAfterEncoding:isBycopy: – encodeUsing: – decodeUsing:

Method Types

Creating an NXPort	+ new + newFromMachPort: + newFromMachPort:dealloc:
Freeing an NXPort	– free
Listening for port deaths	+ worryAboutPortInvalidation
Getting the Mach port	– machPort
Hash-table value for the port	– hash

Class Methods

new

+ **new**

Creates and returns a new NXPort instance. This method allocates a new Mach port that will be deallocated when the instance is freed.

See also: + **newFromMachPort:**, + **newFromMachPort:dealloc:**

newFromMachPort:

+ **newFromMachPort:**(port_t)*port*

Creates and returns a new NXPort instance that wraps an existing port specified by *port*. *port* will not be deallocated when the instance is freed.

See also: + **new**, + **newFromMachPort:dealloc:**

newFromMachPort:dealloc:

+ **newFromMachPort:**(port_t)*port* **dealloc:**(BOOL)*flag*

Creates and returns a new NXPort instance that wraps an existing port specified by *port*. If *flag* is YES, *port* will be deallocated when the instance is freed; otherwise, it won't be deallocated.

See also: + **new**, + **newFromMachPort:**

worryAboutPortInvalidation

+ **worryAboutPortInvalidation**

Forks a thread to listen for port deaths; this thread sleeps until a port dies. If a port death occurs, any objects registered for invalidation notification receive a **senderIsInvalid:** message. This is generally only useful in applications that don't use the Application Kit.

See also: – **senderIsInvalid:** (NXSenderIsInvalid protocol)

Instance Methods

free

– **free**

Decrements the receiver's reference count, returning **self** if the reference count remains greater than 0. If the reference count becomes 0, this method deallocates the receiver's storage and returns **nil**.

See also: NXReference protocol

hash

– (unsigned int)**hash**

Returns a hash-table index for the NXPort. This isn't generally useful.

machPort

– (port_t)**machPort**

Returns the NXPort's Mach port. This can be useful if you need to pass the port to routines that deal with Mach ports rather than NXPorts.

NXProtocolChecker

Inherits From: Object

Declared In: machkit/NXProtocolChecker.h

Class Description

The NXProtocolChecker class defines an object that restricts the messages that can be sent to another object (referred to as the checker's delegate). This can be particularly useful when an object with many methods, only a few of which ought to be remotely accessible, is made available using the Distributed Objects system.

A protocol checker acts as a kind of proxy; when it receives a message that is in its designated protocol, it forwards the message to its delegate, and consequently appears to be the delegate itself. However, when it receives a message not in its protocol, it raises an NX_restrictionEnforcedException exception to indicate that the message isn't allowed, whether or not the delegate implements the method.

Typically, an object that is to be distributed (yet must restrict messages) creates an NXProtocolChecker for itself and returns the checker rather than returning itself in response to any messages. The object might also register the checker as the root object of an NXConnection.

The object should be careful about vending references to **self**; the protocol checker will convert a return value of **self** to indicate the checker rather than the object for any messages that were forwarded by the checker, but direct references to the object (bypassing the checker) could be passed around by other objects.

Instance Variables

id **target**;
Protocol ***protocol**;

target	The checker's delegate
protocol	Indicates the messages the checker will forward

Method Types

Initializing a checker	– initWithObject:forProtocol:
Reimplemented Object methods	
	– forward::
	– descriptionForMethod:
	– free

Instance Methods

descriptionForMethod:

– (struct objc_method_description *)**descriptionForMethod:**(SEL)*aSelector*

Returns an Objective C description for a method in the checker's protocol, or NULL if *aSelector* isn't declared as an instance method in the protocol.

See also: – **descriptionForInstanceMethod:**(Protocol class)

forward::

– **forward:**(SEL)*aSelector* **:**(void *)*args*

Forwards any message to the delegate if the method is declared in the checker's protocol; otherwise raises an NX_restrictionEnforcedException exception. If a delegate method returns **self**, the checker substitutes its own **id** for the return value so that the sender doesn't gain direct access (bypassing the checker) to the delegate.

free

– **free**

If the **free** method is not part of the protocol that the delegate responds to, this message simply frees the checker. If the **free** method is part of the protocol that the delegate responds to, the **free** message is forwarded to the delegate, and the checker is freed if the delegate returns **nil**. This ensures that that the checker is closely coupled to the delegate whether the delegate implements reference counting or not; see the NXReference protocol for more information.

initWithObject:forProtocol:

– **initWithObject:***anObject* **forProtocol:**(Protocol *)*aProtocol*

Initializes a newly allocated NXProtocolChecker instance that will forward any messages in the *aProtocol* protocol to *anObject*, its delegate. Thus, the checker can be vended in lieu of *anObject* to restrict the messages that can be sent to *anObject*. If *anObject* is allowed to be freed or dereferenced by clients, the **free** method should be included in *aProtocol*. Returns the new instance.

NXRecursiveLock

Inherits From: Object

Conforms To: NXLock

Declared In: machkit/NXLock.h

Class Description

An NXRecursiveLock locks a critical section of code such that a single thread can reaquire the lock multiple times without deadlocking, while preventing access by other threads. Note that this implies that a recursive lock will not protect a critical section from a signal handler interrupting the thread holding the lock. Here is an example where a recursive lock functions properly but other lock types would deadlock:

```
// create the lock only once!
NXRecursiveLock *theLock = [[NXRecursiveLock alloc] init];
/* ... other code */
[theLock lock];
/* ... possibly a long time of fussing with global data... */
    [theLock lock];  //possibly invoked in a subroutine
    [theLock unlock];
[theLock unlock];
```

The NXConditionLock, NXLock, NXRecursiveLock, and NXSpinLock classes all implement the NXLock protocol with various features and performance characteristics; see the other class descriptions for more information.

Instance Variables

None declared in this class.

Method Types

Acquire or release a lock	– lock – unlock

Instance Methods

lock

– **lock**

Waits until the lock isn't in use by another thread, then grabs the lock and increments an internal counter indicating how many times the lock is held by the current thread.

unlock

– **unlock**

Decrements the internal count indicating how many times the lock is held by the current thread. If the lock is no longer in use by the thread, it is released for use by the next requestor.

NXSpinLock

Inherits From: Object

Conforms To: NXLock

Declared In: machkit/NXLock.h

Class Description

An NXSpinLock is used to lock short sections of code that take very little time to execute. A lock is created once and is subsequently used to protect one or more regions of code. If a region of code is in use, an NXSpinLock will busy-wait until the lock is released. An NXSpinLock can be acquired very quickly, but will consume CPU resources as long as the lock is held by another party. The following example shows the use of an NXSpinLock:

```
NXSpinLock *theLock = [[NXSpinLock alloc] init];
// done once!
/* ... other code */
[theLock lock];
/* ... short quick section of atomic code... */
[theLock unlock];
```

The NXConditionLock, NXLock, NXRecursiveLock, and NXSpinLock classes all implement the NXLock protocol with various features and performance characteristics; see the other class descriptions for more information.

Instance Variables

None declared in this class.

Method Types

Acquire or release a lock	– lock – unlock

Instance Methods

lock

– lock

Uses **mutex_lock()** to busy-wait until the lock isn't in use and grab the lock.

unlock

– unlock

Releases the lock with **mutex_unlock()**, allowing the next party to access the critical section of code.

Protocols

NXLock

Adopted By: NXConditionLock
NXLock
NXSpinLock
NXRecursiveLock

Declared In: machkit/NXLock.h

Protocol Description

This protocol is used by classes that provide lock objects. The lock objects provided by NeXTSTEP are used only for protecting critical sections—they contain no useful data.

Although an object that isn't a lock could adopt the NXLock protocol, it may be more desirable to design the object so that all locking is handled internally, through normal use rather than requiring that the object be explicitly locked and unlocked.

Four classes conform to the NXLock protocol:

Class	Usage
NXLock	Use NXLock objects to protect regions of code that can consume long periods of time, such as disk I/O or heavy computation.
NXConditionLock	Protects critical sections of code, but can also be used to postpone entry to a critical section until a condition is met. This class is functionally a superset of the NXLock class, though unlocking is slightly more expensive.
NXSpinLock	Use NXSpinLock objects to protect short regions of critical code. Useful in the implementation of drivers or more complex locks. A spin lock may be acquired more quickly than the other locks, but isn't appropriate for long sections of code since blocked spin locks busy-wait.
NXRecursiveLock	Protects critical sections from access by multiple threads, but allows a single thread to acquire a lock several times without deadlocking.

Of these classes, only NXSpinLock busy-waits while the lock is unavailable. The other classes may all be efficiently used for long sections of atomic code. See the class specifications for these classes for further information on their behavior and usage.

Instance Methods

lock

– lock

Acquires a lock. Applications generally do this when entering a critical section of their code.

unlock

– unlock

Releases a lock. Applications generally do this when exiting a critical section of their code.

NXReference

Adopted By: IXFileFinder
IXStoreBlock
NXConnection
NXInvalidationNotifier
NXProxy

Declared In: machkit/reference.h

Protocol Description

The NXReference protocol defines a set of methods for implementing simple reference counting of objects. This allows an object to be referenced multiple times without each client needing to assume that the referenced object may be in use by others. A client of the referenced object can simply send it a **free** message when finished; if the object still has outstanding references, it doesn't free itself.

Method Types

Adding or deleting a reference	– addReference
	– free
Getting the number of references	
	– references

Instance Methods

addReference

– **addReference**

Increments the number of references to the receiver and returns **self**.

free

– **free**

Decrements the receiver's reference count, returning **self** if the reference count remains greater than 0. If the reference count becomes 0, this method deallocates the receiver's storage and returns **nil**.

A typical implementation for a reference counted object that is vended over a Distributed Objects connection might look like this:

```
- free
{
    refs--;
    if (refs > 0) return self;

    [NXConnection removeObject:self];
    return [super free];
}
```

references

– (unsigned int)**references**

Returns the number of references to the receiver.

NXSenderIsInvalid

Adopted By: NXConnection
NXDataLinkManager

Declared In: machkit/senderIsInvalid.h

Protocol Description

This protocol should be implemented by objects that need to be informed of the invalidation of other objects. To receive invalidation messages, the object must send a **registerForInvalidationNotification:** message to an object that may become invalid. An implementation of this method is provided in the NXInvalidationNotifier class, so objects that inherit from NXInvalidationNotifier (such as NXConnection) have the ability to notify other objects of their imminent demise.

Instance Methods

senderIsInvalid:

– **senderIsInvalid:***sender*

This message is sent by an invalidation notifier (such as an NXConnection) whenever it becomes unusable (for example, because its connection has been broken, or because the invalidation notifier is about to be freed). This gives the receiver a chance to take proper action regarding the new status of the invalidation notifier.

An object registers itself with an invalidation notifier by sending it a **registerForInvalidationNotification:** message. It can later unregister itself with **unregisterForInvalidationNotification:**.

Types and Constants

Defined Types

NXMachKitException

DECLARED IN machkit/exceptions.h

SYNOPSIS

```
typedef enum {
        NX_MACH_KIT_EXCEPTION_BASE,
        NX_portInvalidException,
        NX_restrictionEnforcedException,
        NX_referenceAlreadyFreeException,
        NX_MACH_KIT_LAST_EXCEPTION
} NXMachKitException
```

DESCRIPTION These are the exceptions raised by various classes in the Mach Kit.

10 *MIDI Driver API*

10 *MIDI Driver API*

Library: libsys_s.a

Header File Directory: /NextDeveloper/Headers/mididriver

Introduction

This chapter describes the NeXT MIDI driver C functions and supporting header files for MIDI applications. This introduction contains conceptual discussions of the MIDI interface and its implementation on NeXT computers.

The sections "What Is MIDI?" and "Connecting MIDI Devices" provide general information on MIDI on the NeXT. The section "MIDI Driver Overview" outlines how to structure the MIDI support section of an application that uses the MIDI driver functions.

What Is MIDI?

MIDI, the Musical Instrument Digital Interface, defines a software format and a hardware standard for exchanging information among electronic musical instruments (such as synthesizers, samplers, digital pianos, and guitar or wind controllers) as well as other devices (such as computers, sequencers, mixers, signal processors, and even stage lighting). Originally designed to capture the performance gestures of a keyboard player, MIDI normally transmits keyboard-oriented information, such as which key the performer depressed and with what velocity, or which button or slider was adjusted on a synthesizer's control panel. This sort of data is much more compact and more easily edited than the data in a digital audio recording of the same performance. Unlike audio data, MIDI data can easily be used to control other instruments or to create a printed score (using a music notation application).

Connecting MIDI Devices

You can connect MIDI instruments to either of a NeXT computer's serial ports, using an external device known as a MIDI interface. The instruments connect to the MIDI interface (or to each other) with standard MIDI cables, available at most music stores. The MIDI interface adapts these cables' unidirectional 5-pin DIN connectors to the serial port's bidirectional mini-DIN connector. Any number of instruments can be connected to a serial port through the interface, and the two ports can be used simultaneously by a single application. A single serial port can receive and transmit MIDI data at the same time.

The musical instrument must be set up correctly for MIDI communication to work as expected. Because MIDI is a unidirectional protocol, there's no means for an application to verify that the external device is receiving the MIDI data that the application sends. Thus the user is responsible for ensuring that the configuration is correct. For instructions on setting up the MIDI device, see the owner's manual for that device.

In particular, note that most MIDI commands are sent on specific "channels." Unlike the left and right channels of analog audio signals, MIDI channels don't use separate cables, but instead are encoded in the MIDI data itself. The sixteen MIDI channels are used for sending separate streams of commands to different synthesizers on a single MIDI network, or to the distinct sound-generating units within a single multi-timbral synthesizer. There's no MIDI command that asks a device to start using a certain MIDI channel. Instead, the user must manually set the MIDI device to transmit and receive on the channels expected by the software. A typical default is to transmit and receive on channel 1.

The NeXT MIDI Device Driver

The MIDI driver is a loadable Mach device driver that controls the flow of MIDI data to and from the serial ports. The MIDI device driver API contains C functions for direct control of the MIDI driver, giving you control over the buffering and timing of MIDI data. The functions also provide other features—for example, you can manage the size of the MIDI data queue, manipulate the driver's timer, and filter out a few more kinds of MIDI commands—but you'll rarely need these features.

The rest of this document contains information that's useful for programming with the MIDI driver C functions. The sample C programs in **/NextDeveloper/Examples/SoundAndMusic/Drivers/MidiDriver** illustrate some of the functions documented here. Information can also be gleaned from the header files in **NextDeveloper/Headers/mididriver**.

The MIDI Data Format

If you use the MIDI driver functions, you'll be examining MIDI data as hexadecimal values, so you'll need to understand the MIDI data format. Read this section for a synopsis of the data format, if you're not already familiar with the MIDI specification.

MIDI data consists of commands sent in an asynchronous serial stream at 31.25 kBaud. The data is transmitted in ten-bit bytes, but the first and last bits of each byte are start and stop bits, added by the transmitting device and stripped off by the receiving device. Thus, MIDI commands are considered to consist of eight-bit bytes. A typical MIDI command contains:

- One Status byte (whose most significant bit is set to 1). The Status byte defines a type of command, such as Note On or Pitch Bend.
- Zero, one, or two Data bytes (each having its most significant bit set to 0). Data bytes contain values applied by the command, such as "key number" and "velocity," or "amount of pitch bend." The type of command, specified by the preceding Status byte, determines how many Data bytes are expected.

There are two exceptions to the above pattern:

- The Status byte may be omitted, in which case the type of command is given by the most recent Status byte. This condition is called Running Status.
- The Status byte F0 (hexadecimal) is the special System Exclusive command, which is followed by a Data byte identifying a particular manufacturer, and any number of subsequent Data bytes whose meaning the manufacturer is free to determine. Only that manufacturer's instruments are expected to respond to the System Exclusive command.

Status bytes with hexadecimal values from 80 to EF are "channel commands." These MIDI commands are sent on specific MIDI channels, as determined by the rightmost four bits of the Status byte. Most MIDI devices can be configured to respond only to certain channels, making it possible for a single MIDI data stream to deliver different musical information to different devices simultaneously.

Note that although MIDI bytes are classified as Status bytes or Data bytes, the term "MIDI data" refers generically to everything in a stream of MIDI commands, both Status bytes and Data bytes.

The file **mididriver/midi_spec.h** includes a list of Status bytes and other standard MIDI definitions. You can obtain the complete MIDI specification from the International MIDI Association at 11857 Hartsook St., North Hollywood, CA 91607, U.S.A. For an introduction to the MIDI specification, including a summary of commands, see Gareth Loy's article "Musicians Make a Standard: The MIDI Phenomenon" in *Computer Music Journal* Vol. 9, No. 4 (Winter 1985).

MIDI Driver Overview

The MIDI driver is a loadable server residing within the Mach kernel. (For more on loadable servers, see *NeXTSTEP Operating System Software*.) For each serial port, the MIDI driver maintains an input queue (containing MIDI data received from external instruments) and an output queue (for data received from an application). The MIDI driver C functions let you retrieve data from the input queue, place data in the output queue, and perform numerous other operations.

Instead of using a direct message-passing mechanism for forwarding received MIDI data, the driver uses a request/reply interface. This means that data received from a serial port is queued within the driver until the application requests the data. Then the driver asynchronously sends Mach messages containing all the MIDI data that it's received since the last time the application requested data. The application must supply functions that perform the actual work of manipulating the incoming MIDI data in whatever manner is desired. The reply handler acts as a dispatcher by examining each incoming Mach message and routing it in a suitable format to the appropriate one of these application-supplied functions. When the application is ready for the next set of MIDI data, it must make another request for data from the driver.

Output is managed similarly. In addition to the asynchronous messages that contain incoming MIDI data, the driver sends the application a message whenever the output queue has space available for more outgoing data. The reply handler passes these notifications to another application-supplied function, which typically responds by sending more data to the driver.

A stream of MIDI bytes coming in real time from an external instrument doesn't necessarily contain any information about *when* each MIDI command was received. However, to make musical sense of recorded MIDI data, timing information is essential. Thus the driver always timestamps MIDI commands on input. A timer service, included with the driver, serves this purpose. It also schedules each outgoing MIDI command. Additionally, an application can ask this timer service to notify it at a certain time, and the application can stop and restart the timer—or even make it run backwards. The MIDI library has a separate reply handler for messages from the timer service, analogous to the reply handler that manages MIDI input and output.

Functions

The MIDI driver functions enable an application to communicate with the MIDI driver and thus with other MIDI devices. This section documents the specific functions for interaction with the MIDI driver. The discussion begins with an outline of MIDI driver function usage.

Receiving MIDI Data

Before it can begin communicating with the MIDI driver, an application invokes the function **MIDIBecomeOwner**(). Since the MIDI driver can have only one client application at a time, this function returns an error if the driver has already been acquired by another application. Once an application has acquired ownership of the driver, it uses the function **MIDIClaimUnit()** to claim the serial port on which to transfer MIDI data.

The driver converts incoming MIDI data into the MIDIRawEvent format, defined in **mididriver/midi_driver.h**. The raw format has a three-byte timestamp preceding each received MIDI byte. By default, the timestamp measures the number of milliseconds since the device was opened. To start the clock, use **MIDIStartClock**().

After an application has initialized the driver, acquired a serial port, and started its timer, the driver continually receives and enqueues incoming MIDI data. To retrieve the incoming data, the application may repeatedly call either **MIDIAwaitReply**() or **MIDIHandleReply**(). **MIDIAwaitReply**() works by receiving data on the port, then invoking **MIDIHandleReply**().

In an Application Kit-based application, you must make repeated calls to the **MIDIAwaitReply**() function in a separate Mach thread. Alternatively, you can register the application's port set with **DPSAddPort**(), passing that function a handler that receives messages by repeatedly invoking the Mach function **msg_receive**(), and handling the messages by invoking **MIDIHandleReply**(). See **DPSAddPort**() in "Client Library Functions," Chapter 5, "Display PostScript," for more on how to set up and receive messages.

MIDIAwaitReply() and **MIDIHandleReply**() both take as an argument a pointer to a **MIDIReplyFunctions** structure. Among other fields, the **MIDIReplyFunctions** structure contains pointers to four application-supplied functions, one for each reply type. The **MIDIHandleReply**() routine distributes the data to the appropriate one of the four functions, depending on the nature of the reply. These four application-supplied functions are the focus of the MIDI driver input mechanism: They should use the incoming MIDI data in whatever fashion is desired for the particular application.

See **/NextDeveloper/Examples/SoundAndMusic/ Drivers/MidiDriver** for sample code.

Some frequently sent MIDI system commands can clutter the incoming queue, such as "active sensing," a command sent periodically to inform the recipient that the sender is still active and the connection intact, or "timing clock," a synchronization command that the driver currently doesn't use. You can have the driver filter out unwanted MIDI system commands by using the **MIDISetSystemIgnores()** function.

Sending MIDI Data

Sending MIDI data is somewhat similar to receiving it. The function **MIDISendData()** enqueues an array of MIDI data to be sent out the serial port, and returns an errorcode if the queue is full. The capacity of the output queue can be retrieved with the function **MIDIGetAvailableQueueSize()**. The **MIDIRequestQueueNotification()** function can be used to request notification when the queue shrinks to a particular size. The **MIDIClearQueue()** function empties the queue, the **MIDIFlushQueue()** causes all the data to be sent immediately.

This notification message is handled by **MIDIHandleReply()**, just as incoming MIDI data messages are. The application should implement a function that responds to the notification in whatever manner is desired—normally, by sending more MIDI data to the driver. The **MIDIReplyFunctions** structure that the application passes to **MIDIHandleReply()** should contain a pointer to this function, along with the pointers to the three functions that process incoming MIDI data (see "Receiving MIDI Data," above).

MIDI Time Base

The MIDI driver uses a timer to obtain timestamps for incoming MIDI data, as well as to schedule MIDI output. As described under "Receiving MIDI Data," incoming MIDI bytes are given timestamps that indicate the time at which the bytes arrived. Similarly, outgoing MIDI bytes are sent at the times specified by their timestamps. Before outgoing bytes are sent, their timestamps are removed, since the timestamp isn't part of the standard MIDI data format.

A call to the **MIDIStartClock()** function starts up the default timer, using the internal system clock as a time base. To synchronize the clock to a MIDI time signal received on one of the serial ports, use the function **MIDISetClockMode()**. To set the starting time for the clock, use the function **MIDISetClockTime()**.

Time is maintained using seconds and microseconds, but the timer interface also provides arbitrary units called "quanta." A quantum is an unsigned integer representing some number of microseconds, specified by **MIDISetClockQuantum()**. The default is 1000 microseconds, or one millisecond. MIDI commands are time-tagged with quanta, so the value of one quantum represents the resolution of a MIDI event in time.

The timer can be used directly by the process using the MIDI driver. By calling **MIDIRequestAlarm()**, an application can ask to be notified when a certain time is reached. The application handles the notification with the **MIDIAwaitReply()** and **MIDIHandleReply()** functions. These functions accept a **MIDIReplyFunctions** structure argument, which includes a **MIDIAlarmReplyFunction** to handle alarm notification. This notification mechanism gives the application an effective way to stay synchronized with MIDI events or with other applications, even across a network.

An application can control the operation of the timer. MIDI output can be paused by stopping the timer with a call to the function **MIDIStopClock()**. Output is resumed by restarting the timer with **MIDIStartClock()**.

MIDIAwaitReply(), MIDIHandleReply()

SUMMARY Handle replies from the MIDI driver to an application

DECLARED IN mididriver/midi_driver.h

SYNOPSIS kern_return_t **MIDIAwaitReply**(port_t *reply_port*, MIDIReplyFunctions **handlers*, int *timeout*)

kern_return_t **MIDIHandleReply**(msg_header_t **msg*, MIDIReplyFunctions **handlers*)

DESCRIPTION **MIDIAwaitReply()** receives and handles a message from the MIDI driver. *reply_port* is the port set used to receive messages. *handlers* is a MIDIReplyFunctions structure containing pointers to functions for handling replies (see "Types and Constants" for a description of the MIDIReplyFunctions structure). *timeout* represents the amount of time, in milliseconds, the **MIDIAwaitReply()** function will wait before returning if no message is in the MIDI driver's queue. After receiving the message from the MIDI driver as specified, **MIDIAwaitReply()** calls **MIDIHandleReply()**.

MIDIHandleReply() accepts a message received from the MIDI driver and passes it to the appropriate handling function. *msg* is the Mach message received from the MIDI driver on the application's port set. *handlers* is a **MIDIReplyFunctions** structure containing pointers to functions for handling replies.

Before calling one of these functions, you register requests with the MIDI driver by calling one or more of the functions **MIDIRequestData()**, **MIDIRequestAlarm()**, **MIDIRequestExceptions()**, and **MIDIRequestQueueNotification()**. The *handlers* passed in the reply handling functions should include a function for handling each of the responses requested; the *reply_port* set passed to **MIDIAwaitReply()** should include a port for handling each of the request types.

One common use of these functions is to receive MIDI data. The application calls **MIDIRequestData()**, then repeatedly calls one of these reply handling functions in a loop. To do so in an Application Kit application, you must run **MIDIAwaitReply()** in a separate Mach thread. Alternatively, you may register the port set with the **DPSAddPort()** function, use the Mach function **msg_receive()** to receive the response from the MIDI driver, then handle the message with **MIDIHandleReply()**.

RETURN Both functions return KERN_SUCCESS if they successfully handle the reply. If unsuccessful, they return an exception code indicating the reason they couldn't handle the reply.

MIDIBecomeOwner(), MIDIReleaseOwnership()

SUMMARY Acquire and release ownership of the MIDI driver

DECLARED IN mididriver/midi_driver.h

SYNOPSIS kern_return_t **MIDIBecomeOwner**(port_t *driverPort*, port_t *ownerPort*)
kern_return_t **MIDIReleaseOwnership**(port_t *driverPort*, port_t *ownerPort*)

DESCRIPTION **MIDIBecomeOwner**() makes the sending process the owner of the MIDI driver. Before becoming owner of the MIDI driver, an application must look up *driverPort* with a call to the Mach **netname_look_up**() function. It must also allocate, using the Mach **port_allocate**() function, an *ownerPort* to identify it to the MIDI driver in other function calls.

MIDIReleaseOwnership() releases the MIDI driver port from the control of the sending application.

RETURN Both functions return KERN_SUCCESS if they complete successfully, and MIDI_ERROR_BUSY if another process is using the driver.

MIDIClaimUnit(), MIDIReleaseUnit()

SUMMARY Claim and release ownership of serial ports for MIDI driver clients

DECLARED IN mididriver/midi_driver.h

SYNOPSIS kern_return_t **MIDIClaimUnit**(port_t *driverPort*, port_t *ownerPort*, short *unit*)
kern_return_t **MIDIReleaseUnit**(port_t *driverPort*, port_t *ownerPort*, short *unit*)

DESCRIPTION These functions control the access of a MIDI driver client application to the host computer's serial ports.

MIDIClaimUnit() is used to acquire a serial port for MIDI communication. It is called after the MIDI driver has been acquired by the application with the **MIDIBecomeOwner**() function. *driverPort* is the MIDI driver port. *ownerPort* is the port allocated by the process to identify it to the MIDI driver in MIDI function calls, and first registered with the MIDI driver in **MIDIBecomeOwner**(). *unit* may be one of the symbolic constants

MIDI_PORT_A_UNIT and MIDI_PORT_B_UNIT, defined in the header file **mididriver/midi_driver.h**.

MIDIReleaseUnit() is used to release the serial port used in MIDI communication.

RETURN **MIDIClaimUnit()** returns KERN_SUCCESS if it successfully acquires the serial port as requested. **MIDIReleaseUnit()** returns KERN_SUCCESS if it successfully releases the serial port as requested. Both return MIDI_ERROR_NOT_OWNER if the sending process hasn't acquired the MIDI driver and MIDI_ERROR_UNIT_UNAVAILABLE if the specified serial port is busy.

MIDIClearQueue(), MIDIFlushQueue(), MIDIGetAvailableQueueSize()

SUMMARY Manage the MIDI driver queue

DECLARED IN mididriver/midi_driver.h

SYNOPSIS kern_return_t **MIDIClearQueue**(port_t *driverPort*, port_t *ownerPort*, short *unit*)

kern_return_t **MIDIFlushQueue**(port_t *device_port*, port_name_t *ownerPort_port*, short *unit*)

kern_return_t **MIDIGetAvailableQueueSize**(port_t *driverPort*, port_t *ownerPort*, short *unit*, int **theSize*)

DESCRIPTION These functions allow an application to manage the queue in the MIDI driver. *driverPort* is the MIDI driver port. *ownerPort* is the port allocated by the process to identify it to the MIDI driver in MIDI function calls, and first registered with the MIDI driver in **MIDIBecomeOwner()**.

MIDIClearQueue() empties the specified queue without sending any remaining data.

MIDIFlushQueue() returns after sending the data remaining in the queue immediately, bypassing the normal time scheduling mechanism.

MIDIGetAvailableQueueSize() returns, by reference in *theSize*, the amount of space currently available in the queue.

RETURN Each of these functions returns KERN_SUCCESS if the specified operation is performed successfully. Otherwise, they return an error code indicating why the operation wasn't completed.

MIDIFlushQueue() → See MIDIClearQueue()

MIDIGetAvailableQueueSize() → See MIDIClearQueue()

MIDIGetClockTime() → See MIDISetClockMode()

MIDIGetMTCTime() → See MIDISetClockMode()

MIDIHandleReply() → See MIDIAwaitReply()

MIDIReleaseOwnership() → See MIDIBecomeOwner()

MIDIReleaseUnit() → See MIDIClaimUnit()

MIDIRequestAlarm(), MIDIRequestData(), MIDIRequestExceptions(), MIDIRequestQueueNotification()

SUMMARY Request notification from the MIDI driver

DECLARED IN mididriver/midi_driver.h

SYNOPSIS

kern_return_t **MIDIRequestData**(port_t *driverPort*, port_t *ownerPort*, short *unit*, port_t *replyPort*)

kern_return_t **MIDIRequestAlarm**(port_t *driverPort*, port_t *ownerPort*, port_t *replyPort*, int *time*)

kern_return_t **MIDIRequestExceptions**(port_t *driverPort*, port_t *ownerPort*, port_t *replyPort*)

kern_return_t **MIDIRequestQueueNotification**(port_t *driverPort*, port_t *ownerPort*, short *unit*, port_t *replyPort*, int *size*)

DESCRIPTION These functions allow an application to request notification by the MIDI driver in case of specific events.

The reply returned in response to these requests should be handled by an application's corresponding MIDIReplyFunction. For example, the MIDI driver's response to **MIDIRequestExceptions()** should be handled by an application's MIDIExceptionReplyFunction. MIDIReplyFunction types are declared in the header

mididriver/midi_driver.h and described in the section "Types and Constants." After calling one of these functions, call **MIDIAwaitReply()** or **MIDIHandleReply()** to handle the response returned by the MIDI driver.

driverPort is the MIDI driver port. *ownerPort* is the port allocated by the process to identify it to the MIDI driver in MIDI function calls, and first registered with the MIDI driver in **MIDIBecomeOwner**(). *unit* is the serial port associated with the request. *replyPort* is the port on which the response to the request is expected to be sent. This port should be included in the port set passed to **MIDIAwaitReply**() or in the message header passed to **MIDIHandleReply**().

In **MIDIRequestQueueNotification**(), *size* is the queue size below which notification will be sent.

RETURN These functions return KERN_SUCCESS if the specified request is registered with the MIDI driver. Otherwise, they return an error code indicating why the operation wasn't completed.

SEE ALSO **MIDIAwaitReply**()

MIDIRequestData() → See MIDIRequestAlarm()

MIDIRequestExceptions() → See MIDIRequestAlarm()

MIDIRequestQueueNotification() → See MIDIRequestAlarm()

MIDISendData()

SUMMARY Send data using the MIDI driver

DECLARED IN mididriver/midi_driver.h

SYNOPSIS kern_return_t **MIDISendData**(port_t *driverPort*, port_t *ownerPort*, short *unit*, MIDIRawEvent **data*, unsigned int *count*)

DESCRIPTION This function sends data, using the MIDI driver and specified serial port to other MIDI devices. *driverPort* is the MIDI driver port. *ownerPort* is the port allocated by the process to identify it to the MIDI driver in MIDI function calls, and first registered with the MIDI driver in **MIDIBecomeOwner**(). *data* is an array of **MIDIRawEvent** data. *count* is the number of **MIDIRawEvent** structures in the array

RETURN This function returns KERN_SUCCESS if the data is successfully written to the serial port. Otherwise, returns an error code indicating why the operation wasn't completed.

SEE ALSO **MIDIRequestData**()

MIDISetClockMode(), MIDISetClockQuantum(), MIDISetClockTime(), MIDIGetClockTime(), MIDIGetMTCTime()

SUMMARY Control the MIDI driver clock

DECLARED IN mididriver/midi_driver.h

SYNOPSIS

kern_return_t **MIDISetClockMode**(port_t *driverPort*, port_t *ownerPort*, short *synchUnit*, int *mode*)

kern_return_t **MIDISetClockQuantum**(port_t *driverPort*, port_t *ownerPort*, int *interval*)

kern_return_t **MIDISetClockTime**(port_t *driverPort*, port_t *ownerPort*, int *time*)

kern_return_t **MIDIGetClockTime**(port_t *driverPort*, port_t *ownerPort*, int **time*)

kern_return_t **MIDIGetMTCTime**(port_t *driverPort*, port_t *ownerPort*, short **format*, short **hours*, short **minutes*, short **seconds*, short **frames*)

DESCRIPTION These functions let you set and test parameters for the MIDI driver clock. *driverPort* is the MIDI driver port. *ownerPort* is the port allocated by the process to identify it to the MIDI driver in MIDI function calls, and first registered with the MIDI driver in **MIDIBecomeOwner**().

MIDISetClockMode() sets the synchronization mode of the MIDI driver clock. *synchUnit* represents the serial port on which the driver will listen for MIDI time code signals. *mode* is one of the symbolic constants MIDI_CLOCK_MODE_INTERNAL or MIDI_CLOCK_MODE_MTC_SYNC. MIDI_CLOCK_MODE_INTERNAL causes the clock to run on its own internal time, while MIDI_CLOCK_MODE_MTC_SYNC causes the clock to synchronize with the MIDI time code present on *synchUnit*.

MIDISetClockQuantum() sets the interval between clock signals. *interval* represents this quantum in microseconds. The default setting is 1000 (1 millisecond).

MIDISetClockTime() sets the current clock time. *time* is an integer representing the time to which you want to set the MIDI driver clock.

MIDIGetClockTime() returns by reference in *time* the current clock time.

MIDIGetMTCTime() returns the MIDI time code time. *format* represents the MIDI time code format of the current time. *hours, minutes*, and *seconds* represent the chronological value of the current time. *frames* represents the frame number of the current time.

RETURN These functions return KERN_SUCCESS if the operation is performed successfully. Otherwise, they return an error code indicating why the operation wasn't completed.

MIDIGetClockTime() returns, by reference in *time*, the current time.

SEE ALSO **MIDIRequestAlarm**(), **MIDIStartClock**()

MIDISetClockQuantum() → See MIDISetClockMode()

MIDISetClockTime() → See MIDISetClockMode()

MIDISetSystemIgnores()

SUMMARY Sets MIDI system codes the MIDI driver ignores

DECLARED IN mididriver/midi_driver.h

SYNOPSIS kern_return_t **MIDISetSystemIgnores(**port_t *driverPort*, port_t *ownerPort*, short *unit*, unsigned int *ignoreBits*)

DESCRIPTION **MIDISetSystemIgnores**() sets MIDI system codes the MIDI driver ignores. *driverPort* is the MIDI driver port. *ownerPort* is the port allocated by the process to identify it to the MIDI driver in MIDI function calls, and first registered with the MIDI driver in **MIDIBecomeOwner**(). *unit* may be one of the symbolic constants MIDI_PORT_A_UNIT or MIDI_PORT_B_UNIT (defined in the header file

mididriver/midi_driver.h), representing the port on which MIDI system codes should be ignored. *ignoreBits* may be one of the symbolic constants MIDI_IGNORE_CLOCK, MIDI_IGNORE_START, or MIDI_IGNORE_CONTINUE (defined in **mididriver/midi_driver.h**); you may logically OR these constants for multiple settings.

RETURN This function returns KERN_SUCCESS if the operation is performed successfully. Otherwise, it returns an error code indicating why the operation wasn't completed.

MIDIStartClock(), MIDIStopClock()

SUMMARY Start and stop the MIDI clock

DECLARED IN mididriver/midi_driver.h

SYNOPSIS kern_return_t **MIDIStartClock**(port_t *driverPort*, port_t *ownerPort*)
kern_return_t **MIDIStopClock**(port_t *driverPort*, port_t *ownerPort*)

DESCRIPTION **MIDIStartClock**() starts the clock using the current settings. **MIDIStopClock**() stops the clock. *driverPort* is the MIDI driver port. *ownerPort* is the port allocated by the process to identify it to the MIDI driver in MIDI function calls, and first registered with the MIDI driver in **MIDIBecomeOwner**().

RETURN These functions return KERN_SUCCESS if the operation is performed successfully. Otherwise, they return an error code indicating why the operation wasn't completed.

SEE ALSO **MIDIRequestAlarm**(), **MIDISetClockMode**

MIDIStopClock() → See MIDIStartClock()

Types and Constants

Defined Types

MIDIAlarmReplyFunction

DECLARED IN mididriver/midi_driver.h

SYNOPSIS typedef void (***MIDIAlarmReplyFunction**)(port_t *replyPort*, int *requestedTime*,
int *actualTime*);

DESCRIPTION This function is used to handle requests for alarm registered by the **MIDIRequestAlarm()** function. *replyPort* represents the port passed by the **MIDIRequestAlarm()** function. *requestedTime* represents the time passed by the **MIDIRequestAlarm()** function. *actualTime* represents the actual time at which the alarm is sent.

MIDIDataReplyFunction

DECLARED IN mididriver/midi_driver.h

SYNOPSIS typedef void (***MIDIDataReplyFunctio**n)(port_t *replyPort*, short *unit*,
MIDIRawEvent **events*, unsigned int *count*);

DESCRIPTION This function is used to handle requests for data registered by the **MIDIRequestData()** function. *replyPort* represents the port passed by the **MIDIRequestData()** function. *events* represents an array of MIDIRawEvent data. *count* represents the number of elements in *events*.

MIDIExceptionReplyFunction

DECLARED IN mididriver/midi_driver.h

SYNOPSIS typedef void (***MIDIExceptionReplyFunction**)(port_t *replyPort*, int *exception*);

DESCRIPTION This function is used to handle requests for exceptions registered by the **MIDIRequestExceptions()** function. *replyPort* represents the port passed by the **MIDIRequestExceptions()** function. *exception* represents the exception sent by the driver.

MIDIQueueReplyFunction

DECLARED IN mididriver/midi_driver.h

SYNOPSIS typedef void (***MIDIQueueReplyFunction**)(port_t *replyPort*, short *unit*);

DESCRIPTION This function is used to handle requests for queue information registered by the **MIDIRequestQueueNotification()** function. *replyPort* represents the port passed by the **MIDIRequestQueueNotification()** function. *unit* represents the serial port with which the queue is associated.

MIDIRawEvent

DECLARED IN mididriver/midi_driver.h

SYNOPSIS

```
typedef struct {
    int time;
    unsigned char byte;
} MIDIRawEvent;
```

DESCRIPTION *time* is the timestamp associated with the MIDI data.
byte is the actual MIDI data.

MIDIReplyFunctions

DECLARED IN midridriver/midi_driver.h

SYNOPSIS

```
typedef struct _MIDIReplyFunctions {
    MIDIDataReplyFunction dataReply;
    MIDIAlarmReplyFunction alarmReply;
    MIDIExceptionReplyFunction exceptionReply;
    MIDIQueueReplyFunction queueReply;
} MIDIReplyFunctions;
```

DESCRIPTION This structure is used as an argument to the **MIDIAwaitReply()** and **MIDIHandleReply()** functions to allow an application to handle replies to requests to the MIDI driver.

Symbolic Constants

Clock Modes

DECLARED IN mididriver/midi_driver.h

SYNOPSIS

MIDI_CLOCK_MODE_INTERNAL
MIDI_CLOCK_MODE_MTC_SYNC

Controller Definitions

DECLARED IN mididriver/midi_spec.h

SYNOPSIS

MIDI_EXTERNALEFFECTSDEPTH
MIDI_TREMELODEPTH
MIDI_CHORUSDEPTH
MIDI_DETUNEDEPTH
MIDI_PHASERDEPTH
(from original 1.0 MIDI spec)

MIDI_EFFECTS1
MIDI_EFFECTS2
MIDI_EFFECTS3
MIDI_EFFECTS4
MIDI_EFFECTS5
MIDI_DATAINCREMENT
MIDI_DATADECREMENT
(From June 1990 spec)

Error Codes

DECLARED IN mididriver/midi_driver.h

SYNOPSIS
MIDI_ERROR_BUSY
MIDI_ERROR_NOT_OWNER
MIDI_ERROR_QUEUE_FULL
MIDI_ERROR_BAD_MODE
MIDI_ERROR_UNIT_UNAVAILABLE
MIDI_ERROR_ILLEGAL_OPERATION
MIDI_ERROR_UNKNOWN_ERROR

Event Count

DECLARED IN mididriver/midi_driver.h

SYNOPSIS MIDI_MAX_EVENT 100

Event Size

DECLARED IN mididriver/midi_driver.h

SYNOPSIS MIDI_MAX_MSG_SIZE 1024

Exception Codes

DECLARED IN mididriver/midi_driver.h

SYNOPSIS
MIDI_EXCEPTION_MTC_STOPPED
MIDI_EXCEPTION_MTC_STARTED_FORWARD
MIDI_EXCEPTION_MTC_STARTED_REVERSE

General MIDI Constants

DECLARED IN mididriver/midi_spec.h

SYNOPSIS
MIDI_RESETCONTROLLERS
MIDI_LOCALCONTROL
MIDI_ALLNOTESOFF
MIDI_OMNIOFF
MIDI_OMNION
MIDI_MONO
MIDI_POLY
MIDI_NOTEOFF
MIDI_NOTEON
MIDI_POLYPRES
MIDI_CONTROL
MIDI_PROGRAM
MIDI_CHANPRES
MIDI_PITCH
MIDI_CHANMODE
MIDI_CONTROL
MIDI_SYSTEM
MIDI_SYSEXCL
MIDI_TIMECODEQUARTER
MIDI_SONGPOS
MIDI_SONGSEL
MIDI_TUNEREQ
MIDI_EOX
MIDI_CLOCK
MIDI_START
MIDI_CONTINUE
MIDI_STOP
MIDI_ACTIVE
MIDI_RESET
MIDI_MAXDATA
MIDI_MAXCHAN
MIDI_NUMCHANS
MIDI_NUMKEYS
MIDI_ZEROBEND
MIDI_DEFAULTVELOCITY

DESCRIPTION These constants represent various MIDI-specified messages.

Ignores

DECLARED IN mididriver/midi_driver.h

SYNOPSIS MIDI_IGNORE_CLOCK
MIDI_IGNORE_START
MIDI_IGNORE_CONTINUE
MIDI_IGNORE_STOP
MIDI_IGNORE_ACTIVE
MIDI_IGNORE_RESET
MIDI_IGNORE_REAL_TIME

DESCRIPTION Used with the **MIDISetSystemIgnores**() function.

Least Significant Bit for Controller Numbers

DECLARED IN mididriver/midi_spec.h

SYNOPSIS MIDI_MODWHEELLSB
MIDI_BREATHLSB
MIDI_FOOTLSB
MIDI_PORTAMENTOTIMELSB
MIDI_DATAENTRYLSB
MIDI_MAINVOLUMELSB
MIDI_BALANCELSB
MIDI_PANLSB
MIDI_EXPRESSIONLSB

Masks for MIDI Status Bytes

DECLARED IN mididriver/midi_spec.h

SYNOPSIS MIDI_STATUSBIT
MIDI_STATUSMASK
MIDI_SYSRTBIT

Miscellaneous

DECLARED IN mididriver/midi_driver.h

SYNOPSIS MIDI_NO_TIMEOUT

MIDI Controller Numbers

DECLARED IN mididriver/midi_spec.h

SYNOPSIS MIDI_MODWHEEL
MIDI_BREATH
MIDI_FOOT
MIDI_PORTAMENTOTIME
MIDI_DATAENTRY
MIDI_MAINVOLUME
MIDI_BALANCE
MIDI_PAN
MIDI_EXPRESSION
MIDI_EFFECTCONTROL1
MIDI_EFFECTCONTROL2
MIDI_DAMPER
MIDI_PORTAMENTO
MIDI_SOSTENUTO
MIDI_SOFTPEDAL
MIDI_HOLD2

Port Constants

DECLARED IN mididriver/midi_driver.h

SYNOPSIS MIDI_PORT_A_UNIT
MIDI_PORT_B_UNIT

DESCRIPTION Used to identify the port claimed for the application.

11 *NetInfo Kit*

11 *NetInfo Kit*

Library: libni_s.a

Header File Directory: /NextDeveloper/Headers/nikit

Introduction

The NetInfo Kit is a collection of classes and a single function used to provide a connection to and interface with NetInfo domains. The NetInfo Kit provides classes for basic interface with a domain as well as specialized panels.

NetInfo Kit Classes

The NetInfo Kit provides five classes—one for connecting to a domain, and four standard panels.

Domain

The NIDomain class is used to establish or terminate a connection to a NetInfo domain. The connection can be made by specifying a domain name or a host name and domain tag. This class also provides a method for locating a list of specific subdirectories within a domain. If your application will be accessing a NetInfo domain, you'll use this class to establish and maintain the connection.

Panels

The NILoginPanel class provides a mechanism for authenticating a user for access to a NetInfo domain. The panel includes text fields for the user account name and password along with Login and Cancel buttons. This panel can be used to allow the user to authenticate as a user with permission to run an application, as with UserManager and HostManager, or to authenticate as a user with permission to modify a domain, as with NetInfoManager and NFSManager.

The NIDomainPanel class is used to provide the user with a means to select a specific domain from a hierarchy of NetInfo domains. The panel includes a browser for the domain hierarchy, a text field, and OK and Cancel buttons. The Open Domain panel in NetInfoManager is an example of an NIDomainPanel.

The NIOpenPanel class is used to allow the user to open a specific directory (item) within a specific domain. The panel contains an upper browser for selecting the domain and a lower browser to select the item within the selected domain. The Open panels of UserManager and HostManager are examples of NIOpenPanel.

The NISavePanel class is similar to NIOpenPanel, except that it's used to save information to a specific directory within a NetInfo domain. The Save panels of UserManager and HostManager are examples of NISavePanel.

NetInfo Kit Functions

The single NetInfo Kit function is **NIFillDomainHierarchy()**, which fills a column of the domain structure for display in one of the panels.

Classes

NIDomain

Inherits From: Object

Declared In: nikit/NIDomain.h

Class Description

NIDomain provides a connection to and interface with a NetInfo domain.

Instance Variables

char ***fullPath**;
char ***masterServer**;
char ***currentServer**;
char ***domainTag**;
id **parentDomain**;
id **delegate**;
char ***parentDomainName**;
void ***domainHandle**;
ni_status **whatHappened**;
BOOL **connected**;
ni_id **rootDirectory**;
ni_fancyopenargs **fancyStuff**;
struct sockaddr_in **hostSocket**;
struct hostent ***serverHostEnt**;
NXZone ***domainZone**;

fullPath	The fully qualified pathname of the domain.
masterServer	The host name of the master server of the domain.
currentServer	The host name of the current server with which the object is communicating.
domainTag	The domain tag.
parentDomain	The parent domain object, if it's been opened.
delegate	The delegate of the NIDomain object.
parentDomainName	The fully qualified name of the parent domain.
domainHandle	The NetInfo handle to the domain.
whatHappened	The last error condition from a NetInfo call.
connected	Indicates if a domain connection is open.
rootDirectory	The NetInfo directory ID for the root directory of the domain.
fancyStuff	Various parameter settings when a connection is set with arguments.
hostSocket	The socket used when querying for a host name.
serverHostEnt	The hostent used when querying for a host name.
domainZone	Memory allocation zone.

Method Types

Allocating and initializing an NIDomain object
- + alloc
- + allocFromZone:
- – init

Freeing an NIDomain object
- – free

Connecting to or disconnecting from a domain
- – setConnection:
- – setConnection:readTimeout:writeTimeout:canAbort:mustWrite:
- – setTaggedConnection:to:
- – setTaggedConnection:to:readTimeout:writeTimeout:canAbort:
- – disconnectFromCurrent:

Getting data about or from the current domain	
	– getFullPath – getMasterServer – getCurrentServer – getTag – getServerIPAddress – getDomainHandle – findDirectory:withProperty:
Checking the error status	– lastError
Assigning a delegate	– setDelegate:

Class Methods

alloc

+ **alloc**

Returns a new NIDomain instance. You should initialize this object by sending it an **init** message.

allocFromZone:

+ **allocFromZone:**(NXZone *)*zone*

Returns a new NIDomain instance. Memory for the new object is allocated from *zone*. You should initialize this object by sending it an **init** message.

Instance Methods

disconnectFromCurrent

– **disconnectFromCurrent**

Terminates the connection to a domain but retains the NIDomain object. Resets all instance variable values. Returns **self**.

findDirectory:withProperty:

– (ni_entrylist *)**findDirectory:**(const char *)*parentDirectory*
withProperty:(const char *)*property*

Returns a list containing the values associated with the indicated property in the named NetInfo directory. The caller should free this list when it's no longer needed. This method returns NULL if it couldn't read the requested information. You can find the reason for the failure with **lastError**.

free

– **free**

Deallocates the NIDomain object. Returns **nil**.

getCurrentServer

– (const char *)**getCurrentServer**

Returns the host name of the current server of the domain, or NULL if the object isn't currently connected to a domain or the host name couldn't be resolved.

getDomainHandle

– (void *)**getDomainHandle**

Returns the NetInfo handle to the current domain, or NULL if no connection exists. If this function returns NULL, you might be able to find out why with **lastError**.

getFullPath

– (const char *)**getFullPath**

Returns the fully qualified pathname of the current domain, or NULL if the path couldn't be resolved. If this function returns NULL, invoking **lastError** might help you find out the cause.

getMasterServer

– (const char *)**getMasterServer**

Returns the host name of the master server of the current domain, or NULL if the object isn't currently connected to a domain or the host name couldn't be resolved.

getServerIPAddress

– (const struct sockaddr_in *)**getServerIPAddress**

Returns the socket address of the current server of the current domain. If an error occurs, NULL is returned. If the object is connected, invoking **lastError** should return the reason for the failure.

getTag

– (const char *)**getTag**

Returns the tag of the current domain, or NULL if there's no current connection or if it couldn't read the master server property. If the object is connected, invoking **lastError** should return the reason for the failure.

init

– **init**

Initializes a newly allocated NIDomain instance. The new instance isn't connected. Returns **self**.

lastError

– (ni_status)**lastError**

Returns the status code returned by the most recent NetInfo call. This value can be translated to an English error message by the **ni_error()** function, which is described in the **netinfo**(3) UNIX manual page.

setConnection:

– (ni_status)**setConnection:**(const char *)*domain*

Establishes a connection to the named domain. Returns a value indicating status, corresponding to the constants defined in the header file **netinfo/ni_prot.h**. This value can be translated to an English error message by the **ni_error**() function, which is described in the **netinfo**(3) UNIX manual page.

setConnection:readTimeout:writeTimeout:canAbort:mustWrite:

– (ni_status)**setConnection:**(const char *)*domain*
readTimeout:(int)*rtime*
writeTimeout:(int)*wtime*
canAbort:(BOOL)*abortFlag*
mustWrite:(BOOL)*writeFlag*

Establishes a connection to the named domain with arguments corresponding to the ni_fancyopenargs structure described in the UNIX manual page for **netinfo**. Values for *rtime* and *wtime* indicate the timeout, in seconds, for read and write attempts. If *abortFlag* is TRUE, failure will occur after a timeout or other error. Otherwise, attempts will continue forever. If *writeFlag* is TRUE, this method forces a connection to the master server of the domain, since writes can only be made there. Returns a value indicating status, corresponding to the constants defined in the header file **netinfo/ni_prot.h**. This value can be translated to an English error message by the **ni_error**() function, which is described in the **netinfo**(3) UNIX manual page.

setDelegate:

– **setDelegate:***anObject*

Sets the NIDomain object's delegate to *anObject*. Returns **self**.

setTaggedConnection:to:

– (ni_status)**setTaggedConnection:**(const char *)*tag* **to:**(char *)*hostName*

Establishes a connection to a domain by host name and tag rather than domain name. Returns a value indicating status, corresponding to the constants defined in the header file **netinfo/ni_prot.h**. This value can be translated to an English error message by the **ni_error**() function, which is described in the **netinfo**(3) UNIX manual page.

setTaggedConnection:to:readTimeout:writeTimeout:canAbort:

– (ni_status)**setTaggedConnection:**(const char *)*tag*
to:(char *)*hostName*
readTimeout:(int)*rtime*
writeTimeout:(int)*wtime*
canAbort:(BOOL)*abortFlag*

Establishes a connection to a domain by host name and tag with arguments. Same as **setConnection:readTimeout:writeTimeout:canAbort:mustWrite:**, except that it doesn't include the *writeFlag* argument. Since the connection is being made to a specific server, the *writeFlag* argument is irrelevant. Returns a value indicating status, corresponding to the constants defined in the header file **netinfo/ni_prot.h**. This value can be translated to an English error message by the **ni_error**() function, which is described in the **netinfo**(3) UNIX manual page.

Methods Implemented by the Delegate

domain:willCloseBecause:

– **domain:***sender* **willCloseBecause:**(int)*reason*

Indicates that the connection to the current domain will terminate as a result of the **disconnectFromCurrent** method. The value of *reason* is always 0, indicating that the program requested closing.

NIDomainPanel

Inherits From: Object

Declared In: nikit/NIDomainPanel.h

Class Description

NIDomainPanel provides a mechanism for selecting a specific domain in the NetInfo domain hierarchy. The panel includes a browser for the domain hierarchy and a text field at the bottom for entering the path to a domain. An example of this object is the Open Domain panel used in NetInfoManager.

Instance Variables

id **domainBrowser**;
id **okButton**;
id **cancelButton**;
id **domainText**;
id **panel**;
id **groupForm**;
id **fieldEditor**;
id **sharedDomainPanel**;
struct NIHierarchyOfDomains **myDomains**;
ni_status **lastFailure**;
int **exitFlags**;
char **returnPath**[1024];
void ***currentDomain**;
BOOL **domainBrowserLoaded**;
id **panelButton**;
NXZone ***zone**;

domainBrowser	Object to browse NetInfo domains.
okButton	The OK button.
cancelButton	The Cancel button.
domainText	Unused.
panel	The panel object.
groupForm	The text field.
fieldEditor	The editing object for the text field.
sharedDomainPanel	Unused.
myDomains	The domain hierarchy.
lastFailure	The last error condition from a NetInfo call.
exitFlags	Indicates whether the user chose Cancel or OK.
returnPath	Path of domain entered in the text field.
currentDomain	Unused.
domainBrowserLoaded	Indicates if a domain has been loaded into the browser.
panelButton	The icon at the top left of the panel.
zone	A memory allocation zone.

Method Types

Allocating and initializing an NIDomainPanel object	
	+ new + allocWithoutPanelFromZone: – init
Displaying the panel	– runModal – resizePanelBeforeShowing: – panel – windowDidResize:
Getting data	– exitFlags – domain – panelSizeDefaultName

Filling the browser	– loadDomainBrowser – loadDomainBrowserFrom: – browser:fillMatrix:inColumn: – browser:loadCell:atRow:inColumn: – freeLastColumn – fillNextColumn
Text-related methods	– completeDomain – runOk: – text:isEmpty: – textWillChange: – textWillEnd:
Target and action methods	– cellWasHitInBrowser: – cancel: – ok:

Class Methods

allocWithoutPanelFromZone:

+ **allocWithoutPanelFromZone:**(NXZone *)*zone*

Returns a new NIDomainPanel object without the panel. For use with a different panel layout. Use with **init**.

initialize

+ **initialize**

Initializes the NetInfo Kit zone; sent by the run-time system. Don't invoke or override this method.

new

+ **new**

Returns the single NIDomainPanel instance per application. If one doesn't exist, it is created.

Instance Methods

browser:fillMatrix:inColumn:

– (int)**browser:***sender* **fillMatrix:***matrix* **inColumn:**(int)*column*

Sent automatically by the browser when a column needs updating, this NXBrowser delegate method fills the indicated browser column with data.

browser:loadCell:atRow:inColumn:

– **browser:***sender* **loadCell:***cell* **atRow:**(int)*row* **inColumn:**(int)*column*

Sent automatically by the browser, this NXBrowser delegate method fills the indicated cell with data.

cancel:

– **cancel:***sender*

This method is invoked when the Cancel button is clicked. Returns **self**.

cellWasHitInBrowser:

– **cellWasHitInBrowser:**(id)*sender*

This method is invoked when the user clicks in the browser. Returns **self**.

completeDomain

– **completeDomain**

This method is invoked to complete the text field when the user presses the Esc key, when the OK button is pressed, or when the current selection moves out of the text field. Returns **self** if the path was successfully completed; otherwise, returns **nil**.

domain

– (const char *)**domain**

Returns the name of the domain selected in the panel, or a localized string that indicates that the path was invalid.

exitFlags

– (int)**exitFlags**

Returns the exit flags from the panel, indicating whether the user chose OK or Cancel.

fillNextColumn

– **fillNextColumn**

Fills the next column of the domain hierarchy. Sent by **browser:fillMatrix:inColumn:**. Returns **self**, or **nil** if an error occurred.

freeLastColumn

– **freeLastColumn**

Clears the data in the rightmost column of the browser. Returns **self**.

init

– **init**

Initializes the NIDomainPanel object. For use with **allocWithoutPanelFromZone:**. Returns **self**.

loadDomainBrowser

– **loadDomainBrowser**

Loads the current domain information into the browser, filling to match the local domain. Returns **self**, or **nil** if an error occurred.

See also: – **loadDomainBrowserFrom:**

loadDomainBrowserFrom:

– **loadDomainBrowserFrom:**(const char *)*aDomainName*

Loads the browser with information from the named domain rather than the local domain. Returns **self**, or **nil** if an error occurred.

See also: – **loadDomainBrowser**

ok:

– **ok:***sender*

This method is sent when the OK button is clicked. Returns **self**.

panel

– **panel**

Returns the Panel displayed by the NIDomainPanel.

panelSizeDefaultName

– (const char *)**panelSizeDefaultName**

Returns the name of a constant indicating the panel's default size.

See also: – **resizePanelBeforeShowing:**

resizePanelBeforeShowing:

– **resizePanelBeforeShowing:**(const char *)*panelDefaultName*

Resizes the panel to the size indicated by the constant identified with *panelDefaultName*, which can be obtained with the **panelSizeDefaultName** method. Resizes the panel to the larger of the user's last selection or the indicated panel minimum. Useful when changing languages, for example, because the minimum panel size may increase. Returns **nil** if *panelDefaultName* is NULL; otherwise, returns **self**.

See also: – **panelSizeDefaultName**

runModal

– (int)**runModal**

Displays the panel and begins its event loop. Returns the exit flags from the panel, indicating whether the user chose OK or Cancel.

runOk:

– **runOk:***sender*

Sent automatically when Return is pressed or a browser item is double-clicked. Returns **self**.

text:isEmpty:

– **text:***textObject* **isEmpty:**(BOOL)*flag*

Sent automatically when the text field is exited. This Text delegate method enables the OK button if any text is in the text field; otherwise, disables the OK button. Returns **self**.

textWillChange:

– **textWillChange:***textObject*

Sent automatically when text is entered into the text field. This Text delegate method sets the filtering function to be used for the field. Returns zero.

textWillEnd:

– (BOOL)**textWillEnd:** *textObject*

Sent automatically when user has finished editing the text field. This Text delegate method completes the path in the text field, if possible. It then returns NO if the text field contains a valid domain; otherwise, it returns YES.

windowDidResize:

– **windowDidResize:***sender*

Sent automatically when the user finishes resizing the panel. This Window delegate method saves the panel's new size into the defaults system.

NILoginPanel

Inherits From: Panel : Window : Responder : Object

Declared In: nikit/NILoginPanel.h

Class Description

NILoginPanel provides a means of authentication for accessing a NetInfo domain. It can be used to determine authorization to run an application, as with HostManager and UserManager, or to determine if a user can modify a domain, as with NetInfoManager and NFSManager. The panel includes text fields for the user name and password, an icon, and text for instructions to the user.

Instance Variables

id **panel**;
id **userField**;
id **passwordField**;
id **instructionText**;
BOOL **validLogin**;
BOOL **loginSuccess**;
int **bootMode**;
char **currentUser**[16];
char **currentPassword**[16];
id **iconButton**;

panel	Panel object.
userField	Text field for user account name.
passwordField	Text field for password.
instructionText	Text for instructions to the user.
validLogin	Indicates if an authentication attempt was successful.
loginSuccess	Currently means the same as **validLogin**.

bootMode	Indicates whether the delegate should perform authentication.
currentUser	Name of current user.
currentPassword	Password of current user.
iconButton	Icon to display in panel.

Method Types

Creating an NILoginPanel object	+ new
Running the panel	– runModal:inDomain: – runModal:inDomain:withUser:withInstruction: allowChange: – runModalWithValidation:inDomain: withUser:withInstruction:allowChange:
Target and action methods	– ok: – cancel:
Getting data	– isValidLogin: – getPassword: – getUser:

Class Methods

new

+ **new**

Creates, if necessary, and returns the shared instance of NILoginPanel.

Instance Methods

cancel:

– **cancel:***sender*

Sent automatically when the Cancel button is clicked. Returns **self**.

getPassword:

– (const char *)**getPassword:***sender*

Returns the password entered into the password text field. The password is correct only if this method is invoked from **panel:authenticateUser:withPassword:inDomain:**. Otherwise, returns NULL.

getUser:

– (const char *)**getUser:***sender*

Returns the account name entered into the user text field.

isValidLogin:

– (BOOL)**isValidLogin:***sender*

Returns TRUE if the account name and password represent a successful authentication for the domain; otherwise, returns FALSE.

ok:

– **ok:***sender*

Target method for the Login button. Zeroes the password value, for security reasons. Returns **self**.

runModal:inDomain:

– (BOOL)**runModal:***sender* **inDomain:**(void *)*domainID*

Begins a modal event loop for the panel. Runs the panel for the domain indicated by the NetInfo handle *domainID*. You can obtain the NetInfo handle with the **domainHandle** method of the NIDomain class. The user **root** will be used as the default user. Returns TRUE if the user logged in successfully; otherwise, returns FALSE.

See also: – **runModal:inDomain:withUser:withInstruction:allowChange:**,
– **runModalWithValidation:inDomain:withUser:withInstruction:allowChange**

runModal:inDomain:withUser:withInstruction:allowChange:

– (BOOL)**runModal:***sender*
inDomain:(void *)*domainID*
withUser:(const char *)*userName*
withInstruction:(const char *)*warning*
allowChange:(BOOL)*flag*

Begins a modal event loop for the panel for the specified domain and user. The string in *warning* will be displayed in the panel as instructions to the user. If *flag* is TRUE, the user won't be allowed to change the user name in the text field. Returns TRUE if the user logs in successfully; otherwise, returns FALSE.

runModalWithValidation:inDomain:withUser:withInstruction: allowChange:

– (BOOL)**runModalWithValidation:**sender
inDomain:(void *)*domainID*
withUser:(const char *)*userName*
withInstruction:(const char *)*warning*
allowChange:(BOOL)*enableUser*

Same as **runModal:inDomain:withUser:withInstruction:allowChange:**, except that the user will be authenticated by the delegate instead of by the **ni_setuser()** and **ni_setpassword()** functions. Returns TRUE if the user logged in successfully; otherwise, returns FALSE.

See also: **panel:authenticateUser:withPassword:inDomain:** (delegate method)

Methods Implemented by the Delegate

panel:authenticateUser:withPassword:inDomain:

– (BOOL)**panel:***thePanel*
authenticateUser:(const char *)*userName*
withPassword:(const char *)*password*
inDomain:(const void *)*domain*

Sent by **runModalWithValidation:inDomain:withUser:withInstruction: allowChange:**. Should determine whether the combination of *userName*, *password*, and *domain* is valid. Returns TRUE if the user should be authenticated, FALSE otherwise.

NIOpenPanel

Inherits From: NIDomainPanel : Object

Declared In: nikit/NIOpenPanel.h

Class Description

NIOpenPanel is used to allow a user to open an item in a NetInfo domain, such as a user account or host entry. The panel's upper half contains a browser for selecting a NetInfo domain; its lower half contains a browser for selecting a specific item within the domain (a NetInfo directory). Each half has a text field containing a title and an editable text field representing the path of the domain in the upper half and the name of the item in the lower half.

Instance Variables

id **directoryObjectBrowser**;
char ***pathToUse**;
ni_entrylist ***filler**;
id **listTitleField**;
id **panelTitleField**;
id **selectedItemText**;
id **iconButton**;

directoryObjectBrowser	Browser object for lower half of the open panel.
pathToUse	Stores domain path to use when loading domain browser in top half of panel.
filler	Data for browser in lower half of panel.
listTitleField	Field displayed above browser in lower half of panel.
panelTitleField	Field displayed at top of panel.
selectedItemText	Text field at bottom of lower browser.
iconButton	Icon to display in top left corner of panel.

Method Types

Initializing and running a panel	+ new – runModal
Getting data from the panel	– directory – panelSizeDefaultName
Manipulating the panel	– setDirectoryPath: – setListTitle: – setPanelTitle: – refreshLowerData:
Searching	– searchItemList: – searchTextField
Filling the browser	– browser:fillMatrix:inColumn: – browser:loadCell:atRow:inColumn:
Text-related methods	– text:isEmpty: – textWillChange: – completeItemName – completeDomain
Target and action methods	– cellWasHitInBrowser: – cellWasHitInItemList:

Class Methods

new

+ **new**

Creates, if necessary, and returns a new instance of NIOpenPanel. Each application shares just one instance of NIOpenPanel; this method returns the shared instance if it exists.

Instance Methods

browser:fillMatrix:inColumn:

– (int)**browser:***sender* **fillMatrix:***matrix* **inColumn:**(int)*column*

Sent automatically when a column needs updating, this NXBrowser delegate method fills the indicated browser column with data.

browser:loadCell:atRow:inColumn:

– **browser:***sender* **loadCell:***cell* **atRow:**(int)*row* **inColumn:**(int)*column*

Sent automatically by the browser, this NXBrowser delegate method fills the indicated cell with data.

cellWasHitInBrowser:

– **cellWasHitInBrowser:**(id)*sender*

This method is invoked when the user clicks in the upper browser. Returns **self**.

cellWasHitInItemList:

– **cellWasHitInItemList:***sender*

This method is invoked when the user clicks in the lower browser. Returns **self**.

completeDomain

– **completeDomain**

This method is invoked to complete the upper text field (and browser) when the user presses the Esc key, when the OK button is pressed, or when the current selection moves out of the text field. Returns **self** if the path was successfully completed; otherwise, returns **nil**.

completeItemName

– **completeItemName**

Reserved for future use.

directory

– (const char *)**directory**

Returns the name of the directory that's selected in the lower browser, or NULL if no valid directory is selected.

panelSizeDefaultName

– (const char *)**panelSizeDefaultName**

Returns the name of a constant representing the size of the panel. Used in conjunction with the inherited method **resizePanelBeforeShowing:**.

refreshLowerData:

– **refreshLowerData:***sender*

Reloads and redraws browser in lower half of panel. Returns **self**.

runModal

– (int)**runModal**

Displays the panel and begins its event loop. Returns the exit flags from the panel.

searchItemList:

– **searchItemList:***textThing*

Sent automatically to keep the lower browser in sync with what a user types into the lower text field. Don't invoke this method directly. Returns **self**.

searchTextField

– **searchTextField**

Sent automatically to update the lower browser after the user has finished entering text into the lower text field. Don't invoke this method directly. Returns **self**.

setDirectoryPath:

– **setDirectoryPath:**(const char *)*path*

Use this method to set the initial directory path in the lower browser. The contents of the indicated directory will be displayed when the browser is loaded. Returns **self**.

setListTitle:

– **setListTitle:**(const char *)*title*

Use this method to set the title of the lower half of the panel. Returns **self**.

setPanelTitle:

– **setPanelTitle:**(const char *)*title*

Use this method to set the title of the panel. Returns **self**.

text:isEmpty:

– **text:***textObj* **isEmpty:**(BOOL)*flag*

This Text delegate method is invoked when the user types in either text field. It disables the OK button if the text field is empty; otherwise, it enables the OK button.

textWillChange:

– (BOOL)**textWillChange:***textObject*

This Text delegate method is invoked when exiting a text field after an edit has been made.

NISavePanel

Inherits From: NIOpenPanel : NIDomainPanel : Object

Declared In: nikit/NISavePanel.h

Class Description

NISavePanel is a subclass of NIOpenPanel used to allow a user to save information to a NetInfo domain. The panel includes an upper domain browser, a lower browser for NetInfo directories (items), a text field for each browser, and a title for each browser. Examples of this panel are the Save panels in HostManager and UserManager.

Instance Variables

BOOL **frozenBelow**;

frozenBelow	Indicates whether the lower text field can be edited.

Method Types

Creating a new NISavePanel object	+ new
Displaying the panel	– runModal – runModalWithString: – runModalWithUneditableString:
Getting data from the panel	– panelSizeDefaultName – directory
Target and action methods	– cellWasHitInItemList:
Manipulating the panel	– setStartingDomainPath: – refreshLowerData:

Class Methods

new

+ **new**

Returns the single NISavePanel object per application. If one doesn't exist, it is created.

Instance Methods

cellWasHitInItemList:

– **cellWasHitInItemList:***sender*

This method is invoked when the user clicks in the lower browser. Returns **self**.

directory

– (const char *)**directory**

Returns the value of the directory selected by the user in the lower browser.

panelSizeDefaultName

– (const char *)**panelSizeDefaultName**

Returns the name of a constant representing the size of the panel. Used in conjunction with the inherited method **resizePanelBeforeShowing:**.

refreshLowerData:

– **refreshLowerData:***sender*

Reloads and redraws the information in the lower browser of the panel. Returns **self**.

runModal

– (int)**runModal**

Begins a modal event loop for the panel. Returns the exit flags from the panel.

runModalWithString:

– (int)**runModalWithString:**(char *)*initialValue*

Runs the panel, supplying a value to be placed in the text field of the lower half of the panel. The value can be changed by the user. Returns the exit flags from the panel.

runModalWithUneditableString:

– (int)**runModalWithUneditableString:**(char *)*initialValue*

Same as **runModalWithString:**, except that the supplied value can't be modified by the user. Forces the user to save to a specific item and allows the user to cancel if a conflict exists. Returns the exit flags from the panel.

setStartingDomainPath:

– **setStartingDomainPath:**(const char *)*directory*

Sets the path to the domain in the upper browser. This directory will be selected when the browser is loaded. Returns **self** if the path can be resolved; otherwise, returns **nil**.

Functions

NIFillDomainHierarchy()

SUMMARY Fill a column of a domain structure

DECLARED IN nikit/domain.h

SYNOPSIS ni_status **NIFillDomainHierarchy**(struct NIHierarchyOfDomains **domains*, int *level*, const char **toMatch*, int *selectedLevel*)

DESCRIPTION Use this function to fill in the next column (to the right) of a browser in a NetInfo Kit panel, in response to a selection by the user. The return value of this function can be converted to an English error message using the **ni_error()** function. The **ni_error()** function is documented in the **netinfo**(3) UNIX manual page

RETURN A value indicating status, corresponding to the constants defined in the header file **netinfo/ni_prot.h**.

Types and Constants

Symbolic Constants

Connection Status

DECLARED IN nikit/domain.h

SYNOPSIS NI_ALREADYCONNECTED
NI_NOTCONNECTED

DESCRIPTION These constants are used as return values to indicate whether a connection to a NetInfo domain already exists.

Test Modes

DECLARED IN nikit/NILoginPanel.h

SYNOPSIS

NI_USERTESTMODE	0
NI_NETINFOTESTMODE	1

DESCRIPTION These constants are used to set the value of the **bootMode** instance variable. You shouldn't need to use them unless you're subclassing NILoginPanel and are overriding one of the **runModal** methods or implementing a similar method. The method should set **bootMode** to NI_USERTESTMODE if the delegate should validate the authentication. The **bootMode** instance variable should be set to NI_NETINFOTESTMODE if the authentication should be validated by the **ni_setuser()** and **ni_setpassword()** functions, which are documented in the **netinfo**(3) UNIX manual page.

Structures

NIDomainCellData

DECLARED IN nikit/domain.h

SYNOPSIS

```
struct NIDomainCellData {
        char *name;
        BOOL isaLeaf;
}
```

DESCRIPTION Data for a cell of a domain browser.

NIHierarchyOfDomains

DECLARED IN nikit/domain.h

SYNOPSIS

```
struct NIHierarchyOfDomains {
        int numberOfLevels;
        struct NIMultiDomainList *domainListAtLevel;
}
```

DESCRIPTION Hierarchy of NetInfo domains.

NIMultiDomainList

DECLARED IN nikit/domain.h

SYNOPSIS

```
struct NIMultiDomainList{
        int numberOfDomains;
        int activeDomain;
        id activeDomainObject;
        struct NIDomainCellData *topDomain;
}
```

DESCRIPTION Data for a domain browser column.

12 *Networks: Novell NetWare*

12 *Networks: Novell NetWare*

Library: libnwapi_s.a

Header File Directory: /NextDeveloper/Headers/netware

Introduction

NeXTSTEP Release 3 provides programming support for Novell NetWare networking, allowing your application to communicate with other applications on networked PCs, and to access printers on those networks. The NetWare programming interface is documented by Novell.

13 *Phone Kit*

13 *Phone Kit*

Library: libphone_s.a

Header File Directory: /NextDeveloper/Headers/phonekit

Introduction

The Phone Kit offers an easy way for you to connect the application you're developing to a telephone line, to initiate and receive calls over the line, and to transmit and receive data during a call. The phone line must be attached to the user's computer, or to a computer on the user's network, through a Hayes ISDN Extender™ or an equivalent device. A modem is not involved.

The phone line can be a POTS ("plain old telephone service") line or an ISDN (Integrated Services Digital Network) line. An ISDN line is completely digitized end-to-end, from one telephone device to the other. It can therefore be used for the transmission of any kind of digital data. In contrast, the telephones on a POTS line send and receive analog signals, although the information is typically digitized for part of its journey. Without a modem, a POTS line can be used only for voice data.

A basic ISDN line has two bearer channels (B channels) that carry information at 64 kilobits per second and one control channel (D channel) that carries control signals at 16 kilobits per second. A channel is a physical partition of the line's information-carrying capacity. The two B channels can handle calls simultaneously. By using them in concert with each other, you can achieve data transfers at a rate approaching 128 kilobits per second.

A POTS line, on the other hand, has just one channel. It also carries information at 64 kilobits per second, but because of inaccuracies in the analog-to-digital and digital-to-analog conversions that are required, it's suitable only for voice transmission. To send digital data over a POTS line, a modem must specially package the data for analog transmission.

The Telephone Network

The telephone network is a giant system of circuits and switches that can connect one telephone device with any other telephone. Phone users rarely need to know about its many components, but when you substitute a computer for a telephone set, some parts of the network assume greater importance. The network can be diagrammed something like this:

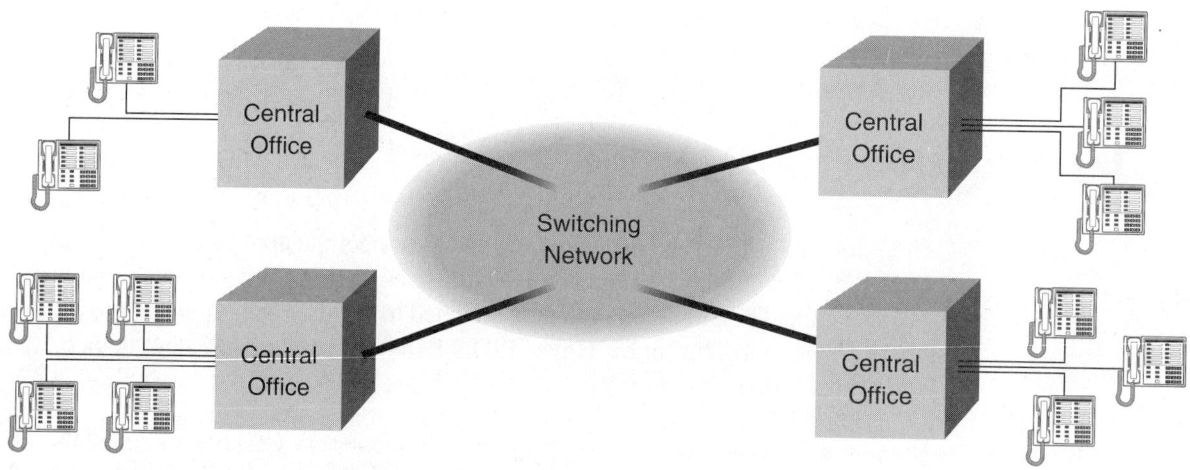

Figure 13-1. Telephone Network

A group of telephones is connected to the first switching station, a "central office," which in turn links those telephones into trunk lines, regional offices, and the rest of the phone system's switching network.

On a POTS telephone line, analog information is passed between the user's telephone and the central office. Between central offices, the information is typically digitized:

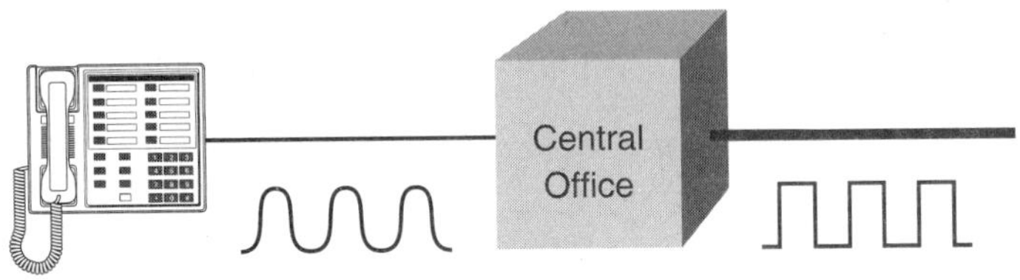

Figure 13-2. POTS Transmission

On an ISDN line, information is also digital between the phone and the central office. So the central office doesn't need to alter it:

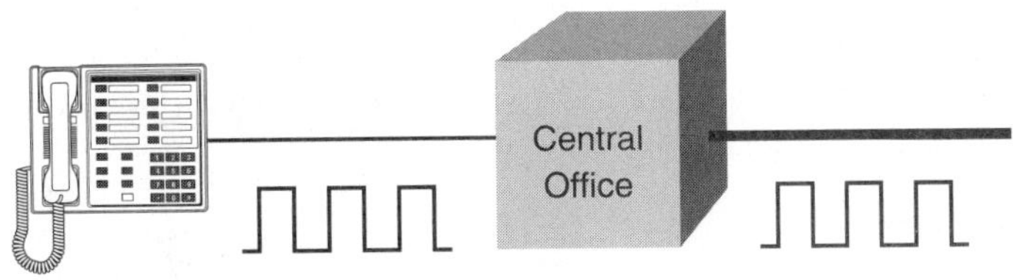

Figure 13-3. ISDN Transmission

Representing Voice as Digital Data

The primary function of the telephone network is to transmit the voice of one phone user to the ears of another. But, as noted above, both POTS and ISDN phone lines carry the human voice as a digital signal, at least for part of the way. The conversion to a digital signal happens at the telephone on an ISDN line and at the central office on a POTS line.

An ISDN phone encodes the speaker's voice using an 8-bit mu-law (nonlinear) quantization at a data rate of 8012.8 samples per second (8 kHz). This encoding favors lower amplitudes—records more distinctions at low amplitudes than at higher ones—and captures frequencies to about one-half the sampling rate (4 kHz).

Although it's not what you'd choose if you were recording music, this digitizing scheme is fast and accurate enough to faithfully reproduce human speech, the purpose for which it was designed.

A central office uses the same 8-bit mu-law encoding to convert an analog signal to a digital one. When a phone call is made between an ISDN telephone at one end of the connection and a POTS phone at the other end, the analog-to-digital and digital-to-analog conversions made at the central office for the POTS line mirror those made by the ISDN phone.

Putting Computers on a Phone Line

When a computer substitutes for a telephone on an ISDN line, there is no human voice, no analog signal, and no need to convert from one form of information to another. The telephone network becomes a kind of computer network, one that just happens to also have some phones on it.

The Phone Kit lets you treat an ISDN line in just this way—as a doorway into a large computer network on which connections are established through normal telephone-call protocols. Of course, if a microphone is attached to the computer, the right software might turn the computer into a phone and send voice data over the ISDN line. This data would be treated just like the digital voice data from any ISDN phone.

When a computer substitutes for a telephone on a POTS line, NeXTSTEP software assumes that any data that's transmitted or received over the line is voice data encoded according to the 8-bit mu-law quantization described above. Data transmitted during a call is converted to an analog signal for the POTS line, and analog data received during a call is converted to digital data. The conversions are done exactly as a central office would do them. The Phone Kit is not a substitute for a modem.

The Phone Server and Phone Kit

The Phone Kit is just one half of NeXTSTEP telephone-management software. The other half is the Phone Server, which monitors the phone line and understands the POTS and ISDN signaling protocols. The Server is an independent process that conveys information to and from the phone line at the behest of client applications

The Phone Server controls input and output on a telephone line much as the Window Server controls input from the keyboard and mouse and output to the screen. Just as the Window Server is able to translate user actions into events and turn PostScript code into visible images, the Phone Server is able to translate information received over the phone line into a form that's useful for applications, and it can take information produced by applications and send it over the line. Applications "talk to" the telephone network through the Phone Server.

The Phone Kit is an object-oriented interface to the Phone Server, in much the same way that the Application Kit is an object-oriented interface to the Window Server. The Phone Kit provides a framework for delivering instructions to the Phone Server and for receiving notifications from the Server of activity on the phone line. Communication between the Kit and the Server is through the mechanism of distributed objects and remote Objective C messages.

Phone Kit Classes

The Phone Kit consists of just three Objective C classes, all direct subclasses of the Object class:

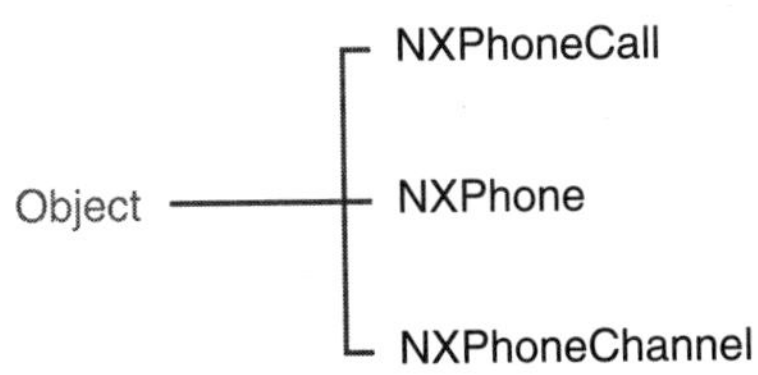

Figure 13-4. Phone Kit Inheritance Hierarchy

An application must have one NXPhone object, one NXPhoneChannel for each channel that it uses, and a separate NXPhoneCall for each call:

- The NXPhone object sets up and maintains the application's connection to the Phone Server. It's also responsible for keeping track of the channels that are used.
- An NXPhoneChannel corresponds to a particular channel on the line. It keeps track of the calls that are associated with a channel and decides how to respond to an incoming call.
- An NXPhoneCall object corresponds to a particular call on a channel. It's responsible for making the call, or answering the phone when a call is received, and for transmitting and receiving data over the line.

The bulk of the work is done by NXPhoneCall objects. Every application must customize the NXPhoneCall class—define an NXPhoneCall subclass—to handle calls in an application-specific manner. The subclass implements methods to respond to notifications received from the Phone Server, much as View subclasses implement methods to respond to event messages.

An application that receives incoming calls also needs to customize the NXPhoneChannel class so that it can provide the appropriate kind of NXPhoneCall to answer incoming calls and decide which calls to answer.

There should never be a need to define an NXPhone subclass.

Getting Set Up

To begin using the Phone Kit, an application first creates an NXPhone instance and an NXPhoneChannel for each channel that will be used. The NXPhone object must be informed about the channels:

```
id thePhone = [[NXPhone alloc] initType:NX_ISDNDevice];
id firstChannel = [[MyChannel alloc] initType:NX_B1Channel];
id secondChannel = [[MyChannel alloc] initType:NX_B2Channel];
[thePhone addChannel:firstChannel];
[thePhone addChannel:secondChannel];
```

Before a channel can be used to make or receive a call, the application must "acquire" it—lock it down for the application's exclusive use:

```
if ( [thePhone acquireChannel:firstChannel] )
    . . .
```

The real work of setting up phone calls and carrying on a conversation falls to custom NXPhoneCall objects (instances of an application-specific subclass of the NXPhoneCall class). The application creates these objects and associates them with a channel as they're needed. The manner in which this is done differs for outgoing calls and incoming calls. See "Making a Call" and "Getting a Call" later in this introduction.

Monitoring the Connection

Phone calls involve the give and take of information. To get information from the Phone Server (and over the phone line), an application must be listening for remote input from that source. Applications that display a user interface and respond to events listen for phone input just as they listen for other remote input—between events. Sending the NXPhone object a **runFromAppKit** message adds a dedicated port for the Phone Server to the list of sources that are checked whenever the application is finished with one event and ready to get another one.

```
[thePhone runFromAppKit];
```

As the name of this method indicates, it enables the Phone Kit to work with the Application Kit. Every Application Kit program turns program control over to the user by sending a **run** message to its Application object. This message initiates the main event loop. Thereafter, the application responds only to user-generated events and, between events, to timed entries and remote messages from other processes. **runFromAppKit** makes the Phone Server one of those processes.

Service applications that have no user interface don't initiate a main event loop; they must therefore monitor the Phone Server port on their own. Sending the NXPhone object, rather than the Application object, a **run** message turns program control over to the Phone Server. Thereafter, the application waits for messages from the Server:

```
[thePhone run];
```

Like the Application class's **run** method, this method enters an endless loop; it doesn't return. The Server becomes the only source of input for the application (unless additional sources are registered by sending **addPort:receiver:method:** messages to the NXPhone object).

Phone Server Messages

All communication between an application and the Phone Server is asynchronous. When a Kit method calls upon the Server to do something—for example to dial a number or transmit some data over the phone line—it doesn't wait for the Server to finish; it returns immediately. Similarly, when the Server sends a message to the application, it doesn't wait for the application to respond.

An asynchronous message can have no valid return. As soon as the message is dispatched to the receiving application, it returns in the sending application. The sender can't get the results of any processing the receiver does, and nothing the receiver returns will ever get back to the sender.

This fact is indicated in the method descriptions by a **void** return type. For example:

– (void)**remotePickup**

A **void** return is a fairly accurate indication of a method that communicates with the Phone Server. In some cases, **void** marks methods that you must implement to respond to remote messages from the Server. In other cases, **void** methods are ones you invoke to send a remote message to the Server.

Making a Call

To make an outgoing call, the application first allocates and initializes an instance of its custom NXPhoneCall subclass, and adds it to the NXPhoneChannel object corresponding to the physical channel that will be used to make the call:

```
id myCall = [[MyPhoneCall alloc] initType:NX_DataCall];
[firstChannel addCall:myCall];
```

Any number of calls can be associated with (added to) a channel, but only one can actively use the channel at a time. The NXPhoneChannel can identify the NXPhoneCall that's currently handling a call:

```
NXPhoneCall *currentCall = [firstChannel activeCall];
```

Once the NXPhone, NXPhoneChannel, and NXPhoneCall objects are in place, the connection to the Phone Server is running, the NXPhoneChannel has been added to the NXPhone and acquired, and the NXPhoneCall has been added to the NXPhoneChannel, you're ready to initiate a call.

The procedure for making a call with the Phone Kit parallels the procedure used when making calls from an ordinary telephone.

- The messages you send the NXPhoneCall object correspond to the actions you would normally take when making a call—picking up the receiver, dialing, talking into the phone, hanging up.

- The notifications the NXPhoneCall object receives from the Phone Server correspond to the kinds of feedback you normally get over the phone line—a dial tone, a busy signal or the sound of the phone ringing at the other end, the noise when the phone is answered and the other party says "hello," and the click when it's hung up again.

This feedback is a necessary part of the process; it signals what it's appropriate to do next. For example, people normally listen for a dial tone before dialing; they wait for someone to answer the phone before starting to talk.

This same sort of interaction is simulated when using the Kit. In an NXPhoneCall subclass, you implement methods that respond to Phone Server notifications in an appropriate manner, normally by taking the next logical step in completing the call. For example, the method that receives a dial tone notification responds by dialing a number.

Notification methods are also implemented to keep users informed of the current state of the call so that they can be prompted for input as necessary.

To initiate a call, you send the NXPhoneCall object a **pickUp** message, telling it to take the phone off-hook:

```
[myCall pickUp];
```

This is the only action you take without waiting for some feedback from the Phone Server. (Note that this message must precede a **run** message to the NXPhone object, since **run** doesn't return.)

After the phone is off-hook, the NXPhoneCall object receives a **dialToneReceived** notification. This lets you know that the phone line and channel are working and that it's OK to begin dialing:

```
- (void)dialToneReceived
{
    [self dialDigits:"18008006398"];
    . . .
}
```

Once the number is dialed, the NXPhoneCall is notified through a **dialingComplete** message. It may then receive either a **remoteBusy** or a **remoteRing** notification. If the number that you called is busy, you need to hang up and let the user know:

```
- (void)remoteBusy
{
    [self hangUp];
    . . .
}
```

If the other party answers the phone, the NXPhoneCall receives **remotePickup** and **callConnected** notifications, in that order. Like **remoteRing**, a **remotePickup** method can be used to inform the user of the current state of the call. The **callConnected** notification is used to begin the transfer of data:

```
- (void)callConnected
{
    [self transmitData:&theData length:numBytes];
    . . .
}
```

If the other party hangs up, the NXPhoneCall should clean up as necessary and also hang up:

```
- (void)remoteHangup
{
    [self hangUp];
    . . .
}
```

The last notification, **callReleased**, announces that the call is over. It can be implemented to free the NXPhoneCall:

```
- (void)callReleased
{
    . . .
    [firstChannel removeCall:self];
    [self free];
}
```

Getting a Call

Incoming phone calls arrive on a particular channel and are first brought to the attention of the NXPhoneChannel object. The NXPhoneChannel has two responsibilities:

- To create or designate an NXPhoneCall object to handle the call.
- To accept or reject the call.

The NXPhoneChannel is notified of the call by an **allocateIncomingCallOfType:** message. A subclass should implement this method to return an application-specific NXPhoneCall object to answer the phone and carry on a conversation with the caller.

```
- allocateIncomingCallOfType:callType
{
   return [[MyPhoneCall alloc] initType:callType];
}
```

Next, the NXPhoneChannel receives an **acceptCall:** message asking it to return YES if it wants the call and NO if it doesn't:

```
- (BOOL)acceptCall:theCall
{
    if ( [theCall type] == NX_DataCall )
        return YES;
    return NO;
}
```

If the answer is YES, the designated NXPhoneCall will receive a **ring** notification. The appropriate response is to answer the phone:

```
- (void)ring
{
     . . .
     [self pickUp];
}
```

The **pickUp** method takes the phone off-hook and makes the connection. The NXPhoneCall then receives a **callConnected** notification telling it that it's OK to begin the conversation.

Sending and Receiving Data

Phone conversations are not always orderly affairs. People can talk at the same time, or ignore and interrupt one another. There can be long silences.

The same is true when you're using the Phone Kit. Incoming information arrives as a continuous bit stream, which the Kit slices up and reports to the NXPhoneCall object in **dataReceived:length:** messages. Outgoing information is sent through **transmitData:length:** messages. Like all other communications between the Phone Server and the application, these messages are asynchronous. Neither the Server nor the application waits for an acknowledgement. Both can be transmitting at once.

It's important, therefore, for both parties to a call to agree on protocols that will keep them coordinated. The nature of the protocols will vary depending on the application and the type of data it processes.

On an open phone line, information is continually being transmitted in both directions. So it's also important to respond to **dataReceived:length:** notifications quickly, before a backlog of unhandled messages builds up. Data will be discarded (messages lost) if your application doesn't keep up.

Even when neither party is transmitting any data, there's constant feedback that the line is open and the other party hasn't hung up. You can hear the silence. Digitally, the other party's silence is received as a stream of uniform bits, each with a value of 1. This filler data is transmitted when no other information is being sent. Like other data, it's reported to the application in **dataReceived:length:** messages.

However, the NXPhoneCall will throw away this filler data if you ask it to use HDLC (High-Level Data Link Control) encoding.

```
[myCall useHDLC:YES];
```

HDLC marks the beginning and end of meaningful data with a byte equal to 0x7E:

```
0 1 1 1 1 1 1 0
```

To ensure the uniqueness of this marker, a 0 is inserted after all sequences of five 1's within the bracketed data:

```
1 1 1 1 1    →    1 1 1 1 1 0
```

In addition, the encoder does a cyclic redundancy check (CRC) and adds a two-byte checksum at the end of the data.

HDLC encoding thus ensures the integrity of the data and makes it easy to distinguish filler data from meaningful data.

When HDLC is used, the Phone Kit encodes the data you transmit and decodes the data you receive. It packages each bracketed sequence of HDLC-encoded data into one **dataReceived:length:** notification and ignores the filler.

When HDLC data is decoded, the marker bytes and inserted 0's are thrown away, the checksum is stripped from the end of the data, and a redundancy check is again made. If the checksums don't match, the data is discarded and no **dataReceived:length:** message is sent. The theory is that it's better not to deliver any data than to deliver bad data.

Classes

NXPhone

Inherits From: Object

Declared In: phonekit/NXPhone.h

Class Description

An NXPhone object corresponds to a telephone line that's connected to the user's computer. When first initialized, it establishes a connection to the Phone Server for that line.

One NXPhone object handles communication over all the channels on the phone line. It maintains a list of NXPhoneChannel objects, one for each channel being used. NXPhoneChannel objects, in turn, manage NXPhoneCall objects, which correspond to actual or potential calls made over the line. An NXPhoneCall object handles the work of making or receiving a call, and transmitting and receiving data during a call.

Communications with the Phone Server are sent and received as remote messages. To get information from the Server, an application has to be listening for remote messages from that source. This can be accomplished in two ways:

- By adding the Server to the list of sources for remote messages that can be received along with events. A **runFromAppKit** message to the NXPhone object means that the connection will be run from within Application Kit event loops.
- By running independently of the event loop. A **run** message to the NXPhone object causes the application to wait for the remote messages that announce activity on the line, and to respond only to that input.

Instance Variables

None declared in this class.

Method Types

Initializing an NXPhone object	– init – initType:
Running the connection to the Phone Server	– run – runFromAppKit: – addPort:receiver:method:
Testing the phone line	– isActive
Managing channels	– addChannel: – removeChannel: – acquireChannel: – releaseChannel:

Instance Methods

acquireChannel:

– (BOOL)**acquireChannel:***aChannel*

Locks down *aChannel* for the exclusive use of the application. The channel must be one that the receiving NXPhone object was previously informed about through an **addChannel:** message. If the channel can be acquired, this method returns YES. If not, it returns NO. A channel can't be acquired if another application is currently using it.

A channel must be acquired before it can be used to make or receive calls.

See also: – **releaseChannel:**, – **addChannel:**

addChannel:

– (void)**addChannel:***aChannel*

Adds a new channel to the NXPhone object's list of channels. *aChannel* must be a kind of NXPhoneChannel object. Its type must correspond to one the channels on the phone line. Adding a channel makes it possible to acquire the channel so that it can be used to make and receive calls.

See also: – **removeChannel:**, – **acquireChannel:**, – **initType:** (NXPhoneChannel)

addPort:receiver:method:

– **addPort:**(port_t)*aPort*
  receiver:*anObject*
  method:(SEL)*aSelector*

Registers *aPort* as a source of remote input in addition to the Phone Server. While the Phone Server is being monitored as the result of a **run** message, *aPort* will also be checked. When a Mach message is received at *aPort*, the Phone Kit notifies *anObject* with an *aSelector* message. *aSelector* should be a method that takes one argument, a pointer to the remote message received at the port. For example:

```
- retrieveMessage:(msg_header_t *)machMessage;
```

Every Mach message begins with a **msg_header_t** structure. This structure is defined in **mach/message.h** and is documented in *NeXTSTEP Operating System Software*.

addPort:receiver:method: works only if the Phone Server is monitored as a result of a **run** message, not a **runFromAppKit** message.

See also: – **run**

init

– **init**

Invokes the **initType:** method to initialize the receiving NXPhone object to be type NX_ISDNDevice, and returns the initialized object.

See also: – **initType:**

initType:

– **initType:**(NXPhoneDeviceType)*deviceType*

Establishes the application's connection to the phone server, initializes the receiving NXPhone object's type to *deviceType*, and returns the initialized object.

NXPhoneDeviceType is defined in **phonekit/phoneTypes.h**. Its permitted values are:

NX_ISDNDevice	for an ISDN phone line
NX_POTSDevice	for a POTS ("plain old telephone service") line

This method is the designated initializer for the class.

isActive

– (BOOL)**isActive**

Returns YES if the phone line is working, and NO if for some reason it's down.

releaseChannel:

– (void)**releaseChannel:***aChannel*

Releases *aChannel* from the exclusive use of the application. *aChannel* should be an channel that was previously acquired by an **acquireChannel:** message to the same receiver.

Releasing a channel while it has an active phone call will lead to errors.

See also: – **acquireChannel:**, – **activeCall** (NXPhoneChannel)

removeChannel:

– (void)**removeChannel:***aChannel*

Removes *aChannel* from the list of channels associated with the NXPhone object. *aChannel* must be a kind of NXPhoneChannel object, and one that was previously added through an **addChannel:** message.

A channel should be released before it is removed.

See also: – **addChannel:**, – **releaseChannel:**

run

– **run**

Runs the connection to the Phone Server, causing the application to wait for notification messages from the Server. This method doesn't return; it terminates only when the application (or the thread that the NXPhone object operates in) does. As it runs, the application (or thread) receives input only from the Phone Server.

Before an application can get remote input from the Phone Server, the NXPhone object must receive either a **run** message or a **runFromAppKit** message. **runFromAppKit** runs the connection from the main event loop.

A **run** message can be sent to the NXPhone object in a separate thread of execution. It's safe to use the Phone Kit in its own thread.

See also: – **runFromAppKit**, – **addPort:receiver:method:**

runFromAppKit

– runFromAppKit

Adds the Phone Server's port, at a priority of NX_MODALRESPTHRESHOLD, to the list of ports that will be monitored during the application's event loop. The application listens for notification messages from the Phone Server in the same way that it listens for events and other remote input. Returns **self**.

For this method to work, the application must enter the main event loop by sending a **run** message to the Application object.

See also: – **run**, – **run** (Application class of the Application Kit)

NXPhoneCall

Inherits From: Object

Declared In: phonekit/NXPhoneCall.h

Class Description

An NXPhoneCall object corresponds to an actual or potential phone call on a channel. It's the object that initiates an outgoing call or answers an incoming call. Once the connection is made, it's responsible for transmitting and receiving data over the line. When the call is terminated, it's the object that hangs up the phone. An NXPhoneCall object is created when the call begins and is typically freed after the call is terminated.

For an outgoing call, a channel must first be selected and acquired. An NXPhoneCall object is then created and added to the channel, as illustrated below. The call is initiated by a message to take the phone off-hook:

```
myCall = [[MyNXPhoneCallSubclass alloc] initType:NX_VoiceCall];
[myChannel addCall:myCall];
[myCall pickUp];
```

For an incoming call, an NXPhoneCall object is created in response to an **allocateIncomingCallOfType:** message sent to the NXPhoneChannel. If the channel accepts the call (by returning YES to an **acceptCall:** message), the NXPhoneCall will receive a **ring** message announcing that the phone is ringing. Its response should be to answer the phone:

```
- (void)ring
{
    . . .
    [self pickUp];
}
```

As this last example illustrates, NXPhoneCall is an abstract class. To make it usable in an application, you must define your own NXPhoneCall subclass and implement methods that will respond to the various notification messages (like **ring**) that an NXPhoneCall receives. It's not necessary to implement a method for each notification, but without some application-specific methods in its repertoire, an NXPhoneCall won't be able to do any useful work.

Instance Variables

None declared in this class.

Method Types

Initializing an NXPhoneCall object	
	– init – initType: – setType: – type
Initiating a call	– pickUp – dialToneReceived – dialDigits: – dialingComplete – remoteBusy – remoteRing – remotePickup
Getting a call	– ring – pickUp
Sending and receiving data	– callConnected – transmitData:length: – dataReceived:length: – useHDLC:
Putting a call on hold	– hold – resume
Detecting a touch-tone	– toneReceived:
Terminating a call	– hangUp – remoteHangup – callReleased
Finding the current state of the call	
	– state
Responding to errors	– error:reason:

Instance Methods

callConnected

– (void)**callConnected**

Implemented by subclasses to respond to a notification that a connection has been made. For outgoing calls, a **callConnected** message is received immediately after a **remotePickup** message. For incoming calls, it's the first notification received after **pickUp** takes the phone off-hook to answer the call.

Typically, this notification is used to begin sending and receiving data over the line.

See also: – **pickUp**, – **remotePickup**

callReleased

– (void)**callReleased**

Implemented by subclasses to respond to a notification that a call has been terminated. A **callReleased** message is received after the NXPhoneCall hangs up (**hangUp**) or the other party does (**remoteHangup**).

This method can be used to free the NXPhoneCall object and do any other cleanup necessary.

See also: – **hangUp**, – **remoteHangup**

dataReceived:length:

– (void)**dataReceived:**(void *)*data* **length:**(int)*numBytes*

Implemented by subclasses to accept data received over the phone line. If the data is being transferred using HDLC encoding, each **dataReceived:length:** message transmits one packet of information. The packet contains *numBytes* bytes of data. The Phone Kit decodes the data (from HDLC) before notifying the NXPhoneCall of its arrival.

If HDLC is not used, each message reports an arbitrary amount of data, *numBytes* in length. The data will be byte-aligned, but there's no guarantee that it will exactly correspond to the packet of information sent in a **transmitData:length:** message. The Phone Kit may divide the stream of data that's received differently and report it in different segments than those used to transmit it.

Received data may include filler (uniform data with all bits set to 1) that's inserted into the bit stream as padding when nothing else is being transmitted. When HDLC is used, the Phone Kit filters out this extraneous data.

During a phone call, data is transferred at up to 64 kilobits per second, so an NXPhoneCall object can expect to receive a continuous stream of **dataReceived:length:** messages. A **dataReceived:length:** method therefore should not initiate any time-consuming processing. The Phone Kit will store incoming data that hasn't yet been read, but the backlog may fairly quickly overwhelm existing resources. If that happens, data will be lost.

This method is responsible for freeing the data it receives using **free()** or **NXZoneFree()**. Do not use **vm_deallocate()**.

See also: – **transmitData:length:**, – **useHDLC:**, **NXZoneFree()** (Common Functions)

dialDigits:

– (void)**dialDigits:**(char *)*digits*

Initiates dialing of the null-terminated string contained in *digits*. The following dialing characters are all acceptable:

```
1 2 3
4 5 6
7 8 9
* 0 #
```

This method returns before the dialing is done. A **dialingComplete** notification will be received when all the characters in *digits* have been dialed.

On a POTS line, it may be necessary to break up the dialing sequence in order to insert delays—for example, after the area code—to allow the switching mechanism time to react. Delays are unnecessary on an ISDN line.

See also: – **dialToneReceived**, – **dialingComplete**

dialingComplete

– (void)**dialingComplete**

Implemented by subclasses to respond to a notification that the entire sequence of digits passed in a previous **dialDigits:** message has been dialed successfully.

See also: – **dialDigits:**

dialToneReceived

– (void)**dialToneReceived**

Implemented by subclasses to respond to a message notifying the NXPhoneCall that the phone line is working and ready for an outgoing call. Typically, subclasses use this method to initiate dialing with the **dialDigits:** method.

A **dialToneReceived** message is the first notification that the NXPhoneCall receives after the **pickUp** method initiates an outgoing call.

See also: – **pickUp**, – **dialDigits:**

error:reason:

– (void)**error:**(SEL)*lastMessage* **reason:**(NXPhoneError)*cause*

Implemented by subclasses to respond to an error. *lastMessage* is the selector for the last Objective C message sent to the NXPhoneCall before the error occurred, and *cause* indicates what type of error it is. Among the possible causes are:

NX_NotEndToEndISDN	Occurs when you try to set up a data call (type NX_DataCall), which implies ISDN data transfers of 64 kilobits per second, but some part of the phone line won't support that rate of transfer.
NX_BufferOverflow	Indicates that data has been lost because the application is trying to transmit it faster than the phone line is able to accept it.
NX_TransmitFailure	Indicates an internal error that prevents data from being transmitted
NX_HardwareFailure	Occurs when a cable has come loose or there's some other disturbance to the hardware.
NX_TemporaryNetworkFailure	Indicates that the telephone network is not responding.
NX_FacilityNotSubscribed	Indicates that the telephone network doesn't believe the user is an ISDN subscriber.

The NXPhoneError type and its values are defined in **phonekit/phoneError.h** and are described in more detail in the "Types and Constants" section of this chapter.

See also: – **channelError:** (NXPhoneChannel)

hangUp

– (void)**hangUp**

Hangs up the phone and terminates the call.

See also: – **state**, – **callReleased**

hold

– (void)**hold**

Puts the phone call on hold. The phone will still be off-hook, but the NXPhoneCall will no longer be the active call for its channel.

Note: This method is not implemented for release 3.0

See also: – **resume**, – **activeCall** (NXPhoneChannel)

init

– **init**

Invokes the **initType:** method to initialize the NXPhoneCall object to type NX_VoiceCall, and returns the initialized object.

See also: – **initType:**

initType:

– **initType:**(NXPhoneCallType)*callType*

Enables the receiving NXPhoneCall to get notification messages from the Phone Server, sets its type to *callType*, and returns the initialized object. *callType* must be either NX_DataCall, which implies ISDN data transfers at 64 kilobits per second, or NX_VoiceCall, for all other kinds of calls. The initial state of the NXPhoneCall is NX_PhoneIdle.

If *callType* is NX_DataCall, the NXPhone object must be of type NX_ISDNDevice, and the NXPhoneChannel must have an ISDN channel type—NX_B1Channel, NX_B2Channel, or NX_AnyISDNChannel. If *callType* is NX_VoiceCall, the NXPhone object can be either NX_ISDNDevice or NX_POTSDevice.

This method is the designated initializer for the class.

NXPhoneCallType and its values are defined in **phonekit/phoneTypes.h**.

See also: – **setType:**, – **type**, – **state**

pickUp

– (void)**pickUp**

Takes the phone off-hook, making the NXPhoneCall object the active call for its channel. This is the first step in initiating an outgoing call or answering an incoming call.

See also: – **activeCall** (NXPhoneChannel)

remoteBusy

– (void)**remoteBusy**

Implemented by subclasses to respond to a notification that a connection can't be made for an outgoing call because the phone being called is busy.

See also: – **remoteRing**

remoteHangup

– (void)**remoteHangup**

Implemented by subclasses to respond to a notification that the other party has hung up the phone. This method can be implemented to give feedback to users that the call has been terminated. It should not be used to free the NXPhoneCall object; that should wait until a **callReleased** notification.

See also: – **callReleased**

remotePickup

– (void)**remotePickup**

Implemented by subclasses to respond to a notification that the party being called answered the phone, taking it off-hook. This method can be implemented to let users know that the call has gone through.

See also: – **pickUp**, – **callConnected**

remoteRing

– (void)**remoteRing**

Implemented by subclasses to respond to a notification that the phone being called is ringing. There's only one **remoteRing** notification, no matter how many times the phone rings.

See also: – **remoteBusy**

resume

– (void)**resume**

Resumes a phone call that had been put on hold. The receiving NXPhoneCall is made the active call for its channel again.

Note: This method is not implemented for release 3.0

See also: – **hold**, – **activeCall** (NXPhoneChannel)

ring

– (void)**ring**

Implemented by subclasses to respond to a notification that the phone is ringing. When an NXPhoneChannel accepts an incoming call, the NXPhoneCall object passed in the **acceptCall:** message gets a **ring** notification. Typically, this method is implemented to answer the phone, as illustrated under "Class Description" above.

Only one **ring** message is sent, no matter how many times the phone rings.

See also: – **pickUp**, – **acceptCall:** (NXPhoneChannel)

setType:

– (void)**setType:**(NXPhoneCallType)*callType*

Sets the type of the NXPhoneCall to *callType*, which must be either NX_DataCall or NX_VoiceCall. Typically, the type is set when the object is initialized immediately after being allocated. See the **initType:** method for more on the possible types.

See also: – **initType:**, – **type**

state

– (NXPhoneCallState)**state**

Returns the current state of the NXPhoneCall. The return value will be one of the following:

NX_PhoneNullState	The NXPhoneCall object is not in a meaningful state.
NX_PhoneIdle	The NXPhoneCall is not handling a call. It doesn't have the phone off-hook.
NX_PhoneOriginating	The NXPhoneCall has taken the phone off-hook and is ready for a call to be made.
NX_PhoneDialing	The NXPhoneCall has initiated a call. The number is being dialed.
NX_PhoneAlerting	The NXPhoneCall is waiting for a connection to be made after dialing.
NX_PhoneConversation	The connection has been made.
NX_PhoneReleasing	Either the other party has hung up but the NXPhoneCall hasn't yet, or the NXPhoneCall has hung up but hasn't received confirmation from the phone system.

These values and the NXPhoneCallState type are defined in **phonekit/phoneTypes.h**.

toneReceived:

– (void)**toneReceived:**(int)*key*

Implemented by subclasses to respond to a notification that a DTMF (Dual-Tone Modulation Frequency) was detected. The tone detected is the one produced by *key* on a touch-tone telephone. *key* will be an integer from 1 through 12, where 10 represents the '*' key, 11 the zero key, and 12 the '#' key.

The Phone Kit sends a separate message to report each DTMF signal that's detected from the other party while the connection is maintained.

Note: This method is not currently implemented for a POTS line.

transmitData:length:

– (void)**transmitData:**(void *)*data* **length:**(int)*numBytes*

Transmits *data* over the phone line. The length of the data in bytes should be reported in the second parameter, *numBytes*.

If the connection is to a POTS line, it's assumed that *data* is mu-law encoded voice data. It will be converted to an analog signal when it's sent over the phone line.

If HDLC encoding is used, *data* is assumed to be one coherent packet of information. The packet sent in a **transmitData:length:** message will match exactly the packet reported at the other end by a **dataReceived:length:** message. If HDLC is not used, the data stream may be segmented differently on the receiving end.

Data cannot be transmitted over a phone line any faster than 64 kilobits per second.

See also: – **useHDLC:**, – **dataReceived:length:**

type

– (NXPhoneCallType)**type**

Returns the call type, either NX_DataCall or NX_VoiceCall

See also: – **initType:**, –**setType:**

useHDLC:

– (void)**useHDLC:**(BOOL)*flag*

Determines whether transmitted data will be HDLC encoded and whether received data is assumed to be HDLC encoded. Errors will result if one party to a conversation uses HDLC encoding but the other doesn't.

The HDLC encoding scheme signals the start and the end of valid data with a byte equal to 0x7E—a sequence of six nonzero bits bounded by zeros:

```
0 1 1 1 1 1 1 0
```

Within the data, it inserts an empty bit after every sequence of five nonzero bits:

```
1 1 1 1 1    →    1 1 1 1 1 0
```

The 0x7E markers and extra zeros are removed when the data is decoded.

HDLC encoding enables data to be sent and received in identical packets. It also makes it easy to distinguish meaningful data from the filler that's transmitted when nothing else is being sent. When HDLC is used, the Phone Kit filters out all filler bytes from the incoming data.

HDLC encoding includes a cyclic redundancy check before the data is sent and after it's received. If the two checksums don't match, the data is discarded; it's not reported to the receiving application.

See also: – **dataReceived:length:**, – **transmitData:length:**

NXPhoneChannel

Inherits From: Object

Declared In: phonekit/NXPhoneChannel.h

Class Description

An NXPhoneChannel corresponds to a particular call-carrying channel on a phone line. A channel is a physical attribute of the line and the way information is transmitted on the line.

A basic-rate ISDN line has two data channels, B1 and B2, and a control channel, D, that can also be pressed into service for data. A POTS line has just one channel.

Phone calls, in the form of NXPhoneCall objects, are associated with a particular channel. They must be added to the channel before they can handle a call. The NXPhoneChannel keeps track of the calls on the channel, much as the NXPhone object keeps track of the channels being used.

When an incoming call arrives, the NXPhoneChannel is responsible first for creating an NXPhoneCall object that can handle the call and then for accepting or rejecting the call. These actions are the responsibility of the **allocateIncomingCallOfType:** and **acceptCall:** methods. Since each application must develop its own NXPhoneCall subclass to handle its calls, and only the application can know whether to accept a particular call, the implementation of these two methods is left to NXPhoneChannel subclasses.

Instance Variables

None declared in this class.

Method Types

Initializing an NXPhoneChannel object	– init – initType: – setType: – type
Tracking calls	– addCall: – removeCall: – activeCall
Setting up an incoming call	– allocateIncomingCallOfType: – acceptCall:
Responding to errors	– channelError:

Instance Methods

acceptCall:

– (BOOL)**acceptCall:***newCall*

Implemented by subclasses to accept or refuse an incoming call. *newCall* is a kind of NXPhoneCall. It's the same object that was previously returned by **allocateIncomingCallOfType:**, but it has been further initialized and is now ready to accept messages.

If this method returns YES, *newCall* is added to the channel and notified of the incoming call by a **ring** message. If this method returns NO, it should first free the *newCall* object.

See also: – **ring** (NXPhoneCall), – **allocateIncomingCallOfType:**

activeCall

– **activeCall**

Returns the NXPhoneCall that's currently using the channel, or **nil** if there is no active call. An NXPhoneCall becomes active when it takes the phone off-hook.

See also: – **pickUp** (NXPhoneCall)

addCall:

– (void)**addCall:***aCall*

Adds *aCall*, which must be a kind of NXPhoneCall, to the list of calls associated with the channel. An NXPhoneCall cannot use the phone line or become active until it has been added to the channel.

See also: – **removeCall:**

allocateIncomingCallOfType:

– **allocateIncomingCallOfType:**(NXPhoneCallType)*callType*

Implemented by subclasses to return an NXPhoneCall object to handle an incoming call. The object returned should be an instance of the NXPhoneCall subclass designed to handle calls for the application. It should be initialized to *callType*.

This method is invoked by the Phone Kit when an incoming call is received on the channel. It should return a valid object whether or not the application intends to accept the call. A second notification, **acceptCall:**, will give the application a chance to reject the call.

See also: – **acceptCall:**

channelError:

– (void)**channelError:**(NXPhoneError)*cause*

Implemented by subclasses to respond to an error. The argument, *cause*, indicates what kind of error it is. For an NXPhoneChannel, *cause* is apt to be NX_NoHardwareAttached, which occurs when the user's computer is not hooked up to a phone line. See the "Types and Constants" section of this chapter for a complete description of the NXPhoneError type and all the possible error values.

See also: – **error:reason:** (NXPhoneCall)

init

– **init**

Invokes the **initType:** method to initialize the type of the receiving NXPhoneChannel to NX_AnyISDNChannel, and returns the initialized object. NX_AnyISDNChannel means that the object will correspond to one of the two ISDN bearer channels, B1 or B2.

See also: – **initType:**

initType:

– **initType:**(NXPhoneChannelType)*channelType*

Initializes the receiving NXPhoneChannel, sets its type to *channelType*, and returns the initialized object. *channelType* must be one of the following constants:

NX_B1Channel	
NX_B2Channel	
NX_DChannel	*not valid for Release 3.0*
NX_POTSChannel	
NX_AnyISDNChannel	

NX_AnyISDNChannel allows the Phone Kit to decide which ISDN channel, either B1 or B2, the NXPhoneChannel will correspond to. Once the correspondence is set, it will not change.

NXPhoneChannelType and these constants are defined in **phonekit/phoneTypes.h**.

This method is the designated initializer for this class.

See also: – **type**, – **setType:**

removeCall:

– (void)**removeCall:***aCall*

Removes *aCall* from the list of calls associated with the NXPhoneChannel. *aCall* must be a kind of NXPhoneCall object that was previously associated with the channel in an **addCall:** message. It's an error to remove the currently active call.

See also: – **addCall:**, – **activeCall**

setType:

– (void)**setType:**(NXPhoneChannelType)*channelType*

Sets the type of the NXPhoneChannel to *channelType*. The type is usually set by **initType:** immediately after the object is allocated. See that method for a description of the possible types.

NXPhoneChannelType and its permitted values are defined in **phonekit/phoneTypes.h**.

See also: – **initType:**, – **type**

type

– (NXPhoneChannelType)**type**

Returns the channel type that was set by **initType:** or **setType:**. See the **initType:** method for a list of the possible types.

See also: – **initType:**, – **setType:**

Functions

NXPhoneErrorString()

SUMMARY Get a string matching an error constant

DECLARED IN phonekit/phoneError.h

SYNOPSIS const char ***NXPhoneErrorString**(NXPhoneError *errval*)

DESCRIPTION This function returns a string that's equivalent to the NXPhoneError constant passed as an argument. In each case, the characters in the string exactly match those in the constant:

String Returned	NXPhoneError Constant
"NX_NotEndToEndISDN"	NX_NotEndToEndISDN
"NX_BufferOverflow"	NX_BufferOverflow
"NX_TransmitFailure"	NX_TransmitFailure
"NX_NoHardwareAttached"	NX_NoHardwareAttached
"NX_HardwareFailure"	NX_HardwareFailure
"NX_TemporaryNetworkFailure"	NX_TemporaryNetworkFailure
"NX_FacilityNotSubscribed"	NX_FacilityNotSubscribed

These constants and the NXPhoneError type are documented in the "Types and Constants" section of this chapter.

If *errval* doesn't match any of the NXPhoneError constants, the string "Invalid error" is returned.

Types and Constants

The Phone Kit has two header files that support the NXPhone, NXPhoneChannel, and NXPhoneCall classes:

phoneError.h	Defines the error values reported by NXPhoneCall's **error:cause:** method and NXPhoneChannel's **channelError:** method.
phoneTypes.h	Defines the types that are passed to the **initType**: methods for each of the three Phone Kit classes, and the values returned by NXPhoneCall's **state** method.

The contents of these header files are documented in this section.

Defined Types

NXPhoneCallState

DECLARED IN phonekit/phoneTypes.h

SYNOPSIS

typedef enum {
  NX_PhoneNullState = –1,
  NX_PhoneIdle = 0,
  NX_PhoneOriginating = 1,
  NX_PhoneDialing = 2,
  NX_PhoneConversation = 3,
  NX_PhoneAlerting = 4,
  NX_PhoneReleasing = 5
} **NXPhoneCallState**;

DESCRIPTION This type is used by just one method in the Phone Kit. NXPhoneCall's **state** method returns NXPhoneCallState constants to report the current status of a call. See that method for a description of what the constants mean.

NXPhoneCallType

DECLARED IN phonekit/phoneTypes.h

SYNOPSIS

typedef enum {
  NX_DataCall = 4,
  NX_VoiceCall = 5
} **NXPhoneCallType**;

DESCRIPTION These constants are used as arguments to NXPhoneCall's **initType:** method to initialize the type of call. NX_DataCall is for ISDN data transmissions at 64 kilobits per second; NX_VoiceCall is for all other calls, including both ISDN and POTS calls. ISDN channels can support either type; POTS channels support only voice calls.

NXPhoneChannelType

DECLARED IN phonekit/phoneTypes.h

SYNOPSIS

typedef enum {
    NX_B1Channel,
    NX_B2Channel,
    NX_DChannel, *not implemented for Release 3.0*
    NX_POTSChannel,
    NX_AnyISDNChannel
} **NXPhoneChannelType**;

DESCRIPTION These constants are used as arguments to NXPhoneChannel's **initType:** method to set the type of channel. A channel for a POTS phone line must be initialized to NX_POTSChannel. A channel on an ISDN line can be initialized to NX_B1Channel or NX_B2Channel, for the two bearer channels, or to NX_AnyISDNChannel, which allows the Phone Kit to pick one of the bearer channels.

NXPhoneDeviceType

DECLARED IN phonekit/phoneTypes.h

SYNOPSIS

typedef enum {
    NX_ISDNDevice,
    NX_POTSDevice
} **NXPhoneDeviceType**;

DESCRIPTION The constants are used to arguments to NXPhone's **initType:** method to set the type of telephone line. NX_ISDNDevice is for ISDN lines, NX_POTSDevice is for all other phone lines.

NXPhoneError

DECLARED IN phonekit/phoneError.h

SYNOPSIS

typedef enum {
    NX_NotEndToEndISDN,
    NX_BufferOverflow,
    NX_TransmitFailure,
    NX_NoHardwareAttached,
    NX_HardwareFailure,
    NX_TemporaryNetworkFailure,
    NX_FacilityNotSubscribed
} **NXPhoneError**;

DESCRIPTION The NXPhoneError type defines a set of constants that are used to report phone errors. All the errors listed, except NX_NoHardwareAttached, occur during a phone call or when a call is attempted. They're reported in a **error:reason:** message to the NXPhoneCall object. NX_NoHardwareAttached errors are reported to the NXPhoneChannel in a **channelError:** message.

The NX_NotEndToEndISDN error occurs when some part of the phone line between the user's computer and the phone or computer the user is connected to at the other end of the line doesn't support ISDN data transmission at 64 kilobits per second. When this is the case, ISDN data transmission is not possible and the call type cannot be NX_DataCall.

NX_BufferOverflow is an error that occurs when you attempt to transmit too much data too quickly. The phone line can accept no more than 64 kilobits of data per second. If your application sends data to the Phone Server at a faster rate, the excess will be buffered and transmitted in due course. However, it's possible to overwhelm the buffers, in which case they'll overflow and data will be lost.

The NX_TransmitFailure error indicates that, for some internal reason, data could not be transmitted. This error should be encountered rarely, if ever. If you do see it, consider it a NeXTSTEP bug.

NX_NoHardwareAttached means that the computer isn't attached to a phone line through the Hayes ISDN Extender or an equivalent device.

NX_HardwareFailure indicates that, while a call is in progress, a cable has become detached, power has been lost, or some other hardware disruption has occurred.

NX_TemporaryNetworkFailure indicates that the phone line is down or the phone network is temporarily not responding.

The NX_FacilityNotSubscribed error occurs when an application attempts a data call but the phone network doesn't believe the user is an ISDN subscriber. This error should be rare; it mainly occurs on Northern Telecom® phone lines when the user fails to enter the required service profile identifier. Users can enter this identifier in the Phone Manager application.

14 *Preferences*

14 *Preferences*

Library:	None, this API is defined by the Preferences application
Header File Directory:	/NextDeveloper/Headers/apps
Import:	apps/Preferences.h

Introduction

The Preferences application lets the user customize system features to agree with personal preferences. By clicking each button in turn at the top of the Preferences window, the user can reveal groups of controls for setting mouse, keyboard, font, and other preferences. Programmatically, these displays are provided by modules that Preferences loads into itself. With the API described in this chapter, you can create additional modules that can be added to the ones that are commonly displayed in Preferences.

A Preferences module contains three components: a TIFF image for the button that represents the new display, a nib file containing the interface for the display, and a file containing the code linking the interface to the Preferences application. When Preferences begins running, it locates modules to be loaded by searching these locations in the order listed:

~/Library/Preferences
/LocalLibrary/Preferences
/NextLibrary/Preferences
/NeXTApps/Preferences.app

It looks for bundles with names of the form "*MyModule*.preferences". When it locates such a bundle, it loads the executable code from the bundle and adds a new button to the scrolling list at the top of the Preferences window. When a user clicks the button, the new module's interface is displayed in the lower portion of the Preferences window. Notice that Preferences checks its own file package for modules; this is in fact how it loads the modules—Mouse Preferences, Keyboard Preferences, Localization Preferences, and so on—that appear on all systems.

The Preferences application and loadable module communicate through the API found in **/NextDeveloper/Headers/apps/Preferences.h**. This API consists of the declarations of the Layout class and a category of Application. The Layout class is an abstract superclass that defines the owner of the module's interface. The methods declared in the Application category make it easier for your module to load its interface and to control Preferences' menu commands.

Building a Preferences Module

Building a module is easy, especially since you're provided with a template (in **/NextApp/Preferences.app/Template.bproj**) to be modified. This template module contains:

File	Description
PB.project	Project file for the loadable module
Template.h	Class interface file
Template.m	Class implementation file
Template.tiff	TIFF image for button in Preferences window
English.lproj/Template.nib	Nib file contain user-interface for this module
Makefile	Instructions used by the **make** utility

To build a Preferences module, make a copy of the template directory and rename the components of the new directory to reflect the nature of the module. For example, for a module that lets the user specify a mantra to be played continuously in the background, you might use these names:

```
Mantra.bproj/
    Mantra.h
    Mantra.m
    Mantra.tiff
    English.lproj
        Mantra.nib
```

Add each of these files to the project in the appropriate place and remove the references to the files having the root name "Template". Next, using Project Builder's Attributes display, change the name of the project to "Mantra". Finally, open the class files and replace any reference to "Template" with "Mantra".

At this point, you can build the project and test the template module. Using Project Builder, build the project. When the process is complete, rename the resultant "Mantra.bundle" file to "Mantra.preferences" and double-click it. Preferences will load the sample module.

Now that process is clear, you can begin adapting the Mantra module to its specific purpose by modifying the project's nib, class, and TIFF files.

Some Requirements and Considerations

Preferences modules are bundle files and so must adhere to the naming requirements for bundles. Specifically, the bundle file package and the executable file within the package must have the same root name. For the Mantra example above, this implies that if the file package is named "Mantra.preferences", the executable file within it is named "Mantra". (See the description of the NXBundle class for more information.)

Preferences also uses this root name to identify the TIFF image for the button that's added to the Perference window and to identify the principal class within the bundle's executable file. (Thus, the example has "Mantra.tiff", and the class is named "Mantra".)

Since the code you write is loaded into the Preferences application, there's a potential for name collisions. For example, if you create a Preferences module called "Mouse.preferences" (which would of course define the Mouse class, **Mouse.tiff**, and **Mouse.nib**), these components would conflict with those in the standard module **/NextApps/Preferences.app/Mouse.preferences**. To be safe, the root name for your module could have a distinctive prefix, for example.

Finally, the subclass of Layout within your module must be the principal class of the bundle—that is, the object file containing the code for this class must be listed first on the **ld** command line that created the bundle. The easiest way to specify this is within Project Builder's Files display. Make sure the the class file (for example, **Mantra.m**) is the first entry under "Classes". If it isn't, Control-drag the class file to the top of the list.

Classes

Application Additions

Inherits From: Responder : Object

Declared In: apps/Preferences.h

Category Description

Preferences.h declares a category that adds four methods to the Application class of the Application Kit. These methods make it easier for your Preferences module to:

- Locate its interface when the module is loaded
- Enable and disable items in the Windows and Edit menus of the Preferences application
- Access the views contained in the Preferences window

Method Types

Loading the interface	– loadNibForLayout:owner:
Controlling menu items	– enableEdit: – enableWindow:
Accessing the Preferences window	– appWindow

Instance Methods

appWindow

– appWindow

Returns the **id** of the Preferences window, enabling you to alter its content view, for example.

enableEdit:

– **enableEdit:**(int)*aMask*

Enables and disables menu items in Preferences' Edit menu. *aMask* specifies which items are to be enabled. For example, this message enables the Cut and Copy commands:

```
[NXApp enableEdit: CUT_ITEM|COPY_ITEM];
```

The permitted values for *aMask* are:

CUT_ITEM
COPY_ITEM
PASTE_ITEM
SELECTALL_ITEM
EDIT_ALL_ITEMS

See also: – **enableWindow:**

enableWindow:

– **enableWindow:**(int)*aMask*

Enables and disables menu items in Preferences' Window menu. *aMask* specifies which items are to be enabled. The permitted values for *aMask* are:

MINIATURIZE_ITEM
CLOSE_ITEM
WINDOW_ALL_ITEMS

See also: – **enableEdit:**

loadNibForLayout:owner:

– **loadNibForLayout:**(const char *)*name* **owner:***anOwner*

Loads the nib file named "*name*.nib" and makes *anOwner* its owner.

This is a convenience method that searches for the nib file in the appropriate language subproject of the bundle from which the class of *anOwner* was loaded.

See also: – **bundleForClass:** (NXBundle common class)

Layout

Inherits From: Object

Declared In: apps/Preferences.h

Class Description

The Layout class defines the link between the Preferences application and a module that's loaded into the application. The principal class of the loadable Preference bundle should be a subclass of Layout. When Preferences loads the bundle, it identifies the View objects to be loaded into the Preferences window by sending this object a **view** message. Once the module is loaded, the object is kept apprised of the state of the Preferences application through notification messages such as **didHide:** and **willSelect:**.

These notification messages allow the Layout object to prepare for the named change (for example, **willHide:**). However, the value the Layout object returns in response to the message is ignored: The Layout object can't prevent the change from occurring. (Also note that being notifications, these methods have one argument, *sender*, which is a private object within Preferences and should not be accessed.)

For your loadable module, create a subclass of Layout and override the inherited methods as needed. For an example of such a subclass, see the Template class files in **/NextApps/Preferences.app/Template.bproj**.

Instance Variables

id **view**;

view	The view that's loaded into the Preferences window.

Method Types

Accessing the root View	– view
Notification of state change	– didHide: – didUnhide: – willSelect: – didSelect: – willUnselect: – didUnselect:

Instance Methods

didHide:

– **didHide:***sender*

Received from the Preferences application when the application hides itself. This gives the Preferences module the opportunity to deallocate resources or do other clean up that might be appropriate (such as removing a timed entry).

See also: – **didUnhide:**

didSelect:

– **didSelect:***sender*

Received from the Preferences application just after this module's interface is displayed in the Preferences window. A **willSelect:** message precedes this message.

See also: – **willSelect:**, – **willUnselect:**, – **didUnselect:**

didUnhide:

– **didUnhide:***sender*

Received from the Preferences application when the application is unhidden. This gives the Preferences module the opportunity to initialize itself, if necessary.

See also: – **didHide:**

didUnselect:

– **didUnselect:***sender*

Received from the Preferences application just after this module's interface ceases to be displayed in the Preferences window. A **willUnselect:** message precedes this message.

See also: – **willUnselect:**, – **willSelect:**, – **didSelect:**

view

– **view**

Returns the View that's loaded into the Preferences window. Typically, this View is the root of a view hierarchy containing the buttons and other controls of your Preferences display.

willSelect:

– **willSelect:***sender*

Received from the Preferences application when this module's interface is about to be displayed in the Preferences window. Immediately following a **willSelect:** message, the module's top-level View (as returned by the **view** method) is made a subview of the Preferences window, and then the Layout object receives a **didSelect:** message.

See also: – **didSelect:**, – **willUnselect:**, – **didUnselect:**

willUnselect:

– **willUnselect:***sender*

Received from the Preferences application when the module's top-level View is about to be removed from the view hierarchy in the Preferences window. Immediately following a **willUnselect:** message, the module's interface is removed, and then the Layout object receives a **didUnselect:** message.

See also: – **didUnselect:**, – **willSelect:**, – **didSelect:**

15 *Run-Time System*

15 *Run-Time System*

Library: libsys_s.a

Header File Directory: /NextDeveloper/Headers/objc

Introduction

The Objective C language pushes many decisions from compile time to run time. For example, objects are dynamically allocated and initialized at run time, messages are dynamically bound to method implementations, and objects assigned to **id** variables are dynamically typed. To correctly and efficiently carry out these tasks as a program executes, the language depends on a *run-time system*—a body of code to operate the object-oriented machinery.

The run-time system consists mainly of:

- Data structures that the compiler develops from class and category definitions and from protocol declarations, and
- The functions that operate on those structures and that are called by compiled Objective C code to produce the desired results.

For example, the compiler translates an Objective C message into a call on a messaging function, usually **objc_msgSend()**, which locates the method implementation that should be invoked in response to the message. The messaging function is what makes dynamic binding work. It and the data structures it requires are part of the run-time system.

For the most part, the run-time system operates behind the scenes. It has a public interface in part to declare common elements that every Objective C program uses—such as the **id** data type. But mainly the interface exists to provide access to run-time code from outside Objective C. Therefore, most of the elements documented here will rarely if ever appear in Objective C programs.

Note: The principal interface to the run-time system is contained in the Object class. Because this class is fundamental to all NeXTSTEP software kits, it's presented at the very beginning of this manual, in Chapter 1, "Root Class."

Classes

Many of the data types that the run-time system defines could equally as well have been implemented as classes. However, only one structure—the one corresponding to protocol declarations—is in fact a class. It differs from other Objective C classes in that its instances are created by the compiler, not by programs. Programs refer to Protocol instances by using the **@protocol**() directive.

Protocol

Inherits From: Object

Declared In: objc/Protocol.h

Class Description

A Protocol object corresponds to a protocol declaration in the Objective C language. It's the data structure that the run-time system uses to keep track of the protocol. Just as the compiler creates one class object for each class declaration it sees, it creates one Protocol object for each protocol declaration it encounters, provided the protocol is used somewhere within the program.

In Objective C, protocols are declared with the **@protocol** directive:

```
@protocol Cartwheels
- turn:(int)numWheels startingFrom:(int)side;
- setRotationSpeed:(float)velocity;
- (BOOL)canStartFromRight;
- (BOOL)canStartFromLeft;
@end
```

The same directive, but with a set of trailing parentheses, is used to refer to a Protocol object in source code. In the following example, the Protocol object for the Cartwheels protocol is assigned to the **wheels** variable:

```
Protocol *wheels = @protocol(Cartwheels);
```

The **@protocol()** directive is the only way to ask for a Protocol object. The Protocol class doesn't define any methods that return or initialize instances of the class.

Because Protocol objects are built by the compiler, not by the application, and are part of the run-time system for the Objective C language, they play a slightly different role within an application that most other objects. In particular, you should not allocate and initialize your own instances of the class. The only valid Protocol objects are those obtained through **@protocol()**.

Incorporation and Adoption

A protocol declaration can incorporate other protocols by listing them within angle brackets:

```
@protocol Tumbling <Cartwheels, WalkOvers, Flips, Aerials>
```

Class declarations use the same syntax to adopt protocols:

```
@interface Gymnast : Object <Tumbling, FloorRoutines>
```

Protocols can also be adopted in categories:

```
@interface Gymnast (BalanceBeam) <Dismounting>
```

The adopting class (or category) must implement all the methods declared in the protocol, including methods declared in any incorporated protocols. In the example above, the Gymnast class is obligated to implement all the methods declared in the Tumbling, Cartwheels, WalkOvers, Flips, Aerials, and FloorRoutines protocols; the BalanceBeam category of Gymnast must implement the methods declared in the Dismounting protocol. If any method is left undefined, the compiler will issue a warning.

You can ask a class if it adheres to a particular protocol by using the **conformsTo:** method defined in the Object class. This method returns YES if the receiving class, or any class above it in the inheritance hierarchy, directly or indirectly adopts the protocol. The same method can also be used to ask an instance if its class conforms:

```
if ( [myObject conformsTo:@protocol(Tumbling)] )
    [myObject turn:4 startingFrom:RIGHTSIDE];
```

Asking whether an object conforms to a protocol is very much like asking whether it responds to a message—except that **respondsTo:** tests whether one particular method is implemented and **conformsTo:** tests whether a group of methods has been adopted (and presumably implemented).

When sent to a Protocol object, a **conformsTo:** message asks if the receiver incorporates another protocol. The following message would return YES:

```
BOOL canFlip = [@protocol(Tumbling) conformsTo:@protocol(Flips)];
```

Type Checking

When a protocol name is included in a type specification, as in

```
id <Cartwheels, Flips> nadia;
```

or in

```
- setGymnast:(id <Tumbling>)anObject;
```

the compiler will check to make sure that only objects that conform to the specified protocols are used in those slots. Thus, protocols provide an added dimension of type checking at compile time.

Protocol Objects

The compiler creates a Protocol object for every protocol declared in source code, provided the protocol is also either:

- Adopted by a class, or
- Referred to by an **@protocol()** directive.

Simply using the protocol name in a type declaration isn't sufficient to cause a Protocol object to be created.

Instance Variables

None declared in this class.

Method Types

Getting the protocol name	– name
Testing for incorporated protocols	
	– conformsTo:
Getting method descriptions	– descriptionForInstanceMethod: – descriptionForClassMethod:

Instance Methods

conformsTo:

– (BOOL)**conformsTo:**(Protocol *)*aProtocol*

Returns YES if the receiving Protocol object directly or indirectly incorporates the *aProtocol* protocol, and NO if it doesn't. One protocol can incorporate another by declaring it within angle brackets:

```
@protocol BalanceBeam <Cartwheels, HandStands>
```

In the following code,

```
[@protocol(BalanceBeam) conformsTo:@protocol(Cartwheels)]
```

conformsTo: would return YES:

See also: + **conformsTo:** (Object)

descriptionForClassMethod:

– (struct objc_method_description *)**descriptionForClassMethod:**(SEL)*aSelector*

Returns a pointer to a structure describing the *aSelector* class method, or NULL if *aSelector* isn't declared as a class method in the receiving Protocol.

The structure has two fields, as illustrated below:

```
struct objc_method_description {
    SEL name;
    char *types;
};
```

The first field contains the method selector (which should be identical to *aSelector*). The second field contains encoded information about the method's return and argument types. Type information is encoded according to the conventions of the **@encode()** directive. For example, type information for this method

```
- (float)returnFloatForInt:(int)number
                 andString:(char *)name
                 andStruct:(struct entry)data;
```

would be encoded as:

```
f28@8:12i16*20{entry=**@}24
```

This method returns a **float** ('f') and pushes 28 bytes onto the stack. Its first two arguments are an object ('@') at an offset of 8 bytes from the stack pointer and a selector (':') at an offset of 12 bytes. These two arguments correspond to **self** (the message receiver) and **_cmd** (the method selector), which are present in every method implementation but are normally hidden by the Objective C language. The three declared arguments are an **int** ('i') at an offset of 16 bytes, a string ('*') at an offset of 20 bytes, and a structure ("{...}") at an offset of 24 bytes. The structure name is "entry" and it consists of two character pointers and an object **id** ("**@").

See also: – **descriptionForInstanceMethod:**, – **descriptionForMethod:** (Object)

descriptionForInstanceMethod:

– (struct objc_method_description *)
  descriptionForInstanceMethod:(SEL)*aSelector*

Returns a pointer to a structure describing the *aSelector* instance method, or NULL if the *aSelector* method isn't declared as an instance method in the receiving Protocol. The structure is described under **descriptionForClassMethod:** above.

See also: – **descriptionForClassMethod:**, – **descriptionForMethod:** (Object)

name

– (const char *)**name**

Returns a null-terminated string containing the name of the protocol.

Functions

This section describes functions and macros that are part of NeXT's run-time system for the Objective C language. Some, such as **sel_getUid()** and **objc_loadModules()**, might be useful when called within an Objective C program. However, most are provided mainly to make it possible to define interfaces to the run-time system other than Objective C. As long as you're programming in Objective C, you shouldn't need to use them. The Objective C language and the Object class are together a sufficient and complete interface to the run-time system. The messages and class definitions in Objective C source files are compiled to execute correctly at run time without the aid of additional function calls.

The functions described here are divided into five groups, each with its own prefix:

- The basic run-time functions have an "objc_" prefix.
- Functions that operate on class objects have a "class_" prefix and take as their first argument a structure of type Class. Class is the defined type (in **objc/objc.h**) for class objects. However, like all other objects, class objects can also be assigned to the more inclusive type **id**.
- Functions that operate on instances have an "object_" prefix and take as their first argument the **id** of the instance.
- Functions that give information about method selectors have a "sel_" prefix.
- Functions that describe method implementations have a "method_" prefix.

NeXT reserves these prefixes for functions in the run-time system.

In addition to these functions, there are also a few macros that operate on the values passed in a message. They begin with a "marg_" prefix (for "message argument").

class_addMethods() → See class_getInstanceMethod()

---

class_createInstance(), class_createInstanceFromZone()

SUMMARY Create a new instance of a class

DECLARED IN objc/objc-class.h

SYNOPSIS id **class_createInstance(**Class *aClass*, unsigned int *indexedIvarBytes*)
id **class_createInstanceFromZone(**Class *aClass*, unsigned int *indexedIvarBytes*,
NXZone **zone*)

DESCRIPTION These functions provide an interface to the object allocators used by the run-time system. The default allocators, which can be changed by reassigning the **_alloc** and **_zoneAlloc** variables, create a new instance of *aClass* by dynamically allocating memory for it, initializing its **isa** instance variable to point to the class, and returning the new instance. All other instance variables are initialized to 0.

The two functions are identical, except that **class_createInstanceFromZone()** allocates memory for the new object from the region specified by *zone* and **class_createInstance()** allocates memory from the default zone returned by **NXDefaultMallocZone()**.

Object's **alloc** and **allocFromZone:** methods use **class_createInstanceFromZone()** to allocate memory for a new object, with **alloc** taking the memory from the default zone. The **new** method uses **class_createInstance()**.

The second argument to both functions, *indexedIvarBytes*, states the number of extra bytes required for indexed instance variables. Normally, it's 0.

Indexed instance variables are instance variables that are not declared or accounted for in the usual way, generally because they don't have a fixed size. Usually they're arrays whose length can't be computed at compile time. Since the components of a C structure can't be of uncertain size, indexed instance variables can't be declared in the class interface. The class must account for them outside the normal channels provided by the Objective C language.

All of the storage required for indexed instance variables must be allocated through one of these two functions. The following code shows how they might be used in an instance-creating class method:

```
+ new:(unsigned int)numBytes
{
    self = class_createInstance((Class)self, numBytes);
    length = numBytes;
    . . .
}

- (char *)getArray
{
    return(object_getIndexedIvars(self));
}
```

Indexed instance variables should be avoided if at all possible. It's a much better practice to store variable-length data outside the object and declare one real instance variable that points to it and perhaps another that records its length. For example:

```
+ new:(unsigned int)numBytes
{
    self = [super new];
    data = malloc(numBytes);
    length = numBytes;
    . . .
}

- (char *)getArray
{
    return data;
}
```

RETURN If successful, both **class_createInstance()** and **class_createInstanceFromZone()** return the new instance of *aClass*. If not successful, they generate an error message and call **abort()**.

class_createInstanceFromZone() → See class_createInstance()

class_getClassMethod() → See class_getInstanceMethod()

class_getInstanceMethod(), class_getClassMethod(), class_addMethods(), class_removeMethods()

SUMMARY Get, add, and remove methods

DECLARED IN objc/objc-class.h

SYNOPSIS Method **class_getInstanceMethod**(Class *aClass*, SEL *aSelector*)
Method **class_getClassMethod**(Class *aClass*, SEL *aSelector*)
void **class_addMethods**(Class *aClass*, struct objc_method_list **methodList*)
void **class_removeMethods**(Class *aClass*, struct objc_method_list **methodList*)

DESCRIPTION The first two functions, **class_getInstanceMethod**() and **class_getClassMethod**(), return a pointer to the class data structure that describes the *aSelector* method. For **class_getInstanceMethod**(), *aSelector* must identify an instance method; for **class_getClassMethod**(), it must identify a class method. Both functions return a NULL pointer if *aSelector* doesn't identify a method defined in or inherited by *aClass*.

The run-time system uses the next function, **class_addMethods**(), to implement Objective C categories. Each function adds the methods in *methodList* to the dictionary of methods defined for *aClass*. To add methods that can be used by instances of a class, *aClass* should be the class object. To add methods that can be used by a class object, *aClass* should be the metaclass object (the **isa** field of the Class structure). All the methods in *methodList* must be mapped to valid SEL selectors before they're added to the class. The **sel_registerName**() function can be used to accomplish this.

The last function, **class_removeMethods**(), removes methods that were previously added using **class_addMethods**(). The run-time system uses it to unload categories that were dynamically loaded at an earlier point in time. Its second argument, *methodList*, must be identical to a pointer previously passed to **class_addMethods**(). To remove instance methods, *aClass* should be the class object. To remove class methods, *aClass* should be the **isa** field of the Class structure.

RETURN **class_getInstanceMethod**() and **class_getClassMethod**() return a pointer to the data structure that describes the *aSelector* method as implemented for *aClass*. If *aSelector* isn't defined for *aClass*, they return NULL.

class_getInstanceVariable()

SUMMARY Get the class template for an instance variable

DECLARED IN objc/objc-class.h

SYNOPSIS Ivar **class_getInstanceVariable**(Class *aClass*, const char **variableName*)

RETURN This function returns a pointer to the class data structure that describes the *variableName* instance variable. If *aClass* doesn't define or inherit the instance variable, a NULL pointer is returned.

class_getVersion() → See class_setVersion()

class_poseAs()

SUMMARY Pose as the superclass

DECLARED IN objc/objc-class.h

SYNOPSIS Class **class_poseAs**(Class *theImposter*, Class *theSuperclass*)

DESCRIPTION **class_poseAs**() causes one class, *theImposter*, to take the place of its own superclass, *theSuperclass*. Messages sent to *theSuperclass* will actually be received by *theImposter*. The posing class can't declare any new instance variables, but it can define new methods and override methods defined in the superclass.

Posing is usually done through Object's **poseAs:** method, which calls this function.

RETURN Normally, **class_poseAs**() returns its first argument, *theImposter*. However, if *theImposter* defines instance variables or is not a subclass of (or the same as) *theSuperclass*, it generates an error message and aborts.

class_removeMethods() → See class_getInstanceMethod()

---

class_setVersion(), class_getVersion()

SUMMARY Set and get the class version

DECLARED IN objc/objc-class.h

SYNOPSIS void **class_setVersion**(Class *aClass*, int *versionNumber*)
int **class_getVersion**(Class *aClass*)

DESCRIPTION These functions set and return the class version number. This number is used when archiving instances of the class.

Object's **setVersion:** and **version** methods do the same work as these functions.

RETURN **class_getVersion**() returns the version number for *aClass* last set by **class_setVersion**(), or 0 if no version has been set.

marg_getRef() → See marg_getValue()

marg_getValue(), marg_getRef(), marg_setValue()

SUMMARY Examine and alter method argument values

DECLARED IN objc/objc-class.h

SYNOPSIS *type-name* **marg_getValue**(marg_list *argFrame*, int *offset*, *type-name*)
type-name ***marg_getRef**(marg_list *argFrame*, int *offset*, *type-name*)
void **marg_setValue**(marg_list *argFrame*, int *offset*, *type-name*, *type-name value*)

DESCRIPTION These three macros get and set the values of arguments passed in a message. They're designed to be used within implementations of the **forward::** method, which is described under the Object class in Chapter 1, "Root Class."

The first argument to each macro, *argFrame*, is a pointer to the list of arguments passed in the message. The run-time system passes this pointer to the **forward::** method, making it available to be used in these macros. The next two arguments—an *offset* into the argument list and the type of the argument at that offset—can be obtained by calling **method_getArgumentInfo**().

The first macro, **marg_getValue**, returns the argument at *offset* in *argFrame*. The return value, like the argument, is of type *type-name*. The second macro, **marg_getRef**, returns a reference to the argument at *offset* in *argFrame*. The pointer returned is to an argument of the *type-name* type. The third macro, **marg_setValue**, alters the argument at *offset* in *argFrame* by assigning it *value*. The new value must be of the same type as the argument.

Because these are macros, the *type-name* must be written as types normally are in source code; it can't be passed as a variable. Therefore, if the type is obtained from **method_getArgumentInfo**(), a **switch** statement would be required to select the correct macro call from a list of predetermined choices. **method_getArgumentInfo**() encodes the argument type according to the conventions of the @**encode**() compiler directive.

RETURN **marg_getValue** returns a *type-name* argument value. **marg_getRef** returns a pointer to a *type-name* argument value.

marg_setValue() → See marg_getValue()

method_getArgumentInfo() → See method_getNumberOfArguments()

method_getNumberOfArguments(), method_getSizeOfArguments(), method_getArgumentInfo()

SUMMARY Get information about a method

DECLARED IN objc/objc-class.h

SYNOPSIS

unsigned int **method_getNumberOfArguments**(Method *aMethod*)
unsigned int **method_getSizeOfArguments**(Method *aMethod*)
unsigned int **method_getArgumentInfo**(Method *aMethod*, int *index*, const char ***type*, int **offset*)

DESCRIPTION

The three functions described here all provide information about the argument structure of a particular method. They take as their first argument the method's data structure, *aMethod*, which can be obtained by calling **class_getInstanceMethod()** or **class_getClassMethod()**.

The first function, **method_getNumberOfArguments()**, returns the number of arguments that *aMethod* takes. This will be at least two, since it includes the "hidden" arguments, **self** and **_cmd**, which are the first two arguments passed to every method implementation.

The second function, **method_getSizeOfArguments()**, returns the number of bytes that all of *aMethod*'s arguments, taken together, would occupy on the stack. This information is required by **objc_msgSendv()**.

The third function, **method_getArgumentInfo()**, takes an *index* into *aMethod*'s argument list and returns, by reference, the type of the argument and the offset to the location of that argument in the list. Indices begin with 0. The "hidden" arguments **self** and **_cmd** are indexed at 0 and 1; method-specific arguments begin at index 2. If *index* is too large for the actual number of arguments, the *type* aand *offset* pointers are set to NULL. Otherwise, the offset is measured in bytes; it depends entirely on the size of arguments preceding the one at *index*. The type is encoded according to the conventions of the **@encode()** compiler directive.

The information obtained from **method_getArgumentInfo()** can be used in the **marg_getValue**, **marg_getRef**, and **marg_setValue** macros to examine and alter the values of an argument on the stack after *aMethod* has been called. The offset can be passed directly to these macros, but the type must first be decoded to a full type name.

RETURN **method_getNumberOfArguments()** returns how many arguments the implementation of *aMethod* takes, and **method_getSizeOfArguments()** returns how many bytes the arguments take up on the stack. **method_getArgumentInfo()** returns the *index* it is passed.

method_getSizeOfArguments() → See method_getNumberOfArguments()

objc_addClass() → See objc_getClass()

---

objc_getClass(), objc_lookUpClass(), objc_getMetaClass(), objc_getClasses(), objc_addClass(), objc_getModules()

SUMMARY Manage run-time structures

DECLARED IN objc/objc-runtime.h

SYNOPSIS
id **objc_getClass**(const char **aClassName*)
id **objc_lookUpClass**(const char **aClassName*)
id **objc_getMetaClass**(const char **aClassName*)
NXHashTable ***objc_getClasses**(void)
void **objc_addClass**(Class *aClass*)
Module ***objc_getModules**(void)

DESCRIPTION These functions return and modify the principal data structures used by the run-time system.

The first two functions, **objc_getClass**() and **objc_lookUpClass**(), both return the **id** of the class object for the *aClassName* class. However, if the *aClassName* class isn't known to the run-time system, **objc_getClass**() prints a message to the standard error stream and causes the process to abort, while **objc_lookUpClass**() merely returns **nil**.

The third function, **objc_getMetaClass**(), returns the **id** of the metaclass object for the *aClassName* class. The metaclass object holds information used by the class object, just as the class object holds information used by instances of the class. Like **objc_getClass**(), it prints a message to the standard error stream and causes the process to abort if *aClassName* isn't a valid class.

objc_getClasses() returns a pointer to the hash table containing all the Objective C classes that are currently known to the run-time system. You can examine the table using the common hashing functions. In the following example, **NXNextHashState()** gets each class from the table in turn, and **object_getClassName()** asks for their names:

```
NXHashTable *classes = objc_getClasses();
NXHashState state = NXInitHashState(classes);
Class thisClass;

while ( NXNextHashState(classes, &state, (void **)&thisClass) )
    fprintf(stderr, "%s\n", object_getClassName((id)thisClass));
```

The NXHashTable type returned by **objc_getClasses()** is defined in the **objc/hashtable.h** header file and is documented in Chapter 3, "Common Classes and Functions." This data structure can be read, as illustrated in the example above, but it should not be modified or freed.

objc_addClass() adds *aClass* to the list of classes known to the run-time system. (The class is added to the hash table that **objc_getClasses()** returns.)

The compiler creates a Module data structure for each file it compiles. The **objc_getModules()** function returns a pointer to the run-time system's list of all current modules, except those that were dynamically loaded. Module structures are described under "Supporting Header Files" later in this chapter.

RETURN **objc_lookUpClass()** returns the class object for *aClassName*, or **nil** if there is no such class. **objc_getClass()** and **objc_getMetaClass()** return the class and metaclass objects for *aClassName*, if such a class exists, and abort otherwise. **objc_getClasses()** returns a pointer to a hash table of all current classes, and **objc_getModules()** returns a pointer to all current modules.

objc_getClasses() → See objc_getClass()

objc_getMetaClass() → See objc_getClass()

objc_getModules() → See objc_getClass()

objc_loadModules(), objc_unloadModules()

SUMMARY Dynamically load and unload classes

DECLARED IN objc/objc-load.h

SYNOPSIS long **objc_loadModules**(char **files*[], NXStream **stream*,
void (**callback*)(Class, Category), struct mach_header ***header*,
char **debugFilename*)
long **objc_unloadModules**(NXStream **stream*, void (**callback*)(Class, Category))

DESCRIPTION **objc_loadModules**() dynamically loads object files containing Objective C class and category definitions into a running program. Its first argument, *files*, is a list of null-terminated pathnames for the object files containing the classes and categories that are to be loaded. They can be full paths or paths relative to the current working directory. The second argument, *stream*, is a pointer to an NXStream where any error messages produced by the loader will be written. It can be NULL, in which case no messages will be written.

The third argument, *callback*, allows you to specify a function that will be called immediately after each class or category is loaded. When a category is loaded, the function is passed both the **Category** structure and the **Class** structure for that category. When a class is loaded, it's passed only the **Class** structure. Like *stream*, *callback* can be NULL.

The fourth argument, *header*, is used to get a pointer to the **mach_header** structure for the loaded modules. It, too, can be NULL. All the modules in *files* are grouped under the same header.

The final argument, which also can be NULL, is the pathname for a file that the loader will create and initialize with a copy of the loaded modules. This file can be passed to the debugger and added to the list of files being debugged. For example:

```
(gdb) add-file debugFilename
```

obj_unloadModules() unloads all the modules loaded by **objc_loadModules**(), that is, all the modules from the *files* list. Each time it's called, it unloads another set of modules, working its way back from the modules loaded by the most recent call to **objc_loadModules**() to those loaded by the next most recent call, and so on.

The first argument to **obj_unloadModules**(), *stream*, is a pointer to an NXStream where error messages will be written. Its second argument, *callback*, allows you to specify a function that will be called immediately before each class or category is unloaded. Both arguments can be NULL.

Note: The NXBundle class, documented in Chapter 3, "Common Classes and Functions," provides a simpler and preferred way to dynamically load classes. NXBundle integrates dynamic loading with localization (using language-specific resources such as strings, images, and sounds).

RETURN Both functions return 0 if the modules are successfully loaded or unloaded and 1 if they're not.

objc_lookUpClass() → See objc_getClass()

---

objc_msgSend(), objc_msgSendSuper(), objc_msgSendv()

SUMMARY Send messages at run time

DECLARED IN objc/objc-runtime.h

SYNOPSIS id **objc_msgSend**(id *theReceiver*, SEL *theSelector*, ...)
id **objc_msgSendSuper**(struct objc_super **superContext*, SEL *theSelector*, ...)
id **objc_msgSendv**(id *theReceiver*, SEL *theSelector*, unsigned int *argSize*,
    marg_list *argFrame*)

DESCRIPTION The compiler converts every message expression into a call on one of the first two of these three functions. Messages to **super** are converted to calls on **objc_msgSendSuper()**; all others are converted to calls on **objc_msgSend()**.

Both functions find the implementation of the *theSelector* method that's appropriate for the receiver of the message. For **objc_msgSend()**, *theReceiver* is passed explicitly as an argument. For **objc_msgSendSuper()**, *superContext* defines the context in which the message was sent, including who the receiver is.

Arguments that are included in the *aSelector* message are passed directly as additional arguments to both functions.

Calls to **objc_msgSend()** and **objc_msgSendSuper()** should be generated only by the compiler. You shouldn't call them directly in the Objective C code you write.

The third function, **objc_msgSendv**(), is an alternative to **objc_msgSend**() that's designed to be used within class-specific implementations of the **forward::** method. Instead of being passed each of the arguments to the *aSelector* message, it takes a pointer to the arguments list, *argFrame*, and the size of the list in bytes, *argSize*. *argSize* can be obtained by calling **method_getArgumentSize**(); *argFrame* is passed as the second argument to the **forward::** method.

objc_msgSendv() parses the argument list based on information stored for *aSelector* and the class of the receiver. Because of this additional work, it's more expensive than **objc_msgSend**().

RETURN Each method passes on the value returned by the *aSelector* method.

objc_msgSendSuper() → See objc_msgSend()

objc_msgSendv() → See objc_msgSend()

---

objc_setMultithreaded()

SUMMARY Make the run-time system thread safe

DECLARED IN objc/objc-runtime.h

SYNOPSIS void **objc_setMultithreaded**(BOOL *flag*)

DESCRIPTION When *flag* is YES, this function ensures that two or more threads of the same task can safely use the run-time system for Objective C. To guarantee correct run-time behavior, it should be called immediately before starting up a new thread.

Because of the additional checking required to ensure thread-safe behavior, messaging will be slower than normal. Therefore, *flag* should be reset to the default NO when there is only one thread using Objective C.

This function cannot guarantee that all parts of the run-time system are absolutely thread-safe. In particular, if one thread is in the middle of dynamically loading or unloading a class (using **objc_loadModules**() or **objc_unloadModules**()) while another thread is using the class, the second thread might find the class in an inconsistent state. Similarly, a thread that gets the class hash table (using **objc_getClasses**()) cannot be sure that another thread won't be modifying it at the same time.

objc_unloadModules() → See objc_loadModules()

object_copy() → See object_dispose()

object_copyFromZone() → See object_dispose()

---

object_dispose(), object_copy(), object_copyFromZone(), object_realloc(), object_reallocFromZone()

SUMMARY Manage object memory

DECLARED IN objc/Object.h

SYNOPSIS

id **object_dispose**(Object **anObject*)
id **object_copy**(Object **anObject*, unsigned int *indexedIvarBytes*)
id **object_copyFromZone**(Object **anObject*, unsigned int *indexedIvarBytes*, NXZone **zone*)
id **object_realloc**(Object **anObject*, unsigned int *numBytes*)
id **object_reallocFromZone**(Object **anObject*, unsigned int *numBytes*, NXZone **zone*)

DESCRIPTION These five functions, along with **class_createInstance**() and **class_createInstanceFromZone**(), manage the dynamic allocation of memory for objects. Like those two functions, each of them is simply a "cover" for—a way of calling—another, private function.

object_dispose() frees the memory occupied by *anObject* after setting its **isa** instance variable to **nil**, and returns **nil**. The function it calls to do this work can be changed by reassigning the **_dealloc** variable.

object_copy() and **object_copyFromZone()** create a new object that's an exact copy of *anObject* and return the new object. **object_copy()** allocates memory for the copy from the same zone as the original; **object_copyFromZone()** places the copy in *zone*. The second argument to both functions, *indexedIvarBytes*, specifies the number of additional bytes that should be allocated to accommodate indexed instance variables; it serves the same purpose as the second argument to **class_createInstance()**.

The functions that **object_copy()** and **object_copyFromZone()** call to do their work can be changed by reassigning the **_copy** and **_zoneCopy** variables.

object_realloc() and **object_reallocFromZone()** reallocate storage for *anObject*, adding *numBytes* if possible. The memory previously occupied by *anObject* is freed if it can't be reused, and a pointer to the new location of *anObject* is returned. **object_realloc()** allocates memory for the object from the same zone that it originally occupied; **object_reallocFromZone()** locates the object in *zone*.

The functions that **object_realloc() and object_reallocFromZone()** call to do their work can be changed by reassigning the **_realloc** and **_zoneRealloc** variables.

RETURN **object_dispose()** returns **nil**, **object_copy()** and **object_copyFromZone()** return the copy, and **object_realloc()** and **object_reallocFromZone()** return the reallocated object. If the attempt to copy or reallocate the object fails, an error message is generated and **abort()** is called.

---

object_getClassName()

SUMMARY Return the class name

DECLARED IN objc/objc.h

SYNOPSIS const char ***object_getClassName**(id *anObject*)

DESCRIPTION This function returns the name of *anObject*'s class, or the string "nil" if *anObject* is **nil**. *anObject* can be either an instance or a class object.

object_getIndexedIvars()

SUMMARY Return a pointer to an object's extra memory

DECLARED IN objc/objc.h

SYNOPSIS void ***object_getIndexedIvars**(id *anObject*)

This function returns a pointer to the first indexed instance variable of *anObject*, if *anObject* has indexed instance variables. If not, the pointer returned won't be valid and should not be used.

SEE ALSO **class_createInstance()**

object_getInstanceVariable() → See object_setInstanceVariable()

object_realloc() → See object_dispose()

object_reallocFromZone() → See object_dispose()

object_setInstanceVariable(), object_getInstanceVariable()

SUMMARY Set and get instance variables

DECLARED IN objc/Object.h

SYNOPSIS Ivar **object_setInstanceVariable**(id *anObject*, const char **variableName*, void **value*)
Ivar **object_getInstanceVariable**(id *anObject*, const char **variableName*, void ***value*)

DESCRIPTION **object_setInstanceVariable()** assigns a new value to the *variableName* instance variable belonging to *anObject*. The instance variable must be one that's declared as a pointer; typically it's an **id**. The new value of the pointer is passed in the third argument, *value*. (Note that the pointer value is passed directly, not by reference.)

object_getInstanceVariable() gets the value of the pointer stored as *anObject*'s *variableName* instance variable. The pointer is returned by reference through the third argument, *value*. For example:

```
int *i;
Ivar var = object_getInstanceVariable(anObject, "num", (void **)&i);
```

These functions provide a way of setting and getting instance variables that are declared as pointers, without having to implement methods for that purpose. For example, Interface Builder calls **object_setInstanceVariable()** to initialize programmer-defined "outlet" instance variables.

These functions cannot reliably be used to set and get instance variables that are not pointers.

RETURN Both functions return a pointer to the class template that describes the *variableName* instance variable. A NULL pointer is returned if *anObject* has no instance variable with that name.

The returned template has a field describing the data type of the instance variable. You can check it to be sure that the value set is of the correct type.

sel_getName() → See sel_getUid()

---

sel_getUid(), sel_getName()

SUMMARY Match method names with method selectors

DECLARED IN objc/objc.h

SYNOPSIS SEL **sel_getUid**(const char **aName*)
const char ***sel_getName**(SEL *aSelector*)

DESCRIPTION The first function, **sel_getUid()**, returns the unique identifier that represents the *aName* method at run time. The identifier is a selector (type SEL) and is used in place of the method name in compiled code; methods with the same name have the same selector. Whenever possible, you should use the **@selector()** directive to ask the compiler to provide the selector for a method. This function asks the run-time system for the selector and should be used only if the name isn't known at compile time.

The second function, **sel_getName()**, is the inverse of the first. It returns the name that was mapped to *aSelector.*

RETURN **sel_getUid()** returns the selector for the *aName* method, or 0 if there is no known method with that name. **sel_getName()** returns a character string with the name of the method identified by the *aSelector* selector. If *aSelector* isn't a valid selector, a NULL pointer is returned.

---

sel_isMapped()

SUMMARY Determine whether a selector is valid

DECLARED IN objc/objc.h

SYNOPSIS BOOL **sel_isMapped**(SEL *aSelector*)

RETURN **sel_isMapped()** returns YES if *aSelector* is a valid selector (is currently mapped to a method implementation) or could possibly be one (because it lies within the same range as valid selectors); otherwise it returns NO.

Because all of a program's selectors are guaranteed to be mapped at start-up, this function has little real use. It's included here for reasons of backward compatibility only.

sel_registerName()

SUMMARY Register a method name

DECLARED IN objc/objc.h

SYNOPSIS SEL **sel_registerName**(const char **aName*)

DESCRIPTION This function registers *aName* as a method name and causes it to be mapped to a SEL selector, which it returns.

No check is made to see if *aName* is already a valid method name. If it is, the same name will be mapped to more than one selector. When the run-time system needs to match a selector to the name, it's indeterminant which one it will find.

RETURN **sel_registerName**() returns the selector it maps to the *aString* method.

Types and Constants

This section documents the types, constants, and structures defined in three header files: **objc/objc-class.h**, **objc/objc-runtime.h**, and **objc/Protocol.h**. For the most part, these definitions are internal to the run-time system and rarely find their way into Objective C source code. More commonly used types and constants are declared in **objc/objc.h** and are documented in Chapter 1, "Root Class."

Defined Types

Cache

DECLARED IN objc/objc-class.h

SYNOPSIS typedef struct objc_cache ***Cache**;

DESCRIPTION This is the defined type for a class's run-time cache of frequently used methods. Each class has its own cache.

Category

DECLARED IN objc/objc-class.h

SYNOPSIS typedef struct objc_category ***Category**;

DESCRIPTION This is the type name for the structure that contains information about a category definition.

Ivar

DECLARED IN objc/objc-class.h

SYNOPSIS typedef struct objc_ivar ***Ivar**;

DESCRIPTION The Ivar type identifies a structure containing information about a single instance variable—including the name of the variable, its type, and its location in the object data structure.

marg_list

DECLARED IN objc/objc-class.h

SYNOPSIS typedef void ***marg_list**;

DESCRIPTION This type is a pointer to the arguments that were passed in a message. It's used by the Object class's **forward::** method.

Method

DECLARED IN objc/objc-class.h

SYNOPSIS typedef struct objc_method ***Method**;

DESCRIPTION The Method type designates a structure containing information about a single method—including its return and argument types, the method selector, and the location of the method implementation.

Module

DECLARED IN objc/objc-runtime.h

SYNOPSIS typedef struct objc_module ***Module**;

DESCRIPTION This data type refers to a file that contributes to an Objective C program. The compiler produces a Module data structure for each file that it encounters.

Symbolic Constants

Type Constants

DECLARED IN objc/objc-class.h

SYNOPSIS

Constant	Meaning	Defined As
_C_ID	**id**	'@'
_C_CLASS	Class	'#'
_C_SEL	SEL	':'
_C_VOID	**void**	'v'
_C_CHR	**char**	'c'
_C_UCHR	**unsigned char**	'C'
_C_SHT	**short**	's'
_C_USHT	**unsigned short**	'S'
_C_INT	**int**	'i'
_C_UINT	**unsigned int**	'I'
_C_LNG	**long**	'l'
_C_ULNG	**unsigned long**	'L'
_C_FLT	**float**	'f'
_C_DBL	**double**	'd'
_C_UNDEF	an undefined type	'?'
_C_PTR	a pointer	'^'
_C_CHARPTR	**char ***	'*'
_C_BFLD	a bitfield	'b'
_C_ARY_B	begin an array	'['
_C_ARY_E	end an array	']'
_C_UNION_B	begin a union	'('
_C_UNION_E	end a union	')'
_C_STRUCT_B	begin a structure	'{'
_C_STRUCT_E	end a structure	'}'

DESCRIPTION These constants identify the character codes used to store method return and argument types. They're the same codes returned by the @**encode()** directive.

Structures

objc_cache

DECLARED IN objc/objc-class.h

SYNOPSIS

```
struct objc_cache {
        unsigned int mask;
        unsigned int occupied;
        Method buckets[1];
};
```

DESCRIPTION This structure stores a class-specific cache of the methods most recently used by instances of the class or by the class object. The Cache data type is defined as a pointer to an **objc_cache** structure.

objc_category

DECLARED IN objc/objc-class.h

SYNOPSIS

```
struct objc_category {
        char *category_name;
        char *class_name;
        struct objc_method_list *instance_methods;
        struct objc_method_list *class_methods;
        struct objc_protocol_list *protocols;
};
```

DESCRIPTION This structure stores the information contained in a category definition. Its fields are:

category_name	The name assigned to the category in source code
class_name	The name of the class that the category belongs to
instance_methods	A list of instance methods defined in the category
class_methods	A list of class methods defined in the category
protocols	A list of the protocols adopted in the category

The Category data type is defined as a pointer to an **obj_category** structure.

---

objc_class

DECLARED IN objc/objc-class.h

SYNOPSIS

```
struct objc_class {
        struct objc_class *isa;
        struct objc_class *super_class;
        const char *name;
        long version;
        long info;
        long instance_size;
        struct objc_ivar_list *ivars;
        struct objc_method_list *methods;
        struct objc_cache *cache;
        struct objc_protocol_list *protocols;
};
```

DESCRIPTION This structure holds information about a class definition. Its fields are:

isa	The metaclass of this class
super_class	The superclass of this class
name	The name of this class
version	The current version of the class (as set by **setVersion:**)
info	The current status of the class
instance_size	The number of bytes to allocate for an instance of the class
ivars	The instance variables declared in the class interface
methods	The instance methods defined in the class implementation
cache	The cache of recently used methods
protocols	The protocols adopted by the class

This structure is also used to store metaclass information, in which case the **methods** field lists class methods rather than instance methods.

The Class data type is defined (in **objc.h**) as a pointer to an **objc_class** structure.

objc_ivar

DECLARED IN objc/objc-class.h

SYNOPSIS

```
struct objc_ivar {
        char *ivar_name;
        char *ivar_type;
        int ivar_offset;
};
```

DESCRIPTION This structure describes a single instance variable. It's fields are:

ivar_name	The name of the instance variable
ivar_type	The data type declared for the instance variable
ivar_offset	The position of the variable in the object (as an offset in bytes)

The Ivar data type is defined as a pointer to an **objc_ivar** structure.

objc_ivar_list

DECLARED IN objc/objc-class.h

SYNOPSIS

```
struct objc_ivar_list {
        int ivar_count;
        struct objc_ivar ivar_list[1];
};
```

DESCRIPTION This structure holds information about the instance variables declared in a class definition. The first field, **ivar_count**, gives the number of variables declared and the second field, **ivar_list**, is a variable-length array of all the variables.

objc_method

DECLARED IN objc/objc-class.h

SYNOPSIS

```
struct objc_method {
        SEL method_name;
        char *method_types;
        IMP method_imp;
};
```

DESCRIPTION This structure describes a single method implemented by the class. The fields are:

method_name	The method selector (not the full name)
method_types	A string encoding the method return and argument types
method_imp	A pointer to the method implementation

The Method data type is defined as a pointer to an **objc_method** structure.

objc_method_description

DECLARED IN objc/Protocol.h

SYNOPSIS

```
struct objc_method_description {
        SEL name;
        char *types;
};
```

DESCRIPTION This structure holds the method information returned by two methods defined in the Protocol class, **descriptionForClassMethod:** and **descriptionForInstanceMethod:**, and by two Object methods, **descriptionForMethod:** and **descriptionForInstanceMethod:**.

objc_method_description_list

DECLARED IN objc/Protocol.h

SYNOPSIS

```
struct objc_method_description_list {
        int count;
        struct objc_method_description list[1];
};
```

DESCRIPTION This structure points to a list of **objc_method_description** structures. Typically the list describes all the methods declared in a particular protocol.

objc_method_list

DECLARED IN objc/objc-class.h

SYNOPSIS

```
struct objc_method_list {
        struct objc_method_list *method_next;
        int method_count;
        struct objc_method method_list[1];
};
```

DESCRIPTION This structure lists all the class or all the instance methods defined within a class or category (within one group bracketed by @**implementation** and @**end**). Its fields are:

method_next	A pointer to another group of methods for the same class
method_count	The number of methods listed in this group
method_list	A variable-length array of method descriptions

Class methods and instance methods are listed in separate structures.

objc_module

DECLARED IN objc/objc-runtime.h

SYNOPSIS

```
struct objc_module {
        unsigned long version;
        unsigned long size;
        const char *name;
        Symtab symtab;
};
```

DESCRIPTION This structure holds information about an object file compiled from Objective C source code. Its fields are:

version	The version of run-time data structures
size	The size of the module in bytes
name	The name of the file
symtab	An obsolete field

The Module data type is defined as a pointer to this structure.

objc_protocol_list

DECLARED IN objc/objc-class.h

SYNOPSIS

```
struct objc_protocol_list {
        struct objc_protocol_list *next
        int count;
        Protocol *list[1];
};
```

DESCRIPTION This structure lists all the protocols adopted by a class in one place. Separate lists are kept for the class interface and for each category that adopts protocols on the class's behalf. The fields of the structure are:

next	A pointer to another list of protocols adopted by the class
count	The number of protocols listed here
list	A variable-length array of Protocol objects

objc_super

DECLARED IN objc/objc-runtime.h

SYNOPSIS

```
struct objc_super {
        id receiver;
        Class class;
};
```

DESCRIPTION This structure helps the messaging function find which method implementation to invoke in response to a message sent to **super**. Its fields are:

receiver	The receiver of the message (the object designated by **super**)
class	The class where the message is sent

Global Variables

Function Pointers

DECLARED IN objc/objc-runtime.h

SYNOPSIS
id (***_alloc**)(Class *aClass*, unsigned int *indexedIvarBytes*)
id (***_dealloc**)(Object **anObject*)
id (***_realloc**)(Object **anObject*, unsigned int *numBytes*)
id (***_copy**)(Object **anObject*, unsigned int *indexedIvarBytes*)
id (***_zoneAlloc**)(Class *aClass*, unsigned int *indexedIvarBytes*, NXZone **zone*)
id (***_zoneRealloc**)(Object **anObject*, unsigned int *numBytes*, NXZone **zone*)
id (***_zoneCopy**)(Object **anObject*, unsigned int *indexedIvarBytes*, NXZone **zone*)
void (***_error**)(Object **anObject*, const char **format*, va_list *ap*)

DESCRIPTION These variables point to the functions that the run-time system uses to manage memory and handle errors. By reassigning a variable, a function can be replaced with another of the same type. The example below shows a temporary reassignment of the **_zoneAlloc** function:

```
id (*theFunction)();
theFunction = _zoneAlloc;
_zoneAlloc = someOtherFunction;
/*
 * code that calls the class_createInstanceFromZone() function,
 * or sends alloc and allocFromZone: messages, goes here
 */
_zoneAlloc = theFunction;
```

- **_alloc** points to the function, called through **class_createInstance()**, used to allocate memory for new instances, and **_zoneAlloc** points to the function, called through **class_createInstanceFromZone()**, used to allocate the memory for a new instance from a specified *zone*.
- **_dealloc** points to the function, called through **object_dispose()**, used to free instances.
- **_realloc** points to the function, called through **object_realloc()**, used to reallocate memory for an object, and **_zoneRealloc** points to the function, called through **object_reallocFromZone()**, used to reallocate memory from a specified *zone*.

- **_copy** points to the function, called through **object_copy()**, used to create an exact copy of an object, and **_zoneCopy** points to the function, called through **object_copyFromZone()**, used to create the copy from memory in the specified *zone*.
- **_error** points to the function that the run-time system calls in response to an error. By default, it prints formatted error messages to the standard error stream (or logs them to the console if there is no standard error stream) and calls **abort()** to produce a core file.

16 *Sound*

16 *Sound*

Library: libNeXT_s.a

Header File Directory: /NextDeveloper/Headers/sound
/NextDeveloper/Headers/soundkit

Import: sound/sound.h
soundkit/soundkit.h

Introduction

This chapter describes the sound software provided by NeXTSTEP. There are three "layers" of software: a sound driver, a set of sound functions, and a Sound Kit. The sound driver is the device that communicates with the sound hardware (including the DSP), allowing sound to be recorded, compressed, converted, and played. The sound functions and Sound Kit provide high-level interfaces to the sound driver. In addition to playing and recording sounds, the Sound Kit also provides classes that let you display sound data.

There are four sections in this chapter:

- "Classes" describes the Objective C classes defined by the Sound Kit.
- "Sound Functions" describes the sound C functions. In general, the operations provided by the sound functions are subsumed by the Sound Kit. However, the sound functions are useful for performing very simple tasks, such as playing a single soundfile.
- "Driver Functions" describes the C functions that give you the most direct access to the sound driver. Although the driver functions have been largely obsolesced by the SoundDevice and SoundStream classes, they're still needed if you want to control a stream of sound into or out of the DSP.
- "Types and Constants" describes the defined types and symbolic constants used by the sound software.

Classes

NXPlayStream

Inherits From: NXSoundStream : Object

Declared In: soundkit/NXPlayStream.h

Class Description

The NXPlayStream class defines methods that initiate and control sound playback. To play sounds with an NXPlayStream object, you must first connect it to an NXSoundOut object and then activate it; these tasks are done through the **initOnDevice:** and **activate** methods (as described in NXSoundStream).

Once it's connected and activated, an NXPlayStream will accept and play buffers of sound data. You supply it with these buffers through the **playBuffer:...** methods. The enqueuing of buffers must be timely and constant—a gap in playback occurs if the underlying sound device isn't supplied with buffers quickly enough (it "underruns"). You can prevent this sort of underrun by using larger buffers; if you're playing a determinate amount of existing data, there's no loss in enqueuing the entire sound in one large buffer. Of course, this isn't possible if you're creating or controlling sound data dynamically; in particular, if you've set the size or number of DMA transfer buffers to yield a better response time (through messages to the NXSoundOut object), then the size of the buffers that you feed to the NXPlayStream should be no greater than DMA buffer size times the DMA buffer count. In any case, you should note that you don't have to wait for a stream buffer to play before enqueuing the next one.

The sound data in the buffers that you enqueue with an NXPlayStream can be one or two channels of 16-bit linear sound samples at either the 44.1 kHz or 22.05 kHz sampling rate. Sounds in other formats and sampling rates must be converted before they can be played through an NXPlayStream.

Scaling and Peak Detection

One of the features of an NXPlayStream is that it allows stream-independent amplitude scaling and peak detection. Amplitude-scaling, or *gain*, is a (stereo) factor that's applied linearly to the left and right channels to increase or decrease the amplitude of a stream before it's mixed with the other coincident playback streams. The **setGainLeft:right:** method sets the left- and right-channel gain factors.

In addition to the general stream-gain factor, each buffer can be given its own stereo gain, set as the buffer is enqueued through the (full-blown) **playBuffer:...** method. When the buffer is played, its data is scaled by its own gain and then by the gain for its stream.

An NXPlayStream's peak detection facility is much like that provided by NXSoundDevice: It holds the (normalized) maximum left- and right-channel amplitudes that it has detected over a certain amount of sound data. For NXPlayStream, the number of samples (or sample frames) that are looked at depends on the NXPlayStream's peak history value (as set through **setPeakHistory:**), the size of a DMA transfer buffer, the sampling rate at which the sound-out hardware is currently running, and the channel count and sampling rate of the NXPlayStream's current buffer. The best way to think of this is to consider the peak history as setting the frequency at which the NXPlayStream's data is examined: If you set the peak history to 1 (the default), the stream is examined after every DMA transfer performed by sound-out. Using the default settings, this means that a stereo 44.1 kHz stream is examined 20 times a second and a stereo 22.05 kHz stream is examined 10 times a second (given that the sound-out hardware is running at these same rates).

As with NXSoundDevice, the peak values aren't sent back to your application—you have to request them by invoking the **getPeakLeft:right:** method. The peak values returned by the method are normalized to fall within (0.0, 1.0), where 0.0 is no amplitude and 1.0 is the maximum amplitude. If you want to continuously monitor the peaks in a stream, you would set up a timed entry that invokes this method at a frequency that matches the rate at which the peaks are detected.

Error Codes

Many of the methods described here access underlying sound devices. Such methods return error codes that declare success or describe failure. A catalog of these error codes can be found in the section "Types and Constants" under the heading "NXSoundDeviceError."

Instance Variables

None declared in this class.

Method Types

Initializing an NXPlayStream	– initOnDevice:
Activating and playing	– activate – playBuffer:size:tag:channelCount:samplingRate: – playBuffer:size:tag:channelCount:samplingRate: bufferGainLeft:right: lowWaterMark:highWaterMark:
Gain and peak detection	– setGainLeft:right: – getGainLeft:right: – getPeakLeft:right: – setDetectPeaks: – isDetectingPeaks – setPeakHistory: – peakHistory

Instance Methods

activate

– (NXSoundDeviceError)**activate**

Activates the NXPlayStream so it can be used to play sounds. This augments the superclass implementation by setting playback-specific attributes. Returns an error code.

See also: – **activate** (NXSoundStream)

getGainLeft:right:

– **getGainLeft:**(float *)*leftScale* **right:**(float *)*rightScale*

Returns, by reference in the arguments, the general scaling factors that are applied to the left and right channels of this NXPlayStream. By default, the gain in both channels is 1.0 (the sound is unmodified). Returns **self**.

See also: – **setGainLeft:right:**

getPeakLeft:right:

– (NXSoundDeviceError)**getPeakLeft:**(float *)*leftAmp* **right:**(float *)*rightAmp*

Returns, by reference in the arguments, the most recently detected peak amplitudes for this NXPlayStream. The peak values are normalized to fall within (0.0, 1.0), where 0.0 is no amplitude and 1.0 is maximum amplitude. You typically set up a timed entry to invoke this method while sound is playing. See the class description, above, for more on peak detection.

See also: – **setPeakHistory:**, – **setDetectPeaks:**, – **isDetectingPeaks**

initOnDevice:

– **initOnDevice:***anObject*

The designated initializer for NXPlayStream, this method invokes the superclass version of **initOnDevice:** and then sets the the gain in both channels to 1.0, and the peak history to 1.

isDetectingPeaks

– (BOOL)**isDetectingPeaks**

Returns YES if the NXPlayStream is detecting peak amplitudes; otherwise, returns NO (the default).

See also: – **setDetectPeaks:**

peakHistory

– (unsigned int)**peakHistory**

Returns the frequency at which the NXPlayStream detects peaks, as explained in the class description.

See also: – **setPeakHistory:**

playBuffer:size:tag:channelCount:samplingRate:

– (NXSoundDeviceError)**playBuffer:**(void *)*data*
size:(unsigned int)*bytes*
tag:(int)*aTag*
channelCount:(unsigned int)*channels*
samplingRate:(float)*rate*

Enqueues a buffer for playback by invoking the grander **playBuffer:...** method (described below) with the following defaults:

Argument	Default Value
leftAmp	1.0
rightAmp	1.0
lowWaterMark	512 kilobytes
highWaterMark	768 kilobytes

Returns an error code.

See also: – **playBuffer:size:tag:channelCount:samplingRate:bufferGainLeft:right: lowWaterMark:highWaterMark:**

playBuffer:size:tag:channelCount:samplingRate:bufferGainLeft:right: lowWaterMark:highWaterMark:

– (NXSoundDeviceError)**playBuffer:**(void *)*data*
size:(unsigned int)*bytes*
tag:(int)*aTag*
channelCount:(unsigned int)*channels*
samplingRate:(float)*rate*
bufferGainLeft:(float)*leftAmp*
right:(float)*rightAmp*
lowWaterMark:(unsigned int)*lowWater*
highWaterMark:(unsigned int)*highWater*

Enqueues a buffer for playback. The arguments are as follows:

Argument	Value
data	A pointer to the buffer that you're enqueuing.
bytes	The size of the buffer, in bytes
aTag	A non-negative integer that's used to identify the buffer in subsequent delegate messages.
channels	The number of channels; must be 1 or 2.
rate	The sampling rate; must be SND_RATE_LOW (22050.0) or SND_RATE_HIGH (44100.0).
leftAmp	An amplitude-scaling factor for the left channel.
rightAmp	An amplitude-scaling factor for the right channel.
lowWater	The minimum number of bytes of data the sound driver will attempt to keep resident in memory (or *wired down*) while the NXPlayStream is playing.
highWater	The maximum number of bytes of data the sound driver will wire down.

The left- and right-channel gain values (*leftAmp* and *rightAmp*) are specific to this buffer. The general stream gain, set through **setGainLeft:right:**, is applied in addition to these.

See also: – **playBuffer:size:tag:channelCount:samplingRate:**

setDetectPeaks:

– (NXSoundDeviceError)**setDetectPeaks:**(BOOL)*flag*

Establishes whether the NXPlayStream detects peak amplitudes. The default is NO. See the class description for more information on peak detection. An error code is returned.

See also: – **isDetectingPeaks,** – **setPeakHistory:,** – **getPeakLeft:right:**

setGainLeft:right:

– (NXSoundDeviceError)**setGainLeft:**(float)*leftAmp* **right:**(float)*rightAmp*

Set the NXPlayStream's general gain. These gains are multiplied by the individual buffer gains (as set through **playBuffer:...**) to get the final amplitude gain for a particular buffer on this NXPlayStream.

See also: – **getGainLeft:right:**

setPeakHistory:

– (NXSoundDeviceError)**setPeakHistory:**(unsigned int)*bufferCount*

Sets the frequency at which the NXPlayStream detects peaks, as explained in the class description. Returns an error code.

See also: – **peakHistory**, – **setDetectPeaks:**

Methods Implemented by the Delegate

soundStreamDidUnderrun:

– **soundStreamDidUnderrun:***sender*

Invoked when the sound driver "underruns," or can't transfer data to the sound hardware quickly enough. Underrun occurs if you're playing too many sounds at the same time, if the DMA transfer buffers are too small or too few, or if the overall system load is too high. It results in a gap in playback.

NXRecordStream

Inherits From: NXSoundStream : Object

Declared In: soundkit/NXRecordStream.h

Class Description

The NXRecordStream class defines methods that retrieve data recorded through the microphone. To use an NXRecordStream object, you must first connect it to an NXSoundIn object and then activate it; these tasks are done through the **initOnDevice:** and **activate** methods, both of which NXRecordStream inherits from its superclass, NXSoundStream.

To record a sound, you must tell the NXRecordStream to enqueue a buffer in which the sound data will be placed by invoking one of the **recordSize:...** methods. You don't have to supply the buffer, just its size (and other specifications); the buffer itself is allocated by the sound driver. If you're recording a determinate amount of data, there's no loss in enqueuing one large buffer to hold the entire recording. In any case, you should note that you don't have to wait for a buffer to be recorded before enqueuing the next one.

As each buffer is recorded, it's returned to the NXRecordStream's delegate through a **soundStream:didRecordData:size:forBuffer:** message. You can force a buffer to return early through the **sendRecordedDataToDelegate** method.

The sound data in the buffers that are returned to the delegate is a single channel of 8-bit mu-law samples at the CODEC sampling rate. You have to convert the format and sampling rate before playing the sound through an NXPlayStream object (as explained in NXPlayStream). If you're using a Sound object or the **SNDStartPlaying()** function to play the sound, these conversions are performed for you.

The sound driver sends recorded data to all NXRecordStreams that are being used simultaneously. This extends to all applications: Any number of applications may recieve record at the same time (each application gets a separate copy of the recorded data). You can reserve the sound-in facilities for your application through NXSoundIn's **setReserved:** method.

Error Codes

Many of the methods described here access underlying sound devices. Such methods return error codes that declare success or describe failure. A catalog of these error codes can be found in the section "Types and Constants" under the heading "NXSoundDeviceError."

Instance Variables

None declared in this class.

Method Types

Enqueueing buffers	– recordSize:tag: – recordSize:tag:lowWaterMark:highWaterMark:
Requesting data	– sendRecordedDataToDelegate

Instance Methods

recordSize:tag:

– (NXSoundDeviceError)**recordSize:**(unsigned int)*bytes* **tag:**(int)*anInt*

Enqueues a recording buffer by invoking **recordSize:tag:lowWaterMark:highWaterMark:** with the default water mark values (48 pages of virtual memory for the low mark, 64 pages for the high mark). Returns an error code.

See also: – **recordSize:tag:lowWaterMark:highWaterMark:**

recordSize:tag:lowWaterMark:highWaterMark:

– (NXSoundDeviceError)**recordSize:**(unsigned int)*bytes*
tag:(int)*aTag*
lowWaterMark:(unsigned int)*lowWater*
highWaterMark:(unsigned int)*highWater*

Enqueues a recording buffer with the given size in bytes. The buffer is identified, when it's returned to the delegate, by *aTag*, an integer that must be greater than or equal to 0. The *lowWater* and *highWater* arguments set the minimum and maximum number of bytes that the sound driver will try to keep resident in memory (or *wired-down*) while the recording is in progress. Note that this means the recording won't start until the driver has wired down memory to the low water mark. When the buffer is filled, it's returned to the NXRecordStream's delegate, through its **soundStream:didRecordData:size:forBuffer:** method. You can force the buffer to be returned before it's filled by sending **sendRecordedDataToDelegate** to the NXRecordStream. Returns an error code.

See also: – **recordSize:tag:**, – **soundStream:didRecordData:size:forBuffer:** (delegate)

sendRecordedDataToDelegate

– (NXSoundDeviceError)**sendRecordedDataToDelegate**

Forces the current buffer to be returned immediately in a **soundStream:didRecordData:size:forBuffer:** message sent to the delegate. The recording continues into the remaining portion of the buffer. An error code is returned.

See also: – **soundStream:didRecordData:size:forBuffer:** (delegate)

Methods Implemented by the Delegate

soundStreamDidOverrun:

– **soundStreamDidOverrun:***sender*

Invoked when memory can't be wired down fast enough, thus causing the driver to drop recorded data. Usually this means that the overall system load is too high. The return value is ignored.

soundStream:didRecordData:size:forBuffer:

– **soundStream:***sender*
  didRecordData:(void *)*data*
  size:(unsigned int)*numBytes*
  forBuffer:(int)*tag*

Returns, in *data*, the most recently recorded buffer of sound data. The size of the data is given by *numBytes*; the *tag* argument is the tag that was placed on the buffer by the **recordSize:...** message that enqueued it. Normally, this is invoked when the driver fills the entire buffer with data. It's also invoked when the NXRecordStream is deactivated, and when it receives a **sendRecordedDataToDelegate** message. When you're finished with *data*, you must free it yourself, through the **vm_deallocate()** function.

NXSoundDevice

Inherits From: Object

Declared In: soundkit/NXSoundDevice.h

Class Description

NXSoundDevice is an abstract superclass; each subclass represents a sound input or output device. Currently, the Sound Kit provides two subclasses of NXSoundDevice:

- NXSoundIn represents sound input (the microphone jack).
- NXSoundOut represents sound output (the speaker, line-out jacks, and headphone jack).

The utility of NXSoundDevice is invested in these subclasses; the NXSoundDevice class itself simply defines methods that are common to them. In addition, you can't create useful subclasses of NXSoundDevice yourself (see "Sound Devices and the DSP," below, for information on accessing the DSP as a sound device).

Many applications needn't bother with NXSoundDevice and its subclasses; in general, the methods provided by the Sound class suffice for applications that record and playback sounds. However, while Sound objects are easy to use, NXSoundDevices let you control sound resources to a much greater degree. The primary advantages of NXSoundDevice objects are that you can:

- Reserve sound devices for exclusive use by your application.
- Specify the host computer of the device that you want to use.
- Specify the size and number of the sound data buffers used by the device.

Initializing and Reserving a Sound Device

You initialize an NXSoundDevice by connecting it to a sound driver. The **init** method connects it to the sound driver on the local host; **initOnHost:** lets you access the sound driver on some other machine. A single NXSoundDevice can be connected to only one sound driver (one host) at a time.

Underneath the two NXSoundDevice subclasses lie two specific sound driver devices: NXSoundIn represents the sound driver's sound-in device, and NXSoundOut represents the sound-out device. You can connect any number of NXSoundOut and NXSoundIn instances to the same sound driver (in other words, you can initialize them on the same host), however, some NXSoundDevice methods, notably **setBufferSize:** and

setBufferCount:, set attributes for the underlying sound driver device, thus sending such a message to one NXSoundOut or NXSoundIn will affect all other instances of its class on that host.

You can reserve a sound driver device for exclusive use by an NXSoundDevice through the **setReserved:** method. While reserved, no other application, nor any other NXSoundDevice within your application, can play or record sounds through the sound device. If it's unreserved, the sound device is shared: For sound-in, this means that more than one application can get a copy of the same recording. For sound-out, more than one application can play sounds at the same time (see the NXSoundOut class description for more on mixing sounds during playback). Note that while you can reserve a sound device, you can't reserve the reservation; **setReserved:YES** will work even if the device has already been reserved by another application (and the previous owner will no longer have access to the device).

Devices and Streams

By themselves, NXSoundDevice objects are of limited use. An NXSoundOut object, for example, lets you manipulate the sound-out device, but it doesn't provide data to the device, thus the object isn't capable of making any sound. For this, you need to connect an NXPlayStream object to the NXSoundOut. This is done by passing the NXSoundOut as the argument to NXPlayStream's **initOnDevice:** method. Similarly, to record sound you must connect an NXRecordStream to an NXSoundIn object, again through an **initOnDevice:** message (sent to the NXRecordStream). NXPlayStream and NXRecordStream inherit from NXSoundStream, an abstract superclass that defines methods for its subclasses in much the same way that NXSoundDevice embodies the common functionality of NXSoundIn and NXSoundOut. You can connect more than one NXSoundStream to the same NXSoundDevice, but the NXRecordStream/NXSoundIn, NXPlayStream/NXSoundOut pairings should be honored; you can't connect an NXPlayStream to an NXSoundIn, for example.

An NXSoundDevice can pause, resume, and abort all the NXSoundStreams that are connected to it. Each NXSoundDevice controls only its own NXSoundStreams; for example, if you create two NXSoundOut objects and connect two NXPlayStreams to each (for a total of four NXPlayStreams), sending a **pauseStreams:** message to one of the NXSoundOuts will pause only the two streams that are connected to it—the other two streams are unaffected, even though both NXSoundOut objects represent the same sound driver device. This ability—to independently control groups of streams connected to the same underlying sound driver device—is the only reason for creating multiple NXSoundDevices for the same driver device. Barring this requirement, you should never need to create more than one NXSoundOut and one NXSoundIn per host machine.

Sound Buffers

The sound-in and sound-out devices transfer sound to or from the associated sound hardware through DMA buffers. These transfer buffers can be no larger than a page of virtual memory, as given by the global variable **vm_page_size**. However, you can make them smaller with the **setBufferSize:** method, if desired. *All* sound streams connected to the device (even those in other applications) will have their sound data broken into pieces of this size for transfer. By default, sound-in DMA buffers are 256 bytes and sound-out buffers are a page of virtual memory.

You can also specify the number of transfer buffers that are used by a device through the **setBufferCount:** method. By default, both sound-in and sound-out use four buffers. DMA buffers are sent as soon as they're filled; by maintaining more than one buffer, the sound driver is able to "run ahead," filling the extra buffers while the first one is being played (or emptied, in the case of recording). This provides a sort of cushion, allowing the buffer-filling process (which is run in a background thread) to procede in jerks and starts while sound is played back (or recorded) without interruption.

For applications that don't depend on user interaction or some other dynamic quality to affect sound recording or playback, the transfer buffer defaults are adequate. However, you may want to make the buffers smaller or fewer in number if you need a quick turn-around between a sound's inception and its capture or realization—this is particularly true for playback that's tightly controlled by the user's actions. If you do resize or renumber the DMA transfer buffers for better response time, you should be aware that all may be for nought unless you similarly adjust the size of the sound data buffers that you enqueue on the NXSoundStream that you're using. In such a case, the NXSoundStream's buffers should be no larger than the DMA buffer size times the DMA buffer count.

Since the changes that you make to the DMA transfer buffer size and count affect the sound driver device, any application that's recording or playing sound will inherit the new settings. However, the buffer attributes for a particular device are reset to their defaults when the last active stream that's connected to that device is closed. Because of this, you should always connect an NXSoundStream to your NXSoundDevice and open the stream (through NXSoundStream's **activate** method) before sending **setBufferCount:** or **setBufferSize:** to the NXSoundDevice.

Furthermore, just as your buffer settings affect other applications, so, too, do the other application's settings affect yours. The only way you can be absolutely sure that your buffer settings will stick is to reserve the sound device.

Peak Detection

You can set an NXSoundDevice to detect the peaks, or maximum absolute amplitudes, witnessed over some number of transfer buffers. To enable this feature, you must send the NXSoundDevice a **detectPeaks:**YES message. The **setPeakHistory:** method then lets you set the number of buffer that you wish to examine. The actual number of samples (or sample frames) that are looked at depends on the sampling rate of the hardware device.

While sound is streaming through the device, you can retrieve the most recent peak amplitudes (in stereo) through the **getPeakLeft:right:** method. The peak values returned by the method are normalized to fall within (0.0, 1.0), where 0.0 is no amplitude and 1.0 is the maximum amplitude supported by the data format. Old peak data is thrown away as the most recent peaks are detected—if you want an on-going and thorough chart of the peaks, you must query for this data promptly and consistently while sound is recording or playing. Typically, you set up a timed entry to invoke **getPeakLeft:right:** at a frequency that matches the rate at which the peaks are detected.

The NXSoundDevice itself doesn't perform the peak detection—it's done by the underlying device. This has a particular significance for sound-out: The data that's returned by **getPeakLeft:right:** is the peak amplitude of all sounds that are being played, *not* just those NXPlayStreams that are connected to the queried NXSoundOut object.

Sound Driver Reply Messages

As it's processing a sound stream, the sound driver sends Mach messages to a reply port that's managed by the NXSoundDevice class object. Each message contains either a status report—whether a sound has started, completed, aborted, and so on—or, in the case of sound-in, a buffer of recorded sound data.

The NXSoundDevice class object interprets each of these driver messages and sends a corresponding Objective C message to the delegate of the appropriate NXSoundStream instance (as described in the class specifications of NXSoundStream, NXPlayStream, and NXRecordStream). For the delegate to be apprised as quickly as possible, you can create a separate thread in which the NXSoundDevice class object will receive messages from the driver. This is done by sending **setUseSeparateThread:YES** to the NXSoundDevice class object.

Although a separate thread increases responsiveness to the sound driver, it may degrade the synchronization between sound and graphics (for example). Also, if you're using a separate thread, your implementation of the delegate methods can't invoke methods or call functions that are non-reentrant or that cause code to be sent to the PostScript interpreter—in other words, they mustn't draw.

If the reply thread isn't separate, you can set the threshold that the Application Kit uses to determine whether to pay attention to driver messages. You specify this threshold with the **setThreadThreshold:** class method. Again, this setting affects all NXSoundDevice objects.

To have an effect, **setUseSeparateThread:** or **setThreadThreshold:** must be invoked *before* any NXSoundDevice objects are initialized.

Sound Device Timeout

The NXSoundDevice and NXSoundStream methods that communicate with the underlying driver do so by sending Mach messages to the driver. Such a method sends the Mach message and then waits for a reply from the driver—the method doesn't return, and your application hangs, until the driver responds. In general, if your application is running, then the sound driver should be running and so should respond. However, if your application is using the sound driver on a remote host, this assurance is less certain; for example, if the remote host is powered off, then your application will hang when a driver-accessing method is invoked.

You can specify the maximum amount of time to wait for the sound driver to respond through NXSoundDevice's **setTimeout:** class method. The method sets, in milliseconds, the time limit for all sound devices. If the sound driver doesn't respond to a Mach message within the given amount of time, the method that caused the message to be sent is forced to return with the error code NX_SoundDeviceErrorTimeout (the sound device error codes are listed in the section "Types and Constants" under the heading "NXSoundDeviceError").

Although you can set the time limit to an excruciatingly specific interval, it's perhaps better thought of as acting as a boolean that determines whether your application can hang forever or not: By default, the timeout is set to NX_SOUNDDEVICE_TIMEOUT_MAX, a number so large that driver-accessing methods will, essentially, never time out and so your application will hang if the sound driver is unresponsive. Setting it to a more reasonable amount of time, say ten seconds or so, will ensure that your application won't hang forever, while allowing enough time for even the sleepiest driver to wake up.

The Sound Kit methods that access the sound driver, and so are liable to the time limit, are those that return an NXSoundDeviceError value (except for NXSoundDriver's **lastError**), plus these additional methods:

Method	Class
isReserved	NXSoundDevice
bufferSize	NXSoundDevice
bufferCount	NXSoundDevice
pauseStreams:	NXSoundDevice
resumeStreams:	NXSoundDevice
abortStreams:	NXSoundDevice
clipCount	NXSoundOut
pause:	NXSoundStream
resume:	NXSoundStream
abort:	NXSoundStream
bytesProcessed	NXSoundStream

Sound Devices and the DSP

As noted above, the Sound Kit currently provides NXSoundIn and NXSoundOut subclasses of NXSoundDevice. Notable by its absence are classes that represent DSP input and output. To use the DSP to process sound—to convert CODEC or compressed sound, for example—you must use the sound driver functions, as described in the "Sound/DSP Driver Functions" section of this chapter. Note that the DSP isn't used for converting monophonic sounds to stereo, as long as the sound format is 16-bit linear and the sampling rate is 22.05 or 44.1 kHz.

Instance Variables

None declared in this class.

Method Types

Initializing and freeing an NXSoundDevice	
	– init – initOnHost: – free
Using a separate thread	+ replyThread + isUsingSeparateThread + setThreadThreshold: + setUseSeparateThread: + threadThreshold
Examining ports	– devicePort + replyPort – streamOwnerPort
Identifying the host computer	– host
Configuring the object	– bufferCount – bufferSize – isReserved – setBufferCount: – setBufferSize: – setReserved: + setTimeout: + timeout

Finding peak amplitudes	– getPeakLeft:right: – isDetectingPeaks – peakHistory – setDetectPeaks: – setPeakHistory:
Controlling streams	– abortStreams: – pauseStreams: – resumeStreams:
Handling errors	– lastError + textForError:

Class Methods

isUsingSeparateThread

+ (BOOL)**isUsingSeparateThread**

Returns YES if the NXSoundDevice is using a separate thread to process messages from the driver to the reply port; otherwise, returns NO.

See also: + **setUseSeparateThread:**

replyPort

+ (port_t)**replyPort**

Returns the port to which the sound driver sends reply messages. You can't set this port yourself, and you normally don't need to note its identity; this method is provided in case you want to pass the reply port as an argument to a function such as **port_status()**.

replyThread

+ (cthread_t)**replyThread**

Returns the thread in which messages from the sound driver are sent to the reply port. If the NXSoundDriver isn't using a separate thread for these messages, this returns NO_CTHREAD. The **cthread_t** type is defined in **mach/cthreads.h**.

See also: + **setUseSeparateThread:**

setThreadThreshold:

+ **setThreadThreshold:**(int)*threshold*

Sets the threshold against which the application's current threshold is compared as messages arrive from the driver. If *threshold* is higher than the current threshold, the message is delivered to the reply port (and so a message is sent to the delegate of the appropriate NXSoundStream), otherwise the message is ignored. By default, *threshold* is NX_MODALRESPTHRESHOLD, as defined in **appkit/Application.h**. If the NXSoundDevice is using a separate thread to receive driver messages, this method has no effect (all messages are received in this case).

This method does nothing and returns **nil** if your application contains any initialized NXSoundDevice objects. Otherwise it returns **self**.

See also: + **threadThreshold,** + **isUsingSeparateThread:**

setTimeout:

+ **setTimeout:**(unsigned int)*milliseconds*

Sets the length of time, in milliseconds, that all sound devices will wait for a method that communicates with the sound driver to return, as explained in the class description, above. Returns **self**.

See also: + **timeout**

setUseSeparateThread:

+ **setUseSeparateThread:**(BOOL)*flag*

If *flag* is YES, the NXSoundDevice class object will use a separate thread for processing messages from the sound driver. The NXSoundDevice class object interprets these Mach messages and sends corresponding Objective-C messages to the delegate of the appropriate NXSoundStream instance. If *flag* is NO, the sound driver messages are processed in the application's main thread.

This method does nothing and returns **nil** if your application contains any initialized NXSoundDevice objects. Otherwise it returns **self**.

See also: + **isUsingSeparateThread**

textForError:

+ (const char *)**textForError:**(NXSoundDeviceError)*errorCode*

Returns a localized string that corresponds to *errorCode*. The sound device error codes are listed in the "Constants and Types" section.

See also: – **lastError**

threadThreshold

+ (int)**threadThreshold**

Returns the threshold that's used to determine whether messages from the sound driver are ignored. The default is NX_MODALRESPTHRESHOLD, as defined in **appkit/Application.h**.

See also: + **setThreadThreshold:**

timeout

+ (unsigned int)**timeout**

Returns the amount of time, in milliseconds, that driver-accessing methods are allowed to hang before being forced to return, as explained in the class description, above. The default is NX_SOUNDDEVICE_TIMEOUT_MAX (essentially forever).

See also: + **setTimeout:**

Instance Methods

abortStreams:

– **abortStreams:***sender*

Aborts all streams that are connected to the NXSoundDevice. You should check the return value of **lastError** after invoking this method to see if an error occurred. Returns **self**.

See also: – **abort:** (NXSoundStream), – **lastError**

bufferCount

– (unsigned int)**bufferCount**

Returns the number of DMA transfer buffers for the sound device. The default is 4 for both sound-in and sound-out. You should check the return value of **lastError** after invoking this method to see if an error occurred while querying the sound driver.

See also: – **setBufferCount:**, – **lastError**

bufferSize

– (unsigned int)**bufferSize**

Returns the size in bytes of each DMA transfer buffer. The default for sound-in is 256 bytes; for sound-out it's a page of virtual memory, as given by the global variable **vm_page_size**. You should check the return value of **lastError** after invoking this method to see if an error occurred while querying the sound driver.

See also: – **setBufferSize:**, – **lastError**

devicePort

– (port_t)**devicePort**

Returns the port that the NXSoundDevice uses to communicate with the sound driver. You can't set this port yourself, and you normally don't need to note its identity; this method is provided in case you want to pass the port as an argument to a function such as **port_status()**.

Warning: This port isn't understood by the old Sound/DSP driver; it shouldn't be used as an argument to the sound driver functions.

free

– **free**

Deallocates the NXSoundDevice's ports and frees the object. If the NXSoundDevice had reserved the underlying sound device, it's made available again.

See also: – **setReserved:**

getPeakLeft:right:

– (NXSoundDeviceError)**getPeakLeft:**(float *)*leftAmp* **right:**(float *)*rightAmp*

Returns the most recent peak amplitudes detected by the NXSoundDevice's underlying sound device. For stereo sounds, peaks are detected independently for the two channels and returned by reference in *leftAmp* and *rightAmp*. For monophonic sounds, the same value is returned in both arguments. The peak values returned in the arguments are normalized to fall within (0.0, 1.0), where 0.0 is no amplitude and 1.0 is the maximum amplitude supported by the data format. See the class description for more information on peak detection. An error code is returned.

See also: – **setPeakHistory:**, – **setDetectPeaks:**, – **isDetectingPeaks,**
– **clipCount** (NXSoundOut)

host

– (const char *)**host**

Returns the name of the computer on which the NXSoundDevice was initialized, or **nil** if it's the local host.

See also: – **initOnHost:**

init

– **init**

Initializes the NXSoundDevice on the machine specified by the NXHost default (normally the local host). Returns **nil** if the sound resources cannot be accessed; otherwise returns **self**.

See also: – **initOnHost:**

initOnHost:

– **initOnHost:**(const char *)*hostName*

Initializes the NXSoundDevice on the machine named *hostName*. Returns **nil** if the sound resources cannot be accessed; otherwise returns **self**.

See also: – **init**

isDetectingPeaks

– (BOOL)**isDetectingPeaks**

Returns YES if the device is detecting peak amplitudes; otherwise, returns NO (the default). See the class description for more information.

See also: – **setDetectPeaks:**

isReserved

– (BOOL)**isReserved**

Returns YES if the device is reserved for exclusive access by this NXSoundDevice; otherwise, returns NO (the default).

See also: – **setReserved:**

lastError

– (NXSoundDeviceError)**lastError**

Returns the most recent sound device error associated with the NXSoundDevice. Many methods don't explicitly return an NXSoundDeviceError, but set an internal variable, which can be retrieved with this method. To retrieve localized text that describes the error, pass the value returned by this method to the **textForError:** class method.

See also: + **textForError:**

pauseStreams:

– **pauseStreams:***sender*

Pauses all streams that are connected to the NXSoundDevice. You should check the return value of **lastError** after invoking this method to see if an error occurred. Returns **self**.

See also: – **pause:** (NXSoundStream), – **lastError**

peakHistory

– (unsigned int)**peakHistory**

Returns the peak history—the number of DMA transfer buffers that the driver examines when detecting peak amplitudes on the device. You should check the return value of **lastError** after invoking this method to see if an error occurred. See the class description for more information on peak detection.

See also: – **setPeakHistory:**, – **lastError**

resumeStreams:

– **resumeStreams:***sender*

Resumes all streams that are connected to the NXSoundDevice. You should check the return value of **lastError** after invoking this method to see if an error occurred. Returns **self**.

See also: – **resume:** (NXSoundStream), – **lastError**

setBufferCount:

– (NXSoundDeviceError)**setBufferCount:**(unsigned int)*count*

Sets the number of DMA transfer buffers for the underlying device to *count*. The default, for both sound-in and sound-out, is 4. Setting the buffer count affects all applications that are currently using the sound driver. See the class description, above, for more on sound buffers. An error code is returned.

See also: – **bufferCount**, – **setBuffersize:**

setBufferSize:

– (NXSoundDeviceError)**setBufferSize:**(unsigned int)*bytes*

Sets the size in bytes of each DMA transfer buffer to *bytes*. The maximum permissible value is the size of a page of virtual memory as given by the global variable **vm_page_size**. The default for sound-in is 256 bytes; for sound-out it's a page of virtual memory. Setting the buffer count affects all applications that are currently using the sound driver. See the class description, above, for more on sound buffers. An error code is returned.

See also: – **bufferSize**, – **setBufferCount:**

setDetectPeaks:

– (NXSoundDeviceError)**setDetectPeaks:**(BOOL)*flag*

Establishes whether the driver detects peak amplitudes on the device. The default is NO. See the class description for more information on peak detection.

See also: – **isDetectingPeaks**, – **setPeakHistory:**, – **getPeakLeft:right:**

setPeakHistory:

– (NXSoundDeviceError)**setPeakHistory:**(unsigned int)*bufferCount*

Sets how many transfer buffers the driver examines when determining the peak amplitude. An error code is returned. See the class description for more information on peak detection.

See also: – **peakHistory**, – **setDetectPeaks:**

setReserved:

– (NXSoundDeviceError)**setReserved:**(BOOL)*flag*

If flag is YES, reserves the underlying device for exclusive access by the NXSoundDevice (even if it's currently reserved by another NXSoundDevice—the current owner is forced to yield). No other application, nor any other NXSoundDevice within your application, will be able access the device while it's reserved. Any currently active streams not connected to this NXSoundDevice instance are aborted. If flag is NO the device is made available to all NXSoundDevices. NXSoundDevices are unreserved by default. An error code is returned.

See also: – **isReserved**,
– **soundStreamDidAbort:deviceReserved:** (NXSoundStream delegate)

streamOwnerPort

– (port_t)**streamOwnerPort**

Returns the port that the NXSoundDevice uses to connect to the sound driver. You can't set this port yourself, and you normally don't need to note its identity; this method is provided in case you want to pass the port as an argument to a function such as **port_status()**.

Warning: This port isn't understood by the old Sound/DSP driver; it shouldn't be used as an argument to the sound driver functions.

NXSoundIn

Inherits From: NXSoundDevice : Object

Declared In: soundkit/NXSoundIn.h

Class Description

NXSoundIn represents the sound-in device of a sound driver on a particular host. All its functionality is provided by its superclass, NXSoundDevice; NXSoundIn's only method, **lookUpDevicePortOnHost:**, is provided primarily to be invoked by NXSoundDevice's **init** methods. See the NXSoundDevice class for a detailed description of classes that represent sound driver devices.

The sound sent to an NXSoundIn object follows the usual rules of microphonology on a NeXT computer: An external microphone plugged into the microphone jack takes precedence over (turns off) the built-in microphone (found on the front of the MegaPixel Display on monochrome systems and in the Sound Box on color systems).

Instance Variables

None declared in this class.

Class Methods

lookUpDevicePortOnHost:

+ (port_t)**lookUpDevicePortOnHost:**(const char *)*hostName*

Returns the sound driver device port for sound-in on the computer named *hostName*. You can't set this port yourself, and you normally don't need to note its identity; this method is provided primarily to satisfy a requirement set forth by the superclass. However, you can use it to pass the device port as an argument to a function such as **port_status()**.

NXSoundOut

Inherits From: NXSoundDevice : Object

Declared In: soundkit/NXSoundOut.h

Class Description

NXSoundOut represents the sound-out device of a sound driver on a particular host. Its superclass, NXSoundDevice, provides most of its functionality; the methods added by NXSoundOut allow you to retrieve and modify the settings specific to the sound-out hardware, as described in the following sections. See the NXSoundDevice class for a detailed description of classes that represent sound driver devices.

To use an NXSoundOut to play sound, you must connect an NXPlayStream object to it. The NXPlayStream is responsible for supplying the NXSoundOut with buffers filled with sound data, as explained in the NXPlayStream class description.

None of the sound-out attributes described below have default settings. An application shouldn't expect any of them to be in a particular state when it plays a sound.

In addition, although the attribute-setting methods are instance methods, you shouldn't take this to mean that they set the attributes independently for each NXSoundOut object. There's only one setting for each attribute per sound-out device, thus it's possible for another NXSoundOut—possibly in another application—to reset the sound-out attributes that a particular NXSoundOut has set. The reason that these are instance methods is because you can create NXSoundOut objects on different hosts, and each host will have its own sound-out device. To guarantee that your settings will hold on a particular host, you must reserve the sound-out device on that host.

Note: You don't need to create an NXSoundOut object to set these attributes; they can also be set through Sound object methods and sound C functions.

Format Conversion

The digital-to-analog converter (DAC; the device that turns sound data into a sound signal that can be broadcast on a speaker) assumes that all data that it receives is two channels of 16-bit linear stereo data sampled at 44.1 kHz. The data that you supply is automatically converted from mono to stereo and 22.05 kHz to 44.1 kHz. Sounds that use quantization formats other than 16-bit linear, or sampling rates other than 22.05 kHz or 44.1 kHz must be converted programmatically before they're sent to an NXSoundOut object.

Mono to stereo conversion is straight-forward: The single channel of data is duplicated to create two channels.

Sampling-rate conversion is more complicated; it admits three schemes:

- If streams of 22.05 kHz data (only) are being played, then the conversion takes place in the sound hardware. The stream is "up-sampled"— a sample frame is inserted between each existing sample frame. The inserted sample frame contains either zeros, or it's a copy of the previous (in other words, the existing) sample frame. You can set your preference through the **setInsertsZeros:** method.
- If you're playing a 44.1 kHz stream and then add a 22.05 kHz stream while the first stream is still playing, the conversion of the added stream is performed by the sound driver (in software); the manner in which the conversion is done is also controlled by the **setInsertsZeros:** method.
- The situation to beware of, if you're concerned with absolute fidelity, is when you're playing a 22.05 kHz stream and then add a 44.1 kHz stream. In this case, the conversion is, once again, performed in hardware. However, the sound hardware accepts only a single stream of data—this means that the 44.1 kHz must be converted to 22.05 kHz and mixed with the first stream (as described below) so the whole thing can then be up-sampled by the hardware. The 44.1 kHz stream is "drop-sampled" by the sound driver: Every other sample is dropped to produce a 22.05 kHz stream.

Stream Mixing

The sound driver mixes the data from all sound output streams that are being played simultaneously. This extends to all applications: The sounds that you're playing may be mixed with sounds from other applications. The number of sounds that can be mixed varies; in general, four sounds at the 44.1 kHz and about twice that at the lower sampling rate can be played simultaneously on a lightly loaded system. You can prevent other applications from mixing in with your playback by reserving the sound-out device, through NXSoundOut's **setReserved:** method (inherited from NXSoundDevice).

Note: Only one of the simultaneously playing sounds can be coming from the DSP.

The sound driver mixes sound streams by blithely adding a sample from each into a single stream that's issued to the sound hardware in DMA transfer buffers (these buffers are described in the NXSoundDevice class description). The driver doesn't try to prevent clipping by, for example, scaling the samples as it adds them. You can scale an individual sound stream (in other words, before it's mixed) through NXPlayStream's **setGainLeft:right:** method.

Ramping

Before passing to the DAC, an extra DMA buffer is attached to the beginning and end of the mixed sound data, if you so request through the **setRampsUp:** and **setRampsDown:** methods. The extra buffer at the beginning is filled with samples to create a linear ramp up from zero amplitude to the value of the first sample in the stream; at the end it creates a ramp down to zero from the last sample. This helps eliminate the clicks that often accompany the beginnings and ends of sounds.

Ramping is performed on the single, mixed sound stream that's sent to the sound hardware; it's not done to individual streams that contribute to the mix. For example, if you initiate one long sound stream and then initiate a short one that ends before the first one is finished, this second, shorter sound won't be ramped, but the beginning and end of the first one will be (assuming that ramping is turned on).

The De-emphasis Filter

The converted, mixed, and ramped sound data is then sent to the DAC. After passing through the DAC, sounds that were recorded with an emphasis filter should be passed through the de-emphasis filter. The de-emphasis filter can be turned on and off through the **setDeemphasis:** method. (The Sound object and sound playback functions automatically turn this filter on when playing sound that have a format SND_FORMAT_EMPHASIZED.) The filter state can also be changed by the user, by pressing the upper volume key on the keyboard while holding down the Command key.

Attenuation and Muting

The (possibly) de-emphasized analog signal then travels to the line-out jacks and to an internal stereo attenuation control. You can set the attenuation level through the **setAttenuationLeft:right:** method. Attenuation is controlled by the user through the familiar volume keys on the keyboard.

After attenuation, the signal is sent to the headphone jacks and to a mute switch that controls the broadcast of the built-in speaker. You can toggle the speaker mute through the **setSpeakerMute:** method.

Error Codes

Many of the methods described here return error codes that declare success or describe failure. A catalog of these error codes can be found in the section "Types and Constants" under the heading "NXSoundDeviceError."

Instance Variables

None declared in this class.

Method Types

Setting attributes for sound output	
	– setAttenuationLeft:right:
	– setDeemphasis:
	– setInsertsZeros:
	– setRampsDown:
	– setRampsUp:
	– setSpeakerMute:
Querying sound output settings	– doesDeemphasize
	– doesInsertZeros
	– doesRampDown
	– doesRampUp
	– getAttenuationLeft:right:
	– isSpeakerMute
	– clipCount
Looking up the device port	+ lookUpDevicePortOnHost:

Class Methods

lookUpDevicePortOnHost:

+ (port_t)**lookUpDevicePortOnHost:**(const char *)*hostName*

Returns the sound driver device port for sound-out on the computer named *hostName*. You can't set this port yourself, and you normally don't need to note its identity; this method is provided primarily to satisfy a requirement set forth by the superclass. However, you can use it to pass the device port as an argument to a function such as **port_status()**.

Instance Methods

clipCount

– (unsigned int)**clipCount**

Returns the number of sample frames that were clipped since the activation of the oldest connected stream (of all streams connected to sound-out, *not* just to this NXSoundOut instance). Clipping occurs when the amplitude of a sample is too great to be represented by a 16-bit signed integer. The clip count is reset to 0 when the last stream is deactivated.

See also: – **getPeakLeft:right:** (NXSoundDevice)

doesDeemphasize

– (BOOL)**doesDeemphasize**

Returns YES if the de-emphasis filter is turned on; otherwise, returns NO.

See also: – **setDeemphasis:**

doesInsertZeros

– (BOOL)**doesInsertZeros**

Returns YES if the sound driver or the sound hardware inserts zeros when it converts 22.05 kHz sound to 44.1 kHz, as explained in the class description, above. Otherwise, returns NO.

See also: – **setInsertsZeros:**

doesRampDown

– (BOOL)**doesRampDown**

Returns YES if the end of a sound stream is ramped down to 0 amplitude, as explained in the class description; otherwise, returns NO.

See also: – **setRampsDown:**

doesRampUp

– (BOOL)**doesRampUp**

Returns YES if the beginning of a sound stream is ramped up from 0 amplitude, as explained in the class description, above; otherwise, returns NO.

See also: – **setRampsDown:**

getAttenuationLeft:right:

– (NXSoundDeviceError)**getAttenuationLeft:**(float *)*leftDB*
right:(float *)*rightDB*

Returns, by reference in the arguments, the attenuation settings of the left and right channels. The range is –84.0 decibels (inaudible) to 0.0 decibels (no attenuation). An error code is returned.

See also: – **setAttenuationLeft:right:**

isSpeakerMute

– (BOOL)**isSpeakerMute**

Returns YES if the internal speaker is muted; otherwise, returns NO.

See also: – **setSpeakerMute:**

setAttenuationLeft:right:

– (NXSoundDeviceError)**setAttenuationLeft:**(float)*leftDB* **right:**(float)*rightDB*

Sets the attenuation level for playback. Attenuation affects the internal speaker and the headphone output, but not the line output. The two channels of the stereo signal are set independent of each other, specified as the values of *leftDB* and *rightDB*. The volume of the internal speaker is the sum of these two values. The arguments should be between –84.0 decibels (inaudible) and 0.0 decibels(no attenuation). The resolution of the attenuation control is currently two decibels. (For finer resolution, adjust the gain of the NXPlayStream, if appropriate.)

The playback attenuation is also adjustable by pressing the volume keys on the keyboard. Each discrete tap on a volume key increments or decrements both the left and the right volume settings by two decibels.

An error code is returned.

See also: – **getAttenuationLeft:right:**, + **setVolume::** (Sound), – **setGain::** (NXPlayStream)

setDeemphasis:

– (NXSoundDeviceError)**setDeemphasis:**(BOOL)*flag*

Sets the state of the de-emphasis filter: YES turns the filter on and NO turns it off. The de-emphasis filter is intended to be used on sounds that were subjected to an emphasis filter during recording.

The filter state can also be changed by toggling the upper volume key on the keyboard while holding down the Command key. The Sound class and sound functions turn the filter on automatically while playing emphasized sounds (format SND_FORMAT_EMPHASIZED). Returns an error code.

See also: – **doesDeemphasize**, **SNDSetFilter()**

setInsertsZeros:

– (NXSoundDeviceError)**setInsertsZeros:**(BOOL)*flag*

Sets the way in which the driver converts a 22.05-kHz sound stream to 44.1 kHz, as explained in the class description, above. For most sounds, sample replication, attained by sending **setInsertsZeros:NO**, is preferable. You should note that CODEC sounds are converted to 22.05 kHz (by the DSP) before being passed to the sound driver and so are affected by this method. Returns an error code.

See also: – **doesInsertZeros**

setRampsDown:

– (NXSoundDeviceError)**setRampsDown:**(BOOL)*flag*

Sets whether the end of sounds are ramped, as explained in the class description. Returns an error code.

See also: – **doesRampDown**, – **setRampsUp**:

setRampsUp:

– (NXSoundDeviceError)**setRampsUp:**(BOOL)*flag*

Sets whether the beginning of sounds are ramped, as explained in the class description. Returns an error code.

See also: – **doesRampDown**, – **setRampsUp**:

setSpeakerMute:

– (NXSoundDeviceError)**setSpeakerMute:**(BOOL)*flag*

If *flag* is YES, the internal speaker is turned off. This doesn't affect the signal to the headphone jack or the line output jacks. If *flag* is NO, the speaker is turned backed on. Returns an error code.

See also: – **isSpeakerMute**

NXSoundStream

Inherits From: Object

Declared In: soundkit/NXSoundStream.h

Class Description

NXSoundDevice is an abstract superclass; each subclass represents a single stream of sound samples. Currently, the Sound Kit provides two subclasses of NXSoundStream:

- NXRecordStream represents sound recorded through the microphone jack.
- NXPlayStream represents sound that's sent to sound output (the speaker, line-out jacks, and headphone jack).

The utility of NXSoundStream is invested in these subclasses; the NXSoundStream class itself simply defines methods that are common to them. In addition, you can't create useful subclasses of NXSoundStream yourself.

Many applications needn't bother with NXSoundStream and its subclasses; in general, the methods provided by the Sound class suffice for applications that record and playback sounds. However, while Sound objects are easy to use, you can only record or play one sound at a time. The primary advantage of using NXSoundStream objects is that they let you record and playback multiple simultaneous sounds.

Streams and Devices

To be of use, an NXSoundStream object must connect it to an instance of an NXSoundDevice subclass: For recording you connect an NXRecordStream to an instance of NXSoundIn, and for playback you connect NXPlayStreams to NXSoundOuts. The connection is formed as the NXSoundStream is initialized, through the **initOnDevice:** method.

Any number of NXSoundStream objects can be connected to the same NXSoundDevice. For recording, this creates multiple copies of the same data—one copy for each NXRecordStream. These copies can even be spread across applications: All NXRecordStreams that are actively listening to the NXSoundIn device will receive the data that's being recorded, regardless of the application that they're in. Similarly, by connecting more than one NXPlayStream to an NXSoundOut object, you can mix several sounds during playback, possibly from different applications. See the NXSoundIn and NXSoundOut classes for more on simultaneous recording and playback.

Using a Sound Stream

Having connected an NXSoundStream to an NXSoundDevice, you must tell the sound driver that you want the NXSoundStream to be involved in a recording or playback. This is done through the **activate** method. Activating an NXSoundStream uses valuable sound driver resources, thus it's best to activate the object just before you want to record or play a sound and deactivate it (through the **deactivate** method) soon after you've finished.

Activating an NXSoundStream doesn't cause it to instantly start recording or playing. For this, you must enqueue sound buffers with the sound device: For recording you enqueue empty buffers that are filled with data and delivered back to your application, for playback you enqueue buffers filled with the data that you want to play. These tasks are performed through methods defined by the respective subclasses. The thing to keep in mind is that you must deliver these buffers constantly and steadily while the stream is running. This is the essential programming difference between using a Sound object and a NXSoundStream: A Sound object can be "turned on" and then ignored; an NXSoundStream demands constant attention. You can ameliorate this by supplying the NXSoundStream with large buffers, although this affords less dynamic control over the data in the stream.

Important: An NXSoundStream's sound data buffers aren't the same as an NXSoundDevice's DMA transfer buffers. The former can be arbitrarily large; the latter is restricted to a page of virtual memory.

As an NXSoundStream delivers sound buffers to the sound driver, the sound driver sends back Mach messages to the NXSoundDevice class, messages that report on a device's status and, for recording, deliver freshly recorded data. The NXSoundDevice class forwards this information to the delegate of the appropriate NXSoundStream. The delegate methods defined by the NXSoundStream class mark general watershed moments in a stream's career: when it starts, ends, pauses, and resumes. NXRecordStream and NXPlayStream augment this collection with record- and playback-specific notification methods.

Sound Stream Errors

Most of NXSoundStream's methods communicate with the sound driver; many of these return NXSoundDeviceError error codes, which enumerate the situations that can thwart this communication. The NXSoundDeviceError codes are listed in NXSoundDevice class specification. NXSoundDevice's **textForError:** method translates these error codes into localized strings that you can display in your application.

Other methods, such as **pause:** and **resume:**, also communicate with the sound driver, but don't return NXSoundDeviceError codes. However, such methods are susceptible to driver-communication errors and maintain a private variable to note their occurences. You should follow these methods (which are listed in NXSoundDevice and noted in the descriptions below) with invocation of **lastError**, a method that returns the last NXSoundDeviceError code that was provoked.

Instance Variables

id **delegate**;

delegate	The receiver of notification messages.

Method Types

Initializing and freeing an NXSoundStream object	
	– init – initOnDevice: – free
Setting the device	– setDevice: – device
Activating and Deactivating	– activate – deactivate
Controlling the stream	– abort: – abortAtTime: – pause: – pauseAtTime: – resume: – resumeAtTime:
Querying the object	– bytesProcessed – isActive – isPaused – streamPort – lastError
Assigning a delegate	– setDelegate: – delegate

Instance Methods

abort:

– **abort:***sender*

Stops the NXSoundStream's playback or recording (after the current DMA transfer buffer has been processed), removes its remaining enqueued buffers, and sends the object's delegate a **soundStreamDidAbort:deviceReserved:** message. The argument is ignored—it's included so the method can be used in Interface Builder as an action method. You should follow this method with an invocation of **lastError** to see if an error occured. If the NXSoundStream isn't currently active, this does nothing. Returns **self**.

See also: – **abortAtTime:**

abortAtTime:

– (NXSoundDeviceError)**abortAtTime:**(NXSoundStreamTime *)*time*

Schedules the NXSoundStream to be aborted (as described in the **abort**: method, above) at the time specified in the structure *time*. The NXSoundStreamTime structure is a cover for the familiar **timeval** structure:

```
struct timeval {
     long tv_sec;    /* seconds */
     long tv_usec;   /* microseconds */
};
```

The value given by *time* is absolute; to abort a stream after a given number of seconds have elapsed, you need to know the present time. This can be retrieved through system calls such as **gettimeofday()**. For example:

```
/* Abort a stream in 2.5 seconds. */
NXSoundStreamTime time;
gettimeofday(&time, NULL);
time.tv_sec += 2;
time.tv_usec += 500;
[aStream abortAtTime:&time];
```

This method returns immediately—it doesn't wait for the stream to abort. A **soundStreamDidAbort:deviceReserved:** message is sent to the NXSoundStream's delegate when the abortion is performed.

You should follow this method with an invocation of **lastError** to see if an error occured. If the NXSoundStream isn't active when this method is invoked or when the specified time is met, this does nothing. If the specified time is in the past, the object is aborted immediately. Returns **self**.

See also: – **abort:**

activate

– (NXSoundDeviceError)**activate**

Adds the NXSoundStream to the sound driver's list of active streams. You must invoke this method before you enqueue buffers on the stream. When you've finished recording or playing, you should send the NXSoundStream a **deactivate:** message. The NXSoundStream must be connected to an NXSoundDevice for this method to have an effect. An error code is returned.

See also: – **deactivate**, – **isActive**

bytesProcessed

– (unsigned int)**bytesProcessed**

Returns the number of bytes of sound that the NXSoundStream has recorded or played since it was most recently activated. Returns 0 if the object is inactive, or if an error occurs. You should follow this method with an invocation of **lastError** to see if an error occured.

deactivate

– (NXSoundDeviceError)**deactivate**

Aborts the NXSoundStream's current activity and removes the object from the sound driver's list of active streams.

See also: – **activate**, – **isActive**

delegate

– **delegate**

Returns the NXSoundStream's delegate.

See also: – **setDelegate:**

device

– **device**

Returns the NXSoundDevice object that the NXSoundStream is connected to.

See also: – **initOnDevice:**, – **setDevice:**

free

– **free**

Deactivates and frees the NXSoundStream.

init

– **init**

Initializes the NXSoundStream without connecting it to an NXSoundDevice. Returns **self**.

See also: – **initOnDevice:**, – **setDevice:**

initOnDevice:

– **initOnDevice:***aDevice*

Initializes the NXSoundStream and connects it to *aDevice*, which should be an instance of an NXSoundDevice subclass. This is the designated initializer for the NXSoundStream class. Returns **self**.

See also: – **init**

isActive

– (BOOL)**isActive**

Returns YES if the NXSoundStream is currently activate; otherwise, NO.

See also: – **activate**

isPaused

– (BOOL)**isPaused**

Returns YES if the NXSoundStream is currently paused; otherwise, NO.

See also: – **pause:**, – **isActive**

lastError

– (NXSoundDeviceError)**lastError**

Returns the most recent sound device error associated with the NXSoundSound. Many methods don't explicitly return an NXSoundDeviceError, but set an internal variable, which can be retrieved with this method. To retrieve localized text that describes the error, pass the value returned by this method to the **textForError:** NXSoundDevice class method.

See also: + **textForError:** (NXSoundDevice)

pause:

– **pause:***sender*

Pauses the NXSoundStream's recording or playback (after the current DMA transfer buffer has been processed) and sends a **soundStreamDidPause:** message to the object's delegate. The argument is ignored—it's included so the method can be used in Interface Builder as an action method. You should follow this method with an invocation of **lastError** to see if an error occured. If the NXSoundStream isn't currently active or if it's already paused, this does nothing. Returns **self**.

See also: – **pauseAtTime:**, – **resume:**

pauseAtTime:

– (NXSoundDeviceError)**pauseAtTime:**(NXSoundStreamTime *)*time*

Schedules the NXSoundStream to be paused (as described in the **pause:** method, above) at the time specified in the structure *time*. See the **abortAtTime:** method for an explanation of the NXSoundStreamTime type. This method returns immediately—it doesn't wait for the stream to pause. A **soundStreamDidPause:** message is sent to the NXSoundStream's delegate at the time that the stream is paused. This does nothing if the NXSoundStream isn't currently active. An error code is returned.

See also: – **pause:**, – **abortAtTime:**

resume:

– **resume:***sender*

Resumes the NXSoundStream's recording or playback (after the current DMA transfer buffer has been processed) and sends a **soundStreamDidResume:** message to the object's delegate. The argument is ignored—it's included so the method can be used in Interface Builder as an action method. You should follow this method with an invocation of **lastError** to see if an error occured. If the NXSoundStream isn't currently active or if it isn't paused, this does nothing. Returns **self**.

See also: – **resumeAtTime:**, – **pause:**

resumeAtTime:

– (NXSoundDeviceError)**resumeAtTime:**(NXSoundStreamTime *)*time*

Schedules the NXSoundStream to be resumed (as described in the **resume:** method, above) at the time specified in the structure *time*. See the **abortAtTime:** method for an explanation of the NXSoundStreamTime type. This method returns immediately—it doesn't wait for the stream to resume. A **soundStreamDidResume:** message is sent to the NXSoundStream's delegate at the time that the stream is resumed. This does nothing if the NXSoundStream isn't currently active. An error code is returned.

See also: – **pause:**, – **abortAtTime:**

setDelegate:

– **setDelegate:***anObject*

Assigns *anObject* as the NXSoundStream's delegate.

See also: – **delegate**

setDevice:

– (NXSoundDeviceError)**setDevice:***aDevice*

Connects the NXSoundStream to *aDevice*, which should be an instance of an NXSoundDevice subclass. If the NXSoundStream is currently active, it immediately starts transferring sound to or from the new device. An error code is returned.

See also: – **initOnDevice:**, – **device**

streamPort

– (port_t)**streamPort**

Returns the port that the NXSoundStream uses to connect to the sound driver. You can't set this port yourself, and you normally don't need to note its identity; this method is provided in case you want to pass the port as an argument to a function such as **port_status()**. (Note that this device port isn't understood by the old Sound/DSP driver, and thus shouldn't be used as an argument to the sound driver functions.)

Methods Implemented By The Delegate

soundStream:didCompleteBuffer:

– **soundStream:***sender* **didCompleteBuffer:**(int)*tag*

Invoked when the driver finishes playing or recording the sound buffer identified by *tag* (as assigned when the buffer was enqueued). The return value is ignored.

See also: – **recordSize:tag:** (NXRecordStream), – **playBuffer:size:tag:channelCount:samplingRate:** (NXPlayStream)

soundStream:didStartBuffer:

– **soundStream:***sender* **didStartBuffer:**(int)*tag*

Invoked when the driver starts playing or recording the sound buffer identified by *tag* (as assigned when the buffer was enqueued). The return value is ignored.

See also: – **recordSize:tag:** (NXRecordStream), – **playBuffer:size:tag:channelCount:samplingRate:** (NXPlayStream)

soundStreamDidAbort:deviceReserved:

– **soundStreamDidAbort:***sender* **deviceReserved:**(BOOL)*flag*

Invoked when the driver aborts the stream. If the stream was aborted because the NXSoundDevice was reserved, *flag* will be YES, otherwise if will be NO. The return value is ignored.

See also: – **abort:**, – **abortAtTime:**, – **setReserved:** (NXSoundDevice)

soundStreamDidPause:

– **soundStreamDidPause:***sender*

Invoked when the NXSoundStream *sender* is paused. The return value is ignored.

See also: – **pause:**, – **pauseAtTime:**

soundStreamDidResume:

– **soundStreamDidResume:***sender*

Invoked when the NXSoundStream *sender* is resumed. The return value is ignored.

See also: – **resume:**, – **resumeAtTime:**

Sound

Inherits From: Object

Declared In: soundkit/Sound.h

Class Description

Sound objects represent and manage sounds. A Sound object's sound can be recorded from CODEC microphone input, read from a soundfile, NXBundle resource, retrieved from the pasteboard or from the sound segment in the application's executable file, or created algorithmically. The Sound class also provides an application-wide name table that lets you identify and locate sounds by name.

Playback and recording are performed by background threads, allowing your application to proceed in parallel. The latency between sending a **play:** or **record:** message and the start of the playback or recording, while within the tolerance demanded by most applications, can be further decreased by first reserving the sound facilities that you wish to use. This is done by calling the **SNDReserve**() C function.

To minimize data movement (and thus save time), an edited Sound may become fragmented; in other words, its sound data might become discontiguous in memory. While playback of a fragmented Sound object is transparent, it does incur some additional overhead. If you perform a number of edits you may want to return the Sound to its natural, contiguous state by sending it the **compactSamples** message before you play it. However, a large Sound may take a long time to compact, so a judicious and well-timed use of **compactSamples** is advised. Note that a fragmented Sound is automatically compacted before it's copied to a pasteboard (through the **writeToPasteboard:** method). Also, when you write a Sound to a soundfile, the data in the file is compact regardless of the state of the object.

A Sound object contains a SNDSoundStruct, the structure that describes and contains sound data and that's used as the soundfile format and the pasteboard sound type. Most of the methods defined in the Sound class are implemented so that you needn't be aware of this structure. However, if you wish to directly manipulate the sound data in a Sound object, you need to be familiar with the SNDSoundStruct architecture, as described in the **SNDAlloc**() function

Instance Variables

SNDSoundStruct ***soundStruct**;
int **soundStructSize**;
int **priority**;
id **delegate**;
int **status**;
char ***name**;

soundStruct	The object's sound data structure.
soundStructSize	The length of **soundStruct** in bytes.
priority	The object's recording and playback priority.
delegate	The target of notification messages.
status	What the object is currently doing.
name	The object's name.

Method Types

Creating and freeing a Sound object	
	+ addName:fromBundle:
	+ addName:fromSection:
	+ addName:fromSoundfile:
	– initFromSection:
	– initFromPasteboard:
	– initFromSoundfile:
	– free
Accessing the Sound name table	+ addName:sound:
	+ findSoundFor:
	+ removeSoundForName:
Accessing the Sound's name	– setName:
	– name
Reading and writing sound data	– readSoundfile:
	– readSoundFromStream:
	– writeSoundfile:
	– writeSoundToStream:
	– writeToPasteboard:

Modifying sound data	– convertToFormat:samplingRate:channelCount: – convertToFormat: – setDataSize:dataFormat:samplingRate: channelCount:infoSize: – setSoundStruct:soundStructSize: – setName: – name
Querying the object	– soundStruct – soundStructSize – data – dataFormat – dataSize – channelCount – samplingRate – sampleCount – duration – info – infoSize – isEmpty – compatibleWith: – processingError
Recording and playing	– pause – pause: – isPlayable – play – play: – record – record: – resume – resume: – stop – stop: – samplesProcessed – status – soundBeingProcessed – soundStructBeingProcessed

Editing sound data	– isEditable – copySamples:at:count: – copySound: – deleteSamples – deleteSamplesAt:count: – insertSamples:at: – needsCompacting – compactSamples
Archiving the object	– finishUnarchiving – read: – write:
Accessing the delegate	– setDelegate: – delegate – tellDelegate:
Accessing the sound hardware	+ getVolume:: + setVolume:: + isMuted + setMute:

Class Methods

addName:fromBundle:

+ **addName:**(const char *)*name* **fromBundle:**(NXBundle *)*aBundle*

Creates a Sound object from the sound resource named *name* in the NXBundle *aBundle*, assigns the name *name* to the object, and places the name on the sound name table. If *name* is already in use, or if the resource isn't found or can't be read, the Sound isn't created and **nil** is returned. Otherwise, the new Sound is returned.

addName:fromSection:

+ **addName:**(const char *)*name* **fromSection:**(const char *)*sectionName*

Creates a Sound object from section *sectionName* in the sound segment of the application's executable file, assigns the name *name* to the object, and places the name on the sound name table. If *name* is already in use, or if the section isn't found or its data can't be copied, the Sound isn't created and **nil** is returned. Otherwise, the new Sound is returned.

addName:fromSoundfile:

+ **addName:**(const char *)*name* **fromSoundfile:**(const char *)*filename*

Creates a Sound object from the soundfile *filename*, assigns the name *name* to the object, and adds it to the named Sound table. If *name* is already in use, or if *filename* isn't found or can't be read, the Sound isn't created and **nil** is returned. Otherwise, the new Sound is returned.

addName:sound:

+ **addName:**(const char *)*name* **sound:***aSound*

Assigns the name *name* to the Sound *aSound* and adds it to the named Sound table. Returns *aSound*, or **nil** if *name* is already in use.

findSoundFor:

+ **findSoundFor:**(const char *)*aName*

Finds and returns the named Sound object. First the named Sound table is searched; if the sound isn't found, then the method looks for "*aName*.snd" in the sound segment of the application's executable file. Finally, the file is searched for in the following directories (in order):

- ~/Library/Sounds
- /LocalLibrary/Sounds
- /NextLibrary/Sounds

where ~ represents the user's home directory. If the Sound eludes the search, **nil** is returned.

getVolume::

+ **getVolume:**(float *)*left* **:**(float *)*right*

Returns, by reference, the stereo output levels as floating-point numbers between 0.0 and 1.0.

isMuted

+ (BOOL)**isMuted**

Returns YES if the sound output level is currently muted.

removeSoundForName:

+ **removeSoundForName:**(const char *)*name*

Removes the named Sound from the named Sound table. If the Sound isn't found, returns **nil**; otherwise returns the Sound.

setMute:

+ **setMute:**(BOOL)*aFlag*

Mutes and unmutes the sound output level as *aFlag* is YES or NO, respectively. If successful, returns **self**; otherwise returns **nil**.

setVolume::

+ **setVolume:**(float)*left* **:**(float)*right*

Sets the stereo output levels. These affect the volume of the stereo signals sent to the built-in speaker and headphone jacks. *left* and *right* must be floating-point numbers between 0.0 (minimum) and 1.0 (maximum). If successful, returns **self**; otherwise returns **nil**.

Instance Methods

channelCount

– (int)**channelCount**

Returns the number of channels in the Sound.

compactSamples

– (int)**compactSamples**

The Sound's sampled data is compacted into a contiguous block, undoing the fragmentation that can occur during editing. If the Sound's data isn't fragmented (its format isn't SND_FORMAT_INDIRECT), then this method does nothing. Compacting a large sound can take a long time; keep in mind that when you copy a Sound to a pasteboard, the object is automatically compacted before it's copied. Also, the soundfile representation of a Sound contains contiguous data so there's no need to compact a Sound before writing it to a soundfile simply to ensure that the file representation will be compact. An error code is returned.

compatibleWith:

– (BOOL)**compatibleWith:***aSound*

Returns YES if the format, sampling rate, and channel count of *aSound*'s sound data is the same as that of the Sound receiving this message. If one (or both) of the Sounds doesn't contain a sound (its **soundStruct** is **nil**) then the objects are declared compatible and YES is returned.

convertToFormat:

– (int)**convertToFormat:**(int)*newFormat*

This is the same as **convertToFormat:samplingRate:channelCount:**, except that only the format is changed. An error code is returned.

convertToFormat:samplingRate:channelCount:

– (int)**convertToFormat:**(int)*newFormat*
  samplingRate:(double)*newRate*
  channelCount:(int)*newChannelCount*

Convert the Sound's data to the given format, sampling rate, and number of channels. The following conversions are possible:

- Arbitrary sampling rate conversion.
- Compression and decompression.
- Floating-point formats (including double-precision) to and from linear formats.
- Mono to stereo.
- CODEC mu-law to and from linear formats.

An error code is returned.

copySamples:at:count:

– (int)**copySamples:***aSound*
  at:(int)*startSample*
  count:(int)*sampleCount*

Replaces the Sound's sampled data with a copy of a portion of *aSound*'s data. The copied portion starts at *aSound*'s *startSample*'th sample (zero-based) and extends over *sampleCount* samples. The Sound receiving this message must be editable and the two Sounds must be compatible. If the specified portion of *aSound* is fragmented, the Sound receiving this message will also be fragmented. An error code is returned.

copySound:

– (int)**copySound:***aSound*

Replaces the Sound's data with a copy of *aSound*'s data. The Sound receiving this message needn't be editable, nor must the two Sounds be compatible. An error code is returned.

data

– (unsigned char *)**data**

Returns a pointer to the Sound's sampled data. You can use the pointer to examine, create, and modify the sound data. To intelligently manipulate the data, you need to be aware of its size, format, sampling rate, and the number of channels that it contains (a query method for each of these attributes is provided by the Sound class). The size of the data, in particular, must be respected; it's set when the Sound is created or given a new sound (through **readSoundfile:**, for example) and can't be changed directly. To resize the data, you should invoke one of the editing methods such as **insertSamples:at:** or **deleteSamplesAt:count:**. To start with a new, unfragmented sound with a determinate length, invoke the **setDataSize:dataFormat:samplingRate:channelCount:infoSize:** method. Keep in mind that the sound data in a fragmented sound is a pointer to a NULL-terminated list of pointers to SNDSoundStructs, one for each fragment. To examine or manipulate the samples in a fragmented sound, you must understand the SNDSoundStruct structure.

dataFormat

– (int)**dataFormat**

Returns the format of the Sound's data. If the data is fragmented, the format of the samples is returned (in other words, SND_FORMAT_INDIRECT is never returned by this method).

dataSize

– (int)**dataSize**

Return the size (in bytes) of the Sound's data. If you modify the data (through the pointer returned by the **data** method) you must be careful not to exceed its length. If the sound is fragmented, the value returned by this method is the size of the Sound's **soundStruct** and doesn't include the actual data itself.

delegate

– **delegate**

Returns the Sound's delegate.

deleteSamples

– (int)**deleteSamples**

Deletes all the samples in the Sound's data. The Sound must be editable. An error code is returned.

deleteSamplesAt:count:

– (int)**deleteSamplesAt:**(int)*startSample* **count:**(int)*sampleCount*

Deletes a range of samples from the Sound: *sampleCount* samples are deleted starting with the *startSample*'th sample (zero-based). The Sound must be editable and may become fragmented. An error code is returned.

duration

– (double)**duration**

Returns the Sound's length in seconds.

finishUnarchiving

– **finishUnarchiving**

You never invoke this method. It's invoked automatically by the **read:** method to tie up loose ends after unarchiving the Sound.

free

– **free**

Frees the Sound and deallocates its sound data. The Sound is removed from the named Sound table and its name made eligible for reuse.

info

– (char *)**info**

Returns a pointer to the Sound's info string.

infoSize

– (int)**infoSize**

Returns the size (in bytes) of the Sound's info string.

initFromPasteboard:

– **initFromPasteboard:**(Pasteboard *)*thePboard*

Initializes the Sound instance, which must be newly allocated, by copying the sound data from the Pasteboard object *thePboard*. (A Pasteboard can have only one sound entry at a time.) Returns **self** (an unnamed Sound) if *thePboard* currently contains a sound entry; otherwise, frees the newly allocated Sound and returns **nil**.

See also: + **alloc** (Object), + **allocFromZone:** (Object)

initFromSection:

– **initFromSection:**(const char *)*sectionName*

Initializes the Sound instance, which must be newly allocated, by copying the sound data from section *sectionName* of the sound segment of the application's executable file. If the section isn't found, the object looks for a soundfile named *sectionName* in the same directory as the application's executable. Returns **self** (an unnamed Sound) if the sound data was successfully copied; otherwise, frees the newly allocated Sound and returns **nil**.

See also: + **alloc** (Object), + **allocFromZone:** (Object)

initFromSoundfile:

– **initFromSoundfile:**(const char *)*filename*

Initializes the Sound instance, which must be newly allocated, from the soundfile *filename*. Returns **self** (an unnamed Sound) if the file was successfully read; otherwise, frees the newly allocated Sound and returns **nil**.

See also: + **alloc** (Object), + **allocFromZone:** (Object)

insertSamples:at:

– (int)**insertSamples:***aSound* **at:**(int)*startSample*

Pastes the sound data in *aSound* into the Sound receiving this message, starting at the receiving Sound's *startSample*'th sample (zero-based). The receiving Sound doesn't lose any of its original sound data—the samples greater than or equal to *startSample* are moved to accommodate the inserted sound data. The receiving Sound must be editable and the two Sounds must be compatible (as determined by **isCompatible:**). If the method is successful, the receiving Sound is fragmented. An error code is returned.

isEditable

– (BOOL)**isEditable**

Returns YES if the Sound's format indicates that it can be edited, otherwise returns NO.

isEmpty

– (BOOL)**isEmpty**

Returns YES if the Sound doesn't contain any sound data, otherwise returns NO. This always returns NO if the Sound isn't editable (as determined by sending it the **isEditable** message).

isPlayable

– (BOOL)**isPlayable**

Returns YES if the Sound can be played, otherwise returns NO. Some unplayable Sounds just need to be converted to another format, sampling rate, or number of channels; others are inherently unplayable, such as those whose format is SND_FORMAT_DISPLAY. To play a Sound that's just been recorded from the DSP, you must change its format from SND_FORMAT_DSP_DATA_16 to SND_FORMAT_LINEAR_16.

name

– (const char *)**name**

Returns the Sound's name.

needsCompacting

– (BOOL)**needsCompacting**

Returns YES if the Sound's data is fragmented. Otherwise returns NO.

pause

– (int)**pause**

Pauses the Sound during recording or playback. An error code is returned.

pause:

– **pause:***sender*

Action method that pauses the Sound. Other than the argument and the return type, this is the same as the **pause** method. Returns **self**.

play

– (int)**play**

Initiates playback of the Sound. The method returns immediately while the playback continues asynchronously in the background. The playback ends when the Sound receives the **stop** message, or when its data is exhausted.

When playback starts, **willPlay:** is sent to the Sound's delegate; when it stops, **didPlay:** is sent. An error code is returned.

Warning: For this method to work properly, the main event loop must not be blocked.

play:

– **play:***sender*

Action method that plays the Sound. Other than the argument and the return type, this is the same as the **play** method. Returns **self**.

processingError

– (int)**processingError**

Returns a constant that represents the last error that was generated. The sound error codes are listed in “Types and Constants.”

read:

– **read:**(NXTypedStream *)*stream*

Reads archived sound data from *stream* into the Sound. Returns **self**.

readSoundfile:

– (int)**readSoundfile:**(const char *)*filename*

Replaces the Sound’s contents with those of the soundfile *filename*. The Sound loses its current name, if any. An error code is returned.

readSoundFromStream:

– **readSoundFromStream:**(NXStream *)*stream*

Replaces the Sound’s contents with those of the sound in the NXStream *stream*. The Sound is given the name of the sound in the NXStream. If the sound in the NXStream is named, the Sound gets the new name. An error code is returned.

record

– (int)**record**

Initiate recording into the Sound. To record from the CODEC microphone, the Sound’s format, sampling rate, and channel count must be SND_FORMAT_MULAW_8, SND_RATE_CODEC, and 1, respectively. If this information isn’t set (if the Sound is a newly created object, for example), it defaults to accommodate a CODEC recording. If the Sound’s format is SND_FORMAT_DSP_DATA_16, the recording is from the DSP.

The method returns immediately while the recording continues asynchronously in the background. The recording stops when the Sound receives the **stop** message or when the recording has gone on for the duration of the original sound data. The default CODEC recording lasts precisely ten minutes if not stopped. To record for a longer time, first increase the size of the sound data with **setSoundStruct:soundStructSize:** or **setDataSize:dataFormat:samplingRate:channelCount:infoSize:**.

When the recording begins, **willRecord:** is sent to the Sound's delegate; when the recording stops, **didRecord:** is sent.

An error code is returned.

Warning: For this method to work properly, the main event loop must not be blocked.

record:

– **record:***sender*

Action method that initiates a recording. Other than the argument and return type, this is the same as the **record** method. Returns **self**.

resume

– (int)**resume**

Resumes the paused Sound's activity. An error code is returned.

resume:

– **resume:***sender*

Action method that resumes the paused Sound. Returns **self**.

sampleCount

– (int)**sampleCount**

Returns the number of sample frames, or channel count-independent samples, in the Sound.

samplesProcessed

– (int)**samplesProcessed**

If the Sound is currently playing or recording, this returns the number of sample frames that have been played or recorded so far. Otherwise, the number of sample frames in the Sound is returned. If the sample frame count can't be determined, –1 is returned.

samplingRate

– (double)**samplingRate**

Returns the Sound's sampling rate.

setDataSize:dataFormat:samplingRate:channelCount:infoSize:

– (int)**setDataSize:**(int)*newDataSize*
  dataFormat:(int)*newDataFormat*
  samplingRate:(double)*newSamplingRate*
  channelCount:(int)*newChannelCount*
  infoSize:(int)*newInfoSize*

Allocates new, unfragmented sound data for the Sound, as described by the arguments. The Sound's previous data is freed. This method is useful for setting a determinate data length prior to a recording or for creating a scratch pad for algorithmic sound creation. An error code is returned.

setDelegate:

– **setDelegate:***anObject*

Sets the Sound's delegate to *anObject*. The delegate may implement the following methods:

- willPlay:
- didPlay:
- willRecord:
- didRecord:
- hadError:

Returns **self**.

setName:

– **setName:**(const char *)*aName*

Sets the Sound's name to *aName*. If *aName* is already being used, then the Sound's name isn't set and **nil** is returned; otherwise returns **self**.

setSoundStruct:soundStructSize:

– **setSoundStruct:**(SNDSoundStruct *)*aStruct* **soundStructSize:**(int)*size*

Sets the Sound's sound structure to *aStruct*. The size in bytes of the new structure, including its sound data storage, must be specified by *size*. This method can be used to set up a large buffer before recording into an existing Sound, by passing the existing **soundStruct** in the first argument while making *size* larger than the current size. (The default buffer holds ten minutes of CODEC sound.) The method is also useful in cases where *aStruct* already has sound data but isn't encapsulated in a Sound object yet. The Sound's status must be NX_SoundInitialized or NX_SoundStopped for this method to do anything. Returns **self**.

soundBeingProcessed

– **soundBeingProcessed**

Returns the Sound object that's being performed. The default implementation always returns **self**.

soundStruct

– (SNDSoundStruct *)**soundStruct**

Returns a pointer to the Sound's SNDSoundStruct structure that holds the object's sound data.

soundStructBeingProcessed

– (SNDSoundStruct *)**soundStructBeingProcessed**

Returns a pointer to the SNDSoundStruct structure that's being performed. This may not be the same structure as returned by the **soundStruct** method—Sound object's contain a private sound structure that may be used for recording playing. If the Sound isn't currently playing or recording, then this will return the public structure.

soundStructSize

– (int)**soundStructSize**

Returns the size, in bytes, of the Sound's sound structure (pointed to by **soundStruct**). Use of this value requires a knowledge of the SNDSoundStruct architecture.

status

– (int)**status**

Return the Sound's current status, one of the following integer constants:

- NX_SoundStopped
- NX_SoundRecording
- NX_SoundPlaying
- NX_SoundInitialized
- NX_SoundRecordingPaused
- NX_SoundPlayingPaused
- NX_SoundRecordingPending
- NX_SoundPlayingPending
- NX_SoundFreed

stop

– (int)**stop**

Terminates the Sound's playback or recording. If the Sound was recording, the **didRecord:** message is sent to the delegate; if playing, **didPlay:** is sent. An error code is returned.

stop:

– **stop:***sender*

Action method that stops the Sound's playback or recording. Other than the argument and the return type, this is the same as the **stop** method. Returns **self**.

tellDelegate:

– **tellDelegate:**(SEL)*theMessage*

Sends *theMessage* to the Sound's delegate (only sent if the delegate implements *theMessage*). You never invoke this method directly; it's invoked automatically as the result of activities such as recording and playing. However, you can use it in designing a subclass of Sound. Returns **self**.

write:

– **write:**(NXTypedStream *)*stream*

Archives the Sound by writing its data to *stream*, which must be open for writing. Returns **self**.

writeSoundfile:

– (int)**writeSoundfile:**(const char *)*filename*

Writes the Sound's contents (its SNDSoundStruct and sound data) to the soundfile *filename*. An error code is returned.

writeSoundToStream:

– **writeSoundToStream:**(NXStream *)*stream*

Writes the Sound's name (if any), priority, SNDSoundStruct, and sound data (if any) to the NXStream *stream*. Returns **self**.

writeToPasteboard:

– (int)**writeToPasteboard:**(Pasteboard *)*thePboard*

Puts a copy of the Sound's contents (its SNDSoundStruct and sound data) on the pasteboard maintained by the Pasteboard object *thePboard*. If the Sound is fragmented, it's compacted before the copy is created. An error code is returned.

Methods Implemented by the Delegate

didPlay:

– **didPlay:***sender*

Sent to the delegate when the Sound stops playing.

didRecord:

– **didRecord:***sender*

Sent to the delegate when the Sound stops recording.

hadError:

– **hadError:***sender*

Sent to the delegate if an error occurs during recording or playback.

willPlay:

– **willPlay:***sender*

Sent to the delegate when the Sound begins to play.

willRecord:

– **willRecord:***sender*

Sent to the delegate when the Sound begins to record.

SoundMeter

Inherits From: View : Responder : Object

Declared In: soundkit/SoundMeter.h

Class Description

A SoundMeter is a view that displays the amplitude level of a sound as it's being recorded or played back. There are two working parts to the meter: A continuously-updated "running bar" that lengthens ands shrinks to depict the current amplitude level, and a "peak bubble" that displays and holds the greatest amplitude that was detected within the last few samples. An optional bezeled border is drawn around the object's frame.

To use a SoundMeter, you must first associate it with a Sound object, through the **setSound:** method, and then send the SoundMeter a **run:** message. To stop the meter's display, you send the object a **stop:** message. Neither **run:** nor **stop:** affect the performance of the meter's sound.

You can retrieve a SoundMeter's running and peak values through the **floatValue** and **peakValue** methods. The values that these methods return are valid only while the SoundMeter is running. A SoundMeter also keeps track of the minimum and maximum amplitude over the duration of a run; these can be retrieved through **minValue** and **maxValue**. All SoundMeter amplitude levels are normalized to fit between 0.0 (inaudible) and 1.0 (maximum amplitude).

Instance Variables

id **sound**;
int **currentSample**;
float **currentValue**;
float **currentPeak**;
float **minValue**;
float **maxValue**;
float **holdTime**;
float **backgroundGray**;

```
float foregroundGray;
float peakGray;
struct {
        unsigned int  running:1;
        unsigned int  bezeled:1;
        unsigned int shouldStop:1;
} smFlags;
```

sound	The object's Sound.
currentSample	The Sound sample currently being displayed.
currentValue	The value of the current sample.
currentPeak	The current value of the peak bubble.
minValue	The minimum sample value so far.
maxValue	The maximum sample value so far.
holdTime	The hold duration of the peak bubble.
backgroundGray	The background color.
foregroundGray	The foreground (average bar) color.
peakGray	The peak bubble color.
smFlags.running	True if the object is currently running.
smFlags.bezeled	True if the object draws a border.
smFlags.shouldStop	True if the object has been sent a **stop:** message.

Method Types

Initializing a SoundMeter instance	– initFrame:
Graphic attributes	– setBezeled: – isBezeled – setBackgroundGray: – backgroundGray – setForegroundGray: – foregroundGray – setPeakGray: – peakGray

Metering attributes	– setSound: – sound – setFloatValue: – setHoldTime: – holdTime
Retrieving meter values	– floatValue – maxValue – minValue – peakValue
Operating the object	– run: – isRunning – stop:
Drawing the object	– drawCurrentValue – drawSelf::
Archiving	– read: – write:

Instance Methods

backgroundGray

– (float)**backgroundGray**

Returns the SoundMeter's background color. The default is dark gray (NX_DKGRAY).

drawCurrentValue

– **drawCurrentValue**

Draws the SoundMeter's running bar and peak bubble. You never invoke this method directly; it's invoked automatically while the SoundMeter is running. You can override this method to change the look of the running bar and peak bubble. Returns **self**.

drawSelf::

– **drawSelf:**(const NXRect *)*rects* **:**(int)*rectCount*

Draws all the components of the SoundMeter (frame, running bar, and peak bubble). You never invoke this method directly; however, you can override it in a subclass to change the way the components are displayed. Returns **self**.

floatValue

– (float)**floatValue**

Returns the current running amplitude value as a floating-point number between 0.0 and 1.0. This is the amplitude level that's displayed by the running bar.

foregroundGray

– (float)**foregroundGray**

Returns the color of the running bar. The default is light gray (NX_LTGRAY).

holdTime

– (float)**holdTime**

Returns the SoundMeter's hold time—the amount of time during which a peak amplitude is detected and displayed by the peak bubble—in seconds. The default is 0.7 seconds.

initFrame:

– **initFrame:**(const NXRect *)*frameRect*

Initializes the SoundMeter, fitting its graphic components within *frameRect*. The object's attributes are initialized as follows:

Attribute	Value
Peak hold time	0.7 seconds
Background gray	NX_DKGRAY
Running bar gray	NX_LTGRAY
Peak bubble gray	NX_WHITE
Border	bezeled

Returns **self**.

isBezeled

– (BOOL)**isBezeled**

Returns YES (the default) if the SoundMeter has a border; otherwise, returns NO. Note that the SoundMeter class doesn't provide a method to change the type of border—it can display a bezeled border or none at all.

isRunning

– (BOOL)**isRunning**

Returns YES if the SoundMeter is currently running; otherwise, returns NO. The SoundMeter's status doesn't depend on the activity of its Sound object.

maxValue

– (float)**maxValue**

Returns the maximum running value so far. You can invoke this method after you stop this SoundMeter to retrieve the overall maximum value for the previous performance. The maximum value is cleared when you restart the SoundMeter.

minValue

– (float)**minValue**

Returns the minimum running value so far. You can invoke this method after you stop this SoundMeter to retrieve the overall minimum value for the previous performance. The minimum value is cleared when you restart the SoundMeter.

peakGray

– (float)**peakGray**

Returns the SoundMeter's peak bubble gray. The default is white (NX_WHITE).

peakValue

– (float)**peakValue**

Returns the most recently detected peak value as a floating-point number between 0.0 and 1.0. This is the amplitude level that's displayed by the peak bubble.

read:

– **read:**(NXTypedStream *)*aStream*

Unarchives the SoundMeter by reading it from *aStream*. Returns **self**.

run:

– **run:***sender*

Starts the SoundMeter running. The object SoundMeter must have a Sound object associated with it for this method to have an effect. Note that this method only affects the state of the SoundMeter—it doesn't trigger any activity in the Sound. Returns **self**.

setBackgroundGray:

– **setBackgroundGray:**(float)*aValue*

Sets the SoundMeter's background color. The default is dark gray (NX_DKGRAY). Returns **self**.

setBezeled:

– **setBezeled:**(BOOL)*aFlag*

If *aFlag* is YES, a bezeled border is drawn around the SoundMeter. If *aFlag* is NO and the SoundMeter has a frame, the frame is removed. Returns **self**.

setFloatValue:

– **setFloatValue:**(float)*aValue*

Sets the current running value to *aValue*. You never invoke this method directly; it's invoked automatically when the SoundMeter is running. However, you can reimplement this method in a subclass of SoundMeter. Returns **self**.

setForegroundGray:

– **setForegroundGray:**(float)*aValue*

Sets the SoundMeter's running bar color. The default is light gray (NX_LTGRAY). Returns **self**.

setHoldTime:

– **setHoldTime:**(float)*seconds*

Sets the SoundMeter's peak value hold time in seconds. This is the amount of time during which peak amplitudes are detected and held by the peak bubble. Returns **self**.

setPeakGray:

– **setPeakGray:**(float)*aValue*

Sets the SoundMeter's peak bubble color. The default is white (NX_WHITE). Returns **self**.

setSound:

– **setSound:***aSound*

Sets the SoundMeter's Sound object. Returns **self**.

sound

– **sound**

Returns the Sound object that the SoundMeter is metering.

stop:

– **stop:***sender*

Stops the SoundMeter's metering activity. Note that this method only affects the state of the SoundMeter—it doesn't trigger any activity in the Sound. Returns **self**.

write:

– **write:**(NXTypedStream *)*aStream*

Archives the SoundMeter by writing it to *aStream*. Returns **self**.

SoundView

Inherits From: View : Responder : Object

Declared In: soundkit/SoundView.h

Class Description

A SoundView object provides a graphical representation of sound data. This data is taken from an associated Sound object. In addition to displaying a Sound object's data, a SoundView provides methods that let you play and record into the Sound object, and peform simple cut, copy, and paste editing of its data. A cursor into the display is provided, allowing the user to set the insertion point and to create a selection over the sound data.

Sound Display

Sounds are displayed on a two-dimensional graph. The amplitudes of individual samples are measured vertically and plotted against time, which proceeds left to right along the horizontal axis. A SoundView's coordinate system is scaled and translated (vertically) so full amplitude fits within the bounds rectangle with 0.0 amplitude running through the center of the view.

For many sounds, the length of the sound data in samples is greater than the horizontal measure of the bounds rectangle. A SoundView employs a reduction factor to determine the ratio of samples to display units and plots the minimum and maximum amplitude values of the samples within that ratio. For example, a reduction factor of 10.0 means that the minimum and maximum values among the first ten samples are plotted in the first display unit, the minimum and maximum values of the next ten samples are displayed in the second display unit and so on.

Lines are drawn between the chosen values to yield a continuous shape. Two drawing modes are provided:

- In NX_SOUNDVIEW_WAVE mode, the drawing is rendered in an oscilloscopic fashion.
- In NX_SOUNDVIEW_MINMAX mode, two lines are drawn, one to connect the maximum values, and one to connect the minimum values.

As you zoom in (as the reduction factor decreases), the two drawing modes become indistinguishable.

Autoscaling the Display

When a SoundView's sound data changes (due to editing or recording), the manner in which the SoundView is redisplayed depends on its **autoscale** flag. With autoscaling disabled, the SoundView's frame grows or shrinks (horizontally) to fit the new sound data and the reduction factor is unchanged. If autoscaling is enabled, the reduction factor is automatically recomputed to maintain a constant frame size. By default, autoscaling is disabled; this is to accommodate the use of a SoundView object as the document of a ScrollView.

Instance Variables

```
id sound;
id reduction;
id delegate;
NXRect selectionRect;
int displayMode;
float backgroundGray;
float foregroundGray;
float reductionFactor;
struct {
        unsigned int disabled:1;
        unsigned int continuous:1;
        unsigned int calcDrawInfo:1;
        unsigned int selectionDirty:1;
        unsigned int autoscale:1;
        unsigned int bezeled:1;
        unsigned int notEditable:1;
        unsigned int notOptimizedForSpeed:1;
} svFlags;
```

sound	The object's Sound.
reduction	The data reduced version of the object's Sound.
delegate	The object's delegate.
selectionRect	The object's current selection.

displayMode	Display mode; NX_SOUNDVIEW_MINMAX by default.
backgroundGray	Background color; NX_WHITE by default.
foregroundGray	Foreground color; NX_BLACK by default.
reductionFactor	The ratio of sound samples to display units.
svFlags.disabled	Does the object (not) respond to mouse events?
svFlags.continuous	Does the object respond to mouse dragged events?
svFlags.calcDrawInfo	Does drawing info need to be recalculated?
svFlags.selectionDirty	Has the object changed (but not been played)?
svFlags.autoscale	Does it rescale the display when the sound data changes?
svFlags.bezeled	Does the object have a bezeled border?
svFlags.notEditable	Is the sound data not editable?
svFlags.notOptimizedForSpeed	Is the object not optimized for fast loading?

Method Types

Initializing a SoundView object	– initFrame:
Freeing a SoundView instance	– free
Modifying the object	– scaleToFit – setBackgroundGray: – setBezeled: – setContinuous: – setDelegate: – setDisplayMode: – setEnabled: – setForegroundGray: – setOptimizedForSpeed: – setSound: – sizeToFit

Querying the object	– backgroundGray – delegate – displayMode – foregroundGray – getSelection:size: – isAutoScale – isBezeled – isContinuous – isEnabled – isOptimizedForSpeed – reductionFactor – sound
Selecting and editing the sound data	– copy: – cut: – delete: – mouseDown: – paste: – selectAll: – setSelection:size: – isEditable – setEditable:
Pasteboard and Services support	– pasteboard:provideData: – readSelectionFromPasteboard: – validRequestorForSendType:andReturnType: – writeSelectionToPasteboard:types:
Modifying the display coordinates	– setAutoscale: – setReductionFactor:
Drawing the object	– drawSelf:: – drawSamplesFrom:to: – hideCursor – showCursor – sizeTo::
Responding to events	– acceptsFirstResponder – becomeFirstResponder – resignFirstResponder

Performing the sound data	– pause: – isPlayable – play: – record: – resume: – soundBeingProcessed – stop:
Archiving the object	– read: – write:
Accessing the delegate	– didPlay: – didRecord: – hadError: – tellDelegate: – willPlay: – willRecord:

Instance Methods

acceptsFirstResponder

– (BOOL)**acceptsFirstResponder**

If the SoundView is enabled, this returns YES, allowing the SoundView to become the first responder. Otherwise, it returns NO. This method is automatically invoked by objects defined by the Application Kit; you should never need to invoke it directly.

backgroundGray

– (float)**backgroundGray**

Returns the SoundView's background gray value (NX_WHITE by default).

becomeFirstResponder

– **becomeFirstResponder**

Promotes the SoundView to first responder. You never invoke this method directly. Returns **self**.

copy:

– **copy:***sender*

Copies the current selection to the pasteboard. Returns **self**.

cut:

– **cut:***sender*

Deletes the current selection from the SoundView, copies it to the pasteboard, and sends a **soundDidChange:** message to the delegate. The insertion point is positioned to where the selection used to start. Returns **self**.

delegate

– **delegate**

Returns the SoundView's delegate object.

delete:

– **delete:***sender*

Deletes the current selection from the SoundView's Sound and sends the **soundDidChange:** message to the delegate. The deletion isn't placed on the pasteboard. Returns **self**.

didPlay:

– **didPlay:***sender*

Used to redirect delegate messages from the SoundView's Sound object; you never invoke this method directly.

didRecord:

– **didRecord:***sender*

Used to redirect delegate messages from the SoundView's Sound object; you never invoke this method directly.

displayMode

– (int)**displayMode**

Returns the SoundView's display mode, one of NX_SOUNDVIEW_WAVE (oscilloscopic display) or NX_SOUNDVIEW_MINMAX (minimum/maximum display; this is the default).

drawSamplesFrom:to:

– **drawSamplesFrom:**(int)*first* **to:**(int)*last*

Redisplays the given range of samples. Return **self**.

drawSelf::

– **drawSelf:**(const NXRect *)*rects* **:**(int)*rectCount*

Displays the SoundView's sound data. The selection is highlighted and the cursor is drawn (if it isn't currently hidden). Returns **self**.

You never send the **drawSelf::** message directly to a SoundView object. To cause a SoundView to draw itself, send it one of the display messages defined by the View class.

foregroundGray

– (float)**foregroundGray**

Returns the SoundView's foreground gray value (NX_BLACK by default).

free

– **free**

Frees the SoundView but not its Sound object nor its delegate. The **willFree:** message is sent to the delegate.

getSelection:size:

– **getSelection:**(int *)*firstSample* **size:**(int *)*sampleCount*

Returns the selection by reference. The index of the selection's first sample (counting from 0) is returned in *firstSample*. The size of the selection in samples is returned in *sampleCount*. The method itself returns **self**.

hadError:

– **hadError:***sender*

Used to redirect delegate messages from the SoundView's Sound object; you never invoke this method directly.

hideCursor

– **hideCursor**

Hides the SoundView's cursor. This is usually handled automatically. Returns **self**.

initFrame:

– **initFrame:**(const NXRect *)*frameRect*

Initializes the SoundView, fitting the object within the rectangle pointing to by *frameRect*. The initialized SoundView doesn't contain any sound data. Returns **self**.

isAutoScale

– (BOOL)**isAutoScale**

Returns YES if the SoundView is in autoscaling mode, otherwise returns NO.

isBezeled

– (BOOL)**isBezeled**

Returns YES if the SoundView has a bezeled border, otherwise returns NO (the default).

isContinuous

– (BOOL)**isContinuous**

Returns YES if the SoundView responds to mouse-dragged events (as set through **setContinuous:**). The default is NO.

isEditable

– (BOOL)**isEditable**

Returns YES if the SoundView's sound data can be edited.

isEnabled

– (BOOL)**isEnabled**

Returns YES if the SoundView is enabled, otherwise returns NO. The mouse has no effect in a disabled SoundView. By default, a SoundView is enabled.

isOptimizedForSpeed

– (BOOL)**isOptimizedForSpeed**

Returns YES if the SoundView is optimized for speedy display. SoundViews are optimized by default.

isPlayable

– (BOOL)**isPlayable**

Returns YES if the SoundView's sound data can be played without first being converted.

mouseDown:

– **mouseDown:**(NXEvent *)*theEvent*

Allows a selection to be defined by clicking and dragging the mouse. This method takes control until a mouse-up occurs. While dragging, the selected region is highlighted. On mouse up, the delegate is sent the **selectionChanged:** message. If **isContinuous** is YES, **selectionChanged:** messages are also sent while the mouse is being dragged. You never invoke this method; it's invoked automatically in response to the user's actions. Returns **self**.

paste:

– **paste:***sender*

Replaces the current selection with a copy of the sound data currently on the pasteboard. If there is no selection the pasteboard data is inserted at the cursor position. The pasteboard data must be compatible with the SoundView's data, as determined by the Sound method **compatibleWith:**. If the paste is successful, the **soundDidChange:** message is sent to the delegate. Returns **self**.

pasteboard:provideData:

– **pasteboard:***thePasteboard* **provideData:**(const char *)*pboardType*

Places the SoundView's entire sound on the given pasteboard. Currently, the *pboardType* argument must be "NXSoundPboardType", the pasteboard type that represents sound data. Returns **self**.

pause:

– **pause:***sender*

Pauses the current playback or recording session by invoking Sound's **pause:** method. If no sound is being processed, returns **nil**; otherwise, returns **self**.

play:

– **play:***sender*

Play the current selection by invoking Sound's **play:** method. If there is no selection, the SoundView's entire Sound is played. The **willPlay:** message is sent to the delegate before the selection is played; **didPlay:** is sent when the selection is done playing. Returns **self**.

read:

– **read:**(void *)*stream*

Unarchives the SoundView by reading it from *stream*. Returns **self**.

readSelectionFromPasteboard:

– **readSelectionFromPasteboard:***thePasteboard*

Replaces the SoundView's current selection with the sound data on the given pasteboard. The pasteboard data is converted to the format of the data in the SoundView (if possible). If the SoundView has no selection, the pasteboard data is inserted at the cursor position. Sets the current error code for the SoundView's Sound object (which you can retrieve by sending **processingError** to the Sound) and returns **self**.

record:

– **record:***sender*

Replaces the SoundView's current selection with newly recorded material. If there is no selection, the recording is inserted at the cursor. The **willRecord:** message is sent to the delegate before the recording is started; **didRecord:** is sent after the recording has completed. Recorded data is always taken from the CODEC microphone input. Returns **self**.

reductionFactor

– (float)**reductionFactor**

Returns the SoundView's reduction factor, computed as

reductionFactor = sampleCount / displayUnits

resignFirstResponder

– **resignFirstResponder**

Resigns the position of first responder. Returns **self**.

resume:

– **resume:***sender*

Resumes the current playback or recording session by invoking Sound's **resume:** method. If no sound is being processed, returns **nil**; otherwise, returns **self**.

scaleToFit

– **scaleToFit**

Recomputes the SoundView's reduction factor to fit the sound data (horizontally) within the current frame. Invoked automatically when the SoundView's data changes and the SoundView is in autoscale mode. If the SoundView isn't in autoscale mode, **sizeToFit** is invoked when the data changes. You never invoke this method directly; a subclass can reimplement this method to provide specialized behavior. Returns **self**.

selectAll:

– **selectAll:***sender*

Creates a selection over the SoundView's entire Sound. Returns **self**.

setAutoscale:

– **setAutoscale:**(BOOL)*aFlag*

Sets the SoundView's automatic scaling mode, used to determine how the SoundView is redisplayed when its data changes. With autoscaling enabled (*aFlag* is YES), the SoundView's reduction factor is recomputed so the sound data fits within the view frame. If it's disabled (*aFlag* is NO), the frame is resized and the reduction factor is unchanged. If the SoundView is in a ScrollingView, autoScaling should be disabled (autoscaling is disabled by default). Returns **self**.

setBackgroundGray:

– **setBackgroundGray:**(float)*aGray*

Sets the SoundView's background gray value to *aGray*; the default is NX_WHITE. Returns **self**.

setBezeled:

– **setBezeled:**(BOOL)*aFlag*

If *aFlag* is YES, the display is given a bezeled border. By default, the border of a SoundView display isn't bezeled. If autodisplaying is enabled, the Sound is automatically redisplayed. Returns **self**.

setContinuous:

– **setContinuous:**(BOOL)*aFlag*

Sets the state of continuous action messages. If *aFlag* is YES, **selectionChanged:** messages are sent to the delegate as the mouse is being dragged. If NO, the message is sent only on mouse up. The default is NO. Returns **self**.

setDelegate:

– **setDelegate:***anObject*

Sets the SoundView's delegate to *anObject*. The delegate is sent messages when the user changes or acts on the selection. Returns **self**.

setDisplayMode:

– **setDisplayMode:**(int)*aMode*

Sets the SoundView's display mode, either NX_SOUNDVIEW_WAVE or NX_SOUNDVIEW_MINMAX (the default). If autodisplaying is enabled, the Sound is automatically redisplayed. Returns **self**.

setEditable:

– **setEditable:**(BOOL)*aFlag*

Enables or disables editing in the SoundView as *aFlag* is YES or NO. By default, a SoundView is editable. Returns **self**.

setEnabled:

– **setEnabled:**(BOOL)*aFlag*

Enables or disables the SoundView as *aFlag* is YES or NO. The mouse has no effect in a disabled SoundView. By default, a SoundView is enabled. Returns **self**.

setForegroundGray:

– **setForegroundGray:**(float)*aGray*

Sets the SoundView's foreground gray value to *aGray*. The default is NX_BLACK. Returns **self**.

setOptimizedForSpeed:

– **setOptimizedForSpeed:**(BOOL)*flag*

Sets the SoundView to optimize its display mechanism. Optimization greatly increases the speed with which data can be drawn, particularly for large sounds. It does so at the loss of some precision in representing the sound data; however, these inaccuracies are corrected as you zoom in on the data. All SoundView's are optimized by default. Returns **self**.

setReductionFactor:

– **setReductionFactor:**(float)*reductionFactor*

Recomputes the size of the SoundView's frame, if autoscaling is disabled. The frame's size (in display units) is set according to the formula

displayUnits = sampleCount / *reductionFactor*

Increasing the reduction factor zooms out, decreasing zooms in on the data. If autodisplaying is enabled, the Sound is automatically redisplayed.

If the SoundView is in autoscaling mode, or *reductionFactor* is less than 1.0, the method avoids computing the frame size and returns **nil**. (In autoscaling mode, the reduction factor is automatically recomputed when the sound data changes—see **scaleToFit:**.) Otherwise, the method returns **self**. If *reductionFactor* is the same as the current reduction factor, the method returns immediately without recomputing the frame size.

setSelection:size:

– **setSelection:**(int)*firstSample* **size:**(int)*sampleCount*

Sets the selection to be *sampleCount* samples wide, starting with sample *firstSample* (samples are counted from 0). Returns **self**.

setSound:

– **setSound:***aSound*

Sets the SoundView's Sound object to *aSound*. If autoscaling is enabled, the drawing coordinate system is adjusted so *aSound*'s data fits within the current frame. Otherwise, the frame is resized to accommodate the length of the data. If autodisplaying is enabled, the SoundView is automatically redisplayed. Returns **self**.

showCursor

– **showCursor**

Displays the SoundView's cursor. This is usually handled automatically. Returns **self**.

sizeTo::

– **sizeTo:**(NXCoord)*width* **:**(NXCoord)*height*

Sets the width and height of the SoundView's frame. If autodisplaying is enabled, the SoundView is automatically redisplayed. Returns **self**.

sizeToFit

– **sizeToFit**

Resizes the SoundView's frame (horizontally) to maintain a constant reduction factor. This method is invoked automatically when the SoundView's data changes and the SoundView isn't in autoscale mode. If the SoundView is in autoscale mode, **scaleToFit** is invoked when the data changes. You never invoke this method directly; a subclass can reimplement this method to provide specialized behavior. Returns **self**.

sound

– **sound**

Returns a pointer to the SoundView's Sound object.

soundBeingProcessed

– soundBeingProcessed

Returns the Sound object that's currently being played or recorded into. Note that the actual Sound object that's being performed isn't necessarily the SoundView's **sound** (the object returned by the **sound** method); for efficiency, SoundView creates a private performance Sound object. While this is generally an implementation detail, this method is supplied in case the SoundView's delegate needs to know exactly which object will be (or was) performed.

stop:

– **stop:***sender*

Stops the SoundView's current recording or playback. Returns **self**.

tellDelegate:

– **tellDelegate:**(SEL)*theMessage*

Sends *theMessage* to the SoundView's delegate with the SoundView as the argument. If the delegate doesn't respond to the message, then it isn't sent. You normally never invoke this method; it's invoked automatically when an action, such as playing or editing, is performed. However, you can invoke it in the design of a SoundView subclass. Returns **self**.

validRequestorForSendType:andReturnType:

– **validRequestorForSendType:**(NXAtom)*sendType*
  andReturnType:(NXAtom)*returnType*

You never invoke this method; it's implemented to support services that act on sound data.

willPlay:

– **willPlay:***sender*

Used to redirect delegate messages from the SoundView's Sound object; you never invoke this method directly.

willRecord:

– **willRecord:***sender*

Used to redirect delegate messages from the SoundView's Sound object; you never invoke this method directly.

write:

– **write:**(void *)*stream*

Archives the SoundView by writing it to *stream*. Returns **self**.

writeSelectionToPasteboard:types:

– **writeSelectionToPasteboard:***thePasteboard* **types:**(NXAtom *)*pboardTypes*

Places a copy of the SoundView's current selection on the given pasteboard. The *pboardTypes* argument is currently ignored. Returns **self**.

Methods Implemented by the Delegate

didPlay:

– **didPlay:***sender*

Sent to the delegate just after the SoundView's sound is played.

didRecord:

– **didRecord:***sender*

Sent to the delegate just after the SoundView's sound is recorded into.

hadError:

– **hadError:***sender*

Sent to the delegate if an error is encountered during recording or playback of the SoundView's sound.

selectionChanged:

– **selectionChanged:***sender*

Sent to the delegate when the SoundView's selection changes.

soundDidChange:

– **soundDidChange:***sender*

Sent to the delegate when the SoundView's sound data is edited.

willFree:

– **willFree:***sender*

Sent to the delegate when the SoundView is freed.

willPlay:

– **willPlay:***sender*

Sent to the delegate just before the SoundView's sound is played.

willRecord:

– **willRecord:***sender*

Sent to the delegate just before the SoundView's sound is recorded into.

Sound Functions

SNDAcquire(), SNDReset(), SNDRelease()

SUMMARY Access sound resources

DECLARED IN sound/accesssound.h

SYNOPSIS int **SNDAcquire**(int *soundResource*, int *priority*, int *preempt*, int *timeout*, SNDNegotiationFun *negFun*, void **arg*, port_t **devicePort*, port_t **ownerPort*)
int **SNDReset**(int *soundResource*, port_t *devicePort*, port_t *ownerPort*)
int **SNDRelease**(int *soundResource*, port_t **devicePort*, port_t **ownerPort*)

DESCRIPTION **SNDAcquire**() attempts to gain ownership of the sound resources specified in *soundResource*, a value that's created by (bitwise) or'ing a combination of the following resource codes:

Code	Resource
SND_ACCESS_OUT	sound-out
SND_ACCESS_IN	sound-in
SND_ACCESS_DSP	the DSP

Alternatively, you can acquire the sound driver device port without gaining ownership of the device by passing 0 as the value of *soundResource*.

Device and ownership ports to a successfully acquired sound resource are returned in *devicePort* and *ownerPort*, respectively. If you pass a previously created port as the value of *devicePort*, that port is used; passing a value of PORT_NULL (0) causes **SNDAcquire()** to create a port for you. The value you pass through *ownerPort* is ignored by the function; a new owner port is always created for you.

Acquiring a resource makes it active, such that other acquisition requests may fail, even if the requests are in the same process. You can grant a priority to the acquisition by setting the value of the *priority* argument—in a subsequent call to **SNDAcquire()**, the acquisition with the higher priority wins. The *preempt* flag is used as a tie-breaker.

The function's *timeout*, *negFun*, and *arg* arguments are currently unused.

SNDReset() and **SNDRelease**() reset to a virgin state and release, respectively, the specified resources. The resources must have been previously acquired through **SNDAcquire**(); the device and owner port arguments are values returned by that function. **SNDRelease**() sets the owner port to PORT_NULL; the device port is unaffected.

RETURN If no error occurs, SND_ERR_NONE is returned. Otherwise, an error code, as described in **SNDSoundError**(), is returned.

ERRORS If **SNDAcquire**() is unable to acquire any one of the resources specified in *soundResource*, none of the resources are acquired.

SNDAlloc(), SNDFree()

SUMMARY Create and free a sound structure

DECLARED IN sound/utilsound.h

SYNOPSIS int **SNDAlloc**(SNDSoundStruct ***sound*, int *dataSize*, int *dataFormat*, int *samplingRate*, int *channelCount*, int *infoSize*)
int **SNDFree**(SNDSoundStruct **sound*)

DESCRIPTION The SNDSoundStruct structure is the data format used by the sound software to encapsulate a sound. It defines the soundfile format and the sound pasteboard type, and it lies at the heart of every Sound object. **SNDAlloc**() creates and returns, in *sound*, a new SNDSoundStruct. The arguments to **SNDAlloc**() correspond to the SNDSoundStruct fields described below. **SNDFree**() frees the SNDSoundStruct pointed to by *sound.* You should always use **SNDFree**() to free a sound structure created through **SNDAlloc**().

The fields of the SNDSoundStruct structure list the attributes of the sound that the structure represents. The sound data itself isn't contained in the structure, but is located by a structure field. Nonetheless, it's often convenient to think of a SNDSoundStruct as containing the sound data that it represents. By convention, the structure is referred to as the sound's "header." It's defined as:

```
typedef struct  {
    int  magic;          /* SND_MAGIC ((int)0x2e736e64) */
    int  dataLocation;   /* Offset or pointer to the raw data */
    int  dataSize;       /* Raw data size in bytes */
    int  dataFormat;     /* The data format code */
    int  samplingRate;   /* The sampling rate */
    int  channelCount;   /* The number of channels */
    char info[4];        /* Textual information about the sound */
SNDSoundStruct;
```

The **magic** field is a magic number that identifies a SNDSoundStruct. It's automatically set when you allocate the structure.

The **dataLocation** field indicates the location of the actual sound data. Usually, the data immediately follows the header. In this case, **dataLocation** is the offset from the beginning of the structure to the first byte of the sound data—in other words, it's the size of the sound's header. However, if you edit the sound through functions such as **SNDDeleteSamples()** or **SNDInsertSamples()**, the sound can become fragmented such that the data no longer follows the header. In this case, **dataLocation** is a pointer to a NULL-terminated block of addresses, each of which points to a separate SNDSoundStruct. The collection of these SNDSoundStructs make up the fragmented data.

dataSize is the size, in bytes, of the memory allocated for the sound data. The memory is initialized to zero.

dataFormat describes the sound data as one of the following codes:

Code	Format
SND_FORMAT_MULAW_8	8-bit mu-law samples
SND_FORMAT_LINEAR_8	8-bit linear samples
SND_FORMAT_LINEAR_16	16-bit linear samples
SND_FORMAT_EMPHASIZED	16-bit linear with emphasis
SND_FORMAT_COMPRESSED	16-bit linear with compression
SND_FORMAT_COMPRESSED_EMPHASIZED	A combination of the two above
SND_FORMAT_LINEAR_24	24-bit linear samples
SND_FORMAT_LINEAR_32	32-bit linear samples
SND_FORMAT_FLOAT	floating-point samples
SND_FORMAT_DOUBLE	double-precision float samples
SND_FORMAT_DSP_DATA_8	8-bit fixed-point samples
SND_FORMAT_DSP_DATA_16	16-bit fixed-point samples
SND_FORMAT_DSP_DATA_24	24-bit fixed-point samples
SND_FORMAT_DSP_DATA_32	32-bit fixed-point samples
SND_FORMAT_DSP_CORE	DSP program
SND_FORMAT_DISPLAY	non-audio display data
SND_FORMAT_INDIRECT	fragmented sampled data
SND_FORMAT_UNSPECIFIED	unspecified format

All but the last five formats identify different sizes and types of sampled data. The others deserve special note:

- SND_FORMAT_DSP_CORE format contains data that represents a loadable DSP core program. Sounds in this format are required by the **SNDBootDSP()** and **SNDRunDSP()** functions. You create a SND_FORMAT_DSP_CORE sound by reading a DSP load file (extension ".lod") with the **SNDReadDSPfile()** function.
- SND_FORMAT_DISPLAY format is used by the Sound Kit's SoundView class. Such sounds can't be played.
- SND_FORMAT_INDIRECT indicates data that has become fragmented due to editing. Only sampled data can become fragmented. You never allocate a sound with this format.
- SND_FORMAT_UNSPECIFIED is used for unrecognized formats.

samplingRate is also given as a code and should be cast into an **int**. The NeXT sound hardware supports the following sampling rates for recording and playback:

Code	Sampling Rate (Hz)
SND_RATE_CODEC	8012.8210513
SND_RATE_LOW	22050
SND_RATE_HIGH	44100

channelCount is the number of channels of sound. Playback of one- and two-channel sounds is supported; a sound with more than two channels is unplayable.

infoSize is the size of a variable-length string that can be used to textually describe the sound. The size is extended to the next 4-byte boundary (the minimum size is 4 bytes). You can't increase the length of the info string once its size has been set.

RETURN If no error occurs, SND_ERR_NONE is returned. Otherwise, an error code, as described in **SNDSoundError()**, is returned.

SNDBootDSP()

SUMMARY Boot the DSP

DECLARED IN sound/accesssound.h

SYNOPSIS int **SNDBootDSP**(port_t **devicePort*, port_t **ownerPort*, SNDSoundStruct **dspCore*)

DESCRIPTION **SNDBootDSP()** boots the DSP using the DSP bootstrap image specified in *dspCore*. This allows you to load all internal RAM and all but the top six words of external RAM on the DSP. The owner and device ports must have been previously acquired through **SNDAcquire()**. The format of *dspCore* must SND_FORMAT_DSP core image should be in loadable (".lod") form, such as is created through the **SNDReadDSPfile()** function.

RETURN If no error occurs, SND_ERR_NONE is returned. Otherwise, an error code, as described in **SNDSoundError()**, is returned.

SNDBytesToSamples() → See SNDSampleCount()

SNDGetCompressionOptions() → See SNDSetCompressionOptions()

SNDCompactSamples() → See SNDInsertSamples()

SNDCompressSound()

SUMMARY Compress or decompress a sound

DECLARED IN sound/convertsound.h

SYNOPSIS int **SNDCompressSound**(SNDSoundStruct **fromSound*, SNDSoundStruct ***toSound*, BOOL *bitFaithful*, int *compressionAmount*)

DESCRIPTION **SNDCompressSound**() creates and returns, in *toSound*, a new SNDSoundStruct that contains a compressed or decompressed version of the sound in *fromSound*:

- If *fromSound's* format is SND_FORMAT_LINEAR_16 or SND_FORMAT_EMPHASIZED, the sound returned in *toSound* is compressed.
- If its format is SND_FORMAT_COMPRESSED or SND_FORMAT_COMPRESSED_EMPHASIZED, the sound is decompressed.

No other formats are allowed; in addition, the sound can't have more than two channels.

The function's *bitFaithful* and *compressionAmount* arguments are used only when compressing:

- *bitFaithful* determines the fidelity with which a compressed sound can be restored to its original state. If *bitFaithful* is YES, the sound returned in *toSound* can be decompressed to exactly match the original sound data; if it's NO, some degradation can be expected.
- The *compressionAmount* argument controls the amount of compression. Its value ranges from 4 to 8 with higher numbers giving more compression but less fidelity. Depending on the signal, a *compressionAmount* of 4 will compress the sound to about half its original size; a value of 8 compresses to about one-sixth the size. For bit-faithful compression, you should set *compressionAmount* to 4.

RETURN If no error occurs, SND_ERR_NONE is returned. Otherwise an error code, as described in **SNDSoundError()**, is returned.

SNDConvertDecibelsToLinear(), SNDConvertLinearToDecibels()

SUMMARY Convert between logarithmic and linear units

DECLARED IN soundkit/NXSoundDevice.h

SYNOPSIS float **SNDConvertDecibelsToLinear**(float *dB*)
float **SNDConvertLinearToDecibels**(float *linear*)

DESCRIPTION These convenience functions convert from units of decibels to a linear value, and vice versa. Decibels express the difference between two quantities in logarithmic units, while on a linear scale the same relationship is expressed as the ratio of the two quantities. For example, a difference of zero decibels is equivalent to a ratio of 1.0. The functions are, in their entirety:

```
float SNDConvertDecibelsToLinear(float dB)
{
    return (float)pow(10.0, (double)dB/20.0);
}

float SNDConvertLinearToDecibels(float linear)
{
    return (float)(20.0 * log10((double)linear));
}
```

SNDConvertLinearToDecibels() → See SNDConvertDecibelsToLinear()

SNDConvertSound(), SNDMulaw(), SNDiMulaw()

SUMMARY Convert a sound's attributes

DECLARED IN sound/convertsound.h

SYNOPSIS int **SNDConvertSound**(SNDSoundStruct **fromSound*, SNDSoundStruct ***toSound*)
unsigned char **SNDMulaw**(short *linearValue*)
short **SNDiMulaw**(unsigned char *mulawValue*)

DESCRIPTION **SNDConvertSound()** copies the sampled data from *fromSound* into *toSound*, converting the copied data to the format, channel count, and sampling rate specified by *toSound*. Memory for the converted data is automatically allocated. The following conversions are possible:

- Arbitrary sampling rate conversion.
- Compression and decompression.
- Floating-point formats (including double-precision) to and from linear formats.
- Mono to stereo.
- CODEC mu-law to and from linear formats.

SNDMulaw() converts a value from 16-bit linear to mu-law: It takes a single linear 16-bit argument and returns the corresponding mu-law value. **SNDiMulaw()** performs the inverse operation: It takes a mu-law argument and returns the 16-bit linear value.

RETURN If no error occurs, **SNDConvertSound()** returns SND_ERR_NONE. Otherwise an error code, as described in **SNDSoundError()**, is returned.

SEE ALSO **SNDAlloc()**, **SNDSamplesToBytes()**

SNDCopySamples() → See SNDCopySound()

SNDCopySound(), SNDCopySamples()

SUMMARY Copy all or part of a sound

DECLARED IN sound/editsound.h

SYNOPSIS int **SNDCopySound**(SNDSoundStruct ***toSound*, SNDSoundStruct **fromSound*)
int **SNDCopySamples**(SNDSoundStruct ***toSound*, SNDSoundStruct **fromSound*, int *startSample*, int *sampleCount*)

DESCRIPTION **SNDCopySound**() creates and returns, in *toSound*, a new SNDSoundStruct that contains a copy of the sound in *fromSound*. This works for any type of sound, including DSP sounds.

SNDCopySamples() also creates a new SNDSoundStruct pointed to by *toSound*, but copies only the specified of *fromSound*, starting with the *startSample* sample (counting from sample 0) and copying *sampleCount* samples. This function works only for sampled sounds.

toSound should eventually be freed with **SNDFree**().

RETURN Both functions return an error code as described in **SNDSoundError**().

ERRORS If an error occurs, the SNDSoundStruct isn't created.

SNDDeleteSamples() → See SNDInsertSamples()

SNDDropATCSamples(), SNDInsertATCSamples()

SUMMARY Speed up or slow down playback of ATC sound

DECLARED IN sound/atcsound.h

SYNOPSIS int **SNDDropATCSamples**(int *numSamples*, int *bySamples*)
int **SNDInsertATCSamples**(int *numSamples*, int *bySamples*)

DESCRIPTION **SNDDropATCSamples()** and **SNDInsertATCSamples()** provide elementary support for synchronizing sound playback to other events. By skipping or repeating selected samples of an ATC sound while it's playing, you can slightly shrink or stretch its duration, as necessary. This mechanism is intended for subtle timing adjustments, not for effects like fast forward. Although dropping or inserting samples shouldn't cause any clicks in the sound, it will cause some distortion. A sound in the ATC (Audio Transform Compression) format must be playing for these functions to have any effect.

If *bySamples* is zero, one sample is chosen randomly out of the next 256 consecutive samples and omitted (in the case of **SNDDropATCSamples()**) or repeated (in the case of **SNDInsertATCSamples()**). This process repeats until *numSamples* samples have been dropped or inserted. If *bySamples* is greater than zero, an attempt is made to drop or add *numSamples* samples before *bySamples* more samples of the original sound have played. Too large a ratio of *numSamples* to *bySamples* may produce unwanted results.

To determine when to drop or insert samples, call **SNDSamplesProcessed()** to obtain an estimate of how many samples have been played thus far. Divide this number by the sampling rate to obtain the elapsed time in seconds, and compare the result to the notion of time with which you want to synchronize.

SEE ALSO **SNDSamplesProcessed()**, **SNDCompressSound()**, **SNDSetATCGain()**, **SNDGetNumberOfATCBands()**

SNDFree() → See SNDAlloc()

SNDGetCompressionOptions() → See SNDCompressSound()

SNDGetDataPointer()

SUMMARY Gain access to sampled sound data

DECLARED IN sound/utilsound.h

SYNOPSIS int **SNDGetDataPointer**(SNDSoundStruct **sound*, char ***ptr*, int **size*, int **width*)

DESCRIPTION The **SNDGetDataPointer**() provides access to *sound*'s sound data. A pointer to the sound data is returned by reference in *sound*, the size of the data is returned in *samples*, and the width (in bytes) of a single sample is returned in *width*. Note that *size* is the total sample count—it isn't a count of the sample frames. The data itself should be unfragmented, sampled data.

RETURN If no error occurs, SND_ERR_NONE is returned. Otherwise, an error code, as described in **SNDSoundError**(), is returned.

SNDGetFilter() → See SNDSetVolume()

SNDGetMute() → See SNDSetVolume()

SNDGetNumberOfATCBands(), SNDGetATCBandFrequencies(), SNDGetATCBandwidths()

SUMMARY Query for frequency bands used by Audio Transform Compression

DECLARED IN sound/atcsound.h

SYNOPSIS int **SNDGetNumberOfATCBands**(int **numBands*)
int **SNDGetATCBandFrequencies**(int *numBands*, float **centerFreqs*)
int **SNDGetATCBandwidths**(int *numBands*, float **bandwidths*)

DESCRIPTION **SNDGetNumberOfATCBands()** returns, by reference in *numBands*, the number of frequency bands that **SNDCompressSound()** uses for compressing sounds with ATC (Audio Transform Compression). Currently, this number is always 40.

SNDGetATCBandFrequencies() fills the array *centerFreqs* with floating-point numbers that specify the center frequency in Hertz of each band. Similarly, the array filled by **SNDGetATCBandwidths()** contains the width in Hertz of each band. The first argument to each of these functions should be the value returned by **SNDGetNumberOfATCBands()**.

The ATC bands correspond roughly to the "critical bands" of hearing. Band zero is centered at zero Hz, and the highest band is centered at half the sampling rate. The bandwidths and spacing are uniform below a certain frequency, above which the bands are progressively wider in Hertz and spaced further apart. For sounds having the standard sampling rate of 44.1 kHz, bands below 1000 Hz have the same bandwidth, while bands above 1000 Hz have bandwidths of approximately 20% of the band's center frequency. For sounds with other sampling rates, the bands' frequencies are scaled so that the same number of bands covers zero Hz to half the sampling rate, whatever the latter may be. **SNDGetATCBandFrequencies()** and **SNDGetATCBandwidths()** assume a 44.1-kHz sampling rate when filling the arrays *centerFreqs* and *bandwidths*, respectively. To obtain the correct values for other sampling rates, multiply each element of the returned arrays by the ratio of the sampling rate to 44.1 kHz.

RETURN 0 is returned unless the host isn't a NeXT computer, in which case ATC is unavailable.

SEE ALSO **SNDCompressSound()**, **SNDSetATCGain()**, **SNDDropATCSamples()**

SNDGetVolume() → See SNDSetVolume()

SNDiMulaw() → See SNDConvertSound()

SNDInsertSamples(), SNDDeleteSamples(), SNDCompactSamples()

SUMMARY Edit a sampled sound

DECLARED IN sound/editsound.h

SYNOPSIS int **SNDInsertSamples**(SNDSoundStruct **toSound*, SNDSoundStruct **fromSound*, int *startSample*)

int **SNDDeleteSamples**(SNDSoundStruct **sound*, int *startSample*, int *sampleCount*)

int **SNDCompactSamples**(SNDSoundStruct ***toSound*, SNDSoundStruct **fromSound*)

DESCRIPTION **SNDInsertSamples**() inserts a copy of *fromSound* into *toSound* at position *startSample* of *toSound* (counting from sample 0). This operation may fragment *toSound*.

SNDDeleteSamples() deletes *sampleCount* samples from *sound*, starting at sample *startSample*. The memory occupied by the deleted segment is freed. The sound may become fragmented.

SNDCompactSamples() creates and returns, in *toSound*, a new SNDSoundStruct that contains a compacted version of *fromSound*. Compaction eliminates the fragmentation that can be caused by inserting and deleting samples.

These functions work only on sounds that contain sampled data.

RETURN If no error occurs, SND_ERR_NONE is returned. Otherwise, an error code, as described in **SNDSoundError**(), is returned.

SNDModifyPriority() → See SNDStartPlaying()

SNDMulaw() → See SNDConvertSound()

SNDPlaySoundfile()

SUMMARY Play a soundfile

DECLARED IN sound/utilsound.h

SYNOPSIS int **SNDPlaySoundfile**(char **path*, int *priority*)

DESCRIPTION **SNDPlaySoundfile()** plays the soundfile named *path*. The function returns immediately while playback continues in a background thread. Playback interrupts a currently playing sound of the same or lower priority.

RETURN If no error occurs, SND_ERR_NONE is returned. Otherwise, an error code, as described in **SNDSoundError()**, is returned.

SNDRead() → See SNDReadSoundfile()

SNDReadDSPfile() → See SNDReadSoundfile()

SNDReadHeader() → See SNDReadSoundfile()

SNDReadSoundfile(), SNDRead(), SNDReadHeader(), SNDReadDSPfile()

SUMMARY Read a sound from a file

DECLARED IN sound/filesound.h

SYNOPSIS int **SNDReadSoundfile**(char **path*, SNDSoundStruct ***sound*)
int **SNDRead**(int *fd*, SNDSoundStruct ***sound*)
int **SNDReadHeader**(int *fd*, SNDSoundStruct ***sound*)
int **SNDReadDSPfile**(char **path*, SNDSoundStruct ***sound*, char **info*)

DESCRIPTION Each of these functions creates and returns, by reference in the *sound* argument, a SNDSoundStruct that contains the sound represented in a specified file.

SNDReadSoundfile() and **SNDRead**() read the entire contents of a soundfile. The *path* argument to **SNDReadSoundfile**() is a pathname; the function opens and closes the file automatically. **SNDRead**() takes a file descriptor *fd* that must be open for reading.

SNDReadHeader() reads only the header portion of the file descriptor *fd*. Storage for the actual sound data isn't allocated. The **dataLocation** field of the new SNDSoundStruct can be interpreted as the size of the header.

SNDReadDSPfile() creates a SNDSoundStruct for the given loadable DSP core file. The file, which is opened and closed by the function, is specified as a pathname and must have a ".lod" extension. The *info* argument is provided as a convenience, allowing you to specify an information string that's written in *sound*'s header. The DSP program is executed by calling **SNDBootDSP**() or **SNDRunDSP**().

For all three functions, *sound* should eventually be deallocated with **SNDFree**().

RETURN If no error occurs, SND_ERR_NONE is returned. Otherwise, an error code, as described in **SNDSoundError**(), is returned.

ERRORS If an error occurs, the SNDSoundStruct isn't created.

SEE ALSO SNDFree()

SNDRelease() → See SNDAcquire()

SNDReserve(), SNDUnreserve()

SUMMARY Reserve sound resources for recording or playback

DECLARED IN sound/accesssound.h

SYNOPSIS int **SNDReserve**(int *soundResource*, int *priority*)
int **SNDUnreserve**(int *soundResource*)

DESCRIPTION **SNDReserve**() attempts to establish the exclusive use of the sound resources specified in **soundResource**, a value that's created by (bitwise) or'ing a combination of the following resource codes:

Code	Resource
SND_ACCESS_OUT	sound out
SND_ACCESS_IN	sound in
SND_ACCESS_DSP	the DSP

The *priority* argument sets the priority of the reservation (0 is the lowest priority). In general, a process has exclusive access to the resources that it reserves. However, another process can overrule a reservation by specifying a higher priority. Use of **SNDReserve()** is optional; prioritized access to the appropriate resource is established when either the **SNDStartPlaying**() or the **SNDStartRecording**() function is called. The process should eventually free its reserved resources by calling **SNDUnreserve**(). Sound resources are automatically freed when the process terminates.

RETURN If no error occurs, SND_ERR_NONE is returned. Otherwise, an error code, as described in **SNDSoundError**(), is returned.

ERRORS If **SNDReserve**() is unable to reserve any one of the resources specified in *soundResource*, it won't reserve any of them.

SNDReset() → See SNDAcquire()

SNDRunDSP()

SUMMARY Run the DSP

DECLARED IN sound/convertsound.h

SYNOPSIS int **SNDRunDSP**(SNDSoundStruct **dspCore*, char **toDSP*, int *toCount*, int *toWidth*, int *toBufferSize*, char ***fromDSP*, int **fromCount*, int *fromWidth*, int *negotiationTimeout*, int *flushTimeout*, int *conversionTimeout*)

DESCRIPTION **SNDRunDSP()** loads and runs the DSP program that you provide. The functions is designed to be used with DSP programs that process sound data—you typically use this function to provide your own sound conversion algorithms. The arguments are as follows:

- The DSP program is represented by *dspCore*; it must implement complex DMA mode for its output, and must be in loadable (".lod") form.
- *toDSP* is a pointer to the data that you wish to feed to the DSP.
- *toCount* is the number of samples to process.
- *toWidth* is the size of a single unprocessed sample.
- *toBufferSize* is the total size, in bytes, of the *toDSP* data.
- *fromDSP* is a pointer to the address of the processed data. The memory to store the data is allocated for you.
- *fromCount* is returned by the function to give the number of samples that it actually processed.
- *fromWidth* is the size, in bytes, of a single processed sample.
- The timeout arguments, *negotiationTimeout*, *flushTimeout*, and *conversionTimeout*, are ignored.

RETURN If no error occurs, SND_ERR_NONE is returned. Otherwise, an error code, as described in **SNDSoundError()**, is returned.

SNDSampleCount(), SNDBytesToSamples(), SNDSamplesToBytes()

SUMMARY Measure samples in a sound

DECLARED IN sound/utilsound.h

SYNOPSIS int **SNDSampleCount**(SNDSoundStruct **sound*)
int **SNDBytesToSamples**(int *byteCount*, int *channelCount*, int *dataFormat*)
int **SNDSamplesToBytes**(int *sampleCount*, int *channelCount*, int *dataFormat*)

DESCRIPTION **SNDSampleCount()** returns the number of sample frames, or channel-independent samples, in *sound*. The sound must contain sampled data.

SNDBytesToSamples() returns the number of samples contained in *byteCount* bytes of sound data with the given channel count and data format. **SNDSamplesToBytes()** performs the inverse operation, returning the number of bytes needed to store *sampleCount* samples. The value returned by **SNDSamplesToBytes()** is useful for computing the *dataSize* argument to **SNDAlloc()**.

RETURN If *sound* doesn't contain sampled data (or if for any other reason the sample count can't be determined), **SNDSampleCount()** returns –1. **SNDBytesToSamples()** and **SNDSamplesToBytes()** return 0 if *dataFormat* isn't a sampled sound format and –1 if *dataFormat* isn't recognized.

SNDSamplesProcessed() → See SNDStartPlaying()

SNDSamplesToBytes() → See SNDSampleCount()

SNDSetATCGain(), SNDGetATCGain(), SNDSetATCEqualizerGains(), SNDGetATCEqualizerGains(), SNDScaleATCEqualizerGains()

SUMMARY Modify volume or equalization for ATC playback

DECLARED IN sound/atcsound.h

SYNOPSIS

int **SNDSetATCGain**(float *level*)
int **SNDGetATCGain**(float **level*)
int **SNDSetATCEqualizerGains**(int *numBands*, float **gains*)
int **SNDGetATCEqualizerGains**(int *numBands*, float **gains*)
int **SNDScaleATCEqualizerGains**(int *numBands*, float **gainScalars*)

DESCRIPTION

Audio Transform Compression (ATC) can be used not only for compression, but also to manipulate a sound's volume or frequency spectrum. These functions determine the playback level of sounds in the ATC format—either their overall gain, or the gains of their individual frequency bands.

SNDSetATCGain() sets the overall sound output level for ATC sound playback. The value for *level* can range from 0.0 (which will silence any ATC sound) to 1.0 (which will play sounds unchanged). The new level setting takes effect starting with the next ATC sound played. **SNDGetATCGain()** returns, in its argument, a pointer to the current level. Note that this volume setting—unlike that specified by **SNDSetVolume()**—affects not only the speaker and headphone output, but also the line-out jacks. This is possible because **SNDSetATCGain()** is implemented as a scaling of the ATC equalizer gains, and so it only affects ATC sounds. For such sounds, the volume at the speaker and headphones is the product of the ATC gain and the global setting returned by **SNDGetVolume()**.

Because ATC manipulates the gain of individual frequency bands, it can be used to implement a graphic equalizer for playback of ATC sounds. An array of "equalizer gains" is provided for this purpose. **SNDSetATCEqualizerGains()** sets the equalizer gains to the values in the array *gains*, and **SNDGetATCEqualizerGains()** returns the current equalizer gains by reference. **SNDScaleATCEqualizerGains()** multiplies each band's gain by the corresponding scalar in the array *gainScalars*. For all three functions, *numBands* should be the value returned by **SNDGetNumberOfATCBands()**. Each element of the *gains* array specifies a factor by which the sound amplitude in the corresponding frequency band will be multiplied during sound playback. The gain should be a nonnegative number between 0.0 and 16.0 (inclusive). Gains greater than 1.0 may cause the output to be clipped. The system default gain for each band is 1.0, meaning that the sound is played without modification. Changes take effect starting with the next sound played; any currently playing sound is unaffected.

RETURN Zero is returned, with one exception: If **SNDSetATCGain()**, **SNDSetATCEqualizerGains()**, or **SNDScaleATCEqualizerGains()** sets the gains of any frequency bands to values less than zero or greater than the 16.0, those values are set to zero or the maximum (respectively), and the function returns the number of bands that were clipped in this way.

SEE ALSO **SNDCompressSound()**, **SNDGetNumberOfATCBands()**, **SNDSetVolume**, **SNDDropATCSamples()**

SNDSetATCSquelchThresholds(), SNDGetATCSquelchThresholds(), SNDUseDefaultATCSquelchThresholds()

SUMMARY Set or get Audio Transform Compression parameters

DECLARED IN sound/atcsound.h

SYNOPSIS int **SNDSetATCSquelchThresholds**(int *numBands*, float **thresholds*)
int **SNDGetATCSquelchThresholds**(int *numBands*, float **thresholds*)
int **SNDUseDefaultATCSquelchThresholds**(void)

DESCRIPTION These functions set or retrieve parameters that control the amount of compression achieved by **SNDCompressSound()** when it uses Audio Transform Compression (ATC).

SNDSetATCSquelchThresholds() and **SNDGetATCSquelchThresholds()** respectively fill and retrieve the array *thresholds*, which specifies the squelch thresholds for each frequency band. The first argument to both functions, *numBands*, should be obtained from **SNDGetNumberOfATCBands()**. (If desired, the frequencies of the bands can be determined by invoking **SNDGetATCBandFrequencies()**.) The thresholds can range from zero to one. A value of 0.0 ensures that frequencies in that band will never be suppressed, while a value of 1.0 almost always squelches them. The default squelch threshold for each band is the estimated threshold of audibility at a normal listening level. The defaults can be restored by calling **SNDUseDefaultATCSquelchThresholds()**. Changes to the thresholds take effect starting with the next sound compressed; any currently compressing sound is unaffected.

RETURN Zero is returned upon success, with one exception: If the *thresholds* array passed to **SNDSetATCSquelchThresholds()** contains any values less than zero or greater than one, those values are set to zero or one (respectively), and the function returns the number of bands that were clipped in this way.

SEE ALSO **SNDCompressSound()**, **SNDGetNumberOfATCBands()**, **SNDGetATCBandFrequencies()**, **SNDSetATCGain()**, **SNDDropATCSamples()**

SNDSetCompressionOptions(), SNDGetCompressionOptions()

SUMMARY Set and get compression attributes used in recording

DECLARED IN sound/preformsound.h

SYNOPSIS int **SNDSetCompressionOptions(**SNDSoundStruct **sound*, int *bitFaithful*, int *compressionAmount***)**

int **SNDGetCompressionOptions(**SNDSoundStruct **sound*, int **bitFaithful*, int **compressionAmount***)**

DESCRIPTION **SNDSetCompressionOptions()** sets the bit-faithfulness and the compression amount that **SNDStartRecording()** uses during subsequent recordings into the sound *sound*. These values are effective only if *sound*'s format specifies compression. By default, such a recording is bit-faithful with a compression amount of 4.

SNDGetCompressionOptions() returns, in its arguments, pointers to the currently established compression options.

RETURN If no error occurs, SND_ERR_NONE is returned. Otherwise an error code, as described in **SNDSoundError()**, is returned.

SNDSetFilter() → See SNDSetVolume()

SNDSetHost()

SUMMARY Set the host computer for subsequent playback or recording

DECLARED IN sound/accesssound.h

SYNOPSIS int **SNDSetHost**(char **newHostname*)

DESCRIPTION **SNDSetHost()** gives you access to the named host for subsequent playbacks or recordings. If *newHostname* is NULL or a zero-length string, the default (the local host) is restored.

RETURN If no error occurs, SND_ERR_NONE is returned. Otherwise, an error code, as described in **SNDSoundError()**, is returned.

SNDSetMute() → See SNDSetVolume()

SNDSetVolume(), SNDGetVolume(), SNDSetMute(), SNDGetMute(), SNDSetFilter(), SNDGetFilter()

SUMMARY Sound playback utilities

DECLARED IN sound/utilsound.h

SYNOPSIS

int **SNDSetVolume**(int *left*, int *right*)
int **SNDGetVolume**(int **left*, int **right*)
int **SNDSetMute**(int *speakerOn*)
int **SNDGetMute**(int **speakerOn*)
int **SNDSetFilter**(int *filterOn*)
int **SNDGetFilter**(int **filterOn*)

DESCRIPTION **SNDSetVolume()** sets the sound playback level for the left and right channels, specified as an integer between 1 and 43 (inclusive). This only affects the signal to the internal speaker and the stereo headphone jack; the line-out level is undisturbed. **SNDGetVolume()** returns, in its arguments, pointers to the playback levels of either channel.

SNDSetMute() mutes and unmutes the internal speaker and headphone level as *speakerOn* is 0 and nonzero, respectively. **SNDGetMute()** returns, in its argument, a pointer to the mute status.

SNDSetFilter() turns the low-pass filter off or on as *filterOn* is 0 or nonzero, respectively. **SNDGetFilter()** returns, in its argument, a pointer to the state of the filter. The filter is automatically turned on while sounds whose format is SND_FORMAT_EMPHASIZED or SND_FORMAT_COMPRESSED_EMPHASIZED are being played.

RETURN If no error occurs, SND_ERR_NONE is returned. Otherwise, an error code, as described in **SNDSoundError()**, is returned.

SNDSoundError()

SUMMARY Describe a sound error

DECLARED IN sound/sounderror.h

SYNOPSIS char ***SNDSoundError**(int *err*)

DESCRIPTION **SNDSoundError()** returns a pointer to a string that describes the given error code. The following are defined as error codes:

Code	String
SND_ERR_NONE	""
SND_ERR_NOT_SOUND	"Not a sound"
SND_ERR_BAD_FORMAT	"Bad data format"
SND_ERR_BAD_RATE	"Bad sampling rate"
SND_ERR_BAD_CHANNEL	"bad channel count"
SND_ERR_BAD_SIZE	"bad size"
SND_ERR_BAD_FILENAME	"Bad file name"
SND_ERR_CANNOT_OPEN	"Cannot open file"
SND_ERR_CANNOT_WRITE	"Cannot write file"
SND_ERR_CANNOT_READ	"Cannot read file"
SND_ERR_CANNOT_ALLOC	"Cannot allocate memory"
SND_ERR_CANNOT_FREE	"Cannot free memory"
SND_ERR_CANNOT_COPY	"Cannot copy"
SND_ERR_CANNOT_RESERVE	"Cannot reserve access"
SND_ERR_NOT_RESERVED	"Access not reserved"
SND_ERR_CANNOT_RECORD	"Cannot record sound"
SND_ERR_ALREADY_RECORDING	"Already recording sound"
SND_ERR_NOT_RECORDING	"Not recording sound"
SND_ERR_CANNOT_PLAY	"Cannot play sound"
SND_ERR_ALREADY_PLAYING	"Already playing sound"
SND_ERR_NOT_IMPLEMENTED	"Not implemented"
SND_ERR_NOT_PLAYING	"Not playing sound"
SND_ERR_CANNOT_FIND	"Cannot find sound"
SND_ERR_CANNOT_EDIT	"Cannot edit sound"
SND_ERR_BAD_SPACE	"Bad memory space in DSP load image"
SND_ERR_KERNEL	"Mach kernel error"
SND_ERR_BAD_CONFIGURATION	"Bad configuration"
SND_ERR_CANNOT_CONFIGURE	"Cannot configure"
SND_ERR_UNDERRUN	"Data underrun"
SND_ERR_ABORTED	"Aborted"
SND_ERR_BAD_TAG	"Bad tag"
SND_ERR_CANNOT_ACCESS	"Cannot access hardware resources"
SND_ERR_TIMEOUT	"Timeout"
SND_ERR_BUSY	"Hardware resources already in use"
SND_ERR_CANNOT_ABORT	"Cannot abort operation"
SND_ERR_INFO_TOO_BIG	"Information string too large"
SND_ERR_UNKNOWN	"Unknown error"

SNDStartPlaying(), SNDVerifyPlayable(), SNDStartRecording(), SNDStartRecordingFile(), SNDWait(), SNDStop(), SNDSamplesProcessed(), SNDModifyPriority()

SUMMARY Recording and playing a sound

DECLARED IN sound/performsound.h

SYNOPSIS

int **SNDStartPlaying**(SNDSoundStruct **sound*, int *tag*, int *priority*, int *preempt*, SNDNotificationFun *beginFun*, SNDNotificationFun *endFun*)
int **SNDVerifyPlayable**(SNDSoundStruct **sound*)
int **SNDStartRecording**(SNDSoundStruct **sound*, int *tag*, int *priority*, int *preempt*, SNDNotificationFun *beginFun*, SNDNotificationFun *endFun*)
int **SNDStartRecordingFile**(char **fileName*, SNDSoundStruct **sound*, int *tag*, int *priority*, int *preempt*, SNDNotificationFun *beginFun*, SNDNotificationFun *endFun*)
int **SNDStop**(int *tag*)
int **SNDWait**(int *tag*)
int **SNDSamplesProcessed**(int *tag*)
int **SNDModifyPriority**(int *tag*, int *newPriority*)

DESCRIPTION

SNDStartPlaying() initiates the playback of *sound*. The function returns immediately while the playback continues in a background thread. During playback, the sound is played on the internal speaker and sent to the stereo line-out jacks.

The *tag* argument is an arbitrary positive integer that the caller supplies to identify the playback session in subsequent calls to **SNDWait**(), **SNDStop**(), **SNDSamplesProcessed**(), and **SNDModifyPriority**(). You should never set a sound's tag to 0.

The value of *priority* establishes the sound's right to use the playback resources. The lowest priority is 0, larger numbers signify higher priorities. Negative priorities are reserved. A call to **SNDStartPlaying()** will interrupt a currently playing sound if the new sound has a higher priority. If the new sound has a lower priority, the old sound continues and the new sound is put in a sound playback queue. Sounds in the queue are sorted by priority.

A nonzero *preempt* flag is used for urgent sounds, such as system beeps. Preemption allows a new sound to interrupt a sound that has the same (or lower) priority. However, if the new sound can't interrupt, it isn't put in the queue.

beginFun and *endFun* are user-defined notification functions that are automatically called when the sound begins playing and when it ends, respectively. A notification function is defined as an integer function with three arguments:

typedef int (*SNDNotificationFun)(SNDSoundStruct **sound*, int *tag*, int *err*);

The *sound* and *tag* arguments are taken directly from the **SNDStartPlaying()** call. The *err* argument is one of the error codes listed in **SNDSoundError()** and is generated automatically to inform the notification function of the state of the playback. The return value is ignored. The value SND_NULL_FUN should be used to specify no function as either *beginFun* or *endFun*.

SNDVerifyPlayable() returns SND_ERR_NONE if *sound* can be played without first being converted to another format, sampling rate, or number of channels. Otherwise, it returns SND_ERR_CANNOT_PLAY.

The arguments to **SNDStartRecording()** are like those to **SNDStartPlaying()**. The sound resource used for recording is implied by information in *sound*'s header; currently, two configurations are allowed:

- If the sound is one channel of mulaw format (SND_FORMAT_MULAW) at the CODEC sampling rate (SND_RATE_CODEC), then the recording is made from the CODEC input (the microphone jack at the back of the monitor).
- If the format is one of the DSP data or compressed formats, the recording is made from the DSP port. In the case of a compressed format, the sound is compressed according to options set by **SNDSetCompressionOptions()**.

Like playback, recording is performed in a background thread. The recording completes when the storage allocated for the sound is filled with data.

SNDStartRecordingFile() is similar to **SNDStartRecording()**, but the sound is written directly to the file *fileName*. The *sound* argument is used for its size and format information.

SNDStop() terminates the playback or recording session that has a tag of *tag*.

SNDWait() returns only when the playback or recording with a tag of *tag* has completed. If *tag* is 0, all sounds in the sound queue are awaited. Note that if you call this function from the main thread of an application that has an asynchronous event-driven user interface, the interface will be effectively frozen until this function returns.

SNDSamplesProcessed() returns the number of samples that have been played or recorded so far in the playback or recording that has the given tag. If the tagged sound isn't currently active, –1 is returned.

SNDModifyPriority() resets the priority, as *newPriority*, of the playback or recording that has a tag of *tag*.

RETURN If no error occurs, SND_ERR_NONE is returned. Otherwise, an error code, as described in **SNDSoundError**(), is returned.

SNDStartRecording() → See SNDStartPlaying()

SNDStartRecordingFile() → See SNDStartPlaying()

SNDStop() → See SNDStartPlaying()

SNDUnreserve() → See SNDReserve()

SNDWait() → See SNDStartPlaying()

SNDWrite() → See SNDWriteSoundfile()

SNDWriteHeader() → See SNDWriteSoundfile()

SNDWriteSoundfile(), SNDWrite(), SNDWriteHeader()

SUMMARY Write a sound to a file

DECLARED IN sound/soundfile.h

SYNOPSIS int **SNDWriteSoundfile**(char **path*, SNDSoundStruct **sound*)
int **SNDWrite**(int *fd*, SNDSoundStruct **sound*)
int **SNDWriteHeader**(int *fd*, SNDSoundStruct **sound*)

DESCRIPTION **SNDWriteSoundfile**() writes the specified sound structure as the soundfile. *path* is a full pathname that should include the ".snd" extension (the convention for soundfiles). The function automatically opens and closes the file.

SNDWrite() also writes a complete soundfile, but its argument is a file descriptor rather than a pathname. The file must be open for writing.

With both **SNDWriteSoundfile()** and **SNDWrite()**, the actual sound data is written as a contiguous block, even if *sound* is fragmented. However, *sound* itself isn't affected—if it's fragmented, it remains fragmented.

SNDWriteHeader() is similar to **SNDWrite()**, but it only writes *sound*'s header to the file.

RETURN If no error occurs, SND_ERR_NONE is returned. Otherwise, an error code, as described in **SNDSoundError()**, is returned.

Sound Driver Functions

These functions access the sound/DSP driver. For simplicity, this driver is referred to as "the sound driver" in the following function descriptions. For sound operations that don't involve the DSP, most of these functions can be replaced by methods of the Sound Kit classes NXSoundDevice, NXSoundStream, and their subclasses.

Warning: There are actually two sound drivers: The sound/DSP driver that was used before the 3.0 version of NeXTSTEP and a sound-in/sound-out only driver introduced in Release 3.0. You should be able to ignore the distinction as long as you don't mix functions described here, which use the old driver, with the Sound Kit methods or the non-dsp "SND" sound functions, which use the new. In particular, ports that are obtained through the new methods and sound functions can't be passed as arguments to the old sound driver functions.

snddriver_dsp_boot(), snddriver_dsp_reset()

SUMMARY Start the DSP

DECLARED IN sound/snddriver_client.h

SYNOPSIS kern_return_t **snddriver_dsp_boot**(port_t *commandPort*, int **bootImage*, int *imageSize*, int *priority*)
kern_return_t **snddriver_dsp_reset**(port_t *commandPort*, int *priority*)

DESCRIPTION **snddriver_dsp_boot**() enqueues a command to boot the DSP. The arguments are as follows:

- *commandPort* is the DSP command port, as retrieved by **snddriver_get_dsp_cmd_port**().
- *bootImage* is a pointer to a DSP program image that's downloaded to the DSP (program memory location 0x0) and immediately executed. The image is created by reading a ".lod" file that's assembled from DSP56001 assembly code.
- *imageSize* is the size of the DSP boot image, in bytes. The image must not exceed 512 words (24-bit DSP words right-justified within 32-bit integers).
- *priority* is one of the three priority constants SNDDRIVER_LOW_PRIORITY, SNDDRIVER_MED_PRIORITY, or SNDDRIVER_HIGH_PRIORITY. The sound driver sorts the commands in its DSP command queue according to priority.

Booting the DSP clears neither external memory nor on-chip data memory.

snddriver_dsp_reset() puts the DSP in its reset state. By this it's meant that the DSP's execution is immediately halted and a bootstrap program is awaited. Booting the DSP automatically resets it, thus you don't need to call this function before calling **snddriver_boot_dsp**().

RETURN Returns an error code: 0 on success, nonzero on failure.

snddriver_dsp_dma_read() → See snddriver_dsp_dma_write()

snddriver_dsp_dma_write(), snddriver_dsp_dma_read()

SUMMARY Transfer data to and from the DSP via DMA

DECLARED IN sound/snddriver_client.h

SYNOPSIS kern_return_t **snddriver_dsp_dma_write**(port_t *commandPort*, int *elementCount*, int *dataFormat*, pointer_t *data*)

kern_return_t **snddriver_dsp_dma_read**(port_t *commandPort*, int *elementCount*, int *dataFormat*, pointer_t *data*)

DESCRIPTION These functions enqueue commands that perform application-initiated DMA transfers to and from the DSP. You must include complex DMA protocol to use these functions. The arguments to the two functions are similar:

- *commandPort* is the DSP command port, as retrieved by **snddriver_get_dsp_cmd_port**().
- *elementCount* is the number of data elements to send during each transfer.
- *dataFormat* is an integer constant that describes the size and packing of an individual data element. These are

DSP_MODE8	1 byte per element
DSP_MODE16	2 bytes per element
DSP_MODE24	3 bytes per element
DSP_MODE32	3 bytes per element, right-justified in 4
DSP_MODE2416	2 bytes per element, packed and right-justified in 4

- *data* is a pointer to the data that you're transferring.

There are three rules regarding the size and alignment of a DMA transfer buffer:

- The size in bytes of a single DMA transfer buffer, reckoned as *elementCount* * bytes-per-element, must be a multiple of 16. Note that bytes-per-element isn't given directly as an argument.
- The data must be "quad-aligned"; in other words, the starting address (*data*) must be a multiple of 16.
- All the data in a transfer buffer must lie on the same page of virtual memory.

If you're writing data, the **snddriver_dsp_dma_write()** function enqueues a command to send the data to the DSP and then immediately returns. **snddriver_dsp_dma_read()**, on the other hand, waits until it has read the prescribed amount of data and returns with *data* filled. DMA-transfer commands are always enqueued with high priority.

RETURN Returns an error code: 0 on success, nonzero on failure.

SEE ALSO **snddriver_dsp_read()**, **snddriver_dsp_write()**, **snddriver_dsp_protocol()**

---

snddriver_dsp_host_cmd()

SUMMARY Enqueue a DSP command

DECLARED IN sound/snddriver_client.h

SYNOPSIS kern_return_t **snddriver_dsp_host_cmd**(port_t *commandPort*, u_int *hostCommand*, u_int *priority*)

DESCRIPTION **snddriver_dsp_host_cmd()** enqueues a command on the sound driver's DSP command queue that interrupts the DSP and causes it to execute one of 32 interrupt routines (or *host commands*). Its arguments are as follows:

- *commandPort* is the DSP command port, as retrieved by **snddriver_get_dsp_cmd_port()**.
- *hostCommand* is an integer that represents the host command you want to execute. The first 22 host commands are already defined (or reserved). The host commands provided by NeXT are represented by constants (prefix "DSP_hc_") that are defined in **/usr/include/nextdev/snd_dsp.h**. Creating your own host command requires a familiarity with DSP programming that lies beyond the scope of this description.
- *priority* is one of the three priority constants SNDDRIVER_LOW_PRIORITY, SNDDRIVER_MED_PRIORITY, or SNDDRIVER_HIGH_PRIORITY. The sound driver sorts the commands in its DSP command queue according to priority.

When the DSP receives a host command, it sets the HC flag in the Command Vector Register. After executing the command, the DSP clears the flag. You should always precede a call to **snddriver_dsp_host_cmd()** with a call to **snddriver_dspcmd_req_condition()** that waits for HC to clear in order to avoid overwriting a previously requested, but as yet unexecuted, host command:

```
/* CVR_HC is defined in <nextdev/snd_dspreg.h> */
err = snddriver_dspcmd_req_condition(commandPort, CVR_HC, 0, ...);
if (err != 0)
    . . .

/* Now enqueue the host command request. */
err = snddriver_dsp_host_cmd(...);
if (err != 0)
    . . .
```

RETURN Returns an error code: 0 on success, nonzero on failure.

SEE ALSO **snddriver_dspcmd_req_condition()**

---

snddriver_dsp_protocol()

SUMMARY Set the sound driver's protocol vis-a-vis the DSP

DECLARED IN sound/snddriver_client.h

SYNOPSIS kern_return_t **snddriver_dsp_protocol(**port_t *devicePort*, port_t *ownerPort*, int *protocol*)

DESCRIPTION **snddriver_dsp_protocol()** lets you establish the manner in which the sound driver communicates with the DSP; specifically, it determines whether to create 0, 1, or 2 DSP-reply buffers and whether DSP interrupts are enabled. The existence of the DSP-reply buffers determines whether you can use streams to transfer data.

The function's first two arguments are the sound driver device port and the DSP owner port, as acquired through **SNDAcquire()**.

protocol is the heart of the matter: It's a code that represents the protocol that you wish to establish. There are two ways to create the appropriate protocol: If you're using streams to access the DSP, then you should pass the protocol variable that's modified by calls to **snddriver_stream_setup()**, as explained (with an example) in the description of that function. Alternatively—or in addition to the foregoing—you can create a protocol code by or'ing the following DSP protocol constants:

- SNDDRIVER_DSP_PROTO_RAW represents the barest protocol. The sound driver makes no assumptions about how the DSP is being used: No DSP-reply buffers are created and the DSP can't interrupt the host. You can't use streams in raw protocol; to transfer data, you use the **snddriver_dsp_write()** and **snddriver_dsp_read()** functions.

All the other protocols create at least one DSP-reply buffer and allow DSP interrupts, thus allowing you to transfer data through a stream:

- SNDDRIVER_DSP_PROTO_DSPMSG ("DSP-message") creates a buffer that can hold 512 DSP-reply messages. A message from the DSP (as it lies in the reply buffer) is a 24-bit word right-justified in 32 bits. To receive the contents of this buffer, you enqueue a request through **snddriver_dspcmd_req_msg()**.
- SNDDRIVER_DSP_PROTO_DSPERR ("DSP-error") creates an additional 512-message DSP-reply buffer that collects error messages sent from the DSP. An error message is identified as having its MSB (bit 23) set. You can request the contents of the error buffer through **snddriver_dspcmd_req_err()**.
- SNDDRIVER_DSP_PROTO_C_DMA ("complex DMA") implies DSP message mode (a single DSP-reply buffer is created) and allows DSP-initiated DMA transfers.
- SNDDRIVER_DSP_PROTO_HFABORT ("host flag abort") causes the driver to take note if the DSP aborts. (The DSP indicates that it has aborted by setting HF2 and HF3.)

To get the documented behavior from these protocols, you *must* include SNDDRIVER_DSP_PROTO_RAW.

Note: A protocol of 0 produces Release 1.0 behavior; this is roughly equivalent to a combination of DSP message, DSP error, and host flag abort modes.

RETURN Returns an error code: 0 on success, nonzero on failure.

SEE ALSO **snddriver_stream_setup()**

snddriver_dsp_read() → See snddriver_dsp_write()

snddriver_dsp_read_data() → See snddriver_dsp_write()

snddriver_dsp_read_messages() → See snddriver_dsp_write()

snddriver_dsp_reset() → See snddriver_dsp_boot()

snddriver_dsp_set_flags()

SUMMARY Set the DSP host flags

DECLARED IN sound/snddriver_client.h

SYNOPSIS kern_return_t **snddriver_dsp_set_flags**(port_t *commandPort*, u_int *flagMask*, u_int *flagValue*, u_int *priority*)

DESCRIPTION **snddriver_dsp_set_flags**() enqueues a command to modify one or both of the DSP host interface flags HF0 (host flag 0) and HF1 (host flag 1).

The *flagMask* argument defines which of the host flags you want to affect. The flags are represented by the constants SNDDRIVER_ICR_HF0 and SNDDRIVER_ICR_HF1. You can set both flags at the same time by or'ing these two constants. (ICR stands for "Interrupt Control Register"; this is the register to which the host flags belong.)

flagValue is the value to which you're setting the flag(s). A host flag can be either on or off, states that are also referred to as "set" and "cleared". To set a flag, you pass its constant identifier; to clear it, you pass 0. The following examples illustrate this concept:

```
/* Set HF0 (turn it on). */
snddriver_dsp_set_flags(..., SNDDRIVER_ICR_HF0,
            SNDDRIVER_ICR_HF0,...)

/* Clear HF1. */
snddriver_dsp_set_flags(..., SNDDRIVER_ICR_HF1,0,...)

/* Set both flags. */
snddriver_dsp_set_flags(...,
        SNDDRIVER_ICR_HF0 | SNDDRIVER_ICR_HF1,
            SNDDRIVER_ICR_HF0 | SNDDRIVER_ICR_HF1, ...)

/* Set HF0 and clear HF1. */
snddriver_dsp_set_flags(...,
        SNDDRIVER_ICR_HF0 | SNDDRIVER_ICR_HF1,
            SNDDRIVER_ICR_HF0, ...)

/* Clear both flags. */
snddriver_dsp_set_flags(...,
        SNDDRIVER_ICR_HF0 | SNDDRIVER_ICR_HF1, 0,...)
```

The other two arguments, *commandPort* and *priority*, are the DSP command port and command-queue priority, respectively. The DSP command port is retrieved through **snddriver_dsp_cmd_port**(); you set the priority to one of SNDDRIVER_HIGH_PRIORITY, SNDDRIVER_MED_PRIORITY, or SNDDRIVER_LOW_PRIORITY.

RETURN Returns an error code: 0 on success, nonzero on failure.

SEE ALSO **snddriver_dspcmd_req_condition**()

---

snddriver_dsp_write(), snddriver_dsp_read(), snddriver_dsp_read_data(), snddriver_dsp_read_messages()

SUMMARY Transfer data to and from the DSP

DECLARED IN sound/snddriver_client.h

SYNOPSIS

kern_return_t **snddriver_dsp_write**(port_t *commandPort*, void **buffer*, int *elementCount*, int *elementSize*, int *priority*)

kern_return_t **snddriver_dsp_read**(port_t *commandPort*, void **buffer*, int *elementCount*, int *elementSize*, int *priority*)

kern_return_t **snddriver_dsp_read_messages**(port_t *commandPort*, void **buffer*, int *elementCount*, int *elementSize*, int *priority*)

kern_return_t **snddriver_dsp_read_data**(port_t *commandPort*, void ***buffer*, int *elementCount*, int *elementSize*, int *priority*)

DESCRIPTION **snddriver_dsp_write**() enqueues a command to perform a one-shot, application-initiated data transfer to the DSP; **snddriver_dsp_read**() brings data back from the DSP in a like manner. You generally use these functions if you have a small amount of data to transfer or if the transfers are infrequent enough that the overhead of the obvious alternative—setting up a DMA stream—would be exorbitant.

The other two functions, **snddriver_dsp_read_messages**() and **snddriver_dsp_read_data**() are auxiliary to **snddriver_dsp_read**(). When you call **snddriver_dsp_read**(), it, in turn, calls one of the auxiliary functions; which of the two functions it calls depends on the current DSP protocol, as described below. You can call these functions yourself by-passing **snddriver_dsp_read**(), although you should adhere to the same protocol rules that **snddriver_dsp_read**() obeys.

The arguments to all four functions are similar:

- *commandPort* is the DSP command port, as retrieved through **snddriver_get_dsp_cmd_port().**
- *buffer*, as used by **snddriver_dsp_write()**, is a pointer to the data you want to send to the DSP. For the **snddriver_dsp_read...()** functions, it's a pointer to the location where you want the retrieved data to be stored. Note that for **snddriver_dsp_read_data()**, *buffer* is the address of a pointer; this allows the function to allocate memory for the data if you haven't allocated it yourself.
- *elementCount* and *elementSize* are the number of data elements to transfer and the size, in bytes, of a single element, respectively.
- *priority* is an integer used to sort the command on the DSP command queue. The sound driver defines three priorities represented by the constants SNDDRIVER_LOW_PRIORITY, SNDDRIVER_MED_PRIORITY, and SNDDRIVER_HIGH_PRIORITY. You normally set all application-initiated data transfers to low priority, thus reserving medium and high priority for operations that need to jump to the head of the DSP command queue.

Of these functions, **snddriver_dsp_write()** is most straightforward: When it's called, a transfer-data-to-the-DSP command is sorted (by priority) into the DSP command queue. If, when its turn comes, the command can't be executed, the driver simply pushes it back on the queue and tries again. No other commands of equal or lower priority can be executed while a frustrated write command is sitting on top of the queue. Note, however, that higher priority commands *will* get through.

As mentioned earlier, **snddriver_dsp_read()** calls one of its two auxiliary functions as determined by the current DSP protocol:

- If your application is in raw protocol, then **snddriver_dsp_read_data()** is used to read data from the DSP transmit registers.
- If DSP message protocol is included, **snddriver_dsp_read_messages()** is used to read data from the DSP-reply buffer.

The difference between the two mechanisms is generally transparent such that you can call **snddriver_read_data()** without regard for the current protocol. However, the manner in which the underlying functions handles incomplete reads is significant: If the read can't be completed (typically because the DSP hasn't generated enough data), **snddriver_dsp_read_data()** blocks the DSP command queue in the fashion of

snddriver_dsp_write(). In the same situation, **snddriver_dsp_read_messages()** waits for more data without blocking the command queue. Thus **snddriver_dsp_read_messages()** can safely be called from a separate thread at any time. This isn't true of **snddriver_dsp_read_data()**; you should be scrupulous about ensuring that sufficient data has been processed by the DSP before you attempt to read it through this function (or through **snddriver_dsp_read()** while in raw protocol).

RETURN Returns an error code: 0 on success, nonzero on failure.

SEE ALSO **snddriver_dsp_dma_read()**, **snddriver_dsp_dma_write()**

---

snddriver_dspcmd_req_condition()

SUMMARY Request a DSP host interface register condition

DECLARED IN sound/snddriver_client.h

SYNOPSIS kern_return_t **snddriver_dspcmd_req_condition**(port_t *commandPort*, u_int *registerMask*, u_int *conditionFlags*, int *priority*, port_t *replyPort*)

DESCRIPTION **snddriver_dspcmd_req_condition()** does two things: It causes the DSP command queue to block until the specified host interface register condition is true, and it registers a request for an asynchronous message to be sent to *replyPort* when the condition is fulfilled. The function returns immediately.

You specify a condition through a combination of the *registerMask* and *conditionFlags* arguments:

- *registerMask* specifies the host interface registers (actually, the bits therein) that you're interested in. It's created by **or**'ing the register-bit constants defined in **nextdev/snd_dspregs.h**. A subset of these are also defined as sound driver constants in **sound/snddriver_client.h**.
- *conditionFlags* encodes the states of the register bits that define a satisfied condition. To specify that you want a register bit set, you **or** the register-bit constant that represents it; if you want it clear, you exclude the constant. If you want all the specified bits to be clear, set *conditionFlags* to 0.

In the following example, the command queue is blocked until HF0 is set and HF1 is clear (both flags are in the Interrupt Control Register):

```
/* Block until HF0 is set and HF1 is clear. */
snddriver_dspcmd_req_condition(...,
        SNDDRIVER_ICR_HF0 | SNDDRIVER_ICR_HF1,
        SNDDRIVER_ICR_HF2, ...)
```

The condition request is sorted into the DSP command queue according to *priority*, which must be one of SNDDRIVER_LOW_PRIORITY, SNDDRIVER_MED_PRIORITY, or SNDDRIVER_HIGH_PRIORITY.

The message that's sent to the reply port when the condition is fulfilled contains the value of the host interface register. By setting the *registerMask* argument to 0, you can use the **snddriver_dspcmd_req_condition**() function to simply poll for this value.

RETURN Returns an error code: 0 on success, nonzero on failure.

SEE ALSO **snddriver_dsp_set_flags()**

snddriver_dspcmd_req_err() → See snddriver_dspcmd_req_msg()

---

snddriver_dspcmd_req_msg(), snddriver_dspcmd_req_err()

SUMMARY Request the contents of the DSP-reply buffers

DECLARED IN sound/snddriver_client.h

SYNOPSIS kern_return_t **snddriver_dspcmd_req_msg**(port_t *commandPort*, port_t *replyPort*)
kern_return_t **snddriver_dspcmd_req_err**(port_t *commandPort*, port_t *replyPort*)

DESCRIPTION The **snddriver_dspcmd_req_msg()** and **snddriver_dspcmd_req_err()** functions are part of the mechanism by which your application retrieves messages from the sound driver's DSP-reply buffers. They request that the contents of the appropriate buffer (as described below) be sent in a Mach message to *replyPort*, a valid port that must already be allocated. Simply requesting a message is only half of the story: You then have to receive the message that's been sent, usually by sitting in a **msg_receive**() loop. You typically process the Mach messages that these functions induce by passing the messages to the **snddriver_reply_handler()** function.

The utility of these functions depends on your application's DSP protocol:

- You should never use these functions in raw protocol since the sound driver doesn't create any DSP-reply buffers.
- By including DSP message protocol, a single DSP-reply buffer is created in which both error and non-error messages are stored; thus **...req_msg()** is of use, but **...req_err()** isn't.
- DSP error protocol deems that two buffers be created, one for error messages and the other for non-error messages. Both functions are useful in this protocol.

DSP protocol and how to set it is explained in the description of the **snddriver_set_dsp_protocol()** function. For both functions, the *commandPort* argument is the DSP command port as retrieved by **snddriver_get_dsp_cmd_port()**.

RETURN Returns an error code: 0 on success, nonzero on failure.

SEE ALSO **snddriver_set_dsp_protocol()**, **snddriver_reply_handler()**

snddriver_get_device_parms() → See snddriver_set_device_parms()

---

snddriver_get_dsp_cmd_port()

SUMMARY Get the DSP command port

DECLARED IN sound/snddriver_client.h

SYNOPSIS kern_return_t **snddriver_get_dsp_cmd_port**(port_t *devicePort*, port_t *ownerPort*, port_t **commandPort*)

DESCRIPTION **snddriver_get_dsp_cmd_port()** attempts to get the *DSP command port*, the port through which the sound driver issues commands to the DSP. If it's successful, the port is returned in the *commandPort* argument, which needn't have been previously allocated.

The first two arguments, *devicePort* and *ownerPort*, are the sound driver device port and the DSP owner port, as acquired through **SNDAcquire()**.

The DSP command port is required as an argument by almost all sound driver functions that communicate with the DSP. The one notable exception, for which you don't have to get the command port as it's gotten implicitly when needed, is if you send and retrieve DSP data via streams after having booted the DSP through the **SNDBootDSP()** sound library function. But even in this case getting the command port as a reflex to getting the DSP owner port won't serve you ill.

RETURN Returns an error code: 0 on success, nonzero on failure.

snddriver_get_volume() → See snddriver_set_device_parms()

---

snddriver_new_device_port()

SUMMARY Reallocate the sound driver device port

DECLARED IN sound/snddriver_client.h

SYNOPSIS kern_return_t **snddriver_new_device_port**(port_t *devicePort*, port_t *superuserPort*, port_t **newDevicePort*)

DESCRIPTION This function deallocates the sound driver device port *devicePort*, as previously acquired through **SNDAcquire()**, then allocates a new port to the device which it returns as *newDevicePort*. When the old device port is deallocated, so, too, are all its resource owner ports and sound streams; thus any currently operating sound driver tasks, such as recording and playing sounds, are aborted. Because of the ruthlessness of this act, you must be the UNIX superuser to call this function, as verified by the *superuserPort* argument, for which you should pass the return value of **host_priv_self()**. The new device port's registration with regard to the Network Name Server is the same as that of the old; in other words, if the old port had been registered (through **netname_check_in()**), the new one will be registered automatically.

RETURN Returns an error code: 0 on success, nonzero on failure.

snddriver_reply_handler()

SUMMARY Respond to asynchronous sound driver messages

DECLARED IN sound/snddriver_client.h

SYNOPSIS kern_return_t **snddriver_reply_handler**(msg_header_t **reply*,
snddriver_handlers_t **handlers*)

DESCRIPTION **snddriver_reply_handler()** helps your application respond to asynchronous sound driver messages. The function is designed around the **snddriver_handlers** structure, which provides a correspondence between the sound driver messages and a list of C functions that you provide. When you receive a message from the sound driver, you pass the message and a **snddriver_handlers** structure to **snddriver_reply_handler()** which then executes the handler function that corresponds to the message.

The definition of the **snddriver_handlers** structure (**typedef**'d, for convenience, as **snddriver_handlers_t**) reveals the nature of the functions that you can register as reply handlers:

```
typedef struct snddriver_handlers {
    void                         *arg;
    int                           timeout;
    sndreply_tagged_t             started;
    sndreply_tagged_t             completed;
    sndreply_tagged_t             aborted;
    sndreply_tagged_t             paused;
    sndreply_tagged_t             resumed;
    sndreply_tagged_t             overflow;
    sndreply_recorded_data_t      recorded_data;
    sndreply_dsp_cond_true_t      condition_true;
    sndreply_dsp_msg_t            dsp_message;
    sndreply_dsp_msg_t            dsp_error;
  } snddriver_handlers_t;
```

The structure's **arg** field is a value that's passed to the reply handlers when they're called by **snddriver_reply_handler()**; you can set it to whatever value best suits your application, but keep in mind that the value must fit within the size of a pointer (four bytes). The **timeout** field is currently unused.

The final ten fields are the heart of the structure: Each corresponds to a particular sound driver message. The first six of these correspond to messages that indicate a change in the state of a stream ("stream-state" messages); in other words, the sound driver sends a specific message when a stream starts processing data, when it completes its processing, when it aborts, and so on. By setting a field to a particular function, you register that function as the handler for the message to which the field corresponds. For example, to establish a function named **handleStreamStart()** as the function that's executed when your application receives a stream-started message from the sound driver, you would do the following:

```
/* Create a snddriver_handlers_t and register the
 * function handleStreamStart() (which we'll assume already
 * exists) to process stream-started messages.
 */
snddriver_handlers_t replyHandlers;
replyHandlers.started = handleStreamStart;
```

While this registers **handleStreamStart()** as the handler for stream-started messages, you must also tell the sound driver that you actually want such messages sent to your application. To do this, you set the *msgStarted* boolean argument to true when you call **snddriver_stream_start_reading()** or **snddriver_stream_start_writing()**. Analogous *msg...* message flags exist for the other five stream-state messages.

When the sound driver sends a stream-state message to your application, it sends it to the port that you specify as the last argument (*replyPort*) to **snddriver_stream_start_reading()** or **snddriver_stream_start_writing()**. To receive the message, you create a **msg_header_t** structure, set its **local_port** field to the stream's reply port, and then wait for the message to arrive by sitting in a message receive (**msg_receive()**) loop. After so capturing the message, you then pass it, along with your handler structure, to **snddriver_reply_handler()**. This is demonstrated by the example below.

Notice, from the definition of **snddriver_handlers**, that the six stream-state handlers are all of type **sndreply_tagged_t**. This type represents a two-argument function protocol that's defined as

```
typedef void (*sndreply_tagged_t) (void *arg, int tag);
```

The functions that you register to handle the stream-state messages must adhere to this protocol. The values of the arguments are set by **snddriver_reply_handler()**:

- *arg* is given the value of the *arg* field of the **snddriver_handlers** structure in which the function is registered. As mentioned earlier, you can set the structure's *arg* field to a (four-byte) value that suits the needs of your application.

- *tag* is the region-identifying tag that you provide as an argument to **snddriver_stream_start_writing()** or **snddriver_stream_start_reading()**.

The seventh of the ten **snddriver_handlers** handler fields—**recorded_data**—also applies to streams. However, unlike the fist six, which are optional, **recorded_data** is essential when you're reading data from a stream. Its importance arises from the way that the sound driver handles read data: It keeps the data in the kernel's virtual memory until you ask to bring it into your application. The only way to bring this data back is to supply a **recorded_data** handler that does so. The following program excerpt demonstrates a typical way to achieve this effect. In the example, details such as acquiring the sound driver and sound resource owner ports are omitted. The read stream shown here is anonymous—the code can be used equally well for a stream that reads from sound-in or from the DSP:

```
/* The code shown in the example requires the following header
   files  */
#import <sound/snddriver_client.h>
#import <mach.h>

/* Define a read stream tag, a read pointer, and a byte count
   variable. */
#define READ_TAG 1
static short *readData;
static int readCount;

/* Create a recorded_data handler; the function's protocol is
 * explained following the example.
 */
static void read_completed(void *arg, int tag, void *kernelData,
                           int size)
{
    /* Make sure this is the read stream. */
    if (tag == READ_TAG) {
        readData = (short *)kernelData;
        readCount = size;
    }
}
```

```
main()
{
    /* Define a read port, a reply port, and a reply structure. */
    port_t readPort, replyPort;
    snddriver_handlers_t replyHandlers;

    /* Allocate a Mach message header. msg_header_t and MSG_SIZE_MAX
     * (and msg_receive, below) are defined in mach.h.
     */
    msg_header_t *reply_msg = (msg_header_t *)malloc(MSG_SIZE_MAX);

    /* Create an error-check variable. */
    int err;

    /* Allocate the reply port. */
    err = port_allocate(task_self(), &replyPort);
    if (err != 0)
        . . .

    /* Set the recorded_data handler. */
    replyHandlers.recorded_data = read_completed;

    /* Set the amount of data you want to read; for the purposes of
     * this example, an arbitrary amount is specified.
     */
    readCount = 1024;

    /* Here, a number of activities -- such as acquiring the sound
     * driver port and sound resource owner port, setting up a read
     * stream through snddriver_stream_setup(), and (possibly)
     * booting the DSP and sending it data -- are omitted.
     */
    . . .

    /* Enqueue a read request.  The six 0 arguments are the message
     * request flags.
     */
    err = snddriver_stream_start_reading(readPort, 0, readCount,
                    READ_TAG, 0,0,0,0,0,0, replyPort);
    if (err != 0)
        . . .
```

```
        /* Sit in a message-receive loop. */
        while(1) {
            /* Set up the reply message.  This must be done inside the
             * loop since msg_receive() may change the message header.
             */
            replyMsg->msg_size = MSG_SIZE_MAX;
            replyMsg->msg_local_port = replyPort;
            err = msg_receive(replyMsg, MSG_OPTION_NONE, 0);
            if (err != 0)
                . . .
        }

        /* Dispatch the message to the reply handlers.*/
        err = snddriver_reply_handler(replyMsg, &replyHandlers);
        if (err != 0)
            . . .
        /* Provide a means to break out of the loop. */
        . . .
        }
    }
```

As implied by the example, you don't need to tell the sound driver that you want a data-recorded message to be sent to your application; the message is always sent automatically. The example also illustrates the rule that the reply port used to receive messages while in the **msg_receive()** loop is that which is specified as the final argument to the **snddriver_stream_start_reading()** function.

The data type of the **recorded_data** field dictates the protocol of the function that you design to bring data back to the application. The type is **sndreply_recorded_data_t**:

```
typedef void (*sndreply_recorded_data_t)(void *arg, int tag,
                void *kernelData, int size);
```

The first two arguments, *arg* and *tag*, are the same as in the **snddreply_tagged_t** type. *kernelData* is a pointer to the recorded data as it resides in the kernel; *size* is the size of the recorded data in bytes.

The final three **snddriver_handlers** fields correspond to messages that are inspired by the DSP:

- The **condition_true** handler is called when a requested DSP host interface register condition comes true. (More accurately, the handler is called when the message that indicates that the condition is true is passed to **snddriver_reply_handler**().)
- **dsp_message** handles general messages that the sound driver receives from the DSP.
- **dsp_error** does the same for DSP error messages.

For each of these three handlers, there is a corresponding sound driver function that enqueues a request for a condition, a DSP message, or a DSP error message, respectively:

- **snddriver_dspcmd_req_condition**() blocks the DSP command queue until the state of the DSP host interface registers satisfies a requested condition.
- **snddriver_dspcmd_req_msg**() requests that the messages in the DSP-reply buffer be sent to your application. You must include DSP-message protocol for this to have an effect.
- **snddriver_dspcmd_req_err**() requests that the 512-byte DSP-reply error buffer be sent in a message. You must include DSP-error protocol for this to have an effect.

As with the **snddriver_stream_start...**() functions, the three DSP request functions require that you provide a reply port as an argument. It's to this reply port that the sound driver sends the requested DSP-inspired messages. A single call to one of these functions causes a single reply message to be sent to your application. Thus, for each call to **snddriver_dspcmd_req_msg**(), for example, your application will receive one message from the sound driver.

The **condition_true** handler is of type **sndreply_dsp_cond_true_t**:

```
typedef void (*sndreply_dsp_cond_true_t)(void *arg, u_int mask,
                u_int flags, u_int registers);
```

arg is the value of the **arg** field. The next two arguments, *mask* and *flags*, are given the values that were passed to **snddriver_dspcmd_req_condition**() (which also has *mask* and *flags* arguments). *registers* encodes the current status of the four DSP host interface registers in a single 32-bit vector. See the description of **snddriver_dspcmd_req_condition**() for more information on how this works.

The **dsp_message** and **dsp_error** are of type **sndreply_dsp_msg_t**:

```
typedef void (*sndreply_dsp_msg_t)(void *arg, int *data, int size);
```

arg is the value of the **arg** field. *data* is a pointer to the contents of the appropriate DSP-message buffer (regular or error, as the handler is **dsp_message** or **dsp_error**). *size* is the size of the buffer contents, in bytes.

snddriver_reply_handler() ignores messages for which you haven't created and registered a handler function.

RETURN Returns an error code: 0 on success, nonzero on failure.

SEE ALSO **snddriver_stream_start_reading()**, **snddriver_stream_start_writing()**, **snddriver_dspcmd_req_condition()**, **snddriver_dspcmd_req_msg()**, **snddriver_dspcmd_req_err()**

---

snddriver_set_device_parms(), snddriver_get_device_parms(), snddriver_set_volume(), snddriver_get_volume(), snddriver_set_ramp()

SUMMARY Set and get sound playback attributes

DECLARED IN sound/snddriver_client.h

SYNOPSIS

kern_return_t **snddriver_set_device_parms**(port_t *devicePort*, boolean_t *speakerOn*, boolean_t *filterOn*, boolean_t *zerofill*)

kern_return_t **snddriver_get_device_parms**(port_t *devicePort*, boolean_t **speakerOn*, boolean_t **filterOn*, boolean_t **zerofill*)

kern_return_t **snddriver_set_volume**(port_t *devicePort*, int *leftVolume*, int *rightVolume*)

kern_return_t **snddriver_get_volume**(port_t *devicePort*, int **leftVolume*, int **rightVolume*)

kern_return_t **snddriver_set_ramp**(port_t *devicePort*, int *rampOn*)

DESCRIPTION These functions set and get attributes of the sound playback system. Each takes, as its first argument, the sound driver device port as acquired through **SNDAcquire()**. You needn't acquire ownership of sound-out to set the playback attributes.

The NXSoundOut class can be used in place of all these functions.

snddriver_set_device_parms() sets three attributes as specified by the values of its boolean arguments:

- The internal speaker is turned on or off as *speakerOn* is true or false. Calling the function with alternating true and false *speakerOn* values is equivalent to toggling the Mute key (Command Mute) on the keyboard.

- Similarly, the value of *filterOn* turns the de-emphasis filter on or off. The filter can be controlled from the keyboard by toggling the louder key while holding down the Command key (this isn't marked on the keyboard). In addition, the de-emphasis filter is automatically turned on when a de-emphasis format sound is played and returned to its previous state when the sound is done playing.

- During playback, low sampling rate (22.05 kHz) sounds are converted to the high sampling rate (44.1 kHz) as they are sent to the DAC (which converts data at 44.1 kHz only). To do this, the sound driver emits an extra sample for every existing sample in the sound data. The value of *zerofill* determines whether these extra samples are set to 0 (true) or if they're copies of the existing samples (false). In almost all cases, copying the samples is preferable, since zerofilling results in a decrease in power. Note that you can't toggle this attribute from the keyboard. Also, keep in mind that CODEC rate sounds are converted to 22.05 kHz before being sent to the DAC and so are also affected by the state of *zerofill*.

snddriver_get_device_parms() returns, by reference in its final three arguments, the values of the attributes described above.

snddriver_set_volume() sets the volume of the internal speaker and similarly adjusts the signal that's sent to the stereo headphone jack (the signal to the line-out jacks is unaffected). The two channels of the stereo signal are set independent of each other, specified as the values of *leftVolume* and *rightVolume*. The volume of the internal speaker is the sum of these two values. Volume values are integers in the range 1 to 43, inclusive, where the unit is equal to 2 decibels. A volume of 1 is inaudible and 43 is full blast. An argument value outside this range will yield some unexpected volume within the range. You can also adjust playback volume by pressing the volume keys on the keyboard. Each discrete tap on a volume key increments or decrements both the left and the right volume settings by 1.

snddriver_get_volume() returns the left and right playback volumes by reference in *leftVolume* and *rightVolume*, respectively.

By default, sounds are ramped during playback: The first few samples are ramped up from zero and the last samples are ramped down. This helps prevent clicks at the beginnings and ends of sounds. **snddriver_set_ramp()** enables or disables this feature as its *rampOn* argument is nonzero or zero. You almost always want ramping enabled; the one obvious case in which it's undesirable is if you're chaining a series of separate sounds that are meant to be played seamlessly, one immediately after the other. In this case, ramping will cause annoying amplitude dips at each seam.

RETURN Returns an error code: 0 on success, nonzero on failure.

SEE ALSO **SNDSetVolume()**, + **setVolume::** (Sound), – **setAttenuationLeft:right:** (NXSoundOut)

---

snddriver_set_dsp_owner_port(), snddriver_set_sndin_owner_port(), snddriver_set_sndout_owner_port()

SUMMARY Acquire ownership of sound resources

DECLARED IN sound/snddriver_client.h

SYNOPSIS kern_return_t **snddriver_set_dsp_owner_port**(port_t *devicePort*, port_t *ownerPort*, port_t **negotiationPort*)
kern_return_t **snddriver_set_sndin_owner_port**(port_t *devicePort*, port_t *ownerPort*, port_t **negotiationPort*)
kern_return_t **snddriver_set_sndout_owner_port**(port_t *devicePort*, port_t *ownerPort*, port_t **negotiationPort*)

DESCRIPTION These functions try to acquire ownership of the DSP, sound-in, or sound-out by setting the resource's owner port to a port that you supply. They duplicate part of the functionality provided by **SNDAcquire()**; the latter should, in most cases, be used to the exclusion of these.

The arguments are the same for all three functions:

- *devicePort* is a valid port to the sound driver device, as acquired through **SNDAcquire()**.
- *ownerPort* is the port that will become the owner port for the requested resource if the function is successful. You must have already allocated *ownerPort* through the function **port_allocate()**.
- If the function successfully acquires ownership of the resource, then the port pointed to by *negotiationPort* is registered as the negotiation port for the resource. However, if the function isn't successful—most likely because ownership of the resource has already been claimed—then the currently registered negotiation port is returned in the

negotiationPort argument. By convention you point *negotiationPort* to *ownerPort* before calling these functions, thereby making the owner port accessible to other tasks. Similarly, if your bid for ownership fails and the current owner has followed this convention, then you can use the port returned in *negotiationPort* as the owner port for the resource. Note, however, that if the function call fails, there's no way to determine if the port pointed to by *negotiationPort* is actually the owner port. If you want to acquire sole ownership of a resource, set *negotiationPort* to something other than the *ownerPort* before calling these functions. This will ensure that only the caller will have access to the resource (assuming that the function is successful).

A single port can be used to claim ownership of more than one device. This is sometimes necessary when setting up a multiple-device stream (as explained in **snddriver_stream_setup**()). In the following example, the same port attempts to own both the DSP and sound-out:

```
err = port_allocate(task_self(), &ownerPort)
. . .

/* Acquire ownership of the DSP. */
err=snddriver_set_dsp_owner_port(devPort, ownerPort, &negPort);
. . .

/* Acquire ownership of sound-out. */
err=snddriver_set_sndout_owner_port(devPort,ownerPort,&negPort);
```

After you've claimed ownership of a resource, you should do something with it. With sound-in you set up a stream port through which you read (record) data. This is done by calling the **snddriver_stream_setup()** and **snddriver_stream_start_reading()** functions. Analogously, with sound-out you set up a stream through which you write (playback) data through the **snddriver_stream_start_writing()** function.

If you claim ownership of the DSP you should also acquire the DSP command port by calling **snddriver_get_dsp_cmd_port()**. Most of the functions that access the DSP require the command port as an argument. You can also set up streams to the DSP as you would to sound-in or sound-out. Successfully setting the DSP's owner port puts the DSP in its reset state.

To relinquish ownership of a resource, you deallocate the owner port by calling **port_deallocate()**:

```
err = port_deallocate(task_self(), ownerPort);
```

Deallocating a resource's owner unregisters the resource's negotiation port. All ports are automatically deallocated when your application exits.

RETURN Returns an error code: 0 on success, nonzero on failure.

SEE ALSO **snddriver_stream_setup()**, **snddriver_get_dsp_cmd_port()**

snddriver_set_ramp() → See snddriver_set_device_parms()

snddriver_set_sndin_owner_port() → See snddriver_set_dsp_owner_port()

---

snddriver_set_sndout_bufcount(), snddriver_set_sndout_bufsize(), snddriver_stream_ndma()

SUMMARY Configure stream transfer buffers

DECLARED IN sound/snddriver_client.h

SYNOPSIS kern_return_t **snddriver_set_sndout_bufcount**(port_t *devicePort*, port_t *sndoutPort*, int *count*)
kern_return_t **snddriver_set_sndout_bufsize**(port_t *devicePort*, port_t *sndoutPort*, int *size*)
kern_return_t **snddriver_stream_ndma**(port_t *streamPort*, int *regionTag*, int *count*)

DESCRIPTION These functions let you control the number and size of the DMA buffers that are used to transfer data in a stream.

snddriver_set_sndout_bufcount() sets the number of buffers that are used when playing back sounds; the *count* argument, which must be greater than 0, establishes the buffer count. Four buffers are used in the default configuration.

snddriver_set_sndout_bufsize() sets the size of the sound-out buffers (in bytes) to the value of the *size* argument. This function is needed only if you're using a linked stream to sound-out (see the **snddriver_stream_setup()** function for more on linked streams). The value of *size* must be no greater than **vm_page_size**, the size of a page of virtual memory; the default is **vm_page_size**. If you're writing directly to the sound-out stream—in other words if the stream to sound-out is configured as SNDDRIVER_STREAM_TO_SNDOUT_22 or ...SNDOUT_44—the size of the sound-out buffers is computed from the *sampleCount* argument to **snddriver_stream_setup()** and the size set here is ignored.

For both of these functions, the *devicePort* and *sndoutPort* arguments are ports to the sound driver device and to sound-out, as acquired through **SNDAcquire()**.

snddriver_stream_ndma() sets, to *count*, the number of DMA transfer buffers that are used to receive data from sound-in, and to transmit and receive data to and from the DSP. The DMA buffer count can be set on a region-by-region basis; the stream and region to which a particular setting applies are identified by the *streamPort* and *regionTag* arguments, respectively. Note that in a linked stream to sound-out, the buffer count to and from the DSP is automatically set to the sound-out buffer count (overruling the setting made through this function).

RETURN Returns an error code: 0 on success, nonzero on failure.

SEE ALSO **snddriver_stream_setup()**

snddriver_set_sndout_bufsize() → See snddriver_set_sndout_bufcount()

snddriver_set_sndout_owner_port() → See snddriver_set_dsp_owner_port()

snddriver_set_volume() → See snddriver_set_device_parms()

---

snddriver_stream_control(), snddriver_stream_nsamples()

SUMMARY Control and query a stream

DECLARED IN sound/snddriver_client.h

SYNOPSIS kern_return_t **snddriver_stream_control**(port_t *streamPort*, int *regionTag*, int *control*)
kern_return_t **snddriver_stream_nsamples**(port_t *streamPort*, int **byteCount*)

DESCRIPTION **snddriver_stream_control()** provides control over an active stream by allowing you to apply a controlling operation to one or more of the stream's enqueued regions. The stream and the regions therein are identified by the function's first two arguments:

- *streamPort* is the stream's port, as created by **snddriver_stream_setup()**.
- *regionTag* is the integer identifier that you gave the region (or regions) in a previous call to **snddriver_stream_start_writing()** or **snddriver_stream_start_reading()**.

A tag value of 0 causes the controlling operation to be applied to all regions enqueued on the stream.

You specify the controlling operation by passing one of the following constants as the control argument:

- SNDDRIVER_PAUSE_STREAM causes the stream to pause. If data is currently being read from or written to the specified region, the read or write is immediately suspended. If the region isn't yet active, the pause takes effect when the region comes to the top of the stream's queue (it's paused just before the first sample is read or written).
- SNDDRIVER_RESUME_STREAM resumes a previously paused stream.
- SNDDRIVER_ABORT_STREAM terminates the stream's activity when the specified region comes to the top of the queue; the queue is then cleared. If the region is currently being acted upon, the stream is terminated immediately.
- SNDDRIVER_AWAIT_STREAM is used to retrieve a partially recorded region from a stream that's reading data—normally, you can't retrieve such data until the entire region has been filled. If the specified region is currently active, a data-recorded message is sent to the reply port that you registered in **snddriver_stream_start_reading()**. You then pass the message to **snddriver_reply_handler()** which calls the **recorded_data** reply handler. The unrecorded portion of the region continues. If the specified region isn't currently active, this has no effect.

While you can use any of these four at the same time by or'ing them in *control*, the only combination that's of use is SNDDRIVER_AWAIT_STREAM or'd with one of the other three. For example, by setting *regionTag* to 0 and *control* to

```
SNDDRIVER_PAUSE_STREAM | SNDDRIVER_AWAIT_STREAM
```

you immediately pause the stream and can then bring back data from the current region.

You can request that a stream-paused, stream-resumed, or stream-aborted message be sent to the reply port when you pause, resume, or abort a stream, respectively, by setting the appropriate *msg*... flag to true in your call to **snddriver_stream_start_...()**.

snddriver_stream_nsamples() returns the number of bytes (*not* samples, despite the name of the function) that have been read from or written to a particular stream. The steam is specified by *streamPort*. The byte count is returned by reference in the *byteCount* argument.

RETURN Returns an error code: 0 on success, nonzero on failure.

SEE ALSO **snddriver_stream_setup()**, **snddriver_stream_start_writing()**, **snddriver_stream_start_writing()**, **snddriver_reply_handler()**

snddriver_stream_nsamples() → See snddriver_stream_control()

---

snddriver_stream_setup()

SUMMARY Configure a sound stream

DECLARED IN sound/snddriver_client.h

SYNOPSIS kern_return_t **snddriver_stream_setup**(port_t *devicePort*, port_t *ownerPort*, int *dataPath*, int *sampleCount*, int *sampleSize*, int *lowWater*, int *highWater*, int **protocol*, port_t **streamPort*)

DESCRIPTION A stream, as it applies to the sound driver, is a path through which an indefinitely long sequence of data passes. One end of a sound driver stream typically lies in your application's memory, while at the other end is a sound device. For example, to record a sound from the microphone you create a stream from sound-in to your application. Analogously, a stream from your application to sound-out is required to play back sound data. A single stream of data can pass through more than one sound device; for example, you can send data from your application to the DSP from whence it issues directly to sound-out. Thus you can DSP-process and play your sound data in one motion, without incurring the overhead of bringing the processed data back into your application.

The **snddriver_stream_setup()** function creates a port to a sound stream. The port, returned in the *streamPort* argument, is used as an identifier in subsequent calls to functions that write to, read from, and otherwise control the stream (as listed at the end of this description).

The function's first two arguments are the usual capability ports: *devicePort* is a port to the sound driver device, and *ownerPort* is the owner port for *all* resources that are touched by the stream, as acquired through **SNDAcquire()**.

You establish the stream's course—the source and destination of its data—by setting *dataPath* to one of constants listed below. There are two types of data paths: "simple" and "linked." The simple data paths (listed below) connect your application to a sound resource:

- SNDDRIVER_STREAM_FROM_SNDIN; read samples from the CODEC microphone.
- SNDDRIVER_STREAM_TO_SNDOUT_44; write samples to the stereo DAC at the high sampling rate (44.1 kHz).
- SNDDRIVER_STREAM_TO_SNDOUT_22; write samples to the stereo DAC at the low sampling rate (22.05 kHz).
- SNDDRIVER_DMA_STREAM_TO_DSP; write data via DMA to the DSP.
- SNDDRIVER_DMA_STREAM_FROM_DSP; read data via DMA from the DSP.

Six linked data paths connect the DSP directly to sound-out:

- SNDDRIVER_STREAM_DSP_TO_SNDOUT_44 and ...SNDOUT_22; DSP-processed samples are sent directly to sound-out at the low or high sampling rate.
- SNDDRIVER_STREAM_THROUGH_DSP_TO_SNDOUT_44 and ...SNDOUT_22; data flows from your application to the DSP and thence directly to sound-out at the high or low sampling rate.
- SNDDRIVER_DMA_STREAM_THROUGH_DSP_TO_SNDOUT_44 and ...SNDOUT_22; data flows from your application to the DSP and thence directly to sound-out using DMA.

Data is transferred through a stream in buffers. The *sampleCount* argument establishes the length of a single transfer buffer in samples (or data elements); the size of a single sample is set by the *sampleSize* argument. The maximum size for a transfer buffer (in bytes) is that of a page of virtual memory, as given by the global read-only variable **vm_page_size**. Typically, the transfer buffer size is set to this limit: If, for example, the samples that you're sending through the stream are two bytes wide, then, to follow this convention, you would set *sampleCount* to **vm_page_size**/2. If the stream uses DMA, then the size of a transfer buffer (in bytes) must be a power of 2 greater than or equal to 16.

For some applications—particularly those in which latency is an issue—setting the number of transfer buffers that are used can be as important as setting the size of the buffers. This is done through the **snddriver_set_sndout_bufcount()** and **snddriver_stream_ndma()** functions.

The range of acceptable values for the *sampleSize* argument depends on the stream's data path:

- If you're reading from sound-in into your application, then *sampleSize* must be set to 1 to accommodate the 8-bit mu-law samples generated by the CODEC microphone input.
- If you're writing from your application to sound-out or from the DSP to sound-out , then *sampleSize* must be 2 since the DAC expects 16-bit interleaved-stereo samples. Note that while the DAC processes data only at the high sampling rate, the sound driver performs the conversion from low to high for you. This isn't true for playback of CODEC-rate sounds for which you typically download a sampling-rate conversion program to the DSP, and then create a stream that goes through the DSP and then directly to sound-out. This is what the **SNDStartPlaying()** function does, for example.
- In all the other paths, your application writes to or reads from the DSP. Here, *sampleSize* can be 1, 2, or 4, according to the sample size expected by or produced by your DSP program.

The *lowWater* and *highWater* arguments are memory threshold values, measured in bytes, that are inspected by the sound driver. During an operation such as recording or playback, successive pages of sound data are locked into physical memory (or "wired down") during which time they're read from or written to. As a page is completed, it's unwired. The driver tries to maintain at least *lowWater* bytes of wired-down memory; if the amount drops below this threshold, the driver wires down pages until it reaches the *highWater* mark.

If your stream touches the DSP, then you need to set the DSP protocol by passing the appropriate value to **snddriver_dsp_protocol()**. The *protocol* argument found here helps you create this value: The function or's the appropriate protocol constants, as determined by the characteristics of the stream that you're setting up, into *protocol* and returns the new value by reference. You then pass the variable to **snddriver_dsp_protocol()**. You should initialize your protocol variable to SNDDRIVER_DSP_PROTO_RAW before calling **snddriver_stream_setup()**, as shown in the following example:

```
/* Initialize the protocol variable. */
    int protocol = SNDDRIVER_DSP_PROTO_RAW;
    int err;

    /* Set up a stream to the DSP. */
    err = snddriver_stream_setup(..., SNDDRIVER_STREAM_TO_DSP,
                                  .., &protocol, ...);
    if (err != 0)
    . . .

    /* Set up a stream from the DSP. */
    err = snddriver_stream_setup(..., SNDDRIVER_STREAM_FROM_DSP,
                                  ..., &protocol, ...);
    if (err != 0)
    . . .

    /* Pass the protocol to the sound driver. */
    err = snddriver_dsp_protocol(..., protocol);
    if (err != 0)
    . . .
```

The protocol constants are described as part of the **snddriver_dsp_protocol()** function.

Having created a stream, you can read from it, write to it, and control it by passing the port returned in *streamPort* to the following functions:

- **snddriver_stream_start_reading()** and **snddriver_stream_start_writing()** read from and write to a stream, respectively. Streams from sound-in or from the DSP can only be read; similarly, streams to sound-out or to the DSP can only be written.
- **snddriver_stream_control()** pauses, resumes, and aborts an active stream.
- **snddriver_stream_nsamples()** measures the amount of data that has passed through the stream.

For sound-in and sound-out, streams are the only way to travel. This isn't true of the DSP; the sound driver provides a one-shot, non-stream DSP read and write mechanism, embodied in **snddriver_dsp_read()**, **snddriver_dsp_dma_read()**, and analogous **...write()** functions, that can be more efficient for short data transfers.

RETURN Returns an error code: 0 on success, nonzero on failure.

SEE ALSO **snddriver_stream_start_reading()**, **snddriver_stream_start_writing()**, **snddriver_set_sndout_bufcount()**, **snddriver_stream_ndma()**

snddriver_stream_start_reading() → See snddriver_stream_start_writing()

→ See snddriver_stream_start_writing()

---

snddriver_stream_start_writing(), snddriver_stream_start_reading()

SUMMARY Send data to and retrieve data fom a stream

DECLARED IN sound/snddriver_client.h

SYNOPSIS kern_return_t **snddriver_stream_start_writing**(port_t *streamPort*, void **data*, int *sampleCount*, int *regionTag*, boolean_t *preempt*, boolean_t *deallocateWhenDone*, boolean_t *msgStarted*, boolean_t *msgCompleted*, boolean_t *msgAborted*, boolean_t *msgPaused*, boolean_t *msgResumed*, boolean_t *msgUnderrun*, port_t *replyPort*)

kern_return_t **snddriver_stream_start_reading**(port_t *streamPort*, char **filename*, int *sampleCount*, int *regionTag*, boolean_t *msgStarted*, boolean_t *msgCompleted*, boolean_t *msgAborted*, boolean_t *msgPaused*, boolean_t *msgResumed*, boolean_t *msgOverrun*, port_t *replyPort*)

DESCRIPTION These two functions cause data to be written to or read from a sound stream identified by *streamPort*, which must have been created by a previous call to **snddriver_stream_setup**(). The two functions operate in much the same manner: Each invocation enqueues a single region of data that's operated on (either read from or written to) asynchronously by the sound driver. However, there's a fundamental difference between the two functions in that **...writing**() enqueues a region that you pass as the *data* argument, while **...reading**() stores the data it reads in a region that it allocates itself. To bring the read data back into your application, you must create and register a reply-handler function that transfers the data when the read is complete. The mechanism for doing this is explained (and an example given) in the **snddriver_reply_handler**() function description.

Note: The **...reading**() argument *filename*—which would imply that the read data is written to a file—is currently unused. Also note that *the* data buffer you pass to **...writing**() is write-protected: Any changes you make to the data after it's been enqueued won't be seen by the driver.

sampleCount is the number of samples in the region that's being written or read. If you're writing to the DSP, *sampleCount* must be a multiple of the *sampleCount* argument to **snddriver_stream_setup**(). In all other cases, *sampleCount* can be any value.

regionTag is an integer that identifies the region. While you can give each region a distinct tag, you usually create a single tag value for each stream that you set up. For example, if you have a stream that reads data from sound-in and another that writes to sound-out, you would create two tag values, one for either stream, and then tag each region with the value associated with its stream.

If the *preempt* flag (**...writing()** only) is true, the sound driver starts writing *data* immediately after the current transfer buffer has been completely processed. When it's finished with the preempting region, the driver returns to its region queue, disregarding the rest of the partially-processed preempted region.

If *deallocateWhenDone* (**...writing()** only) is true, the region's data is deallocated after it's written.

The six *msg...* flags register requests for stream-state messages to be sent asynchronously to the port *replyPort*. The first flags, *msgStarted* and *msgCompleted*, if true, cause messages to be sent just as the driver begins its first and just after it finishes its last transfer of data from the region, respectively. The conditions referred to by the next three arguments, *msgAborted*, *msgPaused*, and *msgResumed*, occur as a result of calls to **snddriver_stream_control**(). The *msgUnderrun* (for **...writing**()) or *msgOverrun* (for **...reading**()) argument, if true, causes a message to be sent if the driver can't transfer data quickly enough to keep up with real time. In general this is only signficant if data is being read from sound-in or written to sound-out: Underrun results in brief pauses in playback; overrun causes incoming samples to be lost. You normally process the asynchronous messages that you receive by passing them to the **snddriver_reply_handler**() function.

RETURN Returns an error code: 0 on success, nonzero on failure.

SEE ALSO **snddriver_reply_handler**, **snddriver_stream_setup**

Types and Constants

Defined Types

NXSoundDeviceError

DECLARED IN soundkit/NXSoundDevice.h

SYNOPSIS

typedef enum _NXSoundDeviceError {
  NX_SoundDeviceErrorNone,
  NX_SoundDeviceErrorKernel,
  NX_SoundDeviceErrorTimeout,
  NX_SoundDeviceErrorLookUp,
  NX_SoundDeviceErrorHost,
  NX_SoundDeviceErrorNoDevice,
  NX_SoundDeviceErrorNotActive,
  NX_SoundDeviceErrorTag,
  NX_SoundDeviceErrorMax
} **NXSoundDeviceError**

DESCRIPTION Error codes returned by Sound Kit methods that access the sound driver.

NXSoundStatus

DECLARED IN soundkit/Sound.h

SYNOPSIS

```
typedef enum {
        NX_SoundStopped,
        NX_SoundRecording,
        NX_SoundPlaying,
        NX_SoundInitialized,
        NX_SoundRecordingPaused,
        NX_SoundPlayingPaused,
        NX_SoundRecordingPending,
        NX_SoundPlayingPending,
        NX_SoundFreed,
} NXSoundStatus;
```

DESCRIPTION These represent the activities of a Sound object, as returned by Sound's **status** method.

NXSoundStreamTime

DECLARED IN soundkit/NXSoundStream.h

SYNOPSIS typedef struct timeval **NXSoundStreamTime**;

DESCRIPTION Used by NXSoundStream objects as arguments to methods such as **pauseAtTime**: and **resumeAtTime:**. The **timeval** structure is defined in **sys/time.h**.

SNDCompressionSubheader

DECLARED IN sound/soundstruct.h

SYNOPSIS

```
typedef struct {
        int originalSize
        int method;
        int numDropped;
        int encodeLength;
} SNDCompressionSubheader;
```

DESCRIPTION This structure describes the attributes of a compressed sound. It immediately follows the general SNDSoundStruct header. If the sound data isn't compressed, this subheader is absent. The structure's fields are

originalSize	The size of the uncompressed data, in bytes
method	The compression format (see "Compression Formats," below)
numDropped	The number of dropped bits, if applicable
encodeLength	The number of samples represented by an encoded block

SNDError

DECLARED IN sound/sounderror.h

SYNOPSIS

```
typedef enum {
        SND_ERR_NONE,
        SND_ERR_NOT_SOUND,
        SND_ERR_BAD_FORMAT,
        SND_ERR_BAD_RATE,
        SND_ERR_BAD_CHANNEL,
        SND_ERR_BAD_SIZE ,
        SND_ERR_BAD_FILENAME,
        SND_ERR_CANNOT_OPEN,
        SND_ERR_CANNOT_WRITE,
        SND_ERR_CANNOT_READ,
        SND_ERR_CANNOT_ALLOC,
        SND_ERR_CANNOT_FREE,
        SND_ERR_CANNOT_COPY,
        SND_ERR_CANNOT_RESERVE,
```

```
        SND_ERR_NOT_RESERVED,
        SND_ERR_CANNOT_RECORD,
        SND_ERR_ALREADY_RECORDING,
        SND_ERR_NOT_RECORDING,
        SND_ERR_CANNOT_PLAY,
        SND_ERR_ALREADY_PLAYING,
        SND_ERR_NOT_IMPLEMENTED,
        SND_ERR_NOT_PLAYING,
        SND_ERR_CANNOT_FIND,
        SND_ERR_CANNOT_EDIT,
        SND_ERR_BAD_SPACE,
        SND_ERR_KERNEL,
        SND_ERR_BAD_CONFIGURATION,
        SND_ERR_CANNOT_CONFIGURE,
        SND_ERR_UNDERRUN,
        SND_ERR_ABORTED,
        SND_ERR_BAD_TAG,
        SND_ERR_CANNOT_ACCESS,
        SND_ERR_TIMEOUT,
        SND_ERR_BUSY,
        SND_ERR_CANNOT_ABORT,
        SND_ERR_INFO_TOO_BIG,
        SND_ERR_UNKNOWN,
} SNDError;
```

DESCRIPTION These are the sound error codes returned by many sound functions. The **SNDSoundError()** function returns a pointer to a string that describes the error given one of these codes as an argument.

SNDNotificationFun

DECLARED IN sound/performsound.h

SYNOPSIS

```
typedef int (*SNDNotificationFun)
        (SNDSoundStruct *s,
        int tag,
        int err);
```

DESCRIPTION This is the notification function required as an argument to methods such as **SNDStartPlaying()** and **SNDStartRecording()**.

SNDSoundStruct

DECLARED IN sound/performsound.h

SYNOPSIS

```
typedef struct {
        int magic;
        int dataLocation;
        int dataSize;
        int dataFormat;
        int samplingRate;
        int channelCount;
        char info[4];
} SNDSoundStruct;
```

DESCRIPTION This structure defines the header for sound data. It's thoroughly explained in the description of the **SNDAlloc()** function.

snddriver_handlers

DECLARED IN sound/sounddriver.h

SYNOPSIS

```
typedef struct snddriver_handlers {
        void *arg;
        int timeout;
        sndreply_tagged_t started;
        sndreply_tagged_t completed;
        sndreply_tagged_t aborted;
        sndreply_tagged_t paused;
        sndreply_tagged_t resumed;
        sndreply_tagged_t overflow;
        sndreply_recorded_data_t recorded_data;
        sndreply_dsp_cond_true_t condition_true;
        sndreply_dsp_msg_t dsp_message;
        sndreply_dsp_msg_t dsp_error;
} snddriver_handlers_t;
```

DESCRIPTION This structure is required as an argument by the **snddriver_reply_handler()** function. It declares, primarily, a series of call-back functions that are used by the sound driver to communicate with your program.

---

sndreply_dsp_cond_true_t

DECLARED IN sound/sounddriver.h

SYNOPSIS typedef void (***sndreply_dsp_cond_true_t**)
(void **arg*,
unsigned int *mask*,
unsigned int *flags*,
unsigned int *regs*);

DESCRIPTION Function type used by the sound driver's reply handler.

---

sndreply_dsp_msg_t

DECLARED IN sound/sounddriver.h

SYNOPSIS typedef void (***sndreply_dsp_msg_t**)
(void **arg*,
int *data,*
int *size*);

DESCRIPTION Function type used by the sound driver's reply handler.

sndreply_recorded_data_t

DECLARED IN sound/sounddriver.h

SYNOPSIS

typedef void (***sndreply_recorded_data_t**)
    (void **arg*,
    int *tag*,
    void **data*,
    int *size*);

DESCRIPTION Function type used by the sound driver's reply handler.

sndreply_tagged_t

DECLARED IN sound/sounddriver.h

SYNOPSIS

typedef void (***sndreply_tagged_t**)
    (void **arg*,
    int *tag*);

DESCRIPTION Function type used by the sound driver's reply handler.

Symbolic Constants

ATC Frame Size

DECLARED IN sound/soundstruct.h

SYNOPSIS ATC_FRAME_SIZE

DESCRIPTION This constant represents the size of a single ATC (Audio Transform Compression) frame.

Compression Formats

DECLARED IN sound/soundstruct.h

SYNOPSIS SND_CFORMAT_BITS_DROPPED
SND_CFORMAT_BIT_FAITHFUL
SND_CFORMAT_ATC

DESCRIPTION These constants represent the three types of sound data compression.

DSP Host Commands

DECLARED IN sound/sounddriver.h

SYNOPSIS SNDDRIVER_DSP_HC_HOST_RD
SNDDRIVER_DSP_HC_HOST_WD
SNDDRIVER_DSP_HC_SYS_CALL

DESCRIPTION These constants represent the DSP host commands that can be passed as an argument to **snddriver_dsp_host_cmd()**.

DSP Protocol Options

DECLARED IN sound/sounddriver.h

SYNOPSIS SNDDRIVER_DSP_PROTO_DSPERR
SNDDRIVER_DSP_PROTO_C_DMA
SNDDRIVER_DSP_PROTO_S_DMA
SNDDRIVER_DSP_PROTO_HFABORT
SNDDRIVER_DSP_PROTO_DSPMSG
SNDDRIVER_DSP_PROTO_RAW

DESCRIPTION These constants represent the DSP protocols that can be passed as an argument to **snddriver_dsp_protocol**().

Executable File Segment Name

DECLARED IN soundkit/Sound.h

SYNOPSIS NX_SOUND_SEGMENT_NAME

DESCRIPTION This represents the segment of an executable file in which sounds are stored.

Null Notification Function

DECLARED IN sound/performsound.h

SYNOPSIS SND_NULL_FUN

DESCRIPTION Used to pass a null **SNDNotificationFun()** function as an argument to functions such as **SNDStartPlaying**() and **SNDStartRecording**().

Sound Device Access Codes

DECLARED IN sound/accesssound.h

SYNOPSIS

Code	Device
SND_ACCESS_IN	Sound-in
SND_ACCESS_DSP	DSP
SND_ACCESS_OUT	Sound-out

DESCRIPTION Used by the sound device access methods, such as **SNDAcquire()** and **SNDReserve()**, to represent specific devices.

Sampling Rates

DECLARED IN sound/soundstruct.h

SYNOPSIS

Code	Rate
SND_RATE_CODEC	8012.8210513 Hz
SND_RATE_LOW	22050.0 Hz
SND_RATE_HIGH	44100.0 Hz

DESCRIPTION These constants represent the three sampling rates that are directly supported by the sound software and hardware.

Sound Device Timeout Limit

DECLARED IN soundkit/NXSoundDevice.h

SYNOPSIS NX_SOUNDDEVICE_TIMEOUT_MAX

DESCRIPTION The default timeout limit for communication with the sound driver. The value is, essentially, infinity. You can reset the timeout limit through NXSoundDriver's **setTimeout:** method.

Sound Device Error Code Limits

DECLARED IN soundkit/NXSoundDevice.h

SYNOPSIS NX_SOUNDDEVICE_ERROR_MIN
NX_SOUNDDEVICE_ERROR_MAX

DESCRIPTION The minimum and maximum NXSoundDeviceError values.

Sound Stream Control Codes

DECLARED IN sound/sounddriver.h

SYNOPSIS SNDDRIVER_AWAIT_STREAM
SNDDRIVER_ABORT_STREAM
SNDDRIVER_PAUSE_STREAM
SNDDRIVER_RESUME_STREAM

DESCRIPTION These constants represent the controlling operations that are specified as an argument to **snddriver_stream_control()**.

Sound Stream Null Time

DECLARED IN soundkit/NXSoundStream.h

SYNOPSIS NXSOUNDSTREAM_TIME_NULL

DESCRIPTION Provides an **NXSoundStreamTime** value that indicates the present time.

Sound Stream Path Codes

DECLARED IN sound/sounddriver.h

SYNOPSIS

SNDDRIVER_STREAM_FROM_SNDIN
SNDDRIVER_STREAM_TO_SNDOUT_22
SNDDRIVER_STREAM_TO_SNDOUT_44
SNDDRIVER_STREAM_FROM_DSP
SNDDRIVER_STREAM_TO_DSP
SNDDRIVER_STREAM_DSP_TO_SNDOUT_22
SNDDRIVER_STREAM_DSP_TO_SNDOUT_44
SNDDRIVER_STREAM_THROUGH_DSP_TO_SNDOUT_22
SNDDRIVER_STREAM_THROUGH_DSP_TO_SNDOUT_44
SNDDRIVER_DMA_STREAM_TO_DSP
SNDDRIVER_DMA_STREAM_FROM_DSP
SNDDRIVER_DMA_STREAM_THROUGH_DSP_TO_SNDOUT_22
SNDDRIVER_DMA_STREAM_THROUGH_DSP_TO_SNDOUT_44

DESCRIPTION These constants represent the sound stream paths that can be specified as an argument to the **snddriver_stream_setup()** function.

Sound Structure Formats

DECLARED IN sound/soundstruct.h

SYNOPSIS
SND_FORMAT_UNSPECIFIED
SND_FORMAT_MULAW_8
SND_FORMAT_LINEAR_8
SND_FORMAT_LINEAR_16
SND_FORMAT_LINEAR_24
SND_FORMAT_LINEAR_32
SND_FORMAT_FLOAT
SND_FORMAT_DOUBLE
SND_FORMAT_INDIRECT
SND_FORMAT_DSP_CORE
SND_FORMAT_DSP_DATA_8
SND_FORMAT_DSP_DATA_16
SND_FORMAT_DSP_DATA_24
SND_FORMAT_DSP_DATA_32
SND_FORMAT_DISPLAY
SND_FORMAT_MULAW_SQUELCH
SND_FORMAT_EMPHASIZED
SND_FORMAT_COMPRESSED
SND_FORMAT_COMPRESSED_EMPHASIZED
SND_FORMAT_DSP_COMMANDS

DESCRIPTION These constants represent the various sound formats in which sound data can be stored. Note that not all formats are playable without conversion.

Sound Structure Magic Number

DECLARED IN sound/soundstruct.h

SYNOPSIS SND_MAGIC

DESCRIPTION This constant is used to identify a sound structure. It's the value of the **magic** field of all valid SNDSoundStruct structures.

SoundView Display Modes

DECLARED IN soundkit/SoundView.h

SYNOPSIS NX_SOUNDVIEW_MINMAX
NX_SOUNDVIEW_WAVE

DESCRIPTION These constants represent the two display modes offered by the SoundView class. See the SoundView class specification for details.

Global Variables

NXSoundPboardType

DECLARED IN soundkit/Sound.h

SYNOPSIS extern NXAtom **NXSoundPboardType**;

DESCRIPTION This is the sound pasteboard type.

17 3D Graphics Kit

17 *3D Graphics Kit*

Library: libMedia_s.a

Header File Directory: /NextDeveloper/Headers/3Dkit

Import: 3Dkit/3Dkit.h

Introduction

The 3D Graphics Kit enables NeXTSTEP applications to model and render 3-dimensional scenes. Much as the Application Kit's 2D graphics capabilities are based on the Display PostScript interpreter, the 3D Kit's capabilities are based on the Interactive RenderMan renderer. There are both similarities and differences in the inner workings of the two implementations.

One similarity is that both are implemented with a client-server model, in which client applications send drawing code to the Window Server, which does the actual drawing. Another similarity is that N3DCamera—the 3D Kit's View—generates *all* drawing code, both 2D and 3D, when its **drawSelf:** method is invoked. This keeps the Application Kit's display mechanism intact for both PostScript and RenderMan drawing.

One difference in the implementations is in the code generated for drawing. For 2D drawing, a View sends PostScript code to the Window Server's Display PostScript interpreter. For 3D drawing, a View sends RenderMan Interface Bytestream (RIB) code to the Window Server's Interactive RenderMan renderer.

The PostScript language is frequently referred to as a *page description language*; The RenderMan language can be thought of as a *scene description language*. It provides graphics primitives, lighting specification, camera controls, and other features required for 3D scene description. This documentation assumes you are familiar with the RenderMan language; for an introduction to the language, see *The RenderMan Companion* by Steve Upstill, published by Addison-Wesley.

The RenderMan Interface and 3D Renderers

The RenderMan Interface is a standard API for 3D scene description. One of the main features of the RenderMan Interface is that it separates *modeling* from *rendering*. A modeling program stores data for the objects in a 3D scene and generates RIB code to describe that scene to a renderer. The level of detail in the model is fixed in the data stored by the modeler. The quality of rendering is determined by the renderer selected and the rendering techniques selected for that renderer.

The 3D Kit uses two separate renderers: the interactive renderer for display and the photorealistic renderer for printed output.

The Interactive Renderer

To draw 3D scenes on-screen, a 3D Kit application sends its RIB output to the Interactive RenderMan renderer. For optimal drawing in response to user actions, the interactive renderer doesn't implement some features of the full RenderMan language. However, it does process all RIB code without error, ignoring attributes and options that it doesn't implement. As one example, shaders written in the RenderMan Shading Language aren't applied to surfaces by the interactive renderer (except for a limited group of standard shaders).

So that multiple applications can render 3D scenes simultaneously, the interactive renderer implements additions to the RenderMan language for creating, selecting, and destroying contexts. Client applications create handles for their rendering contexts, select the appropriate context before they begin generating drawing code, and destroy contexts when they are finished with them. For the most part, interactive rendering contexts are managed by the 3D Kit, so you rarely have to deal with them in your code.

A specification for the interactive renderer, including descriptions of new RenderMan procedures it implements and standard RenderMan procedures it ignores, can be found in the release note **/NextLibrary/Documentation/NextDev/ReleaseNotes/QRMSpec.rtfd**.

The Photorealistic Renderer

The Application Kit's printing mechanism is extended by the 3D Kit to enable RIB output to be correctly incorporated into a print stream. When rendering a 3D image to be printed on a page or saved in a file, 3D Kit applications send their RIB output to the PhotoRealistic RenderMan renderer. The photorealistic renderer generates TIFF image data, which is then incorporated into the PostScript print stream.

The photorealistic renderer supports the full RenderMan standard (with a few minor exceptions), so the images it generates display the detail and features specified in the original model. The photorealistic renderer operates as a separate process. It starts when invoked by a 3D Kit client, and stops when the image based on that RIB has been rendered. For speedier rendering, the 3D Kit supports photorealistic rendering in multiple processes on multiple hosts.

Classes

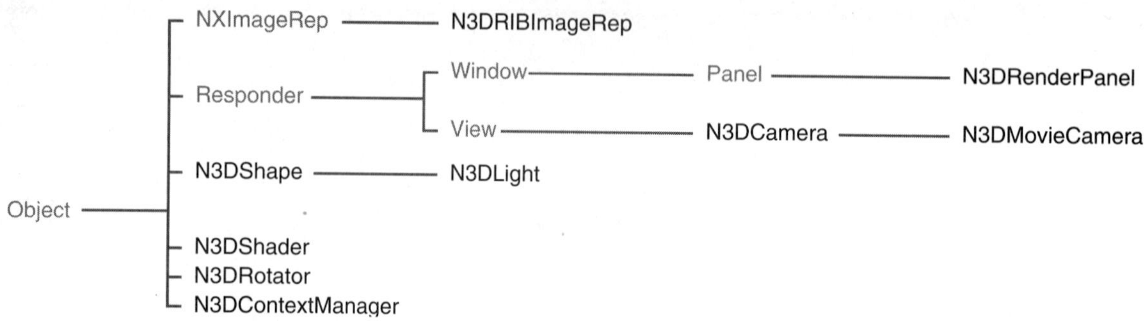

Figure 17-1. The 3D Graphics Kit Inheritance Hierarchy

The classes in the 3D Kit are shown in the inheritance hierarchy above. As you can see, several of these classes inherit from classes in the Application Kit. Here's a brief summary of 3D Kit classes:

N3DCamera	This subclass of View provides a place in the View hierarchy for 3D drawing and event handling. In 3D viewing terms, this class defines camera space. An N3DCamera has a pointer to a single N3DShape object, its world shape. As the name suggests, the world shape defines the origin (0.0, 0.0, 0.0) and base coordinates of the world viewed by the camera. The camera defines its coordinate system in terms of this world coordinate system. Since you can apply a transformation to both the N3DCamera and the world shape, world coordinates can be thought of as existing between the transformation applied to an N3DCamera and that applied to its world shape. Like other Views, N3DCamera provides mechanisms for both displaying and printing a scene.
N3DShape	Objects of this class are used to represent surfaces and transformations in a scene. The N3DShape class defines instance variables for managing a hierarchy of shapes. To represent complex 3D objects with N3DShapes, you define hierarchical relationships among them. Subclasses of N3DShape can be implemented to draw any of the primitive surface types defined in the RenderMan interface. N3DShapes can apply RenderMan Shading Language functions through instances of the N3DShader class.

N3DLight	N3DLight provides light source management in the N3DShape hierarchy. N3DLight is a subclass of N3DShape—thus its instances can be placed in the world and connected to other shapes. Independently of its location in the shape hierarchy, you can set an N3DLight to illuminate the entire scene or just the N3DShape object to which it is directly connected.
N3DMovieCamera	This subclass of N3DCamera supports the rendering of animated sequences of 3D images. Movies can be rendered on-screen by the interactive renderer in the N3DMovieCamera, or off-screen by the photorealistic renderer as a set of TIFF or EPS streams.
N3DRenderPanel	Manages rendering tasks in the print process. Just as the PrintPanel lets users select output devices to receive the PostScript code for a document, the N3DRenderPanel lets users select the renderer to receive the RIB code for a scene. The N3DRenderPanel is brought up automatically by the Application Kit any time the 3D Kit uses the photorealistic renderer.
N3DRIBImageRep	A class for compositing images from RIB files, analogous to the Application Kit's NXEPSImageRep class.
N3DRotator	A class that helps you implement a "virtual sphere" user interface for rotating objects in 3D coordinates.
N3DShader	Manages shader functions written in the RenderMan Shading Language. Every N3DShape can have one each of the six standard shader types (surface, displacement, lightsource, imager, volume, and transformation). A number of standard shaders are included with the 3D Kit in the directory **/NextLibrary/Shaders**. The RenderMan Shading Language (described in *The RenderMan Companion*) can be used to write other shader functions. Interactive RenderMan can represent shading for a limited number of the standard RenderMan shaders. The PhotoRealistic RenderMan renderer can apply any shading language function (except for volume and transformation shaders).

N3DContextManager	Creates and manages rendering contexts for the Interactive RenderMan renderer. An application uses separate contexts for interactive drawing with RIB on the screen and for writing RIB to streams, either for printing or archiving. The N3DContextManager is in a sense analogous to the Application Kit's Application class. For most drawing and printing, you don't use an N3DContextManager directly—N3DCamera manages the context for you.

RenderMan Program Structure in the 3D Kit

The RenderMan Interface includes several functions that must be called in a specific order to properly initialize the rendering environment. The 3D Kit sees to it that these functions are called in the correct order. Because of this, most of the RenderMan code you write goes into the **renderSelf:** methods for N3DCamera, N3DShape, and N3DLight.

However, knowing where the kit calls the RenderMan setup procedures can help if you want to set certain rendering features explicitly. The illustration below shows which classes call the RenderMan setup procedures. For more information on how each RenderMan procedure call is used by the 3D Kit, see the documentation for the classes and methods listed below.

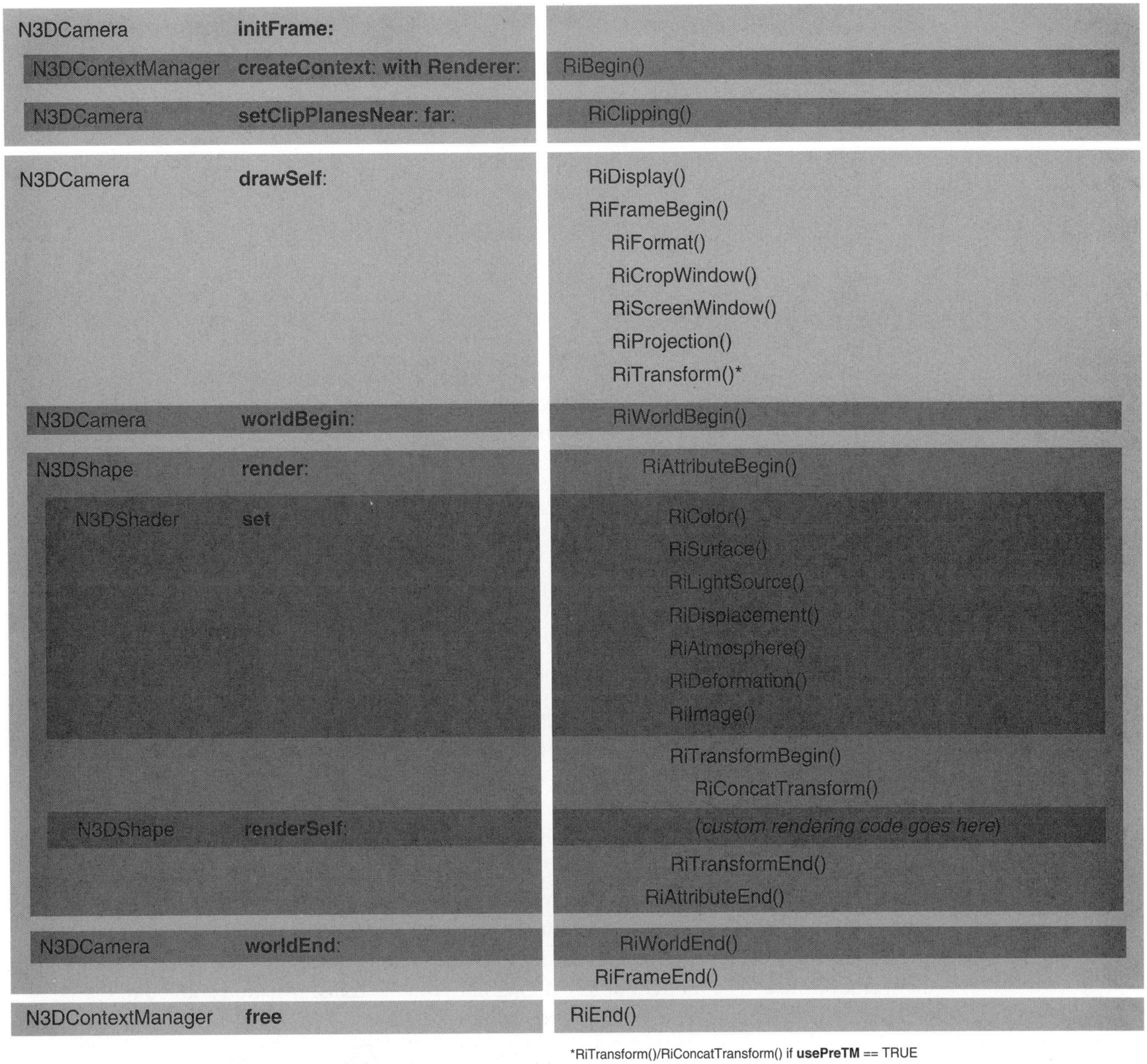

Figure 17-2. RenderMan function calls in the 3D Kit

N3DCamera

Inherits From: View : Responder : Object

Declared In: 3Dkit/N3DCamera.h

Class Description

N3DCamera is the 3D Graphics Kit's link to the Application Kit's event-handling and display mechanisms. N3DCamera is a subclass of View that adds methods for managing and performing both Interactive and PhotoRealistic RenderMan rendering.

PostScript and RenderMan Drawing

An N3DCamera draws both 2D and 3D images in response to a **display** message. The **lockFocus** method focuses both the Display PostScript interpreter and the Interactive RenderMan renderer on the camera. N3DCamera's **drawSelf::** works by synchronizing previous PostScript drawing in the view hierarchy, sending a **render:** message to the camera's world shape (described in the next section), and finally sending itself a **drawPS::** message to perform custom PostScript drawing over the RenderMan rendering.

In other View subclasses, you override the **drawSelf::** method to perform PostScript drawing. In N3DCamera, you override the **drawPS::** method.

The World Shape

The N3DCamera has a pointer to a single N3DShape object—its world shape—that serves as the origin of the coordinate system for the scene viewed by the camera. Since both the camera and the world shape may be transformed (translated, scaled, rotated) independently, the world origin can be thought of as existing between the transformation applied to the N3DCamera and that applied to its world shape.

The world shape is at the top of the hierarchy of shapes potentially visible to the camera. The N3DShape class description includes a discussion of the shape hierarchy, as well as a diagram showing the relationships between camera, world shape, and shape hierarchy.

A camera can be connected to any N3DShape in a shape hierarchy. This allows you to view just a part of a scene by setting the camera's world shape to the shape whose descendants you wish to view. You can also have several cameras viewing the same shapes, from different points of view, by setting each camera's world shape to the same N3DShape.

The Camera Coordinate System

The camera's position is initially defined in terms of the world coordinate system. The camera's view point defines a point in world coordinates at the center of the scene viewed by the camera. The camera's eye point defines the camera's focal point in world coordinates. The line segment connecting the eye point to the view point is referred to as the eye-to-view-point vector.

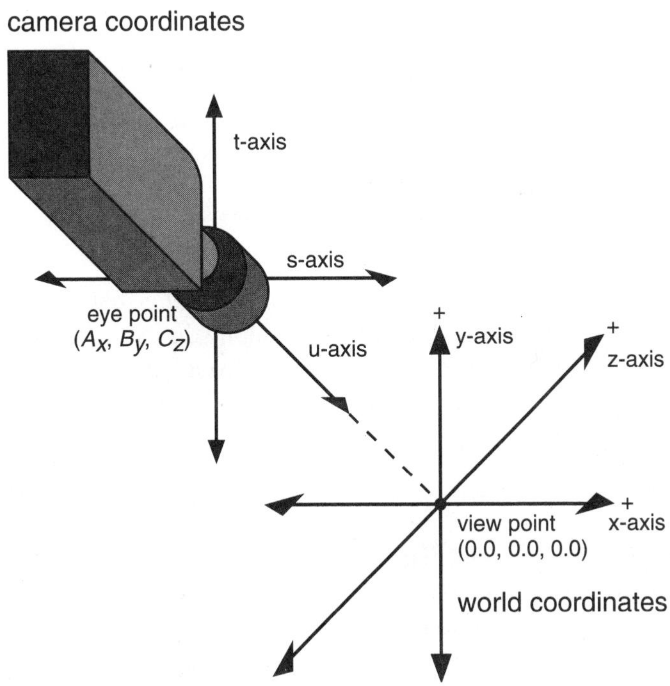

Figure 17-1. World and camera coordinate systems

In the illustration above, the view point is at the origin of the world coordinate system (0.0, 0.0, 0.0) and the eye point is at a point (A_x, B_y, C_z), with A_x being 0.0, B_y being positive, and C_z being negative. By default, the N3DCamera has its eye point positioned at the origin of world space (0.0, 0.0, 0.0) and its view point at (0.0, 0.0, 1.0).

Also shown in the above illustration are the axes of the camera's coordinate system: the s-axis, t-axis, and u-axis. The camera's axes are shown more clearly in the following illustration:

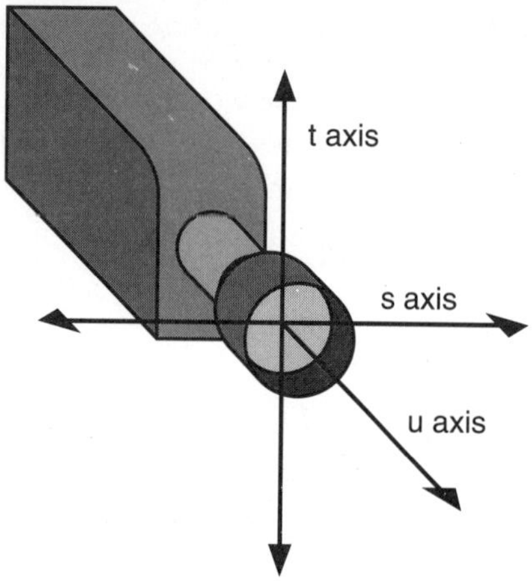

Figure 17-2. Camera coordinates

The origin of the camera coordinate system is always at the eye point. The u-axis is always perpendicular to the camera's focal plane: it points along the eye-to-view-point vector. The s-axis aligns horizontally with the camera, running through the eye point, and the t-axis aligns vertically with the camera through the eye point. (Note that the camera's coordinate system is a left-handed coordinate system.)

The s-basis, u-basis and t-basis are points that define vectors (directed line segments) related to the camera coordinate system. These vectors define the units and orientation of the axes of the camera's coordinate system. The basis points are initialized by N3DCamera with s-basis at (1.0, 0.0, 0.0), t-basis at (0.0, 1.0, 0.0), u-basis at (0.0, 0.0, 1.0). With these settings, units in the camera coordinate system are equal to units in the world coordinate system.

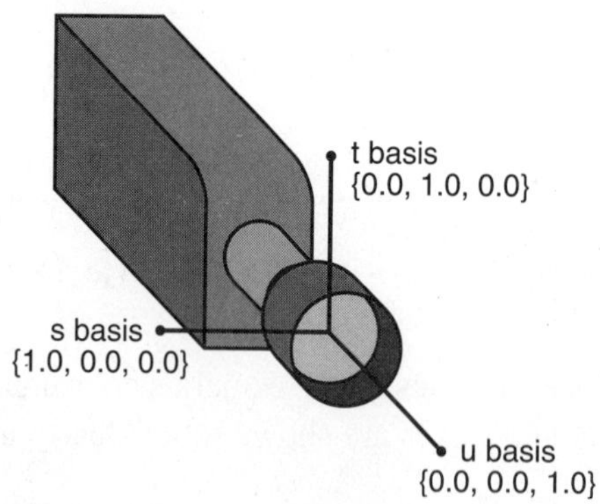

Figure 17-3. Camera bases

The camera's roll defines its rotation about the u-basis. A positive roll angle produces counterclockwise rotation about this axis (as viewed by the camera), negative rotation produces clockwise rotation.

Global Lights

The camera's light list manages N3DLights that illuminate the whole scene viewed by the camera: the world shape, its peers, and its descendants.

Since N3DLight is a subclass of N3DShape, an N3DLight object can be both a descendant or peer of the world shape and a member of the list of global light. Since the light's position is determined by its position in the shape hierarchy, you can place a light at a specific point in the scene viewed by the camera. You can then make it a global light, causing it to illuminate all shapes visible in the scene, even those above it in the shape hierarchy.

A global light need not belong to the shape hierarchy viewed by the camera. You could, for example, create an instance of N3DLight and add it to the global light list. Such a light would by default have a coordinate system that matched the world coordinate system. You could then use a method such as **getEyeAt:toward:roll:** to get the coordinates needed to position this light relative to the camera.

Determining Rendering Order

The camera's hider determines the order in which surfaces are rendered. Which hider is appropriate depends on the type of surface being rendered and the drawing performance desired. The 3D Kit defines three hider types (in the header file **/NextDeveloper/Headers/3Dkit/next3d.h**):

Hider Type	Surface Type	Performance
N3D_HiddenRendering	solids	slower
N3D_InOrderRendering	wireframe, point cloud	faster
N3D_NoRendering	any	fastest

N3D_HiddenRendering performs standard hidden-surface computations using a z-buffer. N3D_InOrderRendering renders objects in the order in which they are defined in the camera's RIB stream; this is the default setting. N3D_NoRendering produces no image. The methods **hider** and **setHider:** manage the hider type used by the camera. The method **setSurfaceTypeForAll:chooseHider:** can be used to select the appropriate hider for a particular surface type.

The Camera's Delegate

The camera's delegate implements a method to handle image streams rendered by the PhotoRealistic RenderMan renderer. The methods **renderAsEPS** and **renderAsTIFF** initiate photorealistic rendering, and the delegate receives the resulting image stream in a message from the 3D Kit when rendering is complete.

Instance Variables

```
unsigned int globalWindowNum;
RtToken windowResource;
N3DProjectionType projectionType;
RtToken contextToken;
id worldShape;
List *lightList;
id delegate;
NXColor backgroundColor;
N3DHider hider;
struct _cameraFlags {
        unsigned int degenerate:1;
        unsigned int windowChanged:1;
        unsigned int needsWindow:1;
        unsigned int basisChanged:1;
        unsigned int canRender:1;
        unsigned int usePreTM:1;
        unsigned int doFlush:1;
        unsigned int inWorldBlock:1;
        unsigned int drawBackground:1;
cameraFlags;
struct _projectionRectangle {
        float l, r, t, b;
} projectionRectangle;
RtPoint eyePoint;
RtPoint viewPoint;
float rollAngle;
float fov;
float pixelAspectRatio;
float nearPlane;
float farPlane;
```

RtPoint **sBasis**;
RtPoint **tBasis**;
RtPoint **uBasis**;
RtMatrix **preTransform**;
RtMatrix **transform**;

globalWindowNum	Server global window number
windowResource	Camera's RenderMan resource token
projectionType	Camera's projection type
contextToken	Camera's RenderMan context token
worldShape	Top of the shape hierarchy viewed by the camera
lightList	Global N3DLight List
delegate	Camera's delegate
backgroundColor	Color filled in bounds behind 3D imaging
hider	The hider used for interactive rendering
cameraFlags.degenerate	YES if the N3DCamera is 0 width or height
cameraFlags.windowChanged	YES if camera changed windows
cameraFlags.needsWindow	YES if camera isn't in a window's view hierarchy
cameraFlags.basisChanged	YES if camera's coordinates changed
cameraFlags.canRender	YES if the camera has all resources for rendering
cameraFlags.usePreTM	YES if **transform** is premultiplied by **preTransform** when rendering
cameraFlags.doFlush	YES if the **render** method sends a **flushRIB** message
cameraFlags.inWorldBlock	YES if inside **WorldBegin()**...**WorldEnd()** block
cameraFlags.drawBackground	YES if **backgroundColor** is filled in before rendering
projectionRectangle.l	Horizontal coordinate of left edge of projection rectangle
projectionRectangle.r	Horizontal coordinate of right edge of projection rectangle
projectionRectangle.t	Vertical coordinate of top edge of projection rectangle
projectionRectangle.b	Vertical coordinate of bottom edge of projection rectangle
eyePoint, viewPoint	Endpoints of viewing vector
rollAngle	Angle of negative rotation about viewing vector

fov	Angle of viewing frustum
pixelAspectRatio	Width/height ratio of pixels
nearPlane	Distance from eye to near clipping plane
farPlane	Distance from eye to far clipping plane
sBasis	Vector defining camera's horizontal axis
tBasis	Vector defining camera's vertical axis
uBasis	Vector defining camera's longitudinal axis
preTransform	Matrix for premultiplication
transform	Matrix for world-to-camera transformation

Method Types

Initializing and freeing	– init – initFrame: – free
Rendering RIB	– render – renderSelf: – setFlushRIB: – doesFlushRIB – flushRIB
Drawing PostScript	– lockFocus – unlockFocus – drawPS:: – drawSelf::
Background color	– setBackgroundColor: – backgroundColor – setDrawBackgroundColor: – doesDrawBackgroundColor
Modifying the frame rectangle	– moveBy:: – moveTo:: – rotateBy: – rotateTo: – setFrame: – sizeBy:: – sizeTo::

Managing the shape hierarchy	– setWorldShape: – worldShape
Managing global lights	– addLight: – removeLight: – lightList
Picking	– selectShapesIn:
Projection rectangle	– setProjectionRectangle:::: – getProjectionRectangle::::
Selecting projection type	– setProjection: – projectionType
Pretransform matrix	– setPreTransformMatrix: – getPreTransformMatrix: – setUsePreTransformMatrix: – usesPreTransformMatrix
Eye position manipulation	– setEyeAt:toward:roll: – getEyeAt:toward:roll: – moveEyeBy::: – rotateEyeBy::about:
Clipping planes	– setClipPlanesNear:far: – getClipPlanesNear:far:
Field of view	– setFieldOfViewByAngle: – setFieldOfViewByFocalLength: – fieldOfView
Pixel aspect ratio	– setPixelAspectRatio: – pixelAspectRatio
Converting coordinates	– convertPoints:count:fromSpace: – convertPoints:count:toWorld:
Frame number	– frameNumber
Printing	– canPrintRIB
Copying RIB	– copyRIBCode:
Setting world attributes	– worldBegin: – worldEnd:
Setting and getting the delegate	– setDelegate: – delegate

Setting the hider	– hider – setHider: – setSurfaceTypeForAll:chooseHider:
Rendering photorealistically	– renderAsEPS – renderAsTIFF – numCropWindows – cropInRects:nRects:
Archiving	– awake – read: – write:

Instance Methods

addLight:

– **addLight:***aLight*

Adds *aLight* to the N3DCamera's light list and sets it to be a global light. Global lights are rendered before all other N3DShapes in the scene viewed by the camera; thus, they potentially illuminate the entire scene (depending on the type of the light). Returns **self**.

If *aLight* is in a shape hierarchy, it remains in that hierarchy, and its origin is determined by any transformations applied by the hierarchy. If not, its origin is the origin of the world coordinate system.

See also: – **lightList**, – **removeLight:**, – **setGlobal:** (N3DLight), – **isGlobal** (N3DLight)

awake

– **awake**

Invoked after unarchiving to allow the N3DCamera to perform additional initialization. Returns **self**.

See also: – **read:**, – **write:**

backgroundColor

– (NXColor)**backgroundColor**

Returns the background color—the color filled behind all drawing, both 2D and 3D, performed by the camera. The default value is NX_COLORBLACK.

See also: – **doesDrawBackgroundColor**, – **setBackgroundColor:**, – **setDrawBackgroundColor:**

canPrintRIB

– (BOOL)**canPrintRIB**

Returns YES. This method is invoked for each View in a View hierarchy when printing to determine if any RIB needs to be rendered by the PhotoRealistic RenderMan renderer.

convertPoints:count:fromSpace:

– **convertPoints:**(RtPoint *)*points*
count:(int)*n*
fromSpace:*aShape*

Converts the elements in *points*, an array of RtPoints specified in the coordinate system of *aShape*, to the two-dimensional (Display PostScript) coordinate system of the receiver. On return, the first two elements of each RtPoint in *points* represents an x-y coordinate pair in the receiver's coordinate system; the third element should be ignored. Returns **self**, and by reference, the transformed points.

This method may be useful for hit detection, for direct manipulation of N3DShapes displayed in the N3DCamera, and for positioning PostScript drawing relative to N3DShapes displayed.

See also: – **convertPoints:count:toWorld:**

convertPoints:count:toWorld:

– **convertPoints:**(NXPoint *)*mcoords*
  count:(int)*pointCount*
  toWorld:(RtPoint *)*wcoords*

Converts each 2D point in *mcoords* from the receiver's coordinate system to a pair of 3D points in world-coordinates. For each 3D point pair returned in *wcoords*, the first point's z-value places it at the near clipping plane, and the second point's z-value places it at the far clipping plane. *wcoords* should point to an array of RtPoints large enough to hold twice *pointCount*.

Returns **self** and, by reference in *wcoords,* the 3D point pairs. A NULL pointer returned in *wcoords* indicates that the N3DCamera has been unable to convert the points.

This method may be useful for hit detection, for direct manipulation of N3DShapes displayed in the N3DCamera, and for positioning shapes relative to PostScript drawing.

See also: – **convertPoints:count:fromSpace:**

copyRIBCode:

– **copyRIBCode:**(NXStream *)*stream*

Copies the RIB code generated by the receiver to *stream*. Use this method to generate data for a ".rib" file or an NX_RIBPasteboardType. The RIB code copied to *stream* includes that generated by the receiver and by any visible shapes in its world shape's hierarchy. Returns **self**.

cropInRects:nRects:

– **cropInRects:**(NXRect *)*theRects* **nRects:**(int)*rectCount*

Returns **self** and, by reference in *theRects*, an array of *rectCount* rectangles representing horizontal strips of the camera's area. This method is used by the kit when rendering on multiple rendering hosts. Override this method if you want an N3DCamera's image to be divided in some other way for rendering on multiple hosts.

See also: – **numCropWindows**

delegate

– **delegate**

Returns the receiver's delegate. An N3DCamera's delegate will be notified by a **camera:didRenderStream:tag:frameNumber:** message when a frame generated by the **renderAsEPS** or **renderAsTIFF** methods has been rendered.

See also: – **renderAsEPS**, – **renderAsTIFF**, – **camera:didRenderStream:tag:frameNumber:** (delegate method)

doesDrawBackgroundColor

– (BOOL)**doesDrawBackgroundColor**

Returns YES if the background color will be drawn in the bounds rectangle by **drawSelf::** before any other rendering or drawing is done in the N3DCamera; returns NO otherwise. The default return value is YES.

See also: – **backgroundColor**, – **setBackgroundColor:**, – **setDrawBackgroundColor:**

doesFlushRIB

– (BOOL)**doesFlushRIB**

Returns YES if the N3DCamera's **render** method flushes the RIB pipeline, waiting to return until all rendering is complete. RIB is flushed by sending a **flushRIB** message after rendering the N3DCamera's global lights, world shape, and shape hierarchy. The default return value is YES.

See also: – **flushRIB**, – **setFlushRIB:**, – **render**

drawPS::

– **drawPS:**(NXRect *)*rects* **:**(int)*nRects*

Abstract method for PostScript drawing in an N3DCamera. Override this method rather than **drawSelf::** to do PostScript drawing in an N3DCamera. This method is invoked by N3DCamera's **drawSelf::** method, which passes along its *rects* and *nRects* arguments; thus you can structure the code in this method exactly as you would the code in a View's **drawSelf::** method. PostScript drawing is done "on the glass" in front of any RenderMan drawing in the view. Returns **self**.

See also: – **drawSelf::**, – **render**, – **renderSelf:**

drawSelf::

– **drawSelf:**(const NXRect *)*rects* **:**(int)*nRects*

Overridden by N3DCamera to perform both PostScript and RenderMan drawing each time the camera is displayed. This method first draws the current background color if the N3DCamera is set to do so. It then redraws all shapes in the N3DCamera's shape hierarchy, clipping the rendering to the first rectangle in *rects*, if any. Finally, it invokes **drawPS::** to do PostScript drawing in the View. Returns **self**.

Unlike other View subclasses, you don't override this method to do custom drawing in a subclass of N3DCamera. Instead, you override the abstract method **drawPS::**. If you override this method, be sure to invoke **drawSelf::** on **super**.

See also: – **drawPS::**, – **render**, – **renderSelf:**, – **backgroundColor**, – **doesDrawBackgroundColor:**, - **setBackgroundColor:**, – **setDrawBackgroundColor:**

fieldOfView

– (float)**fieldOfView**

Returns the field of view for the N3DCamera: the angle in degrees of the viewing frustum. The default field of view is 40 degrees.

See also: – **setFieldOfViewByAngle:**, – **setFieldOfViewByFocalLength:**

flushRIB

– **flushRIB**

Assures that all rendering is completed before execution continues. This method is comparable to the Application Kit function **NXPing()**. Returns **self**.

See also: – **doesFlushRIB**, – **setFlushRIB:**

frameNumber

– (int)**frameNumber**

Returns 1. This method is invoked when rendering to get the value to pass in the RenderMan **RiFrame()** function. It's overridden by N3DMovieCamera for multiple frame animation.

See also: – **frameNumber** (N3DMovieCamera)

free

– **free**

Frees the N3DCamera and its associated storage. Doesn't free the camera's world shape or list of global lights. Invokes **free** on **super** and returns the value returned by that message.

See also: – **initFrame:**

getClipPlanesNear:far:

– **getClipPlanesNear:**(float *)*aNearPlane* **far:**(float *)*aFarPlane*

Returns **self** and, by reference, the distances from the eye point to the clipping planes for the camera's viewing frustum. *aNearPlane* and *aFarPlane* should each be allocated to the size of a single float. The values returned represent the distance in world coordinates along a line extending through the eye-to-view-point vector, with the origin (0.0) at the eye point. The default values are 0.01 (near) and 1000.0 (far). Returns **self**.

See also: – **setClipPlanesNear:far:**

getEyeAt:toward:roll:

– **getEyeAt:**(RtPoint *)*eyePoint*
  toward:(RtPoint *)*viewPoint*
  roll:(float *)*rollAngle*

Returns **self** and, by reference in *eyePoint* and *viewPoint*, the eye-to-view-point vector. The values returned are in world coordinates. *rollAngle* indicates rotation about this vector, with positive values representing counterclockwise rotation (looking through the camera) and negative values representing clockwise rotation. The default *eyePoint* is (0.0, 0.0, 0.0)—the origin of the world coordinate system. The default *viewPoint* is (0.0, 0.0, 1.0)—viewing along the z-axis. The default *rollAngle* is 0.0.

See also: – **setEyeAt:toward:roll:**

getPreTransformMatrix:

– **getPreTransformMatrix:**(RtMatrix)*theMatrix*

Returns **self** and, in *theMatrix*, the camera's pretransform matrix. By default, a camera has no pretransform matrix.

See also: – **setPreTransformMatrix:**, – **setUsePreTransformMatrix:**, – **usesPreTransformMatrix**

getProjectionRectangle::::

– **getProjectionRectangle:**(float *)*left*
  :(float *)*right*
  :(float *)*top*
  :(float *)*bottom*

Returns **self** and, by reference in *left*, *right*, *top*, and *bottom*, the RenderMan screen window extent. These are the values passed to the RenderMan **RiScreenWindow()** function when the camera renders. The default values are -1.0 (*left*), 1.0 (*right*), 1.0 (*top*), and -1.0 (*bottom*).

See also: – **setProjectionRectangle::::**

hider

– (N3DHider)**hider**

Returns the receiver's N3DHider. The returned value represents the technique used to arrange objects in the N3DCamera's image. The 3D Kit defines three hider types (in the header file **3Dkit/next3d.h**):

N3D_HiddenRendering
N3D_InOrderRendering
N3D_NoRendering

See "Determining Rendering Order" in the class description for a discussion of the hider types.

See also: – **setHider:**

init

– **init**

Invokes **initFrame:** with NULL as the argument.

See also: – **initFrame:**

initFrame:

– **initFrame:**(const NXRect *)*fRect*

Initializes the N3DCamera by first invoking **initFrame:** on **super**, then setting instance variables and starting the context for 3D rendering with Interactive RenderMan.

This method sets the N3DCamera's context token to that of the N3DContextManager's main context. It allocates a default world shape, sets the background color to NX_COLORBLACK, sets the global window number to zero, and sets the projection type to N3D_Perspective. It sets the eye point to (0.0, 0.0, 0.0) and sets the view point to (0.0, 0.0, 1.0). This aims the camera directly along the z-axis from the origin of world coordinates, the RenderMan default for camera position. It sets the near clipping plane to 0.01 and the far clipping plane to 1000.0.

This method is the designated initializer for N3DCamera. Returns **self**.

See also: – **initFrame:** (View)

lightList

– **lightList**

Returns the List object that manages the N3DCamera's global light sources—N3DLight objects that illuminate the entire scene viewed by the camera. N3DCamera allocates this list lazily, the first time you invoke **addLight:**. You may want to get at objects in this list for certain lighting effects—like turning lights on or off. You shouldn't add objects to or remove objects from this list using List methods; instead use N3DCamera's **addLight:** and **removeLight:** methods.

See also: – **addLight:**, – **removeLight:**, – **isGlobal** (N3DLight), – **setGlobal:** (N3DLight)

lockFocus

– (BOOL)**lockFocus**

Locks PostScript focus on the View, then invokes the RenderMan **RiDisplay()** function to focus rendering on the window and frame buffer in which the camera is drawn. It also recalculates the projection rectangle to assure that 3D rendering occurs within the correct camera coordinate system. Returns the value returned by **super**'s **lockFocus**.

See also: – **unlockFocus**

moveBy::

– **moveBy:**(NXCoord)*deltaX* **:**(NXCoord)*deltaY*

Overridden to ensure that adjustments to the camera's two-dimensional (PostScript) coordinate system are reflected in its three-dimensional (RenderMan) coordinate system.

This method repositions the view within its superview's coordinate system by invoking super's **moveBy::** method. It then recalculates the 3D coordinate system by invoking **RiDisplay()** and adjusting the projection rectangle to match the new extent of the 2D coordinate system. Returns **self**.

See also: – **moveTo::**

moveEyeBy:::

– **moveEyeBy:**(float)*sDistance* **:**(float)*tDistance* **:**(float)*uDistance*

Moves the camera along its own axes. *sDistance* determines the horizontal movement, *tDistance* determines vertical movement, and *uDistance* determines movement along the axis defined by the eye-to-view-point vector. See the class description for an illustration of these camera axes. Returns **self**.

See also: – **moveBy::**, – **moveTo::**

moveTo::

– **moveTo:**(NXCoord)*x* **:**(NXCoord)*y*

Overridden to ensure that adjustments to the camera's two-dimensional (PostScript) coordinate system are reflected in its three-dimensional (RenderMan) coordinate system.

This method repositions the view within its superview's coordinate system by invoking super's **moveTo::** method. It then recalculates the 3D coordinate system by invoking **RiDisplay()** and adjusting the projection rectangle to match the new origin of the 2D coordinate system. Returns **self**.

See also: – **moveBy::**

numCropWindows

– (int)**numCropWindows**

Returns the number of horizontal rectangles that the camera image will be divided into for PhotoRealistic RenderMan rendering on multiple hosts. This method is invoked by the 3D Kit when printing; the return value is determined by the number of rendering hosts selected.

Override this method if you want the N3DCamera's image to be rendered in some other number of rectangles. You might, for example, want the user to be able to select the number and size of divisions of an image to be rendered.

See also: – **cropInRects:nRects:**, – **numSelectedHosts** (N3DRenderPanel)

pixelAspectRatio

– (float)**pixelAspectRatio**

Returns the pixel aspect ratio for the N3DCamera. The default value is 1.0.

See also: – **setPixelAspectRatio:**

projectionType

– (N3DProjectionType)**projectionType**

Returns the projection type for the N3DCamera. The projection type may be either N3D_Perspective (the default) or N3D_Orthographic, defined in the header file **3Dkit/next3d.h**.

See also: – **setProjection:**

read:

– **read:**(NXTypedStream *)*stream*

Reads an instance of N3DCamera from *stream*. Returns **self**.

See also: – **awake**, – **write:**

removeLight:

– **removeLight:***aLight*

Removes *aLight* from the N3DCamera's light list by invoking List's **removeObject:** method and sending *aLight* a **setGlobal:** message with NO as the argument. Returns **self**.

See also: – **addLight:**, – **lightList**

render

– **render**

Renders the camera, its world shape, and any shapes in the world shape's hierarchy. This method is invoked by N3DCamera's **drawSelf::** method to perform 3D rendering whenever the camera is displayed. Invoke this method directly if you want the camera to perform only 3D drawing; be sure to lock focus on the camera before invoking **render** directly from your code.

This method clips 3D rendering to the rectangle returned by **getVisibleRect:**. It calls **RiFrameBegin()**, invoking the camera's **frameNumber** method for the argument to this function. It sets up the projection type and applies the camera's transformations, then invokes the **worldBegin:** method on **self**. It then does camera-specific rendering by invoking the camera's **renderSelf:** method, and renders the world shape, its descendants, and peers by invoking **render:** on the world shape. After rendering, it invokes **worldEnd:**, calls **RiFrameEnd()**, and returns **self**.

See also: – **getPreTransformMatrix:**, – **setPreTransformMatrix:**, – **frameNumber**, – **worldBegin:**, – **worldEnd:**

renderAsEPS

– (int)**renderAsEPS**

Begins photorealistic rendering of the camera's image, and returns a unique integer tag by which the N3DCamera's delegate can identify the rendering job. This method runs the Render panel before rendering begins. The resulting image contains both PostScript and RenderMan drawing.

A photorealistic image is rendered by a separate process and can take some time to complete. The 3D Kit runs the PhotoRealistic RenderMan renderer asynchronously, and signals the N3DCamera's delegate when EPS image data has been generated, using the delegate's **camera:didRenderStream:tag:frameNumber:** method. The arguments to this method include a tag corresponding to that returned by **renderAsEPS** when the rendering began, the camera that initiated the rendering, and a stream containing the EPS image.

See also: – **renderAsTIFF**, – **camera:didRenderStream:tag:frameNumber:** (delegate method)

renderAsTIFF

– (int)**renderAsTIFF**

Begins photorealistic rendering of the camera's image, and returns a unique integer tag by which the N3DCamera's delegate can identify the rendering job. This method runs the Render panel before rendering begins. The resulting image contains only RenderMan drawing.

A photorealistic image is rendered by a separate process and can take some time to complete. The 3D Kit runs the PhotoRealistic RenderMan renderer asynchronously, and signals the N3DCamera's delegate when TIFF image data has been generated, using the delegate's **camera:didRenderStream:tag:frameNumber:** method. The arguments to this method include a tag corresponding to that returned by **renderAsTIFF** when the rendering began, the camera that initiated the rendering, and a stream containing the TIFF image.

See also: – **renderAsEPS**, – **camera:didRenderStream:tag:frameNumber:** (delegate method)

renderSelf:

– **renderSelf:**(RtToken)*context*

Does nothing, returns **self**. Override this abstract method to do camera-specific rendering in the N3DCamera. This method is invoked by N3DCamera's **render** method before the shapes in the world shape's hierarchy are rendered.

See also: – **drawPS::**, – **drawSelf::**, – **render**

rotateBy:

– **rotateBy:**(NXCoord)*deltaAngle*

Overridden by N3DCamera to prevent the view's 2D (PostScript) coordinate system from being rotated. Does nothing, returns **self**.

See also: – **rotateTo:**

rotateEyeBy::about:

– **rotateEyeBy:**(float)*dElev* **:**(float)*dAzim* **about:**(RtPoint)*pivotPtr*

Rotates the camera horizontally and vertically about the pivot point. This method performs this rotation by first performing an s-axis (horizontal) rotation by *dElev*, followed by a t-axis (vertical) rotation by *dAzim* of the eye vector. Both rotations are about *pivotPtr*, an RtPoint specified in world coordinates. See the class description for an illustration of the camera axes. Returns **self**.

See also: – **moveEyeBy:::**

rotateTo:

– **rotateTo:**(NXCoord)*angle*

Overridden by N3DCamera to prevent the 2D (PostScript) coordinate system from being rotated. Does nothing and returns **self**.

See also: – **rotateBy:**

selectShapesIn:

– **selectShapesIn:**(const NXRect *)*selectionRect*

Returns a List object containing N3DShapes visible in *selectionRect*. Only shapes that return YES in response to **isSelectable** are included in the List. *selectionRect* is in the 2D (PostScript) coordinate system of the receiving camera.

See also: – **isSelectable** (N3DShape class), – **setSelectable:** (N3DShape class)

setBackgroundColor:

– **setBackgroundColor:**(NXColor)*color*

Sets the background color of the N3DCamera. The background color is drawn behind all other drawing—both RenderMan and PostScript—if the **clearFrame** flag is set. By default, the background color is NX_COLORBLACK. Returns **self**.

See also: – **backgroundColor**, – **doesDrawBackgroundColor**, – **setDrawBackgroundColor:**

setClipPlanesNear:far:

– **setClipPlanesNear:**(float)*aNearPlane* **far:**(float)*aFarPlane*

Sets the distances from the eye point to the clipping planes for the camera's viewing frustum. *aNearPlane* and *aFarPlane* represent distances from the eye point along a line extending through the eye-to-view-point vector. RI_EPSILON (a constant defined in the header file **ri/ri.h**) is the minimum value allowed for either argument; if either is smaller, RI_EPSILON is substituted. RI_INFINITY (also defined in **ri/ri.h**) is the maximum value allowed for either argument; if either is larger, RI_INFINITY is substituted. *aNearPlane* should always be less than *aFarPlane*—no 3D drawing can appear in the camera otherwise. Returns **self**.

See also: – **getClipPlanesNear:far:**

setDelegate:

– **setDelegate:***theDelegate*

Sets the N3DCamera's delegate. *theDelegate* implements the method **camera:didRenderStream:tag:frameNumber:**, the method for getting photorealistic images rendered by **renderAsEPS** and **renderAsTIFF** methods. Returns **self**.

See also: – **delegate**

setDrawBackgroundColor:

– **setDrawBackgroundColor:**(BOOL)*flag*

If *flag* is YES, the background color will be drawn in the bounds rectangle before any other drawing is done in the N3DCamera. Returns **self**.

See also: – **backgroundColor**, – **doesDrawBackgroundColor**, – **setBackgroundColor:**

setEyeAt:toward:roll:

– **setEyeAt:**(RtPoint)*fromPoint*
  toward:(RtPoint)*toPoint*
  roll:(float)*aRollAngle*

Establishes the eye-to-view-point vector. *toPoint* is made the camera's view point, and *fromPoint* is set as the eye point. The standard camera transformation is then applied to rotate the camera by *aRollAngle* degrees around its eye-to-view-point vector. See the class description for a discussion of the camera coordinates and the eye-to-view-point vector. Returns **self**.

See also: – **getEyeAt:toward:roll:**

setFieldOfViewByAngle:

– **setFieldOfViewByAngle:**(float)*viewAngle*

Sets the field of view to *viewAngle*, the angle of the camera's viewing frustum in degrees. *viewAngle* should be between 0 and 180 degrees. Returns **self**.

See also: – **fieldOfView**, – **setFieldOfViewByFocalLength:**

setFieldOfViewByFocalLength:

– **setFieldOfViewByFocalLength:**(float)*aFocalLength*

Calculates and sets the field of view as a function of focal length: the distance between the projection rectangle (the *screen window* in RenderMan terminology) and the eye point. The RenderMan standard actually fixes a camera's focal length at 1.0. Thus, if *aFocalLength* is greater than 1.0, this method zooms the camera's lens; if less than 1.0, this method widens the camera's lens. This method achieves the effect of setting focal length by calculating the N3DCamera's field of view from *aFocalLength*. Returns **self**.

See also: – **fieldOfView**, – **setFieldOfViewByAngle:**

setFlushRIB:

– **setFlushRIB:**(BOOL)*flag*

If *flag* is YES, the camera's **render** method sends a **flushRIB** message to **self** after the camera and world shape hierarchy have been rendered. Returns **self**.

See also: – **doesFlushRIB**, – **flushRIB**

setFrame:

– **setFrame:**(const NXRect *)*fRect*

Overridden to ensure that adjustments to the camera's two-dimensional (PostScript) coordinate system are reflected in its three-dimensional (RenderMan) coordinate system.

This method repositions and resizes the view within its superview's coordinate system by invoking **super**'s **setFrame:** method. It then recalculates the 3D coordinate system by invoking **RiDisplay**() and adjusting the projection rectangle to match the new extent of the 2D coordinate system. Returns **self**.

setHider:

– **setHider:**(N3DHider)*theHider*

Sets the receiver's N3DHider. *theHider* represents the technique used to arrange objects in the N3DCamera's image. The 3D Kit defines three N3DHider types in the header file **3Dkit/next3d.h**:

N3D_HiddenRendering
N3D_InOrderRendering
N3D_NoRendering

See "Determining Rendering Order" in the class description for a discussion of the hider types.

See also: – **hider**

setPixelAspectRatio:

– **setPixelAspectRatio:**(float)*theRatio*

Sets the receiver's pixel aspect ratio to *theRatio*. The ratio for images rendered on most displays and printers is 1.0—the default setting. Use this method when rendering images for output on devices with non-square pixels. Values less than 1.0 indicate horizontal stretching of the pixel; values greater than 1.0 indicate vertical stretching. Returns **self**.

See also: – **pixelAspectRatio**

setPreTransformMatrix:

– **setPreTransformMatrix:**(RtMatrix)*theMatrix*

Sets the N3DCamera's pretransform matrix. *theMatrix* represents a 3D transformation that will be applied to the camera before its transform matrix is applied. Returns **self**.

See also: – **getPreTransformMatrix:**, – **setUsePreTransformMatrix:**, – **usesPreTransformMatrix**

setProjection:

– **setProjection:**(N3DProjectionType)*aProjection*

Sets the projection type for the N3DCamera. *aProjection* may be N3D_Perspective or N3D_Orthographic; these are defined in the header file **3Dkit/next3d.h**. Returns **self**.

See also: – **projectionType**

setProjectionRectangle::::

– **setProjectionRectangle:**(float)*left*
    :(float)*right*
    :(float)*top*
    :(float)*bottom*

Sets the camera's projection rectangle (the *screen window* in RenderMan terminology). These values are used in calls to the RenderMan **RiScreenWindow()** function when rendering and when converting points between the camera coordinate system and other coordinate systems. Returns **self**.

See also: – **getProjectionRectangle::::**

setSurfaceTypeForAll:chooseHider:

– **setSurfaceTypeForAll:**(N3DSurfaceType)*surface* **chooseHider:**(BOOL)*flag*

Sets the surface type for all shapes in the world shape's hierarchy. *surface* may be one of the N3DSurfaceTypes, defined in the header file **3Dkit/next3d.h**:

N3D_PointCloud
N3D_WireFrame
N3D_ShadedWireFrame
N3D_FacetedSolids
N3D_SmoothSolids

If *flag* is YES, this method chooses the hider type most appropriate to *surface*: N3D_InOrder for N3D_PointCloud, N3D_WireFrame, and N3D_ShadedWireFrame; N3D_HiddenRendering for N3D_FacetedSolids and N3D_SmoothSolids.

setUsePreTransformMatrix:

– **setUsePreTransformMatrix:**(BOOL)*flag*

If *flag* is YES, sets the receiver to apply its pretransform matrix before applying its transform matrix. When pretransformation is applied to the camera, it is transformed by the pretransform matrix and then by the transform matrix. By default, a camera has no pretransform matrix. Use the **setPreTransformMatrix:** method to set the pretransform matrix, then use this method to apply that matrix.

See also: – **getPreTransformMatrix:**, – **setPreTransformMatrix:**, – **usesPreTransformMatrix**

setWorldShape:

– **setWorldShape:***a3DShape*

Sets the receiver's world shape to *a3DShape*. Returns the previous world shape. This method doesn't apply the surface type set for the world shape and its hierarchy by a previous call to **setSurfaceTypeForAll:chooseHider:**—you must do so explicitly by again invoking that method.

See also: – **setSurfaceTypeForAll:chooseHider:**, – **worldShape**

sizeBy::

– **sizeBy:**(NXCoord)*deltaWidth* **:**(NXCoord)*deltaHeight*

Overridden to ensure that adjustments to the camera's 2D (PostScript) coordinate system are reflected in its 3D (RenderMan) coordinate system.

This method repositions and resizes the view within its superview's coordinate system by invoking **super**'s **sizeBy::** method. It then recalculates the 3D coordinate system by invoking **RiDisplay**() and adjusting the projection rectangle to match the new extent of the 2D coordinate system. Returns **self**.

See also: – **sizeTo::**

sizeTo::

– **sizeTo:**(NXCoord)*width* **:**(NXCoord)*height*

Overridden to ensure that adjustments to the camera's 2D (PostScript) coordinate system are reflected in its 3D (RenderMan) coordinate system.

This method resizes the view within its superview's coordinate system by invoking **super**'s **sizeBy::** method. It then recalculates the 3D coordinate system by invoking **RiDisplay**() and adjusting the projection rectangle to match the new extent of the 2D coordinate system. Returns **self**.

See also: – **sizeBy::**

unlockFocus

– **unlockFocus**

Disables 3D rendering in the camera, then sends an **unlockFocus** message to **super**, returning the value returned by that message.

See also: – **lockFocus**, – **drawPS:**, – **drawSelf::**, – **renderSelf:**, – **render**

usesPreTransformMatrix

– (BOOL)**usesPreTransformMatrix**

Returns YES if the receiver applies its pretransform matrix before applying its transform matrix. Returns NO if the receiver applies only its transform matrix. By default, N3DCamera applies only the transform matrix.

See also: – **getPreTransformMatrix:**, – **setPreTransformMatrix:**, – **setUsePreTransformMatrix**

worldBegin:

– **worldBegin:**(RtToken)*theContext*

Calls the RenderMan function **RiWorldBegin()**. Override this method to place other RenderMan function calls before **RiWorldBegin()**. Returns **self**.

You need to override this method to declare macros for use in photorealistic rendering. Macros are declared between the RenderMan procedures **RiMacroBegin()** and **RiMacroEnd()**.

One simple use of macros in the 3D Kit is to have a world shape load a RIB file as a macro. To do so, you could implement the following **createRIBMacro** method in your N3DShape subclass, and invoke it when setting the camera's world shape:

```
char    *ribFile;  /* name of source file for RIB code */
RtToken ribFileResource, ribMacro; /* tokens for file and macro */
...
- createRIBMacro
{
  ribFileResource = RiResource(ribFile, RI_ARCHIVE, RI_FILEPATH,
    &ribFile, RI_NULL);
  ribMacro = RiMacroBegin(ribFile, RI_NULL);
  RiReadArchive(ribFileResource, NULL, RI_NULL);
  RiMacroEnd();
  return self;
}
```

Your N3DShape's **renderSelf:** method would be implemented as follows:

```
- renderSelf:camera
{
  RiMacroInstance(ribMacro, RI_NULL);
  return self;
}
```

However, the macro would be valid only in the Interactive Renderer context—that is, in the display context. To apply the macro when printing, you'd write a **worldBegin:** method like this:

```
- worldBegin:(RtToken)context
{
  [super worldBegin:context];
  if (NXDrawingStatus != NX_DRAWING)
    [worldShape createRIBMacro];
  return self;
}
```

You can also override **worldBegin:** to call RenderMan functions for setting camera options—such as **RiDepthOfField()**, **RiShutter()**, **RiExposure()**, and so on. Options are declared before the **RiWorldBegin()** call, so a **worldBegin:** method to set depth of field would be coded as follows:

```
- worldBegin:(RtToken)context
{
  RiDepthOfField(myFstop, myFocalLength, myFocalDistance);
  [super worldBegin:context];
  return self
}
```

See also: – **worldEnd:**

worldEnd:

– **worldEnd:**(RtToken)*theContext*

Calls the RenderMan procedure **RiWorldEnd()**. You can override this method to clean up after a camera has rendered.

See also: – **worldBegin:**

worldShape

– **worldShape**

Returns the N3DCamera's world shape. By default, the camera allocates an N3DShape as its world shape.

See also: – **setWorldShape:**

write:

– **write:**(NXTypedStream *)*stream*

Writes the receiving N3DCamera to *stream*. Returns **self**.

See also: – **read:**

Methods Implemented by the Delegate

camera:didRenderStream:tag:frameNumber:

– **camera:***theCamera*
  didRenderStream:(NXStream *)*imageStream*
  tag:(int)*theJob*
  frameNumber:(int)*currentFrame*

Invoked by the 3D Kit when PhotoRealistic RenderMan rendering finishes. Your application initiates photorealistic rendering by invoking N3DCamera's **renderAsEPS** or **renderAsTIFF** method. Each time one of these methods is invoked, it returns a unique integer. The delegate can compare this number with the integer tag *theJob* to identify a rendering job.

Your delegate can handle the image returned by *imageStream* in a number of ways. It can, for example, write *imageStream* to a file or use it to initialize an NXImage:

```
- camera:theCamera didRenderStream:(NXStream *)imageStream
  tag:(int)theJob frameNumber:(int)currentFrame
{
  myImage = [[NXImage alloc] initFromStream:imageStream];
  return self;
}
```

currentFrame represents the number returned by the initiating camera's **frameNumber** method. If *theCamera* is an N3DMovieCamera or subclass thereof, the rendering methods will produce all the frames for the scene; thus *currentFrame* reflects the frame number of the image being returned. If *theCamera* is an N3DCamera or subclass (other than N3DMovieCamera), the rendering methods produce a single frame; thus, *currentFrame* is usually 1.

Photoreal rendering can take some time. If an application exits before a rendering job is finished, this method won't be called and the rendered image will be lost.

See also: – **frameNumber**, – **renderAsEPS**, – **renderAsTIFF**

N3DContextManager

Inherits From: Object

Declared In: 3Dkit/N3DContextManager.h

Class Description

N3DContextManager creates and manages the Interactive RenderMan contexts for all applications using the 3D Graphics Kit. It establishes an application's main connection to the Interactive RenderMan renderer in the Window Server, and releases it when done. It also establishes and releases other interactive rendering contexts on request.

You will rarely need to use this class directly. The 3D Kit—through N3DCamera and N3DImageRep—establishes contexts for interactive rendering as needed.

A context is the portion of a RenderMan program contained within the **RiBegin()** and **RiEnd()** calls. Thus, each time a new context is created, an **RiBegin()** function call is sent to the Interactive RenderMan renderer. Each time a context is destroyed, an **RiEnd()** function call is sent.

An application has only one N3DContextManager object and only one main context. The main context is the context by which the application usually interacts with the Interactive RenderMan renderer. An application's context manager is instantiated and the main context is created the first time an N3DCamera is instantiated. You can get the main context at any time, whether or not it existed previously, with the message:

```
[[N3DContextManager new] mainContext]
```

You can create additional contexts for other purposes—for example, for printing or saving RIB output from the program in a file. Each new context created this way is entered into a HashTable of contexts used by the application. You refer to contexts using the token returned by one of the **create...** methods, or using the name passed to one of those methods.

Interactive RenderMan provides for switching between multiple execution contexts with the **RiContext()** function. Each time the context is set with one of the N3DContextManager methods, an **RiContext()** call is sent to the renderer.

Instance Variables

RtToken **mainContext**;
id **contextTable**;
RtToken **currentContext**;

mainContext	Main context
contextTable	Hash table of contexts
currentContext	Currently selected context

Method Types

Initializing and freeing	+ new – free
Getting the main context	– mainContext
Creating other contexts	– createContext: – createContext:withRenderer: – createContext:toFile:
Managing the current context	– currentContext – setCurrentContext: – setCurrentContextByName:
Destroying a context	– destroyContext: – destroyContextByName:
Archiving	– awake – read: – write:

Class Methods

new

+ **new**

Creates, if necessary, and returns the N3DContextManager for an application. Each application has one and only one N3DContextManager instance, which handles creating, switching, and destroying all Interactive RenderMan contexts for an application.

Instance Methods

awake

– **awake**

Initializes the receiver, a newly unarchived instance of N3DContextManager.

createContext:

– (RtToken)**createContext:**(const char *)*contextName*

Creates and returns the token for a new Interactive RenderMan context with the name *contextName*. The new context is entered into the Interactive RenderMan context dictionary and made the current context. This method works by invoking **createContext:withRenderer:** with RI_DRAFT as the *renderer* argument. If a new context cannot be created for any reason, RI_NULL is returned and the current context remains as before.

See also: – **createContext:withRenderer:**, – **createContext:toFile:**

createContext:toFile:

– (RtToken)**createContext:**(const char *)*contextName*
    toFile:(const char *)*ribFile*

Creates and returns the token for an archiving context with the name *contextName*. The new context is created and entered into the Interactive RenderMan context dictionary. If you pass a null pointer as *contextName*, a unique string is created for the context name.

ribFile should be a full pathname, including a ".rib" extension. If *ribFile* doesn't exist, it is created; if *ribFile* does exist, it is overwritten. If *ribFile* is NULL, the context will be opened on a file **ri.rib** in the application's executable file directory.

When a context is created with this method, making it the current context causes the Interactive RenderMan renderer to send subsequent RIB code from the application to the file *ribFile*.

If a new context cannot be created for any reason, RI_NULL is returned.

See also: – **createContext:**, – **createContext:withRenderer:**

createContext:toStream:

Does nothing, returns NULL. This method is not implemented for NeXTSTEP Release 3.

See also: – **createContext:**, – **createContext:withRenderer:**, – **createContext:toFile:**

createContext:withRenderer:

– (RtToken)**createContext:**(const char *)*contextName*
    withRenderer:(RtToken)*renderer*

Creates and returns the token for a new Interactive RenderMan context with the name *contextName*. The new context is entered into the Interactive RenderMan contexts dictionary and made the current context. If you pass a null pointer as *contextName*, a unique string is created for the context name. If a new context cannot be created for any reason, RI_NULL is returned and the current context remains as before.

renderer can be RI_DRAFT or RI_ARCHIVE. The RI_DRAFT renderer is used to display interactive rendering; you can create an RI_DRAFT context using the **createContext:** method. The RI_ARCHIVE renderer is used to archive RIB code; you can create an RI_ARCHIVE context using the method **createContext:toFile:**.

See also: – **createContext:**, – **createContext:toFile:**

currentContext

– (RtToken)**currentContext**

Returns the token for the current Interactive RenderMan context.

destroyContext:

– (void)**destroyContext:**(RtToken)*aContext*

Destroys *aContext* by making it the current Interactive RenderMan context, sending an **RiEnd()** function call to the Interactive RenderMan renderer, then removing *aContext* from the N3DContextManager's context table. If *aContext* was the current context, the current context is set to NULL. If another context was the current context, it's reset as the current context.

See also: – **createContext:**, – **createContest:toFile:**, – **createContext:withRenderer:**

destroyContextByName:

– (void)**destroyContextByName:**(const char *)*contextName*

Destroys the Interactive RenderMan context referred to by *contextName* by making it the current Interactive RenderMan context, sending an **RiEnd()** function call to the Interactive RenderMan renderer, then removing *contextName* from the N3DContextManager's context table. If the destroyed context was the current context, current context is set to NULL. If another context was the current context, it is reset as the current context.

See also: – **createContext:**, – **createContest:toFile:**, – **createContext:withRenderer:**

free

– **free**

Frees the receiving N3DContextManager after destroying all Interactive RenderMan contexts the manager has created. Returns **nil**.

mainContext

– (RtToken)**mainContext**

Returns the token for the main Interactive RenderMan context. If the main context doesn't exist yet, this method creates it and makes it the current context.

read:

– **read:**(NXTypedStream *)*stream*

Reads the receiver from the typed stream *stream*. Returns **self**.

See also: – **awake**, – **write:**

setCurrentContext:

– (RtToken)**setCurrentContext:**(RtToken)*aContext*

Sets the current Interactive RenderMan context to be *aContext* (if that context is valid). Returns the token for the former current context.

setCurrentContextByName:

– (RtToken)**setCurrentContextByName:**(const char *)*contextName*

Sets the current Interactive RenderMan context to be the context named *contextName* (if it is a valid context). Returns the token for the former current context.

write:

– **write:**(NXTypedStream *)*stream*

Writes the receiver to the typed stream *stream*. Returns **self**.

See also: – **awake**, – **read:**

N3DLight

Inherits From: N3DShape : Object

Declared In: 3Dkit/N3DLight.h

Class Description

N3DLight is a subclass of N3DShape that acts as a cover for the RenderMan **RiLightSource()** function. Like other members of the N3DShape family, an N3DLight can be positioned in a 3D coordinate system and managed as part of a shape hierarchy. When called on to render itself, an N3DLight invokes the **RiLightSource()** function. By this means, an N3DLight applies its lighting effects to its descendants and their peers.

Setting the Light Type

A light's type can be set to one of four enumerated values (defined in the header file **3Dkit/next3d.h**), illustrated in the following figures:

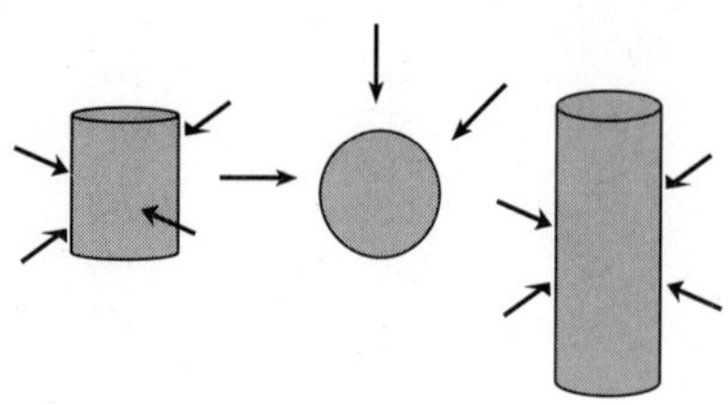

Figure 17-4. N3D_AmbientLight illuminates all surface evenly

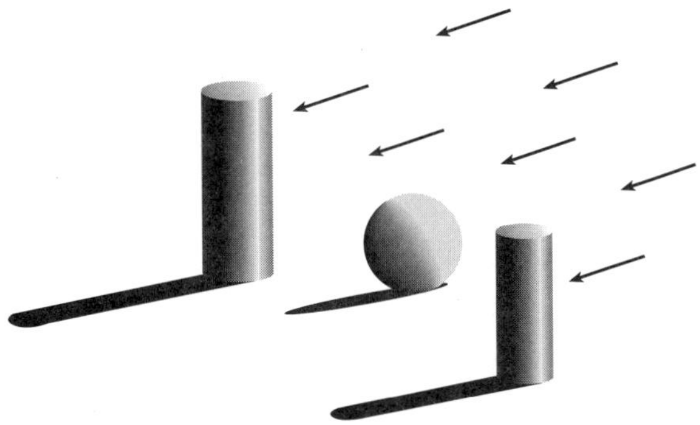

Figure 17-5. N3D_DistantLight illuminates directionally with no falloff over distance

Figure 17-6. N3D_PointLight illuminates from a single point with falloff over distance

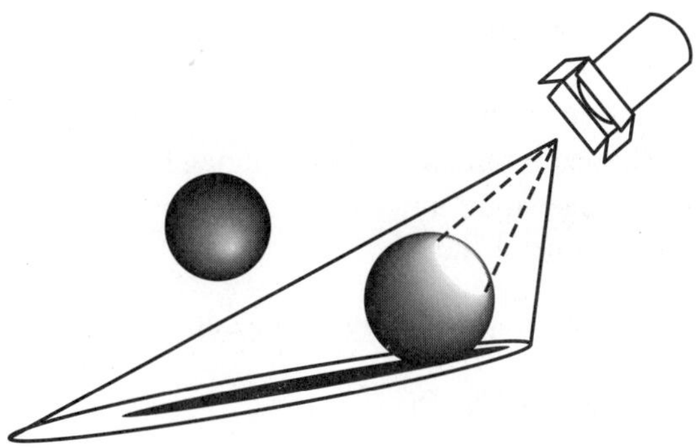

Figure 17-7. N3D_SpotLight illuminates from a single point with falloff over both distance and angle

Each of these types corresponds to an **RiLightSource()** *type* parameter:

N3D_AmbientLight	"ambientlight"
N3D_DistantLight	"distantlight"
N3D_PointLight	"pointlight"
N3D_SpotLight	"spotlight"

The other parameters used in the **RiLightSource()** function call are set using N3DLight methods. Not all parameters apply to all light types: see the method descriptions for specifics on which settings apply to which light types. See *The RenderMan Companion* for more on light types and other parameters used by the **RiLightSource()** function.

Note: N3DLight parameters that specify angles are measured in degrees, not radians.

Lights in the Shape Hierarchy

Because N3DLight is a subclass of N3DShape, it inherits methods for positioning its instances at any point in space. To do so, you add an N3DLight object to the appropriate position in a shape hierarchy, then apply transformations to position it relative to other N3DShapes. By doing so, you can associate the light source with particular surfaces in a scene.

Global and Local Lights

By adding an N3DLight to a camera's global light list, a light source can be made to illuminate all the shapes in a scene. A light that isn't in a camera's global light list remains a local light, illuminating only its descendants and their peers. A light can be in both a shape hierarchy—giving it a position in relation to other objects in a scene—and in a camera's global light list. Alternatively, you can add an instance of N3DLight to the global light list without placing it in a shape hierarchy. A light managed in this way has its origin at the origin of the world coordinate system; any transformations applied will position the light relative to this coordinate system.

Use N3DCamera's **addLight:** method to place a light in a camera's global light list.

Instance Variables

RtToken **lightHandle**;

N3DLightType **type**;

RtPoint **from**;

RtPoint **to**;

```
NXColor color;
RtFloat intensity;
RtFloat coneangle;
RtFloat conedelta;
RtFloat beamdistribution;
struct {
        unsigned int global : 1;
        unsigned int on : 1;
} lightFlags;
```

lightHandle	RenderMan handle for the light
type	Type of light source
from	Position of the light relative to its origin
to	Direction of a directional light
color	Color of the light
intensity	Intensity of the light
coneangle	Angle of distribution of a spotlight
conedelta	Angle at which a spotlight begins to falloff
beamdistribution	Smoothness of a spotlight's angular falloff
lightFlags.global	YES if the light is turned on by N3DCamera
lightFlags.on	YES if the light is on

Method Types

Initializing	– init
Setting light type	– setType: – type – makeAmbientWithIntensity: – makePointFrom:intensity: – makeDistantFrom:to:intensity: – makeSpotFrom:to:coneAngle:coneDelta: beamDistribution:intensity:

Setting light parameters	– setFrom: – setFrom:to: – getFrom:to: – setConeAngle:coneDelta:beamDistribution: – getConeAngle:coneDelta:beamDistribution: – setIntensity: – intensity
Rendering	– renderSelf: – renderGlobal:
Global	– setGlobal: – isGlobal
Switching on and off	– switchLight:
Setting color	– setColor: – color
Archiving	– read: – write: – awake

Instance Methods

awake

– **awake**

Invoked after unarchiving to allow the N3DLight to perform additional initialization. Returns **self**.

See also: – **read:**, – **write:**

color

– (NXColor)**color**

Returns the light's color. The default value is NX_COLORWHITE.

See also: – **setColor:**

getConeAngle:coneDelta:beamDistribution:

– **getConeAngle:**(RtFloat *)*coneAngle* **coneDelta:**(RtFloat *)*deltaAngle* **beamDistribution:**(RtFloat *)*distribution*

Returns **self** and, by reference, the values for the unique parameters of a spotlight. See **makeSpotFrom:to:coneAngle:coneDelta:beamDistribution:intensity:** for a description and illustration of these parameters. By default, *coneAngle* is 30.0 degrees, *deltaAngle* is 5.0 degrees, and *distribution* is 2.0.

See also: – **makeSpotFrom:to:coneAngle:coneDelta:beamDistribution:intensity:**, – **setConeAngle:coneDelta:beamDistribution:**

getFrom:to:

– **getFrom:**(RtPoint *)*fromPoint* **to:**(RtPoint *)*toPoint*

Returns **self** and, by reference, the values of the parameters defining the direction of a distant light or spot light. *fromPoint* represents the **RiLightSource()** *from* parameter and *toPoint* represents the *to* parameter. If the receiver is a point light, *fromPoint* represents the value of the *from* parameter, and *toPoint* may be disregarded. The default settings are (0.0, 0.0, 0.0) for *fromPoint* and (0.0, 0.0, 1.0) for *toPoint*.

init

– **init**

Initializes and returns the receiver, a newly created instance of N3DLight. Creates the light handle used by the RenderMan renderer, and sets the new light's instance variables to the RenderMan parameter default values. The default type is N3D_AmbientLight, while the other settings are:

intensity	1.0
color	NX_COLORWHITE
from	(0.0,0.0,0.0)
to	(0.0,0.0,1.0)
coneAngle	30 degrees
coneDeltaAngle	5 degrees
beamDistribution	2.0

Since the default type is N3D_AmbientLight, the last 5 settings are stored but ignored when the light is rendered.

intensity

– (RtFloat)**intensity**

Returns the intensity of the N3DLight. RenderMan light sources are usually set to values between 0.0 and 1.0. By default, the intensity is set to 1.0.

See also: – **setIntensity:**

isGlobal

– (BOOL)**isGlobal**

Returns YES if the receiver is a global light. Global lights are kept in an N3DCamera's light list; they can illuminate the entire scene viewed by the camera. Because N3DLight is a subclass of N3DShape, global N3DLights can be positioned in a scene and associated with specific N3DShapes by placement in the shape hierarchy. Returns NO if the receiver isn't global; a nonglobal light illuminates only its descendants and their peers. A light's global status is set when N3DCamera's **addLight:** and **removeLight:** methods are invoked.

By default, an N3DLight isn't global.

See also: – **addLight:** (N3DCamera), – **removeLight:** (N3DCamera), – **lightList** (N3DCamera), – **renderGlobal:**, – **setGlobal:**

makeAmbientWithIntensity:

– **makeAmbientWithIntensity:**(RtFloat)*intensity*

Changes the type of the receiver to ambient (N3D_AmbientLight) and sets its intensity to *intensity*. Returns **self**.

See also: – **intensity**

makeDistantFrom:to:intensity:

– **makeDistantFrom:**(RtPoint)*fromPoint*
  to:(RtPoint)*toPoint*
  intensity:(RtFloat)*intensity*

Changes the type of the receiver to N3D_DistantLight, then sets the light's from point, to point, and intensity. Returns **self**.

See also: – **getFrom:to:**, – **intensity**

makePointFrom:intensity:

– **makePointFrom:**(RtPoint)*from* **intensity:**(RtFloat)*intensity*

Changes the type of the receiver to N3D_PointLight, then sets the light's from point and the intensity. Returns **self**.

makeSpotFrom:to:coneAngle:coneDelta:beamDistribution:intensity:

– **makeSpotFrom:**(RtPoint)*fromPoint*
  to:(RtPoint)*toPoint*
  coneAngle:(RtFloat)*coneAngle*
  coneDelta:(RtFloat)*deltaAngle*
  beamDistribution:(RtFloat)*distribution*
  intensity:(RtFloat)*intensity*

Changes the type of the receiver to N3D_SpotLight, then sets the light's from point, to point, cone angle, cone delta, beam distribution, and intensity. *coneAngle* is the angle of distribution of the light in degrees: the angle between the center of the area covered by the light and the edge of the light's coverage. *deltaAngle* is the angle (also in degrees) at which the light's beam begins to fall off. *distribution* is a factor that determines the rate of falloff. (These parameters are described in greater detail in *The RenderMan Companion*.) Returns **self**.

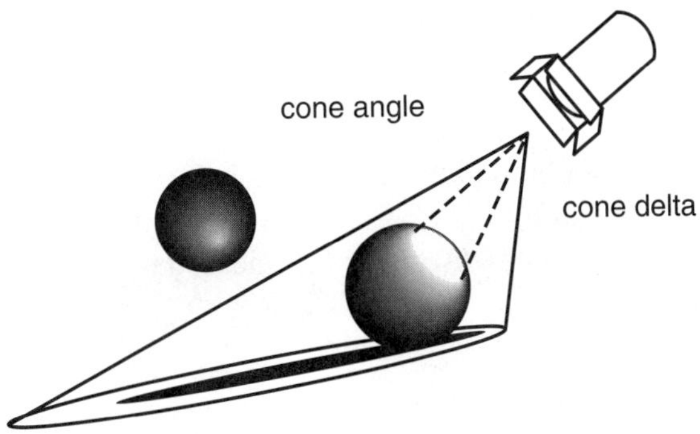

Figure 17-8. N3D_SpotLight's cone angle and cone delta

See also: – **getConeAngle:coneDelta:beamDistribution:**

read:

– **read:**(NXTypedStream *)*stream*

Reads the receiver from the typed stream *stream*. Returns **self**.

See also: – **awake**, – **write:**

renderGlobal:

– **renderGlobal:**(N3DCamera *)*theCamera*

Renders the N3DLight as a global light. **renderGlobal:** is sent to all lights in an N3DCamera's global light list before the world shape is sent a **renderSelf:** message. Override this method to do unique rendering with a global light:

```
renderGlobal:(N3DCamera *)camera
{
    /* rendering before the global light is rendered */
    [super renderGlobal:camera];
    /* rendering after the global light is rendered */
    return self;
}
```

Returns **self**.

renderSelf:

– **renderSelf:**(N3DCamera *)*theCamera*

Renders an N3DLight at its position in the shape hierarchy. If the receiver is global, this method does nothing; otherwise, it uses the parameters set for the light in a call to the RenderMan **RiLightSource**() function. Override this method to do unique rendering with a local light. Returns **self**.

setColor:

– **setColor:**(NXColor)*theColor*

Sets the receiver's color. If *theColor* contains an alpha component, that component is ignored. Returns **self**.

See also: – **color**

setConeAngle:coneDelta:beamDistribution:

– **setConeAngle:**(RtFloat)*coneAngle*
coneDelta:(RtFloat)*coneDelta*
beamDistribution:(RtFloat)*distribution*

Sets the unique parameters for a spot light to the values supplied. See the method **makeSpotFrom:to:coneAngle:coneDelta:beamDistribution:intensity:** for a description and illustration of these parameters. If the receiver isn't a spot light, the arguments are stored but have no effect when the light is rendered. Returns **self**.

See also: – **getConeAngle:coneDelta:beamDistribution:**, – **makeSpotFrom:to:coneAngle:coneDelta:beamDistribution:intensity:**

setFrom:

– **setFrom:**(RtPoint)*fromPoint*

Sets the value of the light's from point to *fromPoint*. This method affects all light types that have a *from* parameter: point lights, distant lights, and spot lights. If the receiver is an ambient light, the argument is stored but has no effect when the light is rendered. Returns **self**.

See also: makePointFrom:intensity:

setFrom:to:

– **setFrom:**(RtPoint)*fromPoint* **to:**(RtPoint)*toPoint*

Sets the value of the light's from and to points. This method affects light types N3D_DistantLight, N3D_SpotLight, and N3D_PointLight (which has only a *from* parameter). The arguments are stored even if they have no effect when the light is rendered. Returns **self**.

setGlobal:

– **setGlobal:**(BOOL)*flag*

Invoked by N3DCamera to set the receiver's **lightFlags.global** instance variable to *flag*. You should never invoke this method directly; instead, invoke N3DCamera's **addLight:** method to add a global light and **removeLight:** to remove a light.

Override this method to adjust the light's parameters or other features when it is added to or removed from the global light list. Returns **self**.

See also: – **addLight:** (N3DCamera), – **removeLight:** (N3DCamera), – **lightList** (N3DCamera), – **renderGlobal:**, – **setGlobal:**

setIntensity:

– **setIntensity:**(RtFloat)*intensity*

Sets the intensity of the N3DLight and returns **self**.

See also: – **intensity**

setType:

– **setType:**(N3DLightType)*aType*

Sets the type of the N3DLight object. *aType* can be one of the following enumerated values (defined in the header file **3Dkit/next3d.h**):

N3D_AmbientLight
N3D_PointLight
N3D_DistantLight
N3D_SpotLight

Returns **self**.

See also: – **type**

switchLight:

– **switchLight:**(BOOL)*flag*

Turns the light on or off. If *flag* is YES, this method turns the light on; if NO, turns the light off. Returns **self**.

type

– (N3DLightType)**type**

Returns the receiver's light type. The return value can be one of the following enumerated values (defined in the header file **3Dkit/next3d.h**):

N3D_AmbientLight
N3D_PointLight
N3D_DistantLight
N3D_SpotLight

The default type is N3D_AmbientLight.

See also: – **setType:**

write:

– **write:**(NXTypedStream *)*stream*

Writes the receiving light to the typed stream *stream*. Returns **self**.

See also: – **awake**, – **read:**

N3DMovieCamera

Inherits From: N3DCamera : View : Responder : Object

Declared In: 3Dkit/N3DCamera.h

Class Description

N3DMovieCamera is a subclass of N3DCamera for managing interactive and photorealistic animation. N3DCamera provides methods for setting the first and last frame, counting frames, and playing a movie on-screen.

In a 3D animation sequence, both the camera and the shapes can move. N3DShape objects get the camera as the argument to their **renderSelf:** method. They can then invoke the camera's **frameNumber** method to determine which frame is being rendered and position themselves appropriately for that frame.

To play a movie on-screen using the interactive renderer, invoke the **displayMovie** method. This method plays the frames of the movie on-screen in sequence, beginning with the first frame, and ending with the last frame. **displayMovie** will skip frames when playing the movie if its frame increment is set greater than 1. Note that N3DMovieCamera doesn't provide a way to set the rate at which frames are displayed, or to synchronize movie display with other events.

To create the frames of a movie with the PhotoRealistic RenderMan renderer, invoke the **renderAsEPS** or **renderAsTIFF** method. For photorealistic rendering, an N3DMovieCamera must have a delegate that implements the **camera:didRenderStream:tag:frameCount:** method. The delegate method should be able to accept the returned images in any sequence and perform the appropriate action with the images (for example, save each in an appropriately named file). See N3DCamera for more description of these photorealistic rendering methods.

Instance Variables

int **frameNumber**;
int **startFrame**;
int **endFrame**;
int **frameIncrement**;

frameNumber	Current frame of camera's movie
startFrame	First frame in movie
endFrame	Last frame in movie
frameIncrement	Amount to increment **frameNumber** between frames

Method Types

Initializing	– initFrame:
RenderMan drawing	– render
Frame counters	– setFrameNumber: – frameNumber – setStartFrame:endFrame:incrementFramesBy: – startFrame – endFrame – frameIncrement
Interactive display	– displayMovie
Rendering photorealistically	– renderAsEPS (N3DCamera) – renderAsTIFF (N3DCamera) – cropInRects:nRects: – getRect:forPage:
Setting up pages	– knowsPagesFirst:last: – numCropWindows
Reading and writing	– read: – write: – awake

Instance Methods

awake

– awake

Performs additional initialization of the receiver after unarchiving. Returns **self**.

See also: **– read:, – write:**

cropInRects:nRects:

– **cropInRects:**(NXRect *)*theRects* **nRects:**(int)*rectCount*

Returns **self** and, by reference in *theRects*, the bounds of the receiving N3DMovieCamera. This method is overridden to prevent the kit from dividing the image into multiple rectangles when rendering on multiple rendering hosts—instead, a movie is rendered one frame per host.

See also: – **numCropWindows**

displayMovie

– **displayMovie**

Displays the frames in the movie beginning with the start frame and ending with the end frame by repeatedly invoking **display** on self. If a frame increment was specified, skips that number of frames between each displayed frame. See the class description for a more complete discussion of playing a movie. Returns **self**.

See also: – **render**, – **setStartFrame:endFrame:incrementFrameBy:**

endFrame

– (int)**endFrame**

Returns the movie's last frame number. By default, the last frame is set to 0.

See also: – **frameIncrement**, – **frameNumber**, – **startFrame**, – **setFrameNumber**, – **setStartFrame:endFrame:incrementFrameBy:**

frameIncrement

– (int)**frameIncrement**

Returns the amount by which the frame counter is incremented between frames when playing a movie. By default, the frame increment is set to 1.

See also: – **frameNumber**, – **startFrame**, – **setFrameNumber:**, – **setStartFrame:endFrame:incrementFramesBy:**

frameNumber

– (int)**frameNumber**

Returns the current frame number. By default, the frame number is set to 0.

See also: – **endFrame**, – **frameIncrement**, – **startFrame**, – **setFrameNumber:**, – **setStartFrame:endFrame:incrementFrameBy:**

getRect:forPage:

– (BOOL)**getRect:**(NXRect *)*theRect* **forPage:**(int)*thePage*

Returns YES if *thePage* corresponds to one of the frames in the camera's movie. Also returns, by reference in *theRect*, the camera's bounds. This method, which is defined in View and invoked by the Application Kit when printing, is overridden by N3DMovieCamera to ensure that movies print correctly.

See also: – **knowsPagesFirst:last:**

initFrame:

– **initFrame:**(const NXRect *)*fRect*

Initializes the receiver, a new instance of N3DMovieCamera. Sets the frame number, start frame, and end frame to 0. Sets the frame increment to 1. Returns **self**.

knowsPagesFirst:last:

– (BOOL)**knowsPagesFirst:**(int *)*firstPage* **last:**(int *)*lastPage*

Returns YES. Also returns, by reference in *firstPage* and *lastPage*, the beginning and ending frame numbers for the movie. Overridden to assure that an N3DMovieCamera can return a rectangle specifying the region that must be displayed to print a specific frame.

See also: – **getRect:forPage:**

numCropWindows

– (int)**numCropWindows**

Returns 1. This method is overridden to prevent the 3D Graphics Kit from dividing the movie camera's image into multiple rectangles when performing photorealistic rendering on multiple hosts—instead, a movie is rendered one frame per host.

See also: – **cropInRects:nRects:**, – **numSelectedHosts** (N3DRenderPanel)

read:

– **read:**(NXTypedStream *)*stream*

Reads the receiver from *stream*. Returns **self**.

See also: – **write:**, – **awake**

render

– **render**

If the receiver is printing, sets the frame number to the page number supplied by the Application's PrintInfo object and renders that frame. Otherwise, renders the current frame number. Returns **self**.

See also: – **render** (N3DCamera class)

setFrameNumber:

– **setFrameNumber:**(int)*aFrameNumber*

Sets the frame number. Returns **self**.

See also: – **endFrame**, – **frameIncrement**, – **frameNumber**, – **startFrame**, – **setStartFrame:endFrame:incrementFramesBy:**

setStartFrame:endFrame:incrementFramesBy:

– **setStartFrame:**(int)*start*
endFrame:(int)*end*
incrementFramesBy:(int)*skip*

Sets the first and last frames in the movie. Also sets the number of frames to skip between frames when playing the movie. Returns **self**.

See also: – **endFrame**, – **frameIncrement**, – **frameNumber**, – **startFrame**, – **setFrameNumber:**

startFrame

– (int)**startFrame**

Returns the first frame of the movie.

See also: – **endFrame**, – **frameIncrement**, – **frameNumber**, – **setFrameNumber**, – **setStartFrame:endFrame:incrementFrameBy:**

write:

– **write:**(NXTypedStream *)*stream*

Writes the receiver to *stream*. Returns **self**.

See also: – **read:**, – **awake**

N3DRenderPanel

Inherits From: Panel : Window : Responder : Object

Declared In: 3Dkit/N3DRenderPanel.h

Class Description

N3DRenderPanel provides a user interface for controlling rendering with the PhotoRealistic RenderMan renderer. The Render panel lets the user select the host or hosts on which to perform rendering and the resolution of that rendering. Each application has at most one instance of N3DRenderPanel.

An N3DRenderPanel is presented anytime RIB is printed (either through an N3DCamera or an N3DRIBImageRep). When an application prints RIB code, the PhotoRealistic RenderMan renderer generates a TIFF image of the 3D scene, which is then merged into the PostScript stream being spooled to the printer. The Render panel is also presented anytime as image is generated using the N3DCamera methods **renderAsTIFF** and **renderAsEPS**.

You generally won't need to use this class directly: The 3D Graphics Kit ensures that an instance of N3DRenderPanel is created and presented to the user at the appropriate times. However, you may want to send messages to that instance to add an accessory view or perform other customization.

Instance Variables

id **browser**
id **nametext**
id **notetext**
id **resolution**
char ****hostnames**
id **accessoryView**

browser	NXBrowser instance that lists rendering host names
nametext	TextField instance that lists the selected host

notetext	TextField instance that displays notes about the host
resolution	TextField instance that displays rendering resolution
hostnames	Pointer to array of names of selected hosts
accessoryView	Optional View added by the application

Method Types

Initializing the class	+ initialize + new
Setting accessory view	– accessoryView – setAccessoryView:
Running modal	– runModal
Setting resolution	– resolution
Host management	– numSelectedHosts – hostNames
Browser delegate method	– browser:fillMatrix:inColumn:

Class Methods

initialize

+ initialize

Initializes the N3DRenderPanel class by reading data from the defaults database. You never invoke this method directly; it is invoked for you the first time an instance of N3DRenderPanel is created by your application.

new

+ new

Creates, if necessary, and returns the application's sole instance of N3DRenderPanel. Use this method to get the **id** of this instance—for example, to add an accessory View to the N3DRenderPanel. It is invoked automatically when an application starts printing a View that generates RIB code, either directly or through a subview.

Instance Methods

accessoryView

– **accessoryView**

Returns the accessory View, an optional View added to the Render panel by the application.

See also: – **setAccessoryView:**

browser:fillMatrix:inColumn:

– (int)**browser:***hostBrowser*
fillMatrix:*matrix*
inColumn:(int)*col*

This method fills the panel's browser with a list of available hosts. The Render panel is *hostBrowser*'s delegate, and NXBrowser objects send this message whenever a column needs to be updated. This method fills *matrix* with the host names and returns the number of names placed in the matrix.

hostNames

– (char **)**hostNames**

Returns an array of selected host names—the list of names in the Render panel's browser that the user has highlighted. The number of entries in this array is returned by **numSelectedHosts**.

See also: – **numSelectedHosts**

numSelectedHosts

– (int)**numSelectedHosts**

Returns the number of rendering hosts that the user has selected in the Render panel's browser. The array of selected host names is returned by **hostNames**.

See also: – hostNames

resolution

– (int)**resolution**

Returns the rendering resolution specified by the user. This value represents the number of pixels per inch for images to be rendered by the PhotoRealistic RenderMan renderer.

runModal

– (int)**runModal**

Presents the Render panel in a modal loop. Before displaying the panel, this method loads the browser with host names and sets the selected host to that previously selected. Returns 1 if the modal loop was ended by the user choosing the Render button, 0 if the modal session was ended by the user choosing Cancel.

setAccessoryView:

– **setAccessoryView:***aView*

Sets the receiver's accessory View to *aView*. Use this method to add a View containing custom user interface features to your application's instance of N3DRenderPanel. Returns **self**.

See also: – **accessoryView**

N3DRIBImageRep

Inherits From: NXImageRep : Object

Declared In: 3Dkit/N3DRIBImageRep.h

Class Description

An N3DRIBImageRep is an object that can render images from RenderMan Interface Bytestream (RIB) files. The file loaded by an N3DRIBImageRep must be a structured RIB file: That is, it must begin with the line:

```
##RenderMan RIB-Structure 1.0
```

The N3DRIBImageRep includes methods for specifying the hider and surface types and for setting the background color. The size of the image is set to the size specified in the RenderMan **Format** call in the RIB file. Other information about the image should be supplied using inherited NXImageRep methods.

Like most other kinds of NXImageReps, an N3DRIBImageRep is generally used indirectly, through an NXImage object. N3DRIBImageRep overrides various NXImageRep methods to ensure that it is automatically instantiated from files with the .rib extension, from pasteboards containing NX_RIBPasteboardType data, and from streams containing RIB code.

Two factors—surface and hider—determine the quality of the rendered image. When displaying a RIB image representation, the interactive renderer uses the selected surface and hider for the image. When printing a RIB image representation, the RenderMan renderer uses shading attributes set in the RIB file; if no surface attributes are set explicitly in the RIB file, the image representation surface and hider factors are applied. These factors are set using the **setSurfaceType:** and **setHider:** methods.

For more information on the use of image representations, see the NXImage and NXImageRep classes in the Application Kit.

Instance Variables

N3DHider **hider**;
N3DSurfaceType **surface**;
NXColor **backgroundColor**;

hider	The hider used when rendering on screen
surface	The surface type used when rendering on screen
backgroundColor	The color drawn behind the rendering

Method Types

Initializing and Freeing	– initFromFile: – initFromStream: – free
Declaring data types	+ imageUnfilteredFileTypes + imageUnfilteredPasteboardTypes + canLoadFromStream:
Drawing	– drawAt: – drawIn: – draw
Size	– getBoundingBox: – getSize:
Background Color	– setBackgroundColor: – backgroundColor
Hidden Surface Removal Type	– hider – setHider:
Surface Type	– setSurfaceType: – surfaceType
Archiving	– read: – write:

Class Methods

canLoadFromStream:

+ (BOOL)**canLoadFromStream:**(NXStream *)*ribStream*

Tests *ribStream* for RIB data. Returns YES if the stream contains RIB data, NO if not. This method is invoked by NXImage to test for the appropriate NXImageRep subclass to handle a particular data stream.

imageUnfilteredFileTypes

+ (const char *const *)**imageUnfilteredFileTypes**

Returns a NULL terminated array of characters whose only member is "rib". Invoked by NXImage's **imageRepForFileType:** method to find the NXImageRep subclass capable of handling files with a particular extension.

imageUnfilteredPasteboardTypes

+ (const NXAtom *)**imageUnfilteredPasteboardTypes**

Returns N3DRIBPasteboardType. Invoked by NXImage's **imageRepForPasteboardType:** method to find the NXImageRep subclass capable of handling pasteboards containing RIB.

Instance Methods

backgroundColor

– (NXColor)**backgroundColor**

Returns the receiver's background color. By default, the background color is NX_COLORBLACK.

See also: – **setBackgroundColor:**

draw

– (BOOL)**draw**

Draws the image at (0.0, 0.0) in the current coordinate system on the current device. This method invokes **drawIn:** with its bounding rectangle as the *rect* argument. Returns YES if successful in rendering the image, and NO if not.

See also: – **drawAt:**, – **drawIn:**

drawAt:

– (BOOL)**drawAt:**(const NXPoint *)*point*

Draws the image at *point* in the current coordinate system of the current device. This method invokes **drawIn:** with the origin of *rect* at *point*, and the size of *rect* set to the size of the image representation. Returns YES if successful in rendering the image, and NO if not.

See also: – **drawIn:**

drawIn:

– (BOOL)**drawIn:**(const NXRect *)*rect*

Draws the image so that it fits inside the rectangle referred to by *rect*. This method returns YES if successful in rendering the image, and NO if not.

free

– **free**

Deallocates the N3DRIBImageRep. Returns **nil**.

getBoundingBox:

– **getBoundingBox:**(NXRect *)*rectangle*

Returns, by reference in *rectangle*, the rectangle that bounds the image. The origin of *rectangle* is at (0.0, 0.0). The size is taken from the RenderMan **Format** call in the RIB from which the N3DRIBImageRep is instantiated. If no **Format** call appears in the RIB, an arbitrary width and height are set (256 wide, 192 high).

getSize:

– **getSize:**(NXSize *)*theSize*

Returns, by reference in *theSize*, the size of the N3DImageRep as described in the **getBoundingBox:** method description.

See also: – **getBoundingBox:**

hider

– (N3DHider)**hider**

Returns the hider used by the N3DRIBImageRep. The 3D Graphics Kit's hider types are listed with the **setHider:** method.

See also: – **setHider:**

init

Generates an error message. This method can't be used to initialize an N3DRIBImageRep. Use one of the other **init**... methods instead.

See also: – **initFromFile:**, – **initFromStream:**

initFromFile:

– **initFromFile:**(const char *)*ribFile*

Initializes the receiver, a newly allocated N3DRIBImageRep object, with the RIB image found in *ribFile*. Some information about the rendering environment is read from the RIB file, but the RIB code won't be read until it's needed to render the image.

If the new object can't be initialized for any reason (for example, *ribfile* doesn't exist or doesn't contain RIB code), this method frees it and returns **nil**. Otherwise, it returns **self**.

This method is the designated initializer for N3DRIBImageReps that read image data from a file.

See also: – **initFromStream:**

initFromStream:

– **initFromStream:**(NXStream *)*ribStream*

Initializes the receiver, a newly allocated N3DRIBImageRep object, with the RIB image read from *ribStream*. If the new object can't be initialized for any reason (for example, *ribStream* doesn't contain RIB code), this method frees it and returns **nil**. Otherwise, it returns **self**.

This method is the designated initializer for N3DRIBImageReps that read image data from a stream.

See also: – **initFromFile:**

read:

– **read:**(NXTypedStream *)*stream*

Reads the N3DRIBImageRep from the typed stream *stream*.

See also: – **write:**

setBackgroundColor:

– **setBackgroundColor:**(NXColor)*aColor*

Sets the receiver's background color to *aColor*. Returns **self**.

See also: – **backgroundColor**

setHider:

– **setHider:**(N3DHider)*aHider*

Sets the hider, returns **self**. The hider determines the hidden-surface algorithm used when rendering the image. *aHider* may be:

N3D_HiddenRendering	Determines hidden surfaces and renders only visible surfaces
N3D_InOrderRendering	Renders objects in the order in which they occur in the RIB stream, regardless of position in the scene
N3D_NoRendering	Produces no output

See "Determining Rendering Order" in the N3DCamera class specification for more on hiders.

See also: – **hider**

setSurfaceType:

– **setSurfaceType:**(N3DSurfaceType)*surfaceType*

Sets the surface type for rendering. *surfaceType* may be:

N3D_PointCloud	Renders the points passed by the RenderMan geometry calls in the RIB stream
N3D_WireFrame	Renders the edges connecting points in the scene, but renders no surfaces
N3D_ShadedWireFrame	Renders edges with depth cueing
N3D_FacetedSolids	Renders a faceted surface on all geometric primitives
N3D_SmoothSolids	Renders a smooth surface on all geometric primitives

See also: – **surfaceType**

surfaceType

– (N3DSurfaceType)**surfaceType**

Returns the surface type set with **setSurfaceType:**.

See also: – **setSurfaceType:**

write:

– **write:**(NXTypedStream *)*stream*

Writes the N3DRIBImageRep to the typed stream *stream*.

See also: – **read:**

N3DRotator

Inherits From: Object

Declared In: 3Dkit/N3DRotator.h

Class Description

N3DRotator provides API for performing rotations on objects in a scene created with the 3D Graphics Kit. The user interface model implemented by the N3DRotator is called a virtual sphere—a trackball-style control for 3D transformations. To the user, the rotator provides direct manipulation of objects in a 3D application. To the programmer, the rotator provides a reusable object for implementing this direct manipulation. Note, however, that the N3DRotator class doesn't provide any on-screen representation to the user: It simply provides a way to convert the offset between two points in 2D coordinates into rotations on 3D matrices.

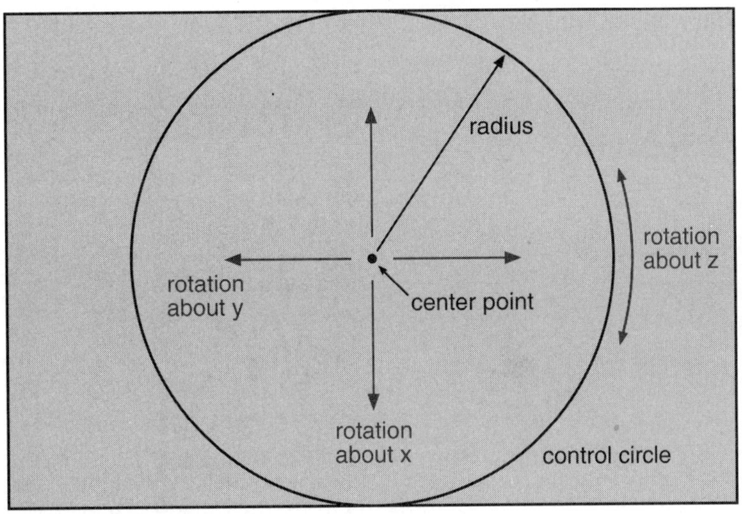

Figure 17-9. N3DRotator

The N3DRotator's *center point* defines the point—in the 2D coordinates of the camera's bounds—about which the effect of cursor movement is centered. With the center point, the *radius* defines the rotator's *control circle*. Cursor movement within this circle controls x- and y-axis rotation; cursor movement outside the circle controls z-axis rotation. The default center point is the center of the rotator's camera's bounds rectangle. By default, the radius is set at one-half the smaller of the width or height of the camera's bounds. Thus, the default control circle fits entirely within the bounds of the rotator's camera. The default center and radius are set when the rotator is first initialized, and are not reset if the camera is resized.

Note that the center point is the center of user manipulation in 2D coordinates, not of the resulting rotation. The origin of the rotation produced by N3DRotator is the origin of the space to which rotation is applied.

The heart of N3DRotator's operation is the **trackMouseFrom:to:rotationMatrix: andInverse:** method. Invoked from within an N3DCamera's **mouseDown:** method, this method accepts two points in the camera's coordinate system and returns two three-dimensional matrices—one representing a rotation, the other an inverse of that rotation. These matrices can be applied to the camera or to the shapes in the scene viewed by the camera. The description for **trackMouseFrom:to:rotationMatrix:andInverse**: includes a code example for rotating the camera and its world shape.

N3DRotator also has methods for setting the center and radius of the virtual sphere, for attaching to a camera, and for setting the axes about which rotations are applied.

Instance Variables

id **camera**;
NXRect **bounds**;
NXPoint **center**;
float **radius**;
N3DAxis **rotationAxis**;

camera	The rotator's N3DCamera
bounds	Bounds of cursor movement effect
center	Center of the control circle
radius	Radius of the control circle
rotationAxis	Axes about which rotation is applied

Method Types

Initializing	– init – initWithCamera:
Setting	– setCamera: – setCenter:andRadius:
Axes of rotation	– setRotationAxis: – rotationAxis
Mouse tracking	– trackMouseFrom:to:rotationMatrix:andInverse:
Archiving	– read: – write:

Instance Methods

init

– **init**

Initializes the receiver, a newly allocated N3DRotator instance with no camera.

initWithCamera:

– **initWithCamera:***aCamera*

Initializes the receiver, a newly allocated N3DRotator instance. Uses the **setCamera:** method to set *aCamera* as the receiver's camera. This method is the designated initializer for N3DRotator. Returns **self**.

See also: – **setCamera:**

rotationAxis

– (N3DAxis)**rotationAxis**

Returns the current axes of rotation for the N3DRotator. The N3DAxis enumerated types returned by this method are defined in the header file **3Dkit/next3d.h** and are listed with the **setRotationAxis:** method.

See also: – **setRotationAxis:**

read:

– **read:**(NXTypedStream *)*stream*

Reads the receiver from the typed stream *stream*.

See also: – **write:**

setCamera:

– **setCamera:***aCamera*

Sets *aCamera* as the receiver's camera. The receiver's bounds is set to the bounds of *aCamera*, its center point is placed at the center of the bounds, and its radius is set to half the smaller of the width or height of the bounds.

See also: – **setCenter:andRadius:**

setCenter:andRadius:

– **setCenter:**(const NXPoint *)*center* **andRadius:**(float)*radius*

Sets the receiver's center point and radius. Together, these define the control circle of the rotator, as described and illustrated in the class description.

setRotationAxis:

– **setRotationAxis:**(N3DAxis)*axis*

Sets the axes about which the receiver's rotations are applied. The N3DAxis enumerated types returned by this method are defined in the header file **3Dkit/next3d.h**. They are:

N3D_AllAxes
N3D_XAxis
N3D_YAxis
N3D_ZAxis
N3D_XYAxes
N3D_XZAxes
N3D_YZAxes

The rotation axes set by this method affect the matrices returned by the **trackMouseFrom:to:rotationMatrix:andInverse:** method. For example, when the rotation axis is set to N3D_AllAxes, the matrices are transformed to represent rotations about all three axes. When set to N3D_Xaxis, the matrices are transformed to represent only rotation about the x axis; that is, the rotator's effect is restricted to the x axis.

See also: – **rotationAxis**, – **trackMouseFrom:to:rotationMatrix:andInverse:**

trackMouseFrom:to:rotationMatrix:andInverse:

– **trackMouseFrom:**(const NXPoint *)*lastPoint*
  to:(const NXPoint *)*thisPoint*
  rotationMatrix:(RtMatrix)*theRotation*
  andInverse:(RtMatrix)*theInverse*

Accepts two points and uses the offset between them to calculate virtual sphere rotations on two matrices. Your application typically invokes this method from within a **mouseDown:** method in a subclass of N3DCamera. In addition to the rotations returned by reference in *theRotation* and *theInverse*, this method returns **self**.

The first two arguments represent cursor positions from NX_MOUSEDOWN or NX_MOUSEDRAGGED events. *lastPoint* is the previous position of the cursor, *thisPoint* is the most recent position of the cursor.

The rotations applied to *theRotation* and *theInverse* may be about one, two, or three axes, depending on the value set by **setRotationAxis:**. By default, rotations are applied to all axes. The direction of mouse movement between *lastPoint* and *thisPoint* determines the affected axes: Horizontal movement inside the control circle rotate about the y-axis, vertical moves inside the circle rotate about the x-axis. Horizontal or vertical moves outside the circle rotate about the z-axis. This behavior is described and illustrated in the class description.

This method does not concatenate the new rotations on existing values in the matrices; any data passed to this method in *theRotation* and *theInverse* is simply ignored.

The way you apply the returned matrices *theRotation* and *theInverse* depends on the effect you want to produce in the space being rotated. For example, to rotate an N3DShape (and its descendants) in its own space, you postmultiply *theRotation*. To rotate a shape (and descendants) in its ancestor's space, you premultiply *theRotation*.

The following code fragment demonstrates the implementation of a **mouseDown:** method within an N3DCamera subclass, using **trackMouseFrom:to:rotationMatrix: andInverse:** to rotate either the camera or its world shape.

```
{
  id   myRotator
  BOOL shouldPreMultiply
  int  applyRotation
}
```

```
...

mouseDown:(NXEvent *)theEvent
{
RtMatrix  theRotation, theInverse, thePreTransform
NXPoint   lastPoint, thisPoint;

[self setUsePreTransformMatrix:YES];
while (/* modal loop tracks mouse-dragged events */) {

  ...

  [myRotator trackMouseFrom:&lastPoint to:&thisPoint
            rotationMatrix:theRotation andInverse:theInverse];
  switch (applyRotation) {
    case TO_CAMERA :
      [self getPreTransformMatrix:thePreTransform];
      if (shouldPreMultiply)
        N3DMultiplyMatrix(thePreTransform,
                          theRotation, thePreTransform);
      else
        N3DMultiplyMatrix(theRotation,
                          thePreTransform, thePreTransform);
      [self setPreTransformMatrix:thePreTransform];
      break;
    case TO_WORLD :
      [worldShape concatTransformMatrix:theRotation
                  premultiply:shouldPreMultiply];
      break;
    }
    [self display];
  }
  [self display];
  return self;
}
```

write:

– **write:**(NXTypedStream *)*stream*

Writes the receiver to the typed stream *stream*.

See also: – **read:**

N3DShader

Inherits From: Object

Declared In: 3Dkit/N3DShader.h

Class Description

N3DShader manages the application of shader functions to N3DShapes. A shader function is written in the RenderMan Shading Language, compiled with the shading language compiler (see the **shader**(1) UNIX manual page), and contained in a shading language object file. The RenderMan Shading Language is described in detail in *The RenderMan Companion*.

Shader Functions and Shading Language Object Files

Each N3DShader instance manages a single shading language function. A shader function is contained in a shading language object file. The name of the shader function and shading language object file are the same (the file name has the extension .slo).

When its shader function is set by the **initWithShader:** or **setShader:** methods, an N3DShader searches for the specified shader language object file in the current directory, and in the directory paths **~/Library/Shaders**, **/LocalLibrary/Shaders**, and **/NextLibrary/Shaders**. If the specified shader is found, the N3DShader's type, along with its arguments and their default values, is set.

The N3DShader class provides methods to determine these arguments for a particular shader function and to assign values for these arguments. When rendering, the argument/value pairs are passed to the shader function. You can reset any of an N3DShader's arguments to their default values using the **resetShaderArg:** method.

Shader Function Arguments

Each shader function can have an open-ended list of arguments. The N3DShader class provides a number of methods for accessing these arguments and setting or retrieving their values.

The method **shaderArgCount** returns the number of arguments for the function. The method **shaderArgNameAt:** returns the name of each argument by zero-based index. The method **shaderArgType:** returns the type of a named argument.

The N3DShader class provides several methods to let you get and set the values for named arguments to a shader function. These methods perform type conversion between the C-language, NeXTSTEP, and RenderMan types used in your application and the RenderMan Shading Language types used in the underlying shading function. The shading language argument types are identified by members of an enumeration, SLO_TYPE, declared in the header file **ri/slo.h**. The following table lists the correspondences between C-language types, shading language types, and methods:

C-language Type	SLO_TYPE	Methods
RtPoint	SLO_TYPE_POINT	**getShaderArg:pointValue:** **setShaderArg:pointValue:**
NXColor	SLO_TYPE_COLOR	**getShaderArg:colorValue:** **setShaderArg:colorValue:**
float	SLO_TYPE_SCALAR	**getShaderArg:floatValue:** **setShaderArg:floatValue:**
const char *	SLO_TYPE_STRING	**getShaderArg:stringValue:** **setShaderArg:stringValue:**

In general, you should use the **shaderArgType:** method to check an argument's type, then use the **getShaderArg:...** and **setShaderArg:...** method appropriate to the type of the argument. While it's recommended that your application enforce these correspondences, the type conversion provided with each of the **getShaderArg:...** and **setShaderArg:...** methods is flexible enough to let you mix ostensibly incompatible data types. The conversion schemes are somewhat complex but are documented with each of the **getShaderArg:...** and **setShaderArg:...** for the sake of completeness.

N3DShader and N3DShape

RenderMan Shading Language functions are applied to specific surfaces in a scene. In the 3D Graphics Kit, N3DShaders are applied by being associated with N3DShapes. As the shapes in a shape hierarchy are rendered, the associated shader functions are called: The shaders are thereby applied to that shape and its descendants. Each N3DShape can apply six different shader types:

surface
displacement
light
imager
volume
transformation

See the description of the **render:** method in N3DShape for an illustration of the order in which a shape's shader functions are invoked.

N3DShader and the Interactive Renderer

While the PhotoRealistic RenderMan renderer can use any shader written with the RenderMan Shading Language, the Interactive RenderMan renderer uses only a limited set of shaders. The surface type shaders that can be used by the interactive renderer are constant, matte, metal, plastic, and none. The atmosphere shaders used by the interactive renderer are depthcue and fog. Other than these, the interactive renderer ignores shading functions for performance reasons.

Instance Variables

NXColor **color**;
float **transparency**;
const char ***shader**;
SLO_TYPE **shaderType**;
int **shaderArgCount**;
SLOArgs ***shaderArgs**;
NXZone ***zone**;

color	Shader color
transparency	Shader transparency
shader	Name of the shader function
shaderType	Type of shader
shaderArgCount	Size of the array of shader arguments
shaderArgs	Array of shader arguments
zone	The zone in which the object's data resides

Method Types

Initializing and freeing	– init – initWithShader: – free
Shader language object file	– setShader: – shader

Shader color	– setColor: – color – setUseColor: – doesUseColor
Shader transparency	– setTransparency: – transparency
Shader function argument handling	– shaderArgCount – shaderArgNameAt: – shaderArgType: – isShaderArg: – setShaderArg:floatValue: – setShaderArg:stringValue: – setShaderArg:pointValue: – setShaderArg:colorValue: – getShaderArg:floatValue: – getShaderArg:stringValue: – getShaderArg:pointValue: – getShaderArg:colorValue: – resetShaderArg:
Shader type	– shaderType
Invoking the shader function	– set
Archiving	– read: – write:

Instance Methods

color

– (NXColor)**color**

Returns the color of the shader.

See also: – **setColor:**, – **setUseColor:**, – **doesUseColor**

doesUseColor

– (BOOL)**doesUseColor**

Returns YES if the shader uses colors; NO if not.

See also: – **color**, – **setColor:**, – **setUseColor:**

free

– **free**

Frees the N3DShader and its data.

getShaderArg:colorValue:

– **getShaderArg:**(const char *)*colorName* **colorValue:**(NXColor *)*colorValue*

Returns by reference the *colorValue* of the shader argument *colorName*. This method should be used for shader function arguments of SLO_TYPE_COLOR. Use the method **shaderArgType:** to check *colorName*'s type before invoking this method. See "Shader Function Arguments" in the class description for a more complete discussion of how to get the type of an argument.

If the argument *colorName* isn't a color type, this method converts the shading language type to an NXColor. If the argument is a float, the argument's value is converted using the **NXConvertGrayToColor()** function. If the argument is a string, the string value is converted to a float and then converted to a color with **NXConvertGrayToColor()**. If the argument is a point, its x-, y-, and z-coordinates are treated as r-, g-, and b-components and converted by the function **NXConvertRGBToColor()**. Returns **self**.

See also: – **shaderArgType:**

getShaderArg:floatValue:

– **getShaderArg:**(const char *)*floatName* **floatValue:**(float *)*floatValue*

Returns by reference the *floatValue* of the shader argument *floatName*. This method should be used for shader function arguments of SLO_TYPE_SCALAR. Use the method **shaderArgType:** to check *floatName*'s type before invoking this method. See "Shader Function Arguments" in the class description for a more complete discussion of how to get the type of an argument.

If the argument *floatName* isn't a float, this method converts the shading language type to a float. If the argument is a color, the value is converted using the **NXConvertColorToGray()** function. If the argument is a string, the string value is converted to a float. If the argument is a point, its x-coordinate is returned. Returns **self**.

See also: – **shaderArgType:**

getShaderArg:pointValue:

– **getShaderArg:**(const char *)*pointName* **pointValue:**(RtPoint *)*pointValue*

Returns by reference the *pointValue* of the shader argument *pointName*. This method should be used for shader function arguments of SLO_TYPE_POINT. Use the method **shaderArgType:** to check *colorName*'s type before invoking this method. See "Shader Function Arguments" in the class description for a more complete discussion of how to get the type of an argument.

If the argument *pointName* isn't a point type, this method converts the shading language type to an RtPoint. If the argument is a color, the the r-, g-, and b-components of the color are assigned to the x-, y-, and z-cooordinates of *pointValue*. If the argument is a float, all three components of *pointValue* return that value. If the argument is a string, the string value is converted to and treated as a float. Returns **self**.

See also: – **shaderArgType:**

getShaderArg:stringValue:

– **getShaderArg:**(const char *)*stringName* **stringValue:**(const char **)*stringValue*

Returns by reference the *stringValue* of the shader argument *stringName*. This method should be used for shader function arguments of SLO_TYPE_STRING. Use the method **shaderArgType:** to check *stringName*'s type before invoking this method. See "Shader Function Arguments" in the class description for a more complete discussion of how to get the type of an argument.

If the argument *stringName* isn't a string type, this method converts the shading language type to a string. If the argument is a point, the string returned contains the x-, y-, and z-coordinates in order. If the argument is a color, the string returned contains the r-, g-, and b-components in order. If the argument is a float, the string returned contains the value. Returns **self**.

See also: – **shaderArgType:**

init

– **init**

Initializes the receiver, a newly allocated instance of N3DShader. The shader name is set to NULL. The receiver's color is set to white and its transparency set to opaque (1.0).

See also: – **initWithShader:**

initWithShader:

– **initWithShader:**(const char *)*aShader*

Initializes the receiver, a newly allocated instance of N3DShader. Invokes **setShader:** to set the receiver's shader to *aShader*.

isShaderArg:

– (BOOL)**isShaderArg:**(const char *)*argName*

Returns YES if *argName* is the name of an argument for the shader owned by the N3DShader.

read:

– **read:**(NXTypedStream *)*stream*

Reads the receiver from the typed stream *stream*. Returns **self**.

See also: – **write:**

resetShaderArg:

– **resetShaderArg:**(const char *)*argName*

Restores the default value for the shader argument *argName*.

set

– **set**

Applies the receiver's shader function during rendering. This method calls the appropriate RenderMan function—**RiSurface()**, **RiAtmosphere()**, and so on—with the N3DShader's shader name and arguments. If the receiver is set to apply its color, this method calls **RiColor()** before calling the shader function.

An N3DShape can have one each of six different N3DShader types. This method is invoked by N3DShape's **render:** method on each of its N3DShader instances before the shape renders itself. Returns **self**.

See also: – **render:** (N3DShape), – **setColor:**, – **setUseColor:**

setColor:

– **setColor:**(NXColor)*aColor*

Sets the color of the N3DShader to *aColor.* Note that the effect produced by this method is distinct from that of **setShaderArg:colorValue:**, which is used to set an argument/value pair for a shader function. Returns **self**.

See also: – **color**, – **setUseColor:**, – **doesUseColor**

setShader:

– **setShader:**(const char *)*aShader*

Sets the receiver's shader function to *aShader. aShader* must be the name of a shader language object file in the default shader search path. Shader language object files are created by the shader compiler; each contains a single shader function.

setShaderArg:colorValue:

– **setShaderArg:**(const char *)*colorName* **colorValue:**(NXColor)*colorValue*

Sets the value of the shader argument *colorName*. This method should be used for shader function arguments of SLO_TYPE_COLOR. Use the method **shaderArgType:** to check *colorName*'s type before invoking this method. See "Shader Function Arguments" in the class description for a more complete discussion of how to get the type of an argument.

If the argument *colorName* isn't a color, this method converts *colorValue* to the appropriate shading language type. If the argument is a float, *colorValue* is converted using the **NXConvertColorToGray()** function. If the argument is a string, *colorValue*'s r-, g-, and b-components are placed in the string in order. If the argument is a point, the r-, g-, and b-components of *colorValue* are set as the x-, y-, and z-components of the argument. Returns **self**.

See also: – **shaderArgType:**

setShaderArg:floatValue:

– **setShaderArg:**(const char *)*floatName* **floatValue:**(float)*floatValue*

Sets the value of the shader argument *floatName*. This method should be used for shader function arguments of SLO_TYPE_SCALAR. Use the method **shaderArgType:** to check *colorName*'s type before invoking this method. See "Shader Function Arguments" in the class description for a more complete discussion of how to get the type of an argument.

If the argument *floatName* isn't a float, this method converts *floatValue* to the appropriate shading language type. If the argument is a color, *floatValue* is converted using the **NXConvertGrayToColor()** function. If the argument is a string, *floatValue* is converted to a string. If the argument is a point, all three coordinates are set to *floatValue*. Returns **self**.

See also: – **shaderArgType:**

setShaderArg:pointValue:

– **setShaderArg:**(const char *)*pointName* **pointValue:**(RtPoint)*pointValue*

Sets the value of the shader argument *pointName*. This method should be used for shader function arguments of SLO_TYPE_POINT. Use the method **shaderArgType:** to check *pointName*'s type before invoking this method. See "Shader Function Arguments" in the class description for a more complete discussion of how to get the type of an argument.

If the argument *pointName* isn't a point, this method converts *pointValue* to the appropriate shading language type. If the argument is a float, *pointValue*'s x-coordinate is assigned to the variable. If the argument is a string, the x-, y-, and z-coordinates of *pointValue* are placed in order in the string. If the argument is a color, this method assigns the x-, y-, and z-coordinates of *pointValue* to the r-, g-, and b-components of the argument. Returns **self**.

See also: – **shaderArgType:**

setShaderArg:stringValue:

– **setShaderArg:**(const char *)*stringName* **stringValue:**(const char *)*stringValue*

Sets the value of the shader argument *stringName*. This method should be used for shader function arguments of SLO_TYPE_STRING. Use the method **shaderArgType:** to check *stringName*'s type before invoking this method. See "Shader Function Arguments" in the class description for a more complete discussion of how to get the type of an argument.

If the argument *stringName* is a float, this method converts *stringValue* to a float. If the argument is a point or color, no conversion is made and the argument's value isn't changed. Returns **self**.

See also: – **shaderArgType:**

setTransparency:

– **setTransparency:**(float)*alphaValue*

Sets the transparency of the shader to *alphaValue*. Returns **self**.

setUseColor:

– **setUseColor:**(BOOL)*flag*

If *flag* is YES, sets the receiver to apply its color when rendering. The color is set with the **setColor:** method, and is applied using the **RiColor()** RenderMan call. Normally, this method is only invoked with *flag* YES for a surface type N3DShader. Note that the effect produced by this method is distinct from that of **setShaderArg:colorValue:**, which is used to set an argument/value pair for a shader function.

See also: – **set**, – **setColor:**

shader

– (const char *)**shader**

Returns the name of the shader function associated with the N3DShader.

shaderArgCount

– (int)**shaderArgCount**

Returns the number of arguments for the shader function associated with the N3DShader.

shaderArgNameAt:

– (const char *)**shaderArgNameAt:**(int)*argIndex*

Returns the name of the argument at position *argIndex* in the list of shader function argument names. To get all argument names, use this method to iterate through the list beginning with an *argIndex* of 0 and ending with an *argIndex* of

```
[self shaderArgCount]-1
```

shaderArgType:

– (SLO_TYPE)**shaderArgType:**(const char *)*argName*

Returns the type of the argument *argName* from the list of shader function argument names. The value returned is an enumerated type, defined in the header file **ri/slo.h**. If *argName* isn't found in the list, returns SLO_TYPE_UNKNOWN.

shaderType

– (SLO_TYPE)**shaderType**

Returns the type of the shader function. The value returned is an enumerated type, defined in the header file **ri/slo.h**. If the receiving N3DShader doesn't have an associated shader function, this method returns SLO_TYPE_UNKNOWN.

transparency

– (float)**transparency**

Returns the transparency (alpha) value set for the receiving N3DShader.

write:

– **write:**(NXTypedStream *)*stream*

Writes the receiving N3DShader to the typed stream *stream*. Returns **self**.

See also: – **read:**

N3DShape

Inherits From: Object

Declared In: 3Dkit/N3DShape.h

Class Description

N3DShape provides techniques for representing 3D transformations, for rendering the standard RenderMan surface primitives, and for creating and managing hierarchically organized structures. Using subclasses of N3DShape, your application can model compound shapes made from hierarchically related N3DShape objects.

Creating an N3DShape Subclass

While N3DShape provides methods for representing 3D transformations and for creating hierarchically organized structures, you need to create a subclass of N3DShape to perform surface modeling. Your subclass must override the abstract method **renderSelf:**, calling one or more of the following RenderMan geometric primitive functions:

Quadric Surfaces

RiSphere()
RiCone()
RiDisk()
RiCylinder()
RiHyperboloid()
RiParaboloid()
RiTorus()

Polygons

RiPolygon()
RiGeneralPolygon()
RiPointsPolygon()
RiPointsGeneralPolygons()

Patches

RiPatch()
RiPatchMesh()
RiNuPatch()

A complete description of these RenderMan geometric primitive functions, including parameter listings and illustrations, can be found in *The RenderMan Companion*. Sample code using the **RiSphere**() function call is included in the description of the **renderSelf:** method.

N3DShapes can be set to render either their surface geometry or their bounding boxes. This ability to switch rendering modes is useful for faster interactive manipulation of shapes. For your N3DShape subclasses to render their bounding boxes, you must provide a way to set the **boundingBox** instance variable, both when the shape is initialized and when its size changes (that is, when values passed to RenderMan geometric primitives in the **renderSelf:** method change).

The Shape Hierarchy

A shape hierarchy is made up by linking shapes in two kinds of relationships: *descendant/ancestor* and *next peer/previous peer*. A shape's descendant inherits its graphics state attributes. A descendant and its peers share the same ancestor, and inherit the same graphics state attributes from that ancestor. In this discussion, the term *descendant* applies to a shape's direct descendant; the term *descendants* applies to the direct descendant, its peers, and all descendants of the direct descendant or peers.

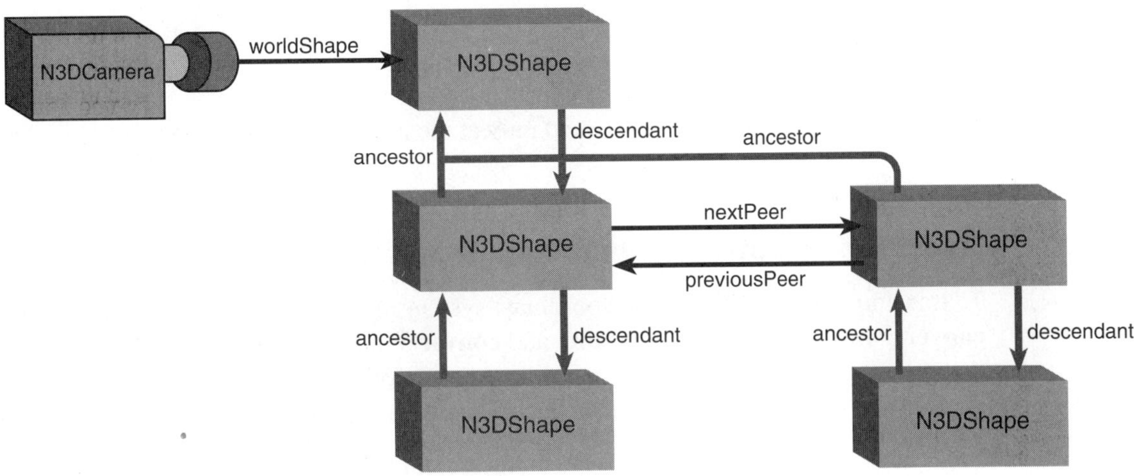

Figure 17-10. A shape hierarchy

Peers share a common ancestor (their **ancestor** methods return the same N3DShape object). However, that ancestor has but one descendant, which is the first peer. Each shape sharing an ancestor can apply its own graphics state attributes, independent of its peers. The two shapes at the bottom of the illustration aren't peers—they have different ancestors.

The graphics state attributes inherited by a shape's descendants include its coordinate system and shaders. You override these inheritances by setting attributes of the descendant explicitly using the appropriate methods. A shape's bounding box isn't explicitly inherited by its descendants. Instead, the box returned by the **getBoundingBox:** method is the union of the receiver's bounding box with those of all its descendants—thus representing the smallest volume capable of containing the receiver and its descendants.

Be sure to use N3DShape methods to place a shape in the shape hierarchy. Methods for shape hierarchy management include **linkPeer:**, **linkDescendant:**, **linkAncestor:**, **unlink**, **group:**, and **ungroup**.

Your application may need to traverse the shape hierarchy to request that each shape apply a setting or respond to a request. To do so, you can add a traversal method such as the following to your subclass of N3DShape:

```
- preTraverse
{
/* do the work here */
if ([self descendant] != nil) {
  descendant preTraverse];
  }
if ([self nextPeer] != nil) {
  [nextPeer preTraverse];
  }
return self;
}
```

Surface modeling is usually performed only at the leaf nodes of a shape hierarchy; that is, by shapes without descendants.

Transforming Between Coordinate Systems

To transform points between the coordinate systems of two N3DShapes, use the methods **convertPoints:count:fromAncestor:** and **convertPoints:count:toAncestor:**. To transform points between the 3D coordinate system of a shape and the 2D (PostScript) coordinate system of its camera, use the method **convertObjectPoints:count:toCamera:**.

You can also transform from one coordinate system to another by applying a matrix to a shape or a camera. A matrix is a two-dimensional array that represents a transformation from one coordinate system to another. The RenderMan standard defines a type, RtMatrix, as a 4 x 4 array of floating point values that represents such a transformation between 3D coordinate systems. Each N3DShape maintains three matrices: the transform, the composite transform, and the inverse of the composite transform. While matrix manipulation concepts are beyond the scope of this discussion, you should understand the meanings of these matrices.

The transform matrix is the matrix the shape applies when its **render:** method is invoked. It represents the transformation from the immediate ancestor's coordinate system to its owner's coordinates. Use the methods **getTransformMatrix:** and **setTransformMatrix:** to access a shape's transform matrix.

The composite transform matrix represents the combined transformations from a distant ancestor—usually the shape at the top of the hierarchy. The composite transform matrix can be used for transforming points from this ancestor's coordinate system to the shape's coordinate system. Use the method **getCompositeTransform:relativeToAncestor:** to access this matrix.

The inverse of the composite transform matrix represents the transformation from its owner's coordinate system to an ancestor's coordinate system. Use the method **getInverseCompositeTransform: relativeToAncestor:** to access this matrix.

The identity matrix represents a *normalized* coordinate system: one to which no transformations are applied. The global constant **N3DIdentityMatrix** is defined in **3Dkit/next3d.h**. The values in the identity matrix are:

```
{{1, 0, 0, 0},
 {0, 1, 0, 0},
 {0, 0, 1, 0},
 {0, 0, 0, 1}}
```

Shaders

Each N3DShape can have one each of the six shader types: surface, displacement, light, imager, volume, and transformation. The shaders belonging to an N3DShape are instances of the N3DShader class; each N3DShader object manages a shading language function. The type of an N3DShader is determined by the shader function which it manages. See the N3DShader class specification for more on shading language functions.

Light shader objects are different than light objects. N3DLight is a subclass of shape whose objects are used to light one or more surfaces in a scene. In most cases, you will illuminate the shapes in a scene using N3DLight objects rather than light shaders.

The Render Delegate

The render delegate is an N3DShape that renders a specific geometry. Render delegates are an efficient way to render multiple versions of a single shape. Say, for example, you want to render all four tires on an automobile. Each N3DShape representing a tire can have the same render delegate. Each time one of the tire shapes gets a **render:** message, it invokes the delegate's **renderSelf:** method. Thus only the render delegate needs to retain the geometric data for the tire. The four shapes using the delegate need only represent the transformation to the origin of the four tire positions.

Instance Variables

```
RtMatrix transform;
RtMatrix compositeTransform;
RtMatrix inverseCompositeTransform;
RtBound boundingBox;
N3DShapeName *shapeName;
N3DSurfaceType surfaceType;
id surfaceShader;
id displacementShader;
id lightShader;
id imagerShader;
id volumeShader;
id transformationShader;
struct _shapeFlags {
 unsigned int selectable:1;
 unsigned int visible:1;
 unsigned int ancestorChanged:1;
 unsigned int compositeDirty:2;
 unsigned int drawAsBox:1;
 unsigned int isInstance:1;
 unsigned int hasShader:1;
}shapeFlags;
id nextPeer;
id previousPeer;
id descendant;
id ancestor;
id renderDelegate;
```

transform	Transformation from ancestor
compositeTransform	Transformation from top of shape hierarchy
inverseCompositeTransform	Transformation to top of shape hierarchy
boundingBox	Three-dimensional bounds of shape
shapeName	Name and **id** of shape
surfaceType	Surface type for interactive rendering
surfaceShader	Surface shader for photorealistic rendering
displacementShader	Displacement shader for photorealistic rendering

lightShader	Light shader for photorealistic rendering
imagerShader	Imager shader for photorealistic rendering
volumeShader	Volume shader for photorealistic rendering
transformationShader	Transformation shader for photorealistic rendering
shapeFlags.selectable	YES if the shape can be selected
shapeFlags.visible	YES if the shape and its descendants are visible
shapeFlags.ancestorChanged	YES if the shape's ancestor changed
shapeFlags.compositeDirty	YES if the composite and inverse transform matrices need updating
shapeFlags.drawAsBox	YES if this shape renders by drawing its bounding box
shapeFlags.isInstance	YES if this shape has a delegate to perform its rendering
shapeFlags.hasShader	YES if this shape has any shaders associated with it
nextPeer	Next shape in the peer group
previousPeer	Previous shape in the peer group
descendant	Shape descended from this one
ancestor	Shape from which this one descends
renderDelegate	Delegate that performs rendering

Method Types

Initializing and freeing	– init – free – freeAll
Rendering the N3DShape	– render: – renderSelf: – renderSelfAsBox:
Traversing the shape hierarchy	– nextPeer – previousPeer – firstPeer – lastPeer – descendant – lastDescendant – ancestor – firstAncestor – isWorld

Managing the shape hierarchy	– linkPeer: – linkDescendant: – linkAncestor: – unlink – group: – ungroup
Shader	– setShader: – shaderType:
Surface	– surfaceType – setSurfaceType:andDescendants:
Bounding box	– getBoundingBox: – setDrawAsBox: – doesDrawAsBox – getBounds:inCamera:
Converting points	– convertObjectPoints:count:toCamera: – convertPoints:count:fromAncestor: – convertPoints:count:toAncestor:
Selection	– setSelectable: – isSelectable
Visibility	– setVisible: – isVisible
Naming shapes	– setShapeName: – shapeName
Delegate for rendering	– setRenderDelegate: – removeRenderDelegate – renderDelegate
Transformation matrices	– setTransformMatrix: – getTransformMatrix: – concatTransformMatrix:premultiply: – getCompositeTransformMatrix:relativeToAncestor: – getInverseCompositeTransformMatrix: relativeToAncestor:

Rotation, scaling, translation	– rotateAngle:axis: – preRotateAngle:axis: – scale::: – preScale::: – scaleUniformly: – preScaleUniformly: – translate::: – preTranslate:::
Archiving	– read: – write: – awake

Instance Methods

ancestor

– ancestor

Returns the receiving object's ancestor—the N3DShape above it in the shape hierarchy. If the receiving shape is at the top of its hierarchy, returns **nil**. The class description includes an illustration and discussion of the shape hierarchy.

See also: **– linkAncestor:**, **– firstAncestor**

awake

– awake

Invoked after unarchiving to reinitialize the N3DShape object. Do not invoke this method directly. Returns **self**.

See also: **– read:**, **– write:**

concatTransformMatrix:premultiply:

– **concatTransformMatrix:**(RtMatrix)*aTransform* **premultiply:**(BOOL)*flag*

Concatenates *aTransform* to the N3DShape's current transform matrix. If *flag* is YES, this method premultiplies the matrix by the *aTransform*; that is, it applies the effect of *aTransform* to the receiving shape's coordinate system before applying the effect of its transform matrix. Otherwise, it postmultiplies the transform matrix by *aTransform*, applying the effect of the transform matrix before applying the effect of *aTransform*. In either case, it places the result in the receiver's **transform** instance variable. Returns **self**.

See also: – **setTransformMatrix:**, – **getTransformMatrix**,
– **getCompositeTransformMatrix:relativeToAncestor:**,
– **getInverseCompositeTransformationMatrix:relativeToAncestor:**

convertObjectPoints:count:toCamera:

– **convertObjectPoints:**(RtPoint *)*points*
count:(int)*n*
toCamera:*camera*

Converts *points* from the receiver's coordinate system to *camera*'s 2D (PostScript) coordinate system. Returns the converted values by reference in the first two (x and y) coordinates of each RtPoint in *points*; you should ignore the z coordinates returned in *points*. Returns **self**.

See also: – **convertPoints:count:fromAncestor:**, – **convertPoints:count:toAncestor:**

convertPoints:count:fromAncestor:

– **convertPoints:**(RtPoint *)*points*
count:(int)*n*
fromAncestor:(N3DShape *)*theShape*

Converts points from *theShape*'s coordinate system to the coordinate system of the receiver. If *theShape* is **nil** or isn't above the receiver in its shape hierarchy, this method converts from the shape at the top of the receiver's shape hierarchy (its first ancestor). Returns the converted values by reference in *points*. Returns **self**. See the class description for a discussion and diagram of the shape hierarchy.

See also: – **convertObjectPoints:count:toCamera:**,
– **convertPoints:count:toAncestor:**, – **firstAncestor**

convertPoints:count:toAncestor:

– **convertPoints:**(RtPoint *)*points* **count:**(int)*n* **toAncestor:**(N3DShape *)*theShape*

Converts points from the receiver's coordinate system to the coordinate system of *theShape*. If *theShape* is **nil** or isn't above the receiver in its shape hierarchy, this method converts to the world shape at the top of the receiver's shape hierarchy. Returns **self**. See the class description for a discussion and diagram of the shape hierarchy.

See also: – **convertShapePointsToWorld:count:**, – **convertShapePoints:count:toCamera:**

descendant

– **descendant**

Returns the receiver's descendant—the N3DShape below it in the object hierarchy. If the receiving shape has no descendant, returns **nil**. See the class description for a discussion and diagram of the shape hierarchy.

See also: – **lastDescendant**, – **linkDescendant:**

doesDrawAsBox

– (BOOL)**doesDrawAsBox**

Returns YES if the receiver is set to draw its bounding box when it renders. For an instance of your subclass of N3DShape to draw its bounding box, you must explicitly set the bounding box when it is initialized and when it is resized (that is, when values passed to RenderMan geometric primitives in the **renderSelf:** method change). By default, returns NO.

See also: – **getBoundingBox:**, – **setDrawAsBox:**

firstAncestor

– **firstAncestor**

Returns the shape at the top of the receiving N3DShape's hierarchy. See the class description for a discussion and diagram of the shape hierarchy.

See also: – **ancestor**, – **linkAncestor:**

firstPeer

– firstPeer

Returns the left-most peer in the receiver's peer group. The first peer is the direct descendant of the receiver's ancestor. See the class description for a discussion and diagram of the shape hierarchy.

See also: **– lastPeer**, **– linkPeer:**, **– nextPeer**, **– previousPeer**

free

– free

Frees the receiving object, its descendants, and the descendants' peers. Unlinks the receiving object from its peer group; if the receiver has a next peer and previous peer, they are set to point to each other; if the receiver has no previous peer, its next peer is set as the direct descendant of the ancestor. Frees the receiver's descendant and its descendants and peers by sending a **freeAll** message to the descendant. See the class description for a discussion and diagram of the shape hierarchy. Returns **nil**.

See also: **– freeAll**

freeAll

– freeAll

Frees the receiver, its next peer (and all subsequent peers) and its descendants. This method first sends a **freeAll** message to the next peer, then sends a **free** message to **self**. See the class description for a discussion and diagram of the shape hierarchy. Returns **nil**.

See also: **– free**

getBoundingBox:

– **getBoundingBox:**(RtBound *)*boundingBox*

Returns, by reference in *boundingBox*, the union of the receiver's bounding box and its descendant's bounding boxes; thus, the six coordinates in *boundingBox* represent the volume of the receiver and all its descendants. The returned values are in the coordinates of the receiving N3DShape.

Note that for your subclass of N3DShape to return the correct value in *boundingBox*, your code must set the **boundingBox** instance variable when an instance is initialized and whenever it changes size (that is, when values passed to RenderMan geometric primitives in the **renderSelf:** method change). Returns **self**.

See also: – **renderSelf:**, – **renderSelfAsBox:**, – **doesDrawAsBox**, – **setDrawAsBox:**

getBounds:inCamera:

– **getBounds:**(NXRect *)*boundingRect* **inCamera:***theCamera*

Returns, by reference in *boundingRect*, the rectangle that bounds the receiver in *theCamera*'s 2D (PostScript) coordinate system. If *theCamera* isn't an N3DCamera object, this method generates an exception. Returns **self**.

getCompositeTransformMatrix:relativeToAncestor:

– **getCompositeTransformMatrix:**(RtMatrix)*theMatrix*
relativeToAncestor:(N3DShape *)*theAncestor*

Returns, by reference in *theMatrix*, the matrix representing the transformation from *theAncestor*'s coordinate system to the receiver's coordinate system. If *theAncestor* is **nil** or if the receiving N3DShape isn't a descendant of *theAncestor*, *theMatrix* represents the transformation from world space to the receiver's coordinate system. See the class description for discussions of the shape hierarchy and transformations. Returns **self**.

See also: – **setTransformMatrix:**, – **getTransformMatrix:**,
– **concatTransformMatrix:premultiply:**,
– **getInverseCompositeTransformationMatrix:relativeToAncestor:**

getInverseCompositeTransformMatrix:relativeToAncestor:

– **getInverseCompositeTransformMatrix:**(RtMatrix)*theMatrix*
relativeToAncestor:(N3DShape *)*theAncestor*

Returns, by reference in *theMatrix*, the matrix representing the transformation from the receiver's coordinate system to *theAncestor*'s coordinate system. If *theAncestor* is **nil** or if the receiving N3DShape isn't a descendant of *theAncestor*, *theMatrix* represents the transformation from the receiver's coordinate system to world space. See the class description for discussions of the shape hierarchy and transformations. Returns **self**.

See also: – **setTransformMatrix:**, – **getTransformMatrix:**, – **concatTransformMatrix:premultiply:**, – **getCompositeTransformMatrix:relativeToAncestor:**

getTransformMatrix:

– **getTransformMatrix:**(RtMatrix)*theMatrix*

Returns, by reference in *theMatrix*, the receiver's transform matrix: the instance variable representing the transformation from the ancestor's space to the receiver's space. This method is invoked by N3DShape's **render:** method to get the transformation matrix for the space in which the shape is rendered. Override this method to apply your own manipulation on the transform matrix—and, thereby, on the receiver's space—when rendering. Returns **self**.

See also: – **concatTransformMatrix:premultiply:**, – **getCompositeTransformMatrix:relativeToAncestor:**, – **getInverseCompositeTransformMatrix:relativeToAncestor:**, – **preRotateAngle:axis:**, – **preScale:::**, – **preScaleUniformly:**, – **preTranslate:::**, – **rotateAngle:axis:**, – **scale:::**, – **scaleUniformly:**, – **setTransformMatrix:**, – **translate:::**

group:

– **group:***toShape*

Makes the receiver a descendant of *toShape* while maintaining its position in world space. Invoking this method on a series of N3DShapes, each with the same N3DShape as *toShape*, causes the receivers to become peers—all descended from *toShape*. This method is useful, for example, to group a set of N3DShapes after they've been selected by the user.

This method modifies the receiver's transform matrix to reflect the transformation from *toShape* to the receiver's current position. If *toShape* has no descendant, the receiver is made its direct descendant using the **linkDescendant:** method. Otherwise, the receiver is linked by invoking **linkPeer:** on *toShape*'s descendant. Returns **self**.

See also: – **linkDescendant:**, – **linkPeer:**, – **ungroup**, – **setSelectable**, – **selectShapesIn:** (N3DCamera)

init

– **init**

Initializes the receiver, a newly allocated instance of N3DShape. The **transform**, **compositeTransform**, and **inverseCompositeTransform** matrices are normalized (see the class description for a discussion of matrices and transformations between coordinate systems). All shaders are set to **nil**, as are the peer, ancestor, and descendant pointers. Returns **self**.

isSelectable

– (BOOL)**isSelectable**

Returns YES if the receiving N3DShape can be selected. Shapes are selected by the N3DCamera method **selectShapesIn:**. By default, N3DShapes aren't selectable.

See also: – **setSelectable:**, – **selectShapesIn:** (N3DCamera)

isVisible

– (BOOL)**isVisible**

Returns YES if the receiving N3DShape has been set to render itself. N3DShapes are visible by default.

See also: – **setVisible:**

isWorld

– (BOOL)**isWorld**

Returns YES if the receiving N3DShape is at the top of its shape hierarchy—that is, it has no previous peer or ancestor. Returns NO otherwise. See the class description for a discussion and diagram of the shape hierarchy.

lastDescendant

– **lastDescendant**

Returns the N3DShape at the end of the receiver's descendant chain. This method searches directly below the receiver; it doesn't search peer branches for deeper descendants. Returns **self** if the receiver has no descendant. See the class description for a discussion and diagram of the shape hierarchy.

See also: – **descendant**, – **linkDescendant:**

lastPeer

– **lastPeer**

Returns the N3DShape at the far right of the receiver's peer group. Searches for the first peer whose next peer is **nil**, beginning with the receiver. See the class description for a discussion and diagram of the shape hierarchy.

See also: – **firstPeer**, – **linkPeer:**, – **nextPeer**, – **previousPeer**

linkAncestor:

– **linkAncestor:***anAncestor*

Sets *anAncestor* as the ancestor of the receiver and its peers. Doesn't reset *anAncestor*'s descendant. Returns the receiver's previous ancestor. See the class description for a discussion and diagram of the shape hierarchy.

See also: – **ancestor**, – **firstAncestor**, – **linkDescendant**

linkDescendant:

– **linkDescendant:***aDescendant*

Inserts *aDescendant* directly below the receiver. *aDescendant* is made the receiver's descendant, and *aDescendant* and its peers set the receiver as their ancestor. The receiver's previous descendant is moved to the bottom of *aDescendant*'s sub-tree, that is, made the descendant of its last descendant. See the class description for a discussion and diagram of the shape hierarchy.

If *aDescendant* isn't an N3DShape (or subclass thereof), no change is made to the receiver's hierarchy. Returns **self**.

See also: – **descendant**, – **lastDescendant**, – **linkAncestor**

linkPeer:

– **linkPeer:***aPeer*

Inserts *aPeer* as the receiver's next peer. *aPeer* brings with it any peers and descendants it may have. The receiver's former next peer is moved to the extreme right of *aPeer*'s peer group, made the next peer of *aPeer*'s last peer. If *aPeer* isn't an N3DShape (or subclass thereof), no change is made to the receiver's hierarchy. See the class description for a discussion and diagram of the shape hierarchy. Returns **self**.

See also: – **firstPeer**, – **lastPeer**, – **nextPeer**, – **previousPeer**

nextPeer

– **nextPeer**

Returns the receiver's next peer—the N3DShape to the right of the receiving N3DShape. If the receiver has no next peer, this method returns **nil**. See the class description for a discussion and diagram of the shape hierarchy.

See also: – **firstPeer**, – **lastPeer**, – **linkPeer:**, – **previousPeer**

preRotateAngle:axis:

– **preRotateAngle:**(float)*angle* **axis:**(RtPoint)*referencePoint*

Rotates the receiver about an axis defined by *referencePoint* and the origin of its coordinate system. The receiving shape's transform matrix is premultiplied by the rotation matrix; that means the rotation is applied to the N3DShape's own coordinate system rather than that of its ancestor. The resulting transformation is stored in the receiver's transform matrix. Both *referencePoint* and the origin are defined in the receiver's coordinate system. Returns **self**.

See also: – **rotateAngle:axis:**

preScale:::

– **preScale:**(float)*xScaleFactor*
:(float)*yScaleFactor*
:(float)*zScaleFactor*

Scales the receiver. A separate scale factor is applied to each of the receiving shape's dimensions. The receiving shape's transform matrix is premultiplied by the scaling matrix; that means the scaling is applied to the N3DShape's own coordinate system rather than that of its ancestor. The resulting transformation is stored in the receiver's transform matrix. Returns **self**.

See also: – **preScaleUniformly:**, – **scale:::**, – **scaleUniformly:**

preScaleUniformly:

– **preScaleUniformly:**(float)*scaleFactor*

Scales the receiver. This method works by invoking **preScale:::** with *scaleFactor* for all three arguments. Returns **self**.

See also: – **preScale:::**, – **scale:::**, – **scaleUniformly:**

preTranslate:::

– **preTranslate:**(float)*xTranslation*
:(float)*yTranslation*
:(float)*zTranslation*

Translates the receiver. A separate translation is applied along each of the receiving shape's axes. The receiving shape's transform matrix is premultiplied by the translation matrix; that is, the translation is applied to the N3DShape's own coordinate system rather than that of its ancestor. The resulting transformation is stored in the receiver's transform matrix. Returns **self**.

See also: – **translate:::**

previousPeer

– **previousPeer**

Returns the receiver's previous peer, the N3DShape to the immediate left of the receiver. If the receiver is the first peer in its peer group, returns **nil**.

See also: – **firstPeer**, – **lastPeer**, – **linkPeer:**, – **nextPeer**

read:

– **read:**(NXTypedStream *)*stream*

Reads the receiver from the typed stream *stream*. Returns **self**.

See also: –**awake**, – **write:**

removeRenderDelegate

– **removeRenderDelegate**

Removes and returns the render delegate for the receiver. See the class description for a discussion of the render delegate.

See also: – **renderDelegate**, – **setRenderDelegate**:

render:

– **render:**(N3DCamera *)*theCamera*

This method renders the N3DShape, its descendants, and its peers. The diagram shows the sequence of 3D Graphics Kit methods and RenderMan functions invoked by **render:**.

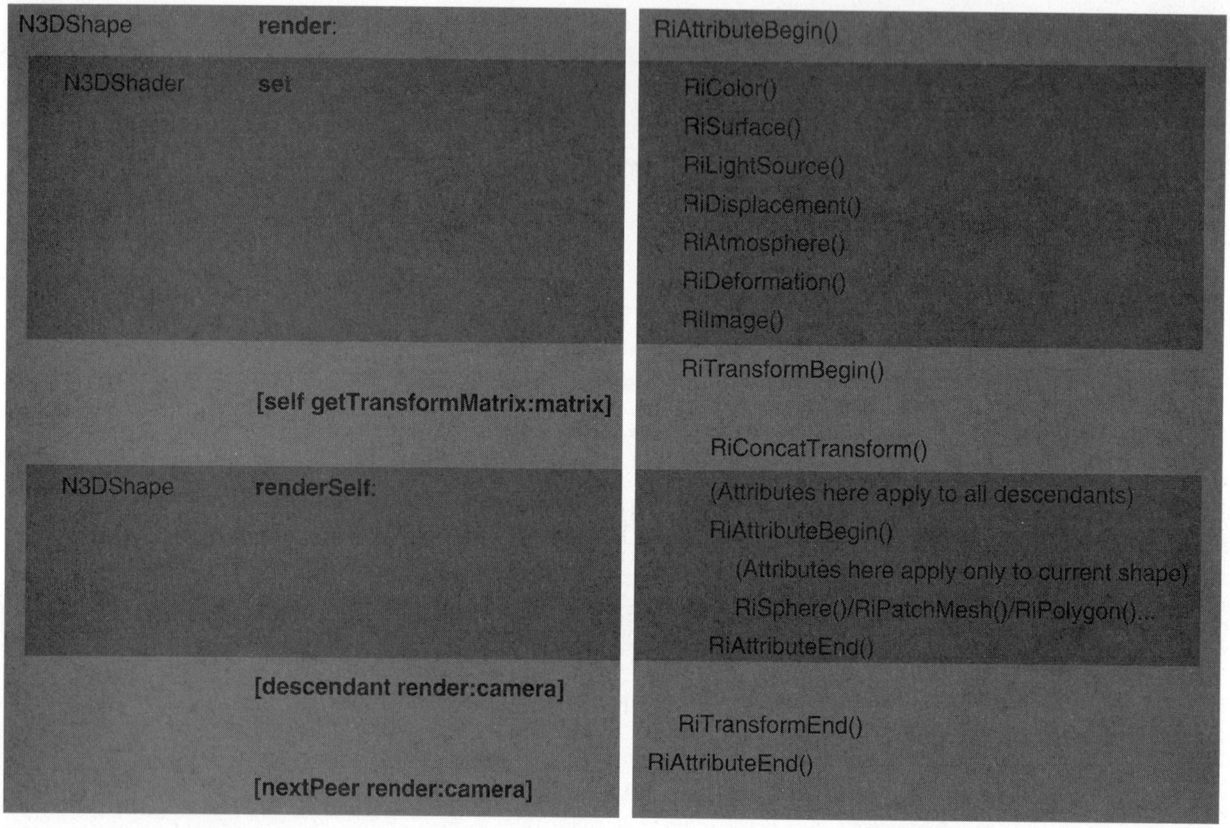

Figure 17-11. Sequence of 3D Kit and RenderMan calls in **render:**

After invoking **RiAttributeBegin()**, this method invokes **set** on each of the N3DShape's N3DShaders, which in turn invoke the appropriate RenderMan shader function. Next, this method applies the shape's transformation by invoking **getTransformMatrix:** on **self** and applying the matrix returned in **RiConcatTransform()**. It then invokes **renderSelf:** (or **renderSelfAsBox:**) to actually render the shape using the transformation and shaders applied.

After rendering the shape, this method invokes **render:** on the N3DShape's descendant, which thus inherits the shading and transformation of the ancestor. This method then invokes **RiTransformEnd()** and **RiAttributeEnd()** to remove the effect of its transformation and shaders, after which it invokes **render:** on the N3DShape's next peer.

You don't invoke this method directly. It is invoked by the N3DShape's ancestor, previous peer, or N3DCamera when rendering. This method returns **self**.

See also: – **renderSelf:**, – **renderSelfAsBox:**, – **getTransformMatrix:**, – **set** (N3DShader)

renderDelegate

– renderDelegate

Returns the receiver's rendering delegate, the N3DShape whose **renderSelf:** method is invoked each time the receiver's **render:** method is invoked.

See also: – **removeRenderDelegate**, – **setRenderDelegate:**

renderSelf:

– renderSelf:(N3DCamera *)*theCamera*

This abstract method does nothing, returns **self**. Override this method to do custom rendering in a subclass of N3DShape. For example, to create a subclass of N3DShape that draws a sphere, you'd implement this method as follows:

```
- renderSelf:(RtToken)context
{
/* attributes here apply to the receiver and descendants */
RiAttributeBegin();
/* attributes here apply only to the receiver */
RiSphere(myRadius, myZMax, myZMin, mySweepAngle, RI_NULL);
RiAttributeEnd();
return self;
}
```

A list of RenderMan geometric primitive functions is included in the class description at the beginning of this discussion. See *The RenderMan Companion* for a complete description of the RenderMan language and its various primitives.

It's recommended that you use N3DShape methods for setting RenderMan attributes rather than placing function calls such as **RiRotate**() and **RiScale**() in **renderSelf:**. Using N3DShape API assures that you can query a shape for an accurate reflection of its state. If you choose to apply attributes directly in **renderSelf:**, make judicious use of **RiAttributeBegin**() and **RiAttributeEnd**(). For example, note that in the above code attributes before **RiAttributeBegin**() apply to the receiver and its descendants; those after **RiAttributeBegin**() apply only to the receiver.

To draw complex shapes, the **renderSelf:** method can include calls to any number and combination of RenderMan geometric primitive functions.

See also: – **render:**, – **renderSelfAsBox:**

renderSelfAsBox:

– **renderSelfAsBox:**(N3DCamera *)*theCamera*

Renders the receiver's bounding box. If the receiver uses a render delegate, renders the delegate's bounding box. This method gets the points to use in drawing the box by invoking **getBoundingBox:** on **self**—thus, the box drawn includes the volume of the receiver and all its descendants. If the N3DShape is set to render itself as a box, this method is invoked instead of **renderSelf:** each time the shape's **render:** method is invoked. Returns **self**.

See also: – **getBoundingBox:**, – **render:**, – **renderSelf:**, – **doesDrawAsBox**, – **setDrawAsBox:**

rotateAngle:axis:

– **rotateAngle:**(float)*ang* **axis:**(RtPoint)*referencePoint*

Rotates the receiver about the axis defined by *referencePoint* and the origin of the receiver's coordinate system. The rotation is postmultiplied on the receiving shape's transform matrix; that means the rotation is applied to the ancestor's coordinate system before any other transformations in the receiver's coordinate system. The resulting transformation is stored in the receiver's transform matrix. Both *referencePoint* and the origin are defined in the receiver's coordinate system. Returns **self**.

See also: – **preRotateAngle:axis:**

scale:::

– **scale:**(float)*xScaleFactor*
    :(float)*yScaleFactor*
    :(float)*zScaleFactor*

Scales the receiver. A separate scale factor is applied along each of the receiving shape's axes. The receiving shape's transform matrix is postmultiplied by the scaling matrix; that means the scaling is applied to the ancestor's coordinate system before any other transformations in the receiver's coordinate system. The resulting transformation is stored in the receiver's transform matrix. Returns **self**.

See also: – **preScale:::**, – **scaleUniformly**, – **preScaleUniformly:**

scaleUniformly:

– **scaleUniformly:**(float)*scaleFactor*

Scales the receiver. This method works by invoking **scale:::** with *scaleFactor* used for all three arguments. Returns **self**.

See also: – **scale:::**, – **preScale:::**, – **preScaleUniformly:**

setDrawAsBox:

– **setDrawAsBox:**(BOOL)*flag*

Sets the receiver to render only its bounding box. If *flag* is YES, **renderSelfAsBox:** is invoked instead of **renderSelf:** each time the N3DShape's **render:** method is invoked; if NO, **renderSelf:** is called. Returns **self**.

For maximum efficiency and minimum screen clutter, you may want to have an N3DShape render itself as a box, while its descendants and their peers remain invisible. This is useful when a user is interactively manipulating the shapes in an N3DCamera. To use this technique on a specific shape, invoke this method with flag YES, then send the message **[descendant setVisible:NO]**.

See also: – **doesDrawAsBox**, – **getBoundingBox:**, – **renderSelfAsBox:**

setRenderDelegate:

– **setRenderDelegate:***aShape*

Sets the receiver's rendering delegate, the N3DShape whose **renderSelf:** method is invoked each time the receiver's **render:** method is invoked. Returns the old render delegate. If *aShape* isn't a subclass of N3DShape, does nothing and returns **nil**.

See also: – **removeRenderDelegate**, – **renderDelegate**

setSelectable:

– **setSelectable:**(BOOL)*flag*

Enables the receiver to be selected. N3DShapes are selected by N3DCamera's **selectShapesIn:** method. Returns **self**.

See also: – **isSelectable**, – **selectShapesIn:** (N3DCamera)

setShader:

– **setShader:***aShader*

Sets *aShader* as the receiver's shader of *aShader*'s type. An N3DShape can have shaders of six types: surface, displacement, light, imager, volume, and transformation. *aShader* must be an object of the N3DShader class (or subclass thereof).

If you want your N3DShape to have various shader types (for example, surface, displacement, and light shaders), you allocate separate instances of N3DShader—each associated with a shader function of the appropriate type. You then invoke this method three separate times, once for each of the N3DShaders.

This method returns the old shader of *aShader*'s type.

See also: – **shaderType:**

setShapeName:

– **setShapeName:**(const char *)*aName*

Sets the receiver's name to *aName*. Returns **self**.

See also: – **shapeName**

setSurfaceType:andDescendants:

– **setSurfaceType:**(N3DSurfaceType)*theSurface* **andDescendants:**(BOOL)*flag*

Sets the surface type used by the interactive renderer. *theSurface* can be one of five enumerated values defined in the header file **3Dkit/next3d.h**:

N3D_PointCloud
N3D_WireFrame
N3D_ShadedWireFrame
N3D_FacetedSolids
N3D_SmoothSolids

Four of these types are shown in the following illustration:

Figure 17-12. N3D_PointCloud, N3D_WireFrame, N3D_FacetedSolids, and N3D_SmoothSolids surface types

N3D_ShadedWireFrame renders an N3D_WireFrame surface with depth cueing.

The surface type set by this method applies to the receiver and, if *flag* is YES, to its descendants and their peers. N3DCamera's **setSurfaceTypeForAll:chooseHider:** method invokes this method on the world shape. The photorealistic renderer uses the surface shader set with the **setShader:** method. Returns **self**.

See also: – **surfaceType**, – **setSurfaceTypeForAll:chooseHider:** (N3DCamera)

setTransformMatrix:

– **setTransformMatrix:**(RtMatrix)*newTransform*

Replaces the receiver's current transform matrix with *newTransform*. Returns **self**.

See also: – **getTransformMatrix:**, – **getCompositeTransformMatrix:relativeToAncestor:**, – **concatTransformMatrix:premultiply:**, – **getInverseCompositeTransformMatrix:relativeToAncestor:**, – **preRotateAngle:axis:**, – **preScale:::**, – **preScaleUniformly:**, – **preTranslate:::**, – **rotateAngle:axis:**, – **scale:::**, – **scaleUniformly:**, – **translate:::**

setVisible:

– **setVisible:**(BOOL)*flag*

If flag is YES, the receiver will be rendered each time its **render:** method is invoked. If NO, the receiver won't be rendered. The N3DShape's descendants (and their peers) also set their visibility to *flag*. Returns **self**.

See also: – **isVisible**, – **render:**

shaderType:

– **shaderType:**(SLO_TYPE)*type*

Returns the id of the receiver's *type* N3DShader object. An N3DShape may have six different shaders, one for each of the standard RenderMan shader types. *type* may be one of the following six constants (defined in the header file **ri/slo.h**):

SLO_TYPE_SURFACE
SLO_TYPE_LIGHT
SLO_TYPE_DISPLACEMENT
SLO_TYPE_VOLUME
SLO_TYPE_TRANSFORMATION
SLO_TYPE_IMAGER

See also: – **setShader:**

shapeName

– (const char *)**shapeName**

Returns the receiver's name.

See also: – **setShapeName:**

surfaceType

– (N3DSurfaceType)**surfaceType**

Returns the receiver's surface type, which can be one of five enumerated values defined in the header file **3Dkit/next3d.h**:

N3D_PointCloud
N3D_WireFrame
N3D_ShadedWireFrame
N3D_FacetedSolids
N3D_SmoothSolids

The default surface type is N3D_WireFrame.

See also: – **setSurfaceType:andDescendants:**

translate:::

– **translate:**(float)*xTranslation*
  :(float)*yTranslation*
  :(float)*zTranslation*

Translates the receiver. A separate translation is applied along each of the receiving shape's axes. The receiving shape's transform matrix is postmultiplied by the translation matrix; that means the translation is applied to the ancestor's coordinate system before any other transformations in the receiver's coordinate system. The resulting transformation is stored in the receiver's transform matrix. Returns **self**.

See also: – **preTranslate:::**

ungroup

– **ungroup**

Removes the receiver from its hierarchy, and promotes its descendant and the descendant's peers to its place. Adjusts the descendant's transformations so that they remain in place relative to the world coordinate system.

If the receiver has a previous peer and next peer, they are set to point to one another. The descendant is then made a peer of the previous peer by the **linkPeer:** method. If the receiver is at the far left of its peer group, the receiver's descendant is made its ancestor's descendant. The receiver's transform matrix is applied to its descendant and the descendants peers: thus, the descendants retain their orientation to the world coordinate system. The receiver's next peer, previous peer, descendant and ancestor are all set to **nil**. Returns **self**.

See also: – **group:**

unlink

– **unlink**

Removes the receiver, its descendants, and the descendants' peers from the shape hierarchy. If the receiver is the direct descendant of its ancestor, its next peer is made the ancestor's descendant. Returns **self**.

See also: – **linkPeer:**, – **linkDescendant:**, – **linkAncestor:**

write:

– **write:**(NXTypedStream *)*stream*

Writes the receiving N3DShape to the typed stream *stream*. Returns **self**.

See also: – **awake**, – **read:**

Functions

These functions provide a C-language interface for manipulating 3D data types defined by the RenderMan interface. These data types include RtPoint, representing points in 3D coordinate systems, RtMatrix, representing transformations between 3D coordinate systems, and RtBound, representing the edges of a 3D bounding box. They're declared in the header file **ri/ri.h**.

N3DIntersectLinePlane()

SUMMARY Returns a point representing the intersection of a line segment and a plane

DECLARED IN 3Dkit/next3d.h

SYNOPSIS void **N3DIntersectLinePlane(**RtPoint **endPoints*, RtPoint *planeNormal*, RtPoint *planePoint*, RtPoint **intersection*)

DESCRIPTION This function accepts two points defining a line segment and two points defining a plane. It calculates and returns by reference the point where the line and the plane intersect.

endPoints is an array of two points defining the line. *planeNormal* and *planePoint* are two points that define a vector normal (perpendicular) to the plane. *planePoint* is on the plane itself, *planeNormal* is a point in space. The line segment between *planePoint* and *planeNormal* is perpendicular to (and thus defines) the plane whose intersection is being tested.

This method treats *endPoints* as the two points defining a line and tests for the intersection of that line with the plane. Thus *intersection* doesn't necessarily represent a point between the points in *endPoints*.

RETURN **N3DIntersectLinePlane()** returns in *intersection* the point where the line defined by *endPoints* intersects the plane defined by *planeNormal* and *planePoint*. If the line and plane are parallel, this function returns NaN for all three values of *intersection*.

N3DInvertMatrix(), N3DMultiplyMatrix()

SUMMARY Perform standard matrix manipulations

DECLARED IN 3Dkit/next3d.h

SYNOPSIS void **N3DMultiplyMatrix(**RtMatrix *preTransform*, RtMatrix *postTransform*, RtMatrix *resultTransform*)
float **N3DInvertMatrix(**RtMatrix *theTransform*, RtMatrix *theInverse*)

DESCRIPTION **N3DMultiplyMatrix()** accepts a *preTransform* matrix, a *postTransform* matrix, and a *resultTransform* matrix. It multiplies *preTransform* by *postTransform* and returns the resulting matrix.

N3DInvertMatrix() accepts *theTransform* matrix and returns its inverse.

RETURN **N3DMultiplyMatrix()** returns the product of *preTransform* and *postTransform* in *resultTransform*.

N3DInvertMatrix() returns the determinant of the matrix and, by reference, the inverse of *theTransform* in *inverseTransform*.

N3DMultiplyMatrix() → See N3DInvertMatrix()

N3DMult3DPoint(), N3DMult3DPoints()

SUMMARY Transform points between coordinate systems

DECLARED IN 3Dkit/next3d.h

SYNOPSIS void **N3DMult3DPoint**(RtPoint *thePoint*, RtMatrix *theTransform*, RtPoint *newPoint*)
void **N3DMult3DPoints**(RtPoint **thePoints*, int *pointCount*, RtMatrix *theTransform*, RtPoint **newPoints*)

DESCRIPTION These functions transform a 3D point or array of 3D points to the coordinate system represented by a 3D matrix.

N3DMult3DPoint() accepts *thePoint*, a single point; *theTransform*, a matrix by which to multiply this point; and *newPoint*, a point in which to place the result.

N3DMult3DPoints() accepts *thePoint*s, an array of points; *pointCount*, the number of points in the array; *theTransform*, a matrix by which to multiply thePoints; and *newPoint*s, an array of points in which to place the results.

RETURN **N3DMult3DPoint()** returns by reference in *newPoint* the transformation of *thePoint* from its coordinate system to the coordinate system represented by *theTransform*.

N3DMult3DPoints() returns by reference in *newPoints* the transformation of *thePoint* from its coordinate system to the coordinate system represented by *theTransform*.

N3D_ConvertBoundToPoints(), N3D_ConvertPointsToBound()

SUMMARY Convert between bounding boxes and points

DECLARED IN 3Dkit/next3d.h

SYNOPSIS void **N3D_ConvertBoundToPoints**(RtBound *theBound*, RtPoint **thePoints*)
void **N3D_ConvertPointsToBound**(RtPoint **thePoints*, RtBound *theBound*)

DESCRIPTION These macros convert between the RtBound and RtPoint data types. *theBound* is a three-dimensional bounding box; *thePoints* is an array of two points.

RETURN **N3D_ConvertBoundToPoints**() returns in *thePoints*[**0**] the origin of *theBound* and in *thePoints*[**1**] the extent of *theBound*.

N3D_ConvertPointsToBound() returns in *theBound* a bounding box whose origin is at *thePoints*[**0**] and whose extent is at *thePoints*[**1**].

N3D_ConvertPointsToBound() → See N3D_ConvertBoundToPoints()

N3D_CopyBound(), N3D_CopyMatrix(), N3D_CopyPoint()

SUMMARY Copy data from one 3D data structure to another

DECLARED IN 3Dkit/next3d.h

SYNOPSIS void **N3D_CopyBound**(RtBound *sourceBounds*, RtBound *destBounds*)
void **N3D_CopyMatrix**(RtMatrix *sourceMatrix*, RtMatrix *destMatrix*)
void **N3D_CopyPoint**(RtPoint *sourcePoint*, RtPoint *destPoint*)

DESCRIPTION These macros efficiently copy the contents of one 3D data structure to another.

RETURN **N3D_CopyBound()** returns, in *destBound*, a copy of the values in *sourceBound*.

N3D_CopyMatrix() returns, in *destMatrix*, a copy of the values in *sourceMatrix*.

N3D_CopyPoint() returns, in *destPoint*, a copy of the values in *sourcePoint*.

N3D_CopyMatrix() → See N3D_CopyBound()

N3D_CopyPoint() → See N3D_CopyBound()

N3D_WComp() → See N3D_XComp()

N3D_XComp(), N3D_YComp(), N3D_ZComp(), N3D_WComp()

SUMMARY Returns the components of a 3D data structure

DECLARED IN 3Dkit/next3d.h

SYNOPSIS RtFloat **N3D_XComp(**RtFloat **theVector*)
RtFloat **N3D_YComp(**RtFloat **theVector*)
RtFloat **N3D_ZComp(**RtFloat **theVector*)
RtFloat **N3D_WComp(**RtFloat **theVector*)

DESCRIPTION These macros return the components of a 3D point or submatrix.

If *theVector* is an RtPoint type, use the macros **N3D_XComp()**, **N3D_YComp()**, and **N3D_ZComp()** to retrieve its elements.

If *theVector* is a row in an RtMatrix (for example, **myMatrix[2]**), use **N3D_XComp()**, **N3D_YComp()**, **N3D_ZComp()**, and **N3D_WComp()** to retrieve its elements.

RETURN **N3D_XComp()** returns the x-component of *theVector*.

N3D_YComp() returns the y-component of *theVector*.

N3D_ZComp() returns the z-component of *theVector*.

N3D_WComp() returns the w-component of *theVector*.

N3D_YComp() → See N3D_XComp()

N3D_ZComp() → N3D_XComp()

Types and Constants

Defined Types

N3DProjectionType

DECLARED IN 3Dkit/next3d.h

SYNOPSIS

```
typedef enum {
        N3D_Perspective,
        N3D_Orthographic
} N3DProjectionType
```

DESCRIPTION Used to set and test the projection type of an N3DCamera.

N3DLightType

DECLARED IN 3Dkit/next3d.h

SYNOPSIS

```
typedef enum {
        N3D_AmbientLight,
        N3D_PointLight,
        N3D_DistantLight,
        N3D_SpotLight
} N3DLightType
```

DESCRIPTION Used to set and test the light type of an N3DLight.

N3DAxis

DECLARED IN 3Dkit/next3d.h

SYNOPSIS

typedef enum {
    N3D_AllAxes,
    N3D_XAxis,
    N3D_YAxis,
    N3D_ZAxis,
    N3D_XYAxes,
    N3D_XZAxes,
    N3D_YZAxes
} **N3DAxis**

DESCRIPTION Used to determine the combination of axes about which a matrix is rotated by N3DRotator objects.

N3DHider

DECLARED IN 3Dkit/next3d.h

SYNOPSIS

typedef enum {
    N3D_HiddenRendering = 0,
    N3D_InOrderRendering,
    N3D_NoRendering
} **N3DHider**

DESCRIPTION Used to set the hider algorithm used by N3DCamera and N3DImageRep objects.

N3DShapeName

DECLARED IN 3Dkit/N3DShape.h

SYNOPSIS

```
typedef struct {
        char  id[6];
        char  name;
} N3DShapeName
```

DESCRIPTION The name and id of the shape as character strings (used for picking shapes).

N3DSurfaceType

DECLARED IN 3Dkit/next3d.h

SYNOPSIS

```
typedef enum {
        N3D_PointCloud = 0,
        N3D_WireFrame,
        N3D_ShadedWireFrame,
        N3D_FacetedSolids,
        N3D_SmoothSolids
} N3DSurfaceType
```

DESCRIPTION Used to set the surface type applied to N3DShape and N3DRIBImageRep objects.

SLOArgs

DECLARED IN 3Dkit/N3DShader.h

SYNOPSIS

```
typedef struct {
    SLO_VISSYMDEF symb;
    union {
        float fval;
        RtPoint pval;
        NXColor cval;
        char *sval;
    } value;
} SLOArgs
```

DESCRIPTION The union that represents shader language function arguments.

Symbolic Constants

Matrix Constants

DECLARED IN 3Dkit/N3DShape.h

SYNOPSIS
N3D_BOTH_CLEAN
N3D_CTM_DIRTY
N3D_CTM_INVERSE_DIRTY
N3D_CTM_BOTH_DIRTY

DESCRIPTION These constants track the status of an N3DShape's composite transformation matrix and its inverse.

Global Variables

N3DIdentityMatrix

DECLARED IN 3Dkit/next3d.h

SYNOPSIS const RtMatrix **N3DIdentityMatrix**

DESCRIPTION Assigned the values representing a normalized matrix when 3D Kit applications are initialized:

```
{{1, 0, 0, 0},
 {0, 1, 0, 0},
 {0, 0, 1, 0},
 {0, 0, 0, 1}}
```

N3DOrigin

DECLARED IN 3Dkit/next3d.h

SYNOPSIS const RtPoint **N3DOrigin**

DESCRIPTION Assigned the value {0, 0, 0} when 3D Kit applications are initialized.

N3DRIBPboardType

DECLARED IN 3Dkit/next3d.h

SYNOPSIS NXAtom **N3DRIBPboardType**

DESCRIPTION Pasteboard for copying RIB data.

18 *Video*

18 *Video*

Library: libMedia_s.a

Header File Directory: /NextDeveloper/Headers/video

Import: video/NXLiveVideoView.h

Introduction

The NXLiveVideoView class provides API for interactive display of live video on the screen of a NeXTdimension Computer. The NXLiveVideoView class specification provides a complete discussion of the NeXTdimension Computer's video capabilities and the API provided by NXLiveVideoView.

Classes

NXLiveVideoView

Inherits From: View : Responder : Object

Declared In: video/NXLiveVideoView.h

Class Description

An NXLiveVideoView is a View that can take video from the input ports of the NeXTdimension board and display it on a MegaPixel Color Display. It can also send drawing to the video output ports of the NeXTdimension board.

The video image is displayed in a *video rectangle* whose lower left corner coincides with the lower left corner of the bounds rectangle of the NXLiveVideoView. The size of the video rectangle is fixed to correspond to the video standard supported by the NeXTdimension board. For NTSC-standard boards, the rectangle is 640 pixels wide by 480 pixels high; for PAL-standard boards, the rectangle is 768 pixels wide by 576 pixels high. The sides of the video rectangle are aligned with the screen coordinate system, no matter what the size or orientation of the NXLiveVideoView. Scaling, rotating, or flipping the coordinate system of the NXLiveVideoView doesn't affect the video rectangle. Translating the coordinate system of the NXLiveVideoView will change which portion of the video rectangle is visible. An NXLiveVideoView can be resized, but the resizing doesn't adjust the video rectangle. Resizing an NXLiveVideoView smaller than the video rectangle effectively clips the video image. Resizing an NXLiveVideoView to be larger than the video rectangle may leave a gap between the top and right of the View and the video rectangle. An NXLiveVideoView can be placed in a ClipView to allow scrolling; only the portion of the video rectangle that's contained within the visible rectangle for the NXLiveVideoView can be seen on-screen.

Note: While the size of the video rectangle is fixed to the video standard, the actual viewing area of the video image output by the NeXTdimension board may appear smaller on a video monitor. This is due to the fact that most monitors "overscan" by about 10-15%; that is, they clip about 5% of the image at the top, bottom, and both sides of the picture. Thus, when producing video intended for output, it's best to keep the image within the area that would be displayed on a video monitor. To compensate for overscan when producing video intended for output, you may want to translate the NXLiveVideoView down and to the left and make its bounds rectangle smaller than the video rectangle—thus representing the output image more accurately.

To draw in an NXLiveVideoView, you can create a subclass and override the **drawSelf::** method, or add one or more subviews to the NXLiveVideoView and draw in the subviews. The effects of drawing in an NXLiveVideoView differ depending on the output mode selected; they are described in the next section.

Video Output Modes

The **setOutputMode:** method determines the source of the image sent to the video output ports of the NeXTdimension board and the image displayed in the NXLiveVideoView (as described below, the two images aren't always the same). There are two arguments for this method: NX_FROMINPUT and NX_FROMVIEW.

In NX_FROMINPUT mode, both the video output ports of the NeXTdimension board and the NXLiveVideoView present video from one of the three video input ports. The input port is selected with the **selectInput:** method. In this mode, the NXLiveVideoView can also draw over the video; this is useful, for example, to place titles over video. Video appears unobscured in the NXLiveVideoView wherever there is no drawing or the drawing has no coverage (alpha value of 0.0). When drawing in the VideoView has partial coverage (alpha greater than 0.0 and less than 1.0) video is dithered with the drawing. The video image in the View can't be manipulated using PostScript operations, since it's displayed by accessing the video memory on the NeXTdimension board rather than by drawing with PostScript code. You can, however, grab individual frames as NXImages and manipulate these images. In NX_FROMINPUT mode, the video output of the NeXTdimension board presents video from the input port, but no drawing from the NXLiveVideoView.

In NX_FROMVIEW mode, the video output of the NeXTdimension board presents drawing from the NXLiveVideoView, but not video from the input port. In this mode, only drawing in the video rectangle of the NXLiveVideoView is sent to the video output. The video input ports of the NeXTdimension board are effectively disconnected from both the NXLiveVideoView and the video outputs. The Window containing an NXLiveVideoView in NX_FROMVIEW mode should be either buffered or retained. If the Window is buffered, only the drawing done by the NXLiveVideoView or its subviews within the video rectangle is sent to the video output ports; if the video rectangle is clipped, only drawing done within the unclipped area of the video rectangle appears on the video output ports. If the Window is retained, anything that overlaps the video rectangle (for example, the cursor, another View, or a Window) will appear on the video output ports. An NXLiveVideoView in a nonretained Window produces unpredictable results.

Starting and Stopping Video

To begin displaying video in NX_FROMINPUT mode or sending drawing to the video output ports in NX_FROMVIEW mode, use the **start:** method. To stop in either mode, use the **stop:** method.

A single NeXTdimension board and MegaPixel Color Display can support any number of NXLiveVideoViews, each of which maintains its own settings for input port, output mode, hue, saturation, brightness, and so on. However, only one NXLiveVideoView can be active—displaying video from the input ports or sending video to the output ports—at a time. The others will be either stopped or suspended (not active and not stopped). There is a simple contention system for ensuring that the NXLiveVideoView the user is interacting with will always be active. When any NXLiveVideoView receives a **start:** message, it becomes active; if another NXLiveVideoView was active, it is suspended. A suspended NXLiveVideoView will become active if it receives a message which affects video (for example, **setHue:**) or if it undergoes a change to its geometry (for example, by scrolling or resizing). If **grabOnStop:** is set when an NXLiveVideoView is stopped or suspended, the last frame of video is grabbed and composited into it.

If you're drawing dynamically over video, you need to be sure that the NXLiveVideoView updates correctly whether video is active or suspended. To do so, you can use the **drawVideoBackground::** method in your dynamic drawing code. If, for example, you're animating over active video, this method fills the update rectangle with transparent paint (alpha value 0.0) to let video show through the area previously occupied the moving image. When video is suspended, this method composites into the update rectangle from the image grabbed on stop. You can respond in other ways to a change in the NXLiveVideoView's active state by creating a delegate that implements the methods **videoDidSuspend:** and **videoDidActivate:**.

If a user has more than one screen attached to a NeXTdimension computer, the Window containing an NXLiveVideoView can be dragged from screen to screen. Video is suspended when the Window containing the View moves off of the screen where playing started. If you drag the Window back onto its original screen, video remains suspended. To enable the NXLiveVideoView to automatically resume playing video, assign the Window a delegate that implements the **windowDidChangeScreen:** method; use this method to send a **start:** message to the NXLiveVideoView, which will restart the video. The screen-changed event causes this message to be sent to the Window's delegate.

Adjusting the Video Image

NXLiveVideoView provides methods for adjusting the quality of the video image displayed. Among these are methods to set the hue, saturation, brightness, and sharpness of the image in the NXLiveVideoView; these are analogous to the controls found on a standard video monitor.

NXLiveVideoView also provides methods for setting the gamma correction for both the input and the output; these settings affect the transfer linearity of the brightness component of the video. Gamma correction is necessary because, when video is represented by a device (for example, taken from a camera or displayed on a monitor), the brightness component may be distorted due to the physical transfer characteristics of the device. Most video sources are gamma corrected for the transfer characteristics of a video monitor. The NeXTdimension board has different transfer characteristics, so the gamma correction usually needs to be adjusted. The **setInputGamma:** method allows this adjustment. The **setOutputGamma:** method allows you to offset the effect of the **setInputGamma:** method, to reinstate the appropriate gamma correction for the video output.

Instance Variables

id **delegate**

delegate	The video view's delegate.

Method Types

Initializing an NXLiveVideoView	– initFrame:
Freeing an NXLiveVideoView	– free
Starting and stopping video display	– start: – stop:
Determining the active state	– isVideoActive

Capturing video as an NXImage	
	– grab – grabIn:fromRect:toRect: – doesGrabOnStop – setGrabOnStop:
Finding the video resource	+ doesRectSupportVideo:standard:size: + doesScreenSupportVideo:standard:size: + doesWindowSupportVideo:standard: size: + videoScreen
Getting the video standard	– getVideoStandard:size:
Getting the video rectangle	– getSourceVideoRect:
Selecting the video input port	– selectInput: – numInputs
Setting the output mode	– setOutputMode:
Controlling input video quality	– setInputBrightness: – inputBrightness – setInputGamma: – inputGamma – setInputHue: – inputHue – setInputSaturation: – inputSaturation – setInputSharpness: – inputSharpness – resetPictureDefaults
Controlling output video quality	
	– setOutputGamma: – outputGamma
Setting output genlock	– setOutputGenlocked: – outputGenlocked
Drawing	– drawSelf:: – drawVideoBackground::
Assigning a delegate	– setDelegate: – delegate
Archiving	– read: – write:

Class Methods

doesRectSupportVideo:standard:size:

+ (BOOL)**doesRectSupportVideo:**(NXRect *)*theRect*
standard:(int *)*theStandard*
size:(NXSize *)*theSize*

Returns YES if *theRect* is located entirely or partially on a screen that supports video, NO otherwise. By reference, returns the video standard (NX_NTSCSIGNAL or NX_PALSIGNAL) supported by the NeXTdimension board and the size of the video rectangle for that standard. If the rectangle lies across two screens, both of which support video, this method returns the main screen. If neither screen is the main screen, this method traverses the list returned by Application's **getScreen:count:** method and returns the first screen in the list that contains part of *theRect* and that supports video.

See also: + **videoScreen:**, – **getVideoStandard:size:**

doesScreenSupportVideo:standard:size:

+ (BOOL)**doesScreenSupportVideo:**(const NXScreen *)*theScreen*
standard:(int *)*theStandard*
size:(NXSize *)*theSize*

Returns YES if *theScreen* supports video, NO otherwise. By reference, returns the video standard (NX_NTSCSIGNAL or NX_PALSIGNAL) supported by the NeXTdimension board and the size of the video rectangle for that standard.

See also: + **videoScreen:**, – **getVideoStandard:size:**

doesWindowSupportVideo:standard:size:

+ (BOOL)**doesWindowSupportVideo:***theWindow*
standard:(int *)*theStandard*
size:(NXSize *)*theSize*

Returns YES if *theWindow* is located entirely or partially on a screen that supports video, NO otherwise. By reference, returns the video standard (NX_NTSCSIGNAL or NX_PALSIGNAL) supported by the video hardware and the size of the video rectangle for that standard. If the Window lies across two screens, both of which support video, this method returns the standard for the main screen. If neither screen is the main screen, this method traverses the list returned by Application's **getScreen:count:** method and returns the first screen in the list that contains part of *theWindow* and that supports video.

See also: + **videoScreen:**, – **getVideoStandard:size:**

videoScreen

+ (const NXScreen *)**videoScreen**

Returns the screen most suited to supporting video; returns NULL if no screen connected to the system supports video. If the NeXTcube computer has two or more screens that support video, this method traverses the list returned by Application's **getScreen:count:** method and returns the first screen in the list that supports video.

See also: + **doesScreenSupportVideo:standard:size:**

Instance Methods

delegate

– **delegate**

Returns the NXLiveVideoView's delegate. See "Methods Implemented By The Delegate" near the end of this specification.

See also: – **setDelegate:**

drawSelf::

– **drawSelf:**(const NXRect *)*rects* **:**(int)*rectCount*

Displays an image as specified by the current output mode and active state of the NXLiveVideoView by invoking **drawVideoBackground::**. Returns **self**.

You never invoke **drawSelf::** directly; it is implemented to ensure that the NXLiveVideoView updates correctly whenever it is redisplayed. If you override this method, your implementation should first send **super** a **drawSelf::** message to ensure that video display will be properly updated to reflect the current state of the NXLiveVideoView.

See also: – **drawVideoBackground::**, – **setGrabOnStop:**, – **setOutputMode:**, – **start:**, – **stop:**

drawVideoBackground::

– **drawVideoBackground:**(const NXRect *)*rects* **:**(int)*rectCount*

Displays an image as specified by the current output mode and active state of the NXLiveVideoView. If the View is in NX_FROMINPUT mode and is active, this method composites transparent paint (alpha value 0.0) into the update rectangles to allow video to appear in them. If the view is in NX_FROMINPUT mode, is suspended or stopped, and is set to grab the last frame on stop, this method composites the grabbed image into the update rectangles. If the NXLiveVideoView has received a **start:** message and hasn't been set to grab the last frame, this method doesn't draw when video is stopped or suspended. If the NXLiveVideoView is in NX_FROMVIEW mode, this method does nothing. Returns **self**.

The **drawSelf::** method invokes this method to ensure that video is updated correctly anytime the NXLiveVideoView is displayed. If you do dynamic drawing over video, you can invoke this method to be sure that the video that appears behind your drawing is appropriate to the current state of the NXLiveVideoView; this method must appear in your code between **lockFocus** and **unlockFocus** messages.

See also: – **drawSelf::**, – **setGrabOnStop:**, – **setOutputMode:**, – **start:**, – **stop:**

doesGrabOnStop

– (BOOL)**doesGrabOnStop**

Returns YES if the NXLiveVideoView grabs the last video frame as an NXImage and composites the image in the video rectangle when it receives a **stop:** message after a **start:** message. Returns NO if the NXLiveVideoView doesn't grab the last frame. The default return value is NO.

See also: – **grab**, – **setGrabOnStop:**, – **start:**, – **stop:**

free

– **free**

Frees the NXLiveVideoView object and its support objects.

getSourceVideoRect:

– **getSourceVideoRect:**(NXRect *)*sourceRect*

Gets the visible portion of the video rectangle by copying it into the structure referred to by *sourceRect*. This method can be used with the **grabIn:fromRect:toRect:** method to capture the exact rectangle in which video is being displayed. Returns **self**.

See also: – **grabIn:fromRect:toRect:**

getVideoStandard:size:

– **getVideoStandard:**(int *)*standard* **size:**(NXSize *)*vidRectSize*

Returns **self** and, by reference, the video standard and the size of the video rectangle supported by the underlying hardware. The value placed in the integer referred to by *standard* may be either NX_NTSCSIGNAL for the NTSC standard or NX_PALSIGNAL for the PAL standard. The values placed in the NXSize structure referred to by *vidRectSize* are 640 pixels by 480 pixels for NTSC and 768 pixels by 576 pixels for PAL.

See also: + **doesRectSupportVideo:standard:size:**,
+ **doesScreenSupportVideo:standard:size:**,
+ **doesWindowSupportVideo:standard:size:**

grab

– (NXImage *)**grab**

Returns an NXImage object for the image displayed in the video rectangle. If the NXLiveVideoView's output mode is currently NX_FROMINPUT and it has received a **start:** message, this method returns an NXImage containing the current frame of video. The frame returned will not be displayed, but video play will continue (the skipped frame will hardly be noticeable). If the NXLiveVideoView has received both **start:** and **stop:** messages and is set to grab the last video frame when it stops (see **setGrabOnStop:**), this method returns the NXImage grabbed when **stop:** was invoked. In other cases, after a stop message, the NXImage returned by this method will either be invalid, or contain an outdated image. The NXImage returned is allocated by the NXLiveVideoView. It includes the entire video rectangle, not just the visible portion of the View.

See also: – **doesGrabOnStop:**, – **setOutputMode:**, – **setGrabOnStop:**, – **start:**, – **stop:**

grabIn:fromRect:toRect:

– **grabIn:**(NXImage *)*theImage*
  fromRect:(NXRect *)*sourceRect*
  toRect:(NXRect *)*destRect*

Grabs an NXImage from the area of the next video frame in the rectangle specified by *sourceRect* and copies it to the coordinates specified by *destRect*. The NXImage is copied by invoking the NXImage method **composite:fromRect:toPoint:** using NX_COPY as the compositing operation and the origin of *destRect* as the point. You must explicitly allocate *theImage* before invoking this method. Returns **self**.

See also: – **grab**, – **getSourceVideoRect:**

initFrame:

– **initFrame:**(const NXRect *)*frameRect*

Initializes and returns the receiver, a newly allocated instance of NXLiveVideoView. **initFrame:** is the designated initializer for the NXLiveVideoView class.

inputBrightness

– (float)**inputBrightness**

Returns the input brightness setting, a value between 0.0 and 1.0. The default setting is 0.5.

See also: – **setInputBrightness:**

inputGamma

– (float)**inputGamma**

Returns the input gamma setting, usually a value in the range of 0.333 and 1.0. Input gamma correction is used to adjust the linearity of the brightness component of the video input to match the transfer characteristics of the NeXTdimension board. The default setting is 0.588, the inverse of the default output gamma setting.

See also: – **setInputGamma:**, – **outputGamma**

inputHue

– (float)**inputHue**

Returns the input hue setting, a value between –180.0 and 180.0. Hue defines the reference orientation of the colors of the input video source. The default setting is 0.0.

See also: – **setInputHue:**

inputSaturation

– (float)**inputSaturation**

Returns the input saturation setting, a value between 0.0 and 1.0. The default setting is 0.5.

See also: – **setInputSaturation:**

inputSharpness

– (float)**inputSharpness**

Returns the input sharpness setting, a value between 0.0 and 1.0. The default setting is 0.5.

See also: – **setInputSharpness:**

isVideoActive

– (BOOL)**isVideoActive**

Returns YES if video is active in the NXLiveVideoView; NO if it's suspended or stopped. The system for selecting the active NXLiveVideoView is described in the class description.

See also: – **videoDidActivate:**, – **videoDidSuspend:** (delegate method), – **start:**, – **stop:**

numInputs

– (int)**numInputs**

Returns the number of video input ports offered by the hardware driving the screen displaying the NXLiveVideoView. Since the NeXTdimension board has three input ports, this method returns 3.

See also: – **selectInput:**

outputGamma

– (float)**outputGamma**

Returns the output gamma setting, usually a value in the range of 1.0 and 3.0. Output gamma correction is used to offset the effect of input gamma correction set with **setInputGamma:** method. The default return value is 1.70, the inverse of the default input gamma setting.

See also: – **setOutputGamma:**, – **setInputGamma:**

outputGenlocked

– (BOOL)**outputGenlocked**

Returns YES if output video is synchronized to the video signal present on the currently selected input port. The value returned by this method is valid only when taking video output from the NXLiveVideoView (NX_FROMVIEW mode). When taking output from the input ports (NX_FROMINPUT mode), the output signal is always synched to the input. The default return value is NO.

See also: – **selectInput:**, – **setOutputGenlocked:**, – **setOutputMode:**

read:

– **read:**(NXTypedStream *)*stream*

Reads the NXLiveVideoView from the typed stream *stream*. Returns **self**.

resetPictureDefaults

– **resetPictureDefaults**

Resets input hue, saturation, brightness, sharpness, gamma, and output gamma to their default settings. Returns **self**.

selectInput:

– **selectInput:**(int)*inputPortNumber*

Selects the video input port from which the NXLiveVideoView will display when it is in NX_FROMINPUT mode. The NeXTdimension board offers three video input ports represented by the constants NX_VIDEOIN1 (Composite-1), NX_VIDEOIN2 (Composite-2), and NX_VIDEOIN3 (SVHS-3). The default selection is NX_VIDEOIN1.

See also: – **numInputs**, – **setOutputMode:**

setDelegate:

– **setDelegate:***anObject*

Sets the NXLiveVideoView's delegate to *anObject*. See "Methods Implemented By The Delegate" near the end of this specification. Returns **self**.

See also: – **delegate**

setGrabOnStop:

– **setGrabOnStop:**(BOOL)*flag*

Determines whether the NXLiveVideoView grabs and displays the last video frame when it receives a **stop:** message after a **start:** message. If *flag* is YES and the NXLiveVideoView receives a **stop:** message, the NXLiveVideoView sends itself a **grab** message to capture the last video frame, then composites the returned image in its video rectangle; the **grab** method returns the displayed NXImage if it is invoked while video is stopped. If *flag* is NO, NXLiveVideoView won't display the last frame when it receives a **stop:** message, and **grab** returns an invalid image. The default setting is NO. Returns **self**.

See also: – **grab**, – **doesGrabOnStop**

setInputBrightness:

– **setInputBrightness:**(float)*brightness*

Sets the input brightness value. The range of values is 0.0 to 1.0. The default setting is 0.5. Returns **self**.

See also: – **inputBrightness**

setInputGamma:

– **setInputGamma:**(float)*inputGamma*

Sets the input gamma value. Input gamma is used to compensate for gamma correction applied to input video signals intended for display directly on a video monitor rather than through a digital display system. *inputGamma* will typically be a value in the range of 0.333 to 1.0. The default setting is 0.588. Returns **self**.

See also: – **inputGamma**, – **setOutputGamma:**

setInputHue:

– **setInputHue:**(float)*hue*

Sets the input hue value. Hue defines the reference orientation of the colors of the input video source. Adjusting the hue by a given amount is similar to rotating all input colors in the HSB (hue, saturation, and brightness) color space by a certain angle. The default value of hue is 0.0; it can range from –180.0 to 180.0. Returns **self**.

See also: – **inputHue**

setInputSaturation:

– **setInputSaturation:**(float)*saturation*

Sets the input saturation value. Saturation determines the color contribution of the input picture. The range of values is 0.0 to 1.0. Adjusting saturation toward 0.0 causes colors to appear washed out; adjusting toward 1.0 causes colors to be artificially emphasized. The default setting is 0.5. Returns **self**.

See also: – **inputSaturation**

setInputSharpness:

– **setInputSharpness:**(float)*sharpness*

Sets the input sharpness value. A higher value for *sharpness* exaggerates transitions between different brightness levels in the video image; a lower value blurs transitions between different brightness levels. The range of values is 0.0 to 1.0. The default setting is 0.5. Returns **self**.

See also: – **inputSharpness**

setOutputGamma:

– **setOutputGamma:**(float)*outputGamma*

Sets the output gamma value to provide gamma correction for the video presented on the NeXTdimension board's video output ports. You may set the output gamma to compensate for the nonlinearity of the device that will display the output video. *outputGamma* will typically be a value in the range 1.0 to 3.0. The default setting is 1.7, the inverse of the default input gamma setting. Together, these defaults assure that the output video will correctly reflect the gamma-correction originally applied to the input video. Returns **self**.

See also: – **outputGamma**, – **setInputGamma:**

setOutputGenlocked:

– **setOutputGenlocked:**(BOOL)*locked*

Locks the video output to the synchronization signal present on the currently selected input port if *locked* is YES. When *locked* is NO, this method causes the NeXTdimension board to generate its own synch signal for output video. This method has effect only when taking video output from the View; when taking output from input, the output signal is always synched to the input. The default setting is NO.

See also: – **outputGenlocked**, – **selectInput:**, – **setOutputMode:**

setOutputMode:

– **setOutputMode:**(int)*outputMode*

Determines the source of the image sent to the video output ports on the NeXTdimension board. *outputMode* can be either NX_FROMINPUT or NX_FROMVIEW. In NX_FROMINPUT mode, both the NXLiveVideoView and the video output ports of the NeXTdimension board present video from the selected video input port. In NX_FROMVIEW mode, the NXLiveVideoView provides the image presented on the NeXTdimension board's video output ports; in this mode, the NeXTdimension board's input ports are effectively disconnected from both the NXLiveVideoView and the video output ports. Returns **self**.

A more complete description of the effects of this method is presented in the class description.

See also: – **selectInput:**

start:

– **start:***sender*

Starts playing video in the NXLiveVideoView. If the output mode is currently NX_FROMINPUT, this method begins displaying the video from the selected input port. If the mode is currently NX_FROMVIEW, it begins sending images drawn in the video rectangle of the NXLiveVideoView to the NeXTdimension's video output ports.

This method invokes the **display** method (and thus the **drawSelf::**) method to draw the receiving NXLiveVideoView and any of its subviews. Using a subview, you can draw over video without creating a subclass of NXLiveVideoView.

Returns **self**.

See also: – **display** (View), – **drawSelf::**, – **isVideoActive**, – **stop:**, – **setOutputMode:**

stop:

– **stop:***sender*

Stops video in the NXLiveVideoView. If the receiving NXLiveVideoView is in NX_FROMINPUT mode, this method stops playing video from the NeXTdimension board's video input ports. If the receiver is in NX_FROMVIEW mode, this method stops sending any images drawn in the NXLiveVideoView's video rectangle to the video output ports. If the receiver is set to grab an NXImage of the last frame, this method sends a **grab** message to **self** and composites the returned NXImage into its video rectangle.

Returns **self**.

See also: – **start:**, – **isVideoActive**, – **setGrabOnStop:**

write:

– **write:**(NXTypedStream *)*stream*

Writes the NXLiveVideoView to the typed stream *stream*. Returns **self**.

Methods Implemented By The Delegate

videoDidActivate:

– **videoDidActivate:***sender*

Notifies the delegate when video is activated in the NXLiveVideoView. This method is included to enable your application to accomodate the acquisition of active video in the View; your implementation shouldn't invoke any of NXLiveVideoView's methods. The system for activating and suspending video in an NXLiveVideoView is described in the class description above.

See also: – **drawVideoBackground::**, – **isVideoActive**, – **start:**, – **stop:**

videoDidSuspend:

– **videoDidSuspend:***sender*

Notifies the delegate when video is suspended in the NXLiveVideoView. This method is included to enable your application to accomodate the loss of video in the View; your implementation shouldn't invoke any of NXLiveVideoView's methods. The system for activating and suspending video in an NXLiveVideoView is described in the class description above.

See also: – **drawVideoBackground::**, – **isVideoActive**, – **start:**, – **stop:**

Types and Constants

Symbolic Constants

Input Selection

DECLARED IN video/NXLiveVideoView.h

SYNOPSIS NX_VIDEOIN1
NX_VIDEOIN2
NX_VIDEOIN3

DESCRIPTION Used with the **selectInput:** method to set the video input source for the NXLiveVideoView.

Output Source

DECLARED IN video/NXLiveVideoView.h

SYNOPSIS NX_FROMINPUT
NX_FROMVIEW

DESCRIPTION Used with the **setOutputMode:** method to set the video output source for the NXLiveVideoView.

Video Standard

DECLARED IN video/NXLiveVideoView.h

SYNOPSIS NX_NTSCSIGNAL
NX_PALSIGNAL

DESCRIPTION Used with the **getVideoStandard:size:** method to identify the video signal standard for the NXLiveVideoView.

19 *Workspace Manager*

19 *Workspace Manager*

Library:	None, this API is defined by the Workspace Manager application
Header File Directory:	/NextDeveloper/Headers/apps
Import:	apps/Workspace.h

Introduction

The Workspace Manager lets the user navigate the file system and manipulate the files and directories therein. Workspace Manager's Inspector panel, with its four displays, gives additional information about a selected item, for example, file ownership and size (Attributes display), applications capable of opening the file (Tools display), and file permissions (Access display). Finally, the Inspector panel's Contents display can give the user information about the contents of certain types of files.

Since there is no limited to the number of file formats, it's impossible for the contents inspector to display the contents of all file types. NeXT provides inspectors for many of the most common formats—RTF, TIFF, EPS, to name a few—and provides a way for you to install a contents inspector for any other file format. It's even possible to replace a standard inspector with one of your own.

Contents inspectors are stored in bundle files that contain the code and interface objects that are loaded into the Workspace Manager. (For more information on bundles, see the class specification for NXBundle, a common class.)

When the Workspace Manager begins running, it locates contents inspector bundles by scanning the application search path (in this order):

~/Apps
/LocalApps
/NextApps

Finally, it searches in its own application file package, where it finds the standard modules.

For each directory that it searches, the Workspace Manager looks for bundles both within the directory and within application file packages (".app" files) in the directory. When it finds a bundle, it checks the executable within it for registry information, information that the Workspace Manager uses to associate an inspector module with a specific file extension. (If more than one module registers for the same file extension, the module later in the search path is ignored.) When the user attempts to inspect the contents of a file, the Workspace Manager consults its registry of file extensions and inspectors and loads the appropriate inspector, if it hasn't been loaded already.

The Workspace Manager application and the contents inspector communicate through the API found in **/NextDeveloper/Headers/apps/Workspace.h**. This API consists of the declaration of the WMInspector class, an abstract superclass that defines the owner of the inspector module's interface. In creating your own contents inspector, you'll create a subclass of WMInspector and an interface that will appear in the Inspector panel.

The principal messages that the Workspace Manager sends your inspector object are **new** and **revert:**. It sends a **new** message whenever it needs to access the inspector object or, through the object, the interface to the inspector. It sends a **revert:** message whenever the inspector might need to be updated, such as when the selection in the File Viewer has changed. Thus, all inspector objects must implement these methods.

The inspector object, in turn, can query the Workspace Manager for information about the selection. The WMInspector class declares a method (**selectionCount**) for determining whether the selection contains a single item or multiple items, and another (**selectionPathsInto:separator:**) that returns the full path to each item in the selection. Your inspector object, therefore, can access this information by sending itself **selectionCount** and **selectionPathsInto:separator:** messages.

The Components of an Inspector Project

Contents inspectors are created as bundle projects; the process is outlined below. Before looking at the process, let's examine the components that are common to all inspector projects. As an illustration, we'll take the example of an inspector that shows the contents of files containing 3D graphics data in RIB format: ".rib" files. Even the simplest RIB inspector would have these components:

File	Description
*.lproj/RIBInspector.nib	A nib file containing the user interface to the contents inspector. (The nib file is stored in a language-specific subdirectory, such as **English.lproj**.)
Makefile	The standard makefile for a bundle project
Makefile.preamble	Additional instructions to the **make** utility to load the information in **bundle.registry** into the executable file.
PB.project	The standard project file for a bundle project.
RIBInspector.h	The class interface file for the subclass of WMInspector.
RIBInspector.m	The class implementation file for the subclass of WMInspector.
bundle.registry	A specification file describing which file extension is associated with this inspector, among other things.

Two files of special interest are **bundle.registry** and **Makefile.preamble**.

The bundle.registry File

This file contains the instructions that the Workspace Manager uses to associate a contents inspector with a specific type of file. Using the example of a RIB file inspector, the **bundle.registry** file would look like this:

```
{type=InspectorCommand; mode=contents; extension=rib;
    selp=selectionOneOnly; class=RIBInspector}
```

The registry information consists of a list of key words and their assigned values. Here are the keys and their possible values. (The quotation marks below are for clarity; don't include them in your registry file):

Key	Description
type	The type of registration. For inspector commands, the value must be "InspectorCommand".
mode	The mode of the Inspector panel. For Release 3.0, this must be "contents".
extension	The file extension to be associated with this inspector. (Don't include the "." in the extension.) You can only list one extension for each inspector module; wildcard characters aren't permitted.
class	The name of the subclass of WMInspector. In general, an instance of this class owns the nib file that contains the inspector's user interface. Workspace Manager instantiates an object of this class when the inspector is loaded.
selp	The *selection predicate*; that is, the requirements concerning the selection. The value can be either "selectionOneOnly" or "selectionOneOrMore".

The **selp** key controls whether your inspector is confined to operating on one file of the given extension at a time (**selectionOneOnly**), or whether it can be displayed if the selection consists of more than one file of the give extension (**selectionOneOrMore**). If you specify **selectionOneOnly** (the usual case), the message "No Contents Inspector for Multiple Selection" appears in the panel when the selection contains multiple files of the given extension.

All six keys must be present in the registry file for your inspector to work properly. The order of these key/value pairs in the registry file isn't important, although the case of the key and value words is.

The Makefile.preamble File

The registry information from **bundle.registry** must be copied into the __ICON segment of the module's Mach object file: This is where the Workspace Manager searches for the information. To accomplish this, you have to create a **Makefile.preamble** file with the proper instructions. These instructions are:

```
BUNDLELDFLAGS = -sectcreate __ICON __header bundle.registry
OTHER_PRODUCT_DEPENDS = bundle.registry
```

The first line instructs the linker to create an **__header** section in the **__ICON** segment of the executable file and to copy the registry information into it. The second ensures that **make** will rebuild the project whenever **bundle.registry** is altered.

Building an Inspector Module

The following steps show you the process for assembling an inspector, using the RIB inspector as an example. (These steps won't show you how to do the actual imaging of RIB files. For that, you'll have to look into the 3D Graphics Kit.)

To build the inspector, follow these steps:

1. Start Project Builder and create a new bundle project. In the New Project panel, make sure that the Project Type pop-up list reads "Bundle". Save the project as **~/RIBInspector**.

2. Start Interface Builder and create a new empty module. (Choose New Empty from the New Module menu). Save the module in **~/RIBInspector/English.lproj/RIBInspector**. When the attention panel appears, confirm that you want to add the nib file to the RIBInspector project.

3. Now, you have to inform Interface Builder of the WMInspector class, as declared in **/NextDeveloper/Headers/apps/Workspace.h**. The easiest way to do this is to drag the file icon for **Workspace.h** from the File Viewer into Interface Builder's File window. Interface Builder will parse the header file and insert the WMInspector class in the Classes browser.

4. Declare a subclass of WMInspector by selecting WMInspector in the Classes browser and dragging to Subclass in the Operations browser. Rename this subclass "RIBInspector".

5. Using the Class inspector, add any outlets and actions that you want to the RIBInspector class. For example, in most cases you would add outlets for the text fields that the inspector uses to display information about the selected file. For this illustration, skip this step.

6. Select the File's Owner object in the Objects display of the Files window. Using the Inspector panel, specify that the File's Owner is of the RIBInspector class.

7. Drag a Panel object from the Palettes window into the workspace. This panel will contain the interface to your contents inspector. When the Workspace Manager displays your contents inspector, it will take the Panel's content view and installs it in the view hierarchy of the Inspector panel. For the purposes of this example, drag a Button or two into the panel. Finally, using Interface Builder's Panel inspector, make sure that the panel is not deferred.

8. Connect the **window** outlet of the File's Owner to the Panel. This outlet must be set so that the Workspace Manager can locate the content view to be displayed in the contents inspector. If your File's Owner had other outlets or actions, you would connect them at this point.

9. Switch to the Classes browser in the Files window and select the RIBInspector class. Using the pull-down list, drag to Unparse and confirm that you want to add the class files to the project.

10. Open the class files and implement the **new** method (see the class specification for WMInspector for an example). You must also implement the **revert:** method for your inspector to take any action based on the selection in the File Viewer. For this example, you can omit the **revert:** method. (Note: You will also have to change the #import line at the top of **RIBInspector.h** from #import "WMInspector.h" to #import <apps/Workspace.h>.)

11. Create **bundle.registry** and **Makefile.preamble** files (as described above) and add them to the Supporting Files suitcase in Project Builder's Files display.

12. Save the project and build it. When done, copy the **RIBInspector.bundle** file into your **Apps** directory.

Registering an Inspector

Workspace Manager must be made aware of this new inspector. If you use Workspace Manager to copy the bundle into **~/Apps** (or anywhere in the application search path, for that matter), it will read the registry information the bundle contains. If you move the file by other means, use Workspace Manager's Update Viewers command to make it recheck for applications and inspectors in the application search path. After Workspace Manager has registered the new inspector, whenever a file of the proper extension (".rib" in the example) is selected and the Contents inspector panel is visible, the custom contents inspector will be displayed.

Once an inspector has been loaded, it can't be unloaded without restarting the Workspace Manager (that is, logging out and back in again). For this and other reasons, it's often better to create a test application to debug a new inspector, as discussed in the next section.

Debugging an Inspector

Your inspector operates within the main thread of execution of the Workspace Manager application, so errors occurring with the inspector can crash the Workspace Manager, bringing down with it all applications launched from the Workspace. Given the severity of the consequences, it's imperative that you ensure the reliability of your inspector's code. Unfortunately, at this time there's no standard way to debug inspectors; you'll have to devise your own test mechanisms.

The best strategy is to create a stand-alone debugging application, one that loads your inspector module into its own window just as the Workspace Manager does. You'll have to create a substitute WMInspector class since the main class in your module must inherit from WMInspector. You could perhaps use an OpenPanel as a means of selecting specific files for your module to inspect.

A debugging application makes it easier, safer, and faster to debug your inspector; however, at times you may find it necessary to debug the inspector after it's been loaded into the Workspace Manager. To do this, you'll need to prevent the inspector's symbol table from being stripped.

By default, when the Workspace Manager loads an inspector bundle, it strips the executable code of its symbols. To prevent this, in a shell window enter:

```
dwrite Workspace StripAfterLoading NO
```

Now, when an inspector is loaded, its symbol data will be preserved. You'll be able to attach to the Workspace Manager process using GDB and trace execution through your inspector's code.

Working Within the Workspace Manager

Some contents inspectors display the actual contents of a file while others show only a synopsis. For example, the contents inspector for TIFF and RTF files shows the complete contents, but the Sound inspector shows only summary information. The Sound inspector, however, does offer the user a button that, when clicked, plays the sound.

Since contents inspectors operate in the Workspace Manager's main thread, it's best to let the user decide whether the panel should embark on time- or resource-intensive operations, as illustrated by the Sound inspector panel. (The RIB inspector example outlined above would no doubt include a Render button.)

Classes

WMInspector

Inherits From: Object

Declared In: apps/Workspace.h

Class Description

The WMInspector class defines the link between the Workspace Manager application and the module that's loaded into the application. When you build a new inspector for the Workspace Manager, you must create a subclass of WMInspector. The inspector you define must load its interface (that is, the nib file containing the interface) in its **new** method. It must also override the inherited **revert:** method to load information about the selection into its display.

Your inspector can query the Workspace Manager for information on the selection in the File Viewer by sending itself **selectionCount** and **selectionPathInto:separator:** messages. It can send itself **okButton**, **revertButton**, and **window** messages to gain access to those features of the Inspector panel.

Although the Contents inspector's principal role is to let the user view the contents of a File Viewer entry, it can also let the user edit the displayed data. It's best not to overuse this capability, however, since the Contents inspector wasn't designed to substitute for normal applications.

An inspector that permits editing should send itself a **touch:** message when the user begins modifying the data. This message enables the inspector's OK and Revert buttons and displays a broken "X" in the panel's close box. (See **textDidChange:** for an alternate way to achieve this result.) The inspector should implement the **ok:** method to commit the modifications the user has made.

Instance Variables

id **window**;
id **okButton**;
id **revertButton**;
id **dirNameField**;
id **dirTitleField**;
id **fileNameField**;
id **fileIconButton**;

window	The Inspector window.
okButton	The Inspector's OK button.
revertButton	The Inspector's Revert button.
dirNameField	The TextField that holds the current directory.
dirTitleField	The TextField that titles **dirNameField.**
fileNameField	The TextField that displays the file name.
fileIconButton	The Button that displays the file's icon.

Method Types

Accessing the inspector object	+ new
Accessing panel controls	– okButton – revertButton – window
Accessing Workspace selection	– selectionCount – selectionPathsInto:separator:
Managing changes	– ok: – revert: – textDidChange: – touch:

Class Methods

new

+ new

Creates a new WMInspector if none exists, or returns the existing one. When the object is created, it must load the nib file that contains the inspector's display.

The Workspace Manager sends a **new** message whenever it needs to access the inspector object. Thus, your subclass of WMInspector should ensure that no more than one instance of its class is created:

```
static id ribInspector = nil;

+ new
{
    if (ribInspector == nil) {
        char path[MAXPATHLEN+1];
        NXBundle *bundle = [NXBundle bundleForClass:self];

        self = ribInspector = [super new];
        if ([bundle getPath:path
                forResource:"RIBInspector"
                ofType:"nib"]) {
            [NXApp loadNibFile:path owner:ribInspector];
        } else {
            fprintf (stderr, "Couldn't load RIBInspector.nib\n");
            ribInspector = nil;
        }
    }
    return ribInspector;
}
```

Instance Methods

ok:

– **ok:***sender*

Implement in your subclass to commit the changes that the user has made to the selected item. The OK button in the Inspector panel sends an **ok:** message when the user clicks it.

This method is optional, but if you implement it, you must send the same message to **super** as part of your implementation:

```
ok:sender
{
    /* your code to commit changes */
    [super ok:sender];
    return self;
}
```

This message to **super** replaces the broken "X" in the panel's close box with the standard "X", indicating that the changes have been saved.

See also: – **revert:**, – **touch:**

okButton

– **okButton**

Returns the **id** of the Inspector's OK button. This can be useful if you want to alter its title, for example.

See also: – **revertButton:**

revert:

– **revert:***sender*

Implement in your subclass to load data into the inspector's display. The Workspace Manager sends this message to the inspector object whenever the inspector's display might need to be updated; for example, when the Inspector panel is opened or when the selection changes in the File Viewer.

Your subclass must implement this method, and it must send the same message to **super** as part of its implementation:

```
revert:sender
{
    /* your code to show contents of selected item(s) */
    [super revert:sender];
    return self;
}
```

This message to **super** replaces the broken "X" in the panel's close box with the standard "X", indicating that the changes have been discarded.

See also: – **ok:**, – **touch:**

revertButton

– **revertButton**

Returns the **id** of the Inspector's Revert button. This can be useful if you want to alter its title, for example.

See also: – **okButton:**

selectionCount

– (unsigned)**selectionCount**

Returns the number of items selected in the File Viewer. You can use this information to determine whether your inspector should be displayed. For example, most inspectors can give information on only one file at a time, so within their **revert:** methods, they would have this test:

```
if ([self selectionCount] != 1) {
    return nil;
} else {
    /* get the path and display the file's contents */
}
```

See also: – **selectionPathsInto:separator:**

selectionPathsInto:separator:

– **selectionPathsInto:**(char *)*pathString* **separator:**(char)*character*

Returns the paths of the files selected in the File Viewer. The paths are place in the string *pathString*; each path is separated from the previous one by *character*. For example, if *character* is ':', *pathString* could contain "/me/test1:/me/test2:/me/test3".

If your inspector acts on only one file at a time (see **selectionCount**), the file's path can be identified using this message:

```
char fullPath[MAXPATHLEN+1];
[self selectionPathsInto:fullPath separator:'\0'];
```

See also: – **selectionCount**

textDidChange:

– **textDidChange:***sender*

Sends the WMInspector a **touch:** message on behalf of some Text object in the Inspector panel.

By making your inspector object the delegate of any Text object in your inspector's display, the Inspector panel will be updated appropriately as the user alters the panel's contents.

See also: – **touch:**

touch:

– **touch:***sender*

Changes the image in the Inspector panel's close box to a broken "X" to indicate that the contents has been edited. Also, enables the OK and Revert buttons.

See also: – **textDidChange:**

window

– **window**

Returns the **id** of the window that contains the user interface for the inspector.

Appendices

A Data Formats

To make it easier for applications to share information, the NeXTSTEP pasteboard supports a number of standard data formats. Each format, or *pasteboard type*, is identified by a global variable:

Variable Name	**Type Description**
NXAsciiPboardType	Plain ASCII text
NXPostScriptPboardType	Encapsulated PostScript code (EPS)
N3DRIBPboardType	RenderMan Interface Bytestream code (RIB)
NXTIFFPboardType	Tag Image File Format (TIFF)
NXRTFPboardType	Rich Text Format (RTF)
NXSoundPboardType	Sound data
NXFilenamePboardType	ASCII text designating a file name
NXTabularTextPboardType	Tab-separated fields of ASCII text
NXFontPboardType	Font and character information
NXRulerPboardType	Paragraph formatting information

Data in other formats can also be placed in the pasteboard. However, the sending and receiving applications must both agree on the structure of the format, its name, and how to interpret it. Other formats may be adopted as standards in the future.

Each of the standard formats is discussed below. In most cases, the discussion is short and consists only of a reference to the primary source document for the format. In some cases, more information is given on modifications to or interpretations of the format in the NeXTSTEP environment.

NXAsciiPboardType

Text in this format consists only of characters from the ASCII character set as extended by NeXTSTEP encoding. None of the characters is given a special interpretation (in contrast to NXTabularTextPboardType and NXFilenamePboardType, for example). Standard ASCII is documented on-line in **/usr/pub/ascii** and the **ascii**(7) manual page. NeXTSTEP encoding is documented in Appendix C, "Keyboard Event Information."

NXPostScriptPboardType

This type is defined as PostScript code in the Encapsulated PostScript Files format (EPS). The PostScript language is documented by Adobe Systems Incorporated, principally in the *PostScript Language Reference Manual*. EPS conventions are documented in *Encapsulated PostScript Files Specification*, also by Adobe.

N3DRIBPboardType

This type is for RenderMan Interface Bytestream (RIB) code. The format of RIB code is documented in *The RenderMan Interface*, by Pixar.

NXTIFFPboardType

This type is for image data in Tag Image File Format (TIFF). TIFF is documented in *Tag Image File Format Specification*, by Aldus Corporation and Microsoft Corporation.

TIFF support in the current NeXTSTEP release follows version 6.0 of the TIFF standard and is based on version 3.0 of Sam Leffler's freely distributed TIFF library. This library provides a good set of routines for dealing with TIFF files that conform to the 6.0 specification.

NeXTSTEP TIFF support is embodied in the Application Kit's NXBitmapImageRep class and the command-line program **tiffutil**. See the class specification for NXBitmapImageRep in Chapter 2, "The Application Kit," and the **tiffutil**(1) manual page for more information.

Unsupported Fields

In the current release, some fields—principally those having to do with response curves—will be read correctly but ignored when imaging the data. Color palettes are not supported except when the palette entries are 8 bits and the stored colors are 24 bits. These files will be read correctly and converted to 24-bit images on the fly.

Multiple Images

Multiple forms of an image can now be stored in the same file—that is, under the same TIFF header. "Multiple forms" might mean the same image at different resolutions (for example, 72dpi and 400dpi) and at different bit depths or colors (for example, 2 bits per sample on a gray scale and 4 bits per sample RGB).

This feature is useful when you want to create color icons for an application and its documents. It's best to create both gray scale and color versions of the icons and store them in the same section of the __ICON segment. Both versions of the icon would be created at 72 dpi and would be 48 pixels wide by 48 pixels high. The gray-scale version would have two components (gray and alpha), with each component stored at 2 bits. The color version would have four components (red, green, blue, and alpha) and each component would be 4 bits deep. (It's recommended that application and document icons be stored at 4 bits per sample, not 8.)

Compression

NeXTSTEP software can both read and write compressed TIFF images. The Compression field in a TIFF file can have any of the following values:

Value	Type
1	No compression
3	CCITT Group 3 compression
4	CCITT Group 4 compression
5	LZW (Lempel-Ziv and Welch) compression
6	JPEG compression
32773	PackBits compression

JPEG compression can be used only for images that have a depth of at least 4 bits per sample; in all cases, the compressed images will be expanded to 8 bits per sample. CCITT Group 3 and Group 4 images can be applied only to monochrome images that have 1 bit per sample.

NXRTFPboardType

This is the pasteboard type for "rich text," text that follows the conventions of the Rich Text Format®, as described in *Rich Text Format Specification* by Microsoft Corporation.

To this specification, NeXT has added a control word to indicate how the user selected the text before copying it to the pasteboard. The control word is

\smartcopy<*num*>

where <*num*> can be 1 or 0. A value of 1 indicates that the user made the selection by double-clicking a word, or double-clicking and dragging over a group of words. The range of text in the pasteboard will be delimited by a word boundary on either side. The pasting application can use this information to correctly adjust the spacing around the word or words that are pasted.

NXSoundPboardType

This format is defined by the SNDSoundStruct structure in the header file **sound/soundstruct.h**. The structure is discussed in detail in Chapter 16, "Sound."

NXFilenamePboardType

This format is a list of tab-separated file names (or pathnames), terminated by a null character ('\0').

NXTabularTextPboardType

This format is ASCII text where tabs (ASCII 0x09) and returns or newlines (ASCII 0x0D) are interpreted as separators between text fields. In a matrix, tabs separate columns and returns separate rows. The text is null-terminated.

NXFontPboardType

This format is used in the font pasteboard to record character properties that are copied and pasted using the Copy Font and Paste Font commands. It consists of RTF control words from the "Font Table" and "Character Formatting Properties" groups.

The following is an example of character data in this format:

```
{\rtf1\ansi{\fonttbl\f0\froman Times;}
\f0\b0\i\ul0\fs48}
```

The first two control words, **\rtf1** and **\ansi**, announce that the information enclosed within the outer braces is RTF version 1 in ANSI character encoding. These two control words, or their equivalent, are required by RTF conventions.

The group within the inner braces defines a font table, here with a single entry specifying font 0 to be Times-Roman. The font is then specified as Times-Roman (font 0), not bold, Oblique (italic), not underlined, and having a font size of 24 points (48 half points).

Among the fonts that can be specified in a font table are these:

```
\fmodern Courier;
\fswiss Helvetica;
\fmodern Ohlfs;
\ftech Symbol;
\froman Times;
```

Several synonyms are recognized for the Times-Roman font. Usually it's written as "Times" or "Times-Roman".

If the font pasteboard contains RTF control words that don't belong to the "Font Table" or "Character Formatting Properties" groups, they should be ignored. If control words specify more than one value for a font characteristic, the last value specified should be used when pasting.

NXRulerPboardType

This format is used in the ruler pasteboard to capture information about how a paragraph is formatted. It consists of RTF control words from the "Paragraph Formatting Properties" group.

The following is an example of this type:

```
{\rtf1\ansi
\pard\ql\tx1252\tx2716\tx4148\tx5592\tx7004\tx11520
\fi-540\li1260}
```

The first two control words are required by RTF conventions, as explained under "NXFontPboardType" above. The next control word, **\pard**, resets the paragraph format to the default. The paragraph is then specified to be left-aligned and a series of six tabs are set. Next, the indentation of the first line is specified and, finally, the left indent. (The example is for a paragraph with a hanging indent.)

If the ruler pasteboard contains RTF control words that aren't in the "Paragraph Formatting Properties" group, they should be ignored. If it includes control words that first set then reset a paragraph property, the final specification should be the one that's used.

B Default Parameters

Default parameters set and store values that affect the behavior of applications at run time. Because their values are read each time an application runs, the parameters are the appropriate vehicle for recording user preferences and for inducing an application to exhibit alternate behavior that's useful during debugging.

Default parameters can be set in application code, on the command line that launches the application, or from a database stored in each user's home directory. Parameter values are read at run time and can be written to the user's database using functions described in Chapter 3, "Common Classes and Functions." See **NXRegisterDefaults()** in that chapter for information on how to use default parameters within a program. Parameters can also be written to the database, read, and removed using the **dwrite**, **dread**, and **dremove** command-line utilities.

Both the names and the values of parameters are passed as character strings. Thus a parameter that sets a numeric value will return a string of numeric characters rather than an integer.

Every pairing of a value to a parameter has an "owner" that designates the domain in which the value is valid. Typically, the owner is an application. For example, if you wanted to set the NXPaperType parameter to "Legal" in the Lawyer application, you could use the **dwrite** utility on the command line as follows:

```
localhost> dwrite Lawyer NXPaperSize Legal
```

If the owner is "GLOBAL" (or "–g" for **dwrite**), the value will apply to all applications except those that specifically own another value for the parameter.

The default parameters documented in this appendix affect the behavior of NeXTSTEP software. Some can be set to aid debugging. Some can be set to affect the way your application works. Others should not be set, but can be read to get information about the user's preferences or the state of the application.

The parameters documented here are useful only in very specific situations, mainly for debugging. For the most part, an application should not use any of them to record user preferences. You must invent your own parameters to store user preferences for the applications you write.

At the beginning of each parameter description, there are two lines, one marked **Value** and the other **Scope**. The **Scope** line reports the part of NeXTSTEP software that's affected by the default parameter. The **Value** line reports the value the parameter has if it's not otherwise set. Often the parameter will have another value when encountered in a running application, because it will have been set on the command line, in program code, by the Preferences application, by the system at startup, or by the Workspace Manager when it launches the application. Don't rely heavily on the values stated.

Debugging Parameters

The following parameters come in handy when debugging an application. They're typically set on the command line to affect the behavior of an application during a debugging session. They should not be written into anyone's defaults database (except perhaps your own for debugging purposes).

NXAllWindowsRetained

Value: NULL
Scope: Application Kit

If set to any value, forces all buffered windows to be retained windows. Since drawing is done directly into an on-screen retained window, you'll be able to watch PostScript code being rendered. (Drawing is rendered in the buffer of a buffered window and then flushed to the screen.)

See also: NXShowAllWindows

NXDebugLanguage

Value: NULL
Scope: Application Kit

If set to "YES", logs warnings when localized resources can't be found. Warnings are issued when a resource file is missing or a requested string is absent from a string table. The **NXLogError**() Application Kit function is used to record the error.

NXDefeatObjectLinkTimeouts

Value: NULL
Scope: Application Kit

If set to any value, removes timeouts for interprocess communications that implement data links. Defeating these timeouts prevents processes from timing out as you're tracking down bugs in the debugger.

NXMallocDebug

Value: "0"
Scope: Application Kit

Sets a value that's passed to **malloc_debug**() to control the amount of error checking done by **malloc**(). Valid values range from "0" through "31", with "31" being the highest level of error checking and "0" being none. See the UNIX manual page for **malloc_debug**() for specifics.

NXPSDebug

Value: NULL
Scope: Application Kit

If set to "YES", causes an alternate PostScript error-handling procedure to be installed. This procedure produces more verbose debugging information than would otherwise be available, including the contents of the operand stack.

See also: NXShowPS

NXShowAllWindows

Value: NULL
Scope: Application Kit

If set to any value, forces all windows to always be on-screen. Windows that are normally hidden, such as windows that store images that are composited to other windows, will be visible as your program runs.

See also: NXAllWindowsRetained

NXShowPS

Value: NULL
Scope: Application Kit

If set to any value, causes all PostScript code sent to the Window Server to also be written to the standard error stream.

See also: NXPSDebug and NXSyncPS

NXSyncPS

Value: NULL
Scope: Application Kit

If set to any value, makes the application wait for the Window Server. Whenever the application sends PostScript code to the Window Server, it will wait for the code to be executed before proceeding. This results in error messages being more closely associated with the code that produced them.

See also: NXShowPS and NXPSDebug

NXTraceEvents

Value: NULL
Scope: Application Kit

If set to any value, causes event-tracing information to be written to the standard error stream.

NXWindowDepthLimit

Value: NULL
Scope: Application Kit

Sets an upper limit on the depth of an application's windows. Windows are created with a depth of two bits per pixel, but promote to a greater depth if it's required to display images in the window. For example, color images would promote a window's depth, as would gray-scale images that use any shade of gray other than the four that are represented in two bits.

A window cannot be promoted to a depth greater than the limit. Normally, the limit is set by what display screens are available. A window won't be promoted to a depth greater than can be displayed on an available screen. This parameter lets you further constrain the limit. Valid settings are:

"TwoBitGray"
"EightBitGray"
"TwelveBitRGB"
"TwentyFourBitRGB"

The depth limit is set to the lesser of this value and the limit imposed by an available screen. If the value is prefixed with "Test", as in "TestTwentyFourBitRGB", the limit will be set to the corresponding value even if it's greater than can be displayed on an available screen.

StripAfterLoading

Value: "YES"
Scope: Workspace Manager

If set to "NO", prevents the Workspace Manager from stripping symbols from the modules it loads. The symbols will therefore be available during debugging. The Workspace Manager can load modules that implement Inspector panels for the contents of files. See Chapter 19, "Workspace Manager," for details.

Localization Parameters

These parameters are used in code that localizes an application (enables it to be used in various languages and various parts of the world). Normally, the Preferences application sets these parameters globally for all applications. You can modify them to affect the behavior of your particular application.

NXDate

Value: "%a %b %d %Y"
Scope: Systemwide

Records the preferred format for presenting a date to the user. The parameter value is a format string that can be passed to the ANSI C function **strftime()**.

See also: NXDateAndTime

NXDateAndTime

Value: "%a %b %d %H:%M:%S %Z %Y"
Scope: Systemwide

Records the preferred format for presenting date and time information to the user. The value of this parameter is a format string that can be passed to the ANSI C function **strftime()**, which translates date and time information recorded in a structure (of type **struct tm**) into a form that humans can read. The format string tells **strftime()** what information is needed and how to present it.

Each formatting character refers to a particular type of information in a particular form. For example, "%a" means a short form of a weekday name (such as "Mon" and "Tue" in English or "Lun" and "Mar" in Spanish) and "%Y" means the last two digits of a year (for example, "92" for 1992). See the specification for **strftime()** for information on all the formatting characters.

The current time can be obtained by **time()** and transformed into the proper structure by **localtime()**.

See also: NXDate and NXTime

NXLanguages

Value: NULL
Scope: Application Kit

Overrides the user's language preferences. The value set should list language names, separated by semicolons, in the order of preference. Use the **systemLanguages** method (defined in the Application class of the Application Kit), not this parameter, to discover the language preferences currently in force.

NXTime

Value: "%H:%M:%S %Z"
Scope: Systemwide

Records the preferred format for presenting a time to the user. The parameter value is a format string that can be passed to the ANSI C function **strftime()**.

See also: NXDateAndTime

System Parameters

The following parameters pass information that is set by the system when an application is launched. They shouldn't be modified by the application, but NXOpen and NXOpenTemp can be used on the command line to pass a file to the application.

NXAutolaunch

Value: "NO"
Scope: Application Kit

If "YES", indicates that the Workspace Manager launched the application automatically at startup.

NXOpen

Value: NULL
Scope: Application Kit

Passes the name of a file for the application to open on launch. When the user double-clicks a file to launch an application, the Workspace Manager uses this parameter to pass the file name to the application.

NXOpenTemp

Value: NULL
Scope: Application Kit

Passes the name of a temporary file for the application to open on launch. The application should delete the file when it's through with it.

NXServiceLaunch

Value: NULL
Scope: Application Kit

If set to any value, indicates that the application wasn't launched directly by the user and therefore should not display an untitled document. For example, the application might have been launched from the Services menu of another application, or it could have been launched to provide link data to another application.

User Preferences

The parameters in this section record user preferences. Most are set by the Preferences application. By reading the parameter and using the value that it contains, your application can be made to conform to the user's wishes.

NXBoldSystemFonts

Value: NULL
Scope: Application Kit

Records the user's preferred bold font for system uses. This is the font used in window title bars. The value is a semicolon-separated list of bold font names such as "Helvetica-Bold". The first font in the list is the user's preference. The other fonts in the list are alternatives if for some reason the user's preference can't be used.

You should use the **boldSystemFontOfSize:matrix:** method (defined in the Font class of the Application Kit) to get the user's preferred bold system font, rather than this parameter.

See also: NXSystemFonts

NXMeasurementUnit

Value: "Inches"
Scope: Application Kit

Records the user's preferred unit of measurement as set in the Preferences application. Possible values are:

"Inches"
"Centimeters"
"Points"
"Picas"

NXPaperType

Value: "Letter"
Scope: Application Kit

Records the default paper size for a page layout. A new PrintInfo object (defined in the Application Kit) will be set to this paper size. The choices are:

"Letter"	"A3"
"Tabloid"	"A4"
"Legal"	"A5"
"Ledger"	"B4"
"Executive"	"B5"

NXSystemFonts

Value: NULL
Scope: Application Kit

Records the user's preferred system fonts for such things as menu commands, button labels, and the text that appears in text fields. This is normally set by the user in the Preferences application. The value is a semicolon-separated list of font names—for example, "Courier;Times-Roman;Helvetica". The first font in the list is the user's preference. The other fonts in the list are alternatives to it, if for some reason it can't be used.

You should use the **systemFontOfSize:matrix:** method (defined in the Font class of the Application Kit) to get the user's preferred system font, rather than this parameter.

See also: NXBoldSystemFonts

Parameters for Expert Programmers

These parameters should be modified with care. No application should use any of them to record user preferences.

NXFontsPaths

Value: "/NextLibrary/Fonts/:~/Library/Fonts/:/LocalLibrary/Fonts/"
Scope: Application Kit

Records the search path for fonts. Applications can modify this path to include other directories if need be. Pathnames should end in a slash ("/") and be separated by a colon.

NXHost

Value: NULL
Scope: Application Kit

If set to the name of a machine on the command line, causes the application to connect to the Window Server running on that machine. The application's user interface will appear on the display attached to the named host.

NXIsJournalable

Value: "NO"
Scope: Application Kit

If set to "YES", makes the application journalable. Through the Application Kit's journaling mechanism, other applications will be able to record the events the application receives. This parameter sets the default value returned by the **isJournalable** method defined in the Application class of the Application Kit. It can be overridden by the **setJournalable:** method.

NXNetTimeout

Value: "60"
Scope: Application Kit

Records how long, in seconds, the application will wait for its communications with other processes to succeed before giving up.

NXObjectLinkUpdateMode

Value: "2"
Scope: Application Kit

Records the default update mode for newly created data links. Permitted values range from "1" through "4":

"1"	The data link is updated continuously.
"2"	The data link is updated when the source document for the link is saved.
"3"	The data link is updated only when the user requests it in the Link Inspector.
"4"	The data link is never updated.

NXUseTrueGrays

Value: NULL
Scope: Application Kit

If set to any value, causes the Application Kit to set a color value for intermediate grays rather than use a pattern. The Kit sometimes uses patterns to keep windows from becoming deeper than they need to be.

For example, when drawing standard user interface devices like scroll bars, the Application Kit normally uses a pattern to represent a 50% gray value midway between black and white. Using the pattern prevents the window displaying the device from promoting from a depth of two bits per pixel to a greater depth capable of showing the intermediate gray as a true color.

When creating artwork from an on-screen display, using a true gray may avoid moire patterns in the result.

Compatibility Parameters

The following parameters are ones that users can set to make applications that were developed with an earlier version of NeXTSTEP software work Release 3. They should be set as individual preferences, not in application code. New applications and updated versions of existing ones should be developed to work with the latest version of NeXTSTEP software.

NXClickForHelpEnabled

Value: "YES"
Scope: Application Kit

If set to "NO", disables click-for-help. On keyboards that don't have a dedicated Help key, the click-for-help feature is controlled by a combination of the Control and Alternate modifier keys. Users of applications that use Control-Alternate combinations for something else may wish to disable this feature.

This parameter sets the default value returned by the **isClickForHelpEnabled** method defined in the NXHelpPanel class of the Application Kit.

NXColorCalibrateLevelOneOps

Value: "YES"
Scope: Application Kit

If set to "NO", turns off all forced calibration of device-dependent PostScript color operators. Device-independent color is a feature of PostScript Level 2. NeXTSTEP Release 3 incorporates PostScript Level 2 and uses a calibrated color space for drawing. When printing, all device-dependent Level 1 operators used in applications based on previous NeXTSTEP releases are reinterpreted to the calibrated color space. (Level 1 operators used in applications based on the current release are not affected.) Setting this parameter to "NO" defeats this feature.

The most likely compatibility problem to occur while this parameter is "YES" is that imported EPS (encapsulated PostScript) files may print with the wrong colors.

NXSave2.0Compatibly

Value: "NO"
Scope: Application Kit

If set to "YES", has the Application Kit write data to a typed stream in a way that's compatible with the previous NeXTSTEP release.

When writing data to a typed stream, the Application Kit is able to include information—notably about PANTONE® Colors—that wasn't available in previous versions of NeXTSTEP software. This new information may not be understood when read by applications that haven't yet been updated to the new release.

When this parameter is "YES", the new information won't be written to the stream and will consequently be lost. For example, PANTONE Color names won't be saved.

NXUseCalibratedColor

Value: "YES"
Scope: Application Kit

If set to "NO", turns off all generation of calibrated colors when printing. If the colors an application displays on the screen or produces from the printer seem wrong or substantially different from what they were under the previous release, and setting the NXColorCalibrateLevelOneOps parameter to "NO" for the application doesn't seem to help, setting this parameter to "NO" should fix the problem.

C Keyboard Event Information

Within NeXTSTEP, event records for keyboard-related events report the character set, character code, and key code. This chapter provides the encoding vectors for the character sets available in NeXTSTEP, and the key codes for some NeXT keyboards.

Encoding Vectors

The encoding vector for a character set maps character codes to particular characters. In the tables below that show the encoding vectors, the digit along the side is the first digit, and the one along the top is the second digit, of the character codes in hexadecimal. The light gray cells in the table denote ASCII control characters, and the dark gray cells are unassigned. The remaining cells are divided horizontally: The bottom portion displays the character's name, and the top shows a representation of the character itself.

The NeXTSTEP encoding vector is a superset of the PostScript language standard encoding vector. The characters that have code assignments in the standard encoding vector have the same assignments in the NeXTSTEP encoding vector. The NeXTSTEP encoding vector makes use of the code points that are unassigned in the standard vector to add characters from the ISOLatin1 character set.

hex	0	1	2	3	4	5	6	7	8	9	A	B	C	D	E	F
0x	NUL	SOH	STX	ETX	EOT	ENQ	ACK	BEL	BS	HT	LF	VT	FF	CR	SO	SI
1x	DLE	DC1	DC2	DC3	DC4	NAK	SYN	ETB	CAN	EM	SUB	ESC	FS	GS	RS	US
2x	space	! exclam	" quotedbl	# numbersign	$ dollar	% percent	& ampersand	’ quoteright	(parenleft	) parenright	* asterisk	+ plus	, comma	- hyphen	. period	/ slash
3x	0 zero	1 one	2 two	3 three	4 four	5 five	6 six	7 seven	8 eight	9 nine	: colon	; semicolon	< less	= equal	> greater	? question
4x	@ at	A A	B B	C C	D D	E E	F F	G G	H H	I I	J J	K K	L L	M M	N N	O O
5x	P P	Q Q	R R	S S	T T	U U	V V	W W	X X	Y Y	Z Z	[bracketleft	\ backslash	] bracketright	^ asciicircum	_ underscore
6x	‘ quoteleft	a a	b b	c c	d d	e e	f f	g g	h h	i i	j j	k k	l l	m m	n n	o o
7x	p p	q q	r r	s s	t t	u u	v v	w w	x x	y y	z z	{ braceleft	| bar	} braceright	~ asciitilde	DEL
8x	figsp	À Agrave	Á Aacute	Â Acircumflex	Ã Atilde	Ä Adieresis	Å Aring	Ç Ccedilla	È Egrave	É Eacute	Ê Ecircumflex	Ë Edieresis	Ì Igrave	Í Iacute	Î Icircumflex	Ï Idieresis
9x	Ð Eth	Ñ Ntilde	Ò Ograve	Ó Oacute	Ô Ocircumflex	Õ Otilde	Ö Odieresis	Ù Ugrave	Ú Uacute	Û Ucircumflex	Ü Udieresis	Ý Yacute	Þ Thorn	µ mu	× multiply	÷ divide
Ax	© copyright	¡ exclamdown	¢ cent	£ sterling	⁄ fraction	¥ yen	ƒ florin	§ section	¤ currency	' quotesingle	“ quotedblleft	« guillemotleft	‹ guilsinglleft	› guilsinglright	ﬁ fi	ﬂ fl
Bx	® registered	– endash	† dagger	‡ daggerdbl	· periodcentered	¦ brokenbar	¶ paragraph	• bullet	‚ quotesinglbase	„ quotedblbase	” quotedblright	» guillemotright	… ellipsis	‰ perthousand	¬ logicalnot	¿ questiondown
Cx	¹ onesuperior	` grave	´ acute	ˆ circumflex	˜ tilde	¯ macron	˘ breve	˙ dotaccent	¨ dieresis	² twosuperior	˚ ring	¸ cedilla	³ threesuperior	˝ hungarumlaut	˛ ogonek	ˇ caron
Dx	— emdash	± plusminus	¼ onequarter	½ onehalf	¾ threequarters	à agrave	á aacute	â acircumflex	ã atilde	ä adieresis	å aring	ç ccedilla	è egrave	é eacute	ê ecircumflex	ë edieresis
Ex	ì igrave	Æ AE	í iacute	ª ordfeminine	î icircumflex	ï idieresis	ð eth	ñ ntilde	Ł Lslash	Ø Oslash	Œ OE	º ordmasculine	ò ograve	ó oacute	ô ocircumflex	õ otilde
Fx	ö odieresis	æ ae	ù ugrave	ú uacute	û ucircumflex	ı dotlessi	ü udieresis	ý yacute	ł lslash	ø oslash	œ oe	ß germandbls	þ thorn	ÿ ydieresis		

ASCII control character

not assigned

Figure C-1. NeXTSTEP Encoding Vector

hex	0	1	2	3	4	5	6	7	8	9	A	B	C	D	E	F
0x	NUL	SOH	STX	ETX	EOT	ENQ	ACK	BEL	BS	HT	LF	VT	FF	CR	SO	SI
1x	DLE	DC1	DC2	DC3	DC4	NAK	SYN	ETB	CAN	EM	SUB	ESC	FS	GS	RS	US
2x	space	! exclam	∀ universal	# numbersign	∃ existential	% percent	& ampersand	∍ suchthat	(parenleft	) parenright	* asteriskmath	+ plus	, comma	− minus	. period	/ slash
3x	0 zero	1 one	2 two	3 three	4 four	5 five	6 six	7 seven	8 eight	9 nine	: colon	; semicolon	< less	= equal	> greater	? question
4x	≅ congruent	Α Alpha	Β Beta	Χ Chi	Δ Delta	Ε Epsilon	Φ Phi	Γ Gamma	Η Eta	Ι Iota	ϑ theta1	Κ Kappa	Λ Lambda	Μ Mu	Ν Nu	Ο Omicron
5x	Π Pi	Θ Theta	Ρ Rho	Σ Sigma	Τ Tau	Υ Upsilon	ς sigma1	Ω Omega	Ξ Xi	Ψ Psi	Ζ Zeta	[bracketleft	∴ therefore	] bracketright	⊥ perpendicular	_ underscore
6x	‾ radicalex	α alpha	β beta	χ chi	δ delta	ε epsilon	ϕ phi	γ gamma	η eta	ι iota	φ phi1	κ kappa	λ lambda	μ mu	ν nu	ο omicron
7x	π pi	θ theta	ρ rho	σ sigma	τ tau	υ upsilon	ϖ omega1	ω omega	ξ xi	ψ psi	ζ zeta	{ braceleft	∣ bar	} braceright	~ similar	DEL
8x	figsp															
9x																
Ax		ϒ Upsilon1	′ minute	≤ lessequal	⁄ fraction	∞ infinity	ƒ florin	♣ club	♦ diamond	♥ heart	♠ spade	↔ arrowboth	← arrowleft	↑ arrowup	→ arrowright	↓ arrowdown
Bx	° degree	± plusminus	″ second	≥ greaterequal	× multiply	∝ proportional	∂ partialdiff	• bullet	÷ divide	≠ notequal	≡ equivalence	≈ approxequal	… ellipsis	⏐ arrowvertex	⎯ arrowhorizex	↵ carriagereturn
Cx	ℵ aleph	ℑ Ifraktur	ℜ Rfraktur	℘ weierstrass	⊗ circlemultiply	⊕ circleplus	∅ emptyset	∩ intersection	∪ union	⊃ propersuperset	⊇ reflexsuperset	⊄ notsubset	⊂ propersubset	⊆ reflexsubset	∈ element	∉ notelement
Dx	∠ angle	∇ gradient	® registerserif	© copyrightserif	™ trademarkserif	∏ product	√ radical	⋅ dotmath	¬ logicalnot	∧ logicaland	∨ logicalor	⇔ arrowdblboth	⇐ arrowdblleft	⇑ arrowdblup	⇒ arrowdblright	⇓ arrowdbldown
Ex	◊ lozenge	〈 angleleft	® registersans	© copyrightsans	™ trademarksans	∑ summation	⎛ parenlefttp	⎜ parenleftex	⎝ parenleftbt	⎡ bracketlefttp	⎢ bracketleftex	⎣ bracketleftbt	⎧ bracelefttp	⎨ braceleftmid	⎩ braceleftbt	⎪ braceleftex
Fx		〉 angleright	∫ integral	⌠ integraltp	⎮ integralex	⌡ integralbt	⎞ parenrighttp	⎟ parenrightex	⎠ parenrightbt	⎤ bracketrighttp	⎥ bracketrightex	⎦ bracketrightbt	⎫ bracerighttp	⎬ bracerightmid	⎭ bracerightbt	

ASCII control character

not assigned

Figure C-2. Symbol Encoding Vector

The standard ASCII abbreviations are shown for the characters with codes 00 through 1F and 7F (such as CR for the Return character, 0D). The characters from 00 through 1F can be generated by holding down the Control key while typing the character whose code is 40 greater; alphabetic characters may be typed in either upper or lower case. For example, 07 is generated by holding down the Control key while pressing the key labeled G, since the character code for G is 47. The following table shows other ways of generating some of these control characters (assuming the standard key mapping):

Code	**Abbreviation**	**Generated by**
00	NUL	Control-space
03	ETX	Enter key (or Command-Return)
08	BS	Shift-Delete (backspace)
09	HT	Tab key
0D	CR	Return key
19	EM	Shift-Tab (backward tab)
1B	ESC	Esc key
7F	DEL	Delete key

Note: Except for Return, Tab, and Shift-Tab, the Application Kit's Text object remaps character codes below 20 to 00.

The character with code 80 is a figure space, a nonbreaking space with the same width as a numeral. A figure space is generated by holding down the Alternate key while pressing the space bar. The figure space should always be a nonbreaking space; in applications (like Edit) that break lines at normal spaces (code 20), lines don't break at nonbreaking spaces. You can't display a figure space with the **show** operator.

The arrow keys generate the codes for the arrow symbols in the Symbol character set (codes AC through AF). With the Shift key down, the arrow keys generate character codes for the double arrows (codes DC through DF). For information on which characters are generated by other character keys, see the *User's Guide*.

Key Codes

The following figures show the key codes of several types of keyboards that can be attached to a NeXT computer.

Note: In the future, computers running NeXTSTEP will have keyboards that generate different key codes.

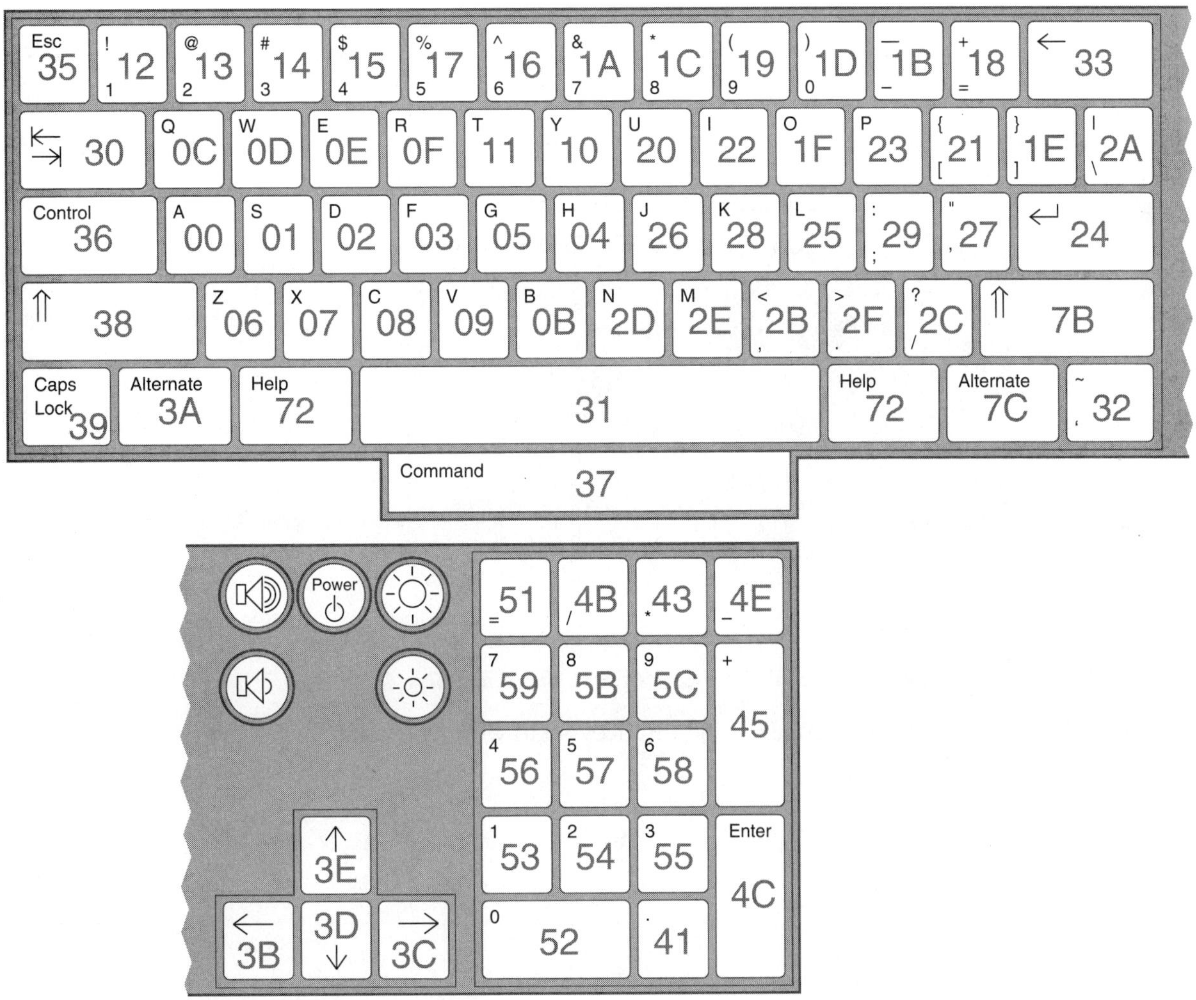

Figure C-3. Key Codes of the U.S. Keyboard with One Command Key

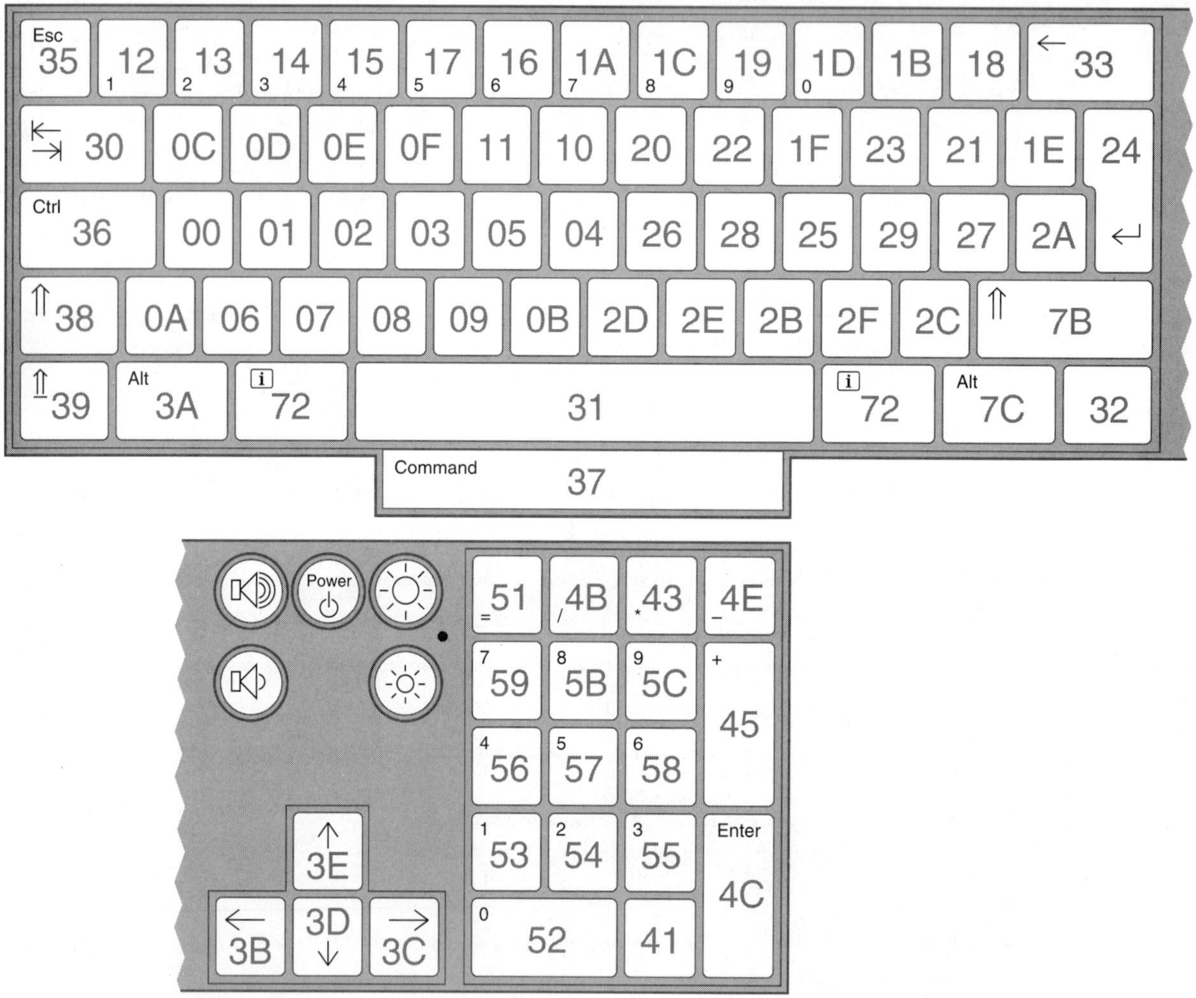

Figure C-4. Key Codes of the ISO Keyboard with One Command Key

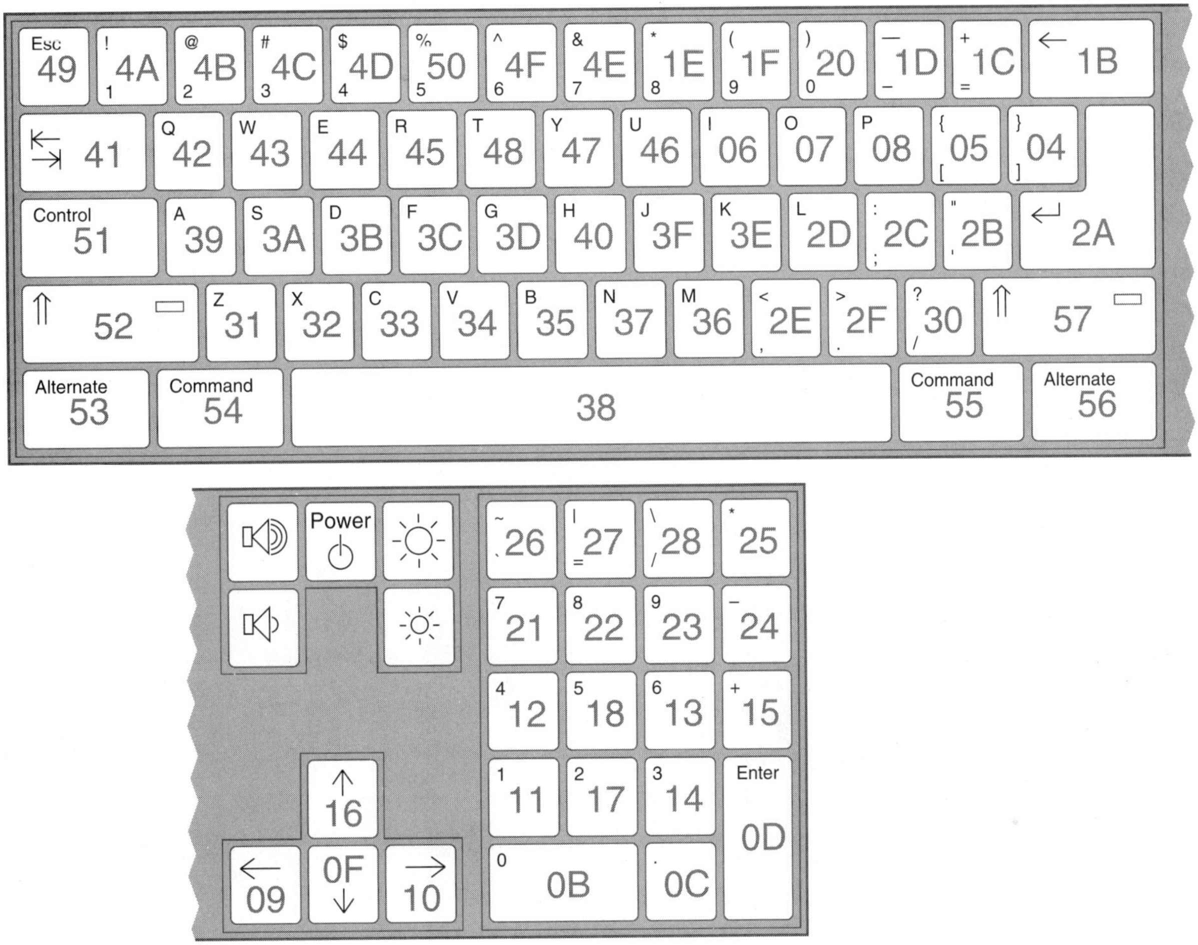

Figure C-5. Key Codes of the ISO Keyboard with Two Command Keys

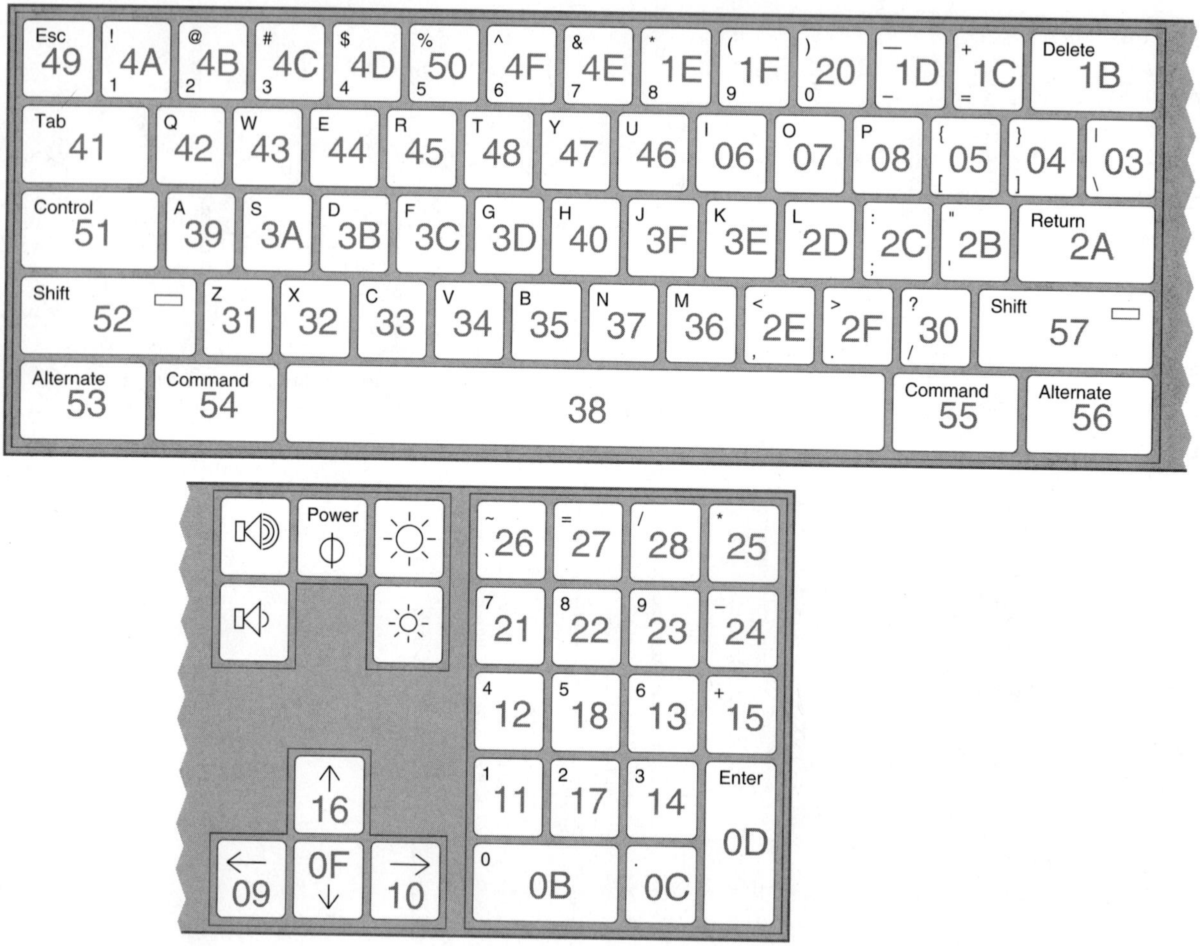

Figure C-6. Key Codes of the Original Keyboard

D System Bitmaps

This appendix shows the bitmaps provided with NeXTSTEP. These bitmaps can be used by the NXImage, Cell, and Cursor classes. They are also available in Interface Builder by typing their names into the "Icon:" field of the inspector. The name and size (in pixels) is listed below each bitmap. For more information, see the class specifications.

The following bitmaps can be used by the NXImage and Cell classes:

NXsquare16
16x16

NXsquare16H
16x16

NXswitch
15x15

NXswitchH
15x15

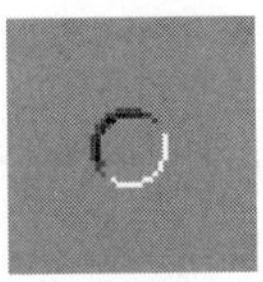

NXradio
16x15

NXradioH
16x15

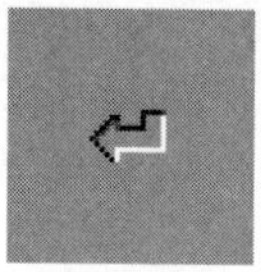

NXreturnSign
16x10

NXmenuArrow
12x9

NXmenuArrowH
12x9

NXscrollDown
16x16

NXscrollDownH
16x16

NXscrollLeft
16x16

NXscrollLeftH
16x16

NXscrollRight
16x16

NXscrollRightH
16x16

NXscrollUp
16x16

NXscrollUpH
16x16

NXLinkButton
12x12

NXLinkButtonH
12x12

NXscrollMenuDown
12x12

NXscrollMenuDownD
12x12

NXscrollMenuDownH
12x12

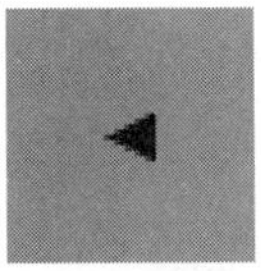

NXscrollMenuLeft
12x11

NXscrollMenuLeftD
12x11

NXscrollMenuLeftH
12x12

NXscrollMenuRight
12x11

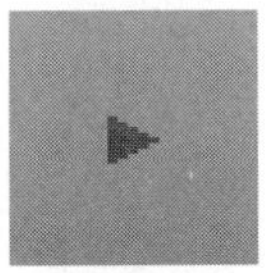

NXscrollMenuRightD
12x11

NXscrollMenuRightH
12x12

NXscrollMenuUp
12x12

NXscrollMenuUpD
12x12

NXscrollMenuUpH
12x12

NXdefaultappicon
48x48

NXdefaulticon
48x48

The following bitmaps are the representations of predefined NXCursor objects:

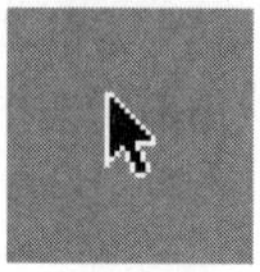

NXarrow
16x16

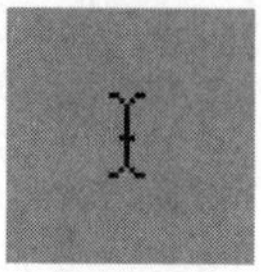

NXibeam
16x16

E Details of the DSP

Memory Map

The following table describes the memory map for the DSP private RAM (8K words).

Start	End	Name
p:0	p:$1FF	On-chip program RAM ('$' denotes hex)
p:$2000	p:$3FFF	Off-chip program RAM, image 1
p:$A000	p:$BFFF	Off-chip program RAM, image 2
x:0	x:$FF	On-chip data RAM, x bank
x:$100	x:$1FF	On-chip data ROM, x bank (Mu-Law, A-law tables)
x:$2000	x:$3FFF	Off-chip data RAM, x bank, image 1
x:$A000	x:$AFFF	Off-chip data RAM, x bank, image 2
y:0	y:$FF	On-chip data RAM, y bank
y:$100	y:$1FF	On-chip data ROM, y bank (Sine wave cycle)
y:$2000	y:$3FFF	Off-chip data RAM, y bank, image 1
y:$A000	y:$AFFF	Off-chip data RAM, y bank, image 2

Off-chip memory exists in two "images" for each space. In image 1, all three memory spaces occupy the same physical memory (in other words, the X/Y~, PS~, and DS~ pins of the DSP56001 are not connected when address line A15 is low). In image 2, x and y are split into separate 4K banks, and p overlays them both with an 8K image (that is, X/Y~ is used as address line A12 and PS~ and DS~ are not connected when A15 is high). External memory starts at 8K ($2000) instead of 512 ($200) because address line A13 in the DSP must be high to enable external DSP RAM. (Note that there is another enable for this RAM in the System Control Register 2.)

DSP D-15 Connector Pinouts

The following describes the output pins of the DSP D-15 connector at the back of the main unit. The left column is the connector pin number, and the right column is the signal name as it appears in the Motorola *DSP56000/DSP56001 Digital Signal Processor User's Manual.*

D-15	DSP
1	SCK
2	SRD
3	STD
4	SCLK
5	RXD
6	TXD
7	+12V, 500mA
8	−12V, 100mA
9	GND
10	GND
11	GND
12	SC2
13	SC1
14	SC0
15	GND

Figure E-1 shows the circuit through which signals are sent from the DSP to the D-15 connector.

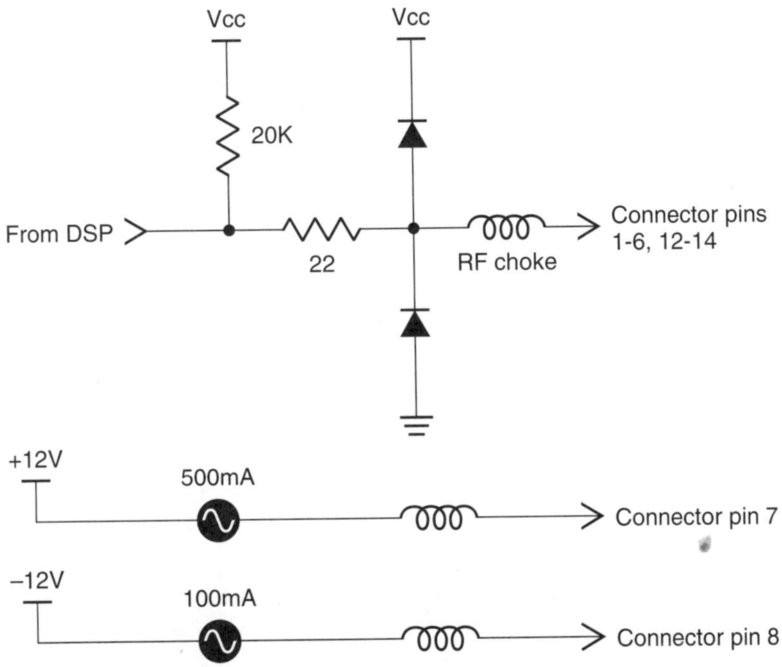

Figure E-1. D-15 Connector

There's a series RF choke on each connector signal that doesn't affect its steady-state level.

DSP56001 Instruction Set Summary

The following notation is used in the summary:

Notation	Denotes
'*'	Instructions that don't allow parallel data moves
[a,b]	One of a or b
<a,b>	Either a,b or b,a
<n>	A nonnegative integer
#I<n>	n-bit immediate value
A<n>	n-bit absolute address
An	A0, A1, or A2 (similarly for Bn)
Xn	X0 or X1 (similarly for Yn)
Rn	R0, R1, R2, R3, R4, R5, R6, or R7 (similarly for Nn, Mn)
AnyEa	Addressing modes (Rn)[−[Nn]], (Rn+Nn), −(Rn) (similarly for An)
AnyXY	[x,y]:AnyEa
AnyIO	[x,y]:<<pp (x or y peripheral address, 6 bits, 1's extended)
Creg	Registers Mn, SR, OMR, SP, SSH, SSL, LA, LC
Dreg	Registers Xn, Yn, An, Bn, A, B
Areg	Registers Rn, Nn
AnyReg	Registers Dreg, Areg, Creg
cc	CC(HS) CS(LO) EC EQ ES GE GT LC LE LS LT MI NE NR PL NN

left-justified moves: → [A,B,Xn,Yn]
right-justified moves: → [An,Bn,Rn,Nn]

Arithmetic Instructions

ABS [A,B]	Absolute Value
ADC [X,Y],[A,B]	Add Long with Carry
ADD [X,Xn,Y,Yn,B,A],[A,B]	Add
ADDL [B,A],[A,B]	Shift Left then Add (D=2*D+S)
ADDR [B,A],[A,B]	Shift Right then Add (D=D/2+S)
ASL [A,B]	Arithmetic Shift Left (D1=D1*2)
ASR [A,B]	Arithmetic Shift Right (D1=D1/2)
CLR [A,B]	Clear Accumulator
CMP [Xn,Yn,B,A],[A,B]	Compare (CCR=Sign(D1–S))
CMPM [Xn,Yn,B,A],[A,B]	Compare magnitude (CCR=Sign(D–S))
*DIV [Xn,Yn],[A,B]	Divide Iteration (D/S iteration)
MAC ±[Xn,Yn],[Xn,Yn],[A,B]	Signed Multiply-Add (no X1*X1, Y1*Y1)
MACR ±[Xn,Yn],[Xn,Yn],[A,B]	Signed Multiply, Accumulate, and Round
MPY ±[Xn,Yn],[Xn,Yn],[A,B]	Signed Multiply (no X1*X1, Y1*Y1)
MPYR ±[Xn,Yn],[Xn,Yn],[A,B]	Signed Multiply-Round (no X1*X1, Y1*Y1)
NEG [A,B]	Negate Accumulator
*NORM [A,B]	Normalize Accumulator Iteration
RND [A,B]	Round Accumulator
SBC [X,Y],[A,B]	Subtract Long with Carry (D = D – S – C)
SUB [X,Xn,Y,Yn,B,A],[A,B]	Subtract (D = D – S)
SUBL [B,A],[A,B]	Shift Left then Subtract (D = 2*D – S)
SUBR [B,A],[A,B]	Shift Right then Subtract (D = D/2 – S)
*Tcc [Xn,Yn,B,A],[A,B]	Transfer Conditionally
TFR [Xn,Yn,B,A],[A,B]	Transfer Data ALU Register
TST [A,B]	Test Accumulator

Logical Instructions

AND [Xn,Yn],[A,B]	Logical AND (D1=D1&S)
*ANDI #I8,[MR,CCR,OMR]	AND Immediate with Control Register
EOR [Xn,Yn],[A,B]	Logical Exclusive OR (D1=D1 XOR S)
LSL [A,B]	Logical Shift Accumulator Left (D1=D1<<1)
LSR [A,B]	Logical Shift Accumulator Right (D1=D1>>1)
NOT [A,B]	Logical Complement on Accumulator (D1=~D1)
OR [Xn,Yn],[A,B]	Logical Inclusive OR (D1=D1S)
*ORI #I8,[MR,CCR,OMR]	OR Immediate with Control Register
ROL [A,B]	Rotate Accumulator Left ([C,D1] ROL)
ROR [A,B]	Rotate Accumulator Right ([D1,C] ROR)

Bit Manipulation Instructions

*BCLR #B5,AnyXY	Bit Test and Clear (C = Selected bit)
*BSET #B5,AnyXY	Bit Test and Set (C = Selected bit)
*BCHG #B5,AnyXY	Bit Test and Change (C = Selected bit)
*BTST #B5,AnyXY	Bit Test on Memory (C = Selected bit)
*JCLR #B5,[AnyXY,AnyIO],xxxx	Jump if Bit Clear
*JSET #B5,[AnyXY,AnyIO],xxxx	Jump if Bit Set
*JSCLR #B5,[AnyXY,AnyIO],xxxx	Jump to Subroutine if Bit Clear
*JSSET #B5,[AnyXY,AnyIO],xxxx	Jump to Subroutine if Bit Set

Loop Instructions

*DO [[x,y]:[AnyEa,A12],AnyReg],L	Start Hardware Loop (L=Label after end)
*ENDDO	Exit from Hardware Loop

Move Instructions

*LUA (Rn)[±[Nn]],[Rn,Nn]	Load Updated Register
MOVE (NOP)	Move Data
*MOVEC <AnyXY,Creg>	Move Control Register
*MOVEC [#I16,#I8],Creg	Move Control Register
*MOVEC <Creg,AnyReg>	Move Control Register
*MOVEM <p:AnyEa,AnyReg>	Move Program Memory
*MOVEP <[AnyReg,AnyXY],AnyIO>	Move Peripheral Data
*MOVEP #I24,AnyIO	Move Peripheral Data

Program Control Instructions

*Jcc [A12,AnyEa]	Jump Conditionally
*JMP [A12,AnyEa]	Jump
*JScc [A12,AnyEa]	Jump to Subroutine Conditionally
*JSR [A12,AnyEa]	Jump to Subroutine
*NOP	No Operation
*REP [AnyXY,#I12,AnyReg]	Repeat Next Instruction
*RESET	Reset Peripherals
RTI	Return from Interrupt
RTS	Return from Subroutine
*STOP	Stop Processing
*SWI	Software Interrupt
*WAIT	Wait for Interrupt

Suggested Reading

Some information you may need or find useful isn't covered in detail in this manual. This section indicates where you can get additional information, whether in printed form or on-line.

Other Books on NeXTSTEP Programming

NeXTSTEP Development Tools and Techniques: Release 3. NeXT Publications. Addison-Wesley, 1992.

NeXTSTEP Programming Interface Summary: Release 3. NeXT Publications. Addison-Wesley, 1992.

NeXTSTEP User Interface Guidelines: Release 3. NeXT Publications. Addison-Wesley, 1992.

NeXTSTEP Operating System Software: Release 3. NeXT Publications. Addison-Wesley, 1992.

See the back cover of this manual for more titles in the *NeXTSTEP Developer's Library*.

The C Language

American National Standard X3.159-1989, Programming Language C. American National Standards Institute, 1989.

This document is the formal and official definition of the C language, its preprocessor, and run-time library. It's available directly from the American National Standards Institute. To order by telephone, call (212)642-4900.

C: A Reference Manual. Third edition. Samuel P. Harbison and Guy L. Steele, Jr. Prentice-Hall, 1991.

Portability and the C Language. Rex Jaeschke. Hayden Books, 1988.

The C Programming Language. Second edition. Brian W. Kernighan and Dennis M. Ritchie. Prentice-Hall, 1988.

C Traps and Pitfalls. Andrew Koenig. Addison-Wesley, 1989.

Programming in ANSI C. Stephen G. Kochan. Hayden Books, 1988.

Object-Oriented Programming

An Introduction to Object-Oriented Programming. Timothy Budd. Addison-Wesley, 1991.

This is a readable introduction that compares several current object-oriented languages, including C++ and Objective C.

Object-Oriented Software Construction. Bertrand Meyer. Prentice-Hall, 1988.

Object Orientation: Concepts, Languages, Databases, User Interfaces. Setrag Khoshafian and Razmik Abnous. John Wiley and Sons, 1990.

Object-Oriented Design: With Applications. Grady Booch. Benjamin/Cummings, 1991.

Designing Object-Oriented Software. Rebecca Wirfs-Brock, Brian Wilkerson, and Lauren Wiener. Prentice-Hall, 1990.

The C++ Programming Language. Second edition. Bjarne Stroustrup. Addison-Wesley, 1991.

C++ Primer. Second edition. Stanley B. Lippman. Addison-Wesley, 1991.

Objective-C: Object-Oriented Programming Techniques. Lewis J. Pinson and Richard S. Wiener. Addison-Wesley, 1991.

Data Formats

Rich Text Format Specification. Microsoft Corporation. To obtain this document, write to the following address:

Microsoft Corporation
One Microsoft Way
Redmond WA 98052-6399
Attention: RTF Program Manager

Tag Image File Format Specification. Aldus Corporation and Microsoft Corporation. Available from Aldus Corporation; for more information, contact the Aldus Developers Desk at (206)628-6593.

Blue Book, Vol. VII.3. CITT, 1988. Describes Group 3 and Group 4 compression.

See "PostScript Language," below, for documents describing PostScript data formats.

PostScript Language

Programming the Display PostScript System with NeXTstep. Adobe Systems Incorporated. Addison-Wesley, 1992. Also known as the "purple book."

PostScript Language Reference Manual. Second edition. Adobe Systems Incorporated. Addison-Wesley, 1990. Also known as the "red book."

PostScript Language Tutorial and Cookbook. Adobe Systems Incorporated. Addison-Wesley, 1985. Also known as the "blue book."

PostScript Language Program Design. Adobe Systems Incorporated. Addison-Wesley, 1988. Also known as the "green book."

Adobe Type 1 Font Format, Version 1.1. Adobe Systems Incorporated. Addison-Wesley, 1990. Also known as the "black book."

Thinking In PostScript. Glenn Reid. Addison-Wesley, 1990.

Real World PostScript. Steven Roth ed. Addison-Wesley, 1988.

Learning PostScript—A Visual Approach. Ross Smith. Peachpit Press, 1990.

The following manuals can be obtained from Adobe's public access file server. For information about using the file server, send an empty electronic mail message with the subject "help" to **ps-file-server@adobe.com**.

Adobe Font Metric Files Specification, Version 2.0. Adobe Systems Incorporated.

Character Bitmap Distribution Format Specification, Version 2.1. Adobe Systems Incorporated.

Display PostScript System: Client Library Reference Manual. Adobe Systems Incorporated.

Display PostScript System: pswrap Reference Manual. Adobe Systems Incorporated.

Encapsulated PostScript Files Specification, Version 2.0. Adobe Systems Incorporated.

Database Query Languages

SQL Language Reference Manual, Version 6, P/N 778-V6.0; Version 7, P/N 778-7.0-0292. Oracle Corporation, 1992. Available from Oracle Corporation, 500 Oracle Parkway, Mail Stop 659308, Redwood Shores, CA, 94065.

*CASE*Method™ Entity Relationship Modeling*. Richard Barker. Addison-Wesley, 1990.

A Guide to Sybase and SQL-Server. David McGovern and C. J. Date. Addison-Wesley, 1991.

Transact-SQL™ User's Guide. Sybase Document 3230–4.0, 1989. Available from Sybase Inc., 6475 Christie Avenue, Emeryville, CA, 94608.

RenderMan Language

The RenderMan Companion: A Programmer's Guide to Realistic Computer Graphics. Steve Upstill. Addison-Wesley, 1990.

The RenderMan Interface. Pixar, 1989. To order by telephone, call (510)236-4000.

Computer Graphics

Computer Graphics: Principles and Practice. Second edition. James Foley, Andries van Dam, Steven K. Feiner, John F. Hughes. Addison-Wesley, 1990.

This is the second edition of the standard text on computer graphics, providing thorough coverage of general concepts in both 2D and 3D image representation.

Compositing

"Compositing Digital Images." Thomas Porter and Tom Duff. *Computer Graphics (SIGGRAPH '84 Conference Proceedings)*, Vol. 18, No. 3, July 1984, pp. 253-259.

"Two-Bit Graphics." David Salesin and Ronen Barzel. *IEEE Computer Graphics and Applications*, Vol. 6, No. 6, June 1986, pp. 36-42.

UNIX 4.3BSD Operating System

The UNIX Programming Environment. Brian W. Kernighan and Rob Pike. Prentice-Hall, 1984.

This book is one of many that describe how to use the UNIX operating system.

Standard UNIX manual pages contain information about UNIX commands and system calls. These are stored on-line, and are accessible in Digital Librarian.

Glossary

abstract class
A class that's defined solely so that other classes can inherit from it. Programs don't use instances of an abstract class, only of its subclasses.

abstract superclass
Same as *abstract class*.

action message
In the Application Kit, a message sent by an object (such as a Button or Slider) in response to a user action (such as clicking the button or dragging the slider's knob). The message translates the user's action into a specific instruction for the application. See also *target*.

activate
In the NeXTSTEP user interface, to cause an application to become active. In the Indexing Kit, to unarchive an object by reading its instance variables directly from storage. See also *passivate* and *transcribe*.

active application
The application currently associated with keyboard events. Menus are visible on-screen only for the active application, and only the active application can have the current key window and main window.

adaptor
In the Database Kit, the software that mediates between an application built from the kit and the database server to which the application connects, handling data transfers and translating from the generic query language of the kit to the specific language required by the database.

ADC
Analog-to-digital converter; a device that samples an audio signal to produce a series of discrete values.

adopt
In the Objective C language, a class is said to adopt a protocol if it declares that it implements all the methods in the protocol. Protocols are adopted by listing their names between angle brackets in a class or category declaration.

alpha value
The value that indicates the coverage of a pixel in an image, ranging from 0.0 for a transparent pixel (no coverage) to 1.0 for an opaque pixel (full coverage). Also, the value set by the **setalpha** operator for the coverage parameter in the current graphics state. See also *color value*.

ALU
Arithmetic-logical unit; the circuit in a microprocessor that performs numeric operations, such as addition and multiplication, on data.

amplitude
The distance from a sound waveform's mean to its furthest displacement; subjectively heard as loudness.

analog-to-digital converter
See *ADC*.

ancestor
In the Application Kit, a View is said to be the ancestor of all the Views below it in the view hierarchy, including its subviews. In the 3D Graphics Kit, an N3DShape's ancestor is the shape from which it inherits both its local coordinate system and its rendering order. Each N3DShape has a pointer to its ancestor; shapes that share the same ancestor are called peers. See also *descendant*.

anchor point
When the user drags to define a range, the position of the cursor when the mouse button is pressed. See also *end point*.

anonymous object
An object of unknown class. The interface to an anonymous object is published through a protocol declaration.

API
Application programming interface; the classes, functions, operators, and other programming elements that let programs make use of NeXTSTEP libraries and applications.

application
A program with a graphical user interface that the user can run from the workspace, such as Edit, FaxReader, or Preferences.

application-activate subevent
A subevent of the kit-defined event. It reports when a user activates an application by clicking in one of its windows.

application-deactivate subevent
A subevent of the kit-defined event. It reports when a user deactivates an application by clicking in another application's window.

application dock
The column holding application icons at the right of the screen.

Application Kit
The Objective C classes and C functions available for implementing the NeXTSTEP window-based user interface in an application. The Application Kit provides a basic program structure for applications that draw on the screen and respond to events.

archiving
The process of preserving a data structure, especially an object, for later use. An archived data structure is usually stored in a file, but it can also be written to memory, copied to the pasteboard, or sent to another application. Archiving involves writing data to a special kind of data stream, called a typed stream. See also *typed stream*.

arithmetic operator
In the Indexing Kit query language, an operator that performs an arithmetic operation on two numbers. See also *operator*.

array processing
A means of performing mathematical computations on large amounts of data extremely quickly.

array processor
A special-purpose digital hardware device capable of performing array processing operations; for example, the Motorola DSP56001 microprocessor.

arrow key
One of the four keys with arrows on them, to the left of the numeric keypad on the NeXT keyboard. They move the insertion point in the indicated direction.

association
In the Database Kit, the mapping between a field in a record list and the object that displays it.

asynchronous message
A remote message that returns immediately, without waiting for the application that receives the message to respond. The sending application and the receiving application act independently, and are therefore not "in sync." See also *synchronous message*.

atom
In the Indexing Kit query language, a scalar data item in an expression.

attach
To choose a menu command that controls a submenu, causing the submenu to appear on-screen next to the supermenu (the menu with the controlling command). Moving or closing a supermenu also moves or closes its attached submenu; choosing the controlling command a second time detaches and hides the submenu.

attention panel
A panel that demands the user's attention. Until the user acts to dismiss the panel from the screen, no other action within the application is possible. Attention panels permit the user to rescind a command (such as Close), ask the user to complete a command (such as Save As), and give warnings that the user must acknowledge. See also *panel*.

attribute
In the Indexing Kit, a characteristic of an object, defined by a name and the return value of a specific message (which takes no arguments). In the Database Kit, the description of one of the properties of an entity; loosely, the name of a field in a table.

attribute parser
In the Indexing Kit, an instance of IXAttributeParser; generally, an object that breaks a stream of text into attribute/value lists.

attribute reader
In the Indexing Kit, an instance of IXAttributeReader or of a subclass; generally, an object that breaks a stream of text into lexemes.

background color
In the Application Kit, the color that fills the content area of a window and provides a background for all the drawing done within the window, or the color that fills a View as a background for any drawing the View or its subviews do.

bar
The part of a slider or a scroller that holds the moveable knob. See also *knob*.

base coordinate system
The reference coordinate system for a window. The origin is in the window's lower left corner of the window, outside the border and resize bar if it has them. The positive x-axis extends to the right and the positive y-axis extends upward; the length of a unit on either axis is one screen pixel.

binder
In the Database Kit, a mechanism for mapping a record in the database to Objective C objects in a container.

blob
In the Indexing Kit, a data item of indeterminate length or structure. A blob is a data item that can't be transcribed. See also *activate*, *passivate*, and *transcribe*.

block
In the Indexing Kit, a unit of storage in an IXStore, identified by a handle.

boolean operator
In the Indexing Kit query language, an operator that performs a boolean or set operation. See also *operator*.

boot block
In the Indexing Kit, the single block in an IXStore from which a store client must be opened or reconstituted. See also *store client*, *open*, *reconstitute*.

bootstrap port
A port to which a new task can send a message that will return any other system service ports that the task needs.

bounds rectangle
In the Application Kit, the smallest rectangle in a View's coordinate system that completely encloses its frame rectangle. Unless the View's coordinate axes have been rotated, the bounds rectangle (stated in the View's own coordinates) and its frame rectangle (stated in its superview's coordinates) enclose exactly the same area on-screen.

buffered window
A window with an input buffer that also acts as a backup buffer for screen pixel values. All images are first rendered in the buffer, then flushed from the buffer to the screen.

busy cursor
The cursor image (a spinning disk) that indicates that an application is busy.

camera coordinate system
In the 3D Graphics Kit, the coordinate system with its origin at the eyepoint of an N3DCamera. The axes of the camera coordinate system are defined in terms of s, t, and u (corresponding to x, y, and z in standard coordinate systems). The s-axis aligns horizontally with the camera, running through the eyepoint, and the t-axis aligns vertically with the camera through the eyepoint. The u-axis is always perpendicular to the camera's focal plane: it points along the eye-to-viewpoint vector.

category
In the Objective C language, a set of method definitions that is segregated from the rest of the class definition. Categories can be used to split a class definition into parts, or to add methods to an existing class.

channel
On a telephone line, the physical capacity to carry a call. An ISDN line has more than one channel, so it can simultaneously carry more than one call.

character code
The code that identifies a character in a given character set; an index into the character set's encoding vector.

character keys
The keys that transmit characters to the computer. This includes not only the usual letters, numbers, and symbols, but also Return, Enter, Delete, Tab, Esc, and the arrow keys.

character set
The set of characters for a particular font or fonts; either the NeXTSTEP character set (an extension of ASCII) or Symbol.

class
In the Objective C language, a prototype for a particular kind of object. A class definition declares instance variables and defines methods for all members of the class. Objects that have the same types of instance variables and have access to the same methods belong to the same class. See also *class object*.

class method
In the Objective C language, a method that can be used by the class object rather than by instances of the class.

class object
In the Objective C language, an object that represents a class and knows how to create new instances of the class. Class objects are created by the compiler, lack instance variables, and can't be statically typed, but otherwise behave like all other objects. As the receiver in a message expression, a class object is represented by the class name.

click
To press and release a mouse button while the cursor is positioned over an object on-screen. Clicking an object may select it or cause it to act in some way. Users can also click to select a particular location (for the insertion point, for example).

clipping path
In the PostScript language, a path enclosing the area where drawing can take place. Areas not within the clipping path aren't affected by PostScript painting operators such as **stroke** and **fill**.

close button
The button that can appear at the far right in a window's title bar. Clicking the button closes the window (removes it from the workspace).

CODEC
A type of analog-to-digital converter (CODEC stands for "coder-decoder"). The CODEC on NeXT computers uses an 8-bit mu-law encoded quantization and a sampling rate of 8012.8 Hz.

color component
One of the parameters that make up a color specification. On a gray scale, there's a single component. A color that's specified by red, green, and blue (RGB) parameters has three components.

color value
The value that indicates the color of a pixel; each color component is assigned a separate value ranging from 0.0 to 1.0. Also, the current value of the color parameter of the graphics state, as set by **setgray**, **setrgbcolor**, or another similar operator. See also *alpha value*.

commit
In the Database Kit, the action of accepting the sequence of modifications grouped in a transaction, so that they take effect in the database and can no longer be rolled back.

compositing
A method of accumulating separately rendered images into a final image. It encompasses simple copying as well as more sophisticated operations that take advantage of transparency.

condition variable
A type of variable provided by the C-thread functions to help synchronize the threads in a task.

conform
In the Objective C language, a class is said to conform to a protocol if it adopts the protocol or inherits from a class that adopts it. An instance conforms to a protocol if its class does. Thus, an instance that conforms to a protocol can perform any of the instance methods declared in the protocol.

console
A special window that displays system log messages, as well as output written to the standard error and standard output streams by applications launched from the Workspace Manager.

container
In the Database Kit, an object used to buffer data being transferred between the database and the application, permitting temporary storage of multiple objects of diverse types.

content area
The area within a window that's available for the application to use. It excludes only the window's border, title bar, and resize bar.

content rectangle
A rectangle surrounding a window's content area, expressed in the screen coordinate system. See also *frame rectangle*.

content view
In the Window class, a View that's exactly the same size as a window's content area and has all the Views that draw within the content area as its subviews and descendants; every Window object has a content view. In the ScrollView class, the ClipView object that encloses the visible portion of a document and provides basic scrolling behavior; see also *document view*.

context number
An integer assigned by the Window Server to identify the PostScript execution context for an application. In the Application Kit, the context number is used to distinguish among running applications.

controls

Graphical objects—such as buttons, sliders, text fields, and scrollers—that the user can operate to give instructions to an application.

coverage

In image representation, how much background shows through a pixel; passed to PostScript operators as a value from 0.0 for no coverage (transparent) to 1.0 for full coverage (opaque). See also *alpha value*.

current coordinate system

The coordinate system reflected in the current transformation matrix (CTM) of an application's current graphics state. It's usually the coordinate system of the View object that's about to draw.

current window

The window that's the current device of a particular PostScript context's current graphics state. The current window receives all drawing directed to the window device of a context's current graphics state. **windowdeviceround** and **currentwindow** set and return the current graphics state's current window.

cursor

In the NeXTSTEP user interface, the small image (usually an arrow) that moves on the screen correspondingly as you move the mouse. In the Database Kit, within a record stream or a record list, the record of current interest.

cursor rectangle

A tracking rectangle that's associated with a particular image for the cursor.

DAC

Digital-to-analog converter; a device that converts a series of digital samples into an audio signal.

database

An organized collection of data. In the Database Kit, often used informally to refer to a database server or a database management system (DBMS), including not only the data but also the server processes that allow access to it, or the language used to state commands or queries, such as SQL.

delegate

In the NeXTSTEP software kits, an object that acts on behalf of another object. Window, Application, Text, Listener, NXBrowser, NXImage, and other objects can be assigned delegates.

demand paging
An operating system facility that causes pages of data to be brought from disk into physical memory only as they're needed.

descendant
In the Application Kit, a View is said to be the descendant of all the Views above it in the view hierarchy, including its superview. In the 3D Graphics Kit, the shape directly below another shape in the shape hierarchy. An N3DShape's descendant—and the descendant's peers—inherits the coordinate system of its ancestor. See also *ancestor.*

designated initializer
The **init...** method that has primary responsibility for initializing new instances of a class. Each class defines or inherits its own designated intializer. Through messages to **self**, other **init...** methods in the same class directly or indirectly invoke the designated intializer, and the designated initializer, through a message to **super**, invokes the designated initializer of its superclass.

destination image
One of the two images that are combined when compositing. The composite replaces the destination image. See also *source image*.

digital signal processing
A branch of array processing concerned primarily with the real-time analysis and processing of digitized analog signals representing physical artifacts such as sounds and images.

digital-to-analog converter
See *DAC*.

directory
A term used in this manual in place of the word *folder* found in other NeXTSTEP documentation. A directory is a collection of files and other directories, sometimes called subdirectories. See also *NetInfo directory.*

dispatch table
A table used to implement run-time messaging for Objective C programs. Each class has a dispatch table that associates method selectors with the addresses of method implementations.

dock
See *application dock.*

docked icon
An icon in the application dock.

document view

A View representing an entire document. A ClipView object contains a document view as its subview. The ClipView translates and clips this subview to allow the user to view a portion of a large document.

document window

A window that displays the contents of a user-created file.

domain

See *NetInfo domain* or *weighting domain*.

domain name notation

One way to identify a specific domain, using a format similar to file pathnames; for example, /boston/earth specifies the domain earth, which is a child of the domain boston, which is a child of the root domain. See also *tagged domain notation*.

double-click

To press and release a mouse button twice in succession while the cursor is positioned over an object on-screen. To count as a double-click rather than as two separate clicks, the mouse cannot move and the mouse button must be pressed the second time within a short interval of the first.

drag

To move the mouse (and the cursor on screen) while a mouse button is held down.

DSP

Digital signal processor, a device that modifies digital signals; for example, the Motorola DSP56001 microprocessor.

DSP system functions

The set of C functions that provide a software interface between the host processor and the DSP.

dspwrap

A program that creates a C function corresponding to a DSP assembly language macro. Functions created with **dspwrap** are normally used in array processing applications.

dynamic binding

Binding a method to a message—that is, finding the method implementation to invoke in response to the message—at run time, rather than at compile time.

dynamic drawing
The drawing that an application does to provide feedback during user actions—for example, highlighting objects that are clicked or pressed, and moving objects that are dragged.

dynamic typing
Discovering the class of an object at run time rather than at compile time. In the Objective C language, all objects of type **id** are dynamically typed. See also *dynamic binding*.

encoding vector
An array that maps character codes to the corresponding characters in a given character set.

end point
When the user drags to define a range, the position of the cursor when the mouse button is released. See also *anchor point*.

entity
In the Database Kit, the description of one of the database's collections of data; loosely speaking, the name and description of a table in the database.

Ethernet
A high-speed local area network technology. Ethernet is considered the industry standard for networking UNIX-based machines because of its reliability and capacity to rapidly transfer large amount of information. Ethernet connectors are built into NeXT computers.

evaluation context
In the Indexing Kit, an object against which a query expression is evaluated. It's usually a container of other objects about which the query is posed.

event
The direct or indirect report of a user's action on the keyboard or mouse. See also *event record* and *event queue*.

event dispatcher
The part of the Window Server that accepts user input such as keyboard and mouse actions and decides which window to assign it to.

event mask
A long integer associated with a window. It controls which types of events will be associated with the window and passed to the application that owns the window. A 1 in the bit corresponding to a particular event type means the window will accept that type of event.

event message
In the Application Kit, a message to perform a method named after an event or subevent. Event messages are used to dispatch events to the objects that will respond to them. See also *action message*.

event procedures
In the Window Server process, PostScript procedures that the Server calls to process events in windows.

event queue
A ring buffer that temporarily stores event records that an application receives from the Window Server.

event record
The structure in which information about an event is passed.

exposure color
The color that's shown in a new area of a window, before any drawing is done in the area.

expression
In the Database Kit, a description of data to be obtained from an entity in a database, stated in terms of one or more of the data's attributes and, optionally, operations on them. For example, "salary – average salary" might be an expression, while "salary" is a minimal expression.

eye-to-viewpoint vector
In the 3D Graphics Kit, the directed line segment that defines the camera coordinate system. This vector is defined by two points, the viewpoint and the eyepoint (both in world coordinates). The viewpoint is the point at which the camera is aiming; the eyepoint is the focal point of the camera.

factory
Same as *class object*.

factory method
Same as *class method*.

factory object
Same as *class object*.

fetch group
In the Database Kit, the set of fields of a single record list, together with a mapping that associates each field with the object that displays it.

file
A collection of related information stored on a disk, such as a document, report, letter, or application.

file package
A directory that the Workspace Manager presents as a file, allowing the user to manipulate a group of files as if they were one file. A file package for an application executable should have the same name as the executable file, plus a ".app" extension. File packages for documents should bear the same extension as the one assigned to the application's document files.

file system
The collection of all the files the user can access through the computer.

first responder
In the Application Kit, the object that will have the first chance to respond to keyboard event messages, mouse-moved event messages, and action messages with user-selected targets. Each Window has its own first responder, which it changes in response to mouse-down events.

flags-changed event
An event that occurs when the user presses an Alternate, Shift, Control, or Command key, or turns Alpha Lock on or off.

floating panel
A panel, such as a palette, that stays in front of standard windows and other panels. See also *tiers*.

flush
To empty a buffer in which information has accumulated, and send the information on to its destination.

foreign key
In the Database Kit, a property in one entity that identifies one or more records in a related entity.

formal protocol
In the Objective C language, a protocol that's declared with the **@protocol** directive. Classes can adopt formal protocols, objects can respond at run time when asked if they conform to a formal protocol, and instances can be typed by the formal protocols they conform to.

frame rectangle
In the Application Kit, the rectangle that defines the location and size of a graphical object, particularly Windows, Views, and Cells. A Window's frame rectangle is stated in the screen coordinate system, a View's frame rectangle is specified in its superview's coordinate system, and a Cell's frame rectangle is specified in the containing View's coordinate system.

frame view
In the Application Kit, the View that fills the Window's frame rectangle and draws its border, title bar, and resize bar. This is a private View; it has the content view as its one public subview. See also *content view*.

freestanding icon
An application icon standing alone in the workspace. Freestanding icons represent running applications and can be dragged into the dock. See also *docked icon*.

frequency
The oscillation rate of a sound vibration. Frequencies are measured in hertz (Hz) or cycles per second (cps), and kilohertz (kHz) or thousands of cycles per second.

gray level
See *gray value*.

gray value
A color value that represents a shade of gray, ranging from 0.0 for black to 1.0 for white.

halftone screen
A pixel pattern that the PostScript interpreter uses to approximate a specified color in an area, if each of the pixels in the area can't be assigned that exact color.

handle
In the Indexing Kit, an identifier for a block of data or a record.

hider
In the 3D Graphics Kit, the algorithm determining the order in which geometry in a 3D scene description is rendered. A hidden-surface removal algorithm causes objects to appear in the natural front-to-back order, regardless of their order in the data describing the scene. An in-order hider algorithm causes objects to be rendered first-in, first-out, regardless of their natural front-to-back order in the scene.

host
The computer that's running (is host to) a particular program. The term is usually used to refer to a computer on a network.

host processor
The microprocessor on which an application program resides. When an application is running, the host processor may call other, peripheral microprocessors, such as the DSP56001, to perform specialized operations.

hot spot
The point in the cursor image whose location on the screen is reported as the cursor's location. The cursor is said to be "over" the location at its hot spot.

id
In the Objective C language, the general type for any kind of object regardless of class. **id** is defined as a pointer to an object data structure. It can be used for both class objects and instances of a class.

informal protocol
In the Objective C language, a protocol declared as a category, usually as a category of the Object class. The language gives explicit support to formal protocols, but not to informal ones.

inheritance
In object-oriented programming, the ability of a superclass to pass its characteristics (methods and instance variables) on to its subclasses. In Mach, the transfer of address space access rights from a parent process to a child process.

inheritance attribute
In Mach, a value indicating the degree to which a parent process and its child process share the parent process's address space. A memory page can be inherited copy-on-write, shared, or not at all.

inheritance hierarchy
In object-oriented programming, the hierarchy of classes that's defined by the arrangement of superclasses and subclasses. Every class (except Object, which is at the root of the hierarchy) has a superclass, and any class may have an unlimited number of subclasses. Through its superclass, each class inherits from those above it in the hierarchy.

in-line data
Data that's included directly in a Mach message, as opposed to referred to by a pointer. See also *out-of-line data*.

insertion point
The point where whatever you type or paste in an application will be inserted. In text, it's typically marked by a blinking vertical bar.

instance
In the Objective C language, an object that belongs to (is a member of) a particular class. Instances are created at run time according to the specification in the class definition.

instance drawing
In the Window Server, temporary drawing done within a window.

instance method
In the Objective C language, any method that can be used by an instance of a class rather than by the class object.

instance variable
In the Objective C language, any variable that's part of the internal data structure of an instance. Instance variables are declared in a class definition and become part of all objects that are members of or inherit from the class.

interactive rendering
In the 3D Graphics Kit, a rendering process that draws directly to the display, enabling the user to interact with the model represented by 3D data. To render images interactively, the renderer may ignore some of geometric details in the model.

Interface Builder
A tool that lets you graphically specify your application's user interface. It sets up the corresponding objects for you and makes it easy for you to establish connections between these objects and your own code where needed.

intersection
When applied to two given rectangles, the area that both have in common. If the two rectangles are expressed in the same coordinate system, their intersection will also be a rectangle. See also *union*.

introspection
The ability of an object to reveal information about itself as an object—such as its class and superclass, the messages it can respond to, and the protocols it conforms to.

I/O
Input/output; the sending and retrieving of information into the memory of a program, usually to and from a file or a peripheral device through an I/O port.

IPC
Interprocess communication; the transfer of information between processes. In Mach, IPC is performed through the use of messages.

ISDN
Integrated Services Digital Network, telephone service that carries information in digital form from one end of the phone line to the other (from one telephone or computer to the other). Because information is digitized for its entire journey over the line, computer data can be sent and received without the intervention of a modem. Commonly contrasted to POTS (plain old telephone service), which sends and receives information in analog form.

join
In relational databases, the action of retrieving data from more than one table by a combination of cross-product and selection constraints. In the Database Kit, relationships are converted into SQL joins by requiring that the foreign key of the main table match primary key fields in a related table. See also *relationship*, *inner join*, *outer join*.

kernel port
A port used to represent a task or thread in Mach function calls. Also known as a task port or thread port.

key
In the Indexing Kit, a data item serving as an identifier for another data item. In the Database Kit, the property or combination of properties that uniquely identifies records in the database. See also *foreign key.*

keyboard alternative
A way of using the keyboard, rather than the mouse, to choose a menu command, operate a button in a panel, or pick an item from a pop-up or pull-down list. While holding a Command key down, the user types a character associated with the command, button, or item. See also *key equivalent*.

key code
A hardware-dependent code that indicates the position of a key on the keyboard.

key-down event
An event that occurs when the user generates a character by pressing a key. Holding the key down generates subsequent key-down events at regular intervals.

key equivalent
In the Application Kit, the character that can be used as the keyboard alternative for a given object.

key space
In the Indexing Kit, the set of possible keys of a specific type.

key-up event
An event that occurs when the user releases any key except Alternate, Shift, Control, Help, or Command.

key window
The window in the active application that receives keyboard events. The title bar of the key window is highlighted in black.

kit-defined event
An event that occurs when the user moves, resizes, or reorders a window or activates or deactivates an application. It includes the window-moved, window-exposed, window-resized, screen-changed, application-activate, and application-deactivate subevents.

knob
The part of a slider or scroller that the user can drag. See also *bar.*

lazy evaluation
A programming philosophy stating that high-overhead operations should be deferred until absolutely necessary. Even then, only the portion of the operation that's unavoidable should be performed.

lexeme
The smallest meaningful unit of a text stream; usually a word, though it may be a phrase, embedded graphic, or other such thing.

linked information
Copied information, such as a graphic image, that can be automatically updated when the original information is modified.

literal
In the Indexing Kit query language, a symbol whose value is equal to its representation; for example, a number or string.

local coordinate system
In the 3D Graphics Kit, the coordinate system belonging to a particular N3DShape. A given N3DShape's local coordinate system is determined by the coordinate system inherited from its ancestor and any transformations the shape applies to that coordinate system.

localize
To adapt an application to work under various local conditions—especially to have it use a local language selected by the user. This entails freeing application code from language-specific and culture-specific references and making it able to import localized resources (such as character strings, images, and sounds). For example, an application localized in Spanish would display "Salir" as the last item in the main menu. In Italian it would display "Esci", in German "Verlassen", and in English "Quit".

Mach
The multitasking operating system used by all NeXT computers. Mach is completely compatible with UNIX 4.3BSD but adds faster interprocess communication, a larger virtual memory space, memory-mapped files, and multiple threads of execution within a single address space.

Mach factor
A measurement of how busy the system is. Unlike the UNIX load average, higher Mach factors mean that the system is less busy.

Mach server
A task that provides services to clients, using a MiG-generated RPC interface.

main event loop
The principal control loop for applications that are driven by events. From the time it's launched until the moment it's terminated, an application gets one event after another from the Window Server and responds to them, waiting between events if the next event isn't ready. In the Application Kit, the Application object runs the main event loop.

main menu
The principal menu in an application, usually identified by the name of the application in its title bar. The main menu lacks a close button and cannot be made the submenu of another menu.

main screen
The screen where the key window is located, or, if there is no key window, the screen where the main menu is located, or, if there's neither a key window nor a main menu on-screen, the screen that has the origin of the screen coordinate system at its lower left corner.

main window
The standard window that's affected by actions in a panel and certain menu commands. If the main window isn't also the key window, its title bar is highlighted in dark gray.

makefile
A specification file used by the program **make** to build an executable version of an application. A makefile details the files, dependencies, and rules by which the application is built.

master NetInfo server
A computer that's the authoritative server of a NetInfo domain.

memory-mapped files
A Mach facility that maps virtual memory onto a physical file. Thereafter, any reference to that part of virtual memory causes the corresponding page of the physical file to be brought into memory.

menu
A small window that displays a list of commands. Only menus for the active application are visible on-screen.

message
In object-oriented programming, the method selector (name) and accompanying arguments that tell the receiving object in a message expression what to do. In Mach, a message consists of a header and a variable-length body; operating system services are invoked by passing a message from a thread to the port representing the task that provides the desired service.

message expression
In object-oriented programming, an expression that sends a message to an object. In the Objective C language, message expressions are enclosed within square brackets and consist of a receiver followed by a message (method selector and arguments).

method
In object-oriented programming, a procedure that can be executed by an object.

MIDI
Musical Instrument Digital Interface; the industry standard used by modern keyboard synthesizers for transmitting and storing musical performance information.

MiG
Mach's message interface generator. MiG provides a procedure call interface to Mach's system of interprocess messaging.

miniaturize button
The button that can appear at the far left in a window's title bar. Clicking the button removes the window from the screen and replaces it with its miniwindow counterpart.

miniwindow
A small, icon-sized window that stands in for a window that has been miniaturized. Double-clicking the miniwindow reverses the miniaturization, returning the full window to the screen.

modal event loop
A temporary event loop that's set up to get events directly from the event queue, bypassing the main event loop. Typically, a mouse-down event initiates the modal loop and the following mouse-up event ends it. The loop gets mouse-dragged events (or mouse-entered and mouse-exited events) to track the cursor's movement while the user holds the mouse button down.

mode
A period of time when the user's actions are interpreted in a special way.

model
In the Database Kit, a description of the data available from a database as it will be seen and used by a database application. The model is produced by the DBModeler application. The model resides in a file having the extension ".dbmodel", in one of several designated directories, so that Interface Builder's database palette is automatically aware of the models available to it.

modifier keys
Keys that change the meaning of other keys or of the user's actions with the mouse; the Shift, Alternate, Command, Control, and Help keys.

module
In the Database Kit, the object that represents a particular *view* of the database (that is, those of the database's entities that the module makes available), with the names by which the module refers to them, and the *properties* that the module defines for them.

mouse-down event
An event that occurs when the user presses a button on the mouse. There's one type of mouse-down event for the left (or only) mouse button and one for the right button.

mouse-dragged event
An event that occurs when the user moves the mouse while holding down a mouse button. There's one type of mouse-dragged event for when the mouse is moved with the left (or only) mouse button down, or with both buttons down, and another type for when it's moved with the right button down.

mouse-entered event
An event that occurs when the cursor enters a tracking rectangle. Depending on instructions given when the rectangle was created, the event may be generated only while one or both of the mouse buttons is being held down.

mouse-exited event
An event that occurs when the cursor leaves a tracking rectangle. Depending on instructions given when the rectangle was created, the event may be generated only while one or both of the mouse buttons is being held down.

mouse-moved event
An event that occurs when the user moves the mouse without holding down a mouse button.

mouse scaling
The responsiveness of the cursor to movements of the mouse. Usually, the faster the mouse is moved, the farther the cursor travels.

mouse-up event
An event that occurs when the user releases a mouse button. There's one type of mouse-up event for the left (or only) mouse button and one for the right button.

multitasking
Describes an operating system that allows the concurrent execution of multiple programs. Mach, the operating system of all NeXT computers, is multitasking.

mutex variable
Mutual exclusion variable; a type of variable provided by the C-thread functions to help protect critical regions in a multiple-thread task.

NetInfo directory
An organizational structure within a NetInfo domain. A NetInfo directory stores properties and sometimes other NetInfo directories.

NetInfo domain
A collection of administrative information including user accounts, host entries, and so on. Information within a domain is organized into NetInfo directories. Domains are organized into a hierarchy.

NetInfo server
A computer that provides storage for and access to a NetInfo domain.

network
A group of hosts that can directly communicate with each other.

network port
In Mach, a port by which local objects communicate with remote objects. A message sent to a network port is received by the local network server, processed, and then sent across the network to a remote network server.

network port identifier
A code by which a network server determines the identity of the recipient local task.

network server
A local operating system representative for tasks on a remote computer. Messages intended for a remote task are processed and redirected by a local network server.

next responder
In the Application Kit, the object that will be sent event and action messages that the intended receiver can't handle. See also *responder chain.*

NeXTSTEP
NeXT's application development and user environment, consisting of the Workspace Manager, the Window Server, various software kits such as the Application Kit and the Database Kit, various applications such as Project Builder and Interface Builder, and other software.

NFS
Network File System. An NFS file server allows users on the network to share files as if they were on their own local disk.

nib file
A file (actually a file package) that stores the specifications for all or part of an application's interface. These files can contain archived objects, information about connections between objects, and sound and image data. You use Interface Builder to create nib files.

nil
In the Objective C language, an object **id** with a value of 0.

NMI
Non-maskable interrupt; the interrupt produced by a particular keyboard sequence.

nonretained window
A window without a backup buffer for screen pixel values.

nonsimple message
In Mach, a message that contains either a reference to a port or a pointer to data.

notify port
In Mach, a port on which a task receives messages from the kernel advising it of changes in port access rights and of the status of messages it has sent.

object
A programming unit that groups together a data structure (instance variables) and the operations (methods) that can use or affect that data. Objects are the principal building blocks of object-oriented programs.

object repository
See *repository.*

open
In the Indexing Kit, to reconstitute a store client from its stored data.

operator
In the Indexing Kit query language, a symbol that performs an action on its arguments and results in a value. See also *arithmetic operator, boolean operator, projection operator, relational operator,* and *search operator.*

outer join
In the Database Kit, setting the outer-join property of a relationship means that all values of the primary key are represented in the return, even when some of the related records have no matching value for the foreign key. For example, if the relationship links "account code" to "salesperson for account," the return will include those that have no assigned salesperson.

outlet
An instance variable that points to another object. Outlet instance variables are a way for an object to keep track of the other objects to which it may need to send messages.

out-of-line data
Data that's passed by reference in a Mach message, as opposed to being included in the message. See also *in-line data.*

package
In the Window Server process, a set of PostScript procedures, shared by all applications, that the Window Server calls to perform various tasks for applications.

panel
A window that holds objects that control what happens in other windows (such as a Font panel) or in the application generally (such as a Preferences panel), or a window that presents information about the application to the user (such as an information panel). See also *attention panel.*

parser
See *attribute parser.*

passivate
In the Indexing Kit, to archive an object by writing its instance variables directly into storage. See also *activate* and *transcribe*.

password
A character string assigned to or chosen by a user that, along with the user name, uniquely identifies that user and allows access to the system.

peer
In the 3D Graphics Kit, a relationship between N3DShapes in a shape hierarchy; an N3DShape's peers all share a single direct ancestor, and thus share a common coordinate system.

period
A single complete cycle of a sound waveform.

periodic waveform
A waveform with a clearly defined period occurring at regular intervals.

photorealistic rendering
In the 3D Graphics Kit, a rendering process that attempts to recreate life-like images from 3D data. Photorealistic rendering allows for such effects as lighting, surface texturing, atmospheric interference, and other details that determine the appearance of true-to-life images.

pixel
The smallest unit that can be assigned a color or coverage value for showing images on the screen or printed page.

plain window
A window with no border, title bar, or resize bar.

policy
In Mach, a thread's scheduling policy determines how the thread's priority is set and under what circumstances the thread runs. See also *priority.*

polymorphism
In object-oriented programming, the ability of different objects to respond, each in its own way, to the same message.

pop-up list
A menu-like list of items that appears over (or next to) an on-screen button when the button is pressed. The user can choose an item by dragging to it and releasing the mouse button. When the mouse button is released, the pop-up list disappears.

port
In Mach, a protected communication channel by which messages are sent to, and received from, operating system objects.

port access rights
In Mach, the ability to send to or receive from a port.

port set
In Mach, a set of zero or more ports. A thread can receive messages sent to any of the ports contained in a port set by specifying the port set as a parameter to **msg_receive**().

posting
In the Indexing Kit, a reference to a data item. A posting consists of a handle and an optional weight.

posting method
An indication to the Window Server of which window or windows an event should be sent to.

power-off subevent
A subevent of the system-defined event. It occurs when the user requests a system shutdown.

predicate
In the Indexing Kit, a single assertion to be tested in a query expression.

press
To press a mouse button and keep it down for a period of time while the cursor is positioned over an object on-screen. Pressing an on-screen object (such as a scroll button) may cause it to take repeated action, or may produce another object (such as a pop-up list) that the user can drag into.

priority
In Mach scheduling, a number between 0 and 31 that indicates how likely a thread is to run. The higher the thread's priority, the more likely the thread is to run. See also *policy.*

process
A program that is at some stage of execution. In Mach, a task containing a single thread of execution is equivalent to a process.

process identifier,* or *process ID
In UNIX, a number that uniquely identifies a process.

program controller
The part of a microprocessor devoted to fetching instructions and updating the program counter.

projection operator
In the Indexing Kit query language, an operator that results in attributes from a given object. See also *operator.*

Project Builder
A tool that lets you create and maintain your application's project and source file hierarchy. Project Builder provides a user interface for building your application from its source files, as well as connections with other NeXT developer applications for interactive debugging.

property
In the Database Kit, a general term for any attribute, relationship, or expression of an entity.

protocol
In the Objective C language, the declaration of a group of methods not associated with any particular class. See also *formal protocol* and *informal protocol.*

pswrap
A program that creates a C function corresponding to a sequence of PostScript code. When this function is called, a binary-encoded version of the PostScript code is sent to the Window Server.

pull-down list
A menu-like list that appears under an on-screen button when the button is pressed. The user can drag into the list to choose an action from it. When the mouse button is released, the pull-down list disappears.

qualifier
In the Database Kit, an expression that filters the records to be retrieved by testing the truth of a proposition, retaining those for which the proposition is true and excluding the rest. In SQL, a clause preceded by "where", as in "name, department, salary where salary > 50000."

quantization
In sound, the rounding up or down of the sampled values of a waveform to fit into a predetermined step size.

quantum
The fixed amount of time a thread can run before being preempted.

query expression
In the Indexing Kit query language, an expression formed of predicates and logical operators, used to select objects from an evaluation context about which the expression is true. In the Database Kit, a statement defining the properties of data to be fetched.

RAM
Random-access memory; memory that a microprocessor can either read or write to.

reader
See *attribute reader.*

real time
A concept of time when using a computer. If the user defines or initiates an event and the event occurs instantaneously, the computer is said to be operating in real time.

receive rights
In Mach, the ability to receive messages on a port. Only one task at a time can have receive rights for any one port. See also *send rights.*

receiver
In object-oriented programming, the object that is sent a message.

reconstitute
In the Indexing Kit, to connect an object to data in an IXStore, essentially recreating the object that stored the data.

record
In the Indexing Kit, an Objective C object used exclusively to store data; often stored in a repository and identified by a handle. In the Database Kit, a set of property values retrieved for an entity; loosely, one row in a table.

record list
In the Database Kit, an object for retrieving, holding, editing, and storing a set of records in a database.

rectangle
In NeXTSTEP, an area that's defined by a point, (x, y), and an extent (width and height).

reference domain
In the Indexing Kit, a weighting domain against which a lexeme's frequency in another domain is compared.

regular expression
In the Indexing Kit, a pattern generated from a string. Indexing Kit search operators look for sequences of text matching the pattern.

relational operator
In the Indexing Kit query language, an operator that performs a value comparison on numbers or strings. See also *operator.*

relationship
In the Database Kit, a property constructed by matching records having the same value for an attribute in one entity with those having the same value for a corresponding attribute in another entity.

remote message
A message sent from one application to an object in another application.

remote object
An object in another application, one that's a potential receiver for a remote message.

renderer
In the 3D Graphics Kit, a program that accepts a description of a three-dimensional scene and interprets it as an image. NeXTSTEP Release 3 includes two separate renderers. The Interactive RenderMan renderer produces images for interactive manipulation on the display. The PhotoRealistic Renderman renderer produces images for printing and for high-resolution display. Both accept 3D data in RIB (RenderMan Interface Bytestream) format. See also *interactive rendering*, *photorealistic rendering*.

reply port
A port associated with a thread that's used in Mach remote procedure calls.

repository
In the Indexing Kit, an object that conforms to the IXRecordReading protocol; usually, any object that archives other objects within itself.

resize bar
The bar, located along the bottom of a window, that the user can grab and drag to resize the window.

resolution
The number of pixels per unit distance along the vertical and horizontal coordinate axes. The greater the resolution in each direction, the more precise an image can be.

responder chain
In the Application Kit, a linked list of Responder objects that's formed by initializing each object's next responder with the **id** of another object. If a Responder can't handle an event message or untargeted action message that it receives, the message is passed to its next responder.

retained window
A window with a backup buffer for screen pixel values. Images are rendered into the buffer for any portions of the window that aren't visible on-screen.

RIB
In the 3D Graphics Kit, the protocol for describing 3D scenes. RIB is short for RenderMan Interface Bytestream, a byte stream representation of the RenderMan Interface. This representation serves as both a network tranpsort protocol for modeling system clients to communicate requests to a rendering server and a compact encoded format which minimizes transmission time and file storage costs.

rollback
In the Database Kit, the action of aborting the sequence of changes in a transaction so that the affected records in the database are restored as they were before the first of the changes was started.

ROM
Read-only memory; memory that a microprocessor can read but not write to.

rotation
A transformation that rotates the origin of the resulting coordinate system relative to the original coordinates. In 2D graphics, the x and y axes can be rotated about their origin. In 3D graphics, any pair of axes can be rotated about the other axis—for example, the x and y axes can be rotated about z, or y and z can be rotated about x.

RPC
Remote procedure call; in Mach, RPC is implemented using MiG-generated messages.

sample
A single digital measurement of the height (or instantaneous amplitude) of a sound waveform.

sample frame
A collection of *n* sound samples where *n* is the number of channels in the sound. Sample frames are ordered just like samples, so the first sample frame contains the first sample from each channel, the second sample frame contains the second sample from each channel, and so on.

sampling rate
The frequency at which a sound waveform is sampled (recorded) or played back; sampling rates are defined in Hz.

screen-changed subevent
A subevent of the kit-defined event. It reports when the user drags a window from one screen to another.

screen coordinate system
The coordinate system used to locate windows on the screen. The origin is in the lower left corner of the screen, the positive x-axis extends to the right, and the positive y-axis extends upward. The length of a unit on either axis is one screen pixel. When the Window Server can display to more than one screen, all screens share the same screen coordinate system; only one of the screens has the coordinate origin at its lower left corner.

screen list
A list maintained by the Window Server that orders windows from front to back, with the frontmost window at the top of the list. If a window isn't on the list, it won't be displayed on the screen.

scroll buttons
Any of the buttons that the user can press to scroll a display, such as the buttons in a scroller. Each scroll button is labeled by a small triangular arrow indicating the direction of scrolling.

search operator
In the Indexing Kit query language, an operator that searches a compound object for specific values. See also *operator.*

selector
In the Objective C language, the name of a method when it's used in a source-code message to an object, or the unique identifier that replaces the name when the source code is compiled. Compiled selectors are of type SEL.

send rights
In Mach, the ability to send messages to a port. Many tasks can have send rights for the same port. See also *receive rights.*

server
In general, a process that provides resources to other processes, or the computer that runs the processes that provide resources.

shader
In the 3D Graphics Kit, a function that defines an effect applied to an element in a 3D scene. The RenderMan Shading Language defines a set of procedures that can be used to write shading functions to simulate various effects in a scene, including lighting, atmosphere, surface textures and patterns, and other components of a realistic image. The N3DShader class provides API for reading shader functions and applying them to N3DShapes.

shape hierarchy
In the 3D Graphics Kit, a directed acyclic graph organizing the N3DShapes belonging to a single scene. A shape hierarchy is made up of two kinds of relationships: descendant-ancestor and peer-to-peer. A descendant inherits the 3D graphics state of its ancestor, including coordinate system, shaders, and other attributes. Peers are shapes that share a common ancestor, and thus inherit a common graphics state; however, only the first member of a peer group is considered to be the descendant of the ancestor.

signal
A continuously varying physical variable.

signal processing
See *digital signal processing.*

signature
In the Indexing Kit, a vector of lexemes, characterizing the word content of a specific body of text.

simple message
In Mach, a message that contains neither references to ports nor pointers to data.

soundfile
A sampled-data storage file used by the Sound Kit.

Sound Kit
The Objective C classes and C functions available for creating sound effects, doing speech analysis, and performing other sound manipulation.

source
In the Indexing Kit, an object acting as a repository with regard to object activation. See also *repository* and *activate*.

source image
One of the two images that are combined when compositing. See also *destination image*.

standard windows
The principal windows of an application; the windows where its primary work is done. All windows are standard windows, except those with specialized functions (menus, panels, pop-up and pull-down lists, miniwindows, and docked and freestanding icons).

static typing
In the Objective C language, giving the compiler information about what kind of object an instance is, by typing it as a pointer to a class.

storage file
In the Indexing Kit, the file that an IXStoreFile keeps its storage in. See also *store file*.

store client
In the Indexing Kit, an object that stores data in an IXStore. A store client is identified by its boot block, and can also be identified by name. See also *store file*.

store context
In the Indexing Kit, an instance of IXStore accessing a particular group of storage; several store contexts may share the same storage.

store file
In the Indexing Kit, a storage file containing an IXStoreDirectory at block 1; the IXStoreDirectory allows store clients to be accessed by name instead of by boot block. See also *storage file* and *store client*.

style
In the Application Kit, the appearance of a window's border, title bar, and resize bar.

subclass
In the Objective C language, any class that's one step below another class in the inheritance hierarchy. Occasionally used more generally to mean any class that inherits from another class, and sometimes also used as a verb to mean the process of defining a subclass of another class.

submenu
Any menu that can be brought to the screen through a command in another menu. All menus except the main menu are submenus of another menu. See also *supermenu*, *main menu*, and *attach*.

subview
In the Application Kit, any View that's located within the coordinate system of another View, its superview. See also *view hierarchy.*

superclass
In the Objective C language, a class that's one step above another class in the inheritance hierarchy; the class through which a subclass inherits methods and instance variables.

supermenu
A menu containing a command that controls another menu, its submenu.

superview
In the Application Kit, any View that has subviews—other Views that are located within its coordinate system. See also *view hierarchy.*

surrogate
In the Indexing Kit, an object created during the evaluation of a query. A surrogate is usually compared against an object from the query's evaluation context.

synchronous message
A remote message that doesn't return until the receiving application finishes responding to the message. Because the application that sends the message waits for an acknowledgement or return information from the receiving application, the two applications are kept "in sync." See also *asynchronous message*.

system control keys
The keys that control the computer's basic functions; the Power, brightness, and volume keys.

system-defined event
An event that occurs when the user requests a system shutdown. A system-defined event can have various subevent types; currently there's only one, the power-off subevent.

table view
In the Database Kit, a matrix-like display of data organized by rows and columns.

tag
A name that identifies a NetInfo database.

tagged domain notation
One of the ways to identify a specific NetInfo domain, where the host serving the domain and the tag of the database are both specified; for example, rhino/network is the database tagged network on host rhino. See also *domain name notation*.

target
In the NeXTSTEP user interface, what the user selects to be acted on by a menu command or a control within a panel—for example, text that's to be deleted by the Cut command. In the Application Kit, the object that receives action messages from a Control.

task
In Mach, a paged virtual address space along with protected access to ports, virtual memory, and system processor(s). A task itself performs no computation; rather, it's a framework for running threads. See also *thread*.

task port
In Mach, a port by which all threads within a task may be addressed. Also known as the task's kernel port.

TCP/IP
Transmission Control Protocol/Internet Protocol. The protocols used to deliver messages between computers over the network. TCP/IP support is included in NeXT computers.

tear off
To drag an attached submenu away from its supermenu. Tearing off a submenu detaches it from its supermenu and gives it an independent life on-screen. Torn-off menus are the only menus with close buttons.

thread
In Mach, the basic unit of program execution. A thread consists of a program counter, a set of registers, and a stack pointer. See also *task*.

thread port
In Mach, a port that represents a single thread within a task. Also known as the thread's kernel port.

thread-safe
Code that can be used safely by several threads simultaneously.

tiers
The sections of the screen list. Each tier is occupied by a different type of window, with attention panels in the frontmost tier, menus in the next two tiers, docked icons in the tier below menus, and floating panels below docked icons. All other windows are in the bottom tier.

timed entry
A function that you specify to be called repeatedly at a given time interval.

title bar
The strip above the content area of a window that users can grab to drag the window to a new location. The title bar holds the window's title, if it has one, and may contain buttons to miniaturize and close the window.

title bar buttons
The miniaturize and close buttons that are located in a window's title bar.

titled window
A window with a border and title bar (and possibly a resize bar). The title bar can be empty.

tracking rectangle
A rectangle that an application can set to track the cursor. The application is notified when the cursor enters or leaves the rectangle. Depending on instructions given when the rectangle is created, the application may be notified only when the left or the right (or both) mouse buttons are held down. See also *mouse-entered event* and *mouse-exited event*.

transaction
In the Database Kit, a sequence of changes to the database that are to be treated as a unit, so that if the entire sequence is not completed successfully, the affected records in the database are restored as they were before the first of the changes was started.

transcribe
In the Indexing Kit, to passivate or activate an object. A fast form of archiving.

transfer function
A procedure that the PostScript interpreter uses to correct color values to compensate for nonlinear response in an output device and the human eye.

transformation
An alteration to a coordinate system (2D or 3D) that defines a new coordinate system. Standard transformations include rotation, scaling, and translation. A transformation is represented by a matrix.

transform operator
In the Indexing Kit query language, an operator that turns its argument into a value of another type. See also *operator.*

triple-click
To press and release a mouse button three times in succession while the cursor is positioned over an object on-screen. The mouse button must be pressed the second time within a short interval of the first, and the third time within a short interval of the second.

two's complement
A binary notation commonly used by computers for storing integers or fractional fixed-point data. Numbers are negated by taking the binary complement (changing each bit to its opposite) and adding 1 in the least-significant position.

type
In the Database Kit, the data type of a particular property or value. This type can be a C data type, an Objective C class, or an entity.

typed stream
A specialized data stream used for archiving. When a typed stream is used, the type of the data is archived along with the data and an object's class hierarchy and version are archived with the object. See also *archiving.*

union
When applied to a set of rectangles, the smallest rectangle that completely encloses them all. See also *intersection.*

user name
The name a user logs in with. Each name must be unique, contain no more than 8 characters, be all lowercase, and contain no spaces.

value
In the Indexing Kit, the data associated with a key; also, the result of sending an attribute's defining message to an object

vector
In the Indexing Kit, a compound item in a query expression; essentially a set of atoms. In the Database Kit, a general term meaning an axis of a data table, equally applicable to a row or a column.

view hierarchy
In the Application Kit, the arrangement of View objects within a window. Each View has a superview and may have any number of subviews. Subviews are located within the coordinate systems of their superviews.

visible rectangle
In the Application Kit, the smallest rectangle in a View's coordinate system that completely covers the visible part of the View—the part falling within all the View's ancestors in the view hierarchy. If the entire area enclosed by a View's frame rectangle is also enclosed by the frame rectangles of each of its ancestors, all of the View is visible and the visible rectangle is identical to the bounds rectangle. If not, the visible rectangle is a portion of the bounds rectangle, or null.

waveform
The motion described by an oscillation; usually associated with sound.

weight
In the Indexing Kit, an indication of the count, frequency, or importance of a lexeme in a body of text. See also *weighting domain.*

weighting domain
In the Indexing Kit, a set of weight statistics for a body of text.

window-exposed subevent
A subevent of the kit-defined event. It occurs when part of a window that was covered becomes exposed to reveal contents not backed by the window buffer. The application has to redraw the contents within a rectangle specified by the event.

window-moved subevent
A subevent of the kit-defined event. It reports when the user moves a window.

window number
In the Window Server, an integer assigned to identify a window; it's never negative or 0. In the Application Kit, a user object that's mapped to the number assigned by the Window Server. The window number used by the Application Kit is said to be "local" to the application; the number assigned by the Window Server is "global."

window-resized subevent
A subevent of the kit-defined event. It reports when a user resizes a window.

Window Server
A process that dispatches user events to applications and renders PostScript code on behalf of applications.

windows
Page-like rectangular areas where applications can draw on-screen. Windows can be moved and reordered front to back.

workspace window
The window that fills the entire workspace on the screen and provides the dark gray background for other windows.

world coordinate system
In the 3D Graphics Kit, the coordinate system from which all other coordinate systems in a scene are derived. The N3DCamera viewing a scene defines its own transformation from world coordinates to the camera coordinate system. The N3DShape being viewed by the camera (its world shape) can define another transformation from world coordinates to its local coordinate system.

zone
A particular region of dynamic memory. Zones are set up in program code and are passed to allocation methods and functions to specify that the allocated memory should come from a particular zone. Allocating related data structures from the same zone can improve locality of reference and overall system performance. For example, all the Views that are displayed in the same window might be clustered in the same zone.

Index